Developing the Curriculum

Developing the Curriculum

Peter F. Oliva
Georgia Southern College

Little, Brown and Company
Boston   Toronto

Library of Congress Catalog Card No. 81–84418

9 8 7 6   ISBN 0-316-64995-3

HAL

Published simultaneously in Canada
by Little, Brown & Company (Canada) Limited

Printed in the United States of America

CREDITS

Numbers preceding each entry refer to the footnote, table, or box number in the text.

Chapter 1. From *Dictionary of Education,* 3rd ed. by Carter V. Good, p. 157. Copyright © 1959, 1973 by McGraw-Hill, Inc. Copyright © 1945 by McGraw-Hill, Inc. Copyright renewed 1979 by Carter V. Good. Used with permission of McGraw-Hill Book Company. 3. From Hollis L. Caswell and Doak S. Campbell, *Curriculum Improvement* (New York: American Book Company, 1935), p. 66. Reprinted with permission. 4. From *Curriculum Planning for Better Teaching and Learning* by J. Galen Saylor and William M. Alexander, pp. 4–5. Copyright © 1954 by J. Galen Saylor and William M. Alexander. Reprinted by permission of Holt, Rinehart and Winston. 5. From *Planning Curriculum for Schools,* Third Edition, by J. Galen Saylor and William M. Alexander, p. 6. Copyright © 1974 by Holt Rinehart and Winston, Inc. Reprinted by permission of Holt, Rinehart and

Winston. 6, 7. Excerpts from *Curriculum Development: Theory and Practice* by Hilda Taba, pp. 11, 10. © 1962 by Harcourt, Brace and Jovanovich, Inc. and reprinted by permission of the publisher. 8. Ronald C. Doll, *Curriculum Improvement: Decision Making and Process,* 4th ed. (Boston: Allyn and Bacon, 1978), p. 6. Reprinted with permission. 9. Reprinted with permission of Macmillan Publishing Company from *Curriculum Development: Theory Into Practice,* 2nd ed., by Daniel Tanner and Laurel N. Tanner, p. 43. Copyright © 1980, Macmillan Publishing Co., Inc. 10. Specified excerpt from *Curriculum Improvement: A Guide to Problems, Principles, and Process,* 2nd ed. by Albert I. Oliver, p. 8. Copyright © 1977 by Albert I. Oliver. By permission of Harper & Row, Publishers, Inc. 15. W. James Popham and Eva L. Baker, *Systematic Instruction,* p. 48. © 1970 by

(continued on page 524)

**To Cory, the newest in the family,
whose curriculum is just starting to develop.**

Preface

This text is designed to be a comprehensive analysis of the process of curriculum development. It is intended for students in courses such as Curriculum Development, Curriculum Planning, and Curriculum Improvement. Moreover, curriculum coordinators, assistant principals for curriculum, departmental chairpersons, instructional team leaders, and grade coordinators will find the book to be a practical guide to curriculum development.

The text begins with an examination of the theoretical dimensions of curriculum development. After curriculum is defined and its relationship to instruction is discussed, the text looks at the roles of various personnel who have primary responsibility for developing the curriculum. The various models of curriculum development are then described and the use of one integrated model is suggested. A step-by-step process for utilizing this model is delineated. This process is carried all the way from stating broad aims of education, to listing curriculum and instructional goals and objectives, to implementing instruction, and to evaluating instruction and curriculum.

Each chapter begins with a number of cognitive objectives (competencies) to be achieved by the student on completion of each chapter and a number of issues or problems (largely affective in nature) that require the student to formulate personal positions on topics presented in the chapter. The supplementary exercises at the end of each chapter serve to reinforce the goals and content of each chapter and to extend the treatment of topics beyond the material presented. To further enhance the usefulness of the text, each chapter concludes with a bibliography of pertinent books, journal articles, and other media.

At the end of the textbook are four appendixes. Appendix A is a list of Exit Competencies, a summary of behaviors students should be able to demonstrate at the end of the course. Appendix B lists ERIC Clearinghouses; Appendix C, facilitators of the National Diffusion Network; and Appendix D, regional educational laboratories and research and development centers.

Many people have contributed to the writing and publishing of this book. Through their insights into curriculum and instruction, teachers, administrators, and students with whom I have worked helped shape my thinking. Also, I am particularly grateful to colleagues who reviewed the manuscript during its development. I wish to thank Charles M. Clarke, North Texas State University; Raymond B. Fox, Northern Illinois University; Alvin J. Stuart, Indiana University of Pennsylvania; Gordon F. Vars, Kent State University; and Truman Whitfield, Murray State University. Lastly, I wish to express my appreciation to Mylan Jaixen and Dana Norton, my editors at Little, Brown.

Brief Contents

Part I The Curriculum: Theoretical Dimensions   **1**
1 Curriculum and Instruction Defined   3
2 Principles of Curriculum Development   23

Part II Curriculum Development: Roles of School Personnel   **47**
3 Curriculum Planning: A Multilevel, Multisector Process   49
4 Curriculum Planning: The Human Dimension   102

Part III Curriculum Development: Components of the Process   **151**
5 Models for Curriculum Development   153
6 Aims of Education   175
7 Needs Assessment   207
8 Curriculum Goals and Objectives   248
9 Organizing and Implementing the Curriculum   276
10 Instructional Goals and Objectives   347
11 Selecting and Implementing Strategies of Instruction   374
12 Evaluating Instruction   402
13 Evaluating the Curriculum   427

Part IV Curriculum Development: Problems and Products   **453**
14 Problems in Curriculum Development   454
15 Curriculum Products   492

Appendix A   Exit Competencies   508

Appendix B   ERIC Clearinghouses   510

Appendix C   National Diffusion Network   513

Appendix D   Regional Educational Laboratories and
              Research and Development Centers   522

Index   531

Contents

Part I   The Curriculum: Theoretical Dimensions   **1**

1   Curriculum and Instruction Defined   **3**
Conceptions of Curriculum   4
    Certification and Curriculum   5   Interpretations of
    Curriculum   5   Definitions by Purposes, Contexts, and
    Strategies   8   Curriculum as a Plan for Experiences   10
Relationships Between Curriculum and Instruction   10
    Models of the Curriculum-Instruction Relationship   11
Curriculum as a Discipline   14
    The Characteristics of a Discipline   14
Curriculum Practitioners   18
    Curriculum Specialists   18   Teachers   19   Supervisors   19
    Role Variations   20
Summary   20

2   Principles of Curriculum Development   **23**
Clarification of Terms   24
Types of Curriculum Developers   26
Sources of Curriculum Principles   27
    Common Sense   27
Types of Principles   28
    Whole Truths   28   Partial Truths   29   Hypotheses   29
Ten Axioms   30
    Inevitability of Change   30   Curriculum as a Product of Its
    Time   31   Concurrent Changes   33   Change in People   36
    Cooperative Endeavor   37   Decision-Making Process   38
    Continuous Process   40   Comprehensive Process   40
    Systematic Development   41   Starting from the Existing
    Curriculum   42
Summary   42

Part II   Curriculum Development: Roles of School Personnel   47

3   Curriculum Planning: A Multilevel, Multisector Process   49

Illustrations of Curriculum Decisions   50
  *Variations Among Schools   50   Simultaneous
  Developments   51*

Levels of Planning   53
  Importance of Classroom Level   53   A Revised Step Model   55

Sectors of Planning   56
  *A Hierarchical Structure   57   Limitations of Hierarchical
  Structure   57*

Curriculum Efforts at the Various Levels   58
  *The Classroom Level   60   The Team, Grade, and Department
  Level   63   The School Level   70   The School-District
  Level   79   The State Level   85*

Sectors of Planning   89
  *The Regional Sector   89   The National Sector   90
  The International Sector   96*

Summary   99

4   Curriculum Planning: The Human Dimension   102

The School as a Unique Blend   103
  Differences Among Faculty   104   Dependent Variables   105

The Cast of Players   106
  *Role of the Administrator   106   Role of Students   110   Role
  of the Adult Citizens of the Community   112   Role of the
  Curriculum Workers   116   Role of the Teachers   117   Role
  of the Curriculum Leader   118*

The Curriculum Leader and Group Process   119
  *The Change Process   119   Interpersonal Relations   125
  Leadership Skills   134
  Communication Skills   141*

Summary   147

Part III   Curriculum Development: Components of the Process   151

5   Models for Curriculum Development   153

Selecting Models   154
  Variation in Models   154

Models of Curriculum Development 155
The Tyler Model 155 The Leyton Soto Model 159 The Taba Model 161 The Saylor and Alexander Model 164 Similarities and Differences Among Models 167 The Oliva Model 168
Summary 171

6 Aims of Education 175
Using the Proposed Article 176
Aims of Education 177
Proliferation of Terms 177 Global Aims 178 Statements of Purposes 179 Derivation of Aims 180 Statements by Prominent Individuals and Groups 182
Philosophies of Education 184
Reconstructionism 185 Perennialism 186 Essentialism 187 Progressivism 190
Formulating a Philosophy 198
Value in Writing a Philosophy 199 Problems in Developing and Implementing a Philosophy 200
Examples of School Philosophies 200
Summary 203

7 Needs Assessment 207
Categories of Needs 208
A Classification Scheme 209 Interests and Wants 210
Needs of Students: Levels 211
Human 211 National 212 State or Regional 212 Community 213 School 213 Individual 213
Needs of Students: Types 214
Physical 214 Sociopsychological 214 Educational 215 Developmental Tasks 215
Needs of Society: Levels 216
Human 216 International 216 National 217 State 219 Community 219 Neighborhood 220
Needs of Society: Types 221
Social Processes 221
Needs Derived from the Subject Matter 224
New Programs in the Disciplines 225 Minimal Competencies 227
Needs Assessment 228
Perceived Needs Approach 229 Data Collection 236 Steps in Conducting a Needs Assessment 237 A District-wide Assessment 239
Summary 244

8   Curriculum Goals and Objectives   **248**
Hierarchy of Outcomes   249
    Aims, Goals, and Objectives   250
Defining Goals and Objectives   252
    Curriculum Goals   252   Curriculum Objectives   254
    Examples of Curriculum Goals   254
Locus of Curriculum Goals and Objectives   254
    State Curriculum Goals and Objectives   256
Constructing Statements of Curriculum Goals   264
    Characteristics of Curriculum Goals   264
Constructing Statements of Curriculum Objectives   265
    Elements of Curriculum Objectives   265
Validating and Prioritizing Goals and Objectives   266
    Function of Curriculum Committee   267
Summary   272

9   Organizing and Implementing the Curriculum   **276**
Necessary Decisions   277
    A Hypothetical Setting   277   Hypothetical Steps   277
    Assessing Curriculum Organization   278
Where We Have Been   280
The Elementary School   280
    The Graded School   280   The Activity Curriculum   282
    The Nongraded Elementary School   286
The Junior High School   290
    The School in the Middle   290   The Core Curriculum   292
The Senior High School   298
    The Subject Matter Curriculum   298   Broad-Fields
    Curriculum   304   Team Teaching   306   Flexible
    Scheduling   309   The Nongraded High School   314
Where We Are   317
The Elementary School   317
    Open Education and Open Space   317
The Junior High School   326
    A School in Transition   326
The Senior High School   328
    A Comprehensive High School   328
Where We Are Going   331
The Elementary School   331
    Return to Traditional Modes   331
The Junior High School   331
    The Middle School   331
The Senior High School   335
    Some Alternatives   335   What Is in the Distant Future   340
Summary   341

10   Instructional Goals and Objectives   **347**
Planning for Instruction   348
  The Instructional Model   349
Instructional Goals and Objectives Defined   350
  Stating Objectives   351
The Use of Behavioral Objectives   352
  Problems with Behavioral Objectives   353
Guidelines for Preparing Instructional Goals and Objectives   354
  Relationship to Curriculum Goals and Objectives   354
  Domains of Learning   356
Taxonomic Levels   358
  Cognitive Taxonomy   360   Affective Taxonomy   360
  Psychomotor Taxonomies   362
Rules for Writing   363
  Three Elements of an Instructional Objective   364
Validating and Prioritizing Instructional Goals and Objectives   368
Summary   369

11   Selecting and Implementing Strategies of Instruction   **374**
Deciding on Instructional Strategies   375
Sources of Strategies   376
  Objectives As Source   376   Subject Matter As Source   377
  Student As Source   378   Community As Source   379
  Teacher As Source   380   Guidelines for Selecting
  Strategies   380
Styles of Teaching   381
Styles of Learning   383
Models of Teaching   385
  Need for Variety   387
Teaching Skills   388
  Generic Competencies   389
Organizing for Instruction   391
  Unit Plans   392   Lesson Plans   393
Summary   397

12   Evaluating Instruction   **402**
Assessing Instruction   403
  Assessing Student Achievement   403   Cycle Within a
  Cycle   404
An Era of Assessment   404
  The National Assessment of Educational Progress   406   State
  Assessment Programs   406   Definition of Terms   407
Stages of Planning for Evaluation   408
  Expanded Model of Instruction   408   Three Phases of
  Evaluation   409

Norm-Referenced and Criterion-Referenced Measurement   411
   Norm-Referenced Measurement 411   Criterion-Referenced
   Measurement 412   Comparison of the Two Types of
   Measurement 413
Evaluation in Three Domains   415
   Psychomotor Domain 416   Cognitive Domain 417
   Affective Domain 419
Other Means of Evaluation   421
   Feedback 421
Summary   422

13   **Evaluating the Curriculum**   **427**
Purposes and Problems of Curriculum Evaluation   428
   Problems in Evaluation 428
Delimiting Evaluation   431
   Differences Between Instructional and Curriculum Evaluation 431
   Difference Between Evaluation and Research 432
Evaluation Models   433
   The Saylor and Alexander Model 434   The CIPP Model 441
   Model with Types of Evaluation 446   Standards for
   Evaluation 448
Summary   449

Part IV   Curriculum Development: Problems and Products   453

14   **Problems in Curriculum Development**   **454**
Continuing Problems   455
   Scope 455   Relevance 460   Balance 462
   Integration 466   Sequence 468   Continuity 472
   Articulation 473   Transferability 475   Implications of the
   Continuing Curriculum Problems 477
Current Curriculum Problems   478
   The Back-to-Basics Movement 478   Minimal
   Competencies 479   Integration of the Races 480
   Sexism 481   Programs for the Handicapped 482
   Bilingual Education 483   Censorship 484
The Impact of Professional Problems upon Curriculum   485
   Teacher Organizations 485   Improved Dissemination 486
   Improved Research 487   Improved Preparation 487
Summary   487

15 Curriculum Products   **492**
Tangible Products   493
Curriculum Guides, Courses of Study, and Syllabi   494
    Curriculum Guide   495
Resource Unit   500
Sources of Curriculum Materials   501
Summary   501

Appendix A   Exit Competencies   **508**

Appendix B   ERIC Clearinghouses   **510**

Appendix C   National Diffusion Network   **513**

**Appendix D   Regional Educational Laboratories and Research
and Development Centers**   **522**

Index   **531**

Part I

The Curriculum:
Theoretical Dimensions

1

Curriculum and Instruction Defined

After studying this chapter you should be able to:
1. Define curriculum.
2. Define instruction.
3. Explain in what ways curriculum can be considered a discipline.
4. Create a model of the relationship between curriculum and instruction and describe your creation.

You should also be able to formulate and give reasons for your views on the following issues:
1. Whether it makes any difference which definition of curriculum planners adopt.
2. Whether you believe curriculum should be an area of specialization certifiable by the state.

CONCEPTIONS OF CURRICULUM

Marcus Tullius Cicero and his cohorts of the first century before Christ had no idea that the oval track upon which the Roman chariots raced would bequeath a word used almost daily by educators twenty-one centuries later. That track — *the curriculum* — has become one of the key concerns of today's school personnel and its meaning has expanded from a race course to an abstract concept.

In the world of professional education, the word "curriculum" has taken on an elusive, almost esoteric connotation. This poetic, neuter word does possess an aura of mystery. By contrast other dimensions of the world of professional education like administra*tion,* instruc*tion,* and supervi*sion* are strong, action-oriented words. Administration is the *act* of administering; instruction is the *act* of instructing; and supervision is the *act* of supervising. Everyone both inside and outside the profession understands at least in broad terms what it is to administer, what it is to instruct, and what it is to supervise.

But in what way is "curriculum" an act? While administrators administer, instructors instruct, and supervisors supervise, no school person curricules and it is only a rare individual who curricularizes.

The quest for a definition of curriculum has taxed many an educator. Dwayne Huebner ascribed ambiguity and a lack of precision to the term "curriculum."[1] Indeed, curriculum seems at times analogous to the blind men's elephant. It is the pachyderm's trunk to some; its thick legs to others; its pterodactyl-like flopping ears to some people; its massive, rough sides to other persons; and its ropelike tail to still others.

Though it may be vehemently denied, no one has ever seen a curriculum, not a real, total, tangible, visible entity called a curriculum. The interested observer may have seen a written plan that may have been called a curriculum. Somehow the observer knows, probably by word of mouth, that in every school in which teachers are instructing students a curriculum exists. A written plan provides the observer with an additional clue to the existence of a certain something called a curriculum. But if by some bit of magic the observer could lift the roof of a school in session and examine the cross-section thereof, the curriculum would not be apparent. What the observer would immediately perceive would be many instances of teacher-pupil interaction which we call *instruction.*

The search for evidence of the mysterious creation that we call curriculum is not unlike efforts to track down Bigfoot, the Yeti, or the Loch Ness Monster. Both Bigfoot and the Yeti have left their tracks in the mud and the snow and Nessie has rippled the waters of its lagoon but no cameraperson has yet succeeded in photographing these suspected monsters. Nor has anyone ever pho-

---

[1] Dwayne Huebner, "The Moribund Curriculum Field; Its Wake and Our Work," *Curriculum Inquiry* 6, no. 2 (1976): 156.

tographed a curriculum. Shutterbugs have instead photographed pupils, teachers, and other school personnel. Perhaps if someone photographed every instance of behavior in every classroom, corridor, office, and auxiliary room of a school every day and then investigated this record as thoroughly as military leaders analyze air reconnaisance photos, a curriculum could be deduced.

Certification and Curriculum

State certification laws compound the problem of defining curriculum, as few if any professionals can become certified in "curriculum." Whereas all professionals in training must take courses of one type or other called "curriculum," there is not a certifiable field labeled "curriculum." Professionals are certified in administration, guidance, supervision, school psychology, elementary education, and many fields of teaching. But in "curriculum" per se? Not as a rule, although preparation in the field of curriculum is a required part of certification for certain fields of specialization, as administration and supervision.

Despite this phenomenon, numbers of curriculum workers, consultants, coordinators, and even professors of curriculum can be identified. These specialists, even though they may be certified in one or more fields, cannot customarily hang on the wall a certificate which shows that state approval has been granted in a field called "curriculum."

While a certifiable field of specialization called curriculum may be lacking, the word itself is treated as if it had tangible substance, for it can undergo a substantial variety of processes. Curriculum — or its plural, curricula or curriculums (depending on the user's penchant or abhorrence for the Latin) — is built, planned, designed, and constructed. It is improved, evaluated, and revised. Like photographic film and muscles, the curriculum is developed. It is also organized and, like a wayward child, reformed. With considerable ingenuity the curriculum planner — another specialist — can mold, shape, and tailor the curriculum.

Interpretations of Curriculum

The amorphous nature of the word curriculum has given rise over the years to many interpretations. Depending on their philosophical beliefs, persons have conveyed these interpretations, among others.

- □ Curriculum is that which is taught in school.
- □ Curriculum is a set of subjects.
- □ Curriculum is content.
- □ Curriculum is a program of studies.
- □ Curriculum is a set of materials.
- □ Curriculum is a sequence of courses.
- □ Curriculum is a set of performance objectives.
- □ Curriculum is a course of study.

□ Curriculum is everything that goes on within the school, including extra-class activities, guidance, and interpersonal relationships.
□ Curriculum is that which is taught both inside and outside of school directed by the school.
□ Curriculum is everything that is planned by school personnel.
□ Curriculum is a series of experiences undergone by learners in school.
□ Curriculum is that which an individual learner experiences as a result of schooling.

In the foregoing definitions it is apparent that curriculum can be conceived in a narrow way (as subjects taught) or in a broad way (as all the experiences of learners both in school and out directed by the school). The implications for the school to be drawn from the differing conceptions of curriculum can vary considerably. The school that accepts the definition of curriculum as a set of subjects faces a much simpler task than the school that takes upon itself responsibilities for experiences of the learner both inside and outside of school.

A variety of nuances *is* perceived when the professional educators define curriculum. The first definition, for example, given in Carter V. Good's *Dictionary of Education* describes curriculum as "a systematic group of courses or sequences of subjects required for graduation or certification in a major field of study, for example, social studies curriculum, physical education curriculum...." [2]

Hollis L. Caswell and Doak S. Campbell viewed curriculum not as a group of courses but as "all the experiences children have under the guidance of teachers." [3] J. Galen Saylor and William M. Alexander in 1954 defined curriculum in a light that could be interpreted even more broadly. They said:

> ... the school curriculum is the total effort of the school to bring about desired outcomes in school and in out-of-school situations. ... The curriculum is the sum total of the school's efforts to influence learning, whether in the classroom, on the playground or out of school. [4]

It is of interest to note that Saylor and Alexander refined their definition of curriculum in later years, for they said in 1974:

> Specifically, we define curriculum as the plan for providing sets of learning opportunities to achieve broad goals and related specific objectives for an identifiable population served by a single school center. [5]

---

[2] Carter V. Good, ed. *Dictionary of Education,* 3rd ed. (New York: McGraw-Hill, 1973), p. 157.
[3] Hollis L. Caswell and Doak S. Campbell, *Curriculum Development* (New York: American Book Company, 1935), p. 66.
[4] J. Galen Saylor and William M. Alexander, *Curriculum Planning for Better Teaching and Learning* (New York: Holt, Rinehart and Winston, 1954), pp. 4–5.
[5] J. Gaylen Saylor and William M. Alexander, *Planning Curriculum for Schools* (New York: Holt, Rinehart and Winston, 1974), p. 6.

The more recent Saylor and Alexander definition parallels the one given by Hilda Taba in a discussion of criteria for curriculum development: "A curriculum is a plan for learning." [6] She defined curriculum by listing its elements:

All curricula, no matter what their particular design, are composed of certain elements. A curriculum usually contains a statement of aims and of specific objectives; it indicates some selection and organization of content; it either implies or manifests certain patterns of learning and teaching, whether because the objectives demand them or because the content organization requires them. Finally, it includes a program of evaluation of the outcomes.[7]

Ronald C. Doll defined the curriculum of a school as:

. . . the formal and informal content and process by which learners gain knowledge and understanding, develop skills, and alter attitudes, appreciations, and values under the auspices of that school.[8]

Daniel Tanner and Laurel N. Tanner proposed the following definition:

The authors regard curriculum as *that reconstruction of knowledge and experience, systematically developed under the auspices of the school (or university), to enable the learner to increase his or her control of knowledge and experience.*[9]

Albert I. Oliver equated curriculum with the educational program, and divided it into four basic elements: "(1) the program of studies, (2) the program of experiences, (3) the program of services, and (4) the hidden curriculum." [10]

The program of studies, experiences, and services are readily apparent. To these elements Oliver has added the concept of a hidden curriculum, which encompasses values promoted by the school, differing emphases given by different teachers within the same subject areas, the degree of enthusiasm of teachers, and the physical and social climate of the school.

Arthur W. Foshay identified not one but three curricula of the school: the academic disciplines and extraclass activities, which are given the most

---

[6] Hilda Taba, *Curriculum Development: Theory and Practice* (New York: Harcourt, Brace, Jovanovich, 1962), p. 11.

[7] Taba, p. 10.

[8] Ronald C. Doll, *Curriculum Improvement: Decision Making and Process,* 4th ed. (Boston: Allyn and Bacon, 1978), p. 6.

[9] Daniel Tanner and Laurel N. Tanner, *Curriculum Development: Theory Into Practice,* 2d ed. (New York: Macmillan, 1980), p. 43.

[10] Albert I. Oliver, *Curriculum Improvement: A Guide to Problems, Principles, and Process,* 2d ed. (New York: Harper & Row, 1977), p. 8.

attention; problems of participation in social decisions; and activities related to self-development.[11]

A different approach to defining curriculum was taken by Robert M. Gagné, who wove together subject matter (content), the statement of ends (terminal objectives), sequencing of content, and preassessment of entry skills required of students when they begin the study of the content.[12] Mauritz Johnson Jr. agreed basically with Gagné when he defined curriculum as a "structured series of intended learning outcomes." [13] Johnson perceived curriculum as "the output of a 'curriculum development system' and as an input into an 'instructional system'." [14]

Definitions by Purposes, Contexts, and Strategies

Differences in substance of definitions of curriculum, while they exist, are not as great or as common as differences in what the curriculum theorists include in their conceptions of the term. Some theorists elaborate more than others. Some combine elements of both curriculum and instruction, a conceptual problem that this chapter later examines. Others find a definition of curriculum in (1) purposes or goals of the curriculum, (2) contexts within which the curriculum is found, or (3) strategies used throughout the curriculum.

Purposes. The search for a definition of curriculum is clouded when the theoretician responds to the term not in the context of what curriculum *is* but what it *does* or *should do,* that is, its purpose. On the purposes of the curriculum we can find many varying statements.

When curriculum is conceptualized as "the development of reflective thinking on the part of the learner" or as "the transmission of the cultural heritage," purpose is confused with entity. This concept could be stated more correctly: "The purpose of the curriculum is transmission of the cultural heritage" or "The purpose of the curriculum is the development of reflective thinking on the part of the learner." A statement of what the curriculum is meant to achieve does little to help us sharpen a definition of what curriculum is.

Contexts. Definitions of curriculum sometimes state the settings within which it takes shape. When theoreticians speak of an essentialist curriculum, a child-centered curriculum, or a reconstructionist curriculum, they are signalling two characteristics of the curriculum at the same time — purpose and context.

---

[11] Arthur W. Foshay, *Curriculum for the 70's: An Agenda for Invention* (Washington, D. C.: National Education Association, 1970), pp. 28–32.

[12] See Robert M. Gagné, "Curriculum Research and the Promotion of Learning," *AERA Monograph Series on Evaluation: Perspectives of Curriculum Evaluation,* no. 1. (Chicago: Rand McNally, 1967), p. 21.

[13] Mauritz Johnson, Jr., "'Definitions and Models in Curriculum Theory," *Educational Theory* 17, no. 2 (April 1967): 130.

[14] Johnson, p. 133.

For example, an essentialistic curriculum is designed to transmit the cultural heritage, to school young people in the organized disciplines, and to prepare boys and girls for the future. This curriculum arises from a special philosophical context, that of the essentialistic school of philosophy.

A child-centered curriculum clearly reveals its orientation — the learner, who is the primary focus of the progressive school of philosophy. The development of the individual learner in all aspects of growth may be inferred but the plans for that development may vary considerably from school to school. The curriculum of a school following reconstructionist philosophical beliefs aims to educate youth in such a way that they will be capable of solving some of society's pressing problems and therefore change society for the better. Again we see a particular orientation or context within which the curriculum is lodged.

Strategies. While purpose and context are sometimes offered as definitions of curriculum, an additional complexity arises when the theoretician equates curriculum with instructional strategy. Some theoreticians isolate certain instructional variables such as processes, strategies, and techniques and then proceed to equate them with curriculum. The curriculum as a problem-solving process illustrates an attempt to define curriculum in terms of an instructional process — problem-solving techniques, the scientific method, or reflective thinking. The curriculum as group living, for example, is an effort at definition built around certain instructional techniques that must be used to provide opportunities for group living. The curriculum as individualized learning and the curriculum as programmed instruction are, in reality, specification of systems by which the learners encounter curricular content through the process of instruction. Neither purpose, context, nor strategy provides a clear basis for defining curriculum.

In a class by itself is the definition of curriculum as ends or terminal objectives. W. James Popham and Eva L. Baker classified curriculum as ends and instruction as means when they said: "Curriculum is all the planned learning outcomes for which the school is responsible." [15] In designing the curriculum, planners would cast these outcomes or objectives in operational or behavioral terms.

The operational or behavioral objectives are, in effect, instructional objectives. According to the proponents of behavioral objectives, a compilation of all the behavioral objectives of all the programs and activities of the school would constitute the curriculum. The curriculum then would be the sum total of all instructional objectives. As we will see in Chapter 8, distinguishing between curricular goals and objectives and instructional goals and objectives is an important preparatory step for designing curriculum.

---

[15] W. James Popham and Eva L. Baker, *Systematic Instruction* (Englewood Cliffs, N.J.: Prentice-Hall, 1970), p. 48.

Both curriculum goals and objectives and instructional goals and objectives can be specified in behavioral terms. Some advocates of behavioral objectives seem comfortable with the notion that once the terminal objectives (the ends) are clearly specified, the curriculum has been defined. From that point on instruction takes over. This view of curriculum as specification of objectives is quite different, for example, from the concept of the curriculum as a plan, a program, or a sequence of courses.[16]

Curriculum as a Plan for Experiences

In an earlier work, I defined curriculum for elementary and secondary schools as "all the experiences a young person encounters under the direction of the school." [17] To convey the concept of the curriculum as a plan and to include the adult learner, this definition could be modified slightly to view curriculum as "a plan or program for all the experiences which the learner encounters under the direction of the school." This modification injects the notion of a curriculum as a plan or more realistically, plans, which should be, however tentative, in written form and not simply in the head of the planner. While the curriculum should encompass "all experiences under the direction of the school," a number of plans of varying scope will be necessary to achieve that goal. The curriculum, therefore, may be a unit, a course, a sequence of courses, the school's entire program of studies — and may take place outside of class or school when directed by the personnel of the school.

RELATIONSHIPS BETWEEN CURRICULUM AND INSTRUCTION

In the search for clarifying the meaning of curriculum we have found uncertainty about the distinctions between curriculum and instruction and their relationships to each other. We may simplistically view curriculum as that which is taught and instruction as the means used to teach that which is taught. Even more simply, curriculum can be conceived as the "what" and instruction, the "how." We may think of the curriculum as a program, plan, content, and learning experiences whereas we may characterize instruction as methodology, the teaching act, implementation, and presentation.

Distinguishing instruction from curriculum, Johnson defined instruction as "the interaction between a teaching agent and one or more individuals intending to learn." [18] James B. Macdonald viewed curricular activity as the production of plans for further action and instruction as the putting of plans

---

16 See, for example, Gagné, *Curriculum Research.*
17 Peter F. Oliva, *The Secondary School Today,* 2d ed. (New York: Harper & Row, 1972), p. 81.
18 Johnson, p. 138. See also Saylor, Alexander, and Lewis, *Curriculum Planning for Better Teaching and Learning,* 4th ed. (New York: Holt, Rinehart and Winston, 1981), pp. 9–10 for definition of instruction.

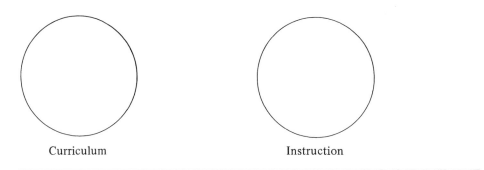

FIGURE 1-1   The dualistic model

into operation. Thus, according to Macdonald, curriculum planning precedes instruction.[19]

In the course of planning for either the curriculum or instruction, decisions are made. Decisions about the curriculum relate to plans or programs and thus are *programmatic,* while those about instruction (and thereby implementation) are *methodological.* We may consider both curriculum and instruction as two subsystems or subdimensions of a larger system or enterprise called schooling or education.

Models of the Curriculum-Instruction Relationship

Definitions of the two terms are valuable but can obscure the interdependence of these two subsystems. They may be recognized as two entities but like Siamese twins who are joined together, one may not function without the other. That the relationship between the "what" and the "how" of education is not easily determined can be seen in several different models of this relationship. For lack of better terminology, the following labels are coined for these models: (1) dualistic model; (2) interlocking model; (3) concentric models; (4) cyclical model.

Dualistic Model. We might depict the dualistic model as shown in Figure 1-1. Curriculum sits on one side and instruction on the other and never the twain shall meet. Between the two entities lies a great gulf. What takes place in the classroom under the direction of the teacher seems to have little relationship to what the master plan says should go on in the classroom. The planners ignore the instructors and in turn are ignored by them. Discussions of curriculum are divorced from their practical application to the classroom. Under this model the curriculum or the instructional process may change without significantly affecting one another.

19 James B. Macdonald and Robert R. Leeper, eds., *Theories of Instruction* (Alexandria, Va.: Association for Supervision and Curriculum Development, 1965), pp. 5–6.

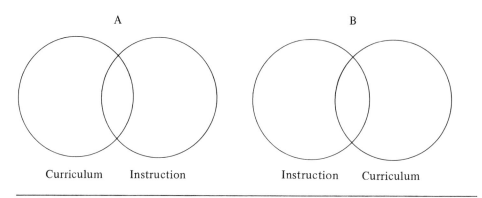

FIGURE 1-2   The interlocking model

Interlocking Model. When curriculum and instruction are shown as systems entwined, an interlocking relationship exists (see Figure 1-2).

We can depict this model in one of two ways as indicated by sketches A and B.

No particular significance is given to the position of instruction or curriculum in each version of this model. The same relationship is implied whether one appears on the left or the right. These models clearly demonstrate an integrated relationship between these two entities. The separation of one from the other would do serious harm to both.

It would be difficult for a curriculum planner to regard instruction as paramount to curriculum and to determine teaching methods before program objectives. Nevertheless, some faculties proceed as if instruction were primary by dispensing with advance planning of the curriculum and by letting it more or less develop as it unfolds in the classroom.

Concentric Models. The preceding models of the relationship between curriculum and instruction reveal varying degrees of independence from complete detachment to interlocking relationships. Mutual dependence is the key feature of concentric models. Two conceptions of the curriculum-instruction relationship can be sketched that show one as the subsystem of the other (see Figure 1-3). Both variation A and B convey the idea that one of the entities occupies a superordinate position while the other is subordinate.

Concentric model A makes instruction a subsystem of curriculum, which is itself a subsystem of the whole system of education. Concentric model B subsumes curriculum within the subsystem, instruction. A clear hierarchical relationship comes through in both these models. Curriculum is superior in model A while instruction is superior in model B. In model A instruction is not a separate entity but a very dependent portion of the entity, curriculum. Model B makes curriculum subservient to and derivative from the more global instruction.

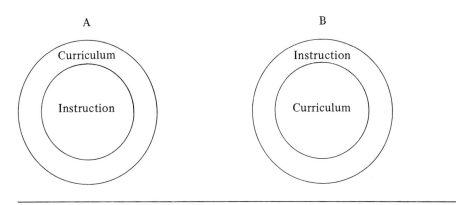

FIGURE 1-3   Concentric models

Cyclical Model. The cyclical conception of the curriculum-instruction relationship is a simplified systems model which stresses the essential element of feedback. Curriculum and instruction are separate entities with a continuing circular relationship. Curriculum makes a continuous impact on instruction and, vice versa, instruction impacts on curriculum. This relationship can be schematically represented as in Figure 1-4. This cyclical model implies that instructional decisions are made after curricular decisions which in turn are modified after instructional decisions are implemented and evaluated. This process is continuous, repetitious, and never-ending. The evaluation of instructional procedures affects the next round of curricular decision making, which again affects instructional implementation. While curriculum and instruction are diagrammed as separate entities, following this model they are not to be conceived as separate entities but as parts of a sphere — a circle that revolves, causing continuous adaptations and improvements of both entities.

Each curriculum-instruction model has its champions who espouse it in part or in whole, in theory or in practice. Yet how can we account for these numerous conceptions and how do we know which is the "right" one to hold?

FIGURE 1-4   The cyclical model

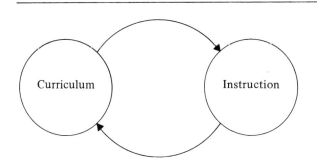

Common Beliefs. As newer developments occur in education, as research adds new insights on teaching and learning, as new ideas are developed, and as times change, beliefs about curriculum and instruction also undergo transformation. The "rightness" or "wrongness" of concepts like curriculum and instruction cannot be established by an individual educator or even by a group of educators. One index of "correctness" might be the prevailing opinion of most educators at a particular stage in history — a rather pragmatic but nevertheless viable and defensible position. Though no one to my knowledge has made a count of prevailing postulates regarding curriculum and instruction, it appears that most theoreticians today agree that:

- Curriculum and instruction are related but different.
- Curriculum and instruction are interlocking and interdependent.
- Curriculum and instruction may be studied and analyzed as separate entities but cannot function in mutual isolation.

The dualistic conceptual model of the relationship between curriculum and instruction with its separation of the two entities and concentric models that make one a subsystem of the other pose, in my judgment, serious problems.

Some curriculum workers feel comfortable with an interlocking model since it shows a close relationship between the two entities. Of all the curriculum-instruction models that have crossed my path, however, the cyclical has much to recommend it for its simplicity and for its stress on the need for continuous feedback of each entity on the other.

CURRICULUM AS A DISCIPLINE

In spite of its elusive character, curriculum is viewed by many, including myself, as a discipline — a subject of study — and even, on the graduate level of higher education, as a teaching field. Curriculum is then both a field within which people work and a subject to be taught. Graduate students take courses in curriculum development, curriculum theory, curriculum evaluation, secondary school curriculum, elementary school curriculum, middle school curriculum, junior high school curriculum, community college curriculum, and on rare occasions, university curriculum.

Can there be a discipline called curriculum? Are the many college courses in curriculum mere frosting, as some of the critics of teacher education maintain, or is there cake beneath the surface? Is there a curriculum field or occupation in which and to which persons can devote their lives?

The Characteristics of a Discipline

To arrive at a decision as to whether an area of study is a discipline, the question might be raised, "What are the characteristics of a discipline?" If the characteristics of a discipline could be spelled out, it could be determined whether curriculum, for example, was a discipline or not.

Principles. *Any discipline worthy of study has an organized set of theoretical constructs or principles that govern it.* Certainly, the field of curriculum has developed a significant number of principles, tried and untried, proved and unproved, many of which are appropriately the subjects of discussion in this text. Balance in the curriculum, discussed in Chapter 14, is a construct or concept. Curriculum itself is a construct or concept, a verbalization of an extremely complex idea or set of ideas. Using the constructs of balance and curriculum, we can derive a principle or rule which, stated in simple terms, says, "A curriculum that provides maximum opportunities for learners incorporates the concept of balance." Sequencing of courses, career education, open-space education, behavioral objectives, and a systems approach to teaching reading are examples of constructs incorporated into one or more curriculum principles.

A major characteristic of any theoretical principle is its capacity for being generalized and applied in more than one situation. Were curriculum theories but one-shot solutions to specific problems, it would be difficult to defend the concept of curriculum as a discipline. But the principles of curriculum theory are often successful efforts to establish rules which can be repeated in similar situations and under similar conditions. It is not difficult to secure agreement, for example, that the concept of balance should be incorporated into every curriculum. There is more controversy over a principle which might be stated as "The first step in curriculum planning is the specification of behavioral objectives." Though some maintain that this principle has become universal practice and therefore might be labeled "truth," it is being tested, validated, and argued in schools throughout the country. It has been rejected by some schools, tried and accepted by others, and tried and abandoned by still others.

Knowledge and Skills. *Any discipline encompasses a body of knowledge and skills pertinent to that discipline.* The field of curriculum has adapted and borrowed subject matter from a number of pure and derived disciplines. Figure 1-5 schematically shows the areas from which the field of curriculum has borrowed constructs, principles, knowledge, and skills. Selection of content for study by students, for example, cannot be done without referring to the disciplines of sociology, psychology, philosophy, and subject areas. Organization of the curriculum depends upon knowledge from organizational theory and management, which are aspects of administration. The fields of supervision, systems theory, technology, and communications theory are called on in the process of curriculum development. Knowledge from many fields is selected and adapted by the curriculum field.

The "child-centered curriculum" as a concept draws heavily on what is known about learning, growth, and development (psychology and biology), on philosophy (particularly from one school of philosophy, progressivism),

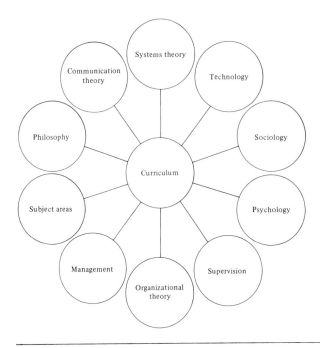

FIGURE 1-5   Sources of the curriculum field

and on sociology. The "essentialist curriculum" borrows from the subject areas philosophy, psychology, and sociology.

It might be asked whether the field of curriculum contributes any knowledge of its own to that borrowed from other disciplines. Certainly, a good deal of thinking and research is going on in the name of curriculum. New curricular ideas are being generated continuously. These ideas, whether they be the systems approach, computer-assisted instruction, or behavioral objectives, to mention but three fairly recent concepts, borrow heavily from other disciplines.

The skills utilized by curriculum specialists are also borrowed from other fields. Let's take an example from the field of social psychology. It is generally accepted that a curriculum changes only when the people affected have changed. This principle, drawn from the field of social psychology and applied in the field of curriculum development, was, perhaps, most dramatically demonstrated by the Western Electric researches conducted by industry in the 1930s.[20] Here researchers discovered that factory workers assembling telephone relays were more productive when they were consulted and made to

---

[20] See F. J. Roethlisberger and William J. Dickson, *Management and the Worker* (Cambridge, Mass.: Harvard University Press, 1939) for discussion of the Western Electric researches.

feel of value to the organization. Making the workers feel important resulted in greater productivity than manipulating the physical environment, e.g., lighting in the factory. The feeling of being a part of the research studies also created its own aura, which we call the Hawthorne Effect, named for Western Electric's Hawthorne plant in Chicago. Since the feeling of involvement can in itself contribute to high productivity, this effect is one which researchers learn to discount for it can obscure the hypothesized or real causes for change. It is worth pointing out, however, that the educational practitioner aware of the Hawthorne Effect may take advantage of it to promote learning.

As an added illustration, it can be postulated that an instructional leader, let's call him or her a supervisor, is the person who acts as a catalyst or agent for bringing about change in people. How does the supervisor do this? He or she makes use of knowledge and skills from a number of fields: communications theory, psychology of groups, and other areas. How does the supervisor help teachers to carry out the change once they have subscribed to it? He or she applies principles and skills from management, from knowledge of the structure of disciplines, and from other areas.

Consequently, we can conclude that the field of curriculum requires the use of an amalgamation of knowledge and skills from many disciplines. That curriculum theory and practice are derived from other disciplines does not in any way diminish the importance of the field. The observation of its derived nature simply characterizes its essence. Curriculum's synthesis of elements from many fields in some ways makes it both a demanding and exciting area in which to work.

In a cyclical fashion the derived discipline of "curriculum" in turn makes its own potent impact upon the disciplines from which it is derived. Through curricular research, experimentation, and application, subject areas are modified; learning theories are corroborated, revised, or rejected; administrative and supervisory techniques are implemented or changed; and philosophical positions are subjected to examination.

Theoreticians and Practitioners. *A discipline has its theoreticians and its practitioners.* Certainly, the field of curriculum has an array of workers travailing in its name. We have already mentioned some of the titles these workers go by: planners, consultants, coordinators, directors, professors of curriculum, to recall but a few. We can include them all under the generic title of curriculum worker or curriculum specialist.

The curriculum specialist makes a number of distinctive contributions to his or her field. The specialist knows what types of curricula have worked in the past, under what conditions, and with what success. Since the name of the game is improvement, the specialist must be well-grounded in the historical development of the curriculum and must possess the capacity to use that knowledge to help the schools avoid historic pitfalls.

The curriculum specialist generates or helps to generate new curriculum concepts. In this capacity the specialist draws on the past and conceives new arrangements, new combinations, and recombinations of programs, adaptations of existing approaches, or completely new approaches. Alternative forms of schooling, for example, are new arrangements and approaches for the same general goal-education of the young.

While curriculum specialists are indulging in the "big think," hoping to bring to light new theories — a worthy goal not to be dismissed lightly — other, and perhaps more, curriculum specialists are experts in application. They know techniques of curriculum planning that are most likely to result in higher achievement on the part of learners. They are familiar with variations in organizational patterns. Not only must they be knowledgeable but creative and able to spark innovations that give promise of bringing about higher achievement in learners.

In its day the "core" curriculum, for example, was a promising, creative innovation. In one of its shapes the core curriculum, which we will discuss in Chapter 9, fused English and social studies into a block of time — ordinarily two to three periods — at the junior high school level, using content based on adolescent needs and interests. But was this innovative concept truly original, unique to the field of curriculum or was it adapted and drawn from a variety of disciplines? Examination of the subconcepts of the core curriculum shows that it owed a great deal to other disciplines. The adolescent needs base followed in some core programs came from student-centered, progressive learning theories as did the problem-solving approach utilized in instruction. One reason for the inauguration of the core curriculum in schools in the 1930s and 1940s could be attributed to dissatisfaction with the subject matter curriculum as evidenced by, among other factors, the low holding power of schools of the times.

CURRICULUM PRACTITIONERS

Curriculum Specialists

Curriculum specialists often make a unique contribution by creatively transforming theory and knowledge into practice. Through their efforts a new, at first experimental, approach gradually becomes a widespread practice. Curriculum specialists also examine and reexamine theory and knowledge from their field and related fields. Aware of past successes and failures, today they will rarely recommend a core curriculum as a current response to demands for a relevant education.

The curriculum specialist is in the best position to stimulate research on curricular problems. The possibility of research is another characteristic of a discipline. The specialist carries out and encourages study of curricular problems, comparisons of plans and programs, results of new patterns of curriculum organization, and history of curriculum experiments, to indicate but a few areas of research. The specialist encourages the use of results of research to continue efforts to improve the curriculum.

While classroom teachers daily concern themselves with problems of curriculum and instruction, the curriculum specialist is charged with the task of providing leadership to the teachers. Since there are so many different types of specialists in so many different locations, it is difficult to generalize their roles. Some curriculum workers are generalists whose roles may be limited to leadership in curricular or programmatic planning or whose roles may also encompass instructional planning and decision making.

Some curriculum workers confine their spheres of action to certain levels or subjects, as secondary school curriculum, elementary school curriculum, community college curriculum, special education, science education, early childhood education, and others. What can be observed is that the roles the curriculum specialist plays are shaped by the job, by the specialist's administrator, and by the specialist himself or herself. At varying times the curriculum specialist must be:

- □ a philosopher
- □ a psychologist
- □ a sociologist
- □ a supervisor
- □ a human relations expert
- □ a conceptual idea person (theoretician)
- □ an historian
- □ a scholar in one or more disciplines
- □ an evaluator
- □ a researcher
- □ an instructor
- □ a systems analyst

Teachers

Up to this point we have talked mainly of the curriculum specialists and their place in the scheme of a field called curriculum. We must not deemphasize that even numerically larger group of professionals — the teachers. Just as the curriculum specialist works primarily in the curriculum realm of that continuum which we call curriculum-instruction and secondarily in the instructional realm, so too the teacher works primarily in one realm (instructional) and secondarily in the other (curriculum).

The teacher, too, is a curriculum worker who engages in curriculum planning in varying degrees in varying settings, on different occasions, generally under the leadership of a specialist, be that person a coordinator, consultant, supervisor, team leader, department head, or assistant principal. How the teacher-instructor and the curriculum specialist work together in the two fields of curriculum and instruction is a recurrent theme of this book.

Supervisors

An additional clarification should be made at this point — that is, the relationship between the roles of persons designated as curriculum workers or specialists and those persons who are called supervisors. Some consider the titles synonymous.

In this text a *supervisor* is perceived as a specialist who works in three domains: instructional development, curriculum development, and teacher development.[21] When the supervisor works in the first two domains, he or she is a curriculum specialist. Thus, the curriculum worker or specialist is a particular type of supervisor, one with more limited responsibilities than a "complete" supervisor. Both the curriculum specialist and the supervisor fulfill similar roles when they work with teachers in curriculum development and instructional development, but the curriculum specialist is not primarily concerned with such activities as organizing inservice programs and evaluating teachers, which are more properly responsibilities of the supervisor.

Role Variations

As with so many jobs within the field of education it is difficult to draw firm lines that apply under all conditions and in all situations. To understand more fully the roles and functions of educational personnel, local practice must be examined. Teachers, curriculum specialists, and supervisors all engage in activities to improve both the curriculum and instruction. At times their roles are different and at other times their roles are similar. These personnel, all specialists in their own right, frequently trade places to accomplish the task of improvement. Sometimes they are one and the same person — the teacher who is his or her own curriculum specialist and supervisor. Other times they are two persons — the teacher and curriculum specialist/ supervisor. At still other times they are a team of three — the teacher, the curriculum specialist, and the supervisor. Whatever the structure of leadership for the improvement of curriculum and instruction, all teachers and all specialists must ultimately participate in this challenging task. Since curriculum and instruction are the mind and heart of schooling, all personnel, all students, and the community as well participate in the improvement of what is offered in the school and how it is implemented.

In Chapters 3 and 4 we will examine at length roles of personnel involved in curriculum development, including teachers, students, department heads, team leaders, administrators, curriculum specialists, supervisors, and lay persons.

SUMMARY

Curriculum and instruction are viewed as separate but dependent concepts. Curriculum is defined in a variety of ways by theoreticians. This text follows

---

[21] See Peter F. Oliva, *Supervision for Today's Schools* (New York: Harper & Row, 1976).

the concept of curriculum as a plan or program for the learning experiences that the learner encounters under the direction of the school.

Instruction is perceived in these pages as the means for making the curriculum operational: the techniques that teachers use to make the curriculum available to the learners. In short, curriculum is program and instruction is methodology.

A number of models showing the relationship between curriculum and instruction have been discussed. While all models have their strengths and weaknesses, the cyclical model seems to have particular merit for its emphasis on the reciprocity between curriculum and instruction.

It is advocated that planning begin with the programmatic, that is, with curricular decisions, rather than with instructional decisions. Appropriate planning begins with the broad aims of education and proceeds through a continuum that leads to the most detailed objectives of instruction.

Curriculum is perceived as a discipline, albeit a derived one that borrows concepts and principles from many disciplines.

Many practitioners work in the field of curriculum, including specialists who make a career of curriculum planning and development. Teachers, curriculum specialists, and supervisors share leadership responsibilities in efforts to develop the curriculum.

As a discipline, curriculum possesses an organized set of principles, a body of knowledge and skills, and its theoreticians and practitioners.

SUPPLEMENTARY EXERCISES

1. Describe the characteristics of a discipline.
2. Decide whether curriculum is a discipline, a pseudodiscipline, a derived discipline, or not a discipline and state your reasons for the decision.
3. Make a brief presentation on the distinctions between a curriculum specialist and a supervisor, using selected quotes from the professional literature.
4. Define: curriculum worker, curriculum specialist, curriculum planner, curriculum coordinator, curriculum consultant, and instructional supervisor.
5. Locate in the literature and describe one or more models of the relationship between curriculum and instruction different from those which appear in this chapter.
6. Locate and report three definitions of curriculum found in books other than those quoted in this chapter.
7. Take each of the disciplines from which the field of curriculum borrows and state at least one contribution (principle, construct, or skill) borrowed from that discipline.

8. State what is meant by the terms: curriculum planning, curriculum development, curriculum revision, curriculum improvement, curriculum reform, and curriculum evaluation.
9. Report on the Western Electric researches mentioned in this chapter and explain their significance for curriculum development. Include in your answer your description of the Hawthorne Effect.

BIBLIOGRAPHY

Caswell, Hollis L. and Campbell, Doak S. *Curriculum Development.* New York: American Book Company, 1935.

Doll, Ronald C. *Curriculum Improvement: Decision Making and Process,* 4th ed. Boston: Allyn and Bacon, 1978.

Eisner, Elliot W., ed. *Confronting Curriculum Reform.* Boston: Little, Brown, 1971.

———. *The Educational Imagination: On the Design and Evaluation of School Programs.* New York: Macmillan, 1979.

——— and Vallance, Elizabeth, eds. *Conflicting Conceptions of Curriculum.* Berkeley, Cal.: McCutchan, 1974.

Foshay, Arthur W. *Curriculum for the 70's: An Agenda for Invention.* Washington, D. C.: National Education Association, 1970.

Frymier, Jack R. and Hawn, Horace C. *Curriculum Improvement for Better Schools.* Worthington, Ohio: Charles A. Jones, 1970.

Johnson, Mauritz, Jr. "Definitions and Models in Curriculum Theory." *Educational Theory* 17, no. 2 (April 1967): 127–140.

Kelly, A.V. *The Curriculum: Theory and Practice.* New York: Harper & Row, 1977.

Macdonald, James B. and Leeper, Robert R., eds. *Theories of Instruction.* Alexandria, Va.: Association for Supervision and Curriculum Development, 1965.

Oliver, Albert I. *Curriculum Improvement: A Guide to Problems, Principles, and Process,* 2d ed. New York: Harper & Row, 1977.

Pratt, David. *Curriculum: Design and Development.* New York: Harcourt, Brace, Jovanovich, 1980.

Roethlisberger, F. J. and Dickson, William J. *Management and the Worker.* Cambridge, Mass.: Harvard University Press, 1939.

Saylor, J. Galen and Alexander, William M. *Curriculum Planning for Better Teaching and Learning.* New York: Holt, Rinehart, and Winston, 1954; 4th ed. (with Arthur J. Lewis, 1981).

———. *Planning Curriculum for Schools.* New York: Holt, Rinehart, and Winston, 1974.

Schwab, Joseph J. *The Practical: A Language for Curriculum.* Washington, D. C.: National Education Association, 1970. Auxiliary Series, *Schools for the 70's.*

Taba, Hilda. *Curriculum Development: Theory and Practice.* New York: Harcourt, Brace, Jovanovich, 1962.

Tanner, Daniel and Tanner, Laurel N. *Curriculum Development: Theory Into Practice.* New York: Macmillan, 1975; 2d ed., 1980.

Tyler, Ralph W. *Basic Principles of Curriculum and Instruction.* Chicago: University of Chicago Press, 1949.

Wiles, Jon and Bondi, Joseph. *Curriculum Development: A Guide to Practice.* Columbus, Ohio: Charles E. Merrill, 1979.

Zais, Robert S. *Curriculum: Principles and Foundations.* New York: Harper & Row, 1976.

2

Principles of
Curriculum Development

After studying this chapter you should be able to:
1. Describe the ten axioms for curriculum development discussed in this chapter.
2. Formulate and support one or two additional axioms pertaining to curriculum development. These may be original ones that you will be able to defend or they may be axioms drawn from the professional literature.
3. Illustrate in what way the curriculum is influenced by changes in society.
4. Describe limitations affecting curriculum changes in a school system and within which curriculum workers must function.

You should also be able to formulate and give reasons for your views on the following issues:
1. The necessity for change in the curriculum
2. The necessity for a given curriculum to be satisfactorily adapted to the needs and learners of the times.
3. The necessity and extent of cooperation in curriculum development.

CLARIFICATION OF TERMS

Education is one of the institutions the human race has created to serve certain needs and like all human institutions responds or should respond to changes in the environment. The institution of education is activated by a curriculum that itself changes as forces affecting it cause it to change. The curriculum of the caveman, albeit informal and unstructured, was quite different from increasingly more formal types of schooling that the human race invented over subsequent periods of history. With acknowledgment to J. Abner Peddiwell, techniques for coping with the woolly mammoth may well have been of paramount concern to prehistoric man.[1] But the woolly mammoth has disappeared, and men and women today must learn to cope with other sources of anxiety like decreasing natural resources, decreasing living space, cost of housing, drug addiction, pollution, unemployment, crime, health problems, malnutrition, and the military and industrial hazards of nuclear power. At the same time humankind must learn to apply the technological tools at its disposal to solve these and other problems.

While no educator — teacher, curriculum coordinator, administrator, or professor — would dream of arguing that techniques of coping with the woolly mammoth should be a part of the curriculum of schools at the dawn of the twenty-first century A.D. in third-century America, the woolly mammoth syndrome still persists. Schools "woolly mammoth" children when they offer a curriculum that:

  □ allows learners to leave school without an adequate mastery of the basic skills
  □ omits exposure to the fine arts, including the development of local aesthetic appreciation
  □ portrays the average American child as living with a father, mother, and one sibling of the opposite sex, of Caucasian extraction, residing in a $100,000 single-family home equipped with all modern conveniences and two cars in the garage
  □ utilizes materials that show all children as members of healthy, happy, white, Anglo-Saxon Protestant families joyously living in suburbs
  □ ill equips its learners to find employment when they leave school
  □ fails to promote attitudes of concern for others, cooperation with others, responsibility for one's actions, tolerance of others, and conservation of resources
  □ leaves out the practical knowledge and skills necessary for survival and success in a complex society, such as knowledge about insurance and income taxes, writing a letter of application for a job, interviewing for a job, typing, discussion and listening skills

---

[1] For delightful reading the little classic by Harold Benjamin (J. Abner Peddiwell) entitled *The Saber-Tooth Curriculum* (New York: McGraw-Hill, 1939) is recommended.

□ appeals to short-term interests of students and ignores long-range needs, and, vice versa, when it appeals to long-range needs and ignores short-term interests

□ distorts truths of the past ("Honest Abe had no faults"), the present ("Every person who is willing to work can find a job"), and the future ("There is no need for residents of growing sections of the United States to worry about running out of potable water")

If the curriculum is perceived as a plan for the learning experiences that young persons encounter under the direction of the school, its purpose is to provide a vehicle for ordering and directing these experiences. This process of providing the vehicle and keeping it running smoothly is known as curriculum development.

It may be helpful at this point to review the slight distinctions among the following terms: curriculum development, curriculum planning, curriculum implementation, curriculum improvement, and curriculum evaluation. *Curriculum development* is the more comprehensive term, which includes planning, implementation, and evaluation. Since curriculum development implies change and betterment, *curriculum improvement* is often used synonymously with curriculum development, though in some cases improvement is viewed as the result of development.

Curriculum planning is the preliminary phase of curriculum development when the curriculum workers make decisions and take actions to establish the plan that teachers and students will carry out. Planning is the thinking or design phase whereas implementation is the action phase.

Curriculum implementation is translating plans into action. During the stage of curriculum planning, certain patterns of curriculum organization or reorganization are chosen. These patterns are put into operation at this stage. Ways of delivering the learning experiences, for example, using teaching teams, are taken out of the planning context and made operational. Since curriculum implementation translates plans into action in the classroom, thereby transforming the realm of curriculum into the realm of instruction, the role of the teacher changes from curriculum worker to instructor.

Curriculum evaluation is the final phase of development in which results are assessed and successes of both the learners and the programs (sometimes referred to as the "treatments") are determined. On occasion, *curriculum revision* is used to refer to the process for making changes in the curriculum or to the changes themselves and is substituted for curriculum development or improvement. We shall return to the distinctions among curriculum planning, implementation, and evaluation when models of curriculum development are diagrammed and discussed in Chapter 5 of this text.

Through the process of curriculum development, new ways are discovered for providing more effective pupil learning experiences. The curriculum developer continuously strives to find newer, better, and more efficient means to accomplish the task of educating the young.

TYPES OF CURRICULUM DEVELOPERS

Some curriculum developers excel in the conceptualizing phase (planning), others in carrying out the curricular plan (implementation), and still others in measuring results of curriculum treatments (evaluation). Over the centuries the human race has had no shortage of curriculum developers. In a positive vein Moses, Jesus, Buddha, Confucius, and Mohammed could all be called curriculum consultants. They had their respective conceptions of the goals of the human race and recommended behavior that must be learned and practices to achieve these goals. On the negative side Hitler, Stalin, Mussolini, and Mao Tse-Tung at a later period in history had definite notions and programs to train the young in what to believe and how to behave in a totalitarian society.

The ranks of the politicians in a democracy have produced curriculum consultants, some more astute than others. To the weary professional curriculum worker, it sometimes seems that every federal, state, and local legislator is a self-appointed, self-trained curriculum consultant who has his or her own pet program to promulgate. The statutes of the state legislatures, as we shall see in Chapter 3, provide numerous examples of legislative curriculum making.

It would be difficult to single out all the politicians-turned-curriculum consultants through the years. But the kite-flier who experimented with electricity, invented a stove, created a new educational institution called the Academy, and in between found time to participate in a revolution, Benjamin Franklin, made some farsighted curriculum proposals for his academy. Franklin's statement of recommendations almost seems to have been drawn out of a report on a high school's program of studies by a present-day visiting evaluation committee. Franklin proposed for his academy (later to become the University of Pennsylvania) a curriculum much more suited to its time than its predecessor, the Latin Grammar School.[2]

Curriculum advisers have been found not only among politicians but academicians, journalists, the clergy, and the public at large. Professional educators have received a great deal of both wanted and unwanted help in shaping their curricula. An unending procession of advisers from both within and outside the profession of education over the years has not been at a loss to advocate curriculum proposals. No matter how significant or minor these proposals, no matter how mundane or bizarre, all proposals have shared one common element: advocacy of change.

What has led so many people to be dissatisfied with so much of what education is all about? Why is the status quo rarely a satisfactory place to be? And why does it turn out, as will be illustrated, that yesterday's status quo is sometimes tomorrow's innovation? For answers to these questions some gen-

---

[2] For discussion of the Academy see Nelson L. Bossing, *Principles of Secondary Education* (Englewood Cliffs, N.J.: Prentice-Hall, 1955), pp. 97–107.

eral principles of curriculum development must be considered by teachers and specialists who participate in efforts to improve the curriculum.

SOURCES OF CURRICULUM PRINCIPLES

Principles serve as guidelines to direct the activity of persons working in a particular area. Curriculum principles are derived from many sources: (1) empirical data based on observation, (2) experimental data, (3) the folklore of curriculum, composed of unsubstantiated beliefs, philosophical positions, and attitudes, and (4) common sense. In an age of science and technology, the attitude often prevails that all principles must be scientifically derived from either empirical or experimental data. Yet, even folklore and common sense can have their usage. The scientist has discovered, for example, that some truths underlie ancient folk remedies for human maladies and that old wives' tales are not always the ravings of demented witches. While a garland of garlic hung around the neck may or may not fend off werewolves and asafetida on the end of a fishline may or may not lure fish onto the hook, the aloe plant does, after all, yield a soothing ointment for burns and the peppermint herb has relieved many a stomachache.

Common Sense

Common sense, which is often distrusted, combines folklore, generalizations based on observation, and learnings discovered through experimentation. It can function not only as a source of curriculum principles but as a methodology as well. For example, Joseph J. Schwab proposed a common-sense process he called "deliberation," to deal with curriculum problems. Minimizing the search for theoretical constructs and principles, his method depends more on practical solutions to specific problems.[3] Schwab pointed out the pitfalls of relying on theory alone. He rejected ". . . the pursuit of global principles and comprehensive patterns, the search for stable sequences and invariant elements, the construction of taxonomies of supposedly fixed or recurrent kinds" and recommended "three other modes of operation . . . the practical, the quasi-practical, and the eclectic." [4]

Of particular interest is Schwab's contrast of the theoretical and practical modes. Schwab explained:

> The end or outcome of the theoretical is knowledge, general or universal statements which are supposed to be true, warranted, confidence-inspiring. Their truth, warrant, or untrustworthiness is held, moreover, to be durable and extensive. . . . The end or outcome of the practical, on the other hand, is a *decision,* a selection and guide to possible action. Decisions

---

[3] Joseph J. Schwab, *The Practical: A Language for Curriculum* (Washington, D. C.: National Education Association, Center for the Study of Instruction, 1970).

[4] Schwab, p. 2.

are never true or trustworthy. Instead, a decision (before it is put into effect) can be judged only comparatively, as probably better or worse than alternatives. . . . A decision, moreover, has no great durability or extensive application. It applies unequivocally only to the case for which it is sought.[5]

When curriculum planning is based on deliberation, judgment or common sense are applied to decision making. Some professional educators have faulted the application of common sense or judgment as a methodology, so imbued are they with a scientific approach to problem solving. Franklin Bobbitt in 1918 took note of scientific methodology in curriculum making, citing the application of measurement and evaluation techniques, diagnosis of problems, and prescription of remedies.[6] Arthur W. Combs at a later date was moved to warn against too great a reliance on science for the solution of all educational problems.[7] Whereas science may help us find solutions to some problems, not all answers to educational problems of the day can be found this way. Certainly, hard data are preferred over beliefs and judgments. But there are times in the absence of hard data when curriculum workers must rely on their intuition and make judgments on the best available evidence.

Unless a principle is established that is irrefutable by reason of objective data, some degree of judgment must be brought into play. Whenever judgment comes into the picture, the potential for controversy also arises. Consequently, some of the principles for curriculum development provoke controversy while others are generally accepted as reasonable guidelines. Controversy occurs as often as a result of differing philosophical orientations of curriculum workers as it does from lack of hard data for making decisions.

TYPES OF PRINCIPLES

Curriculum principles may be viewed as whole truths, partial truths, or hypotheses. While all function as operating principles, they are distinguished by their known effectiveness or by degree of risk. It is important to understand these differences before examining the major guiding principles for curriculum development.

Whole Truths

Whole truths are either obvious facts or are concepts proved through experimentation and are usually accepted without challenge. Few will dispute, for example, that students will be able, as a rule, to master an advanced body of content only after they have developed the prerequisite skills. From this prin-

---

[5] Schwab, pp. 2–3.

[6] See Franklin Bobbitt, *The Curriculum* (Boston: Houghton Mifflin Company, 1918), pp. 11 12.

[7] See Arthur W. Combs, *The Professional Education of Teachers* (Boston: Allyn and Bacon, 1965), p. 74.

ciple come the practices of preassessment of entry skills and sequencing of content.

Partial Truths

Partial truths are based on limited data and can apply to some, many, or most situations but are not always universal. Some educators assert, for example, that student achievement is higher when students are grouped homogeneously for instruction. Some learners may achieve better results when placed in groups of like ability while others may not. The practice of homogeneous or ability grouping may be successful with some groups but not with others. It may permit schools to achieve certain goals of education, such as mastery of content, but prevent them from achieving other goals, such as learning to live and work with persons of differing levels of ability. Partial truths are not "half-truths," containing falsehoods, but they do not tell the whole story.

Hypotheses

Finally, some principles are neither whole nor partial truths but are *hypotheses* or tentative working assumptions. Curriculum workers base these ideas on their best judgments, folklore, and common sense. As one example, teachers and administrators have talked for many years about optimum size for classes and for schools. The magic ratio of one teacher to twenty-five pupils has been repeatedly advocated as a standard for class size. Educators have been less certain as to how many pupils should be housed in a single school. Figures used as recommendations for class and school size are but estimates based on best judgments. School planners have reasoned that for purposes of economy and efficiency, class and school sizes can be too small. They also know from intuition or experience that class and school sizes can grow so large as to create situations which reduce educational productivity. Yet, the research recalls no magic number that will guarantee success.

While practice based on whole truth is a desideratum, the use of partial truths and the application of theories contribute to the development of the field. Growth would be stymied if the field waited until all truths were discovered before any changes were made. Judgments, folklore, and common sense make the curriculum arena a far more stimulating place to work than if everything were already predetermined. It should be considered the joint responsibility of both the proponents of unproved positions and practitioners to undertake tests of judgments, folklore, and common sense. The goal, of course, would be to relegate beliefs to the status of whole truth or falsehood. Ideally, all theories, beliefs, and hypotheses would be either proved or disproved, and those that were proved would become whole truths. If this were to happen and Nirvana were attained — a most unlikely event — we would have reached that condition of perfection that would make life among the curriculum developers exceedingly dull. Given the inventiveness of the human mind, the rapid growth of knowledge, and the continuing changes taking place in society, it is far from likely that curriculum planners will ever discover all truths. Rather it will be fortuitous if the planners move fast enough to learn enough truths to enable them to provide viable solutions, however temporary, to curricular problems.

TEN AXIOMS

Instead of talking in terms of whole truths and partial truths, since so many of the principles practitioners subscribe to have not been fully tested, we might be more accurate if we speak of "axioms." *Webster's New Collegiate Dictionary* Eighth Edition defines an axiom as "1. a maxim widely accepted on its merit 2a: a proposition regarded as a self-evident truth b: POSTULATE." [8] Or perhaps "axiom" should be replaced with "theorem," which this dictionary defines as . . . . . . "an idea accepted or proposed as a demonstrable truth often as part of a general theory: PROPOSITION" . . . . . .[9] As students of mathematics know well, even though an axiom may be a postulate and a theorem may be a proposition, both axioms and theorems serve the field well. They offer guidelines that establish a frame of reference for workers seeking ways of operating and resolving problems. Several generally accepted axioms that apply to the curriculum field may serve to guide efforts that curriculum workers make for the purpose of improving the curriculum.

Inevitability of Change

Axiom 1: As a point of departure, it has already been postulated that *change is both inevitable and necessary, for it is through change that life forms grow and develop.* Human institutions like human beings themselves grow and develop in proportion to their ability to respond to change and to adapt to changing conditions. Society and its institutions continuously encounter problems to which they must respond or perish. Glen Hass includes these factors in his summary of major contemporary problems facing society:

- □ the preservation of our environment
- □ the energy crisis
- □ changing values and morality
- □ changes in family life and structure
- □ urban and suburban crises
- □ the movement of minorities, females, and the handicapped for equal rights
- □ rising crime rates, including violence and vandalism in the schools
- □ feelings of alienation and anxiety on the part of many people[10]

---

[8] By permission. From *Webster's New Collegiate Dictionary* © 1981 by G. & C. Merriam Co., Publishers of Merriam-Webster Dictionaries.

[9] By permission. From *Webster's New Collegiate Dictionary* © 1981 by G. & C. Merriam Co., Publishers of the Merriam-Webster Dictionaries.

[10] Glen Hass, *Curriculum Planning: A New Approach,* 3rd ed. (Boston: Allyn and Bacon, 1980), pp. 40–42.

The public school, one of our society's fundamental institutions, faces a plethora of contemporary problems, some of which threaten its very existence. We need cite only the intense and growing competition from private schools, the creation of alternative forms of schooling, and even serious proposals for "deschooling" to illustrate the scope of problems currently confronting the public school.[11] Change in the form of responses to contemporary problems must be foremost in the minds of curriculum developers.

Curriculum as a Product of Its Time

Axiom 2: The second axiom is a corollary of the first axiom. Quite simply, *a school curriculum not only reflects but is a product of its time*. Though it may seem to some that the curriculum is a tortoise moving infernally slo-o-w-l-y, it has really undergone more transformations than the number of disguises assumed by a skilled master-change artist.

David Turney, for example, commented on the slowness of change when he said:

> Real social change is painfully slow. It proceeds like a glacier whose movement is measured in feet per year. Educational and especially curriculum change is a part and parcel of social change and proceeds at about the same rate.[12]

Turney felt that at least a decade must be allowed as a minimum period of time for a basic change in education to be made. The reader has no doubt heard the comment (itself now an axiom) that it takes fifty years to effect an innovation in the school's curriculum. Many also believe it takes an additional fifty years before the innovation is universally adopted by the schools. The fifty-year axiom excellently illustrates that axioms, which are created by human beings, are themselves subject to change as conditions change. Prior to the advent of the television, the computer, and sophisticated media, this axiom may have had an element of truth; but today news and ideas flash across the country instantaneously. Fifty years were certainly not required for thousands of schools across the country to try out team teaching, open-space education, values clarification, and behavioral objectives, to mention only a few relatively recent innovations. But as a word of caution, although an innovation may not require fifty to one hundred years, it may require three, five, or ten years or more — to some a long period of time — before it becomes a relatively common practice.

It is clear that the curriculum responds to and is changed by social forces, philosophical positions, psychological principles, accumulating knowledge, and educational leadership at its moment in history. The impact of the rapid

---

[11] See Ivan Illich, *Deschooling Society* (New York: Harper & Row, 1971).

[12] David Turney, "Sisyphus Revisited," *Perspectives on Curriculum Development 1776–1976,* 1976 ASCD Yearbook (Alexandria, Va.: Association for Supervision and Curriculum Development, 1976), p. 232.

accumulation of knowledge may be one of the more dramatic illustrations of forces affecting the curriculum. Certainly some adaptations in the school's program ought to be made as a result of discoveries of lifesaving vaccines, inventions such as the photocopy machine and the calculator, and scientific accomplishments like the Moon landings, the Mars flights, and the Venus, Jupiter, Uranus, and Saturn probes.

The presence of persuasive educational groups and individuals has been responsible for the adoption of curricular innovations at given moments in history and in numerous cases has caused permanent and continuing curriculum change. The famous pronouncements known as the Seven Cardinal Principles of Secondary Education by the Commission on the Reorganization of Secondary Education[13] and the Ten Imperative Needs of Youth by the Educational Policies Commission[14] are but two illustrations of the impact persuasive groups can have on the curriculum.

We may even point to individuals over the course of history who can be credited (or blamed, depending on one's perspective) for changes that have come about in the curriculum. Who can calculate the impact on education, for example, of Benjamin Franklin in the eighteenth century or Horace Mann in the nineteenth? What would the progressive education movement of the early twentieth century have been without John Dewey, William H. Kilpatrick, and Boyd Bode? How many secondary schools in the late fifties and early sixties literally "Conantized" their programs on the recommendations of James B. Conant, the former president of Harvard University? What responses of the curriculum in the latter half of the twentieth century can be traced to the teachings of Jean Piaget and of B. F. Skinner?

We could fashion for ourselves a little chart — see Table 2-1 — to illustrate the effects of several forces during periods of history on both the curriculum and instruction. In barest skeletal form we might break American educational history into three historical periods: 1650–1750, 1750–1850, and 1850 to the present. We might then chart some of the curricular and instructional responses to philosophical, psychological, and sociological forces of their time as the table shows. The arrow to the left of the chart indicates that forces and responses often overlap from one period to the next.

We could embellish the chart by refining the period of history and by adding other elements, but this skeletal description serves to illustrate that a curriculum is the product of its own time. James B. Macdonald made this point in this way:

> It should be clear to most knowledgeable and thoughtful observers of
> the American scene during the past twenty-five years, that any reforms in

---

[13] Commission on the Reorganization of Secondary Education, *Cardinal Principles of Secondary Education* (Washington, D. C.: U.S. Office of Education, Bulletin 35, 1918). See Chapter 3 of this text.

[14] Educational Policies Commission, *Education for All American Youth* (Washington, D. C.: National Education Association, 1944). See Chapter 3 of this text.

institutional setting, whether in education, occupations, churches, families, recreation, or whatever, are intricately related to multiple social pressures and set in the context of a general cultural ethos.[15]

Consequently, the curriculum planner of today must identify and be concerned with forces that impinge on the schools and must carefully decide how the curriculum should change in response to these often conflicting forces.

Concurrent Changes

Axiom 3: *Curriculum changes made at an earlier period of time can exist concurrently with newer curriculum changes at a later period of time.* The classical curriculum of the Latin Grammar School was continued, in spite of the reluctance of Benjamin Franklin, in the Academy. Indeed, even the first high school, established in Boston in 1821 was known as the English Classical School. It was not until three years later that the English Classical School became the English High School.

Curriculum revision rarely starts and ends abruptly. Changes coexist and overlap long periods of time. Ordinarily, curricular developments phase in gradually and phase out the same way. Since competing forces and responses occur at different periods of time and continue to exist, curriculum development becomes a frustrating yet challenging task.

Philosophical positions that differ on the nature of humankind, the destiny of the human race, good and evil, and the purposes of education have existed at every period of history. The powerful schools of essentialism and progressive thought continually strive to capture the allegiance of the profession and the public. The college preparatory curriculum, for example, vies with the vocational curriculum for primacy. Instructional strategies that are targeted at the development of the intellect compete with strategies for treating the child in body, mind, and spirit.

The competing responses to changing conditions have almost mandated an eclecticism. Curriculum developers select the best responses from previous times or modify them for future times. Either-or choices except at the most trivial level are almost impossible to make in complex social areas like education. Yet, some people continue to look for and argue for either-or solutions. To some, education will perish if all teachers do not write behavioral objectives. To others, the growth of preadolescents will surely be stunted unless they are educated in a middle school. Some elementary school administrators seek to provide a quality education through open-space schools. Others hold firmly to the traditional self-contained classroom.

Some themes are repeated through history. Critics have, for example,

---

[15] James B. Macdonald, "Curriculum Development in Relation to Social and Intellectual Systems," in *The Curriculum: Retrospect and Prospect*, ed. Robert M. McClure, 70th Yearbook, Part I, National Society for the Study of Education. (Chicago: University of Chicago Press, 1971), pp. 98–99.

TABLE 2-1   Forces affecting curriculum and instruction

PERIOD	FORCES	CURRICULAR RESPONSES	INSTRUCTIONAL RESPONSES
1650–1750	*Philosophy*	Latin Grammar School:	Strict discipline
			Rote learning
	Essentialism	School for boys	Use of sectarian
		The Bible	materials
		The 3 R's	Mental disci-
		Classical curriculum	pline
	Psychology		
	Faculty psychology –		
	mind as a muscle		
	Sociology		
	Theocracy-Calvinist		
	Male chauvinism		
	Agrarian society		
	Rich-poor dichotomy		
1750–1850	*Philosophy*	Academy:	Mental disci-
	Essentialism	Education for girls	pline
	Utilitarianism	Instruction in:	Recitation
		English	Strict discipline
		Natural history	Some practical
		Modern languages	applications
		plus 3 R's and classical	
		curriculum	
	Psychology		
	Faculty psychology		
	Sociology		
	Industrial Revolution		
	Westward Movement		
	Rise of middle class		
	Increased urbanization		

lambasted the schools periodically for what they conceive as failure to stress subject matter.[16] The history of curriculum development is filled with illustrations not only of recurrent philosophical themes, like the subject matter cacophony, but also with recurrent and cyclical curricular responses. Many of our schools have changed from an essentialistic to a progressive curriculum and back to the former.

---

[16] See Arthur Bestor, *Educational Wastelands: The Retreat from Learning in Our Public Schools* (Urbana, Ill.: University of Illinois Press, 1953); Hyman Rickover, *Swiss Schools and Ours: Why Theirs Are Better* (Boston: Little, Brown, 1962).

TABLE 2-1 continued

PERIOD	FORCES	CURRICULAR RESPONSES	INSTRUCTIONAL RESPONSES
1850 to present		**1850–1925:**	
	Philosophy	High schools	Practical applications
			Electives
	Essentialism	**1925–1950:**	
	Pragmatism	Child-centered curriculum	Problem-solving methods
		Experimentalism	Attention to whole child
		Life adjustment	
	Psychology	**1950 to present:**	
	Behavioristic	Career education	Individualization of instruction
	Experimental	Open-space education	
	Gestalt	Alternative schools	Technology
	Perceptual	plus basic skills	Opportunities for self-discipline
	Sociology		
	Mechanized society		
	Internationalism		
	Urbanization		
	Immigration		
	Settling the West		
	Civil rights		
	Big business		
	Big labor		
	Equal rights		
	Changes in family		
	Protecting the environment		
	Diminishing resources		

Schools have moved from self-contained to open-space to self-contained; they have taught "old math," then "new math," and reverted to the former; they have followed the phonics method of teaching reading, shifted to "look/say" methods, then reverted to phonics; they have stressed modern languages, then abandoned them, then reincorporated them into the curriculum. Significantly, on the other hand, some schools, particularly the essentialistic, have remained unchanged while social change has swirled around them.

The schools of the early days in America stressed basic skills taught in a strict disciplinary climate. The early twentieth century schools went beyond

basic skills — some would stay away from basic skills — to concern for pupils'
diverse needs and interests appealed to in a more permissive environment.
By the tail end of the twentieth century we see signs of schools reverting to
stress on the basic skills (the "back-to-basics" movement) and the return of
stricter discipline, including corporal punishment. It is of interest that one of
the current "innovations" on the educational scene is the designation of
"Traditional Basic Skills" schools, which emphasize the three R's, subject
matter, homework, academic achievement, deportment, and decorum.

As curricular themes are often recapitulated, some teachers and curriculum developers are disposed to maintain the status quo, concluding that their
current mode of operation, while it may be out of favor at the present moment, will be in style again sometime in the future. Why change and then
have to change back? they ask.

When the status quo has come out of synch and new responses are
needed, the maintenance of the status quo in the face of new demands for
new responses is inexcusable, for it denies the learners responses appropriate
to their times. Even if prior responses return at a later date, they should
result from a reexamination of the forces of that particular time. Thus, the
reemergence of prior responses will be *new* responses, not *old* in the sense
of being unchanging and unchangeable.

Change in People

Axiom 4: *Curriculum change results from changes in people.* Thus, curriculum developers should begin with an attempt to change the people who must
ultimately effect curriculum change. This effort implies involving people in
the process of curriculum development to gain their commitment to the
change. It has been learned from sad experience over a long period of time
that changes handed down from on high to subordinates do not work well
as a rule. Not until the subordinates have internalized the change and accepted
it as their own can the changes be effective and long-lasting. Many school
personnel lack commitment because they are denied this involvement in
change and their contribution to that change has been deprecated.

The importance of effecting change in people has been stressed by the
curriculum experts for many years. Vernon Anderson, for example, advised
curriculum developers that no curriculum change would be lasting without a
change in the way people think. He gave this principle paramount importance.[17] Jack Frymier and Horace Hawn spoke to the same theme:

> Tinkering with the minutiae in curriculum may cause some minor
> changes to occur in the educational process, but for anyone seriously in-

---

[17] See Vernon E. Anderson, *Curriculum Guidelines in an Era of Change* (New York:
The Ronald Press Company, 1969), p. 19.

terested in effecting significant change, the people who are involved must be themselves changed.[18]

An interested observer does not have to look far in most school systems to find evidence of curricular decisions being made without participation of those affected by the decisions. How many school buildings, for example, that impact heavily on curriculum are planned in cooperation with the teachers and curriculum workers?

When curricular prescriptions are handed down and mandated, programs may exist and even grow but, as a rule, those who must translate the mandated programs into action — the teachers — do so with less than enthusiasm. This lack of enthusiastic support spills over to the students who often adopt negative attitudes as a result.

Some curriculum planners interpret this axiom to mean that one hundred percent commitment of all affected parties must be achieved before a curriculum change can be implemented. Would that it were possible to obtain one hundred percent consensus on any issue in education! Somewhere between a simple majority and universal agreement would appear to be a reasonable expectation. Involvement of persons affected in the process itself will succeed in garnering some support even from those who may disagree with the final curricular product.

The curriculum planner should ensure that all persons have an opportunity to contribute to a proposed change before it is too far along and irreversible. No persons should be involved in the charade practiced in some school systems whereby teachers and others are brought into the planning process for window-dressing when it is a foregone conclusion that the curriculum change will be implemented whether the participants accept it or not. The "curriculum planner knows best" attitude has no place in curriculum design and implementation. Chapter 4 expands on the process for instituting and effecting curriculum change.

Cooperative Endeavor

Axiom 5: *Curriculum improvement is effected as a result of cooperative endeavor on the part of groups.* Oliver underscored the group nature of curriculum development when he said:

> It cannot be stressed too strongly that curriculum improvement is a cooperative endeavor. In the past, action on the curriculum was often limited to small-group work or to administrative decree; today, on the other hand, many groups and individuals are being encouraged to participate in a spirit of genuine cooperation.[19]

---

[18] Jack R. Frymier and Horace C. Hawn, *Curriculum Improvement for Better Schools* (Worthington, Ohio: Charles A. Jones, 1970), p. 24.

[19] Albert I. Oliver, *Curriculum Improvement,* 2d ed. (New York: Harper & Row, 1977), p. 37.

While an individual teacher working in isolation might conceivably effect changes in the curriculum by himself or herself, large and fundamental changes are brought about as a result of group decision.

Several groups or constituencies are involved in curriculum development in differing roles and with differing intensities. Students and laypersons often, though perhaps not as frequently as might be desired, join forces with educational personnel in the complex job of planning a curriculum.

Teachers and curriculum specialists constitute the professional core of planners. These professionally trained persons carry the weight of curriculum development. They work together under the direction of the school administrator whose task it is to oversee their activities and to facilitate their efforts at all stages of development. The administrator may take the bows for the school personnel's successful activities but by the same token will also encounter criticism for efforts gone awry.

Students enter the process of curriculum development as direct recipients of both benefits and harm which result from curriculum change, and parents are brought in as the persons most vitally concerned with the welfare of their young. More often and more willingly than in days gone by, administrators invite students and parents to participate in the process of curriculum planning. Some school systems go beyond parents of children of their schools and seek representation from the total community, parents and nonparents alike. Persons from the community are asked more frequently now what it is they feel the schools should offer and what they believe the schools are omitting from their programs.

Generally, any significant change in the curriculum should involve all of the aforementioned constituencies such as clerical staff and maintenance crews. The more persons affected by the change, the greater its complexity, and the greater its costs, the larger the number of persons and groups that should be involved. The roles of various individuals and groups in curriculum development are examined in Chapter 4.

While some limited gains certainly take place through independent curriculum development within the walls of a classroom, significant curriculum improvement comes about through group activity. Results of group deliberation are not only more extensive than individual efforts but the process by which the group works together allows group members to share their ideas and to reach group consensus. In this respect group members help each other to change and to achieve commitment to change.

Decision-Making Process

Axiom 6: *Curriculum development is basically a decision-making process.* The curriculum planner in cooperation with those involved must make a variety of choices, including:

1. Choices among disciplines. The absence of philosophy, anthropology, Chinese, even art and music from the curriculum of schools indicates that

choices have been made about the subjects to which students will be exposed.

2. Choices among competing viewpoints. Planners must decide, for example, whether they agree that bilingual education best serves the needs of segments of society. They must make decisions about programs such as interscholastic athletics for girls, whether pupils with learning disabilities should be assigned to special classes, whether to group pupils by ability, and whether a program of sex education should be offered.

3. Choices of emphases. Shall a school system, for example, give extra help to poor readers? Shall school systems provide programs for the gifted? Shall extra efforts be made for disadvantaged youngsters? Should school funds be diverted from one group of students to aid another group?

4. Choices of methodology. What is the best way, for example, of teaching reading? phonics? look/say? "systems" reading? What are the more effective materials to use? How is cultural bias eliminated from the program?

5. Choices in organization. Is a nongraded school, for example, the better approach to an organizational arrangement that will provide maximum opportunities for learners? Should alternative forms of schooling within and outside the system be provided? Shall elementary programs be delivered in an open-space setting, with totally self-contained classrooms, or with the use of resource persons to assist a teacher in a self-contained classroom?

It is apparent that two necessary characteristics of a curriculum planner are the ability to effect decisions after sufficient study of a problem and the willingness to make decisions.[20] The indecisive person who is unable to make a decision had best not gravitate to a career as a curriculum planner. Those persons for whom every *i* must be dotted and every *t* crossed before a move can be made are far too cautious for curriculum planning. Every decision involves calculated risk, for no one — in spite of what some experts may claim — has all the answers to all the problems or a single panacea for every problem. Some decisions will end in dismal failure. But unless the test is made, it can never be known what will succeed and what will not. The most that can be expected of a fallible human being is that decisions will be made on available evidence which suggests success for the learners and which promises no serious harm for them as a result of a decision taken. In the history of curriculum development we can find evidence of many roads which were not taken. Those roads might have turned out to be expressways to learning, though, of course, the pessimistic champion of the status quo would assure us that the roads not taken would have been overgrown ruts which

---

[20] For description of a decision-making process, see Chapter 3 of this text regarding material from Phi Delta Kappa National Study Committee on Evaluation, Daniel L. Stufflebeam, Committee Chairman, *Educational Evaluation and Decision Making* (Itasca, Ill.: F. E. Peacock Publishers, 1971).

ended at the brink of a precipice or circular paths which would lead us right back to where we were.

While the task of making curricular choices may be difficult in complex, advanced societies, the opportunity to make choices from among many alternatives is a luxury not found in every country.

Continuous Process

Axiom 7: *Curriculum development is a continuous, never-ending process.* The curriculum planner constantly strives for the ideal, yet the ideal eludes him or her. John R. Verduin, Jr. made this point succinctly: "Continuous examination, evaluation, and improvement of the curriculum is, therefore, of vital importance." [21] Dogmatic as it may sound, perfection in the curriculum will never be obtained. The curriculum can always be improved and better solutions can always be found to accomplish specific objectives. As the needs of learners change, as society changes, and as new knowledge appears, the curriculum must grow and develop.

Comprehensive Process

Axiom 8: *Curriculum development is a comprehensive process.* Historically, much of curriculum development has been a hit-or-miss procedure: patching, cutting, adding, plugging in, shortening, lengthening, and trouble-shooting. In agreeing with the necessity for comprehensive planning, Taba explained:

> Some commentators have pointed out that the whole history of curriculum revision has been piecemeal — a mere shifting of pieces from one place to another, taking out one piece and replacing it with another without a reappraisal of the whole pattern. The curriculum has become "the amorphous product of generations of tinkering" — a patchwork. This piecemeal approach is continuing today, when additions and revisions in certain areas are made without reconsidering the entire pattern, and when acceleration in one part of the school system is recommended without corresponding changes in the next.[22]

Curriculum planning has often been too fragmentary rather than comprehensive or holistic. Too many curriculum planners have focused on the trees and not seen the forest.

Curriculum development spills not only into the forest but beyond the forest. A comprehensive view includes an awareness of the effects of curriculum development not only on the students and teachers directly affected by a programmatic change but also on the innocent bystanders, those not directly involved in the curriculum planning but affected in some way by the results

---

[21] John R. Verduin, Jr., *Cooperative Curriculum Improvement* (Englewood Cliffs, N.J.: Prentice-Hall, 1967), p. 33.

[22] Hilda Taba, *Curriculum Development: Theory and Practice* (New York: Harcourt, Brace, Jovanovich, 1962), p. 8.

of planning.[23] Sex education, for example, may affect not only teachers, students, and parents of students involved but also students, teachers, and parents of those not involved. These latter groups may like to be included, may object to becoming included, or may reject the subject as inappropriate for schools.

The comprehensive approach to curriculum planning requires a generous investment of physical and human resources. Curriculum workers must engage in, without meaning to be redundant, planning for curriculum planning or what some people might refer to as "preplanning." Some predetermination must be made prior to initiating curriculum development as to whether the tangible resources, the personnel, and sufficient time will be available to allow a reasonable expectation of success. Not only must personnel be identified but their sense of motivation, energy level, and other commitments must be taken into consideration by the curriculum leaders. Perhaps one of the reasons why curriculum development has historically been fragmentized and piecemeal is the demand the comprehensive approach places on the school's resources.

Systematic Development

Axiom 9: *Systematic curriculum development is more effective than trial-and-error.* Curriculum development should ideally be comprehensive by looking at the whole canvas and be systematic by following an established set of procedures. That set of procedures should be agreed upon and known by all those who participate in the development of the curriculum. Curriculum planners are more likely to be productive and successful if they follow an agreed-upon model for curriculum development.

If the curriculum worker subscribes to the foregoing axioms and consents to modeling his or her behavior on the basis of these axioms, will success be inevitable? The answer is an obvious "no," for there are many limitations on curriculum workers, some of which are beyond their control. Among the restrictions on the curriculum planner are the style and personal philosophy of the administrator, the resources of the school system, the degree of complacency in the school system and community, the presence or absence of competent supervisory leadership, the fund of knowledge and skills possessed by the participants in curriculum development, and the availability of professional materials and resource persons.

One of the great limitations — sometimes overlooked because it is so obvious and encompassing — is the existing curriculum. Many treatises have been written by the curriculum experts on the characteristics of different types of curriculum. The earmarks of an activity curriculum, a subject matter curriculum, a broad-fields curriculum, and variations of core curricula are de-

---

[23] See Michael Scriven, "The Methodology of Evaluation," *Perspectives of Curriculum Evaluation,* AERA Monograph Series on Curriculum Evaluation no. 1 (Chicago: Rand McNally, 1967), p. 77.

scribed in the literature in detail.[24] From a purely cognitive base such discussions are useful. But the inference is sometimes drawn that the choice of a type of curriculum is an open one, that if the planners know and believe in the characteristics of an activity curriculum, for example, they will have the option of organizing and implementing that type of curriculum. It is as if a curriculum planner could start from scratch and design a totally new curriculum, which is rarely the case, and which leads us to the tenth axiom.

Starting from the Existing Curriculum

Axiom 10: *The curriculum planner starts from where the curriculum is just as the teacher starts from where the students are.* Curriculum change does not take place overnight. There are few overnight quantum leaps in the field of curriculum, which may be a positive value rather than a negative one, for slow but steady progress toward change allows time for testing and reflection.

Since curriculum planners begin with already existing curricula, it would be more accurate if, instead of talking about curriculum organization, we talked about curriculum reorganization. The investment of thought, time, money, and work put in by previous planners cannot be thrown out even if such a drastic remedy appeared to a new set of planners as valid. The curriculum worker might well follow the advice in the *Book of Common Prayer* where the believer is told to "hold fast to that which is good."

SUMMARY

The system that we call education responds to change as conditions in its suprasystem, society, change. Curriculum change is a normal, expected consequence of changes in the environment.

The curriculum worker's responsibility is to seek ways of making continuous improvement in the curriculum. The task of the curriculum worker is facilitated if the worker follows some generally accepted principles for curriculum development. Ten general principles or axioms are presented. The principles stem not only from disciplines outside of professional education but also from the folklore of curriculum, observation, experimental data, and common sense.

Axioms suggested as guides to curriculum developers are:

- Curriculum change is inevitable and desirable.
- The curriculum is a product of its time.
- Curriculum changes of earlier periods often coexist with and overlap curriculum changes of later periods.
- Curriculum change results only as people are changed.

---

[24] See B. O. Smith, William O. Stanley, and J. Harlan Shores, *Fundamentals of Curriculum Development,* rev. ed. (New York: Harcourt, Brace, Jovanovich, 1957). See also Chapter 9 of this text.

☐ Curriculum development is a cooperative group activity.

☐ Curriculum development is basically a process of making choices from among alternatives.

☐ Curriculum development never ends.

☐ Curriculum development is more effective if it is a comprehensive, not piecemeal process.

☐ Curriculum development is more effective when it follows a systematic process.

☐ Curriculum development starts from where the curriculum is.

Both teachers and curriculum specialists fill roles as curriculum workers in cooperation with other school personnel. Teachers, curriculum specialists, supervisors, administrators, students, parents, and other community representatives can all play significant roles in effecting curricular change.

Curriculum developers start from the given and work within specific parameters. Change is relatively slow, limited, and gradual.

SUPPLEMENTARY EXERCISES

1. Develop your own chart of the effects of forces on curriculum and instruction by periods of history of the United States. Your chart should expand on the periods of history and present additional details.

2. Write a paper on the contributions of one of the following persons to the development of curriculum thought or practice: Horace Mann, William James, John Dewey, William H. Kilpatrick, Boyd Bode, B. F. Skinner, Jean Piaget, Ralph Tyler, and Robert Hutchins.

3. Write a paper on one of the following groups and describe its impact on curriculum development in the United States: The Commission on the Reorganization of Secondary Education, The Committee of Ten, The Educational Policies Commission, and The National Science Foundation.

4. Choose three social developments, events, pressures, or forces in the United States within the last fifteen years that have caused changes in the school's curriculum and briefly describe those changes.

5. Read Ivan Illich's *Deschooling Society* (New York: Harper & Row, 1971) and report to the curriculum class on Illich's recommendations.

6. Look up one or more books or articles by an author who has been critical of public education (such as Arthur Bestor, Rudolph Flesch, Paul Goodman, John Holt, John Keats, James D. Koerner, Jonathan Kozol, Max Rafferty, Hyman Rickover, and Mortimer Smith in the 1950s and 1960s and Charles E. Silberman in 1970) and make a critique of the criticisms in a written report or oral presentation.

7. Read *The Practical: A Language for Curriculum* by Joseph J. Schwab and explain to the class what Schwab means by three modes of operation for curriculum development: the practical, the quasipractical, and the

eclectic. Tell what Schwab means when he says, "The field of curriculum is moribund" and state whether you agree with Schwab. (See reference to Schwab's book in the bibliography following.)

8. Consult some books on the history of American education and prepare comparative descriptions of the curriculum of (1) the Latin Grammar School, (2) the Academy, and (3) the English High School.

BIBLIOGRAPHY

Anderson, Vernon E. *Curriculum Guidelines in an Era of Change.* New York: Ronald Press, 1969.

———. *Principles and Procedures of Curriculum Improvement,* 2d ed. New York: Ronald Press, 1965.

Benjamin, Harold R. W. [Peddiwell, J. Abner]. *The Saber-Tooth Curriculum.* New York: McGraw-Hill, 1939.

Bobbitt, Franklin. *The Curriculum.* Boston: Houghton Mifflin, 1918. Also, New York: Arno Press and *The New York Times,* 1975.

Charters, W. W. *Curriculum Construction.* New York: Macmillan, 1923. Also, New York: Arno Press and *The New York Times,* 1971.

Combs, Arthur W. *The Professional Education of Teachers: A Perceptual View of Teacher Preparation.* Boston: Allyn and Bacon, 1965.

Davis, O. L., Jr., ed. *Perspectives on Curriculum Development 1776–1976,* 1976 Yearbook. Alexandria, Va.: Association for Supervision and Curriculum Development, 1976.

Doll, Ronald C. *Curriculum Improvement: Decision Making and Process,* 5th ed. Boston: Allyn and Bacon, 1982.

Firth, Gerald R. and Kimpston, Richard D. *The Curricular Continuum in Perspective.* Itasca, Ill.: F. E. Peacock Publishers, 1973.

Frymier, Jack R. and Hawn, Horace C. *Curriculum Improvement for Better Schools.* Worthington, Ohio: Charles A. Jones, 1970.

Gagné, Robert M. *The Conditions of Learning,* 2d ed. New York: Holt, Rinehart and Winston, 1970; 3rd ed., 1977.

Gwynn, J. Minor and Chase, John B., Jr. *Curriculum Principles and Social Trends,* 4th ed. New York: Macmillan, 1969.

Hass, Glen. *Curriculum Planning: A New Approach,* 3rd ed. Boston: Allyn and Bacon, 1980.

Herrick, Virgil E. and Tyler, Ralph W. *Toward Improved Curriculum Theory.* Supplementary Educational Monograph, no. 71, March, 1950. Chicago: University of Chicago Press, 1950.

Knezevich, Stephen J. *Administration of Public Education,* 3rd ed. New York: Harper & Row, 1975.

McClure, Robert M., ed. *The Curriculum: Retrospect and Prospect,* 70th Yearbook. Chicago: National Society for the Study of Education, University of Chicago Press, 1971.

Macdonald, James B., Anderson, Dan W., and May, Frank B. *Strategies of Curriculum Development: Selected Writings of the Late Virgil E. Herrick.* Columbus, Ohio: Charles E. Merrill, 1965.

Oliver, Albert I. *Curriculum Improvement: A Guide to Problems, Principles, and Process,* 2d ed. New York: Harper & Row, 1977.

Orlofsky, Donald E. and Smith, B. Othanel. *Curriculum Development: Issues and Insights.* Chicago: Rand McNally, 1978.

Rubin, Louis, ed. *Curriculum Hand-*

book: The Disciplines, Current Movements, and Instructional Methodology. Boston: Allyn and Bacon, 1977.

————. *Curriculum Handbook: Administration and Theory.* Boston: Allyn and Bacon, 1977.

————. *Curriculum Handbook: The Disciplines, Current Movements, Instructional Methodology, Administration and Theory,* Abridged ed. Boston: Allyn and Bacon, 1977.

Saylor, J. Galen and Alexander, William M. *Planning Curriculum for Schools.* New York: Holt, Rinehart and Winston, 1974.

Saylor, J. Galen, Alexander, William M., and Lewis, Arthur J. *Curriculum Planning for Better Teaching and Learning,* 4th ed. New York: Holt, Rinehart and Winston, 1981.

Schwab, Joseph J. *The Practical: A Language for Curriculum.* Washington, D.C.: National Education Association, Center for the Study of Instruction, 1970.

Short, Edmund C. and Marconnit, George D., eds. *Contemporary Thought on Public School Curriculum.* Dubuque, Iowa: William C. Brown, 1968.

Taba, Hilda. *Curriculum Development: Theory and Practice.* New York: Harcourt, Brace, Jovanovich, 1962.

Tanner, Daniel and Tanner, Laurel N. *Curriculum Development: Theory Into Practice,* 2d ed. New York: Macmillan, 1980.

Unruh, Glenys H. *Responsive Curriculum Development: Theory and Action.* Berkeley, California: McCutchan, 1975.

Verduin, John R., Jr. *Cooperative Curriculum Improvement.* Englewood Cliffs, N.J.: Prentice-Hall, 1967.

Wiles, Jon and Bondi, Joseph. *Curriculum Development: A Guide to Practice.* Columbus, Ohio: Charles E. Merrill, 1979.

Zais, Robert S. *Curriculum: Principles and Foundations.* New York: Harper & Row, 1976.

Part **II**

Curriculum Development: Roles of School Personnel

3

Curriculum Planning: A Multilevel, Multisector Process

After studying this chapter you should be able to:

1. Describe types of curriculum planning that are conducted at five levels and in three sectors.
2. Design an organizational pattern for curriculum development at the individual school level.
3. Design an organizational pattern for curriculum development at the school district level.

You should also be able to formulate and give reasons for your views on the following issues:

1. The extent of planning necessary for successful curriculum development.
2. The degree to which teachers should be involved in curriculum planning at one or more levels and in one or more sectors.

ILLUSTRATIONS OF CURRICULUM DECISIONS

Daily, curriculum decisions like the following are being made in some school district somewhere in our land:

- □ An elementary school has decided to replace its reading series with that of another publisher.
- □ An entire school district has decided to put a program of sex education into the curriculum at all levels.
- □ A junior high school has decided to incorporate more material on the achievements of various ethnic groups in its social studies program.
- □ A senior high school has instituted more individualized physical activities of the type that will carry over into adult life.
- □ Several elementary schools in a school district have been designated "traditional basic skills" schools.
- □ The English department of a senior high school has added a course in creative writing.
- □ A school system has approved a plan by which several elementary schools will offer a bilingual education program.
- □ The secondary schools of a district have put into operation a plan for increasing opportunities for girls to participate in team sports and for placing these sports on a par with boys' athletic activities.

Variations Among Schools

Countless curricular decisions like the preceding examples are made constantly. Some decisions are relatively simple — adding a course here, deleting a course there, or making some minor change of content. Other decisions are sweeping and far-reaching as, for example, the institution or abandonment of open-education plans or the conversion of a 6–3–3 plan for school organization (six years of elementary school, three of junior high, and three of senior high) to a 4–4–4 plan (four years of elementary school, middle school, and high school). These changes are both administrative and curricular decisions.

Some of the more dynamic school systems engage in a lively pace of curriculum decision making and are continuously effecting changes in the curriculum as a result of these decisions. Often more than one type of change occurs simultaneously in some districts and schools.

Some systems follow a reasoned, measured process for arriving at planning decisions and carrying out those decisions; others enter into an almost frenzied, superheated process in which dozens of curricular ideas are dancing around without decision or resolution, whereas other school districts demonstrate lethargy and apathy toward curricular decision making and are, for all intents and purposes, stagnant.

The foregoing illustrations of curriculum decisions are typical examples occurring within individual school districts. These illustrations might have been stated to show that the same kinds of decisions were being made at the same time in more than one school district. Our illustrations of curriculum decisions could apply to multiple school districts scattered throughout the United States and might be reported as follows:

- □ A number of elementary schools have decided to replace their reading series with that of another publisher. We might extend this illustration by pointing out that they have all chosen the same publisher!
- □ Several school districts have decided to put a program of sex education into the curriculum at all levels.
- □ Several junior high schools have decided to incorporate more material on the achievements of various ethnic groups in their social programs, etc.

How can we account for the simultaneous development of curriculum plans in different parts of the country? Shall we attribute it to legal pressures from federal or state sources? Among the foregoing illustrations only two — bilingual education programs and increased opportunities for girls to participate in team sports — may be said to have evolved as a result of legal processes. In 1974 the United States Supreme Court opened the doors to bilingual education programs with its decision in the *Lau* v. *Nichols* case.[1] As a consequence of this decision the San Francisco school system was required to provide special instruction to children of Chinese ancestry who were having difficulty with the English language. Furthermore, federal funds have been appropriated to assist school systems to develop and implement bilingual education programs. The participation of girls in team sports has been advanced through the U. S. Congress's enactment of Title IX of the Educational Amendments of 1972, which bars discrimination on the basis of sex. Certainly, federal and state legislation and court decisions have brought about curricular change as we will explore more fully later. But we must also look elsewhere for other causes or partial causes of simultaneous development of curricular plans.

Simultaneous Developments

Though unlikely, similar curriculum developments in different school systems may unfold at the same time in an unplanned way, by pure chance. This situation resembles that of two astronomers, unknown to each other and separated by oceans and continents, who suddenly discover the same star, or two scientific researchers who find within days or weeks of each other a cure for a disease plaguing humankind.

More likely, our country's efficient systems of transportation and communication can be pointed to as principal reasons for concurrent curriculum

---

[1] *Lau* v. *Nichols,* 414 U. S. 563 (1974).

development. These pervasive technological systems make possible the rapid transmission of the beneficial pollen (or not so beneficial virus, depending on one's point of view) of curricular ideas.

These giant systems have an impact on all the constituencies of a school district — the administrators, teachers, students, parents, and other members of the community. Transportation makes it possible for people from all parts of the country to get together in formal and informal settings and discuss contemporary problems of the schools. It would be interesting, for example, to measure the effects of national professional education conferences on the spread of curricular innovation. While the pessimist would assert that a great deal of drivel flows at many professional conferences, enough kernels of wisdom are shared that are taken back home where they are planted and brought to fruition. Could not several of the preceding illustrations have come about through the exchange of ideas on a person-to-person basis at a state, regional, or national meeting?

With possibly an even greater impact, communication systems permit the dissemination of reports of educational and social problems in various parts of the country and descriptions of how communities have sought to cope with those problems. The commercial press and television consistently make the public aware of social problems that call for some curricular responses, such as drug abuse, unemployment, racial problems, environmental problems, and the lack of basic skills on the part of young people. The media have been instrumental in revealing widespread citizen dissatisfaction with the public schools to the point where lay constituencies are demanding that curricular changes be made.

While the commercial media are pointing up social problems and, on occasion, educational responses to these problems, the professional media are engaged in healthy dialogue. The United States is blanketed with professional journals filled with educators' philosophical positions, proposals for change, and reports of projects, research, and experimentation. National and state professional organizations, the United States Department of Education, and state departments of education frequently release monographs, guides, and research reports of promising curricular projects. Both popular and professional books on education make their contributions to the quest for curricular solutions to many social and educational problems. Who is to assay, for example, the impact made on the schools by writers and educators such as Earl Kelley who stressed the importance of an individual's self-concept; [2] Ralph Tyler who suggested a systematic way of arriving at instructional objectives; [3] Benjamin Bloom and his associates who offered a way of classify-

---

[2] Earl C. Kelley, *Education for What Is Real* (New York: Harper & Row, 1947).
[3] Ralph W. Tyler, *Basic Principles of Curriculum and Instruction* (Chicago: University of Chicago Press, 1949).

ing educational objectives and advocated mastery learning; [4] James Conant who made recommendations that were widely adopted by secondary schools; [5] Jerome Bruner who wrote on the structure of disciplines; [6] and Charles Silberman who painted a grim picture of today's schools? [7]

Through modern means of communication and transportation, curriculum innovations — good, bad, and indifferent — are transmitted rapidly to a world thirsty for new and better ways of meeting its educational obligations to children and youth. It is extremely difficult in an enterprise as large as education to pinpoint the source of a particular curriculum change, and it is not usually necessary to do so. What is important to the student and practitioner in curriculum planning is to understand that processes for effecting change are in operation. These processes extend beyond the classroom, the school, even the school district.

LEVELS OF PLANNING

Curriculum planning occurs on many levels and curriculum workers — teachers, supervisors, administrators, or others — may be engaged in curriculum efforts on several levels at the same time. The levels of planning on which teachers function can be conceptualized as shown in Figure 3-1.[8] All teachers are involved in curriculum planning at the classroom level, most teachers participate in curriculum planning at the school level, some take part at the district level, and fewer and fewer engage in the planning process at state, regional, and national levels. A few teachers, however, do participate in curriculum planning at all levels.

Importance of Classroom Level

The model in Figure 3-1 with its ascending stairs and even with its use of the term "levels" may lead you to some erroneous conclusions. You might conclude, since the steps clearly sketch a hierarchy, that planning at the classroom level is least important while planning at the national level is most important. Nothing could be further from the truth. If we are concerned about

---

[4] Benjamin S. Bloom, ed., *Taxonomy of Educational Objectives: The Classification of Educational Goals: Handbook I: Cognitive Domain* (New York: Longman, 1956).

Benjamin S. Bloom, J. Thomas Hastings, and George F. Madaus, *Handbook on Formative and Summative Evaluation of Student Learning* (New York: McGraw-Hill, 1971).

[5] James B. Conant, *The American High School Today* (New York: McGraw-Hill, 1959).

[6] Jerome Bruner, *The Process of Education* (Cambridge, Mass.: Harvard University Press, 1960).

[7] Charles E. Silberman, *Crisis in the Classroom: The Remaking of American Education* (New York: Random House, 1970).

[8] Peter F. Oliva, *The Secondary School Today*, 2d ed. (New York: Harper & Row, 1972), p. 280.

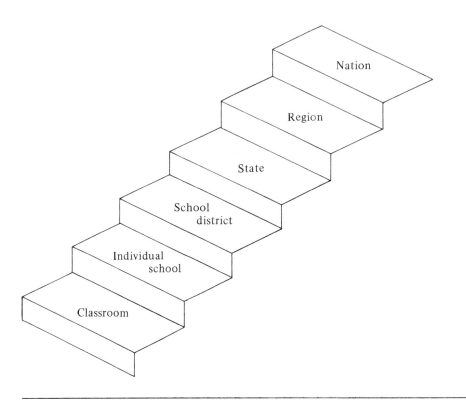

FIGURE 3-1   Levels of planning

levels of importance, and indeed we are, classroom planning should be conceded as being far more important than any of the successive steps. At the classroom level, the results of curriculum planning make their impact on the learners.

In some ways, it would appear more pertinent if we turned the model around and placed classroom planning at the top and national planning at the bottom. Unfortunately, reversing the ladder model would introduce another possible misinterpretation. Since the classroom is the focal point for curriculum planning and the main locale for curriculum development efforts, this stage is shown as the first step. It would be extremely inaccurate to designate the national level as the initial step since relatively few teachers or curriculum specialists work at that level and then usually only after they have demonstrated experience and competence at the other levels.

The step model may convey to some readers that curriculum workers move through each stage or level in a fixed sequence. Although most teachers are involved in curriculum planning at both the classroom and school levels, some will proceed no further than these two levels. Some teachers and curriculum specialists work in sequence from one level to the next or simultaneously at all levels, whereas others may skip whole levels. Though curriculum planning usually begins in the classroom, it may begin at whatever level curriculum workers feel a need to initiate change.

A Revised Step Model

Since the steps in the ladder model are of equal width and rise, the model can give the impression that curriculum planners have an equal opportunity to participate at all levels and spend equal amounts of time in planning at each level. Opportunities for curriculum planning become fewer in number at each successive step of the ladder.

The persons with whom we are most concerned in this textbook — the curriculum workers at the school and district levels — will be able to devote only limited time to curriculum planning at levels beyond the district. Consequently, if we retain the step model to show the levels of planning, we should picture the rise between steps as progressively higher and the width of each step as progressively narrower, as shown in Figure 3-2.

FIGURE 3-2   Levels of planning in relation to opportunity and time

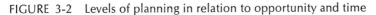
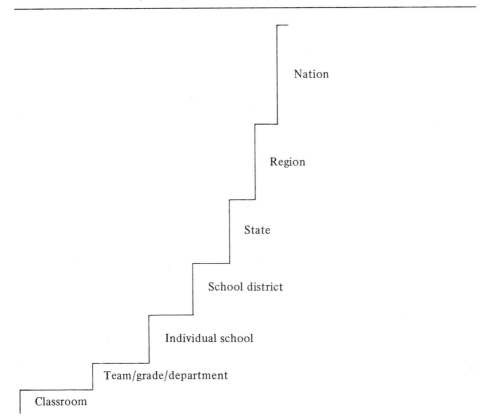

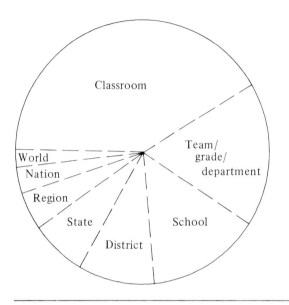

FIGURE 3-3   Sectors of planning

To make our ladder model of curriculum planning complete, we should add a tier above the national level with a higher rise and even narrower width — the international level, in which some few teachers and curriculum workers engage. As long as we conceptualize levels of planning as loci of work rather than of importance and understand that curriculum specialists do not necessarily work at all levels or in a fixed sequence of levels, the concept of levels of planning is valid and useful.

SECTORS OF PLANNING

Some curriculum theorists might feel somewhat more comfortable if, instead of speaking of levels of planning, we talked of sectors of planning. The model above eliminates the hierarchical and sequence problems of the step model and says simply that curriculum planning goes on in eight sectors: the classroom, the team/grade/department, the individual school, the school district, the state, the region, the nation, and the world. The sector model, illustrated in Figure 3-3, shows teachers and curriculum workers spending the largest part of their planning time in the individual school and in the school district with decreasing amounts of their time in sectors beyond the district boundaries. The broken lines signify that an individual teacher or curriculum planner may work at separate times or simultaneously in more than one sector. On the other hand, the teacher or curriculum planner may confine himself or herself to the classroom sector.

Models of levels or of sectors of planning address the question of where decisions are made and speak to the organizational processes for developing plans. These models do not, of course, answer the question of why decisions are made, a topic explored in later chapters.

In discussing levels or sectors of planning, we should distinguish between levels or sectors in which individual planners work and those where decisions are actually made. These are not necessarily the same. Let's take, for example, the case of a fifth grade teacher. This teacher may possess sufficient leadership skills, motivation, and knowledge to become involved in curriculum planning either at successive times or simultaneously in the classroom, team/grade/department, school, and district levels. This individual may be involved at each level in making curriculum decisions that affect him or her as well as others in the school system.

On the other hand, this fifth grade teacher may be engaged in curriculum planning at only the classroom level and not actively involved in the process above that level. Nevertheless, decisions about classroom curriculum which the individual teacher wishes to make must often be referred to a higher level of decision making especially if these decisions will have an impact on other teachers. For example, the individual teacher cannot unilaterally replace an adopted textbook that is part of an articulated series used at several grade levels. Decision making, then, will and must take place at higher levels whether or not the individual teacher actively participates in them.

A Hierarchical Structure

Since many curriculum decisions must be, in effect, ratified at successive levels, we do have a hierarchical structure up through and including the state level. Each successive level possesses the power to approve or reject curriculum proposals of the level below it.

In practice, curriculum planning is the responsibility primarily of the school district and its sublevels. Whereas teachers and curriculum specialists may participate in curriculum projects at the state level, their curriculum efforts at that level are purely advisory. Only the state board of education, the state department of education, or the state legislature can mandate incorporating the projects' results in the schools' program. As long as school districts follow specific state regulations and statutes, they are generally free to demonstrate initiative in curriculum planning.

Limitations of Hierarchical Structure

Beyond the state level the hierarchical structure does not hold true. In our decentralized system of education, authority for education is reserved to the states. The regional, national (with appropriate qualifications), and international sectors may seek to bring about curriculum change only through persuasion by working through state and local levels.

The national level represents a unique blend of control through both authority and persuasion. Some maintain that in spite of our decentralized system the federal government exercises too much control over the schools, including the curriculum of those schools.

The history of federal legislation in support of vocational education and education of the handicapped, for example, reveals that the national level exerts a potent influence on the curriculum of schools throughout the country. The dollar, disseminated by the federal government, is, of course, in itself a powerfully persuasive instrument. However, officials at the national level can intervene in state and local school matters only subsequent to federal legislation which they are empowered and required to enforce.

It is a moot question, however, whether the enactment of federal legislation and the enforcement of federal decisions can be called curriculum planning in its true sense. Whereas school districts must comply with federal legislation, for example, which bans all forms of discrimination in the schools' programs, they are under no obligation to submit grant proposals for optional types of aid.

Consequently, we might design a model that shows the levels of curriculum planning through the state level and the sectors beyond the state level. Such a model is shown in Figure 3-4.

CURRICULUM EFFORTS AT THE VARIOUS LEVELS

When the graduates of teacher education programs with degrees and state certificates fresh in hand sign contracts for their first teaching positions, they generally have only the vaguest of notions of the extent to which they will be involved in curriculum planning and development. Rarely do teacher education institutions require courses in curriculum development at the undergraduate level. A typical preservice training program, ignoring the problem of differing delivery systems, consists of general education (liberal studies), foundations of education (social, psychological, philosophical, and/or historical) or introduction to education, methods of teaching (both general and specific), and student teaching. On occasion, teacher candidates are exposed to an undergraduate course in curriculum, which provides them with an overview of the sources of the curriculum, presents a survey of programs in elementary and secondary education, and raises some curriculum issues. Despite this lack of training, the teacher engages in instructional and curricular decision making from day one. The novice teacher is, as a rule, reasonably well trained to make the instructional or methodological decisions but is less well equipped to make the curricular or programmatic decisions.

Teachers and curriculum specialists work within and across many levels and sectors. Each level performs distinct curricular efforts and has its own

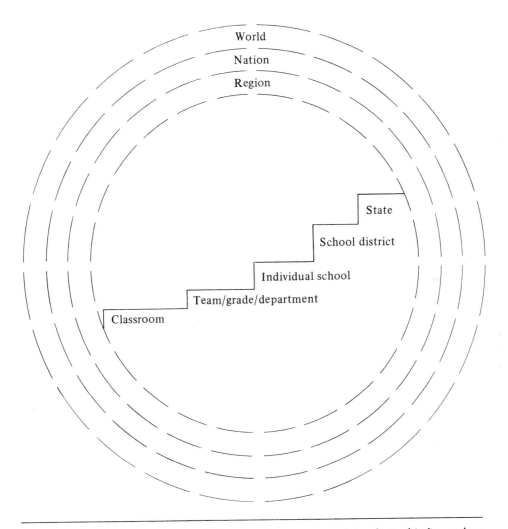

World

Nation

Region

State

School district

Individual school

Team/grade/department

Classroom

FIGURE 3-4   Levels and sectors of planning. For purposes of simplicity this figure does not show two levels — the area level that is a subdivision of the district and the intermediate unit that is a level between the district and the state. The area level is found in large urban school systems and the intermediate level, primarily a service unit, in some states.

organizational processes for making curriculum decisions. By examining these levels in depth, we will learn of the internal structures professionals have created themselves to improve the curriculum. By contrast, Chapters 4 and 7 explore how external structures — those outside the teaching profession itself — impinge on internal structures.

For curriculum decision making to take place, appropriate organizational structures are essential. In the following pages of this chapter we will examine such structures in some detail. In Chapter 4 we will consider more fully the roles of various individuals and groups in the curriculum development process.

The Classroom Level

At first blush it seems that all programmatic decisions have been made for the teacher at the time he or she is employed. A full-blown program is already in operation at the school where the teacher is to be assigned. The principal contracts with the applicant to fill an advertised position, be it early childhood education, sixth grade, junior high school English, or senior high school chemistry; designates the grade or subject(s) to be taught; and informs the teacher about school policies and regulations. If the school is large enough to require the services of supervisory personnel other than the principal, the teacher may be referred to one of the supervisors for further orientation. The supervisory person designated by the principal, for example, the assistant principal, a grade coordinator, or a department head, acquaints the teacher with the adopted textbooks and whatever other curriculum materials are used, such as statements of objectives, syllabi, and curriculum guides.

The new teacher begins to feel as if all the important decisions about the curriculum have been made. Perhaps the life of the teacher would be easier and certainly less complicated were that the case. On the other hand, it is safe to say that the teacher's life would be immensely duller were there no curriculum decisions to be made. If the teacher subscribes to the axioms that change is inevitable and never-ending, he or she will come to view his or her role first and foremost as a decision maker. The teacher then not only makes decisions or participates in shared decision making but also gathers data on which to base decisions, implements decisions, and evaluates programs. In what specific curriculum endeavors, we may ask, is the individual classroom teacher likely to participate? Let's respond to that question in two ways.

Two Cases. First, let us take the hypothetical cases of two high-powered, experienced, highly motivated teachers — a fourth grade teacher and a ninth grade teacher of social studies. We will further posit that (1) the fourth grade teacher is a male and the ninth grade teacher a female, (2) both are employed in the same school district, and (3) both participate in curriculum planning at all levels and in all sectors. Our fourth grade teacher, whom we will refer to as Teacher F, is the leader of a team of three teachers who have responsibility for a group of ninety students in an open-area setting. Our ninth grade teacher, Teacher N, is a member of a social studies department numbering eight faculty members. We will examine their curriculum development activities at one point in time — the cool and windy month of March.

During this period Teacher F was reviewing with the other teachers the next day's mathematics lesson for the slower students in the class and examining a new fourth-grade reading program (team/grade level). He was also participating in making recommendations for implementing a new human growth and development program in the school (school level); serving on a committee studying ways to implement federal legislation regarding the handicapped (district level); participating in a committee to define minimal competencies in reading (state level); taking part in a panel discussion at a regional conference on open-space schools (regional sector); finishing a proposal for federal funding of a Title I project (national sector and local levels); and planning activities for the Parent-Teacher Association's celebration of the International Year of the Child (international sector and local levels).

Teacher F's activities can be seen as fairly direct, immediate decision making to solve specific curricular problems, e.g., writing developmental reading activities and recommending ways to implement a new human growth and development program. His other activities bear more indirect implications for curriculum development, e.g., participation in a panel on open-space schools and planning P.T.A. activities to celebrate the International Year of the Child. Yet even from these last two activities, curricular revisions, learning experiences for children in his and other teachers' classes, and new programs may be derived. Study, discussion, and demonstration of one's ideas are integral parts of the process of curricular decision making.

While Teacher F has been making his contribution toward keeping the curriculum of his school system lively, Teacher N has been no less occupied. She has just finished resequencing the content of a course in geography which she regularly teaches (classroom level); is planning together with all the other ninth grade teachers a new course in consumer economics (grade level); will attend later in the week as her grade representative a meeting of the school's curriculum committee to discuss ways of utilizing community resources more effectively (school level); has been serving on the same district committee as Teacher F which is charged with the task of making recommendations for implementing curricula for the handicapped (district level); has been invited to participate in a committee to consider changes in the state's minimal requirements for high school graduation (state level); served a week ago on the visiting committee for a distant high school that is seeking regional accreditation (regional sector); has been notified by the United States Department of Education that the proposal which she will codirect on increasing children's global awareness will be funded (national sector and local levels); and has been invited by UNESCO to present a paper at a conference to be held in June at its headquarters in Paris (international sector). While relatively few teachers have the opportunity, ability, or perhaps the inclination to participate in curriculum efforts at all the levels and sectors suggested in these two hypothetical cases, none of these curricular activities is beyond the realm of possibility. Teachers have engaged in all these activities at some time somewhere in these United States.

A second way to respond to the question, "In what specific endeavors is the individual classroom teacher likely to participate?", is to survey typical curriculum efforts that take place at each level and in each sector. When we consider some of the curriculum responsibilities of the classroom level, it becomes apparent that the individual teacher has a rather large task cut out for him or her. A number of tasks in curriculum development may be identified at the classroom level. They can be classified into three categories: curriculum planning or design, curriculum implementation, and curriculum and instructional evaluation.

Tasks of Teachers. Teachers carry out activities in curriculum design when they write curricular goals and objectives; select subject matter (content); choose materials; identify resources in the school and community; sequence or resequence the subject matter; decide on the scope of the topics or course; revise the content; decide on types of instructional plans to use; construct the plans; try out new programs; create developmental and remedial programs in reading or other subject matter; seek ways to provide for all kinds of individual differences in the classroom; incorporate content mandated by levels above the classroom; and develop their own curricular materials.

Curriculum implementation is equated by some curriculum experts with instruction. Some hold the view that curriculum implementation does not start until the teacher interacts with the students. I would include in this concept the final stages of curriculum planning or design when the nitty-gritty decisions are made about how programs will be put into operation and how instruction will be designed and presented. Within this context teachers are occupied at the classroom level when they select appropriate emphases within the subjects; decide which students will be confronted with what subject matter; allot times for the various topics and units to be taught; determine if the facilities are appropriate and how they may be modified, if necessary; decide on how materials and resources may best be made available to the learners; assign duties to volunteer aides; write instructional goals and objectives; and select and carry out strategies for classroom presentation and interaction.

Teachers have the responsibility of evaluating both the curriculum and instruction. In some ways it is difficult to separate the two dimensions of evaluation and to tell where instructional evaluation ceases and curriculum evaluation begins. In a very real sense evaluating instruction is evaluating curriculum implementation. We may clarify the distinctions between the two dimensions if we define *curriculum evaluation* as the assessment of programs, processes, and curricular products (material not human) and *instructional evaluation* as the assessment of student achievement before, during, and at the end of instruction and the assessment of the effectiveness of the instructor. Thus, teachers work at the task of curriculum evaluation when they seek to find out if the programs are meeting the curriculum objectives; try to learn if the programs are valid, relevant, feasible, of interest to the learners, and in keeping with the learners' needs; review the choices of delivery systems, materials, and resources; and examine the finished curriculum products, e.g. guides, units, and modules, which they have created. Teachers conduct instructional evaluation when they assess the learners' entry skills before the start of instruction; give progress tests; write, administer, score, and interpret final achievement tests; and permit students to evaluate their performance as instructors.

These examples of activities transpiring at the classroom level demonstrate that curriculum planning and development are complex and demanding responsibilities for the teacher.

The Team, Grade, and Department Level

One of the axioms in Chapter 2 stated that curriculum development is essentially a group undertaking. Once the teacher leaves the sanctuary of the self-contained elementary or secondary school classroom and joins other teachers, curriculum development takes a new turn. It calls for a cooperative effort on the part of each teacher, places a limit on solitary curriculum planning, and calls for a more formal organizational structure. It is at the team, grade, or department level that curriculum leadership begins to emerge and leaders come to be distinguished from followers.

For decades the graded school system with its orderly hierarchical structure and self-contained classrooms has been the prevailing model of school organization. In the late seventies, however, the self-contained classroom was jostled by the appearance of open-space or open-area schools. Scores of elementary, middle, and junior high schools were built as or converted into open-space facilities. In the place of the walled, self-contained classrooms came large open spaces in which the learning activities of a large group of youngsters were directed by a team of teachers assisted in some cases by paraprofessionals. A semblance of territoriality was created by assigning each of the team members to a particular group of youngsters whose home base was a sector of the large open area. In theory and in practice, groups and subgroups were formed and reformed continuously depending on their learning needs, goals, and interests.

Specific curriculum innovations are discussed in this text primarily to delineate the process of curriculum development and to help the curriculum worker to effect and evaluate curriculum change.[9] Two organizational pat-

---

[9] See Chapter 9 of this text for a discussion of the graded school, open-space schools, and other organizational arrangements.

terns — the self-contained classroom and open space — are mentioned in this chapter to point out that teachers in an open-space school, unlike their counterparts in the self-contained classroom, participate in curriculum planning at the team level. In cases where there is more than one team at the same grade level, teachers in open-space schools engage in planning on two levels: team and grade. When only one team exists at a particular grade level, as, for example, one fourth grade team consisting of three teachers for ninety students, teachers serve as planners at both the team and grade level simultaneously. Teachers in both open-space schools and in the self-contained classroom participate in curriculum planning at the grade level.

Elementary school teachers in open-space schools, therefore, participate in curriculum planning at both the team and grade levels, whereas secondary school teachers join with their colleagues in curriculum planning at both the grade and department levels. With the children for whom they are specifically responsible in mind, the teachers in a team, a given grade, or a particular department are called on to make curriculum decisions like the following:

☐ adapting instruction for exceptionalities
☐ establishing team, grade, or departmental objectives
☐ selecting materials and resources suitable to the children under their supervision
☐ creating groupings of learners
☐ adapting instruction for exceptionalities
☐ establishing a means of coordinating progress of students in the various sections and classrooms
☐ writing tests to be taken by all students of the team, grade, or department
☐ writing curriculum materials for use by all teachers
☐ agreeing on team-wide, grade-wide, and department-wide programs that all students and teachers will attend
☐ agreeing on ways students can learn to demonstrate socially responsible behavior and self-discipline
☐ agreeing on minimal standards which pupils must demonstrate in the basic skills
☐ cooperating in the establishment and use of laboratories and learning centers
☐ agreeing on marking practices
☐ agreeing on the institution of new programs and abandonment of old programs within their area of jurisdiction
☐ evaluating their own programs, students, and instructors

These are but a sampling of the many kinds of cooperative decisions members who constitute the team, grade, or department must make. Individual classroom teachers are generally free to make many, though not all, decisions that affect only their classes. When a decision is likely to have an impact on teachers other than the individual classroom teacher, this decision becomes a matter for joint deliberation by the parties to be affected or, at higher levels, by their representatives.

To make the decision-making process more efficient, curriculum leaders either emerge or need to be designated. Team leaders or lead teachers, grade coordinators or chairpersons, and department heads or chairpersons are appointed by the principal or elected by the teachers themselves. Those administrators who are inclined to a bureaucratic approach to administration prefer the former system while those who are disposed to a collegial approach permit the latter system. In either case, if the most experienced and skilled teachers are chosen for these leadership positions, they may establish themselves as curriculum specialists, key members of a cooperating group of curriculum workers.

Decisions and Organizational Patterns. Working together, members of a team, grade, or department cooperatively decide on such matters as:

- □ offerings for each semester or year
- □ sequencing of subject matter
- □ satisfying unmet curricular needs
- □ providing remedial work for students
- □ sharing resources and ideas
- □ writing curricular materials
- □ preparing tests
- □ reviewing textbooks
- □ choosing media
- □ establishing ways of evaluating the curriculum

Although many schools have their own unique organizational arrangements, we might diagram common organizational patterns for curriculum planning through the team, grade, and departmental levels. Later in this chapter we will look at parallel patterns of organization for curriculum development on a school-wide and district-wide basis.

Patterns 1 through 5 reveal ways in which individual classroom teachers, teams, grades, and departments are organized for carrying out their assigned tasks, a major one of which is curriculum development. Each pattern should be viewed in the mind's eye as expanded to include all teachers, teams, grades, and departments in the school. It is apparent that the channels shown in the charts can be followed for both administrative and curricular decision making, limited, of course, in these illustrations to decisions affecting only one teacher, team, grade, or department. In a moment we will look at the means of organizing on a school-wide basis and for making decisions that affect more than one teacher, team, grade, or department.

The arrowheads at both ends of the lines in the diagrams convey a philosophy and practice of collegiality. This element of collegiality extends even to the various leaders' relationships with the administrator. Many charts, es-

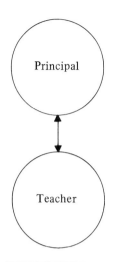

PATTERN 1   Individual classroom teacher in a small school. There is only one section of that grade, self-contained.

pecially showing administrative decision making in a bureaucratic model, include lines with no arrows or arrows in only one direction — from the top down. Interchange among all participants is absolutely essential to intelligent and effective curriculum planning.

Pattern 1 posits an uncommon, small school with one class of each grade with one teacher in a self-contained unit. The individual teacher is the curriculum leader (and follower, for that matter) and has sole responsibility for making curriculum decisions (with the administrator's cooperation and approval) for the classroom and grade levels, in this case identical. The teacher and principal relate to each other directly. Were we to show the pattern from the standpoint of the principal rather than the teacher, we would need to sketch one teacher for each class-grade, each relating independently to the principal. Whereas the absence of multiple sections of grades prevents cooperative curriculum planning within grade levels, cooperation is possible, if the principal permits, at the school level and across grade levels.

This illustration is an historic pattern for organizing curricular development. For cost-effectiveness and other reasons, school systems build schools to house sizable enrollments. Yet a pattern similar to this small school's exists in some large schools today.

In schools housing multiple sections of each grade, the principal sometimes eschews school level organization for curriculum planning and attempts to relate to each teacher on an individual basis. The principal does not encourage cooperative planning by the faculty within grade levels and across grade levels.

Pattern 2 shows an open-space team arrangement in a small school in which this one team also constitutes the grade faculty. Since there is but one team-taught section of the grade in this school, the team leader is, in effect, the grade coordinator. All members of the team interact with each other while the team leader serves as the team's liaison person to the principal's office. If we wished to visualize the extension of this pattern school-wide, we might in a simplistic fashion, hypothesizing one section at each grade level, K through 6, figuratively add five more identical teams.

The organizational arrangements for curriculum planning become more complex and at the same time more common as we find multiple sections at the various grade levels. Pattern 3 depicts the structure in an open-space school that has two sections of a particular grade, each made up of a team of three teachers. In this model we see two team leaders, one of whom happens to be serving also as grade coordinator. Members of each team interact with each other and with the grade coordinator.

The broken lines between Teams I and II are significant. Although there may be no walls between groups of children of one team, there are walls

PATTERN 2   Team in an open-space school. There is only one of this grade level in the school.

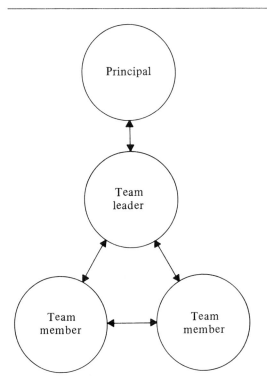

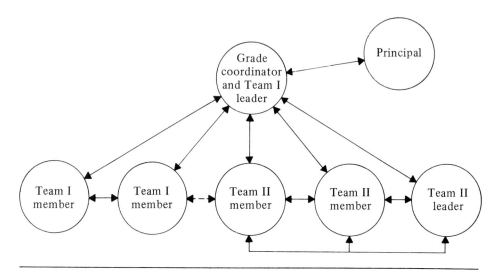

PATTERN 3   Two teams of one grade level in an open-space elementary school

between teams. Furthermore, the interaction among teachers is more limited across than within teams.

Alternately, we might have charted a situation that is less complicated and even more common: the grade level organization in an elementary school with self-contained classrooms. For example, the pattern for one grade consisting of three sections, each in a self-contained unit under a single teacher, would be identical to the diagram for Team I, Pattern 3, with only the labels changed. We would have one teacher who is grade coordinator and two grade teachers. The three teachers would interact with each other and the grade coordinator would serve as the link to the principal.

Two ways of organizing grade and departmental faculty of a secondary school for administrative purposes and for curriculum planning are represented by Patterns 4 and 5. Of these two models Pattern 5 is the typical, traditional, standard vehicle by which much of the work of the secondary school is conducted. Pattern 4 is utilized only when the grade structure becomes particularly significant, as in the case of schools implementing team concepts such as the core curriculum, interdisciplinary team teaching, differentiated staffing,[10] and the school-within-the-school.[11]

---

[10] For discussion of the core curriculum, team teaching, and differentiated staffing, see Chapter 9 of this text.

[11] See David W. Beggs, III, ed., *Team Teaching: Bold New Venture* (Indianapolis: Unified College Press, 1964), p. 20; *Education by Choice,* 16 mm. film which shows seven schools within Quincy (Illinois) High School (Media Five, 1011 North Cole Avenue, Hollywood, Cal., 1976); and Peter F. Oliva, *The Secondary School Today,* 2nd ed. p. 193.

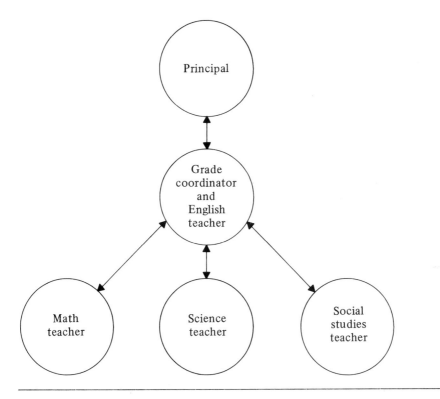

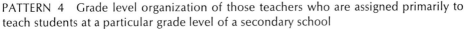

PATTERN 4   Grade level organization of those teachers who are assigned primarily to teach students at a particular grade level of a secondary school

These latter two patterns can exist concurrently in the same school. Departmental organization, however, is the prevailing pattern in the secondary school and most high school administrators would feel at a loss without it. Grade-level organization in the secondary school, unless provided for specific and innovative undertakings such as those just mentioned, tends to be weak, loose, and relatively nonexistent as far as curriculum planning is concerned. As an added block to grade-level planning in the secondary school as opposed to departmental planning, many teachers teach at more than one grade level.

There will be times when the principal of a secondary school will wish to meet with the faculty of one grade level — ninth grade teachers, for example — to discuss matters pertinent to just that level. Unless plans are consciously drawn to provide for curriculum planning, grade-level faculty meetings, like meetings of the entire faculty of a school, generally offer only limited opportunity for curriculum decision making. Patterns 2 through 5 show four ways curriculum development may be carried on at the team,

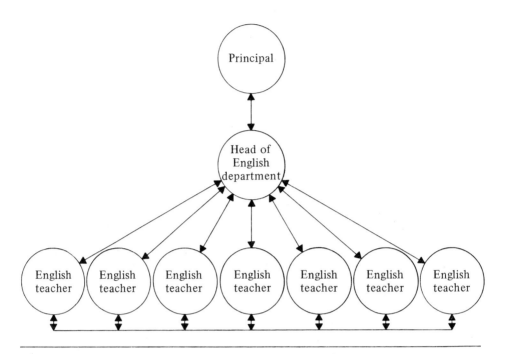

PATTERN 5   Organizational pattern of all members of a secondary school department. One faculty member happens to be also a grade coordinator.

grade, and/or department level. Curriculum matters that can be settled and contained within a team, grade, or department are handled at that level. Yet, curriculum planning sends out waves that affect, sometimes even engulf, persons beyond the planners and the client group for whom the plans were made. Hence, we must look to the next level — the school level — for curriculum decision making that transcends the team, grade, or department level.

The School Level

Although many curriculum decisions may be made at the classroom or team/grade/department level, other decisions can only be reached at a school-wide level. The institution must provide some mechanism by which the curriculum is articulated and integrated. The administrator must assure a process whereby the implications of curriculum decisions made anywhere within the institution will be understood and, hopefully, agreed to by the faculty as a whole.

Of all the levels and sectors of curriculum planning, the individual school has emerged as the most critical. Current administrative philosophy promotes an approach to school administration known generally as "school-based management" in which authority is decentralized and the school principal is granted considerable autonomy over not only curriculum planning but also the budget, hiring and firing of school personnel, inservice education of staff, supervision of personnel, and evaluation of staff.[12]

The previous chapter demonstrated that curriculum specialists conceive of curriculum development as a group, cooperative undertaking. Given the many dimensions of the school administrator's job, intensified by the concept of school-based management, a participatory approach to administration is sound not only philosophically but also practically. Shared decision making, whether in respect to curriculum planning or other aspects of the administrator's job, makes for a more efficient and effective school.

Foreign observers are often disturbed, if not jolted, by the uniqueness of each American school. Two elementary schools in the same community, for example, may be completely different in environment, student body, staffing, and composition of the neighborhood. Achievement levels, motivation of the students, enthusiasm of the faculty, leadership skills of the principal, and curricular emphases differ school by school. Consequently, we may anticipate that organizational arrangements for curriculum development will differ school by school.

Constituencies of the School. The democratic process is accepted more and more to varying degrees in school systems across the country. Nowhere is its presence more clearly felt than in the participatory procedures that seek to involve the major constituencies of the school in curriculum development. Usually identified as the principal constituencies are the administrators and their staffs, teachers, students, and citizens of the community. On occasion, non-professional employees of the school system are acknowledged in this way and become involved in the planning process — but rarely as major participants.

Frymier and Hawn stated a principle that summarizes their belief in the necessity for involving persons in curriculum planning on a broad scale:

> *People Who Are Affected Must Be Involved.* Involvement is a principle fundamental to democracy and to learning theory. The very essence of democracy is predicated upon the assumption that those who are affected by any change should have some say in determining just what that change shall be. This is guaranteed in our political-social system through citizen participation and through our efforts to persuade elected representatives once they have been chosen. Devising ways of involving people in decision-making is a difficult and time-consuming chore, but *unless decisions are made democratically they will be less than the best....* Significant and lasting change can only come about by such involvement. All

---

[12] See Barbara Parker, "School Based Management: Improve Education by Giving Parents, Principals More Control of Your Schools," *American School Board Journal* 166, no. 7 (July 1979): 20–21. School-based management materials are available from National Commission for Citizens in Education, Suite 410, Wilde Lake Village Green, Columbia, Maryland 20144.

who are affected by curriculum development and change must have a genuine opportunity to participate in the process.[13]

Robert S. Zais raised a question about the validity of the participatory model of curriculum decision making. Speaking of the democratic "grass-roots model,"[14] Zais said:

> The grass-roots model of curriculum engineering[15] . . . is initiated by teachers in individual schools, employs democratic group methods of decision making, proceeds on a "broken front," and is geared to the specific curriculum problems of particular schools or even classrooms.
>
> The intensely democratic orientation of the grass-roots model is responsible for generating what have probably become the curriculum establishment's two least-questioned axioms: First, that a curriculum can be successfully implemented only if the teachers have been intimately involved in the construction and development processes, and second, that not only professional personnel, but students, parents, and other lay members of the community must be included in the curriculum planning process. To deny the validity of either of these claims (neither of which has been satisfactorily demonstrated) is not necessarily to deny *any* role to teachers or lay participants; rather it is to suggest the need to define more precisely the *appropriate* role that administrators, teachers, curriculum specialists. and nonprofessionals should play in curriculum engineering.[16]

Decisions and Organizational Patterns. It is within the purview of the school's curriculum committee to meet and make recommendations on such matters as:

- adding new programs for the school, including interdisciplinary programs
- deleting existing programs
- revising existing programs
- conducting school-wide surveys of teacher, student, and parental opinion
- evaluating the school's curriculum
- planning ways to overcome curricular deficiencies
- planning for school accreditation
- choosing articulated series of textbooks
- utilizing library and learning centers
- planning for exceptional children

---

[13] Jack R. Frymier and Horace C. Hawn, *Curriculum Improvement for Better Schools* (Worthington, Ohio: Charles A. Jones, 1970), pp. 28–29.

[14] Zais attributes the classification "grass-roots model" to B. Othanel Smith, William O. Stanley, and J. Harlan Shores, *Fundamentals of Curriculum Development* (New York: Harcourt, Brace, Jovanovich, 1957). See Zais, *Curriculum: Principles and Foundations* (New York: Harper & Row, 1976), p. 448.

[15] Zais refers to the definition of "curriculum engineering" by George A. Beauchamp, *Curriculum Theory,* 2d ed. (Wilmette, Ill.: The Kagg Press, 1968) and uses the term to encompass "curriculum construction," "curriculum development," and "curriculum implementation," Zais, pp. 18 and 445.

[16] Zais, pp. 448–449.

□ verifying the school's compliance with state mandates and federal legislation

□ sanctioning school-wide events like career days, science fairs, etc.

□ supervising assessment of student achievement

□ reviewing recommendations of accrediting committees and planning for removal of deficiencies

□ reducing absenteeism

□ increasing the holding power of the school

While curriculum specialists may not agree to what degree to encourage or permit the involvement of various constituencies, how each group will be constituted, and which group has the primary role, the literature on curriculum development almost unanimously endorses the concept of the democratic, participatory approach. Although it is possible that the collective judgment of specialists in the field could be in error, their judgments based on experience, training, observation, and research provide a foundation for accepting the validity of the democratic approach to curriculum development.

There are several organizational arrangements on the school level for considering curriculum matters. In Patterns 1, 2, and 3, the administrator(s) shares decision making with the group that most curriculum experts agree is of primary importance in curriculum development — the teachers. Patterns 4 and 5 expand cooperation into collaborative models that include other groups in addition to teachers.

It should not be forgotten that in any organizational model in which decision making is shared, groups other than the duly appointed administrators serve only in advisory capacities. Both professionally and legally the administrator does not and cannot surrender his or her "line" authority for making ultimate decisions and supervising the staff.

Amitai Etzioni would reverse the traditional line-and-staff relationship that places the administrator in a superordinate position and others in subordinate roles. Said Etzioni, ". . . to the extent that there is a staff-line relationship at all, professionals should hold the major authority and administrators the secondary staff authority." [17] It is doubtful that even the professional organizations to which Etzioni was addressing his comments are ready for such a reversal of roles. The following patterns of organizing for curriculum development at the local school level maintain the customary line-and-staff relationship which we have already seen at the team/grade/department level and will see again at the school district level. They also serve as illustrations of ways schools may be organized for carrying out curriculum development and convey a sense of the variations possible for accomplishing this task.

---

[17] Amitai Etzioni, *Modern Organizations* (Englewood Cliffs, N.J.: Prentice-Hall, 1964), p. 81.

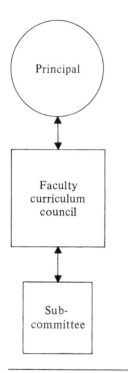

PATTERN 1   Principal works with a faculty curriculum council. Subcommittees of the faculty curriculum council are appointed as needed.

The principals in Patterns 1 and 2 utilize a faculty curriculum council, which some schools refer to as faculty council or faculty curriculum committee. In practice, faculty committees that serve to advise school administrators on curriculum matters are constituted either by election of teachers by their colleagues or by appointment of teachers by school administrators. In some cases, team leaders or department heads, elected in some schools, appointed in others, may make up the faculty curriculum committee. I would advocate the democratic election of representatives to curriculum committees and councils at all levels of the school system.

The principal in Pattern 2 has provided a systematic way by which the total faculty acting as a body approves or disapproves decisions of the faculty curriculum council. Although only one subcommittee is pictured in each of these figures, it is understood that the faculty curriculum council would appoint as many subcommittees of the faculty as needed.

Pattern 3 is a modification of Patterns 1 and 2 in that the principal delegates curriculum leadership responsibilities to the assistant principal for curriculum or the curriculum coordinator. The block with the label "total faculty" is also incorporated into this pattern. Citizens of the community and students join forces with the faculty and administrators to produce collaborative Patterns 4 and 5. The principal of Pattern 4 keeps the three constituencies separate. The model shows, however, the possibility of interaction among the several working groups.

The principal serves as the pivotal point and decides what matters go before each of the groups. Pattern 5 integrates all three constituencies into one expanded curriculum committee. Both Patterns 4 and 5 incorporate the total faculty within the model.

Pattern 5, an integrated, collaborative model appears the most democratic and it might be wrongfully concluded that it is therefore the most efficient. As anyone who has grappled with the concept of "parity" as dictated by some federal programs — public school teachers, university specialists, and lay people working together as equal partners from proposal stage to final evaluation — has discovered, "parity" is not necessarily the most efficient way to do business. In reference to the expanded curriculum committee the professionals — the teachers and administrators — must often talk a language filled with concepts which must be explained to lay citizens and students and

PATTERN 2   Principal works with a faculty curriculum council and involves total faculty.

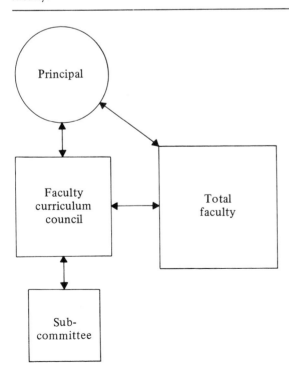

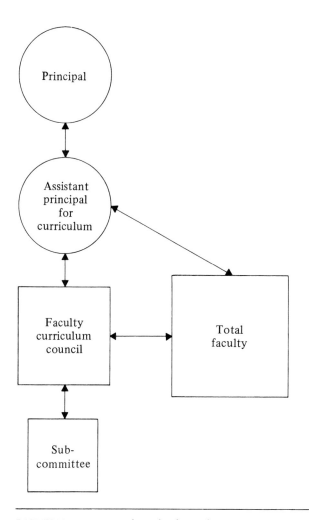

PATTERN 3   Principal works through an assistant principal.

must make distinctions between desired outcomes and processes. Technical decisions that must be made are often beyond the competence of lay citizens and students. Only if an expanded curriculum committee is composed of persons who are well informed about the processes of education and are highly motivated can this pattern meet with any degree of success.

Students and lay persons often participate with teachers and administrators on school-level curriculum committees. We will examine the roles of these constituent groups in curriculum development in the next chapter. We might ask at this point: What are typical curriculum tasks of the school-wide curriculum committee? The school curriculum committee or council must articulate with curriculum development efforts at the classroom and team/grade/department levels. In effect, the school-wide committee coordinates the work of these lower levels. It receives proposals for curricular change from the lower levels, especially proposals that affect more than one team, grade, or department or that are interdisciplinary in nature.

The school curriculum council considers proposals that require human and material resources, budgetary expenditures, and changes in staffing. The council conducts or supervises assessment of the educational needs of pupils. It coordinates the development of a statement of school philosophy. It specifies and regularly reviews curriculum goals and objectives for the school.

The curriculum council plans the evaluation of the curriculum. It studies results of student assessment and proposes changes based on the data gathered. The council studies the educational needs of the community and implements programs to meet legitimate needs. The council seeks solutions to short-range curricular problems while also establishing and refining long-range plans.

PATTERN 4   Principal involves lay citizens and students as well as faculty.

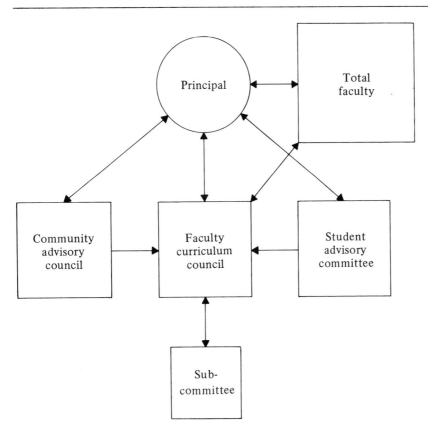

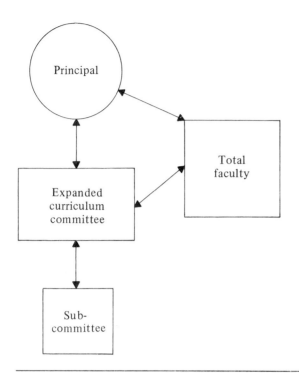

PATTERN 5   Principal involves lay citizens, students, and faculty in a combined curriculum committee.

The council is both proactive and reactive in its manner of operating. Whereas it may react to proposals presented by both the principal and the faculty, it also generates its own proposals and solutions to curricular problems. At the time of a pending school evaluation by a regional accreditation team, the curriculum council may act as a steering committee and assign specific tasks to various committees. The council coordinates an intensive self-study prior to the visit of an accrediting team.

The council must assure articulation between and among the various grades and departments of the school, making certain that teachers are following agreed-upon sequences and meeting minimal prescribed objectives. Requests from higher levels and various sectors for the school's cooperation on curriculum projects are routed to the curriculum council.

The local school curriculum council occupies a strategic position and fulfills a key role in the process of curriculum development. Of all groups at all levels and sectors of planning, the school-wide curriculum council is in the position to make the most significant contributions to curriculum improvement.

The School-District Level

None of the previously discussed levels — classroom, team/grade/department, or individual school — can work as isolated units. They function within the context of the school district under the direction of the duly elected school board and its administrative officer, the superintendent. Their efforts must be coordinated among themselves and with the central district office. Goals and objectives of the subordinate units must mesh with those of the district level. Consequently, the superintendent must provide a mechanism whereby district-level curriculum planning may be conducted.

Curriculum planning on a district-wide level is often conducted through the district curriculum council composed of teachers, administrators, supervisors, lay persons, and, in some cases, students. The size of the district curriculum council and the extent of its representation depend upon the size of the school district. Representatives may be either elected by members of their respective groups or appointed by district-level administrators, frequently on the recommendation of school principals.

Decisions and Organizational Patterns. District-wide committees meet to consider problems such as:

- adding new programs for the district
- abandoning district-wide programs
- reviewing student achievement in the various schools and recommending ways to improve programs of deficient schools, if any
- writing or reviewing proposals for state and federal grants
- gathering data on student achievement for presentation to parent groups and lay advisory councils
- supervising district compliance with state mandates and federal legislation
- evaluating programs on a district-wide basis
- articulating programs between levels

The patterns that follow show typical organizational arrangements for curriculum development at the district level. The patterns increase in complexity as the size of the school district increases. The district represented in Pattern 1 utilizes a curriculum council composed of professionals only — administrators and supervisors named by the superintendent and teachers selected by their principals or elected by their faculties to represent them on the council. Subcommittees of professionals from anywhere in the school system are appointed by the curriculum council to conduct specific phases of curriculum development. The community advisory council serves in an advisory capacity to the superintendent and may or may not consider curriculum matters. Subordinate school units are responsible to the superintendent through the principals. Pattern 2 is essentially like Pattern 1 except this

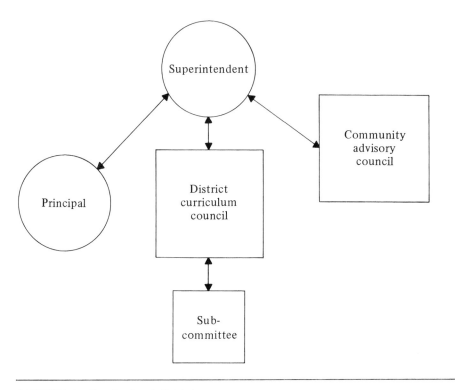

PATTERN 1   Small school district

school district extends membership on the curriculum council to students and lay persons.

The superintendent of the district depicted in Pattern 3 delegates curriculum leadership responsibility to the assistant superintendent for curriculum and instruction. This assistant superintendent makes use of a steering committee, which oversees all phases of curriculum development. This committee, which is created through appointment, election, or a combination thereof, appoints task forces of professional persons in the school system and lay committees to serve as sounding boards for curriculum matters. The community council advises the superintendent on educational matters that are of concern to the citizens whom it represents. The principals and their subordinate units report to the assistant superintendent.

Pattern 4 charts the organizational structure for curriculum development in a large county system administratively broken down into four areas, each of which is placed under the control of an area superintendent. The area superintendents report on matters of curriculum and instruction to the assistant superintendent for curriculum and instruction who, in turn, is responsible to the superintendent. Each area superintendent charges a director of instruction or a director of elementary and secondary schools with the job of leadership in curriculum development. In each of the four areas, a curriculum council, made up of administrators, supervisors, and teachers representative of the area, works with the director of instruction in the vital task of improving the curriculum in their subdivision of the district. Subcommittees are appointed by the curriculum councils as they are needed in their areas. Principals and their subordinate units are supervised by the directors of instruction. In some cases the directors of instruction supervise only in curriculum and instruction; in other cases, in all areas, including administrative matters. The area superintendents enlist the aid of community advisory councils, which advise them on curricular and other matters. To maintain coordition among the four areas of the district, the assistant superintendent has established a district-wide curriculum coordinating council.

Decisions made at the area level, which is a subdistrict of the larger school district, affect all the schools within that area while decisions made at the district level are binding on all schools of the entire system. The district curriculum council serves in a coordinating capacity. It acts on proposals from subordinate levels; develops or causes to be developed statements of district philosophy, goals, and objectives; and establishes minimal competencies to be achieved by all students in the entire district. It recom-

PATTERN 2   Small school district with expanded curriculum council composed of administrators, teachers, students, and lay people

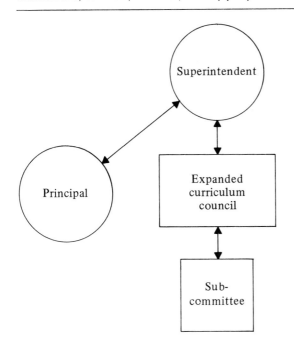

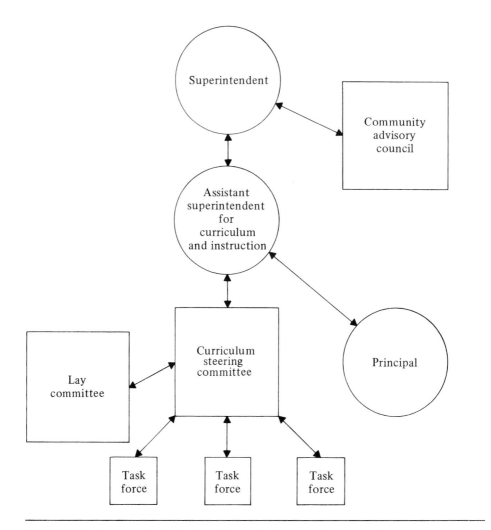

PATTERN 3   Larger school district with curriculum steering committee

mends on district-wide programs and projects, develops plans to secure federal moneys, and reviews district efforts to cooperate with state, regional,
national, and other outside agencies on curriculum matters. The district curriculum committees, such as the curriculum steering committee shown in
Pattern 3 and the curriculum coordinating council of Pattern 4, can be extremely influential groups; they, in the last analysis, make the final recommendations on curriculum to the chief administrator who, upon approval,
takes them to the school board for action.

Sequence for Decision Making. We might summarize the sequence for decision making by the curriculum groups at the various levels within a school

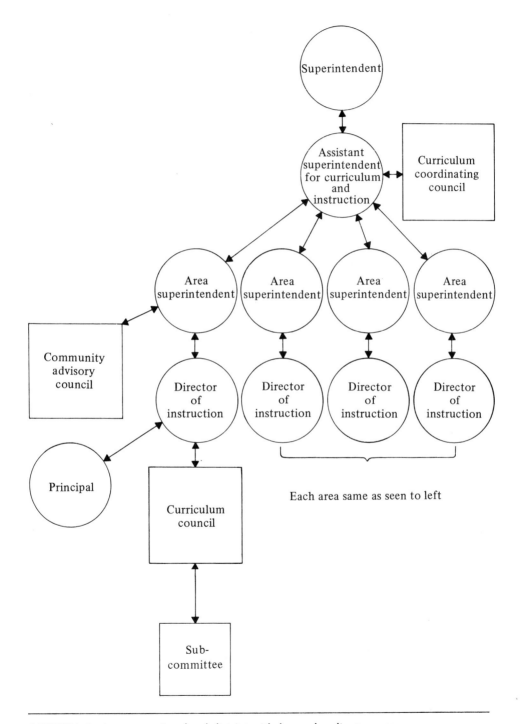

PATTERN 4   Large county school district with four subordinate areas

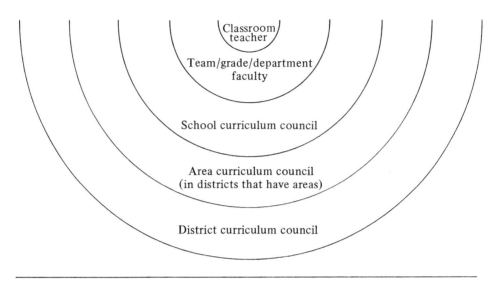

FIGURE 3-5   Sequence of decision making

system in the form of waves starting in the individual teacher's classroom and terminating with the district curriculum coordinating council, as pictured in Figure 3-5. Teachers new to a school system should be informed, perhaps through a faculty handbook or other means, of the district's structures for curriculum development. Teachers should be aware not only of the process of curriculum development in the district but also of the opportunities for curricular leadership.

Each level receives information, ideas, and proposals from the lower levels and, in turn, sends information, ideas, and proposals to them. Each level acts within the limitations of its own "territory." Councils at any level may initiate action as well as react to suggestions made to them. Councils must be responsive to both subordinate and higher levels. If a council wishes to initiate a plan that affects levels below it, it must involve persons from those levels from the earliest planning stage. If a council wishes to initiate or endorse a plan that goes beyond its "territory" or that might likely create repercussions anywhere in the system, it must seek approvals of higher levels.

Before discussing curriculum development at the next level — the state level — the following observations should be made about the previously discussed organizational patterns for curriculum development.

□ Although administrators — the principal or superintendent — have been shown at the top of each model, the patterns should not be considered simply administrative models in which orders are given by the administrator to his or her subordinates. The arrows at both ends of the lines from administrator to curriculum committees signify that exchange is a two-way rather than a one-way process. The administrator is shown in the patterns because, like Everest, he or she is there. The administrator holds the power for final decision making and must take the consequences if decisions prove to be wrong. The administrator's presence at the top of each pattern does not in itself make the pattern an undemocratic one.

The key difference between a democratic and an undemocratic process is the involvement of people. No administrator worth his or her keep can turn over the decision-making process completely to others. Yet, every administrator can seek to obtain the widest possible participation of persons in that process.

□ The patterns presented are rather typical arrangements that permit the work of curriculum development to be carried out by the professionals in the school system and by others whose aid they solicit. Other patterns also exist. Zais, for example, analyzed a number of existing and proposed models of curriculum development.[18]

□ Realistically, we must admit that a significant amount of curriculum change is brought about *outside* of the established structure. Individual teachers and small committees often effect changes that are well received and disseminated throughout the school system and sometimes beyond. B. Frank Brown pointed out that a few teachers, by their example, may be instrumental in bringing about curriculum revision, a process he referred to as "spinning out."[19] The public and teachers' organizations are often ahead of the designated curriculum leaders.[20]

□ The patterns described in this chapter are models of structure — the organizational arrangements whereby the professionals and those who assist them may apply their knowledge and skills to curriculum improvement. We should distinguish these organizational patterns from models for the process of curriculum development, which we will consider in Chapter 5.

The State Level

Curriculum development beyond the boundaries of the school district seems like a remote undertaking to most school personnel. Administrators, teachers, and others are aware, sometimes painfully, that curriculum development does go on outside the school district and that it has an impact on schools of the district. Yet, relatively few school personnel in proportion to the number of employees are actively involved in curriculum making outside the district and then rarely on a sustaining basis.

---

18 Zais, Chapter 19.

19 B. Frank Brown, *The Nongraded High School* (Englewood Cliffs, N.J.: Prentice-Hall, 1963), pp. 209–210.

20 See Peter F. Oliva, "In Search of the Curriculum Leader," *FASCD Journal,* no. 2 (February 1980): 29–33.

As we move further and further away from the district level, the percentage of school personnel actively and continuously participating in curriculum development shrinks in size. Were the state not in a superordinate position over the local school districts and were the state not directly responsible for the educational system within its borders, we should classify the state as a sector rather than as a level. It is clear, however, that by Amendment X of the United States Constitution and by the state constitutions, the state holds the primary power over education in this country.

Channels Within Education. The state also operates in the arena of curriculum development through channels within the profession of education. The state department of education — an agency of the executive branch of the state government — headed by a chief state school officer, his or her staff, and school personnel from the various districts of the state who are called on to assist the state department of education constitute the professional channel for curriculum development under the aegis of the state.

State Departments of Education. The state department of education, often a large bureaucracy, exercises direct responsibility over the curriculum of the schools of the state. Led by a chief state school officer (superintendent or commissioner of education), the state department consists of a number of assistant superintendents, heads of branches, curriculum specialists, and other staff members. The state department of education provides leadership generally to the schools; interprets, enforces, and monitors legislated regulations as well as its own which attain the force of law.

The state department of education wields great power over the districts of the state. In curriculum matters it accredits school programs, disburses state and federal-through-state moneys for specific programs, approves standards for high school graduation, and sets specifications for amounts of time to be devoted to specific content areas. The state department of education develops statewide statements of philosophy, goals, and objectives. Additionally, the state department of education makes available a limited amount of consultant help to the individual schools and districts and conducts evaluations of school programs.

At times, decisions are made on the state level without advance consultation with the local school personnel of the state. At other times, however, the state department of education seeks advice and assistance from individuals and from ad hoc committees which they create for the purpose of studying specific problems and recommending solutions. Administrators and teachers are often asked to participate in organizing, conducting, or attending conferences and workshops held throughout the state on specific topics, e.g., drug abuse, programs for the handicapped, eliminating sexism; writing curriculum guides; conducting research studies; identifying teacher competencies; specifying minimal competencies that students should be expected to achieve at each grade level; and selecting textbooks for state adoption.

The state department of education takes a leadership role in disseminating information regarding curriculum innovations and practices among the schools of the state. It issues both regular and periodic bulletins, monographs, and newsletters, frequently containing articles written by persons from local school districts, to keep local school personnel up-to-date on recent developments in curriculum, instruction, and other matters.

The state's presence in all school matters is a commanding one. Yet, bureaucratic as it may be, local school personnel do find limited opportunity to participate in curriculum decision making through established state channels.

State Professional Organizations. In a less formal way curriculum workers find opportunities for curriculum planning and consideration of curriculum problems through activities of the state professional organizations. Conference programs of such organizations as the state chapters of the National Council for the Social Studies, the National Council of Teachers of English, and the Association for Supervision and Curriculum Development customarily focus on curriculum concerns. Although the participants may engage in curriculum planning in only the most rudimentary and often passive way, the sharing of curriculum ideas often lays groundwork for subsequent curriculum planning. This type of curriculum activity cannot, of course, be equated with more structured efforts under the state department of education. Nor can we truly label the examination of curriculum problems by state professional organizations as a level of planning as no element of authority exists in this type of voluntary activity. More appropriately, the state professional organizations constitute a state sector that seeks to effect curriculum change through example and persuasion. Nevertheless, we would be remiss if we did not credit state professional organizations for the influence they often have in bringing about changes in the curriculum of the local school systems of the state.

Channels Outside of Education. Other departments of the executive branch, the state legislature, and the state judicial branch form channels outside the profession of education. Within the executive branch are the governor and state board of education who wield tremendous power over the state educational system. The governor presents a budget to the legislature in which he or she recommends supporting or curtailing programs.

Legislative Decisions. State legislatures throughout the country consistently demonstrate a penchant for curriculum making. The legislature of the state of Florida is an excellent case as the following statute reveals:

> Members of the instructional staff of the public schools, subject to the rules and regulations of the state board and of the school board, shall teach efficiently and faithfully, using the books and materials required, following the prescribed courses of study, and employing approved methods of instruction the following: The essentials of the United States Constitution,

flag education, including proper flag display and flag salute, the elements of civil government, the elementary principles of agriculture, the true effects of all alcoholic and intoxicating liquors and beverages and narcotics upon the human body and mind, kindness to animals, the history of the state, conservation of natural resources, and such additional materials, subjects, courses, or fields in such grades as may be prescribed by law or by regulations of the state board and the school board. . . .[21]

The legislature became very specific when it required a high school course in Americanism versus Communism, stipulating:

The public high schools shall each teach a complete course of not less than 30 hours, to all students enrolled in said pubic high schools entitled "Americanism versus Communism."

The course shall provide adequate instruction in the history, doctrines, objectives and techniques of Communism and shall be for the primary purpose of instilling in the mind of the students a greater appreciation of the democratic processes, freedom under law, and the will to preserve that freedom.

The course . . . shall emphasize the free-enterprise-competitive economy of the United States as the one which produces higher wages, higher standards of living, greater personal freedom and liberty than any other system of economics on earth.

The course shall lay particular emphasis upon the dangers of Communism, the ways to fight Communism, the evils of Communism, the fallacies of Communism, and the false doctrines of Communism.[22]

Perhaps even more sweeping is the statute of the Florida legislature directing the commissioner (state superintendent) to:

Develop and administer in the public schools a uniform, statewide program of assessment to determine, periodically, educational status and progress and the degree of achievement of approved minimum performance standards. The uniform statewide program shall consist of testing in grades 3, 5, 8 and 11 and may include the testing of additional grades and skill areas as specified by the commissioner.[23]

While some legislation is a result of grass-roots movements within the state and some statutes evolve from recommendations made by the state superintendent and the state department of education, many acts of the state legislature stem from the personal beliefs and desires of the legislators themselves. Even the state judicial branch finds itself entangled in curriculum decision making from time to time. Two famous cases may serve to illustrate involvement of the state courts in curriculum making.

The Supreme Court of Michigan ruled in 1874 in a case brought against

---

[21] Florida Statute 233.061, *Florida School Laws* (1979), p. 83.
[22] Florida Statute 233.064, *Florida School Laws*, p. 83.
[23] Florida Statute 229.565, *Florida School Laws*, p. 19.

the school district of Kalamazoo by a taxpayer of that community that the school board of Kalamazoo could, indeed, spend public funds to provide a secondary school education for youth of their district.[24]

In 1927 the Supreme Court of Tennessee replied to the appeal of the defense attorneys of John Thomas Scopes of the world famous "monkey trial" by upholding the constitutionality of the Tennessee law that forbade teaching in the public schools any theory which denied the creation of man by a Divine Being.[25] It is both interesting and pertinent to this discussion to note that in 1979, legislatures in Iowa, Minnesota, and Florida attempted to mandate the teaching of "scientific creationism" in the public schools as a counterbalance to the theory of evolution.

SECTORS OF PLANNING

When the curriculum planner leaves the state level and moves onto the broader scene, he or she works in quite a different context. Participation in planning in the regional, national, and international sectors is ordinarily a voluntary activity. Except in the case of federal legislation, information sharing and persuasion rather than statutory power are the powerful tools of the regional, national, and international sectors. No assurance of any kind exists that curriculum decisions reached in these sectors will or can be put into operation in the schools.

Fewer opportunities exist for curriculum workers to engage in planning in the regional, national, and international sectors. Yet, the opportunities that do arise can be exciting for the participants.

The Regional Sector

Participation in planning in the regional, national, and international sectors is not comparable to that in the previously described levels. It is true that on occasion curriculum specialists of a particular region of the United States, from around the nation, or even from a number of foreign countries may assemble and develop curriculum materials which they will then disseminate or try out in their own schools. Most notable illustrations of this type of cooperative endeavor were those of the scholars from various parts of the country who in the late fifties developed the so-called "new math" and "new science" programs.

As a general rule, curriculum activities in the regional, national, and international sectors consist more of sharing problems, exchanging practices, reporting research, and gathering information. Conferences of the professional organizations, like the South Atlantic Modern Language Association,

---

24 *Stuart v. School District No. 1, Village of Kalamazoo,* 30 Mich. 69 (1874).
25 See Lyon Sprague de Camp, *The Great Monkey Trial* (Garden City, New York: Doubleday, 1968).

are the most common vehicle whereby school personnel participate in regional curriculum study.

With considerable frequency school personnel — teachers, administrators and curriculum specialists — are invited to take part in the activities of the regional associations (New England, Middle States, Southern, North Central, Northwest, and Western), which accredit schools and colleges. This participation consists of three types. First, school personnel are invited to serve on various committees and commissions of the associations, e.g., Commission on Elementary Schools and the regional association's committee within each state. Second, committees of professionals review, revise, and write for each subject area the criteria that schools must meet to be accredited by the associations. Third, and most extensive of the three types of participation, is service on accreditation committees that go into a school in the region to discover the strengths and weaknesses of its programs and to make recommendations for improvements and accreditation of the school.

Much of the participation in which school personnel take part in the regional sector falls into the category of curriculum evaluation as opposed to planning or implementation.

The National Sector

U. S. Department of Education. The national scene is peppered with a variety of public, private, and professional curriculum activities in some of which school personnel from the state level and below play key roles. In the public, governmental sector, the Department of Education exercises a strong influence. Formerly called the United States Office of Education until education was separated from the U. S. Department of Health, Education, and Welfare in 1980, the Department of Education with its large bureaucracy gathers data, disseminates information, provides consultant assistance, sponsors and conducts research, funds projects, and disburses money appropriated by the Congress. Local school personnel find the opportunity to participate in national curriculum efforts by writing and submitting proposals for grants to conduct curricular research or to put particular programs into operation in their school systems.

Federal Funding. To choose recipients of funds for proposals awarded competitively, the Department of Education calls in readers who are specialists in the particular fields in which grants are being given, such as bilingual education. These readers evaluate and make recommendations on proposals to be awarded by the specific office within the Department of Education. Several persons from all over the United States journey to Washington (or sometimes to other sites) to read proposals. In so doing, they grow professionally and bring back new ideas for curriculum development in their own communities.

Federal funding permits numerous committees to carry out curriculum projects which the United States Congress deems significant, e.g., Title I of the Elementary and Secondary Education Act, for programs aiding the culturally disadvantaged. Thus, local school personnel in communities that receive federal moneys not only develop proposals but actually put them into operation.

Funds from the federal government have enabled national study groups to prepare curriculum materials, some of which have been used extensively, such as the Glastonbury (Connecticut) audio-lingual materials for teaching modern languages, which became known as *A-LM*.[26]

Federal aid has stimulated and resulted in the involvement of curriculum workers both directly as participants and indirectly as consumers of products of the Educational Resources Information Centers (ERIC) clearinghouses, e.g., ERIC Clearinghouse for Science, Mathematics, and Environmental Education at The Ohio State University, and the Regional Educational Laboratories, e.g., the Northwest Regional Educational Laboratory in Portland, Oregon.[27]

The publicly funded National Science Foundation joined with the United States Office of Education to assist social studies and humanities specialists led by Jerome S. Bruner[28] to develop *Man: A Course of Study,* a multimedia curriculum for elementary school pupils.[29] Heralded by many, *Man: A Course of Study* presents an interesting case of problems of curriculum development on a national scale. Imbued with the ambitious goal of analyzing the human condition, *Man: A Course of Study* became controversial subject matter in contrasting life in the United States with life among members of an Eskimo tribe.

John D. McNeil pointed out that criticisms of *Man: A Course of Study* (MACOS) came from several quarters — from humanists who "criticized Bruner for failing to recognize MACOS' potential for fostering emotional growth," from "social reconstructionists opposed [to] MACOS on grounds that it was created by a scholarly elite" and from the U. S. Congress, where a Congressman "said the material was full of references to adultery, cannibalism, killing of female babies and old people, trial marriage, wife-swapping, and violent murders." [30]

Historically, the leadership of the United States Department of Education in curriculum planning for the schools of this nation can be traced back many years. One of the more significant attempts at curriculum decision mak-

---

26 *A-LM,* (New York: Harcourt, Brace, Jovanovich). Available in French, German, Italian, Russian, and Spanish.

27 See Appendices B, C, and D of this text.

28 Author of *The Process of Education* (Cambridge, Mass.: Harvard University Press, 1960).

29 *Man: A Course of Study* (Washington, D. C.: Curriculum Development Associates, 1970).

30 John D. McNeil, *Curriculum: A Comprehensive Introduction,* 2d ed. (Boston: Little, Brown, 1981), p. 60.

ing was the appointment of the Commission on the Reorganization of Secondary Education following World War I. In 1918 this Commission stated the purposes of secondary education in the United States in the form of Seven Cardinal Principles.[31] These principles were:

1. health
2. command of fundamental processes (currently known as the basic skills)
3. worthy home membership
4. vocation
5. citizenship
6. worthy use of leisure
7. ethical character

The Commission's report, possessing no authority other than its persuasiveness, was widely received and accepted as a valid statement of goals for secondary education of its time. Many high schools over the years have attempted to operationalize the Commission's Cardinal Principles. Many educators feel that this statement of the purposes of secondary education is as relevant today as it was when first issued so many years ago.[32]

Development of curricula in specialized fields has been made possible by the National Science Foundation in cooperation with professional associations. The National Science Foundation, the American Mathematical Society, the National Council of Teachers of Mathematics, and the Mathematical Association of America joined forces in the fifties to produce the School Mathematics Study Group (SMSG) program for grades four through twelve. Involved in the production of this program were mathematicians, mathematics educators, and high school teachers. At about the same time and through a similar collaborative effort, the American Institute of Biological Sciences with financial backing by the National Science Foundation brought forth the Biological Sciences Curriculum Study (BSCS) programs (in three versions) for high school biology.

Local schools in various regions of the country have participated in curriculum evaluation on a national scale through the National Assessment of Educational Progress, based in Denver and funded by the National Center for Education Statistics of the U. S. Department of Education. Under the direction of the National Assessment of Educational Progress, objectives have been specified, criterion-referenced measurement instruments have been created, and assessments have been conducted in ten subject areas: art, career and occupational development, citizenship, literature, mathematics, music, science, social studies, reading, and writing. Although test scores made by individual

---

[31] Commission on the Reorganization of Secondary Education, *Cardinal Principles of Secondary Education* (Washington, D. C.: United States Office of Education, Bulletin no. 35, 1918).

[32] For recent criticism of the Seven Cardinal Principles, see Chapter 9 of this text.

schools are not divulged, the National Assessment of Educational Progress reports data by geographical area, size and type of community, race, age-groups, and the educational attainment of parents. From these data curriculum developers in the local school systems can draw inferences about appropriate objectives of the areas tested, achievements of pupils in their region as compared to other regions, and their own state and local assessment programs.

Private Foundations. Several private foundations, notably the Ford and Kellogg Foundations, have demonstrated a keen interest in supporting projects designed to improve education in the United States. Ford has given generous backing to experimentation with novel staff patterns in the schools and the use of educational television, whereas Kellogg has zeroed in on studies of educational administration. As examples of foundations' interest in the curriculum of the schools we might mention the Carnegie Corporation's support in the field of mathematics and the Alfred P. Sloan Foundation's aid in the field of science. The Carnegie Corporation financially backed professors in arts and sciences, education and engineering at the University of Illinois to develop a school mathematics program for grades nine through twelve, which has become known as the University of Illinois Committee on School Mathematics (UICSM) math. Shortly thereafter, in the late 1950s, the Carnegie Corporation funded another mathematics project: the development of a program for grades seven and eight by teachers of mathematics, mathematicians, and mathematics educators at the University of Maryland.

The Alfred P. Sloan Foundation entered into curriculum development in the late 1950s by supporting, along with the National Science Foundation and the Ford Foundation's Fund for the Advancement of Education, the production of a new program for high school physics known as Physical Science Study Committee (PSSC) physics.

Several observations can be made about these illustrations of national curriculum development in mathematics and science. First, these programs were developed through the collaboration of scholars and practitioners, professors and teachers, combinations which have been tried with rather low frequency, unfortunately. Second, all of these undertakings took considerable effort and cost a significant amount of money. Without the largesse of the federal government, public and private foundations, and professional organizations, these materials would most probably have never seen the light of day. Third, as you may have already noted, all these developments occurred in the decade of the fifties and continued into the early sixties. The fifties were a time when there was great ferment in education and money flowed into educational pursuits as if from the proverbial horn of plenty. As a response to Russian technology and in the name of national defense, the availability of funds for educational projects and research made the fifties a heady time for educators. No such concerted collaborative activity on such a broad scale has occurred since, and we may well ponder whether it is ever likely to occur again. Finally and most significantly, in spite of the curriculum fervor of the fifties (Could it be *because* of the fervor of the fifties?), some of the "new math" and the "new science" programs have gone into eclipse, causing us to muse with François Villon, "Where are the snows of yesteryear?"

The professional education associations afford opportunities for educators to engage in curriculum deliberations. Over the years the National Education Association has repeatedly called together influential groups to evaluate purposes and programs of the schools. The NEA's Committee of Ten issued a report in 1893 that recommended the same courses (foreign languages, history, mathematics, and science) and the same allotment of time for each course for both college bound and noncollege bound students.[33] Gerald R. Firth and Richard D. Kimpston commented on the influence of the Committee of Ten's report:

> The recommendations of courses to be taught, coupled with a statement that the courses should be offered in the same manner to both the college-bound and the non-college bound, became a powerful force influencing the secondary school curriculum well into the 20th century.[34]

Between 1938 and 1961 the prestigious Educational Policies Commission of the National Education Association formulated statements of the purposes of education. Three of these statements have had an enduring effect on American education. In 1938 the Educational Policies Commission defined the purposes of education as fourfold: self-realization, human relationship, economic efficiency, and civic responsibility.[35] Six years later in the midst of World War II the Educational Policies Commission released its report on *Education for All American Youth* which set forth ten imperative educational needs of American youth.[36]

Refining the earlier Seven Cardinal Principles, the Educational Policies Commission in 1944 saw the purposes of secondary education as follows:

1. All youth need to develop salable skills.
2. All youth need to develop and maintain good health, physical fitness, and mental health.
3. All youth need to understand the rights and duties of the citizen of a democratic society.
4. All youth need to understand the significance of the family.

---

[33] National Education Association, *Report of the Committee of Ten on Secondary School Studies* (New York: American Book, 1894).

[34] Reproduced by permission of the publisher, F. E. Peacock Publishers, Inc., Itasca, Illinois. From Gerald R. Firth and Richard D. Kimpston, *The Curricular Continuum in Perspective,* 1973 copyright, p. 70.

[35] Educational Policies Commission, *The Purposes of Education in American Democracy* (Washington, D. C.: National Education Association, 1938).

[36] Educational Policies Commission, *Education for All American Youth* (Washington, D. C.: National Education Association, 1944).

5. All youth need to know how to purchase and use goods and services intelligently.
6. All youth need to understand the methods of science.
7. All youth need opportunities to develop their capacities to appreciate beauty in literature, art, music, and nature.
8. All youth need to be able to use their leisure time well.
9. All youth need to develop respect for other people, to grow in their insight into ethical values and principles, to be able to live and work cooperatively with others, and to grow in the moral and spiritual values of life.
10. All youth need to grow in their ability to think rationally, to express their thoughts clearly, and to read and listen with understanding.[37]

Once again, this time in 1961, the Educational Policies Commission turned its attention to the purposes of education and decided that the central purpose of American education was to develop the ability to think.[38]

On the current scene, the Association for Supervision and Curriculum Development, a professional association with a special interest in curriculum improvement, engages its members and others in numerous curriculum studies. It disseminates the results of studies through its journal, *Educational Leadership,* its yearbooks, and its monographs. Of special help to persons interested in the curriculum field are the ASCD's National Curriculum Study Institutes in which participants under the leadership of recognized experts focus on particular curriculum problems.

In this discussion of curriculum efforts on a national scale we have mentioned the executive branch of the U. S. government (the Department of Education) and the legislative branch (the U. S. Congress). We should not neglect to mention that on occasion the judicial branch of the federal government assumes the role of curriculum maker. For example, the United States Supreme Court has ruled that public schools may not conduct sectarian practices,[39] that released time for religious instruction under certain conditions is permissible,[40] that the theory of evolution may be taught,[41] that special instruction in English must be given to non-English speaking pupils,[42] and that prayer in the public school is a violation of the First Amendment of the U. S. Constitution.[43] Needless to say, the U. S. Supreme Court justices do not seek the role of curriculum specialists but by virtue of the cases that come before them sometimes find themselves in that role.

---

[37] Educational Policies Commission, *American Youth,* pp. 225–226.
[38] Educational Policies Commission, *The Central Purpose of American Education* (Washington, D. C.: National Education Association, 1961).
[39] *Illinois ex rel McCollum* v. *Board of Education,* 333 US 203, 68 S. Ct. 461 (1948).
[40] *Zorach* v. *Clauson,* 343 US 306, 72 S. Ct. 679 (1952).
[41] *Epperson* v. *Arkansas,* 393 US 97, 89 S. Ct. 266 (1968).
[42] *Lau* v. *Nichols,* 414 US 663 (1974).
[43] *School District of Abington Township, Pa.* v. *Schemp & Murray* v. *Curlett,* 374 US 203, 83 S. Ct. 1560 (1963).

Tests and Texts. Before we leave the national sector, we should explore an aspect of curriculum development that has evoked considerable discussion. Standardized tests of achievement and textbooks used in the schools have played a great part in molding the contemporary curriculum. Combined with the movement toward specification of minimal competencies for high school graduation, achievement tests profoundly affect what is being taught and how it is being taught. Under these conditions, curriculum decisions have been, in effect, put into the hands of the test makers and the textbook writers. Some curriculum experts see the reliance on tests and textbooks as constituting a "national curriculum." [44] Elliot W. Eisner expressed concern about the influence of the testing movement:

> One may wax eloquent about the life of the mind and the grand purposes of education, but must face up to the fact that school programs are shaped by other factors, as well. Communities led to believe that the quality of education is represented by the reading and math scores students receive come to demand that those areas of the curriculum be given highest priority. When this happens, teachers begin to define their own priorities in terms of test performance. Indeed, I do not believe it an exaggeration to say that test scores function as one of the most powerful controls on the character of educational practice. [45]

Considerable activity in planning, implementing, and evaluating curriculum transpires in the national sector. While curriculum activities on the national scene are many and diverse, opportunities for personal involvement in planning are rather limited for the rank-and-file teacher and curriculum specialist. Their roles are more often as recipients of curriculum plans developed by others, implementors of plans, and sometimes evaluators.

The International Sector

World Council for Curriculum and Instruction. Involvement of curriculum workers on the international scene is made possible through membership in international professional associations, primarily those based in the United States. The International Reading Association, for example, attracts reading specialists from around the world but primarily from the United States and Canada. One of the more pertinent international organizations for those interested in curricular activities on an international scale is the World Council for Curriculum and Instruction (WCCI). [46] With its Secretariat at Teachers College, Columbia University, the World Council is open to all educators who have an interest in "global fellowship." This organization, comprised of

---

[44] Other educators identify textbooks that are used throughout the country and federal aid for specific categories as types of national curricula.

[45] Elliot W. Eisner, *The Educational Imagination: On the Design and Evaluation of School Programs* (New York: Macmillan, 1979), p. 2.

[46] World Council for Curriculum and Instruction Secretariat, Box 171, Teachers College, Columbia University, New York, New York 10027.

members from more than seventy countries, provides advice and assistance on curricular matters, carries out transnational projects, and sponsors triennial conferences in various locations throughout the world.

If teachers and administrators are willing to spend a period of time abroad, they can become intimately involved in curriculum development overseas by accepting employment in the U. S. Department of Defense Schools[47] or in the private American Community/International Schools whose curricula are mainly those offered statewide. Or they may become active in developing curricula of national schools through employment with the Peace Corps or the Agency for International Development.

UNESCO. The United Nations Educational, Scientific, and Cultural Organization with headquarters in Paris affords opportunities for curriculum study, research, teaching, and technical assistance to educators from the member United Nations. The Institute of International Education in New York City directs an international exchange of students and teachers supported in part by Fulbright funds. The Council for International Exchange of Scholars in Washington, D. C., administers Fulbright grants that enable faculty from institutions of higher education to conduct research and teach in foreign countries.

Opportunities for firsthand participation in actual curriculum construction on a cross-national basis are rare, which is, perhaps, to be expected. The curricular needs and goals of education in various countries are so divergent as to make impractical the building of a particular curriculum that will fit the requirements of the educational system of each country.

Comparative Studies of Student Achievement. Significant efforts primarily in the realm of curriculum evaluation should be mentioned. Funded by the U. S. Office of Education and the Ford Foundation, the International Association for the Evaluation of Educational Achievement (IEA) conducted cross-national studies of student achievement in mathematics, science, literature, reading comprehension, foreign languages (English and French), and civic education.[48] Carried out on a grand scale, the study surveyed some 250,000 students and 50,000 teachers in twenty-two countries. The study of achievement in mathematics alone surveyed more than 130,000 students taught by over 13,000 teachers in more than 5,000 schools of twelve countries.[49] For

---

47 These schools may be placed under the administration of the U.S. Department of Education.

48 See T. Neville Posthlethwaite, "International Educational Surveys," *Contemporary Education* 42, no. 2 (November 1970): 61–68.

Joseph Featherstone, "Measuring What Schools Achieve: Learning and Testing," *The New Republic* 169, no. 24 (December 15, 1973): 19–21.

"International Study Brings Coleman Report into Question," *Phi Delta Kappan* 55, no. 5 (January 1974): 358.

49 See Torsten Husén, ed., *International Study of Achievement in Mathematics,* vols. 1 & 2 (New York: John Wiley & Sons, 1967).

the United States the results of the IEA studies were both encouraging and discouraging. If the IEA research accomplished anything, it revealed how difficult it is to make comparisons across cultures.[50]

U.S.-U.S.S.R. Textbook Project. One of the more interesting international curriculum studies of recent years is the U.S.-U.S.S.R. Textbook Project in which educators of the United States and the Soviet Union have examined history and geography textbooks used in the secondary schools of each other's countries.[51] These educators have been searching for errors of fact and distortions in the textbooks. Through a planned joint report, they hope to correct these faults so that a more accurate picture of each other's country may be presented to students. This exciting approach to international curriculum study might well furnish a model that the United States could replicate with other countries.

Global Awareness. To this point we have concentrated on opportunities for collaborative cross-cultural curriculum research and development. A somewhat different curriculum activity is the current funding by the United States Department of Education of programs in the schools for the development of global awareness among American children and youth. In spite of international tensions, American commitment to the development of students' and teachers' understanding of foreign nations remains high as evidenced by the recommendations of the President's Commission on Foreign Languages and International Studies.[52] Among its many recommendations were:

□ regional centers for upgrading competencies for foreign language teachers
□ summer institutes abroad for foreign language teachers and others
□ reinstatement of foreign language requirements in schools and colleges
□ the integration of international studies throughout the school curricula
□ expansion of international exchanges of students, teachers, administrators, and policymakers
□ requirement of two to three courses in international studies for all bachelor's degree candidates
□ establishment of regional international studies centers at colleges and universities

---

[50] See also L. C. Comber and John P. Keeves, *Science Education in Nineteen Countries* (New York: John Wiley & Sons, 1973); Alan C. Purves, *Literature Education in Ten Countries* (New York: John Wiley, 1973); Robert L. Thorndike, *Reading Comprehension Education in Fifteen Countries* (New York: John Wiley & Sons, 1973).

[51] See G. K. Hodenfield, "The U.S.-U.S.S.R. Textbook Project," *American Education* 15, no. 1 (January-February, 1979): 27–29.

[52] See Malcolm G. Scully, "Require Foreign-Language Studies, Presidential Panel Urges Colleges," *The Chronicle of Higher Education* XIX, no. 11 (November 13, 1979): 1 ff.

If inflation does not defeat these well-intentioned recommendations, teachers, curriculum specialists, and others may find increased occasions for participation in curriculum development on a worldwide scale.

SUMMARY

Curriculum planning is viewed as occurring on five levels: classroom, team/grade/department, individual school, school district, and state. Each level in ascending order exercises authority over levels below it.

Planning takes place additionally in regional, national, and world sectors. Sectors are distinguished from levels since powers of the sectors over the five levels are either nonexistent or limited.

Teachers and curriculum specialists will find their most frequent opportunities to participate actively in curriculum development at the first four levels. Some curriculum workers are called on by the state to serve on curriculum projects. A limited number of school-based persons take part in a variety of curriculum efforts sponsored by regional, national, and international organizations and agencies.

This chapter diagrams a variety of organizational patterns for carrying out curriculum development activities in the individual school and school district. A teacher or curriculum specialist may be requested to serve on a number of curriculum committees and councils within a school system.

Forces outside the schools also influence curriculum decision making. Curriculum development is perceived as a multilevel, multisector process and as a collaborative effort.

SUPPLEMENTARY EXERCISES

1. Chart the organizational pattern for curriculum development in your school and district.
2. Write a short paper describing the extent to which the organizational patterns operating in your school system can be called participatory.
3. Tell how curriculum committees and councils are selected and constituted in your school district.
4. Account for any program changes in the last three years that resulted from curriculum development activities in the school district.
5. Describe activities of the faculty of a team, grade, or department in the area of curriculum development.
6. Describe any curriculum developments that have come about as a result of regional activities.
7. Describe any programs that exist in the schools as a result of federal assistance or legislation.

8. Describe any curriculum development in your school system that might be attributed to international influences.
9. Report on any national curriculum studies that you would call significant.
10. Report on any international curriculum studies that you would call significant.
11. Report on several programs that have come about or been affected as a result of state legislation.
12. Report on several programs that have come about or been affected as a result of federal legislation.
13. Report on the purposes and recent activities of at least two state, two national, and two international professional organizations concerned with curriculum development.
14. Report on the purposes and activities of the accrediting association of your region.
15. Report on at least two state and two federal court decisions that have had an impact on the curriculum of your school system.
16. Write a description of the processes, including political pressures, by which textbooks are selected in your state/district.

BIBLIOGRAPHY

Beauchamp, George A. *Curriculum Theory,* 3rd ed. Wilmette, Ill.: The Kagg Press, 1975.

Bruner, Jerome S. *The Process of Education.* Cambridge, Mass.: Harvard University Press, 1977.

Commission on the Reorganization of Secondary Education. *Cardinal Principles of Secondary Education.* Washington, D. C.: United States Office of Education, Bulletin no. 35, 1918.

Doll, Ronald C. *Curriculum Improvement: Decision Making and Process,* 4th ed. Boston: Allyn and Bacon, 1978. 5th ed., 1982.

Educational Policies Commission. *The Central Purpose of American Education.* Washington, D. C.: National Education Association, 1961.

————. *Education for All American Youth.* Washington, D. C.: National Education Association, 1944.

————. *The Purposes of Education in American Democracy.* Washington,

D. C.: National Education Association, 1938.

Eisner, Elliot W. *Confronting Curriculum Reform.* Boston: Little, Brown, 1971.

————. *The Educational Imagination: On the Design and Evaluation of School Programs.* New York: Macmillan, 1979.

Featherstone, Joseph. "Measuring What Schools Achieve," *Phi Delta Kappan* 55, no. 7 (March 1974): 448–450.

Firth, Gerald R. and Kimpston, Richard D. *The Curricular Continuum in Perspective.* Itasca, Ill.: F. E. Peacock Publishers, 1973.

Frymier, Jack R. and Hawn, Horace C. *Curriculum Improvement for Better Schools.* Worthington, Ohio: Charles A. Jones, 1970.

Hass, Glen, ed. *Curriculum Planning: a New Approach,* 3rd ed. Boston: Allyn and Bacon, 1980.

Husén, Torsten, ed. *International*

Study of Achievement in Mathematics, vols. 1 and 2. New York: John Wiley, 1967.

Kimbrough, Ralph B. and Nunnery, Michael Y. *Educational Administration: An Introduction.* New York: Macmillan, 1976.

McNeil, John D. *Curriculum: A Comprehensive Introduction,* 2d ed. Boston: Little, Brown, 1981.

Oliva, Peter F. *The Secondary School Today,* 2d ed. New York: Harper & Row, 1972.

Oliver, Albert I. *Curriculum Improvement: A Guide to Problems, Principles, and Process,* 2d ed. New York: Harper & Row, 1977.

Rubin, Louis, ed. *Curriculum Handbook: The Disciplines, Current Movements, and Instructional Methodology.* Boston: Allyn and Bacon, 1977.

Saylor, J. Galen and Alexander, William M. *Planning Curriculum for Schools.* New York: Holt, Rinehart and Winston, 1974.

Saylor, J. Galen; Alexander, William M.; and Lewis, Arthur J. *Curriculum Planning for Better Teaching and Learning,* 4th ed. New York: Holt, Rinehart and Winston, 1981.

Zais, Robert S. *Curriculum: Principles and Foundations.* New York: Harper & Row, 1976.

4

Curriculum Planning: The Human Dimension

After studying this chapter you should be able to:
1. Describe the roles of (a) the principal, (b) the curriculum leader, (c) the teachers, (d) the students, and (e) the parents and other citizens in curriculum development.
2. Describe the knowledge and skills needed by the curriculum leader.

You should also be able to formulate and give reasons for your views on the following issues:
1. The degree to which you possess leadership skills.
2. The degree to which you possess interpersonal skills.
3. The degree to which you possess communication skills.
4. The desirability of continual change in the curriculum.

THE SCHOOL AS A UNIQUE BLEND

Let us for a few moments step into the shoes of the superintendent of a school district. It is mid-May. The school year is almost over and summer school plans are ready to be implemented. The superintendent has just concluded a meeting with his principals on the budget and staffing needs for next year. In thirty minutes he will meet with an assistant superintendent and one of the principals of the district, who intend to bring charges of insubordination against one of the teachers in the principal's school. For a half hour he muses on what improvements in curriculum and instruction have been accomplished in the school district this year. Since his energies have been channeled into public relations, budgeting, personnel problems, transportation, new buildings, and other administrative matters, he has delegated responsibility for curriculum and instruction in the school district to the assistant superintendent for curriculum and instruction. He holds in his hands a report updating developments in the district this year.

The superintendent is struck by the large amount of time and effort that the school district is expending toward improving curriculum and instruction. He is impressed by the sizeable number of people involved in this activity. He notes that most teams of teachers meet practically daily; most grade faculties or departments meet as groups regularly, some of them on a weekly basis; every school has its own curriculum council, which meets at least once a month; and a number of curriculum committees meet at various times on district-wide problems of curriculum and instruction. The superintendent can certainly not fault the quantity of effort expended by the professionals in curriculum development.

As to quality he is less certain. He reviews some of the accomplishments to date and is struck by the unevenness of developments from school to school. It is evident that the accomplishments of some schools far outshine those of others. Several innovative programs are in experimental stages in some schools. Other schools have defined their philosophies, goals, and objectives. Some have conducted thorough re-examinations of their curricula whereas others have been content with the status quo. Several groups of teachers have revised their particular curricula. Other groups have developed some new curriculum guides. Some schools have responded to previously unmet curricular needs of their students while others have failed to come up with solutions to some of their more pressing curricular problems. The superintendent is surprised, though he realizes that he should not be, that a few schools obviously surpass the others in both quantity and quality of curriculum output. A few schools have tackled curriculum development with a vigor that has effected significant change. He finds repeated references in the assistant superintendent's report to positive changes made by a few schools. He concludes that some schools are imbued with the spirit of change and are willing to move forward and out, while others find the established ways of operating more comfortable. The superintendent wonders why such great variations in curriculum development exist from school to school. Whom should he credit in those schools that seem to be engaged in productive curriculum efforts? The principals? The teachers? The curriculum leaders, whoever they are? The students? The parents? The signs of the zodiac? Lady Luck? Or, a combination of all these factors?

The superintendent is aware that schools differ considerably from one another. Their physical facilities, resources, and locales all differ. Yet these more or less tangible factors do not explain the great differences in strides made by schools in curriculum and instruction. Yes, we may say that schools differ in many ways, but schools are only brick, concrete, mortar, steel, wood, glass, and a host of other building materials. It is not the schools that differ but the people who either support or operate within them. The superintendent must credit not the schools in the abstract but the people who make them tick. In his short period of reflection, the superintendent reinforces a long-held, verified belief — that curriculum development is a "people" process, a human endeavor. Curriculum development is a process in which the human players accept and carry out mutually reinforcing roles. Given a predisposition to change and a subtle blending of skills and knowledge, a faculty can achieve significant successes in curriculum improvement even in a substandard physical environment. The "people" setting far outweighs the physical setting.

Differences Among Faculty

Let's leave the meditating superintendent and focus our attention on another place, another time. It is early in the school year. The principal of a medium size secondary school is presiding over the initial organizational meeting of the school's curriculum council. Representatives of the nine departments of the school are about to elect their chairperson. With freshness, high spirits, and a modicum of levity, the curriculum council is getting under way. The principal wonders what progress the school will make this year in curriculum improvement. He realizes as he looks around the room that success in improving the curriculum depends largely on human differences among individual curriculum workers and between curriculum groups.

Each school is characterized by its own unique blend of persons, each with his or her own skills, knowledge, experience, and personality. The principal mentally lists some of the ways individuals within the curriculum council, which represents the faculty, differ. Certainly, the philosophical beliefs of the various council members diverge greatly. It will take considerable effort to reach some kind of consensus on the goals of this school, let alone the general goals of education. The council members differ in their knowledge about and ability to apply learning theory. Some are outstanding instructors, others only passable. Variations exist in the members' knowledge of curriculum history and theory and in experience in curriculum development.

Some younger members, new to teaching and the particular school, are less knowledgeable about children in general and in this setting than older teachers who have taught several years, many of them in this school. It also becomes apparent as soon as the council settles down to work that there are great differences in individuals' skills in interacting with others, in the leadership skills of the various council members, in followership skills, in organizational skills, in writing skills, and in oral skills.

Some of the council members will show themselves as being more perceptive of parental roles and the needs of the community. Personal traits like friendliness, reliability, motivation, sense of humor, enthusiasm, and frustration level are significant differences among individuals that contribute to the success or failure of group efforts like curriculum development. Outside commitments, family obligations, and allocations of time differ from person to person and can affect the process of curriculum planning.

The human variables in the process are many and complex. Success or failure will depend to a great extent on how the council members relate to each other; on how each member relates to other teachers on the faculty and how they, in turn, relate to one another. The way the council and faculty interact with parents, others in the community, and the students can make or break curriculum efforts.

Dependent Variables

The differences among individuals and groups participating in curriculum development are dependent rather than independent variables. The presence or absence of a particular skill or trait and the degree to which an individual possesses it have an impact on all other individuals who partake of the process. Not only are the leaders' leadership skills and the followers' followership skills significant in themselves but the manner in which they come together is even more important. Competence in leadership must ideally be met with competence in followership. Whether in military service, industry, or education, a superb leader is going nowhere without committed followers. In the same manner superb followers are going nowhere without competent leadership.

In accounting for success or failure in a cooperative enterprise, we should also look to differences among groups as well as individuals. It is trite but pertinent to say that the whole is greater than the sum of its parts. A group is not simply the addition of each individual member to make a sum but something more than the sum, something special created by an inexplicable meshing of the human elements. Working together, the group must become unified as it moves toward common goals in a spirit of mutual respect. Thus, a curriculum council *as a group* can demonstrate leadership skills and a faculty *as a group* can demonstrate competence in leadership. Success in curriculum development is more likely to be achieved when the leadership skills of the council interface with those of the faculty, resulting in a total team approach to the solution of curriculum problems. When we compare schools' achievements in curriculum improvement, we quickly discover great variations in the leadership skills of (1) the person or persons directing the curriculum study, (2) the curriculum committees or councils, (3) the total faculty, and (4) the preceding three entities working together. Enhancing the work of the professionals are the contributions to curriculum improvement that may be made by students, parents, and others from the community.

THE CAST OF PLAYERS

We would not be far off the mark if we perceived the process of curriculum development as a continuing theatrical production in which actors play specific roles. Some of these roles are determined by society and the force of law; others are set by players themselves. Some roles are mandated, whereas others spring out of the personalities of the players themselves.

When discussing roles of various groups, Saylor and Alexander applied the analogy of drama to the process of curriculum planning:

> In addition to leading roles of students and teachers in the curriculum planning drama, important supporting actors include the members of lay advisory groups, curriculum councils and committees, teacher teams, and curriculum development units.... all of these roles are affected by their interaction with various groups and agencies outside the curriculum theatre....[1]

Whereas we can overwork the metaphor of curriculum planning as drama, we must admit that a good deal of playacting does occur, much of it unconsciously, in the group process itself. For the moment, let's talk about the conscious roles the curriculum participants are called on to play. For purposes of analysis we will focus our attention on roles of constituent groups (administrators, students, lay people, and curriculum workers-teachers, curriculum consultants, and supervisors). To achieve clarity we will focus on the individual school level.

Role of the Administrator

Whether the chief administrator of the school, the principal, serves actively as curriculum leader or passively by delegating leadership responsibilities to subordinates, curriculum development is doomed to failure without his or her support. In these times the role of the administrator is in a period of transition. While some school administrators still take the position that they are instructional leaders, others realistically admit that today they are only or primarily managers.

Some years ago the Southern States Cooperative Program in Educational

---

[1] J. Galen Saylor and William M. Alexander, *Planning Curriculum for Schools* (New York: Holt, Rinehart and Winston, 1974), p. 59.

Administration listed the tasks of educational administration. Sponsored by the W. K. Kellogg Foundation this study group specified the following as critical tasks:

1. instruction and curriculum development
2. pupil personnel
3. community-school leadership
4. staff personnel
5. school plant
6. school transportation
7. organization and structure
8. school finance and business management[2]

Interestingly, instruction and curriculum development head this list. Yet, instruction and curriculum development today rarely rank as the number one priority of the school principal.

William H. Roe and Thelbert L. Drake observed that the principal is torn between his or her desired role as instructional leader and his or her actual role as administrator and manager:

> By reading the literature, attending state and national meetings, and discussing the position with present incumbents, one gets the mental picture of a professional person torn apart on the one hand by intense interest and desire to lead in instruction and learning, and on the other hand by the responsibility to "keep school" through the proper administration and management of people and things as expected by the central administration. In this little drama the eternal struggle takes place and in the end the strong instructional leadership role is set aside because of the immediacy and press of everyday administrative duties.[3]

The reasons for the low priority assigned by principals to what used to be their main raison d'être are found both within the personality of the principal and in the pressure from outside forces. Some of the factors that lead principals away from spending time on instructional leadership are the priority that the higher officers place on efficiency of operation, limitations placed on principals' fields of operation by teachers' organizations, and preservice programs for administrators that stress business and personnel management, minimizing curriculum and instructional development.

The principal's movement from a curriculum and instructional leader to a manager continues unabated today. Several factors reveal this change in role: the rash of textbooks and articles in the professional literature on educational management; the emphasis on the "systems" approach to administration, which is borrowed from military and industrial models; and the

---

[2] Southern States Cooperative Program in Educational Administration, *Better Teaching in School Administration* (Nashville, Tenn.: McQuiddy, 1955), pp. 125–177.

[3] William H. Roe and Thelbert L. Drake, *The Principalship*, 2d ed. (New York: Macmillan, 1980), p. 11.

nationwide establishment of inservice training programs for administrators under the rubric of Management Training Academies.

Perceptions of Parents. The new managerial direction in administration apparently opposes the perceptions of parents about the manner in which the principal should be occupying his or her time. Roe and Drake reported a study of priorities parents would set on the duties of principals. They rated as top priorities the following:

1. Initiate improvements in teaching techniques and methods.
2. Make certain that curricula fit the needs of students.
3. Direct teachers to motivate students to learn at their optimal levels.
4. Afford teachers the opportunity to individualize programs.
5. Direct teachers to coordinate and articulate the subject matter taught on each grade level.[4]

Although parents and principals perceive the principal's role differently, we must conclude that the principal will probably play an indirect role in curriculum development and will delegate responsibility for curriculum leadership to subordinates like the assistant principal for curriculum, the curriculum coordinator, or the chairperson of the school's curriculum council.

Whether the principal plays a direct or an indirect role, his or her presence is always keenly felt by all the players. The participants are aware that the principal by both tradition and law is charged with responsibility for running all the affairs of the school and for decision making in that school. In that sense, all curriculum groups and subgroups of the school are advisory to the principal.

"Theory X" and "Theory Y." In his or her own style the principal exerts a force on all operations within the school. The success of the curriculum developers may depend to some extent on whether the principal is a "Theory-X" or a "Theory-Y" type person. Douglas McGregor has classified two sets of assumptions that he believes managers have about people into categories Theory X and Theory Y.[5] These theories are widely quoted in the literature on management. According to McGregor, managers following Theory X believe:

□ The average person dislikes work and tries to avoid it.
□ Most people must be forced to work and threatened with punishment to get them to work.
□ The average person lacks ambition and avoids responsibility.
□ The average person must be directed.
□ The need for security is the chief motivation of the average person.

---

[4] Roe and Drake, p. 132.
[5] Douglas M. McGregor, *The Human Side of Enterprise* (New York: McGraw-Hill, 1960).

Authority, control, task maintenance, and product orientation dominate the thinking of the Theory-X administrator. On the other hand, the administrator who subscribes to Theory Y follows a human relations approach for he or she believes:

□ The average person welcomes work.
□ The average person seeks responsibility.
□ Most people will demonstrate self-reliance when they share a commitment to the realization of common objectives.
□ The average person will be committed to an organization's objectives if he or she is rewarded for that commitment.
□ Creativity in problem solving is a trait found rather widely among people.

Whereas the typical administrator will be more inclined toward one theory, he or she will manifest behavior in practice that will at times lean toward the other. There are occasions, for example, when the Theory-Y administrator must exercise authority and follow Theory-X principles. Nevertheless, the position among current specialists in curriculum development, supervision, and administration counsels a human relations approach. Thomas J. Sergiovanni and Fred D. Carver expressed this position well:

> In our view, the unique role of the school as a humanizing and self-actualizing institution requires that school executives adopt the assumptions and behavior manifestations of Theory Y.[6]

The human-relations–oriented principal nurtures the curriculum development process by establishing a climate in which the planners feel valued and in which they can satisfy, to use Abraham Maslow's term, "self-fulfillment needs." [7] The principal must encourage and facilitate the process. Since he or she holds the power for final decision making within the school, the principal must give serious consideration to recommendations made by the school's curriculum study groups. Further, the principal must always demonstrate sincere interest in the curriculum development process. Personal traits such as a negative attitude or indifference by the school's chief administrator will effectively block progress in improving the school's curriculum. It could be observed that the principal's personality may be a more powerful determinant of progress than his or her training, knowledge, or conscious intentions.

Regardless of their style or approach — and here we may generalize to all levels of the school system — administrators and their assistants must assume responsibility for providing leadership in many areas. They must establish the organizational framework so curriculum development may proceed; secure facilities and needed resources, coordinate efforts of the various groups;

6 Thomas J. Sergiovanni and Fred D. Carver, *The New School Executive: A Theory of Administration,* 2d ed. (New York: Harper & Row, 1980), p. 49.

7 Abraham H. Maslow, *Motivation and Personality* (New York: Harper & Row, 1954).

offer consultative help; keep the groups on task; resolve conflicts; communicate school needs to all groups; maintain a harmonious working climate; assure collection of needed data; provide for communication among groups; advise groups on latest developments in education; and make final decisions for their particular level.

Role of Students

Before turning our attention to the main participants in the curriculum development process (the curriculum leaders and their fellow workers), let's briefly consider the roles of two supporting groups — the students and the adult citizens from the community. With increasing frequency, students, depending upon their maturity, are participating both directly and indirectly in the task of improving the curriculum. In some few cases, notably at the high school level (and above), students are accorded membership on curriculum councils. More commonly, student input is sought in a more indirect fashion. There are still many administrators and teachers who take a dim view of sharing decision making with the student clientele of the school. On the other hand, it is becoming increasingly more common for administrators and faculties to solicit student reactions to the curriculum. Surveys are conducted to obtain student perceptions of their programs; individual students and groups are interviewed. Suggestions for improvement in the curriculum and for ways of meeting their perceived needs are actively sought.

The recipient of the program — the student — is often in the best position to provide feedback about the product — the curriculum. Advice from the student constituency of the school may well provide clues for intelligent curriculum decision making.

Some schools seek information and advice from the chosen student leaders — the student government — whereas others look toward sampling opinion about programs more widely. Even in those schools in which student input is not actively sought and in which channels have not been established for gathering data from students, the learners speak loudly by their achievements in class. When standardized and state assessment test scores are consistently below level in a given school, it can be concluded that some adjustments are necessary in respect to either the curriculum or instruction. When diagnostic tests reveal deficiencies on the part of learners, something is being conveyed about the school's program.

John McNeil pointed out how students can silently make an impact on the curriculum:

> Informally, however, students have much influence over what is taught. Often they can "vote with their feet" by refusing to enroll in courses that feature the curriculum of academic specialists. The failure of students to respond to the Physical Science Study Committee's "Physics," was an

argument for curriculum change. Alternative schools and underground newspapers are other instances of student power.[8]

In Chapter 7 we will consider the student as a source of the curriculum. Here we are primarily concerned with the student's role as a participant in curriculum development.

Student Involvement. Student involvement in curriculum improvement has been connected with the growing movements toward student rights and the stress on humanism in the schools.[9] Doll spoke of the connection between student participation in curriculum development and the student rights movement as follows:

> Great changes have occurred in the role of pupils, especially at secondary school level, in planning the curriculum. The revolutionary movement in colleges of the sixties had almost immediate effect on many high schools and indeed on some elementary schools. "Student rights" came to include the right to participate with adults in planning the uses to which pupils' time in schools was to be put. Though this right had existed in some better-known schools for many years and had been advocated to a limited extent by authors in the curriculum field, it now meant permission to speak freely and at length in curriculum meetings often on a footing equal to that of experienced adults. To some teachers and principals, pupils' newly acquired status represented a refreshing view of human potential and a deserved position in the educational hierarchy; to others it seemed an especially time-consuming and plaguing form of contemporary insanity.[10]

Students can help out greatly by indicating to the professional curriculum planners how they perceive a new proposal or program. They can provide input from the standpoint of the recipients of the program, the persons for whom the program was designed. The more alert students can point out pitfalls that the professional planners might be able to avoid. The students can communicate to the professional planners reactions of their peers and they can further communicate the nature and purpose of curricular changes to their parents and other citizens of the community. Students can excel in the area of the affect, relating to the professional planners how they perceive a development and how they feel about it.

The degree to which students may participate and the quality of that participation depend on a number of variables such as intelligence, motivation, and knowledge. The most significant variable is the student's maturity. For

---

[8] John D. McNeil, *Curriculum: A Comprehensive Introduction,* 2d ed. (Boston: Little, Brown, 1981), pp. 305–306.

[9] See, for example, Albert I. Oliver, *Curriculum Improvement: A Guide to Problems, Principles, and Process,* 2d ed. (New York: Harper & Row, 1977), p. 46.

[10] Ronald C. Doll, *Curriculum Improvement: Decision Making and Process,* 4th ed. (Boston: Allyn and Bacon, 1978), p. 327.

that reason students in senior high schools and in higher education find more opportunities for participating in curriculum development than students in elementary, middle, and junior high schools.

A particularly valuable contribution to curriculum improvement that students can make is to evaluate the teacher's instruction. Although some teachers resist student evaluations of their performance — as one senior high school principal was heard to comment, "Students have no business evaluating teachers" — evaluations done anonymously by the learners can provide valuable clues for modifying a curriculum and improving methods of instruction.

Although students do enter actively into the process of curriculum development in some school systems, their involvement by and large still tends to be sporadic and ancillary.

Role of the Adult Citizens of the Community

The roles of parents and other members of the community in the affairs of the school have changed considerably over the years. Originally, the community *was* the school. Parents tutored their young at home for lack of or in preference to a formal school. Or, the well-to-do imported tutors from Europe to live in their homes and to instruct their children. The church provided instruction in its religious precepts, and young men learned trades as apprentices on the job. Ladies in Colonial America would often bring youngsters into their homes and for a small payment from each of their families teach them the 3 R's.[11]

As formal schools evolved, the community turned the task of educating the young (for many years only young white males) over to the school. A cleavage developed between the community and the school. Both the community and the institution it established developed the attitude that the community should get on with its business and leave teaching to those who know how to do it best — the school personnel. An invisible wall was erected between community and school, resembling the one between church and school.

Erosion of Wall Between School and Community. Although some school administrators prefer to cling to an outmoded concept of community-school relationships, the wall separating school from community has crumbled. The process of erosion began slowly and has accelerated in recent years. The involvement of parents and other community members can be readily observed in school affairs today. The literature on professional education is filled with discussions of the necessity for involving the community in the educational process.

Community involvement was initially interpreted as passive support to the schools. The school would send bulletins and notices home to inform parents

---

[11] Commonly referred to in the literature on educational history as "the dame school" or "kitchen school."

about issues and activities. The Parent-Teacher Association would meet and, in its best mood, discuss educational issues, hear about the school's achievements, and plan a rummage sale to raise funds for some school improvement. The school would conduct a "Back to School Night" with much fanfare, which brought parents in record numbers. Booster clubs would raise money for athletics and the band. During this period the community rarely participated in decision making even of an advisory nature. The old sentiment still prevailed that school matters were best left to the school people. The community's role was to support and strengthen decisions made by the school.

Erosion of the wall between school and community was hastened when administrators and teachers began to realize that parents might supply them with certain types of information that might aid in decision making. Consequently, still resorting to a somewhat passive technique, the school sent home questionnaires for parents to fill out and return. While the school and community were taking careful, modest steps toward repairing the cleavage, American society in the twentieth century was bubbling. First the sociologists and then the educators began to subject the American community to intense study, identifying networks of influential persons who are referred to in the literature as "the power structure." [12] Educators started to give attention to the politics of education as they realized the school is as much a part of the total political structure as other social institutions. The astute school administrator became intensely conscious of public relations and sought to involve community members in support of the school. Some might say that the educators' attention to community concerns was more effect than cause as discontent, anxiety, and pressure on educators from outside the schools had been growing and increasing in intensity for several decades.

Social Problems. Four major wars, several revolutions, a number of sociological movements, and an ailing economy changed the tapestry of twentieth-century America. The technological revolution, the sexual revolution, the heightened divorce rate, the change in family structure, the equal rights movement, the student rights movement, the declaration of unconstitutionality of segregation, and the severe inflation all created problems for the schools, problems which they could no longer solve by themselves. With America's social and economic problems came a disenchantment with the programs of the school and the achievement of the pupils.

Today, community involvement in school activities is widespread, en-

---

[12] See the following: Robert S. Lynd, *Middletown: A Study in American Culture* (New York: Harcourt, Brace, Jovanovich, 1929) and Robert S. Lynd and Helen M. Lynd, *Middletown in Transition: A Study in Cultural Conflicts* (New York: Harcourt, Brace, Jovanovich, 1937).

Ralph B. Kimbrough, *Community Power Structure and Analysis* (Englewood Cliffs, N. J.: Prentice-Hall, 1964).

Ralph B. Kimbrough and Michael Y. Nunnery, *Educational Administration: An Introduction* (New York: Macmillan, 1976), Chapter 12.

couraged, and valued. Members of the community aid in curriculum development in a variety of ways. Parents and other citizens serve on numerous advisory committees.

It is always a dilemma for a school principal to decide how lay people should be involved and who these people should be. Some principals seek the participation of parents of children in their own schools. Some try to involve a representative stratum of the community, including parents and nonparents and representatives from all socioeconomic levels of the area served by the schools. Some limit participation by plan or by default to parents who happen to be available to attend meetings during the day. The chief participants under this condition tend to be middle-class, nonworking housewives. Some principals seek out the community decision makers from among the citizens who make up the power structure.

State and National Initiatives. Supplementing local initiatives to involve the community in school affairs have been state and national efforts. Roald F. Campbell and others pointed out that commissions in several states recommended the participation of citizens in the affairs of the school.[13] In 1976 the Florida legislature not only established school advisory councils but also charged the principal of every public school in the state with the responsibility of publishing by November first of each year an annual report of school progress that must be distributed to the parent or guardian of each student in the school.[14]

Campbell and others noted the impact of federal legislation on citizen involvement in the affairs of the local schools:

> Most federal legislation enacted since the early 1970's requires citizen consulting and advisory mechanisms. The number of federally mandated advisory councils is staggering: there are approximately 14,000 district-wide Title I Parent Advisory Committees and 44,000 building-level committees with a total of nearly 900,000 members; another 150,000 persons serve on Head Start, Follow Through, and other district and building-level groups.[15]

Thus, local, state, and federal initiatives have promoted the involvement of members of the community in affairs of the school.

The universal use of program advisory groups in connection with federally funded vocational education programs, for example, has exerted a significant influence on the curriculum of local school systems.

Looking to the future, Campbell and others predicted:

---

[13] Roald F. Campbell, Luvern L. Cunningham, Michael D. Usdan, and Raphael O. Nystrand, *The Organization and Control of American Schools,* 4th ed. (Columbus, Ohio: Charles E. Merrill, 1980), p. 149.

[14] Florida Statute 229.575 (3), *Florida School Laws,* 1979, pp. 19–20.

[15] Campbell et al., p. 149.

Interest groups representing blacks, American Indians, and other ethnic groups will continue to focus on the schools as a major mechanism for equalizing educational, social, and economic opportunities for their constituencies. Taxpayer groups, manifesting their concerns about inflation, recession, and energy shortages in a troubled economy, will continue to scrutinize school expenditures. . . . The political power of Hispanic communities will escalate dramatically in the next decade or so.[16]

The wise administrator realizes that strong community support can make his or her job much simpler and for that reason devotes considerable time to building that support. Some schools have been turned into community schools in which the resources of the school are shared with the community and vice versa.

Models for citizen participation in school affairs differ widely from community to community. In some communities citizens play a purely advisory role; in others they share directly in the decision-making process. In some localities members of the community serve on standing committees that meet regularly; in other locations they serve on ad hoc groups that undertake a specific task and are then disbanded. In some school districts parents and others are invited to address themselves to any and all problems of the schools, whereas in other communities their areas of responsibility are clearly delimited.

Community Involvement. Saylor and Alexander envisioned persons from the community as helping in four stages of curriculum planning: goal setting, designing, implementing, and evaluating.[17] As examples of community participation at the goal-setting stage, they pointed to:

□ groups of community representatives appointed by the school board to advise on educational goals
□ groups appointed by the school board to advise on a particular area of the curriculum
□ Parent-Teacher Association committees at the local school
□ homeroom parents' organizations
□ dads' clubs

Members of the community are consulted in the curriculum designing stage to arrange for work-experience type programs. Saylor and Alexander suggested the possible need for councils to coordinate the educational experiences that take place outside the school and with the cooperation of persons in the community.

At the implementation stage citizens of the community are called on to serve as resource persons, volunteer tutors, and school aides. The resources

---

[16] Campbell et al., pp. 377, 379.
[17] Saylor and Alexander, *Planning Curriculum for Schools*, pp. 67–69.

of individuals, businesses, institutions, and other agencies are tapped to enhance the learning experiences of the students.

Parents and others share in curriculum evaluation by responding to opinion polls, providing feedback about their children's school work, and supervising work experiences. Parents are able to describe the impact of new programs on their children and can be very specific in telling teachers about problems their children are encountering. They can serve as resource persons and voluntary aides to the teacher. They may invite children to their places of work and thereby contribute to the children's knowledge of the world around them.

Parents and others can inform the professional planners about potential conflicts likely to arise in the community over the teaching of controversial topics and programs. They can help the school authorities review materials for bias and distortion. Parents and other citizens of the community are often able to suggest programs that would help meet certain educational needs in the community. By actively seeking citizen participation, the principal is able to develop a reservoir of good will toward the school, which will stand him or her in good stead when problems inevitably develop. The principal is more readily able to gain support for new programs and to defuse potential controversies if parents and others perceive the school as their institution and as a place where their voices may be heard and their opinions valued. Community participation in curriculum development is a natural consequence of the public's legal power over education in our democratic society.

Role of the Curriculum Workers

Primary responsibility for curriculum development is assigned to teachers and their elected or appointed leaders, both of whom we will refer to as "curriculum workers." This group of persons working together carry the heaviest burden in seeking to improve the curriculum. In Chapter 3 we pointed out that curriculum groups function at several levels and in several sectors. To make the following discussion clearer, however, let's conceptualize the curriculum council of a particular school. Let's choose an elementary school with grades K through 6 that is fortunate enough to have a full-time curriculum coordinator on its staff (in this case bootlegged by the principal under the guise of a classroom teacher). By agreement of the total faculty, the grade coordinators (seven of them) join with the curriculum coordinator (appointed by the principal) to form the school's curriculum council. In our hypothetical school, by tacit understanding between the principal and the faculty, the coordinator serves as chairperson or leader of the council.

Let's imagine that we are neutral observers watching this council at its first session of the year. We watch the group get organized; we listen to its discussion; we study the faces of the council members; we observe the interplay between the coordinator and the council members and among the council members. We cannot help but speculate as to whether this curriculum group will have a productive year. The question crosses our mind, "What conditions make for a productive year in curriculum development?" We wonder, "Could we predict whether a curriculum council is likely to be productive?"

After a great deal of thought, we might conclude that success in terms of productivity is more likely to come about if the group:

- □ sets its goals at the beginning of its work
- □ is made up of compatible personalities
- □ has members who bring to the task expertise, knowledge, and technical competence
- □ is composed of persons who are motivated and willing to expend time and energy
- □ accepts its appropriate leadership and followership roles
- □ has persons who can communicate with each other
- □ has developed skills in decision making
- □ has members who keep their own personal agendas in appropriate relationship to the group's goals

What are the roles, we may ask, of those persons whom we call curriculum workers? How do teachers function in curriculum development? What role does the curriculum leader play?

Role of the Teachers

Throughout this text teachers are repeatedly seen as the primary group in curriculum development. Numerous examples are given of teacher involvement in curriculum development. The teachers constitute either the majority or the totality of the membership of curriculum committees and councils. Teachers participate at all stages in curriculum development. They initiate proposals and carry them out in their classrooms. They review proposals, gather data, conduct research, make contact with parents and other lay people, write and create curriculum materials, evaluate resources, try out new ideas, obtain feedback from learners, and evaluate programs. Teachers serve on committees at all levels and in all sectors of planning.

New teachers typically view themselves primarily as instructors and are often scarcely aware of the responsibilities that are likely to be expected of them in the curriculum arena. Beginning teachers' lack of awareness of their professional obligations in curriculum development is not surprising given that preservice teacher education programs, as a rule, emphasize the mastery of instructional skills over curriculum development competencies.

At the very least, preservice teachers should be oriented to the obligations and opportunities they will encounter in curriculum development. Becoming aware that they will serve on various councils and committees, that curriculum development takes place in many levels and sectors, and that instruction and curriculum are different domains, both worthy of involvement, should all be part of their training. Thus, the teachers, in cooperation with the administrators and other professionals, can bring appropriate knowledge and skills to bear in efforts to improve the curriculum. *Only* the teachers, by being at the classroom level, can assure that curricular plans are carried out.

Role of the Curriculum Leader

As we consider the complexities in carrying out curriculum development, we become keenly aware of the curriculum leader's responsibility for the success or failure of the work of a curriculum committee or council. The curriculum leader most often is a member of the faculty but can be an outsider. It is perhaps inaccurate here to refer to a curriculum leader as *the* curriculum leader. A person may serve as a leader for a period of time and then be displaced by another leader for any number of sound reasons. Some teachers may serve as leaders at one level, e.g., the grade, whereas others may serve as leaders at another level, e.g., the school. In a democratic organization individuals serve as either leaders or followers as the situation demands.

The curriculum leader (coordinator) may also come from outside the teacher group, as in the case of central office supervisors, curriculum consultants, directors of instruction, and assistant principals for curriculum. Perhaps even in these cases it would be useful to think of the teachers and leaders from outside the faculty as comprising the "extended family," for they are all colleagues, albeit with different functions and duties. The leadership position is filled either by appointment by an administrator or supervisor, election by the group's members, or self-selection from the group.

The principles we will now discuss apply to all curriculum leaders regardless of whether they come from inside or outside of the teacher group. We may begin to look at the role of the curriculum leader by asking ourselves what special knowledge and skills he or she must bring to the task. The curriculum coordinator must

- ◻ possess a good general education
- ◻ have good knowledge of both general and specific curricula
- ◻ be knowledgeable about resources for curriculum development
- ◻ be skilled in research and knowledgeable about locating pertinent research studies
- ◻ be knowledgeable about the needs of learners, the community, and the society
- ◻ be a bit of a philosopher, sociologist, and psychologist
- ◻ know and appreciate the individual characteristics of his or her participating colleagues

Most significantly, the curriculum coordinator must be a specialist in the group process, possessing a unique set of skills. Many treatises on the functioning of groups reveal that managing groups effectively is not a trivial task. It is an enormously complicated effort that brings into play all the subtleties of environment and personality. Curriculum development is an exercise in group process, a human endeavor that leads to joy and frustration.

Success in curriculum improvement depends, of course, on the concerted effort of both group members and leaders. We will focus our attention, however, on the curriculum leader; no matter how well-intentioned, motivated, and skilled the followers of a group are, group effort cannot succeed without competent leadership.

THE CURRICULUM LEADER AND GROUP PROCESS

Neither technical expertise nor knowledge about curriculum theory can substitute for a curriculum leader's knowledge of and aptitude for group process. What, then, might we ask, are some basic principles from the research on group process that would help the curriculum leader? This section will discuss key concepts about the group process and aspects of the literature that the curriculum leader may wish to pursue.

The curriculum leader should possess the following four sets or clusters of skills and knowledge about group process:

1. *The change process.* The curriculum leader must be knowledgeable about the process of effecting change and be able to implement that knowledge with the group. He or she must demonstrate effective decision-making skills and be able to lead group members in demonstrating them.
2. *Interpersonal relations.* The curriculum leader must be knowledgeable about group dynamics. He or she must exhibit a high degree of human relations skills, be able to develop interpersonal skills among members of the group, and be able to establish a harmonious working climate.
3. *Leadership skills.* The curriculum leader must demonstrate leadership skills, including organizational skills and ability to manage the process. He or she must seek to develop leadership skills from within the group.
4. *Communication skills.* The curriculum leader must communicate effectively and be able to lead members of the group in communicating effectively. He or she must be a proficient discussion leader.

The Change Process

Axiom 1 in Chapter 2 presented the proposition that change is both inevitable and desirable. Human institutions like human beings must change if they are to continue growing and developing. Neither the status quo nor regression are defensible positions for living institutions like the schools.

As stated, curriculum development is the planned effort of a duly organized group or groups that seek to make intelligent decisions to effect planned change in the curriculum. Planned change, far different from trial and error or natural evolution, implies a systematic process to be followed by all participants. Let's begin our examination of the change process by looking at the variables that exist within organizations and that have an impact upon the change process.

Four Variables. Harold J. Leavitt identified four variables: "task," "people," "structure," and "technology." [18]

Regarding *task*, Robert G. Owens and Carl R. Steinhoff spoke about the purpose of organizations as follows:

> By definition, an organization exists for the purpose of achieving something: reaching some goal or set of goals, by accomplishing certain *tasks*. ... The main goal of a business firm, for example, is to make profits for its entrepreneurs and investors. In order to achieve such a goal, the firm must perform certain tasks; it must manufacture and sell products, or buy and sell products, or provide certain services.[19]

The school performs many tasks in a number of curriculum development areas and provides a vital service — the education of the young. Although the school is not engaged in the tasks of manufacturing and selling products for profit, it does, however, turn out products — a quite different kind of product — the learners themselves, human beings whose behavior is modified as a result of exposure to the school curriculum.

The human element — the *people* — sets the operation in motion and carries out the task. The differences in people make each school's efforts at curriculum development a unique undertaking. The persons essential to the curriculum development process have been discussed. Experts in the social science of human behavior refer to the main characters in the change process as *the change agent* and *the client system*. In their language a change agent is a person trained in the behavioral sciences who helps an organization change. The client system consists of those persons in the organization with whom the change agent works and who may, themselves, undergo change. To stress this point, refer to Axiom 4, Chapter 2, which postulates that curriculum change results from changes in people.

Behavioral scientists argue whether the change agent must come from within or without the system. In practical terms schools will ordinarily utilize their own personnel for developing the curriculum. William H. Lucio and John D. McNeil attested that personnel from within the system are charged with the responsibility for bringing about change.[20]

Robert J. Alfonso, Gerald R. Firth, and Richard F. Neville identified change theory as one of four theoretical fields assumed to have implications

---

[18] Harold J. Leavitt, *Managerial Psychology: An Introduction to Individuals, Pairs, and Groups in Organizations,* 2d ed. (Chicago: The University of Chicago Press, 1964).

[19] Robert G. Owens and Carl R. Steinhoff, *Administering Change in Schools* (Englewood Cliffs, N.J.: Prentice-Hall, 1976), p. 60.

[20] See William H. Lucio and John D. McNeil, *Supervision: A Synthesis of Thought and Action,* 2d ed. (New York: McGraw-Hill, 1969), p. 208.

for the behavior of instructional supervisors.[21] John T. Lovell devoted a chapter in a text on supervision to demonstrate that curriculum development is one of the major responsibilities of the instructional supervisor and affirmed that supervisors must be guided by a theory of change.[22]

Alfonso, Firth, and Neville clearly showed that the supervisor from within the system must serve as a change agent:

> If change is to occur, a school system must value it enough to give some person or group the responsibility for it, and not leave it to chance occurrence. Supervisors, if they desire change, must make this a priority, or else it will not occur. They should not expect to be agents of change unless they devote a significant amount of time, effort, and creative thought to the change process.[23]

Even when the services of an outside change agent are sought Alfonso, Firth, and Neville advised:

> If a supervisor wishes to use the services of an outside change agent or consultant, the external agent must be perceived as enhancing the work of the supervisor. If such linkage can take place, or if, in fact, the external agent can be at least temporarily joined to the system, the total change effort will be more successful. Simply "importing" a change agent will not assist the supervisor markedly unless teachers perceive such a person as connected to the system or to the supervisor in some acceptable way.[24]

What are the typical functions of a change agent? Warren G. Bennis listed the following normative goals of change agents:

- improving interpersonal competence of managers;
- effecting a change in values so that human factors and feelings come to be considered legitimate;
- developing increased understanding among and within working groups to reduce tensions;
- developing "team management";
- developing better methods of "conflict resolution" than suppression, denial, and the use of unprincipled power;
- viewing the organization as an organic system of relationships marked by mutual trust, interdependence, multi-group membership, shared responsibility, and conflict resolution through training and problem solving.[25]

---

[21] See Robert J. Alfonso, Gerald R. Firth, and Richard F. Neville, *Instructional Supervision: A Behavior System,* 2d ed. (Boston: Allyn and Bacon, 1981), Chapter 8.

[22] See Kimball Wiles and John T. Lovell, *Supervision for Better Schools,* 4th ed. (Englewood Cliffs, N.J.: Prentice-Hall, 1975), p. 270 and Chapter 7. Kimball Wiles, *Supervision for Better Schools,* 3rd ed., was revised by John T. Lovell for the 4th ed.

[23] Alfonso, Firth, and Neville, p. 283.

[24] Alfonso, Firth, and Neville, p. 284.

[25] Reproduced by special permission from *The Journal of Applied Behavioral Science,* "Theory and Method in Applying Behavioral Science to Planned Organizational Change," by Warren G. Bennis, Volume 1, Number 4, p. 348, copyright 1965, NTL Institute.

Every organization establishes its own *structure*. In Chapter 3 we considered some of the organizational patterns that schools have adopted to carry out curriculum development. As stated, structures differ considerably among school systems and among individual schools. "It is the structure that gives an organization order, system, and many of its distinctive characteristics," said Owens and Steinhoff.[26] Organizational structures are shaped not only by the tasks to be accomplished but also by the idiosyncrasies of administrators, supervisors, and teachers. No single organizational structure will satisfy the personal and professional needs of participants in every school system. Determination of the appropriate organizational structure is one of the prior decisions that the curriculum developers must make.

The fourth variable — in addition to task, people, and structure — is *technology*. Owens and Steinhoff defined technology in the following manner:

> The organization must have technological resources or, in other words, the tools of the trade. Technology, used in this sense, does not only include such typical hardware items as computers, milling machines, textbooks and chalk, and electron microscopes. Technology may also include program inventions: systematic procedures, the sequencing of activities, or other procedural inventions designed to solve problems that stand in the way of organizational task achievement.[27]

Owens and Steinhoff perceived the interdependence of these four variables as the key factor in choosing strategies for change in organizations. They explained:

> These four factors — *task, structure, technology,* and *people* — are variables that differ from time to time and from one organization to the next. Within a given organization these four factors are highly interactive, each tending to shape and mold the others. They can be considered the key elements to be dealt with in attempting to change the organization. As in any system, the interdependence of the variable factors means that a significant change in one will result in some adaptation on the part of the other factors. *This is the key to selecting strategies and tactics for organizational change.*[28]

Owens and Steinhoff charge the administrator with the responsibility of developing organizational structures that "assure the development of more adaptive ways of integrating people, technology, task, and structure in a dynamic, problem-solving fashion."[29]

Kurt Lewin perceived organizations as being in a state of balance or equilibrium when forces of change (driving forces) and forces of resistance (re-

[26] Owens and Steinhoff, p. 60.
[27] Owens and Steinhoff, p. 60.
[28] Owens and Steinhoff, pp. 61–62.
[29] Owens and Steinhoff, p. 142.

straining forces) are equal in strength.[30] Changes occur when the organization is forced into a state of disequilibrium. This state of imbalance may be accomplished by augmenting the driving forces or by reducing the restraining forces — either action breaking the force field that maintains the organization in equilibrium.

Following his concept of the force field, Lewin proposed a simple strategy consisting of three steps. Or was it so simple? Lewin suggested that existing targets of change be unfrozen, then changes or innovations made, and finally the new structures refrozen until the start of a new cycle.

How shall we go about unfreezing old programs and practices, in effect, changing old habits? How would we move, for example, from the junior high school to the middle school, from "old math" to "new math," from the self-contained classroom to open classrooms, from exclusive stress on cognitive learning to provision for cognitive, affective, and psychomotor learning, from emphasis on convergent thinking to stress on divergent thinking, or from rote learning to problem solving? How do we thaw out old patterns?

By identifying the barriers or impediments to change, the organization can be set into disequilibrium by eliminating those barriers. Table 4-1 lists several commonly encountered barriers and suggests tactics for overcoming them.

Decision Making. Axiom 6 of Chapter 2 takes the position that curriculum development is basically a decision-making process. The lack of skills in decision making by a curriculum leader and group can be a formidable barrier to change. Are there any principles of decision making that could be helpful to curriculum study groups? Let's turn to Daniel L. Stufflebeam and the Phi Delta Kappa National Study Committee on Evaluation, which Stufflebeam chaired, for guidance on the process of decision making.[31]

Stufflebeam and his committee ventured that the process of decision making consists of four stages — awareness, design, choice, and action — during which four kinds of decisions must be made — planning, structuring, implementing, and recycling.

Planning decisions are made "to determine objectives." They "specify *major changes that are needed in a program."* Structuring decisions are made "to design procedures." They "specify the *means to achieve the ends* established as a result of planning decisions." Implementing decisions are made "to utilize, control and refine procedures." Decisions on implementation are "those involved in *carrying through the action plan."* Recycling decisions are made "to judge and react to attainments." "These are decisions used in deter-

---

[30] See Kurt Lewin, *Field Theory in Social Science* (New York: Harper-Torch Books, 1951). Also in Kurt Lewin, "Frontiers in Group Dynamics," *Human Relations* 1 (1947): 5–41.

[31] Daniel L. Stufflebeam et al., Committee Chairman, *Educational Evaluation and Decision Making* (Itasca, Ill.: F. E. Peacock, 1971), especially chapter 3.

TABLE 4-1 Common barriers to change

BARRIERS	TACTICS
Fear of change on the part of those likely to be affected	The group should proceed slowly. Leader gives repeated reassurance to those affected by change. Involvement of those affected in decision making. The changed status must be made more attractive than the old pattern.
Lack of clear goals	The group must set clear goals before proceeding further.
Lack of competent leadership	Superiors must appoint or peers must elect persons as leaders who are most qualified. Leaders who prove to be incompetent should be removed.
Lack of ability of group members to function as a group	Training in group process should be conducted.
Lack of research on problems before the group	The leader should have the ability to conduct research, to locate pertinent research data, and to interpret research studies to the group.
A history of unsuccessful curriculum efforts	The group must be made to feel progress is being made continuously.
Lack of evaluation of previous curriculum efforts	Efforts should be made to evaluate previous efforts, and an evaluation plan for current efforts must be designed.
Negative attitudes from the community	School personnel must call parents and citizens in for discussion, must involve them in the process, and try to change their attitudes.
Lack of resources	Adequate resources both to carry out curriculum planning and to implement plans decided upon must be available. Personnel needed must be available.
External pressures such as state and federal legislation, regional accreditation, and regulations of the state department of education	Efforts must be made to work within the framework of laws and regulations or to try to get the laws and regulations changed. Responses to laws and regulations, which are broad and general, may vary from school to school.
Lack of experience or knowledge about a particular curricular problem	The group may call in consultants for assistance or the school may provide training for some of its personnel.

mining the relationship of attainments to objectives and whether to continue, terminate, evolve, or drastically modify the activity." [32]

From the time a perceptive staff member in a school first starts to feel uneasy about a program and senses that something is not right and change is needed, decisions must be made constantly. Since decision making never ends, skills in the process need to be developed.

Creative Individuals. While the literature on change stresses the necessity for group involvement, it must be pointed out that change can be and is often brought about by creative individuals and small groups of individuals working independently. Many of our great inventors, for example, have been individualists.

What sometimes happens is that an individual experiments with a new idea; a few others who like the idea adopt it; success with the idea builds on success and the idea is translated widely into practice. Creative individual enterprise should be encouraged by administrators and faculty as long as the implications of the activity do not invade areas outside the individual's own sphere. When creative endeavor begins to force demands on others without their sanction or involvement, independence must give way to cooperation.

In summary, curriculum leaders guide cooperating workers in bringing about change. In so doing they must exhibit skill in directing the change process. Skill in decision making by both leaders and followers is essential if positive curricular changes are to be effected.

Interpersonal Relations

The principal's reminder, "faculty meeting today at 3:30 p.m.," is normally greeted with less than enthusiasm. The typical teacher responses are likely to be "Oh, no, not again!", "I hope it's short," and "Faculty meetings are such a waste of time." At best these group meetings are received with a quiet resignation. Why does a group effort like a faculty meeting, which should be such a potent instrument for group deliberation, provoke such widespread dissatisfaction?

Let's try to answer that question by picturing a typical secondary school faculty meeting. Some thirty faculty members shuffle into a classroom and take their seats while the principal stands at the desk at the front of the room. We observe the faculty meeting in session and take some notes:

- The classroom is crowded and the pupils' desks-in-rows are uncomfortable for some of the faculty, particularly the heavier teachers.
- The straight rows are not conducive to group discussion.
- Some refreshments would help set a pleasant tone for the meeting.
- It is difficult to understand the purpose of the meeting. Was it infor-

---

[32] Stufflebeam, pp. 80–84.

mation-giving on the part of the principal? A sermon from the principal on responsibilities? An effort to gain faculty approval of policies? An attempt to get faculty opinion on an issue?

- One teacher in the back was reading the daily newspaper.
- One teacher by the window was grading papers.
- Two teachers were talking about an incident that took place in one of the teacher's classrooms that day.
- One teacher, tired, sat with her eyes closed during the meeting.
- The football coaches were absent.
- The principal spoke for thirty of the forty-five minutes of the meeting.
- A couple of teachers spoke repeatedly whereas the majority remained silent.
- Several teachers watched the clock on the wall.
- The principal became visibly annoyed with the comment of one teacher.
- A restlessness among the teachers was apparent after the first thirty minutes.
- The group rushed out of the room as soon as the meeting ended.

None of the behaviors at this hypothetical meeting was unusual. The behaviors were quite predictable and to a great extent preventable. The general faculty meeting is but one of many group configurations in which teachers and administrators will participate. If the administrator fosters a collegial approach to administration, teachers will find themselves working on a number of committees for a variety of purposes, including curriculum development.

It is reasonably safe to generalize that most new teachers do not fully realize the extent to which teaching is a group-oriented career. Training in group process, for example, is conspicuous by its absence in preservice programs. The mind-set novice teachers have developed about teaching pictures the teacher as an *individual* planner, presenter, evaluator, and curriculum developer. When they begin teaching, they are unaware of the degree to which these activities are group tasks in which responsibilities are shared.

Whereas beginning teachers realize from student teaching that they work with groups of children, they are often not ready to work cooperatively with their professional colleagues. A training program for teachers should seek to develop an appreciation of the necessity for working in groups, an attitude of willingness to work cooperatively, an understanding of the working or dynamics of a group, and skills as group members. If these cognitive and affective objectives are not achieved in preservice teacher education, their attainment should be sought in inservice training programs.

Let's try to improve our understanding of the composition and functioning of groups by examining some of the salient characteristics of group dynamics. We shall not belabor the question of defining *group* but will call two or more persons working together for a mutual purpose a group. In all human institutions of which the school is one example, we find both formal and informal groups.

Formal groups are established to carry out tasks officially designated by the organization. Created by the administrative structure, they are usually shown in the institution's table of organization. The faculty as a body, curriculum councils, departments, advisory committees, teams, and cabinets are illustrations of formal groups.

Informal groups are self-constituted, ad hoc, and impromptu collections of individuals who gather together for some immediate purpose and later disband. Protest groups and cliques of teachers are illustrations of informal groups. Although we are primarily concerned with the functioning of formally constituted groups, we should not overlook the possible impact of informal groups. It is quite possible, for example, for the formal and informal groups within a school to be working at cross purposes. The wise curriculum leader seeks to identify informal groups that may have an impact on curriculum development efforts and to channel their energies into the deliberations of the formal structure.

Recall that in the illustration of the hypothetical secondary school faculty meeting, the sense of purpose was unclear. Both the general purpose and the specific goals of the group must be known. Groups are organized most frequently for the following purposes:

- □ to receive instructions or information. Faculty meetings are often used for this purpose.
- □ to help individuals develop personally or professionally. Sensitivity groups, study groups, and workshops in pedagogy are examples of groups with this purpose.
- □ to recommend solutions to problems. This is a major purpose of curriculum improvement groups.
- □ to produce something. Curriculum committees, for example, may be charged with the task of creating new programs or writing curriculum guides.
- □ to resolve conflicts. Curriculum development efforts sometimes result in disagreements among factions, necessitating new groups to resolve these differences.

To some extent all these purposes operate in curriculum development. However, the latter three are the primary purposes, which make curriculum committees action- or task-oriented groups rather than ego- or process-oriented groups. In all human groups we find individuals who are there to serve the social needs of the organization, that is, the fulfillment of the group's task, and others who are there to satisfy their own ego needs.

One of the great difficulties for the curriculum leader is keeping a group "on task." Challenging this goal are the many individuals who are impelled to satisfy their own personal needs in a group setting, behavior referred to as "processing." Some processing is essential in any group, particularly early in the group's activity when individuals are getting to know each other and trying to analyze the task. The leader must assure some balance between "task orientation" and "process orientation." He or she must assure that a group move on with its task while permitting individuals to achieve personal satisfaction as members of the group. Excessive stress on either approach can lead to frustration and withdrawal.

The curriculum leader, who is, of course, a key — or the key — member of a curriculum planning group, must be aware of the presence of three types of behavior within a group. First, each group is composed of individuals who bring their own individual behaviors to the group. Some will maintain these behaviors, sometimes consciously and other times subconsciously, regardless of the group setting. Thus, the teacher who is habitually punctual, conscientious, confident, or complaining is likely to bring this trait into the group setting. Some traits impact positively on the group, others negatively.

Individuals bring their motivations, often covert, into group efforts — their personal desires, feelings, or goals, commonly referred to as the "hidden agenda." Individuals may react negatively to a curriculum proposal, for example, not because they object to the proposal per se but because they dislike the person who made the proposal. Individuals may attack a proposal because they feel their ideas have not been adequately considered. Individuals may strive to ask a group member embarrassing questions because they perceive that person as a potential rival for a leadership position. The curriculum leader must constantly attempt to channel negative behaviors into constructive paths or to eliminate them where possible. He or she must often act as mediator to assure that the individuals' hidden agendas do not sabotage the official agenda.

Second, individuals in groups often behave in ways that are quite different from their individual behaviors. We have only to turn to studies of mob psychology to demonstrate that individuals change their behavior in group situations. Have we never observed, for example, a group of otherwise sweet, innocent elementary school youngsters taunting a fellow classmate? Have we never seen an otherwise cautious adolescent driver become reckless when driving a car filled with friends? The presence of fellow human beings who read and evaluate an individual's behavior causes that individual to behave in a way in which he or she perceives the group members wish him or her to act.

We see great contrasts in behavior between the individual who relies on his or her own inner resources (the inner-directed personality) and the individual who takes cues from those around him or her (the outer-directed personality). While few individuals are immune from outer-direction in our society, some individuals are more adept than others at weighing external influences before acting on them. Some individuals are aware when they are being manipulated by others whereas others are highly subject to suggestion.

Not only do personal behaviors sometimes change in a group setting, but individuals assume, as we shall soon see, special roles that they do not or cannot perform in isolation.

Third, the group itself assumes a personality of its own. The cliché that describes this situation is, "The whole is greater than the sum of its parts." The functioning of the group is more than the sum of the functioning of each of the individuals who make up the group. The individuals interact with and reinforce each other, creating a unique blend. In this respect some departments of a school are perceived as being more productive (pick your own word: creative, enthusiastic, reactionary, innovative, obstreperous) than others, just as schools are perceived as being different from one another.

The curriculum leader must try to develop pride in the group as a team organization by promoting group morale and by helping the group feel a sense of accomplishment. The group concept is fostered when:

- interaction among group members is frequent, on a high professional level, friendly, and harmonious
- personal conflicts among group members are infrequent or nonexistent
- leadership is allowed to develop from within the group so that the group capitalizes on the strengths of its members
- constructive dissent is encouraged
- the group realizes that it is making progress toward meeting its goals, which points out again the necessity for clearly specifying the goals the group expects to attain
- the group feels some sense of reward for accomplishment

Perhaps the most satisfying reward for a group is to see its recommendations translated into practice. A word of appreciation from the administrator also goes a long way in securing the continuous motivation of teachers to participate in curriculum development.

Roles Played by Group Members. A number of years ago Kenneth D. Benne and Paul Sheats developed a classification system for identifying functional roles of group members.[33] They organized their classification system into three categories: group task roles, group building and maintenance roles, and individual roles. Group members take on task roles when they seek to move the group toward attaining its goals and to solving its problems. Group members play group building and maintenance roles when they are concerned with the functioning of the group. Individual roles of group members are indulged to satisfy certain personal needs.

Since the Benne-Sheats classification system stands as one of the most creative and comprehensive expositions of roles played by group members, its categories and roles are reproduced:

---

[33] Kenneth D. Benne and Paul Sheats, "Functional Roles of Group Members," *The Journal of Social Issues* 4, no. 2 (Spring 1948): 43–46.

GROUP TASK ROLES

a. Initiator-contributor. Suggests ideas, ways of solving problems, or procedures.

b. Information seeker. Seeks facts.

c. Opinion seeker. Asks for opinions about the values of suggestions made by members of the group.

d. Information giver. Supplies facts or facts as he/she sees them.

e. Opinion giver. Presents his/her own opinions about the subject under discussion.

f. Elaborator. States implications of suggestions and describes how suggestions might work out if adopted.

g. Coordinator. Tries to synthesize suggestions.

h. Orienter. Lets group know when it is off task.

i. Evaluator-critic. Evaluates suggestions made by group members as to criteria which he/she feels important.

j. Energizer. Spurs the group to activity.

k. Procedural technician. Performs the routine tasks which have to be done such as distributing materials.

l. Recorder. Keeps the group's record.

GROUP BUILDING AND MAINTENANCE ROLES

a. Encourager. Praises people for their suggestions.

b. Harmonizer. Settles disagreements among members.

c. Compromiser. Modifies his/her position in the interests of group progress.

d. Gate keeper. Tries to assure that everybody has a chance to contribute to the discussion.

e. Standard setter or ego ideal. Urges the group to live up to high standards.

f. Group-observer and commentator. Records and reports on the functioning of the group.

g. Follower. Accepts suggestions of others.

INDIVIDUAL ROLES

a. Aggressor. Attacks others or their ideas.

b. Blocker. Opposes suggestions and group decisions.

c. Recognition-seeker. Seeks personal attention.

d. Self-confessor. Expresses personal feelings not applicable to the group's efforts.

e. Playboy. Refrains from getting involved in the group's work with sometimes disturbing behavior.

f. Denominator. Interrupts others and tries to assert own superiority.

g. Help-seeker. Tries to elicit sympathy for himself/herself.

h. Special interest pleader. Reinforces his/her position by claiming to speak for others not represented in the group.

A group will be more effective if the individual and negative roles are minimized or eliminated. Groups can be helped by the leader or by an outside consultant by exposing them to group dynamics theory and a classification system such as the Benne-Sheats model. Help of a more personal nature can be achieved through group interaction that permits feedback to its members. This feedback could be in the form of simple analysis of interaction skills by the various members or could be derived from sensitivity training or encounter sessions. Certainly, a group will be more productive if its members already possess a high degree of interaction skill. If, however, a group appears to lack skills in interaction or human relations, it may be advisable to depart from the group's task long enough to seek to develop some fundamental interpersonal skills.

A trained observer who records the performance of individuals participating in a group can provide valuable feedback. Thomas J. Sergiovanni and Robert J. Starratt suggested in the first edition of their book on supervision an observation sheet that used the Benne-Sheats roles.[34] On the observation sheet (shown in Figure 4-1 in a form expanded by this author), the observer would record the frequency of role performance by the members of the group. After the observation period members would be furnished feedback about their performance.

The observer must exercise great tact in how he or she presents the information. Some of the individual roles are particularly unflattering, and it will be difficult for some individuals to accept that they behave in this way. Therefore, negative feedback should be supplied to individuals only on request and in confidence.

Task-oriented Groups. Curriculum development groups are or should be essentially task-oriented groups. They are given a specific job to do, carry it out, and then either accept another job or cease to function. Their productivity should be measured first in the quality of improvement that takes place in the curriculum and secondly in the personal and professional growth of the participants.

Curriculum development consists of a continuing series of interpersonal experiences. Both leaders and followers are obligated to study the process of group decision making and of working together to make the process successful. Professional persons should be able with a modicum of training to bury their hidden agendas and to eliminate or suppress negative behaviors that disrupt the group's effort. Fortunately, some human beings have learned during their formative years to demonstrate human relations skills like warmth, empathy, valuing of others' opinions and beliefs, intellectual honesty, patience, mutual assistance, and respect for others as persons. They have learned to accept responsibility and to refrain from blaming others for their own deficiencies. They have learned to put aside their own ego needs in deference to the needs of the group. They have learned to enjoy and take pride in group accomplishments. Others who demonstrate a low level of per-

---

[34] Thomas J. Sergiovanni and Robert J. Starratt, *Emerging Patterns of Supervision: Human Perspectives* (New York: McGraw-Hill, 1971), p. 199.

	Members								
	A	B	C	D	E	F	G	H	I
Task roles Initiator-contributor									
Information seeker									
Opinion seeker									
Information giver									
Opinion giver									
Elaborator									
Coordinator									
Orienter									
Evaluator-critic									
Energizer									
Procedural technician									
Recorder									
Building/maintenance roles Encourager									
Harmonizer									
Compromiser									
Gate keeper									
Standard setter									
Group-observer									
Follower									
Individual roles Aggressor									
Blocker									
Recognition-seeker									
Self-confessor									
Playboy									
Dominator									
Help-seeker									
Special interest pleader									

FIGURE 4-1   Record of behavior of individuals in groups

formance in these skills should be encouraged to participate in a human relations training program to improve their interpersonal skills.

     Remember that curriculum development is ordinarily a voluntary undertaking. Curriculum workers might ask themselves what motivated them to agree to serve in a group devoted to curriculum improvement. They might uncover motives like the following:

- □ a desire to please the administrator
- □ a desire to work with certain colleagues
- □ a desire to be where the action is
- □ a desire to grow professionally
- □ a desire to make a professional contribution to the school system
- □ a desire to make use of one's skills and talents
- □ a desire for a new experience
- □ a desire to socialize
- □ a desire to use the group as a sounding board for personal beliefs and values

The reasons why individuals agree to participate in group activity are many and varied, sometimes verbalized but often not; sometimes valid in terms of the group's goals, sometimes not. Individuals who are motivated and possess the necessary personal and professional skills should be encouraged to take part in curriculum development.

Characteristics of Productive Groups. From examining the wealth of literature on group dynamics and group process, how might we summarize the characteristics that make for group effectiveness or productivity? We have already noted in Chapter 1 that research conducted in the Hawthorne plant of the Western Electric Company in Chicago produced evidence that involvement of workers in planning and carrying out a project led to greater productivity. Research by Kurt Lewin, Ronald Lippitt, and Ralph K. White on groups of eleven-year-old children showed their productivity to be greater in a democratic group climate than in an authoritarian or laissez-faire one.[35] Rensis Likert saw a supportive environment, mutual confidence and trust among group members, and sharing of common goals as contributing to group effectiveness.[36] Ned A. Flanders's studies of classroom verbal interaction led users of his instrument for observing this process to conclude that group leaders need to decrease their own verbal behavior and stimulate members of the group to interact more.[37] John Dewey[38] and Daniel L. Stufflebeam[39] wrote of the importance of the skill of problem solving or decision making. Warren G. Bennis, Kenneth D. Benne, and Robert Chin advocated skill in planning for change.[40] Fred E. Fiedler concentrated on the effectiveness

---

[35] Kurt Lewin, Ronald Lippitt, and Ralph K. White, "Patterns of Aggressive Behavior in Experimentally Created Social Climates," *Journal of Social Psychology* 10 (May 1939): 271–299.

[36] Rensis Likert, *New Patterns of Management* (New York: McGraw-Hill, 1961).

[37] Ned A. Flanders, *Analyzing Teacher Behavior* (Reading, Mass.: Addison-Wesley, 1970).

[38] John Dewey, *How We Think*, rev. ed. (Lexington, Mass.: D. C. Heath, 1933).

[39] Stufflebeam, et al., *Educational Evaluation and Decision Making.*

[40] Warren G. Bennis, Kenneth D. Benne, Robert Chin, eds. *The Planning of Change*, 2d ed. (New York: Holt, Rinehart and Winston, 1969).

of the leader[41] and Kimball Wiles gave attention to skill in communication[42] as essential to group effectiveness. These latter two sets of skills will now be discussed in depth.

Based on the foregoing principles, we might conclude that a group is effective when:

- leaders and members support each other
- trust is apparent among members
- goals are understood and mutually accepted
- adequate opportunity for members to express their own feelings and perceptions is possible
- roles played by group members are essentially positive
- hidden agendas of members do not disrupt the group
- leadership is competent and appropriate to the group
- members possess the necessary expertise
- members have the necessary resources
- members share in all decision making
- communication is at a high level
- leadership is encouraged from within the group
- progress in accomplishing the task is noticeable and significant
- the group activity satisfies members' personal needs
- leaders seek to release potential of the members
- the group manages its time wisely

Leadership Skills

Let's attend the meeting of a school's curriculum committee as guest of the curriculum coordinator who is serving as chairperson. It is early in the year. We take a seat in the back of the room and in the course of less than an hour we observe the following behaviors:

- Two teachers are discussing an action of the principal.
- Each person speaks as long as he or she wishes, sometimes going on at length.
- The coordinator engages in dialogue with one individual, ignoring the group.
- Several members ask whether this discussion is in keeping with the group's purposes.
- The coordinator pushes his ideas and is visibly annoyed when someone disagrees with him.
- Two teachers become involved in arguing.

---

[41] Fred E. Fiedler, *A Theory of Leadership Effectiveness* (New York: McGraw-Hill, 1967).

[42] Kimball Wiles, *Supervision for Better Schools*, 3rd ed. (Englewood Cliffs, N.J.: Prentice-Hall, 1967). Also Wiles and Lovell, 4th ed.

▫ The coordinator steers the group toward a proposal that he has offered.

▫ The meeting breaks up without closure and without identifying next steps.

We might conclude that this session of the curriculum committee was less than productive. Would we attribute this lack of productivity to deficiencies on the part of the group members? To lack of leadership skills on the part of the coordinator? To both? Certainly, group productivity arises from a harmonious blend of skills by group members and the group leader. Yet, a heavy burden for the productivity of groups rests with the leader. This person has been chosen to set the pace, to provide expertise, and to channel the skills of others. The skilled leader would have been able to avoid and resolve some of the unproductive situations that developed in this curriculum committee.

Traits of Leaders. When asking ourselves and others what traits a leader should possess, we would probably garner the following responses:

▫ intelligent
▫ experienced
▫ assertive
▫ articulate
▫ innovative
▫ dynamic
▫ charismatic

Some would say, "You must be in the right place at the right time." Others, perhaps more cynical, would say a leader must be:

▫ a politician
▫ a climber
▫ a friend of a person in power

Like Laurence J. Peter, Jr., some people would observe that persons rise to their level of incompetence.[43]

What the research has found, however, is that it is almost impossible to ascribe any single set of traits to all persons in positions of leadership. Ralph B. Kimbrough and Michael Y. Nunnery offered four generalizations about leaders and leadership which they believe to be reasonably valid.

1. Leaders tend to be slightly higher in intelligence than the average of the group led.
2. Leaders tend to be emotionally mature, to exhibit self-confidence, to be goal oriented, to initiate action, to be dependable in exercising responsibilities, to have insight into problems faced by the group, and to have a strong continuing drive to succeed.

---

[43] See Laurence J. Peter, Jr., and Raymond Hull, *The Peter Principle: Why Things Always Go Wrong* (New York: William Morrow, 1969).

3. Leaders realize that people are essential for goal achievement. Therefore they attempt to communicate with others, tend to be sociable, show consideration for people, and seek cooperation of others.
4. The presence of such traits and characteristics does not guarantee effective performance as a leader, nor does their absence preclude effective performance; rather, the presence of these traits and characteristics enhances the probability of effective performance as a leader.[44]

Two Approaches. Leaders tend to lean toward one of two basic approaches to administration: the traditional, monocratic, bureaucratic approach or the emerging, pluralistic, collegial approach. The first approach has been labeled autocratic; the second, democratic. Edgar L. Morphet, Roe L. Johns, and Theodore L. Reller discussed the assumptions that underlie these two approaches. Leaders following the traditional, monocratic, bureaucratic approach, according to Morphet, Johns, and Reller believe that:

□ Leadership is confined to those holding positions in the power echelon.
□ Good human relations are necessary in order that followers accept decisions of superordinates.
□ Authority and power can be delegated but responsibility cannot be shared.
□ Final responsibility for all matters is placed in the administrator at the top of the power echelon.
□ The individual finds security in a climate in which the superordinates protect the interests of subordinates in the organization.
□ Unity of purpose is obtained through loyalty to the administrator.
□ The image of the executive is that of a superman.
□ Maximum production is attained in a climate of competition.
□ The line-and-staff plan of organization should be utilized to formulate goals, policies, and programs as well as to execute policies and programs.
□ Authority is the right and privilege of a person holding a hierarchical position.
□ The individual in the organization is expendable.
□ Evaluation is the prerogative of superordinates.[45]

On the other hand, leaders who follow the emerging, pluralistic, collegial approach believe that:

□ Leadership is not confined to those holding status positions in the power echelon.
□ Good human relations are essential to group production and to meeting the needs of the individual members of the group.
□ Responsibility, as well as power and authority, can be shared.
□ Those affected by a program or policy should share in decision making with respect to that program or policy.

---

[44] Kimbrough and Nunnery, p. 141.
[45] Edgar L. Morphet, Roe L. Johns, and Theodore L. Reller, *Educational Organization and Administration: Concepts, Practices, and Issues,* 3rd ed. (Englewood Cliffs, N.J.: Prentice-Hall, 1974), pp. 106–108.

☐ The individual finds security in a dynamic climate in which he shares responsibility for decision making.

☐ Unity of purpose is secured through consensus and group loyalty.

☐ Maximum production is attained in a threat-free climate.

☐ The line-and-staff organizations should be used exclusively for the purpose of dividing labor and implementing policies and programs developed by the total group affected.

☐ The situation and not the position determines the right and privilege to exercise authority.

☐ The individual in the organization is not expendable.

☐ Evaluation is a group responsibility.[46]

In contrasting these two approaches to administration Morphet, Johns, and Reller noted that the traditional approach operates in a closed climate, whereas the democratic approach functions in an open climate. The traditional approach relies on centralized authority with a fixed line-and-staff structure. Authority is spread out and shared under the pluralistic approach and the structure, while sometimes more complex than the traditional structure, is more flexible to allow for maximum participation of members of the organization. The flow of communication is much different under these two approaches. Under the autocratic or authoritarian approach, persons are imbued with the philosophy of going through channels. Messages may originate from the top of the echelon, which is most common, or from the bottom. Messages from the top down pass through intermediate echelons but may not be stopped by these echelons. On the other hand, messages originating from the bottom proceed through intermediate echelons and may be stopped by any echelon. Subordinates are required to conduct business through channels and may not with impunity "go over the head" of their immediate superior. Under a pluralistic approach communications may flow in any direction — up, down, circularly, or horizontally. They may skip echelons and may be referred to persons outside the immediate chain of command. The pluralistic administrator is not "hung up" on channels and personal status. It is the traditional approach that begets the "organization man."

Morphet, Johns, and Reller cautioned, in comparing these two approaches, "It should not be inferred, however, that democratic administration is *ipso facto* good and that authoritarian administration is *ipso facto* bad. History provides numerous examples of successful and unsuccessful democratic administration and successful and unsuccessful authoritarian administration." [47] They noted, however, that some studies reveal monocratic organizations to be less innovative than pluralistic ones.

Leadership style is a potent factor in the productivity of groups. A classic

---

[46] Morphet, Johns, and Reller, pp. 111–114.
[47] Morphet, Johns, and Reller, p. 117.

study of the impact of leadership is the previously mentioned research conducted by Kurt Lewin, Ronald Lippitt, and Ralph K. White. Lewin, Lippitt, and White studied the effects of three different styles of adult leadership on four groups of eleven-year-old children. They examined the effects of "authoritarian," "democratic," and "laissez-faire" leadership and found:

> Under the authoritarian leadership, the children were more dependent upon the leader, more discontent, made more demands for attention, were less friendly, produced less work-minded conversation than under the democratic leadership. There was no group initiative in the authoritarian group climate.
>
> The laissez-faire atmosphere produced more dependence on the leader, more discontent, less friendliness, fewer group-minded suggestions, less work-minded conversation than under the democratic climate. In the absence of the laissez-faire leader, work was unproductive. The laissez-faire group was extremely dependent upon the leader for information.
>
> The converse of these situations was true for the democratic group climate. In addition, relations among the individuals in the democratic leadership atmosphere were friendlier. Those under the democratic leadership sought more attention and approval from fellow club members. They depended upon each other for recognition as opposed to recognition by the leader under the authoritarian and laissez-faire systems. Further, in the absence of the leader the democratic groups proceeded at their work in productive fashion.[48]

Thus, if a curriculum leader seeks commitment from a group, the authoritarian and laissez-faire approaches are not likely to be effective. The curriculum leader's power (what little there is) is conferred by the group, especially if the leadership is encouraged from *within* the group. The democratic approach is, indeed, the only viable approach open to the curriculum leader who is a staff and not a line person propped up by an external authority.

Task- and Relationship-oriented Leaders. Fred E. Fiedler studied the age-old question as to whether successful leadership results from personal style or from the circumstances of the situation in which the leader finds himself or herself.[49] Fiedler spoke of the need for an appropriate match between the leader's style and the group situation in which he or she must exercise leadership. Developing what is called a "contingency model," Fiedler classified leaders as task-oriented or relationship-oriented. We might substitute human–relations–oriented for the latter term. In some respects this classi-

---

[48] Kurt Lewin, Ronald Lippitt, and Ralph K. White, "Patterns of Aggressive Behavior in Experimentally Created Social Climates," *Journal of Social Psychology* 10 (May 1939): 271–299. Quoted from Peter F. Oliva, "High School Discipline in American Society," *NASSP Bulletin* 40, no. 26 (January 1956): 7–8.

[49] See Fred E. Fiedler, *A Theory of Leadership Effectiveness* (New York: McGraw-Hill, 1967). Also, Fred E. Fiedler, "Style or Circumstance: The Leadership Enigma," *Psychology Today* 2, no. 10 (March 1969): 38–43.

fication resembles the dichotomy between the autocratic and democratic leader. The task-oriented leader keeps the goals of the organization always in front of him or her and the group. The needs of the organization take precedence over the needs of individuals. The superordinate-subordinate relationship is always clear. The relationship-oriented leader is less task-oriented and more concerned with building harmonious relationships among the members of the organization. He or she possesses a high degree of human relations skill and is less conscious of status.

Persons exhibiting either of these two styles may find themselves in organizations that are either structured or unstructured, or in mixed situations possessing elements of both structure and lack of structure. Successful leadership depends upon the fortuitous combination of both style and circumstance. Fiedler found that task-oriented leaders perform better than relationship-oriented leaders at both ends of the continuum from structure to lack of structure. They perform well in structured situations where they possess authority and influence and in unstructured situations where they lack authority and influence. Relationship-oriented persons function best in mixed situations in which they possess moderate authority and influence.

Sergiovanni and Starratt were inclined to support relationship-oriented leadership in school situations. They said:

> Unstructured situations are typical in educational policy development, in curriculum decision making, in instructional improvement, in in-service education, and the like. . . . If [leader-member personal relationships are good], then by and large the relationship-oriented style will bring educational supervisors closer to group effectiveness. The contingency model suggests that if such relationships are poor, the task-oriented leader will be more successful. We propose, however, that groups of professionals brought together in unstructured situations with weak position power for the leader and poor leader-member relations, who are subject to task-oriented styles for *long periods of time,* will become increasingly less effective. This deterioration is likely to continue until (1) leader-member relations are improved, (2) members co-opt leadership functions, or (3) the leader is replaced.[50]

In a truly democratic situation, leadership will be nurtured, developed, and shared. As the group progresses in its work, the original leader may give way temporarily or permanently to leaders from within the group who possess a particular expertise or who serve the group's purposes more closely.

Leadership, then, arises from the exigencies of a situation. Stephen J. Knezevich, for example, espoused a situational view of leadership in the following way:

> Leadership can arise out of any given situation. This view is almost, but not quite, a contradiction of the trait theory. A person is not chosen to

---

[50] Sergiovanni and Starratt, p. 203.

lead simply on the basis of intelligence or originality, but rather may become a leader if personal characteristics such as intelligence or originality are seen as a means of satisfying group purposes. He is followed because he promises to get — or actually gets — what his followers want. A leader is a product, not of specific or universal characteristics possessed by all such persons, but of his functional relations to specific individuals in a specific situation.[51]

It should be pointed out that when a group member who has been in the role of follower assumes the role of leader that person is then expected to demonstrate democratic behaviors associated with his or her new status of leadership. If the original leader remains a part of the group, he or she then assumes the role of follower. Some status leaders find it difficult to surrender power and are compelled to be constantly on center stage. Such behavior will effectively prevent leadership from developing within the group and is likely to impede its progress. When the original leader resists being replaced, the leader's superior with executive power may have to correct the situation by urging changes in the original leader's behavior or by removing him or her from the scene.

The research on leadership thus suggests that the leader in curriculum development should:

- seek to develop a democratic approach
- seek to develop a relationship-oriented style
- move between a task-oriented and relationship-oriented style as the situation demands (Jacob W. Getzels, James M. Lipham, and Roald F. Campbell called this flexible style "transactional.")[52]
- keep the group on task and avoid excessive processing
- avoid a laissez-faire approach
- encourage the development of leadership from within the group
- maintain an openness and avoid a defensive posture
- fulfill his or her role as a change agent by serving as:

advisor	interpreter
expert	reinforcer
mediator	spokesperson
organizer	intermediary
explainer	summarizer
discussion leader	team builder

Even with the best leadership some groups experience great difficulties in moving toward accomplishment of their goals. Without effective leadership little can be expected of groups in terms of productivity.

---

[51] Stephen J. Knezevich, *Administration of Public Education,* 3rd ed. (New York: Harper & Row, 1975), p. 87.

[52] Jacob W. Getzels, James M. Lipham, and Roald F. Campbell, *Educational Administration as a Social Process* (New York: Harper & Row, 1968).

Communication Skills

Curriculum development is primarily an exercise in verbal behavior — to some degree written but to a greater degree oral. Through the miraculous gift of language one human being is able to communicate his or her thoughts and feelings to another. Much of the world's business — particularly in a democratic society — is transacted through group discussion. Sometimes it seems as if most administrators, including school personnel, spend the majority of their hours participating in groups, for the standard response to callers is "Sorry, he's [she's] in a meeting."

Thoughts are communicated verbally in the form of oral activity, handwritten and printed documents, pictures, diagrams, charts, etc., and nonverbally in the form of gestures and actions. Styles of oral communication and writing differ from individual to individual and from group to group. Styles vary among ethnic, regional, and national groups.

The choice of words, the loudness or softness of speech, and the rapidity of the spoken language differ from person to person and from group to group. We find differences in "accent" and in tone or intonation. The flexibility of language, both a strength and a problem, can be seen in a simple example. By using the same words but by varying the intonation or stress pattern, a speaker can convey different meanings, as follows:

□ *They* said that.
□ They *said* that.
□ They said *that*.
□ They said *that?*

Individuals from some cultures are said to "talk with their hands," indicating frequent use of nonverbal behavior, while individuals from other cultures are taught not to be so expressive. Proficiency in communication skills by both the leader and the group members is essential to successful curriculum development. They must demonstrate proficiency in both oral and written communication. At the same time, they must be aware of their own nonverbal behavior and be skilled at reading other people's.

The leader must demonstrate proficiency in two ways: he or she must possess a high degree of communication skill and be able to help group members to increase their proficiency in communicating.

For purposes of our discussion, we will assume that the school or district curriculum committees, in which we are most interested, operate through the medium of the English language and that, although they represent a variety of ethnic groups and national origins, they possess at least average proficiency in English language usage. What we have to say about communication goes beyond the mere mechanics of grammar, syntax, spelling, vocabulary, and sentence structure. Deficiencies in the linguistic aspects of communication can be remedied perhaps more easily than some of the more complex psychological, social, and cultural aspects.

It is safe to conjecture that even in a group in which all members possess an excellent command of the language, communication leaves something to be desired. Have you ever sat in, for example, on group meetings where:

☐ two people talk at the same time?
☐ one member consistently finishes sentences for people?
☐ one member jumps into the discussion without recognition from the chair, elevates his or her voice, and continues to do so until he or she has forced others to be silent?
☐ one member, angered with the way the discussion is going, gets up and stomps out of the room?
☐ members snicker and make snide remarks whenever a particular member of the group speaks?
☐ one member drones on ad infinitum?
☐ one member cannot resist displaying his or her advanced knowledge of the subject under discussion?
☐ one member becomes sullen when another disagrees with his or her ideas?
☐ the leader has to explain a point three times before all group members seem to understand?

Do you recognize any of these people? Some of them are, of course, playing the group roles discussed earlier. It is possible that many, even most, of the members thought they were communicating something to the group while they were speaking. It is highly probable that what they were communicating was much different from what they thought they were.

Two people vying for the floor may communicate that they both are individuals who demand attention, Or shall we say that they possess a trait, lauded by some, called "assertiveness"? The member who finishes others' sentences may communicate that it is necessary for him or her to think for others. The member who stomps out of the room might attempt to convey that he or she is a person who sticks to his or her principles. More likely, in rejecting the group, this person will be perceived as a "sore loser." We communicate not only through words but through our actions as well.

Common Misunderstandings. We should clear up some common misunderstandings about communication. First, articulateness is sometimes mistaken for communication. The ability to respond quickly and fully — to "think on one's feet" — is an attribute desired, some say required, of a leader. Yet articulation does not assure that a message is getting across. One need only listen to some political leaders to make the distinction between the ability to articulate and to communicate. Americans place great stress on oral facility often to the point that they are unaware that they are accepting form in place of substance. While a soft answer may turneth away wrath, a glib tongue may also obfuscate a topic under discussion. A speaker should strive to be both articulate and communicative.

Second, group interaction is sometimes mistaken for communication. Comments like "We had a lively discussion" are meaningless unless we know whether the discussion led to understanding and decision making. Processing, the sharing of personal feelings and opinions, is sometimes equated with communication. Interaction for interaction's sake cannot be accepted as a legitimate activity for work in curriculum development.

Third, the assumption is often made without sufficient evidence that communication is full, clear, and completely understood. Alfonso, Firth, and Neville advised supervisors against making such an assumption:

> Communication will always be inaccurate because sender and receiver can never share common perceptions. Supervisors often operate on the assumption that communication is perfect. Instead, they should function on the basis that communication is imperfect and must always be so.[53]

How many times have we heard the words of a speaker, understood them all, yet not comprehended what the speaker was saying? How many times have we heard a member of a group tell another, "I hear you," but mean, "Even though I hear you, I do not know what you are saying"?

What are some common problems people experience in trying to communicate and what can be done to solve them? Let's create three categories: (1) problems with oral communication or those that oral and written communication share, (2) problems with written communication, and (3) problems brought about by nonverbal behavior or the absence thereof.

Oral Communication. Difficulties in oral communication can arise in the following situations:

1. *Members of the group either unintentionally or deliberately fail to come to the point.* They "talk around" instead of "to" an issue. Sometimes they engage in avoidance behavior, that is, resisting to come to grips with the issue. The curriculum leader must help group members to address the issues and to come to the point. When some group members prattle on, others in the group become bored and frustrated. The burden of keeping the group's attention on the issues falls on the group leader.

2. *Members of the group use fuzzy, imprecise language.* They use words with many interpretations, like "relevance," without defining them. They use "psychobabble," like "Tell me where you're coming from" and "I'm into behavioral objectives." They employ words of low frequency like "nomothetic," "synergy," and "androgogy," which some members of the group may not understand. They lapse into pedagese, like "Each child must develop his or her personal curriculum," without venturing how this may be done. They borrow Madison Avenue jargon, like "Let's run it up the flagpole," or turn to sports analogies, like "It's in your court now" and "What's the game plan?" The group leader must be alert to difficulties

---

[53] Alfonso, Firth, and Neville, p. 175.

members may have in following a discussion. He or she must ask speakers to repeat and clarify statements and questions as necessary. The leader must keep in mind that some members hesitate to ask for clarifications themselves, feeling that in so doing they may expose their own ignorance.

3. *Members of the group select out of a discussion those things that they wish to hear.* It is a well-known fact that we hear and see selectively. We hear and see things that we wish to hear and see and reject those that we do not want to hear or see. The leader must help group members to see all facets of a problem, calling attention to points they may have missed.

4. *Members fail to express themselves, particularly if they disagree with what has been said.* Some persons hold back their views from a sense of insecurity. They feel that their opinions are not worthwhile. Or, they fear embarrassment or ridicule. They may not wish to seem in disagreement with status persons who are in a position to reward or punish them. The group leader must assure members that dissent is possible and encouraged. The leader must foster a climate in which each person can express himself or herself without fear.

5. *Members fail to follow an orderly process of discussion.* Communication is impossible when group members are unwilling to discipline themselves, taking turns in discussing, listening to each other, and respecting each other's views. The group leader must enforce order during the discussion process to assure that everyone who wishes to be heard has an opportunity.

6. *Discussion is shut off and the group presses for a premature vote.* The group should be striving to reach consensus on issues. The goal is commitment of as many persons as possible. The group leader should keep the goal of consensus in front of the group. Close votes on issues should be re-examined, if possible.

7. *Sessions break up without some sort of closure.* If next steps are not clear, members leave the group sessions confused and frustrated. The leader has the responsibility for seeking closure on issues when possible, for summarizing the group's work, and for calling the group's attention to next steps.

8. *The communication flow is primarily from leader to members.* The leader should resist the temptation to dominate a discussion and to foist his or her views on the group. He or she should assure that communication is initiated by members of the group to the leader and to each other as well as from the leader to group members.

9. *Acrimony, hostility, and disharmony exist within a group.* When these conditions occur, the leader must spend time developing a pleasant, harmonious group climate before positive communication can take place among members. Members must learn to work together in an atmosphere

of trust and mutual respect. The leader should seek to promote a relaxed, threat-free atmosphere.

Written Communication. In the course of a group's activity there will be occasions on which the leader and members of the group will wish and need to communicate in written form between group sessions. They will also need to communicate in writing with persons outside the work group. Difficulties arise with this form of communication when the following situations occur:

1. *The writer cannot sense the impact of his or her words in a written communication.* Extra care needs to be taken when structuring a written message. Writers of memos must weigh their choice of words and manner of phrasing their thoughts. Some messages are unintentionally blunt or curt and cause negative responses in the receivers. A message when put in writing may give a far different impression from what the writer intended. The writer should review any written communication in the light of the impact it would have on him or her if he or she were the recipient.
2. *Written communications are excessive in number.* Some persons indulge in memorandum writing with almost the same frequency as some individuals write letters to the editor of a newspaper. Some vent their own frustrations in memo after memo. Some people believe that every thought, word, and deed must be committed to writing in order to (1) preserve them for posterity, (2) maintain an ongoing record for current use, or (3) cover one's posterior, as is crudely suggested. Some recipients — or intended recipients — will not take any action unless they have word in written form. In some organizations we have almost immobilized ourselves with the ubiquitous memo to the point where we have many communiqués but little communication. The leader should encourage the use of memoranda and other written communications as needed and discourage their excessive use. Courtesy, clarity, and brevity should be earmarks of written communications.
3. *The use of English is poor.* Many memoranda, particularly from professional people, lose their impact because of poor English. Inaccurate spelling and improper grammar can detract from the message contained in the memoranda and can subject the writers to unnecessary criticism.

The writing of intelligible memoranda that do not create negative responses on the part of recipients is an art, which, at least in a cooperative activity like curriculum development, should serve only to supplement, not replace, oral communication.

Face-to-face communication is ordinarily — barring the need for complex or technical data — a far more effective means of conveying ideas among members of small groups of peers such as a typical curriculum development group. Even in the case of complex or technical data presented in written form, follow-up discussion is usually necessary.

Nonverbal Behavior. Human beings communicate with each other without the use of words. A smile, a frown, a wave, and a wink all say something to the recipient. Who among those watching the television set at the time can forget the Premier of the Soviet Union, Nikita Krushchev, seated at a meeting of the United Nations in New York banging the top of his desk with his shoe! Did Mario Puzo's *Godfather* convey any message when he planted the kiss of death on the cheek of his formerly trusted associate? Does the behavior of children and adolescents change when they detect pleasant aromas emanating from the school cafeteria?

Nonverbal behavior is shaped both biologically and culturally. All human beings start out life with basically the same physiological equipment — two eyes, arms, legs, etc. But what they do with that equipment is shaped by the culture in which they grow and develop. Thus, it is possible for every human being to smile but some individuals within a single culture are more prone to smile than others and members of a particular culture are more prone to smile than members of another. South American Indians, for example, are much more stoic and reserved than the more expressive Latinos of Spanish origin.

Nonverbal behavior is less studied and less understood than verbal behavior. We have great need in our teacher education programs for training in understanding differences in nonverbal behavior between members of the United States culture and foreign cultures; among members of diverse cultures in the United States; and among members of a single culture in the United States.

In our pluralistic society many social and work groups are composed of persons from varying subcultures, white, black, Hispanic, Indian, and Asian, among others. Every individual brings to a group his or her culturally determined ways of behaving. While some cultures prize assertiveness, others stress deference. Signs of respect are accorded to age, status, and experience more often in some cultures than in others. Attitudes of both males and females toward children and of one sex toward the other vary among cultures and these attitudes are shown in both verbal and nonverbal behavior.

We need to learn to perceive what our colleagues are trying to communicate to us by the expressions on their faces, by the look in their eyes, by the way they hold their mouths or their heads, by the movement of their hands, and by the fidgeting of their legs. A group leader should be able to detect fatigue, boredom, hostility, and sensitivity on the part of members of the organization. He or she should be able to sense when one individual is stepping on another's toes and turn the discussion to constructive paths. He or she should strive to effect more signs of pleasure than pain among members of the group. The leader must be especially cautious of the nonverbal signals he or she gives and must make every effort to assure that those signals are positive. Finally, for successful curriculum development both the leader and group members must exhibit a high degree of skill in all modes of communication.

SUMMARY

In this chapter we focused on the roles played by various persons and groups participating in curriculum development at the individual school level. Some principals perceive themselves as instructional leaders and take an active part in curriculum development whereas others delegate that responsibility. A Theory-X administrator emphasizes authority and control whereas a Theory-Y administrator follows a human relations approach.

Students in some schools, depending on their maturity, participate in curriculum improvement by serving on committees and by providing data about their own learning experiences.

Parents and other citizens participate in curriculum work by serving on advisory committees, responding to surveys, providing data about their children, and serving as resource persons in school and out.

The professional personnel — teachers and specialists — share the greatest responsibility for curriculum development. Both leaders and followers need to develop skills in group process. Among the competencies necessary for the curriculum leader are skills in producing change, in decision making, in interpersonal relationships, in leading groups, and in communicating.

SUPPLEMENTARY EXERCISES

1. Write a paper stating the pros and cons and showing your position on the role of the principal as instructional leader.
2. List qualities and qualifications needed by a curriculum leader.
3. Explain what is meant by Theory X and Theory Y and draw implications of these theories for curriculum development.
4. Report on ways pupils are involved in curriculum development in a school district with which you are familiar.
5. Report on ways parents and others from the community are involved in curriculum development in a school district with which you are familiar.
6. Explain the meaning of the term, "power structure," and draw implications of the power structure for curriculum development.
7. Write an essay on the curriculum leader as change agent.
8. Write a brief paper on ways to unfreeze an existing curricular pattern.
9. Identify roles played by group members and how the curriculum leader copes with each. You should make an effort to describe roles in addition to those mentioned in this chapter.
10. Describe common barriers to educational change and suggest ways the curriculum leader may work to eliminate them.
11. List steps in the decision-making process.

12. Observe a discussion group in action and apply the observation chart based on the Benne-Sheats classification system discussed in this chapter.
13. Observe a discussion group in action and record evidences of task orientation and process orientation. Conjecture on hidden agendas present in the group.
14. Observe a discussion group in action and evaluate the effectiveness of the leader, using criteria discussed in this chapter.

BIBLIOGRAPHY

Alfonso, Robert J.; Firth, Gerald R.; and Neville, Richard F. *Instructional Supervision: A Behavior System,* 2d ed. Boston: Allyn and Bacon, 1981.

Benne, Kenneth D. and Sheats, Paul. "Functional Roles of Group Members," *The Journal of Social Issues* 4, no. 2 (Spring 1948): 43–46.

Bennis, Warren G.; Benne, Kenneth D.; and Chin, Robert, eds. *The Planning of Change,* 2d ed. New York: Holt, Rinehart and Winston, 1969.

Bennis, Warren G.; Benne, Kenneth D.; Chin, Robert; and Corey, Kenneth E., eds. *The Planning of Change,* 3rd ed. New York: Holt, Rinehart and Winston, 1976.

Campbell, Roald F.; Cunningham, Luvern L.; Usdan, Michael D.; and Nystrand, Raphael O. *The Organization and Control of American Schools,* 4th ed. Columbus, Ohio: Charles E. Merrill, 1980.

Doll, Ronald C. *Curriculum Improvement: Decision Making and Process,* 4th ed. Boston: Allyn and Bacon, 1978.

Fiedler, Fred E. *A Theory of Leadership Effectiveness.* New York: McGraw-Hill, 1967.

Getzels, Jacob W; Lipham, James M.; and Campbell, Roald F. *Educational Administration as a Social Process.* New York: Harper & Row, 1968.

Goodlad, John I. *The Dynamics of Educational Change: Toward Responsive Schools.* New York: McGraw-Hill, 1975.

Haiman, Franklyn S. *Group Leadership and Democratic Action.* Boston: Houghton Mifflin, 1951.

Herriott, Robert E. and Gross, Neal, eds. *The Dynamics of Planned Educational Change.* Berkeley, Cal.: McCutchan, 1976.

Kimbrough, Ralph B. and Nunnery, Michael Y. *Educational Administration: An Introduction.* New York: Macmillan, 1976.

Knezevich, Stephen J. *Administration of Public Education,* 3rd ed. New York: Harper & Row, 1975.

Leavitt, Harold J. *Managerial Psychology: An Introduction to Individuals, Pairs, and Groups in Organizations,* 2d ed. Chicago: The University of Chicago Press, 1964; 3rd ed., 1972; 4th ed., 1978.

Leese, Joseph. *The Teacher in Curriculum Making.* New York: Harper & Row, 1961.

Lewin, Kurt. *Field Theory in Social Science: Selected Theoretical Papers,* edited by Dorwin Cartwright. New York: Harper Torch Books, 1951.

Lewin, Kurt; Lippitt, Ronald; and White, Ralph K. "Patterns of Aggressive Behavior in Experimentally Created Social Climates," *Journal of Social Psychology* 10 (May 1939): 271–299.

Lucio, William H. and McNeil, John D. *Supervision: A Synthesis of Thought and Action,* 2d ed. New York: McGraw-Hill, 1969.

Lynd, Robert S. *Middletown: A Study in American Culture.* New York: Harcourt, Brace, Jovanovich, 1929.

Lynd, Robert S. and Lynd, Helen M. *Middletown in Transition: A Study in*

Cultural Conflicts. New York: Harcourt, Brace, Jovanovich, 1937.

McGregor, Douglas M. *The Human Side of Enterprise.* New York: McGraw-Hill, 1960.

McNeil, John D. *Curriculum: A Comprehensive Introduction,* 2d ed. Boston: Little, Brown, 1981.

Madeja, Stanley S. "Where Have All the Disciplines Gone?" *Educational Leadership* 38, no. 8 (May 1981): 602–604.

Maslow, Abraham H. *Motivation and Personality,* 2d ed. New York: Harper & Row, 1970.

Miel, Alice. *Changing the Curriculum: A Social Process.* New York: Appleton-Century-Crofts, 1946.

Morphet, Edgar L.; Johns, Roe L; and Reller, Theodore L. *Educational Organization and Administration: Concepts, Practices, and Issues,* 3rd ed. Englewood Cliffs, N.J.: Prentice-Hall, 1974.

Oliver, Albert I. *Curriculum Improvement: A Guide to Problems, Principles, and Process,* 2d ed. New York: Harper & Row, 1977.

Owens, Robert G. and Steinhoff, Carl R. *Administering Change in Schools.* Englewood Cliffs, N.J.: Prentice-Hall, 1976.

Peter, Laurence J., Jr. and Hull, Raymond. *The Peter Principle: Why Things Always Go Wrong.* New York: William Morrow, 1969.

Roe, William H. and Drake, Thelbert L. *The Principalship,* 2d ed. New York: Macmillan, 1980.

Roethlisberger, F. J. and Dickson, William J. *Management and the Worker.* Cambridge, Mass.: Harvard University Press, 1939.

Saylor, J. Galen and Alexander, William M. *Planning Curriculum for Schools.* New York: Holt, Rinehart, and Winston, 1974.

Saylor, J. Galen; Alexander, William M.; and Lewis, Arthur J. *Curriculum Planning for Better Teaching and Learning,* 4th ed. New York: Holt, Rinehart and Winston, 1981.

Sergiovanni, Thomas J. and Carver, Fred D. *The New School Executive: A Theory of Administration,* 2d ed. New York: Harper & Row, 1980.

Sergiovanni, Thomas J. and Starratt, Robert J. *Emerging Patterns of Supervision: Human Perspectives.* New York: McGraw-Hill, 1971.

———. *Supervision: Human Perspectives,* 2d ed. New York: McGraw-Hill, 1979.

Stufflebeam, Daniel L. et al. *Educational Evaluation and Decision Making.* Itasca, Ill.: F. E. Peacock Publishers, 1971.

Toffler, Alvin. *Future Shock.* New York: Random House, 1970.

———. *The Third Wave.* New York: William Morrow, 1980.

Wiles, Jon and Bondi, Joseph, Jr. *Curriculum Development: A Guide to Practice.* Columbus, Ohio: Charles E. Merrill, 1979.

Wiles, Kimball. *Supervision for Better Schools,* 3rd ed. Englewood Cliffs, N.J.: Prentice-Hall, 1967.

Wiles, Kimball and Lovell, John T. *Supervision for Better Schools,* 4th ed. Englewood Cliffs, N.J.: Prentice-Hall, 1975.

FILMS

Leadership: Style or Circumstance? 30 min. color. CRM/McGraw-Hill Films, Del Mar, California 92014. 1975. Identifies and differentiates two types of leaders: the relationship-oriented and the task-oriented leader. Shows how each type of leader can work effectively depending on the job situation.

Theory X and Theory Y: Work of Douglas McGregor. 25 min. color. BNA Communications, Inc., 9401 Decoverly Hall Rd., Rockville, Maryland 20850. 1969. Two basic sets of assumptions about human nature that characterize management style.

VIDEOTAPE

Selecting Appropriate Leadership Styles for Instructional Improvement. 30 min. color. 1978. Association for Supervision and Curriculum Development, 225 N. Washington St., Alexandria, Va. 22314. Dr. Gordon Cawelti, Executive Director, Association for Supervision and Curriculum Development narrates this taped program that synthesizes studies on leader behavior and develops the Situational Leadership Model of Philip E. Gates, Kenneth H. Blanchard, and Paul Hersey.

Part **III**

Curriculum Development: Components of the Process

5

Models for
Curriculum Development

After studying this chapter you should be able to:
1. Analyze each model for curriculum development in this chapter and to decide which models, if any, meet the necessary criteria for such a model.
2. Choose one model and carry out one or more of its components in your school.
3. Design your own model for curriculum development following criteria you first select for creating the model.

You should also be able to formulate and give reasons for your views on the following issues:
1. The model for curriculum development that you would be most inclined to follow.
2. The agreements or disagreements you may have with the principles of each of the models described.

SELECTING MODELS

The current literature of education is replete with discussions of "modeling." Models, which are essentially patterns serving as guidelines to action, can be found for almost every form of educational activity. The profession has models of instruction, of administration, of evaluation, of supervision, and others. At last count, there were some ninety-nine models of observational analysis.[1] We can even find models of *curriculum* as opposed to models of *curriculum development*.[2]

Unfortunately, the term "model" rates with "scenario" as one of the most abused words in current English usage. While a scenario may turn out to be any plan or series of events, a model may be a tried or untried scheme. It may be a proposed solution to a piece of a problem; it may be an attempt at a solution to a specific problem; or it may be a microcosmic pattern proposed for replication on a grander scale.

Some faculties have been "modeling" for years. They have been devising their own patterns for solving educational problems or establishing procedures, though they may not have labeled their activity as "modeling."

Variation in Models

Some of the models found in the literature are simple; others are very complex. The more complex border on computer science with charts made up of squares, boxes, circles, rectangles, arrows, etc. Within a given area of specialization (as administration, instruction, supervision, or curriculum development), models may differ but bear great similarities. The similarities may outweigh the differences. Individual models are often refinements or revisions, frequently major, often minor, of already existing models.

The educational consumers, i.e., the practitioners to whom a model is directed, therefore have the heavy responsibility of selecting one model in their particular field from the often bewildering variety in the literature. If the practitioners are not disposed to apply models they discover, they may either design their own, by no means a rare event, or may reject all models that prescribe order and sequence. They may thus proceed intuitively without the apparent limitations imposed by a model. After proceeding intuitively, the practitioners may then "put it all together" and come out with a working model at the end of the process instead of starting with a model at the beginning.

The proliferation of models in many aspects of education is almost a malady to which I must admit I have succumbed. Five models of curriculum development are presented in this chapter, one of which is my own. I believe that

---

[1] See Anita Simon and E. Gil Boyer, *Mirrors for Behavior III: An Anthology of Observation Instruments* (Philadelphia, Pa.: Research for Better Schools, 1974).

[2] For a model of *curriculum,* see Mauritz Johnson, Jr., "Definitions and Models in Curriculum Theory," *Educational Theory* 17, no. 2 (April 1967): 127–140.

using a model in such an activity as curriculum development can result in greater efficiency and productivity.

By examining models for curriculum development, we can analyze the phases their originators conceived as essential to the process of curriculum development. The purpose in presenting five models is to acquaint the reader with some of the thinking that has gone on or is going on in the field. Three of the chosen models were conceived by persons well known in the curriculum and/or instructional design fields: William M. Alexander, J. Galen Saylor, Hilda Taba, and Ralph W. Tyler. Whereas the model by Mario Leyton Soto is less well known to North American readers, it is included to show how Tyler's model could be refined and expanded. My own model is presented as an effort to tie together essential components in the process of curriculum development.

All of these models specify or depict major phases and a sequence for carrying out these phases. The models, including mine, show *phases* or *components,* not *people.* The various individuals and groups involved in each phase are not included in the models per se. To do so would require a most cumbersome model, for we would have to show the persons involved in every component. For example, if we showed the people involved in the component, specification of curriculum goals, we would need to chart a progression of steps from departmental committee to school faculty curriculum committee or extended school committee to principal to district curriculum committee to superintendent to school board. The roles of individuals and groups in the process are discussed elsewhere in this text.

MODELS OF CURRICULUM DEVELOPMENT

Curriculum development is seen here as the process for making programmatic decisions and for revising the products of those decisions on the basis of continuous and subsequent evaluation.

A model can give order to the process. As Taba stated, "If one conceives of curriculum development as a task requiring orderly thinking, one needs to examine both the order in which decisions are made and the way in which they are made to make sure that all relevant considerations are brought to bear on these decisions." [3]

The Tyler Model

Perhaps the best or one of the best known models for curriculum development with special attention to the planning phases is Ralph W. Tyler's in his classic little book, *Basic Principles of Curriculum and Instruction.*[4] "The Tyler Ra-

---

[3] Hilda Taba, *Curriculum Development: Theory and Practice* (New York: Harcourt, Brace, Jovanovich, 1962), pp. 11–12.

[4] Ralph W. Tyler, *Basic Principles of Curriculum and Instruction* (Chicago: University of Chicago Press, 1949), p. 3.

tionale," a process for selecting educational objectives, is widely known and practiced in curriculum circles. Although Tyler proposed a rather comprehensive model for curriculum development, the first part of his model, the selection of objectives, received the greatest attention from other educators.

Tyler recommended that curriculum planners identify general objectives by gathering data from three sources: the learners, contemporary life outside the school, and the subject matter. After identifying numerous general objectives the planners refine these by filtering them through two screens: the educational and social philosophy of the school and the psychology of learning. The general objectives that successfully pass through the two screens become specific instructional objectives. In describing general objectives Tyler referred to them as "goals," "educational objectives," and "educational purposes." [5]

The curriculum worker begins his or her search for educational objectives by gathering and analyzing data relevant to student needs and interests. The total range of needs — educational, social, occupational, physical, psychological, and recreational — is studied. Tyler recommended observations by teachers, interviews with students, interviews with parents, questionnaires, and tests as techniques for collecting data about students.[6] By examining the needs and interests of students, the curriculum developer identifies a set of potential objectives.

Analysis of contemporary life in both the local community and in society at large is the next step in the process of formulating general objectives. Tyler suggested that curriculum planners develop a classification scheme that divides life into various aspects such as health, family, recreation, vocation, religion, consumption, and civic roles.[7] From the needs of society flow many potential educational objectives. It is apparent that the curriculum worker must be somewhat of a sociologist to make an intelligent analysis of needs of social institutions. After considering this second source, the curriculum worker has lengthened his or her set of objectives.

For a third source the curriculum planner turns to the subject matter, the disciplines themselves. It should be remembered that many of the curricular innovations of the 1950s — the new math, audio-lingual foreign languages, and the plethora of science programs — came from the subject matter specialists. From the three aforementioned sources curriculum planners derive a multiplicity of general or broad objectives, which lack precision and which I would prefer to call instructional goals. These goals may be pertinent to specific disciplines or may cut across disciplines.

Johnson held a different perspective about these sources. He commented that the "only possible source [of the curriculum] is the total available culture" and that only organized subject matter, i.e., the disciplines, not the needs and

---

[5] Tyler, p. 3.
[6] Tyler, pp. 12–13.
[7] Tyler, pp. 19–20.

interests of learners or the values and problems of society can be considered a source of curriculum items.[8]

Once this array of possibly applicable objectives is determined, a screening process is necessary, according to Tyler's model to eliminate unimportant and contradictory objectives. He advised the use of the school's educational and social philosophy as the first screen for these goals.

Philosophical Screen. Tyler advised teachers of a particular school to formulate an educational and social philosophy. He urged them to outline their values and illustrated this task by emphasizing four democratic goals:

- ☐ the recognition of the importance of every individual human being as a human being regardless of his race, national, social or economic status;
- ☐ opportunity for wide participation in all phases of activities in the social groups in the society;
- ☐ encouragement of variability rather than demanding a single type of personality;
- ☐ faith in intelligence as a method of dealing with important problems rather than depending upon the authority of an autocratic or aristocratic group.[9]

Interestingly, in his discussion of formulating an educational and social philosophy, Tyler personifies the school. He talks about "the educational and social philosophy to which the school is committed," "when a school accepts these values," "many schools are likely to state," and "if the school believes." [10] Thus, Tyler makes of the school a dynamic, living entity. The curriculum worker will review the list of general objectives and omit those that are not in keeping with the faculty's agreed-upon philosophy.

Psychological Screen. The application of the psychological screen is the next step in the Tyler model. To apply the screen, teachers must clarify the principles of learning that they believe to be sound. "A psychology of learning," said Tyler, "not only includes specific and definite findings but it also involves a unified formulation of a theory of learning which helps to outline the nature of the learning process, how it takes place, under what conditions, what sort of mechanisms operate and the like." [11] Effective application of this screen presupposes adequate training in educational psychology and in human growth and development by those charged with the task of curriculum development.

Tyler explained the significance of the psychological screen:

- ☐ A knowledge of the psychology of learning enables us to distinguish changes in human beings that can be expected to result from a learning process from those that can not.

---

8 Johnson, "Definitions and Models," p. 132.
9 Tyler, p. 34.
10 Tyler, pp. 33–36.
11 Tyler, p. 41.

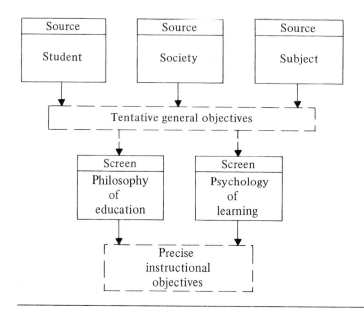

FIGURE 5-1   Tyler's curricular rationale

    □ A knowledge of the psychology of learning enables us to distinguish goals that are feasible from those that are likely to take a very long time or are almost impossible of attainment at the age level contemplated.

    □ Psychology of learning gives us some idea of the length of time required to attain an objective and the age levels at which the effort is most efficiently employed.[12]

After the curriculum planner has applied this second screen, his or her list of general objectives will be reduced, leaving those that are the most significant and feasible. Care is then taken to state the objectives in behavioral terms, which turns them into instructional, classroom objectives. We will return to the writing of behavioral objectives in Chapters 7, 8, and 10.

Tyler did not make use of a diagram in describing the process he recommended. However, Popham and Baker cast the model into the illustration shown in Figure 5-1.[13]

For some reason, discussions of the Tyler model often stop after examining the first part of his model — the rationale for selecting educational objectives. Actually, Tyler's model goes beyond this process to describe three more steps in curriculum planning: selection, organization, and evaluation of learning experiences. He defined learning experiences as "the interaction between

    [12] Tyler, pp. 38–39.

    [13] W. James Popham and Eva L. Baker, *Establishing Instructional Goals* (Englewood Cliffs, N.J.: Prentice-Hall, 1970), p. 87.

the learner and the external conditions in the environment to which he can react." [14]

He suggested teachers give attention to learning experiences

- □ to develop skill in thinking
- □ helpful in acquiring information
- □ helpful in developing social attitudes
- □ helpful in developing interests[15]

He explained how to organize the experiences into units and described various evaluation procedures.[16] Although Tyler did not devote a chapter to a phase called direction of learning experiences (or implementation of instruction), we can infer that instruction must take place between the selection and organization of the learning experiences and the evaluation of student achievement of these experiences.

Expanded Model. We could, therefore, modify the diagram of Tyler's model by expanding it to include steps in the planning process after specifying the instructional objectives. Figure 5-2 shows how such an expanded model might appear.

When observing that writers before Tyler identified similar sources of general objectives, Daniel and Laurel Tanner commented that the Tyler rationale "actually represents a systematic resynthesis of progressive educational thought spanning earlier decades." [17] One of the more serious difficulties in the Tyler rationale, in the Tanners' view, is that Tyler presented the three sources as separate entities, not showing their interaction. If curriculum planners consider the components to be separate and fail to understand the interaction between the sources, curriculum development can become too mechanical a process. The Tanners noted, however, that the Tyler rationale "stands to this day as the definitive conceptual scheme for curriculum development." [18]

The Leyton Soto Model

With the collaboration of Ralph Tyler, Mario Leyton Soto revised and expanded upon the model presented by Tyler.[19] Leyton Soto observed the linear nature of the Tyler model and the separation of the three sources of objectives. He included in his schematic representation of Tyler's model the understanding that the two screens — philosophy and psychology — were not necessarily to be applied in a preferred sequence but that either one might precede the other.

---

[14] Tyler, p. 63.

[15] Tyler, Chapter 2.

[16] Tyler, Chapters 3 and 4.

[17] Daniel Tanner and Laurel N. Tanner, *Curriculum Development: Theory Into Practice* (New York: Macmillan, 1975), p. 60.

[18] Tanner and Tanner, p. 60.

[19] Mario Leyton Soto and Ralph W. Tyler, *Planeamiento Educacional* (Santiago, Chile: Editorial Universitaria, 1969).

FIGURE 5-2   Tyler's curricular rationale (expanded)

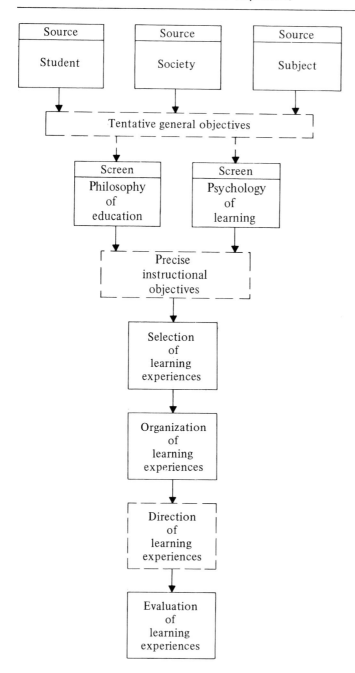

An Integrated Model. Leyton Soto eliminated some of the objections to the Tyler model and added some of his own refinements and clarifications. Leyton Soto's Integrated Model appears in Figure 5-3.[20]

Leyton Soto's model charted three basic elements: philosophy, psychology, and sources; three basic processes: selection, organization, and evaluation; and three fundamental concepts: objectives, activities, and experiences. Significantly, Leyton Soto clearly showed the interrelationships among the various components of the model.

This model starts with the two screens rather than the three sources. It is evident that the sources themselves are influenced by the philosophical and psychological screens and vice versa. Whereas Tyler himself described (1) the selection of objectives and (2) the selection, organization, and evaluation of learning experiences, Leyton Soto distinguished between learning experiences and learning activities. He defined objectives as the combination of experiences that the learner tries to achieve. *Experiences,* in Leyton Soto's terminology, are the behaviors that are written into the objectives, whereas *activities* are those experiences that the learner undertakes to achieve the expected behaviors. For this reason Leyton Soto maintained and indicated by arrows in his model that *objectives,* i.e., the expected behaviors, and *activities* are selected and organized, but only *experiences,* i.e., the terminal behaviors, are evaluated.

Thus, Leyton Soto has presented an integrated or comprehensive, albeit relatively complex model for curriculum development from the point of selecting objectives to the point of evaluating experiences.

The Taba Model

Taba took what is known as a grass-roots approach to curriculum development. She believed that the curriculum should be designed by the teachers rather than handed down by higher authority. Further, she felt that teachers should begin the process by creating specific teaching-learning units for their students in their schools rather than by engaging initially in creating a general curriculum design. Taba, therefore, advocated an inductive approach to curriculum development, starting with specifics and building up to a general design as opposed to the more traditional deductive approach of starting with the general design and working down to the specifics.

Five-Step Sequence. Eschewing graphic exposition of her model, Taba listed a five-step sequence for accomplishing curriculum change, as follows:[21]

1. *Production by teachers of pilot teaching-learning units representative of the grade level or subject area.* Taba saw this step as linking theory and

---

[20] Soto and Tyler, p. 55.
[21] Taba, pp. 456–459.

FIGURE 5-3   Leyton Soto's integrated model

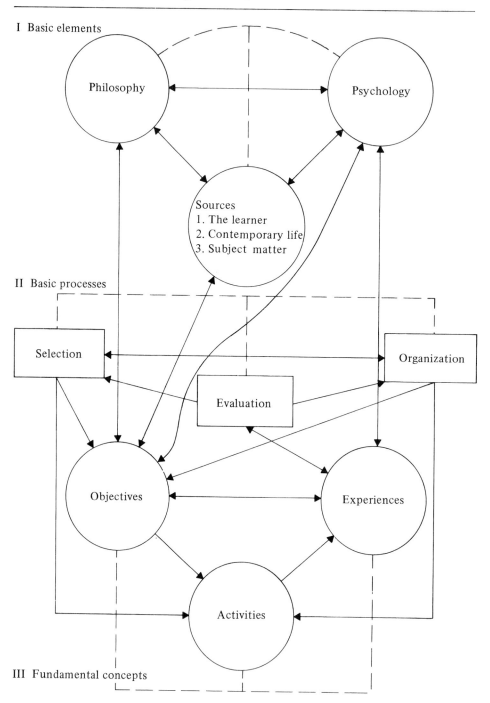

practice. She proposed the following eight-step sequence for curriculum developers who are producing pilot units.[22]

    a. *Diagnosis of needs.* The curriculum developer begins by determining the needs of the students for whom the curriculum is being planned. Taba directs the curriculum worker to diagnose the "gaps, deficiencies, and variations in [students'] backgrounds." [23]

    b. *Formulation of objectives.* After student needs have been diagnosed, the curriculum planner specifies objectives to be accomplished. Interestingly, Taba uses the terms "goals" and "objectives" interchangeably, a point to which we will return later.

    c. *Selection of content.* The subject matter or topics to be studied stem directly from the objectives. Taba pointed out that not only must the objectives be considered in selecting content but also the "validity and significance" of the content chosen.[24]

    d. *Organization of content.* With the selection of content goes the task of deciding at what levels and in what sequences the subject matter will be placed. Maturity of learners, their readiness to confront the subject matter, and their levels of academic achievement are factors to be considered in the appropriate placement of content.

    e. *Selection of learning experiences.* The methodologies or strategies by which the learners are involved with the content must be chosen by the curriculum planners. Pupils internalize the content through the learning activities selected by the planner-teacher.

    f. *Organization of learning activities.* The teacher decides how to package the learning activities and in what combinations and sequences they will be utilized. At this stage the teacher adapts the strategies to the particular students for whom he or she has responsibility.

    g. *Determination of what to evaluate and of the ways and means of doing it.* The planner must decide whether objectives have been accomplished. The instructor selects from a variety of techniques appropriate means for assessing achievement of students and for determining whether the objectives of the curriculum have been met.

    h. *Checking for balance and sequence.* Taba counseled curriculum workers to look for consistency among the various parts of the teaching-learning units, for proper flow of the learning experiences, and for balance in the types of learning and forms of expression.

2. *Testing experimental units.* Since the goal of this process is to create a curriculum encompassing one or more grade levels or subject areas and since teachers have written their pilot units with their own classrooms in

---

    [22] Taba, pp. 345–379. On page 12 of her book Taba lists the first seven steps. See Chapter 11 of my text for a discussion of the creation of units.

    [23] Taba, p. 12.

    [24] Taba, p. 12.

mind, the units must now be tested "to establish their validity and teachability and to set their upper and lower limits of required abilities." [25]

3. *Revising and consolidating.* The units are modified to conform to variations in student needs and abilities. available resources, and different styles of teaching so that the curriculum may suit all types of classrooms. Taba would charge supervisors, the coordinators of curricula, and the curriculum specialists with the task of "stating the principles and theoretical considerations on which the structure of the units and the selection of content and learning activities are based and suggesting the limits within which modifications in the classroom can take place." [26] Taba recommended that such "considerations and suggestions might be assembled in a handbook explaining the use of the units." [27]

4. *Developing a framework.* After a number of units have been constructed, the curriculum planners must examine them as to adequacy of scope and appropriateness of sequence. The curriculum specialist would assume the responsibility of drafting a rationale for the curriculum which has been developed through this process.

5. *Installing and disseminating new units.* So that the teachers may effectively put the teaching-learning units into operation in their classrooms, Taba called on administrators to arrange appropriate inservice training.

Taba's inductive model may not appeal to curriculum developers who prefer to consider the more global aspects of the curriculum before proceeding to specifics. Some planners might wish to see a more comprehensive model that includes steps both in diagnosing the needs of society and culture and in deriving needs from subject matter, philosophy, and learning theory. Taba elaborates on these points in her fine text.[28]

The Saylor and Alexander Model

Saylor and Alexander conceptualized the *curriculum planning process* in the model shown in Figure 5-4.[29] To understand this model for curriculum planning, it is necessary to first analyze their concepts of "curriculum" and "curriculum plan." Their definition of curriculum was quoted earlier in this text — "a plan for providing sets of learning opportunities to achieve broad educational goals and related specific objectives for an identifiable population served by a single

---

[25] Taba, p. 458.
[26] Taba, p. 458.
[27] Taba, pp. 458–459.
[28] Taba, Part One.
[29] J. Galen Saylor and William M. Alexander, *Planning Curriculum for Schools* (New York: Holt, Rinehart and Winston, 1974), p. 27. This figure also appears in slightly different form in J. Galen Saylor, William M. Alexander, and Arthur J. Lewis, *Curriculum Planning for Better Teaching and Learning,* 4th ed. (New York: Holt, Rinehart and Winston, 1981), p. 30.

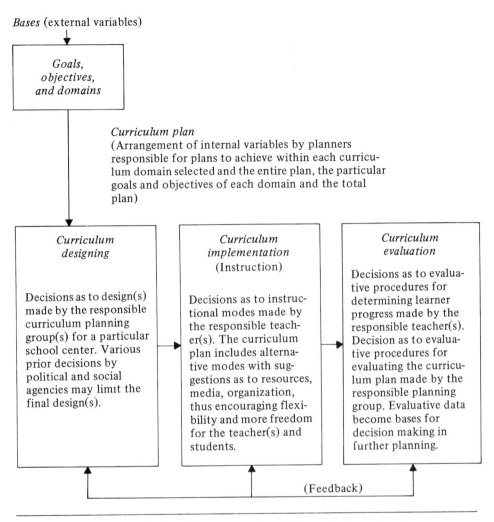

Bases (external variables)

Goals,
objectives,
and domains

Curriculum plan
(Arrangement of internal variables by planners
responsible for plans to achieve within each curriculum domain selected and the entire plan, the particular
goals and objectives of each domain and the total
plan)

*Curriculum
designing*

Decisions as to design(s)
made by the responsible
curriculum planning
group(s) for a particular
school center. Various
prior decisions by
political and social
agencies may limit the
final design(s).

*Curriculum
implementation*
(Instruction)

Decisions as to instruc-
tional modes made by
the responsible teach-
er(s). The curriculum
plan includes alterna-
tive modes with sug-
gestions as to resources,
media, organization,
thus encouraging flexi-
bility and more freedom
for the teacher(s) and
students.

*Curriculum
evaluation*

Decisions as to evalua-
tive procedures for
determining learner
progress made by the
responsible teacher(s).
Decision as to evalua-
tive procedures for
evaluating the curricu-
lum plan made by the
responsible planning
group. Evaluative data
become bases for
decision making in
further planning.

(Feedback)

FIGURE 5-4   Saylor and Alexander's conception of the curriculum planning process

school center." [30] Yet, the curriculum plan is not to be conceived as a single document but rather as "many smaller plans for particular portions of the curriculum." [31]

Goals, Objectives, and Domains. The model indicates that the curriculum planners begin by specifying the major educational goals and specific objectives they wish to be accomplished. Each major goal represents a curriculum do-main. While Saylor and Alexander advocate four major goals or domains (per-

[30] Saylor and Alexander, p. 24.
[31] Saylor and Alexander, p. 24.

sonal development, human relations, continued learning skills, and specialization), they fully expect that some of the domains they have suggested will not be accepted by all schools and that additional domains will be defined.[32]

The goals, objectives, and domains are selected after careful consideration of external variables, among which are legal requirements, educational research, regional accreditation standards, views of community groups, etc.[33] Saylor and Alexander refer to the three blocks in the model, curriculum designing, curriculum implementation, and curriculum evaluation, as internal variables with regard to which curriculum planners must make numerous choices.[34] Once the goals — and may we infer subgoals and objectives — and domains have been established the planners move into the process of designing the curriculum. The curriculum workers decide on the appropriate learning opportunities for each domain and how and when these opportunities will be provided. Will the curriculum be designed along the lines of academic disciplines, according to a pattern of social institutions, or in relation to student needs and interests, as examples?

Instructional Modes. After the designs have been created — and there may be many — all teachers affected by a given part of the curriculum plan must create the instructional plans. They select the methods through which the curriculum will be related to the learners.[35] At this point in the model it would be helpful to see the term "instructional objectives" introduced. Teachers would then specify the instructional objectives before selecting the strategies or modes of presentation.

Evaluation. Finally, the curriculum planners and teachers engage in evaluation. They must choose from a wide variety of evaluation techniques. Saylor and Alexander urge a comprehensive approach to evaluation.[36] They would like to see an evaluation design that would permit assessment of the total educational program of the school and that would include the curriculum plan, the effectiveness of instruction, and the achievement of learners. Through the evaluation processes, curriculum planners can determine whether or not the goals of the school and the objectives of instruction have been met.

Saylor and Alexander supplemented this model of the curriculum planning process with companion models depicting the elements of the curriculum system and the process of defining the purposes of the school.[37] To fully understand the model of the curriculum planning process, the student should examine the two companion models as well.

Although a highly useful approach to the designing of a model for cur-

---

[32] Saylor and Alexander, pp. 37, 41.
[33] Saylor and Alexander, pp. 30–33.
[34] Saylor and Alexander, p. 24.
[35] See Saylor and Alexander, Chapter 6.
[36] See Saylor and Alexander, Chapter 7.
[37] Saylor and Alexander, pp. 23, 153.

riculum improvement, the Saylor and Alexander model when accompanied by the companion models is rather complex. Curriculum planners might find some synthesis of the models desirable, if possible.

Similarities and Differences Among Models

The models just discussed reveal both similarities and differences. Taba, Tyler, and Leyton Soto outlined a sequence of steps to be taken in curriculum development. Saylor and Alexander charted the components of the curriculum development process (design, implementation, and evaluation) as opposed to actions taken by the curriculum workers (diagnosis of needs, formulation of objectives, etc.). Tyler's concepts of sources and screens stand out in his model. Leyton Soto sought to improve on Tyler's model by depicting reciprocal and cyclical aspects of the process as opposed to Tyler's linear approach.

Models are inevitably incomplete; they do not and cannot show every detail and every nuance of a process as complicated as curriculum development. In one sense the originator of a model is saying, sometimes in graphic form, "These are the features you should not forget." To depict every detail of the curriculum development process would require an exceedingly complex drawing or several models. One task in building a model for curriculum improvement is to determine what the most salient components in the process are — no easy task — and to limit the model to those components. Model builders find themselves between the Scylla of oversimplification and the Charybdis of complexity to the point of confusion.

In looking at various models we cannot say that any one model is inherently superior to all other models. Some curriculum planners have followed the Tyler model, for example, for years with considerable success. On the other hand, this does not mean that the Tyler model represents the ultimate in models for curriculum improvement or that all educators are satisfied with it.[38] As we continue to study the complex nature of curriculum development, it becomes apparent that refinements of earlier models can be made.

Before choosing a model or designing a new model — certainly a viable alternative — curriculum planners might attempt to outline the criteria or characteristics they would look for in a model for curriculum improvement. They might agree that this model should show:

1. major components of the process
2. customary, but not inflexible, "beginning" and "ending" points
3. the relationship between curriculum and instruction
4. distinctions between curricular and instructional goals and objectives
5. reciprocal relationships between components

---

[38] See "Is the Tyler Rationale a suitable basis for current curriculum development?" *ASCD Update* 22, no. 6 (December 1980): 4–5. Replies to the question from Fenwick English, Dwayne Huebner, Rodgers Lewis, James Macdonald, Laurel Tanner, and Marilyn Winters.

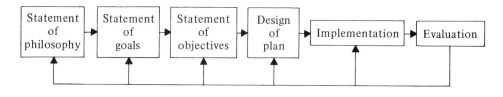

FIGURE 5-5   A model for curriculum development (Oliva, 1976)

6. a cyclical rather than a linear pattern
7. feedback lines
8. the possibility of entry at any point in the cycle
9. an internal consistency and logic
10. enough simplicity to be intelligible
11. components in the form of a diagram or chart

To this end, a model incorporating these guidelines will now be proposed. The model will accomplish two purposes: (1) to suggest a system that curriculum planners might wish to follow and (2) to serve as the framework for explanations of phases or components of the process for curriculum improvement.

The model is not presented as the be-all and end-all of models of curriculum development but rather as an attempt to implement the aforementioned guidelines. The proposed model may be acceptable in its present form to curriculum planners. It may, at the same time, stimulate them to improve the model or to create another that would better reflect their goals, needs, and beliefs.

The Oliva Model

Several years ago I set out to chart a model for curriculum development that met three criteria: the model had to be simple, comprehensive, and to follow a systems approach. The design is shown in Figure 5-5.[39] Although this model represents the most essential components, it can be readily expanded into an extended model that provides additional detail and shows some processes which the simplified model assumes. In this chapter we will look at an extended model and briefly describe its components. The subsequent chapters of Part III elaborate on each component. The extended model that we will discuss in detail appears in Figure 5-6.

The Twelve Components. The model charted in Figure 5-6 is a comprehensive, step-by-step process that takes the curriculum planner from the sources of the curriculum to evaluation. In Chapters 6 through 13, we will examine

[39] Peter F. Oliva, *Supervision for Today's Schools* (New York: Harper & Row, 1976), p. 232.

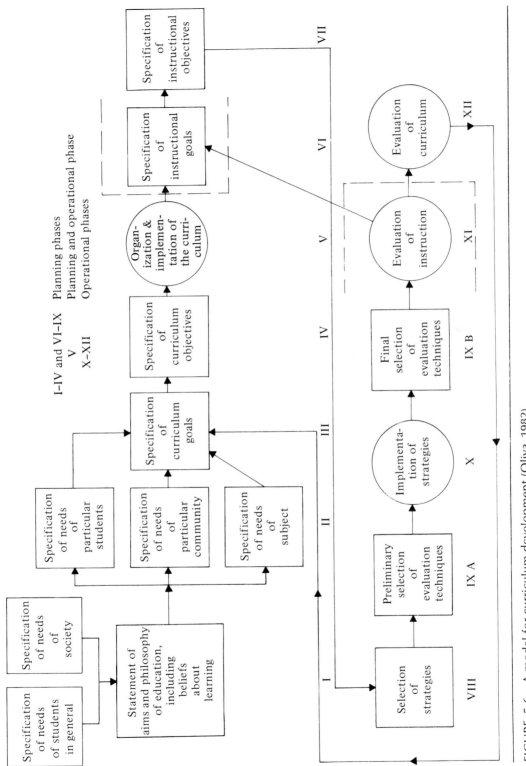

FIGURE 5-6 A model for curriculum development (Oliva, 1982)

each part of the model. Each component (designated by Roman numerals I through XII) will be described, and illustrations will be given to guide curriculum planners and their co-workers. We will now undertake a cursory overview of the model.

The reader will note that both squares and circles are used in the model. The squares are used to represent planning phases and the circles, operational phases. The process starts with component I, at which time the curriculum developers state the aims of education and their philosophical and psychological principles. These aims are beliefs that are derived from the needs of our society and the needs of individuals living in our society. This component incorporates concepts similar to Tyler's "screens."

Component II requires an analysis of the needs of the community in which the school is located, the needs of students served in that community, and the exigencies of the subject matter that will be taught in the given school. Sources of the curriculum are seen as cutting across components I and II. While component I treats the needs of students and society in a more general sense, component II introduces the concepts of needs of particular students in particular localities, since the needs of students in particular communities are not always the same as the general needs of students throughout our society.

Components III and IV call for specifying curricular goals and objectives based on components I and II. A distinction that will be clarified later with examples is drawn between goals and objectives. The tasks of component V are to organize and implement the curriculum, to formulate and establish the structure by which the curriculum will be organized.

In components VI and VII an increasing level of specification is sought. Instructional goals and objectives are stated for each level and subject. Once again we will distinguish between goals and objectives and will show by illustration how the two differ.

After specifying instructional objectives, the curriculum worker moves to component VIII at which point he or she chooses instructional strategies for use with students in the classroom. Simultaneously, the curriculum worker initiates phase A of component IX, Preliminary Selection of Evaluation Techniques. At this stage the curriculum planner thinks ahead and begins to consider ways he or she will assess student achievement. The implementation of instructional strategies — component X — follows.

After the students have been provided appropriate opportunity to learn (component X), the planner returns to the problem of selecting techniques for evaluating student achievement and the effectiveness of the instructor. Component IX, then, is separated into two phases: the first *precedes* the actual implementation of instruction (IXA) and the second *follows* the implementation (IXB). The instructional phase (component X) provides the planner with the opportunity to refine, add to, and complete the selection of means to evaluate pupil performance.

Component XI is the stage when evaluating instruction is carried out.

Component XII completes the cycle with evaluation not of the student or the teacher but rather of the curricular program. It can be seen from the model that components I-IV and VI-IX are planning phases, whereas components X-XII are operational phases. Component V is both a planning and operational phase.

Like some other models, this model combines both a scheme for curriculum development (components I-V and XII) and a design for instruction (components VI-XI).

The curricular components (I-V and XII) constitute one subcycle of the model and the instructional components (VI-XI) constitute another subcycle. To distinguish between the curriculum and the instructional components, the instructional subcycle is enclosed within broken lines.

Important features of the model are the feedback lines that cycle back from the evaluation of the curriculum to the curriculum goals and from the evaluation of instruction to the instructional goals. These lines indicate the necessity of continuous revision of the components of their respective subcycles.

Use of the Model. The model can be used in a variety of ways. First, the model offers a process for the complete development of a school's curriculum. The faculty of each special area, e.g., language arts, can, by following the model, fashion a plan for the curriculum of that area and design ways in which it will be carried out through instruction. Or, the faculty may develop school-wide, interdisciplinary programs that cut across areas of specialization such as career education, guidance, and extraclass activities.

Second, a faculty may focus on the curricular components of the model (components I-V and XII) to make programmatic decisions. Third, a faculty may concentrate on the instructional components (VI-XI).

Two Submodels. This twelve-phase model integrates a general model for curriculum development with a general model for instruction. When the curricular submodel is followed, the curriculum planners must keep in mind that the task has not been completed until the curricular goals and objectives are subsequently translated by them or others into instruction. Further, when the instructional submodel is followed the instructional planners must be aware of the curriculum goals and objectives of the school as a whole and/or of a given subject area or areas.

In order to keep the model as uncluttered as possible at this point I have not attempted to show all the nuances of the model. At several places in subsequent chapters certain refinements and embellishments of the model will be shown.

SUMMARY

Five models of curriculum development are presented in this chapter. Models can help us to conceptualize a process by showing certain principles and procedures. Whereas some models are embellished with diagrams, others are simply lists of steps that are recommended to curriculum workers.

Those who take leadership in curriculum development are encouraged to become familiar with various models, to try them out, and to select or develop a model that is most understandable and feasible to them and to the persons with whom they are working.

I have presented a model for consideration consisting of twelve components. This model is comprehensive in nature, encompassing both curricular and instructional development.

SUPPLEMENTARY EXERCISES

1. Define "sources" and "screens" as used by Ralph W. Tyler.
2. Explain why Tyler's model has been referred to as "linear" in nature and identify the presence or absence of linearity in each of the other models.
3. Write a brief position paper, giving reasons for your position, on the question: "Is the Tyler Rationale a suitable basis for current curriculum development?"
4. Describe the refinements Leyton Soto made in the Tyler model and state whether you feel these refinements are improvements on the model.
5. Cast Taba's steps for curriculum development into a diagrammed model.
6. Identify one or more domains in addition to the four suggested by Saylor and Alexander or, alternately, design your own pattern of domains.
7. Explain the meaning of the broken lines in the diagram of the Oliva model.
8. Explain why components X, XI, and XII of the Oliva model are shown as circles whereas the other components, except for component V, are shown as squares. Explain why component V is depicted with both a square and a circle.
9. Describe the four models of curriculum planning found in Geneva Gay's chapter in the 1980 Yearbook of the Association for Supervision and Curriculum Development (see bibliography). These models are the academic model, the experiential model, the technical model, and the pragmatic model.
10. Distinguish between an inductive and a deductive model of curriculum development. Find one illustration of each in the literature.
11. Define curriculum engineering as used by Robert S. Zais (see bibliography) and report on one of the following models for curriculum engineering discussed by Zais:
    a. The Administrative (Line-Staff) Model
    b. The Grass-Roots Model
    c. The Demonstration Model
    d. George Beauchamp's System
    e. Carl Rogers' Interpersonal Relations Model

12. Robert M. Gagné maintains that there is no such step in curriculum development as "selection of content" (see bibliography). State whether you agree, give reasons, citing quotes from the literature that support your position.
13. Describe the model of curricular and instructional planning and evaluation proposed by Mauritz Johnson in *Intentionality in Education* (see bibliography).

BIBLIOGRAPHY

Beauchamp, George A. *Curriculum Theory,* 2d ed. Wilmette, Illinois: The Kagg Press, 1968.

Bloom, Benjamin S., ed. *Taxonomy of Educational Objectives: The Classification of Educational Goals: Handbook I: Cognitive Domain.* New York: Longman, 1956.

Foshay, Arthur W., ed. *Considered Action for Curriculum Improvement,* 1980 Yearbook. Alexandria, Va.: Association for Supervision and Curriculum Development, 1980.

Gagné, Robert M. "Curriculum Research and the Promotion of Learning." *AERA Monograph Series on Evaluation: Perspectives of Curriculum Evaluation,* no. 1. Chicago: Rand McNally, 1967, pp. 19–23.

Gay, Geneva. "Conceptual Models of the Curriculum-Planning Process." In *Considered Action for Curriculum Improvement,* 1980 Yearbook. Alexandria, Va.: Association for Supervision and Curriculum Development, 1980, pp. 120–143.

Golby, Michael; Greenwald, Jane; and West, Ruth, eds. *Curriculum Design.* London: Croom Helm in association with The Open University Press, 1965.

Herrick, Virgil E. and Tyler, Ralph W., eds. *Toward Improved Curriculum Theory.* Papers presented at the Conference on Curriculum Theory, University of Chicago, 1947. Chicago: University of Chicago Press, 1950.

Johnson, Mauritz, Jr. "Definitions and Models in Curriculum Theory," *Educational Theory* 17, no. 2 (April 1967): 127–140.

————. *Intentionality In Education.* Albany, New York: Center for Curriculum Research and Services, 1977.

Krathwohl, David R.; Bloom, Benjamin S.; and Masia, Bertram B. *Taxonomy of Educational Objectives: The Classification of Educational Goals: Handbook II: Affective Domain.* New York: Longman, 1964.

Leyton Soto, Mario and Tyler, Ralph W. *Planeamiento Educacional.* Santiago, Chile: Editorial Universitaria, 1969.

McNeil, John D. *Designing Curriculum: Self-Instructional Modules.* Boston: Little, Brown, 1976.

Nicholls, Audrey and Nicholls, S. Howard. *Developing a Curriculum: A Practical Guide,* 2d ed. London: George Allen & Unwin, 1978.

Oliva, Peter F. *Supervision for Today's Schools.* New York: Harper & Row, 1976. Part 3.

Popham, W. James. *Evaluating Instruction.* Englewood Cliffs, N.J.: Prentice-Hall, 1973.

Saylor, J. Galen and Alexander, William M. *Planning Curriculum for Schools.* New York: Holt, Rinehart and Winston, 1974.

Saylor, J. Galen; Alexander, William M.; and Lewis, Arthur J. *Curriculum Planning for Better Teaching and Learning,* 4th ed. New York: Holt, Rinehart and Winston, 1981.

Schaffarzick, Jon and Hampson,

David H., eds. *Strategies for Curriculum Development.* Berkeley, Cal.: McCutchan, 1975.

Taba, Hilda. *Curriculum Development: Theory and Practice.* New York: Harcourt, Brace, Jovanovich, 1962.

Tanner, Daniel and Tanner, Laurel N. *Curriculum Development: Theory Into Practice.* New York: Macmillan, 1975; 2d ed., 1980.

Tyler, Ralph W. *Basic Principles of Curriculum and Instruction.* Chicago: University of Chicago Press, 1949.

Zais, Robert S. *Curriculum: Principles and Foundations.* New York: Harper & Row, 1976. Chapter 19.

FILMSTRIP-TAPE PROGRAM

A Curriculum Rationale, 1969, Vimcet Associates, P.O. Box 24714, Los Angeles, California 90024.

6

Aims of Education

After studying this chapter you should be able to:
1. Explain how aims of education are derived.
2. Cite commonly voiced statements of the aims of education.
3. Write statements of the aims of education.
4. Outline major beliefs of four well-known schools of philosophy.
5. Draft a school philosophy that could be submitted to a school faculty for discussion.

You should also be able to formulate and give reasons for your views on the following issues:
1. The acceptance or rejection of the commonly voiced aims of education in our society.
2. The value to be derived from clarifying your philosophical beliefs.
3. Your school's statement of philosophy.
4. The desirability of sharing with your peers your beliefs about the aims of education.
5. Your own philosophy of education.
6. The question of whether it is worthwhile for a school faculty to formulate a school philosophy of education.

USING THE PROPOSED MODEL

A comprehensive model for the process of curriculum development, consisting of twelve phases or components, was presented in Chapter 5. For a moment, let's take another look at it (see Figure 5-6, p. 169) and then we will underscore some of its characteristics.

Examining the model reveals the following special characteristics:

1. *The model flows from the most general (aims of education) to the most specific (evaluation techniques).* Beginning here and in the remaining chapters of Part III, we will describe each component and define its terms in such a way as to show this flow.

2. *The model can be followed by curriculum planning groups (or even to some extent by individuals) in whole or in part.* The model allows for a comprehensive, holistic study of the curriculum. Given the many demands on the time of teachers, administrators, and others, it is likely that a complete look at the curriculum from the aims of education (component I) to evaluation of the curriculum (component XII) will be carried out only periodically. Although somewhat arbitrary, reassessment and revision of the various phases might be considered on the following schedule:

Aims of education	In depth: every 10 years Limited: every 5 years
Assessment of needs	In depth: every 3 years Limited: every year
Curriculum goals	In depth: every 2 years Limited: every year
Curriculum objectives	In depth: every 2 years Limited: every year
Instructional goals	In depth: every year Limited: continuously
Instructional objectives	In depth: every year Limited: continuously
Organization and implementation of the curriculum	In depth: every 10 years Limited: every year
Other components	Continuously

Faculties will wish to set their own schedules for considering the various components.

3. *A single curriculum group, like the curriculum committee of an individual school, department, or grade will not carry out all phases of the model by itself.* Various groups, subgroups, and individuals will assume responsibility

for different parts of the model. One group (for example, the school's curriculum council) may work on the first component, the aims of education. A subgroup may be conducting a needs assessment and studying the derivation of curricular needs. The school's curriculum council may attempt to define school-wide curriculum goals and objectives while committees within the various disciplines identify curriculum goals and objectives within particular fields. Individual faculty members and groups in various grades and departments will be engaged in specifying instructional goals and objectives. Decisions at any phase that have relevance to the entire school may be presented to the total faculty for its information and support or rejection. Throughout the process, decisions made by any of the subgroups must be shared so that relationships between the various components are clearly understood. In this respect the curriculum council of the school will serve as a coordinating body.

4. *With modifications, the model can be followed at any level or sector of curriculum planning.* Or, parts of the model may be applied at the various levels and sectors that we discussed in Chapter 3.

AIMS OF EDUCATION

Proliferation of Terms

The educational literature uses a proliferation of terms, rather loosely, often interchangeably, to signify terminal expectations of education. Educators speak of "outcomes," "aims," "ends," "purposes," "functions," "goals," and "objectives." Whereas these terms may be used synonymously in common language, it is helpful if distinctions are made in pedagogical language.

In this book the term "outcome" applies to terminal expectations generally. "Aims" are equated with "ends," "purposes," and "functions." The aims of education are the very broad, general statements of the purposes of education; they are meant to give general direction to education universally throughout the country.

In this text we speak of "curriculum goals," "curriculum objectives," "instructional goals," and "instructional objectives" as separate entities. Curriculum goals are defined as general, programmatic expectations without criteria of achievement or mastery, whereas curriculum objectives are specific, programmatic targets with criteria of achievement and, therefore, are measurable. The curriculum objectives stem from the curriculum goals.[1] Both curriculum goals and curriculum objectives trace their sources to the statement of aims of education.

---

[1] See Chapter 8 of this text for discussion of curriculum goals and objectives.

Instructional goals are statements of instructional targets in general, non-observable terms without criteria of achievement, whereas instructional objectives are expected learner behaviors formulated, with possible exceptions for those in the affective domain, in measurable and observable terms.[2] Instructional objectives are derived from instructional goals, and both instructional goals and instructional objectives originate from the curriculum goals and objectives.

The aims of education have special relevance to the nation as a whole. We will talk about aims for our educational system, society, and country. Presumably, in former days we could have set forth regional aims — for the North, South, Midwest, and West. Yet, in the fast-approaching twenty-first century, it would seem an anachronism to promote regional aims as if the broad purposes of education are different in California, for example, from those in New York.

Global Aims

It is possible, even desirable, and sometimes attempted to define aims of education on a global scale. The United Nations Educational, Scientific, and Cultural Organization (UNESCO) is the foremost exponent of attempts on a worldwide scale to state aims of education for humanity. Among the aims of education that UNESCO seeks to promote are:

- □ fostering international understanding among all peoples of the world
- □ improving the standard of living of people in the various countries
- □ solving continuing problems that plague humanity, such as war, disease, hunger, and unemployment

Similar organizations, such as the Organization of American States, are also concerned with the aims of education on an international scale. The few Americans who participate in such organizations find some opportunity for expressing aims of education that can apply across national boundaries. More common are statements of aims of education by the respective nations of the world to guide the development of their own educational systems.

In any discipline, the field of curriculum notwithstanding, the specialist seeks to find or develop generalizations or rules that apply in most situations. On the other hand, the specialist must always be aware that exceptions may be found to most rules. Whereas we hold to the view that curriculum development is a group process and is more effective as a result of that process, we must admit that individuals can carry out any of the components of the suggested model of curriculum development. It would seem at first sight, for example, that defining aims of education to which our country might subscribe would certainly be a group project. Yet, as we will see, several significant statements of aims of education have been made over the years by prominent

---

[2] See Chapter 10 of this text for discussion of instructional goals and objectives.

individuals. When statements are generated by individuals instead of groups, members of the social structure, for which the aims were intended, become, in effect, consumers and interpreters of the ideas of the individuals — a not entirely untenable procedure.

That statements of aims, goals, and objectives may originate from individuals rather than groups should not invalidate them. It might be said that "While individuals propose, the group will dispose." Groups should react to coherent statements in a deliberative manner. The model of curriculum development should not be construed to eliminate spontaneous, individual efforts at curriculum development. Some of the most successful innovations in schools have been effected as the result of the work of independently motivated mavericks on the school's staff.

Statements of Purposes

We are confronted with aims of education when we read various societies' statements of purposes:

- □ to inculcate adult values in the behavior of the young
- □ to prepare youth to fit into a planned society
- □ to promote free enterprise
- □ to further the glorious revolution
- □ to create citizens who will serve the fatherland
- □ to prepare an enlightened citizenry
- □ to nurture the Islamic heritage
- □ to correct social ills
- □ to promote the Judeo-Christian heritage

We encounter aims of education in a descriptive form when someone declares:

- □ Education is life, not preparation for life.
- □ Education is the molding of the young to the values of the old.
- □ Education is the transmission of the cultural heritage.
- □ Education is vocational training.
- □ Education is the liberal arts.
- □ Education is training in socialization.
- □ Education is intellectual development.
- □ Education is personal development.

We can even find implied aims of education in slogans such as:

- □ If you think education is expensive, try ignorance.
- □ If you can read this sign, thank a teacher.

Presumably ever since the caveman and his common law wife discovered that the flint axe was more effective for killing game than a wooden club, that animal skins made better protection against the elements than fig leaves, and that roast boar was superior to raw, they continually discussed what training they must provide their Neanderthal young so that they could cope with their environment. In their own primitive way they must have dealt with the heady topic, the purposes of education in Neanderthal land.

Today, several thousand years later, men and women still affirm coping with the environment as a central purpose of education. The in-vogue term to express this purpose is "survival skills." Instead of learning survival skills like stealing a wife from a neighboring tribe, stalking a gazelle, frightening a tiger, and spearing a fish, today's children and youth must master the basic skills, learn to conserve resources, learn to live on a more densely populated planet, and know how to earn a legitimate living. And every so often when our civilized veneer wears off and the Neanderthal in us shows through, the martial arts become survival skills once again. Not only do the martial arts become a priority when a nation is confronted by an enemy from beyond its borders but it is an unfortunate commentary on today's civilization that men and women are flocking to training in self-defense so that they can protect themselves from predators on the streets of many urban areas.

Derivation of Aims

The aims of education are derived from examining the needs of children and youth in our American society, from analyzing our culture, and from studying the various needs of our society. Given the historic development of nations with their own institutions, mores, values, and often, language, no two countries exhibit exactly the same needs. One need not be an anthropologist to recognize that the needs of Japanese, Chinese, Russian, English, Mexican, or Tahitian youngsters are not identical to those of American youth. The automobile, for example, has become a "need" of American high school youth if we judge by the school parking lots crammed with vehicles of students. A male high schooler, when asked how he could continue to afford the rising cost of gasoline averred that he would buy it no matter what the cost because the automobile was a part of his "lifestyle."

Few countries have such a heterogeneous population as the United States. To extend a comment often heard about people in the sunbelt cities of America, "Everybody here is from someplace else," we might say the same thing about America in toto. We are a nation of immigrants who have brought, as some say, both the best and worst traits of the societies that we left. We cannot even claim the American Indian, who was here first, as indigenous to America, for theory holds that they themselves migrated out of Asia across the Bering Strait.

With such heterogeneity it is extremely difficult to reach consensus on aims of education and particularly on values central to aims. Some years ago the National Education Association attempted to identify moral and spiritual values that it believed should be taught in the public schools.[3] They listed the following ten values:

1. human personality
2. moral responsibility
3. institutions as the servants of men
4. common consent
5. devotion to truth
6. respect for excellence
7. moral equality
8. brotherhood
9. the pursuit of happiness
10. spiritual enrichment

The assumption was made that these are common values held by a majority of the people of the society at that particular time. On how many of these values could we still reach consensus? It is significant that educators and educational groups have ceased to attempt to identify common moral and spiritual values that should be promoted. The spectre of indoctrination has loomed so large that the search for broad-based, common, secular values to which we as a people can subscribe has been pretty much abandoned. None of the professional organizations has in recent years come out with a significant statement on values that education should promote, as if the concept itself were passé.

Instead we read about "moral education" without identification of the values themselves. We have programs of "values clarification" in which children clarify their own values. We find programs of "moral discussion" in which children are confronted with dilemmas for which they must recommend solutions. Yet, there is often hesitation about coming out flat-footedly and saying that justice is better than injustice, that honesty is better than dishonesty, that democracy is better than autocracy.

Salad Bowl versus Melting Pot. As our heterogeneous population reveals plural rather than common values, the "salad bowl" concept now challenges the old "melting pot" idea. It is argued that since we have few, if any, common values, we should no longer strive to assimilate values but should collect and assemble the plural values in a saladlike concoction that preserves the essence of each, as, for example, a tasty fruit salad.[4] If we make this dilemma an either-or question, we create a false dichotomy. We need the salad bowl concept to preserve the values on which men and women are divided such as materialistic versus nonmaterialistic goals, pro-abortion versus "right to life,"

---

[3] Educational Policies Commission, *Moral and Spiritual Values in the Public Schools* (Washington, D. C.: National Education Association, 1951), pp. 17–34.

[4] See Theodore R. Sizer, "Education and Assimilation: A Fresh Plea for Pluralism," *Phi Delta Kappan* 58, no. 1, (September 1976): 31–35.

pro-ERA versus anti-ERA, and sectarian versus secular goals. On the other hand, we need the melting pot concept to preserve fundamental, overarching values that promote the welfare of all. As we examine statements of aims of education, it becomes apparent that these statements are, in effect, philosophical positions based on some set of values and are derived from an analysis of society and its children and youth.

Statements by Prominent Individuals and Groups

To gain a perception of statements of educational aims, let's sample a few of the better known ones proferred by various individuals and groups over the years. In 1916 John Dewey described the functions of education in a number of ways, including its socialization of the child and its facilitation of personal growth.[5] Putting these concepts into the form of aims of education we could say that, according to Dewey, the aims of education are:

1. to socialize the young, thereby transforming both the young and the society
2. to develop the individual in all his or her physical, mental, moral, and emotional capacities

Dewey made it clear that the school is an agency for socializing the child:

> I believe that all education proceeds by the participation of the individual in the social consciousness of the race . . . the only true education comes through the stimulation of the child's powers by the demands of the social situations in which he finds himself. . . . this educational process has two sides — one psychological and one sociological — and that neither can be subordinated to the other, or neglected, without evil results following. Of these two sides, the psychological is the basis . . . knowledge of social conditions, of the present state of civilization, is necessary in order properly to interpret the child's powers. . . . In sum, I believe that the individual who is to be educated is a social individual, and that society is an organic union of individuals. . . . I believe that the school is primarily a social institution.[6]

Dewey elaborated on his conception of education as growth in the following terms:

> One net conclusion is that life is development, and that developing, growing is life. Translated into its educational equivalents, that means (i) that the educational process has no end beyond itself; it is its own end; and that (ii) the educational process is one of continual reorganizing, reconstructing, transforming. . . . Normal child and normal adults alike, in other words, are engaged in growing. . . . Since in reality there is nothing to

[5] John Dewey, *Democracy and Education: An Introduction to the Philosophy of Education* (New York: Macmillan, 1916), chapters 2 and 4.

[6] John Dewey, *My Pedagogic Creed* (Washington, D. C.: Progressive Education Association, 1929), pp. 3–6.

which growth is relative save more growth, there is nothing to which education is subordinate save more education.[7]

The National Education Association's Commission on the Reorganization of Secondary Education in 1918 spoke to the role of education in our democratic society in this way:

> ... education in a democracy, both within and without the school, should develop in each individual the knowledge, interests, ideals, habits, and powers whereby he will find his place and use that place to shape both himself and society toward even nobler ends.[8]

The Educational Policies Commission of the National Education Association in 1937 related the aim of education to democracy as follows:

> In any realistic definition of education for the United States, therefore, must appear the whole philosophy and practice of democracy. Education cherishes and inculcates its moral values, disseminates knowledge necessary to its functioning, spreads information relevant to its institutions and economy, keeps alive the creative and sustaining spirit without which the letter is dead.[9]

In 1943 — in the midst of the Second World War — James B. Conant, president of Harvard University, appointed a committee of professors from the fields of education and the liberal arts and sciences to examine the place of general (i.e., required, liberal) education in our society. The Harvard Committee took the position that the aim of education was:

> ... to prepare an individual to become an expert both in some particular vocation or art and in the general art of the free man and the citizen.[10]

To accomplish this aim the Harvard Committee recommended a prescribed set of subjects, including English, science, mathematics, and the social studies for all secondary school pupils.[11]

Statements of aims of education repeatedly address great themes like democracy and the progress of humanity. The National Education Association's Educational Policies Commission in 1961 elaborated on the role of education in solving the problems of humanity:

> Many profound changes are occurring in the world today, but there is a fundamental force contributing to all of them. That force is the expand-

---

7 Dewey, *Democracy and Education,* pp. 49–51. (Free Press)

8 Commission on the Reorganization of Secondary Education, *Cardinal Principles of Secondary Education* (Washington, D. C.: United States Office of Education, Bulletin 35, 1918), p. 9.

9 Educational Policies Commission, *The Unique Function of Education in American Democracy* (Washington, D. C.: National Education Association, 1937), p. 89.

10 Harvard Committee on General Education, *General Education in a Free Society* (Cambridge, Mass.: Harvard University Press, 1945), p. 54.

11 Harvard Committee on General Education, pp. 99–100.

ing role accorded in modern life to the rational powers of man. By using these powers to increase his knowledge, man is attempting to solve the riddles of life, space, and time which have long intrigued him.[12]

Before the Committee on Appropriations of the United States House of Representatives of the Eighty-Seventh Congress in 1962, Vice-Admiral Hyman G. Rickover, generally acknowledged as the father of the nuclear submarine, testified on distinctions between American and British educational systems and formulated for the Committee the aims of education as he saw them. He observed:

> The school's major objective should be to send its graduates into the world equipped with the knowledge they will need to live successfully, hence happily. . . . A school system performs its proper task when it does a first-rate job of equipping children with the requisite knowledge and intellectual skill for successful living in a complex modern society. . . . There is general agreement abroad that a school must accomplish three difficult tasks: First, it must transmit to the pupil a substantial body of knowledge; second, it must develop in him the necessary intellectual skill to apply this knowledge to the problems he will encounter in adult life; and third, it must inculcate in him the habit of judging issues on the basis of verified fact and logical reasoning.[13]

These statements of aims of education vary from advocacy of cognitive competence alone to a concern for the development of cognitive, affective, and psychomotor competencies.

PHILOSOPHIES OF EDUCATION

Statements of aims of education are positions taken that are based on a set of beliefs — a philosophy — of education. Clearly, the authors of the illustrations of aims just cited held certain assumptions about education, society, and how young people learn. An aim of education then is a statement of belief central to the author's philosophical creed which is directed to the mission of the school.

We will now examine four major philosophies of education that have demanded the attention of educators, only two of which appear to have great significance for today's schools. Although these philosophies are known by various names and there are schools of philosophy within schools, we shall refer to these four philosophies as reconstructionism, progressivism, essentialism, and perennialism.

We might chart the four philosophies from most liberal to most conservative as shown in Figure 6-1. At the far left is the most liberal of these four

---

[12] Educational Policies Commission, *The Central Purpose of American Education* (Washington, D. C.: National Education Association, 1961), p. 89.

[13] H. G. Rickover, *Education for All Children: What We Can Learn From England, Hearings before the Committee on Appropriations, House of Representatives, 87th Congress, Second Session* (Washington, D. C.: U.S. Government Printing Office, 1962), pp. 14, 17, 18.

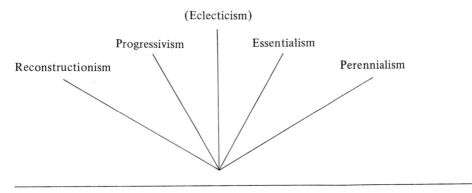

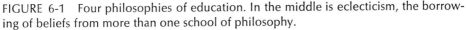

FIGURE 6-1 Four philosophies of education. In the middle is eclecticism, the borrowing of beliefs from more than one school of philosophy.

philosophies, reconstructionism, and at the far right, the most conservative, perennialism. Although essentialism and progressivism have been widely accepted and practiced by educators, neither reconstructionism nor perennialism has found widespread endorsement in the schools. It appears that the American public is far too conservative to espouse reconstructionism and at the same time far too liberal to accept perennialism as a prevailing philosophy. Since reconstructionism and perennialism have had less impact on the schools than the two other philosophies, we will discuss them first, then come back to the two more pervasive philosophies: essentialism and progressivism.

Reconstructionism

Taba pointed out that John Dewey "consistently saw the function of the school in both psychological and social terms." [14] She explained:

> A flowering of the idea that education is a social process, the primary and the most effective instrument of social reconstruction, came with the work and writings of Dewey and his followers. The main thesis of this group was that the school is not merely a residual institution to maintain things as they are: education has a creative function to play in the shaping of individuals and through them in the shaping of the culture. . . . In subsequent development one fork of this dual orientation of Dewey on the function of education matured into an elaboration of the social responsibilities of the school, while the other centered more emphatically on individual development.[15]

Branching out from Dewey's philosophy, the reconstructionists followed a path that led them to propose using the school to achieve what they considered

---

[14] Hilda Taba, *Curriculum Development: Theory and Practice* (New York: Harcourt, Brace, Jovanovich, 1962), p. 23.

[15] Taba, p. 23.

to be improvements in society. In essence, reconstructionism holds that the school should not simply transmit the cultural heritage or simply study social problems but should become an agency for solving political and social problems. The subject matter to which all youngsters should be exposed consists of the unsolved, often controversial, problems of the day such as unemployment, health needs, housing needs, and ethnic problems. Group consensus is the methodology by which solutions to the problems are sought.

Theodore Brameld made clear the values of the reconstructionists. Most people want:

a. sufficient nourishment
b. adequate dress
c. shelter and privacy
d. sexual expression
e. physiological and mental health
f. steady work, steady income
g. companionship, mutual devotion, belongingness
h. recognition, appreciation, status
i. novelty, curiosity, variation, recreation, adventure, growth, creativity
j. literacy, skill, information
k. participation, sharing
l. fairly immediate meaning, significance, order, direction[16]

Some educators agree that young people should consider pressing social, economic, and political problems and even attempt to reach consensus on possible solutions. They do take exception when teachers propose their own specific solutions.

Reconstructionism with its heavy emphasis on controversial social issues and its major premise to make the school a primary agency for social change has not made great inroads into our largely middle class, centrist schools.

Perennialism

In the tradition of Plato, Aristotle, and the scholasticism of the Catholic thinker, St. Thomas Aquinas, the contemporary perennialist sees the aims of education as the disciplining of the mind, the development of the ability to reason, and the pursuit of truth. Unlike progressivists who, as we shall see later, hold that truth is relative and changing, the perennialists believe that truth is eternal, everlasting, and unchanging. In their pursuit of truth the secular perennialists joined hands with the sectarian perennialists. The secular perennialists advocated a highly academic curriculum with emphasis on grammar, rhetoric, logic, classical and modern languages, mathematics, and — at the heart of the perennialist curriculum — the great books of the Western world. In the great books of the past, one could find truth, which in perennialist thinking is the

---

[16] Theodore Brameld, *Patterns of Educational Philosophy: A Democratic Interpretation* (Yonkers-on-Hudson, New York: World Book Company, 1950), pp. 477–478.

same today as it was then and always shall be. To these academic disciplines the sectarian perennialists would add study of *The Bible* and theological writings.

Robert M. Hutchins, former President of the University of Chicago, is perhaps the best known exponent of the philosophy of perennialism in America. Hutchins and other perennialists eschewed immediate needs of the learners, specialized education, and vocational training. Hutchins made these points clear when he stated:

> The ideal education is not an ad hoc education, not an education directed to immediate needs; it is not a specialized education, or a preprofessional education; it is not a utilitarian education. It is an education calculated to develop the mind.[17]

The perennialist agrees with the essentialist that education is preparation for life but opposes the progressivist who holds that education *is* life. If taken seriously, perennialism would afford an education suitable to that small percentage of students who possess high verbal and academic aptitude.

The perennialist looks backward for the answers to social problems. We must wonder, for example, how useful Lucretius's *De Rerum Natura* is in helping twentieth-century men and women solve the energy problem. One criticism that appears to be overlooked in most critiques of perennialism is its ethnocentricity. The perennialist showcase features the great books of the Western world, considered by some as the greatest works of all humanity. Excluded are great books of the Middle East, Egypt, China, India, and Japan — those of the Eastern world of which many of us are abysmally ignorant. An outstanding curriculum project would bring together, perhaps under the auspices of UNESCO, a group of world scholars who would draw up a set of great books of the world. Perhaps East and West might have something to say to each other.

In conclusion, perennialism has not proved an attractive philosophy for our educational system.

Essentialism

Historically, essentialism and progressivism succeeded in commanding the allegiance of the American public. Both have been and remain potent contenders for public and professional support. In longevity and durability, essentialism is clearly the victor. With only slight inaccuracies, we can mark the periods of supremacy of one school over another. From 1635 with the establishment of Boston Latin School to 1896 with the creation of John Dewey's Laboratory School at the University of Chicago — a period of 261 years — the doctrines of essentialism (with a patina of sectarian perennialism from 1635 to the ad-

---

17 Robert M. Hutchins, *On Education* (Santa Barbara, Cal.: Center for the Study of Democratic Institutions, 1963), p. 18.

vent of the English High School in 1824) held sway. Starting in 1896, moving slowly, and gathering steam in the 1930s and 1940s until 1957, the year of Sputnik, progressivism emerged for a short time as the more popular educational philosophy. Its path was somewhat rocky, however, strewn as it was with the loss of the Progressive Education Association and essentialist criticisms from sources like the Council on Basic Education, Arthur Bestor, Max Rafferty, John Keats, Albert Lynd, and Mortimer Smith. From 1957 essentialism has reclaimed its predominant position.

The aim of education, according to essentialistic tenets, is the transmission of the cultural heritage. Unlike the reconstructionists who would actively change society, the essentialists seek to preserve it. Again, unlike the reconstructionists who would seek to adjust society to its populace, the essentialists seek to adjust men and women to society.

Cognitive Goals. The goals of the essentialist are primarily cognitive and intellectual. Organized courses are the vehicle for transmitting the culture, and emphasis is placed on mental discipline. The 3 R's and the "hard" (i.e., academic) subjects form the core of the essentialist curriculum. In one sense the essentialist tailors the child to the curriculum whereas the progressivist tailors the curriculum to the child.

The subject matter curriculum, which we will examine in Chapter 9, is an essentialist plan for curriculum organization and the techniques of Assign-Study-Recite-Test are the principal methodology. Erudition, the ability to reproduce that which has been learned, is highly valued, and education is perceived as preparation for some future purpose — for college, vocation, life.

In spite of the mitigating influence of Jean-Jacques Rousseau, Johann Pestalozzi, and Friedrich Froebel, essentialism has for generations dominated European education and all the areas of the globe to which it has been exported. Essentialist thinking fits in well with centralized administrative structures as represented in the European and most colonial ministries of education. The ministries, following essentialist concepts, can select, promote, and control the content to which their young people are exposed. They can promote and reward the young in respect to their mastery of subject matter. They can screen youth for the universities on the basis of stringent examinations that call for recapitulation of subject matter.

William C. Bagley, one of the foremost advocates of essentialistic philosophy, strongly criticized the child-centered approach and urged teachers to follow essentialistic principles.[18]

James B. Conant, in a series of reports on the junior and senior high school, conducted in the late fifties and midsixties, revealed an essentialist outlook in

---

[18] See William C. Bagley, "An Essentialist's Platform for the Advancement of American Education," *Educational Administration and Supervision* XXIV, no. 4 (April 1938): 251–252.

his major recommendations.[19] Conant championed stress on the academic disciplines.[20]

Behavioristic Principles. The essentialists found the principles of the behaviorist school of psychology as particularly harmonious to their philosophical beliefs. V. T. Thayer called attention to the urbanization of America and immigration taking place in the late 1800s and early 1900s and explained the reason for the essentialists' espousal of behavioristic principles. Said Thayer:

> The changes in American society to which we have drawn attention affected education on all levels. But the contrast between programs of education keyed, on the one hand, to the inner nature of the young person and, on the other, to the demands of society were most obvious on the junior high school level. Here genetic psychology was emphasizing the dynamic and distinctive potentialities of the young person, with the clear implication that nature was to be followed; whereas life outside the school, in the home and community, in business and industry, stressed the importance of education for adjustment, one that would give specific and detailed attention to the formation of desirable habits and skills and techniques. Confronted with this necessity of choice, educators turned to a psychology that would further education for adjustment.[21]

Behaviorism casts the learner in a passive role as the recipient of the many stimuli to which he or she must respond. Known in its variants as connectionism, association, S-R (Stimulus-Response) bond, and conditioning, behaviorism brought into the classroom drill, programmed instruction, teaching machines, standardized testing, and, of course, behavioral objectives. The whole current competencies movement in both general and teacher education owe a debt to the behaviorists. Selection of content by the adult for the immature learner and reinforcement, preferably immediate and positive, are central to behaviorist thought. Noted among the behaviorists are Ivan Pavlov, the Russian scientist, who performed the classic experiment in which a dog was taught to salivate at the ringing of a bell; John B. Watson who maintained that with the right stimuli he could shape a child into whatever he wished; Edward L. Thorndike who is considered by many to be the father of the controversial standardized test; and B. F. Skinner who popularized teaching machines.

Teachers of the behaviorist-essentialist school fragment content into logical, sequential pieces and prescribe the pieces the learner will study. Typically, they begin instruction by giving the learners a rule, concept, or model (for ex-

---

[19] See James B. Conant, *The American High School Today* (New York: McGraw-Hill, 1959).

———, *Recommendations for Education in the Junior High School Years* (Princeton, N.J.: Educational Testing Service, 1960).

———, *The Comprehensive High School* (New York: McGraw-Hill, 1967).

[20] See Chapter 9 for further discussion of the Conant reports.

[21] V. T. Thayer, *The Role of the School in American Society* (New York: Dodd, Mead, 1960), pp. 251–252.

ample, the formula for finding the area of a rectangle) and then provide many opportunities to practice (drill) using this guide. With adequate practice the learner can presumably use the rule, concept, or model whenever he or she needs it. The learning has become a habitual part of the individual's behavior. Though human beings are prone to forget content not used regularly, the behaviorists and essentialists maintain that if the content has been thoroughly mastered, it can be easily retrieved.

The present call for a return to the basic skills and the establishment of so-called traditional basic skills schools clearly derive from the essentialists. Thus, the educational pendulum continues its swing to the right begun in 1957.

Progressivism

In the late nineteenth and early twentieth centuries progressivism, also known as pragmatism, swept through the educational structure of America challenging the time-honored doctrines of essentialism. Led by John Dewey, William H. Kilpatrick, John Childs, George S. Counts (faculty members at Teachers College, Columbia University), and Boyd Bode, the progressivists maintained that it was time to subordinate subject matter to the learner. Borrowing from some European philosophers like Rousseau, who advocated rearing a child in a relaxed environment without forcing learning, the progressivists created the child-centered school. Its prototype was the University of Chicago Laboratory School. Moving east from Chicago to New York, John Dewey formulated progressive beliefs in a series of publications that included among others *Democracy and Education*,[22] *Experience and Education*,[23] *How We Think*,[24] and *My Pedagogic Creed*.[25] By insisting that the needs and interests of learners must be considered and by recognizing that learners bring their bodies, emotions, and spirits to school with their minds, progressivism captured the attention and allegiance of educators for a time.

Dewey clearly stated the differences between the essentialist and the progressive curriculum:

> The fundamental factors in the educative process are an immature, underdeveloped being; and certain social aims, meanings, values incarnate in the matured experience of the adult. The educative process is the due interaction of these forces.... From these elements of conflict grow up different educational sects. One school fixes its attention upon the importance of the subject-matter of the curriculum as compared with the contents of the child's own experience.... Hence the moral: ignore and minimize the child's individual peculiarities, whims, and experiences.... As educators our work is precisely to substitute for these superficial and casual

---

[22] Macmillan Publishing, 1916.
[23] Macmillan Publishing, 1938.
[24] D. C. Heath, 1933.
[25] Progressive Education Association, 1929.

affairs stable and well-ordered realities; and these are found in studies and lessons.

Subdivide each topic into studies; each study into lessons; each lesson into specific facts and formulae. Let the child proceed step by step to master each one of these separate parts, and at last he will have covered the entire ground.... Problems of instruction are problems of procuring texts giving logical parts and sequences, and of presenting these portions in class in a similar definite and graded way. Subject matter furnishes the end, and it determines method. The child is simply the immature being who is to be matured; he is the superficial being who is to be deepened; his is narrow experience which is to be widened. It is his to receive, to accept....

Not so, says the other sect. The child is the starting-point, the center, and the end. His development, his growth, is the ideal. It alone furnishes the standard. To the growth of the child all studies are subservient; they are instruments valued as they serve the needs of growth. Personality, character, is more than subject matter. Not knowledge or information, but self-realization, is the goal.... Moreover, subject matter never can be got into the child from without. Learning is active. It involves reaching out of the mind. It involves organic assimilation starting from within.... It is he and not the subject matter which determines both quality and quantity of learning.

The only significant method is the method of the mind as it reaches out and assimilates. Subject matter is but spiritual food, possible nutritive material. It cannot digest itself; it cannot of its own accord turn into bone and muscle and blood. The source of whatever is dead, mechanical, and formal in schools is found precisely in the subordination of the life and experience of the child to the curriculum. It is because of this that "study" has become a synonym for what is irksome, and a "lesson" identical with a task.[26]

To the progressivists then, education is not a product to be learned, e.g., facts and motor skills, but a process that continues as long as one lives. To their way of thinking a child learns best when actively experiencing his or her world as opposed to passively absorbing preselected content. If experiences in school are designed to meet the needs and interests of individual learners, it follows that no single pattern of subject matter can be appropriate for all learners. Brameld explained this point:

The subject matter of a curriculum, say such progressivists as Rugg,[27] is properly any experience that is educative. This is to say, with Dewey, that the good school is concerned with every kind of learning that helps students, young and old, to grow. There is no single body of content, no system of courses, no universal method of teaching, that is appropriate to

---

[26] John Dewey, *The Child and the Curriculum* (Chicago: The University of Chicago Press, 1902), pp. 7–14.

[27] Harold Rugg, et al., *Foundations for American Education* (Yonkers, New York: World Book Company, 1947).

every kind of school. For, like experience itself, the needs and interests of individuals and groups vary from place to place, from time to time, and from culture to culture.[28]

The progressivist position that the child should undergo educative experiences in the here and now has led to the clichélike indicators of progressive philosophy: "education is life" and "learn by doing." The progressivists urged schools to provide for learners' individual differences in the broadest sense of the word, encompassing mental, physical, emotional, spiritual, social, and cultural differences.

At the heart of progressive thinking is an abiding faith in democracy. Hence the progressivists see little place for authoritarian practices in the classroom and the school. They do not hold with the essentialists that the learners are immature subjects of adult preceptors and administrators but rather are partners in the educational process. Teachers influenced by progressive thinking see themselves as counselors to pupils and facilitators of learning rather than expounders of subject matter. Cooperation is fostered in the classroom rather than competition. Individual growth in relationship to one's ability is considered more important than growth in comparison to others.

A concern for the many unresolved problems of democracy led to a split in the progressive camp with reconstructionists advocating that the schools become the instrument for building a new social order. It has been mentioned that the perennialist considers truth to be absolute, enduring, and found in the wisdom of the past; the essentialist presents the cultural heritage as truth whereas the progressive pragmatist regards truth as relative, changing, and in many cases as yet to be discovered. Education, for the pragmatist, is a continuing search for the truth utilizing whatever sources are needed to discover that truth.

Scientific Method. The scientific method, known also as reflective thinking, problem solving, and practical intelligence, became both a goal and a technique in the progressive school. The scientific method was both a skill to be achieved and a means of finding solutions to problems. In its simplest elements the scientific method consists of five steps:

- □ identifying a problem
- □ forming an hypothesis or hypotheses
- □ gathering data
- □ analyzing the data
- □ drawing conclusions

The progressivists proposed the scientific method as a general methodology to be applied in any area of human endeavor. It is generally accepted for both unsophisticated problem solving and for sophisticated research. Taba offered a

---

[28] Brameld, p. 149.

very legitimate caution about accepting this methodology of problem solving as complete training in the ability to think:

> But to maintain that all aspects of thinking are involved in problem solving or in the process of inquiry is one thing. To assume that following these steps also provides sufficient training in all elements of thinking is something else. For training purposes it is important both to master the various aspects of elements of thinking — such as generalizing, concept formation, analysis of assumptions, application of principle — and to use these processes in an organized sequence of problem solving. . . . If these elements are not consciously recognized and mastered, problem solving can turn into a ritualistic process of defining any kind of question, collecting any kind of data, hypothesizing any variety of solutions, and so on.
>
> Subsuming all reflective thinking under the category of problem solving has also caused certain elements of thinking to be neglected, especially those which, although involved in problem solving, are not fully attended to *while* solving problems. Among these are such mental processes as concept formation, abstracting, and various methods of induction.[29]

Experimentalist Psychology. In behaviorism the essentialists found learning theories compatible with their philosophy. The progressivists did not have to look far for theories of learning compatible with their views on education. They found a wealth of ideas in the experimentalist psychology of Charles S. Pierce and William James; in the field (gestalt) psychology of Max Wertheimer, Wolfgang Köhler, Kurt Koffka, and Kurt Lewin; and in the perceptual psychology of Earl Kelley, Donald Snygg, Arthur Combs, Abraham Maslow, and Carl Rogers.

The experimentalists encourage the active involvement of the learner in all his or her capacities in the educational process. Brameld credited James's efforts to promote experimentalist-progressive thought, saying:

> The influence of James has, of course, been gigantic throughout the twentieth century. His famous *Principles of Psychology* is still, in various respects, the single greatest achievement in this field by any American scholar-scientist. . . . the dominant viewpoint is one of living organisms that function through experience, action, flowing feelings, habit patterns. Concern is nearly always with the total self viewed in a range of overlapping perspectives — spiritual, emotional, bodily.[30]

Gestalt Psychology. In contrast to the behaviorist's presentation of subject matter in parts, the gestaltists concentrated on wholes, "the big picture," so to speak. They advised teachers to organize subject matter in such a way that learners could see the relationships among the various parts. This advice fit in perfectly with the progressivist's concern for "the whole child." The unit method of teaching in which content from all pertinent areas is organized into

---

[29] Taba, p. 184.
[30] Brameld, p. 103.

a holistic plan in order to study a particular topic or problem became a popular and enduring instructional technique. It is common now to find teachers writing unit plans. For example, the topic The Victorian Era provides a unifying theme for the study of the history, philosophy, government, literature, science, and fine arts of the period.

The gestaltists pointed out that the learners achieve insight when they discern relationships among elements in a given situation. In order to sharpen the skill of insight the gestaltists encourage inquiry or discovery learning. Both the experimentalists and gestaltists agree that the closer content to be mastered is to real-life situations and the closer problems are to the previous experiences of the learner, the more likelihood there is for successful mastery of the material.

Perceptual Psychology. Of more recent vintage, perceptual psychology focused on the development of the learner's self-concept. The goal of the perceptualists is the development of the "self-actualizing" or "fully functioning" personality. Maslow defined self-actualization as follows:

> Self-actualization is defined in various ways, but a solid core of agreement is perceptible. All definitions accept or imply: (a) acceptance and expression of the inner core or self, i.e., actualization of these latent capacities and potentialities, "full functioning," availability of the human and personal essence; and (b) minimal presence of ill health, neurosis, psychosis, or loss or diminution of the basic human and personal capacities.[31]

The perceptualists concentrate their efforts on developing persons who are adequate. Combs listed the following "four characteristics of the perceptual field which always seem to underlie the behavior of truly adequate persons:" [32] (a) a positive view of self, (b) identification with others, (c) openness to experience and acceptance and (d) possession of a rich field of perceptions gained from both formal schooling and informal sources.[33]

According to the perceptual psychologists, teachers must help young people to develop an adequate concept of themselves and must be willing to deal both with their perceptions of the world and the world as it is. The perceptualist maintains that it is more important to know how the learner perceives the facts than what the facts of a given situation are. It is known that we all have a tendency to selectively perceive our environment. We recognize familiar faces before we pay attention to unfamiliar persons. We pick out words we know and ignore those that we do not know. We are sure that our version of the

---

[31] A. H. Maslow, "Some Basic Propositions of a Growth and Self-Actualization Psychology," *Perceiving, Behaving, Becoming,* 1962 Yearbook (Alexandria, Va.: Association for Supervision and Curriculum Development, 1962), p. 36.

[32] Arthur W. Combs, "A Perceptual View of the Adequate Personality," in *Perceiving, Behaving, Becoming,* 1962 Yearbook (Alexandria, Va.: Association for Supervision and Curriculum Development, 1962), p. 51.

[33] Combs, pp. 51–62.

truth of any situation is the right one, for that is the way we perceive it. The perceptualists emphasize dealing with people's perceptions of the world around them.

An individual's feeling of adequacy or inadequacy can often be attributed to other people's perceptions. If a child is told by a parent that he or she is a weakling, the child may agree that this is so. If a child is told by teachers that he or she has an artistic talent, the child may seek to develop that ability. If a child is told that he or she is a poor reader, lacks aptitude for mathematics, or is short on musical talent, the child may accept these perceptions and internalize them. The child is exemplifying then what is referred to in the literature as the self-fulfilling prophecy. We are not only what we eat, as the health food devotees tell us, we are what others have made us, as the perceptual psychologists maintain. Combs described how the self-concept is learned in the following passage:

> ... People *learn* who they are and what they are from the ways in which they have been treated by those who surround them in the process of their growing up. ... People discover their self-concepts from the kinds of experiences they have had with life; not from telling, but from experience. People develop feelings that they are liked, wanted, acceptable and able from *having been* liked, wanted, accepted and from *having been* successful. One learns that he is these things, not from being told so, but only through the experience of *being treated as though he were so*. Here is the key to what must be done to produce more adequate people. To produce a positive self, it is necessary to provide experiences that teach individuals they are positive people.[34]

The perceptualists attacked the notion that children must experience failure. Said Combs, "Actually, the best guarantee we have that a person will be able to deal with the future effectively is that he has been successful in the past. People learn that they are able, not from failure, but from success." [35]

The progressive philosophers identified readily with the experimentalist, gestalt, and perceptual schools of psychology. Their combined efforts to humanize education captured the imagination of educators, particularly those in teacher education, flourished for a relatively brief period, peaked, but left an indelible mark on our educational system. Because of progressivism essentialism will never be the same.

The Eight-Year Study. The cause of the progressives was boosted by the Eight-Year Study, conducted by the Progressive Education Association between 1933 and 1941. Many educators recognize this study as one of the most significant pieces of educational research ever conducted in the United States. There have been few longitudinal studies that followed subjects over a period

---

[34] Combs, p. 53.
[35] Combs, p. 53.

of years. Few studies have been as sweeping or have involved as many people. Students, high school teachers and administrators, curriculum consultants, researchers, and college professors all played significant roles in the study.

The Progressive Education Association was disenchanted with the typical high school college preparatory curriculum with its customary prescribed constants required for college admission. The Association wanted to see more flexibility in the secondary school curriculum but realized that would not be possible as long as the colleges demanded a prescribed set of courses. It therefore enlisted the cooperation of more than 300 colleges and universities, which agreed to accept graduates from a limited number of high schools without regard to the usual college entrance requirements. Obtaining the cooperation of so many colleges and universities for an experiment of this nature, which might shatter traditional notions of what is needed to succeed in college, was a feat in itself. Wilford M. Aikin, H. H. Giles, S. P. McCutchen, Ralph W. Tyler, and A. N. Zechiel brought it about and were instrumental in the conduct of the study.[36]

The colleges and universities consented to admit graduates from thirty public and private schools regardless of their programs for a five-year period, from 1936 to 1941. Beginning in 1933 these thirty experimental schools were able to modify their programs in any way they saw fit.

Once admitted to cooperating colleges or universities, graduates of the experimental schools were matched with counterparts in the same institution who came from conventional high schools and their performance in college was analyzed. More than 1400 matched pairs of students were involved in this study. The findings of the Eight-Year Study are summarized as follows:

> The graduates of the experimental schools, as it turned out, did as well as or better than their counterparts in college in all subjects except foreign languages. The graduates of the experimental schools excelled their counterparts in scholastic honors, leadership positions, study habits, intellectual curiosity, and extraclass activities. The Eight-Year Study showed rather conclusively that a single pattern of required courses is not essential for success in college.[37]

The Eight-Year Study gave impetus to novel curriculum experiments like the core curriculum, which along with the progressivist experience curriculum will be discussed in Chapter 9.

Decline of Progressivism. In spite of its contributions — placing the child at the center of the educational process, treating the whole child, appealing to children's needs and interests, providing for individual differences, and emphasizing reflective thinking — progressivism has declined in acceptance by both

---

[36] See Wilford M. Aikin, *The Story of the Eight-Year Study* (New York: Harper & Row, 1942).

[37] Peter F. Oliva, *The Secondary School Today*, 2d ed. (New York: Harper & Row, 1972), p. 120.

the public and educators. It is probably not too far from the truth to maintain that the public was never completely enamored of progressive doctrines.

It was not Sputnik per se followed by the panicky rush to the "substantive" courses — science, mathematics, and foreign languages — that caused the turn away from progressivism. Trouble had been brewing for a number of years prior to the Russian achievement in space.

The essentialist curriculum has always been the easiest to understand and the simplest to organize and administer. It appears clear-cut and can be readily preplanned by teachers and administrators drawing on their knowledge of the adult world. We must not overlook the force that tradition plays in our society. The essentialist curriculum has been the one to which most Americans have been exposed and which, therefore, they know best and wish to retain.

There can be no doubt that some of the so-called progressive schools went to extremes in catering to the needs and interests of children. The high school graduate who must write in block printing because he or she was not required to master cursive writing caused raised eyebrows among the American public. Appealing to the child's immediate needs and interests, the progressive school seemed to sacrifice long-range needs and interests of which the immature learner was scarcely aware.

A feeling developed that the graduates of the progressive school were not learning the basic skills or the elements of our cultural heritage. The public was uncomfortable with assertions from educators such as "The child should be taught to read only after he or she expresses a felt need for reading" (even if the child does not express that need until high school) or "There's no need to memorize the multiplication tables, you can always look them up or [today] use a calculator."

Compared to the apparent tidiness of the essentialist curriculum and the relative ease of measuring achievement of subject matter, the progressivist curriculum appeared at times disorganized and impossible to evaluate. In attempting to deal with the whole child, the progressive school seemed to many parents to be usurping some of the functions of the home and many harried teachers agreed with them.

Some of the more zealous progressivists led even Dewey to warn:

> Apart from the question of the future, continually to appeal even in childhood to the principle of interest is eternally to excite, that is, distract, the child. Continuity of activity is destroyed. Everything is made play, amusement. This means overstimulation; it means dissipation of energy. Will is never called into action. The reliance is upon external attractions and amusements. Everything is sugar-coated for the child, and he soon learns to turn from everything that is not artificially surrounded with diverting circumstances.[38]

---

[38] John Dewey, *Interest and Effort in Education* (Boston: Houghton Mifflin, 1913), pp. 4–5.

Mass education alone has contributed to the decline of progressive practices. What might work in a class of twenty-five will not necessarily work in
classes of thirty-five and above. No one has yet demonstrated satisfactorily
how a high school English teacher can provide for the cognitive differences
among 150 pupils per day, let alone the affective. As long ago as 1959 James
B. Conant was advocating a maximum of one hundred pupils per high school
English teacher — a standard yet to be realized in many schools.[39]

Criticisms from the essentialists, the behaviorists, and the supernaturalists
converged to resurrect essentialism to its currently strong position.

FORMULATING A PHILOSOPHY

In a holistic approach to curriculum development, the curriculum committee
designated to lead the process examines statements of aims of education,
chooses those that appear most significant, and tries its skill at fashioning its
own statements.

The curriculum committee should be cognizant of the major principles of
the leading schools of philosophy, particularly essentialism and progressivism.
They should know where they stand as individuals and as a group in the philosophical spectrum. They may discover that they have adopted, as have perhaps
a majority of educators, an eclectic approach to philosophy, choosing the best
from several philosophies. They may find that there is no such thing as a pure
essentialist or a pure progressivist but rather, more commonly, one is an essentialist who leans toward progressive thinking (a progressive essentialist) or
conversely, a progressivist who leans toward essentialist ideas (an essentialistic
progressivist).

Curriculum workers should take the time to think through their own philosophies and to formulate them into some kind of coherent statement. The
formulation of philosophy is not an activity that most Americans — pragma-
tists as they are — engage in with either zeal or frequency. Unlike European
schools that include the study of philosophy at the secondary level, philosophy
is conspicuous in our secondary schools by its absence. Even on the college
level philosophy professors rarely have to beat off hordes of students clamoring at their doors.

Schools would do well to draw up a statement of philosophy, review and
revise it every five years, and thoroughly re-examine and revise it every ten
years. This recommendation follows the requirements of the National Study
of School Evaluation for schools that seek accreditation by the regional associations of colleges and schools.[40] Whether or not a school seeks regional accreditation, it should formulate a school philosophy to establish a framework

---

[39] Conant, *The American High School Today,* p. 51.
[40] National Study of School Evaluation, Falls Church, Virginia. See Chapters 7 and
13 of this text for discussion of the *Evaluative Criteria* published by this organization.

for the practices of that school. A school's philosophy should always be the result of cooperative efforts by teachers and administrators and preferably with the additional help of parents and students. Statements of philosophy are often written and promulgated by a school administrator as the philosophy of that school. Such an activity might be engaged in to meet the terms for a report to the accreditation association, yet it misses the spirit of the exercise. The writing of a school philosophy should be an effort to gain consensus among divergent thinkers and to find out what aims and values the group holds in common. For this reason even a statement of philosophy drawn up by a faculty committee should be presented to the total faculty for acceptance, rejection, or modification. In a very real sense, the faculty's statement of philosophy becomes a manifesto signifying "This is what we believe" or "This is where we stand."

Value in Writing a Philosophy

Some hold that writing statements of philosophy is a waste of time, that such an effort takes up too much valuable time which could be better spent in other ways, and that most efforts wind up with empty platitudes. It is true that philosophical statements can become meaningless slogans, but they do not have to be. Should we call the following phrases of political philosophy from the *Declaration of Independence* — "all Men are created equal" and "they are endowed by their Creator with certain unalienable rights," including "Life, Liberty, and the Pursuit of Happiness," — empty platitudes? Why, we might ask, did our forefathers not just sever relations between the motherland and the colonies instead of prattling about unalienable rights? Perhaps, they recognized that they must set the stage and provide a rationale to which other likeminded persons might rally.

A school's philosophy is not of the same order or in the same class as the *Declaration of Independence.* Yet, it does set the stage and does offer a rationale that calls for the allegiance of the school's faculty. If a statement of philosophy is to serve this purpose, it must be a truthful one and not simply platitudinous window dressing. If a school faculty believes that the major purpose of its school is to develop cognitive skills; to preserve the social status quo; or to direct the growth and development of the gifted and academically talented, it should say so. A frank statement of philosophical beliefs is much more defensible than a sanctimonious statement of platitudes which many faculty may not support and which many do not translate into classroom practice.

As curriculum workers we must disabuse ourselves of the purely American notions that it is somehow indecent to expose our beliefs and that we must feel either silly or guilty when setting forth ideals. The formulation of a school philosophy can be a valuable inservice educational experience, giving teachers and administrators a chance to exchange views and to find a common meeting ground.

A school's philosophy should include statements of belief about the purpose of education, our society, and the learner. Statements of philosophy written by school personnel will soon be presented. Though gathered from Florida schools, the statements are typical of philosophies written by faculties throughout the country. They speak about democracy, the individual, and the learning process. Some of the statements are brief; others are lengthy. The statements of some schools also include goals or goals and objectives. Here we reproduce only the "philosophy." In Chapter 8, however, we will discuss the writing of goals and objectives and will provide examples of these.

These statements of philosophy reveal the schools of thought to which the faculties subscribe. Interestingly, in spite of the essentialistic turn in American education, progressive beliefs are still strong. Despite the current stress on developing the intellect, these examples show concern for the whole child. In spite of the increased emphasis on the development of cognitive abilities, the examples provided give attention to the affect.

Problems in Developing and Implementing a Philosophy

Before examining the examples of school philosophies, we should mention that curriculum workers often encounter two sets of problems in developing and implementing a school's philosophy. First, those who are charged with drafting a statement usually enter into the process with differing assumptions, sometimes unexpressed, about the learning process, the needs of society, and the roles of individuals in that society. The various participating individuals may well espouse differing and conflicting philosophies of life, which color their beliefs about education. Somehow the differing views need to be aired and reconciled. If consensus cannot be reached, perhaps no statement of philosophy can be drafted or that which is drafted will be so inconsequential as to be useless.

A second set of problems arises from the statement of philosophical beliefs in rather general, often vague, terms, which permit varying interpretations. When a statement of philosophy has been completed and, presumably, consensus has been reached on the *wording,* curriculum leaders will experience the continuing problem of striving to achieve consensus (sometimes even among those who drafted the statement) on *interpretations* of the wording.

EXAMPLES OF SCHOOL PHILOSOPHIES

Let's now look at a small sampling of school philosophies. A district-wide statement (St. Lucie County Public Schools) is shown in Box 6-1, and a school statement (Henry M. Flagler Elementary School, in the Dade County Public School System) is given in Box 6-2. You will notice references to democratic concepts, to respect for the individual, and to the necessity of providing programs to develop the pupil in all his or her capacities. You will note also references to the basic skills, intellectual growth, and the structure of subject matter. Although some may fault the style or prose of a given school philosophy, what we have to keep in mind is the purpose of the statement — to communicate to

BOX 6-1

PHILOSOPHY OF EDUCATION
OF
ST. LUCIE COUNTY SCHOOLS

Since our country was founded upon democratic concepts, loyalty to these principles naturally necessitates our placing all education within a democratic frame of reference. Consequently, we of the St. Lucie County School System believe we must try to ingrain in our students the following democratic ideals:

1. The individual citizen has individual rights only insofar as they do not impinge upon the rights of others.

2. The individual citizen has respect for authority and understands the need for authority.

3. The individual citizen has an obligation to himself and to society to become a useful productive member of that society.

4. The individual citizen has an obligation to uphold and promote the ideals of democracy.

Operating within this democratic framework, then, we are committed to the belief that each student has an intrinsic value and worth, and, in an effort to bolster each student's feelings of self-esteem, we must give full consideration to individual differences in the growth rate of physical, mental, social, creative, emotional, and ethical development. Further, we believe that each individual must be accepted by the school, community, and nation on his own merit regardless of race, creed, or color; and that we, as educators, can best promulgate this acceptance by acting in a positive manner on our own convictions.

It is also our belief that the school should be a place where a student can satisfy his innate curiosity, develop his abilities and talents, pursue his interests, and from the adults and other students around him, get a glimpse of the great variety and richness in life. If we can foster an intelligent, alert, wholehearted participation in life, then we will be truly educating.

SOURCE: St. Lucie County, Florida, Public Schools. Reprinted by permission.

---

professionals and the public the beliefs held by the personnel of a school or a school system. A philosophy serves its purpose when significant beliefs are successfully communicated.

From our beliefs about education, schooling, learning, and society, we can proceed to subsequent steps of the curriculum development process. Component I of the suggested model for curriculum development calls for a statement of educational aims and philosophy. In respect to aims of education, curriculum workers should

□ be aware that educational aims are derived from and are a part of one's educational philosophy

BOX 6-2

SCHOOL PHILOSOPHY
HENRY M. FLAGLER ELEMENTARY SCHOOL

The focus of the Dade County Public Schools is on the individual learner. Our democracy is based on the recognition of the dignity and worth of the individual and his right to participate in those experiences which will enable him to develop his potential to the fullest extent in harmony with his environment. By performing this service we feel Henry M. Flagler serves our area, district, state and nation.

We believe:

□ that it is our responsibility to provide for the maximum mental, moral, physical, social and emotional growth and development of children and youth in our community commensurate with their capabilities.

□ in the right of the individual to participate in learning experiences which will assure him (with effort) success in developing his unique capabilities.

□ that it is our responsibility to provide opportunities for all children to acquire a mastery of the basic skills required to obtain and express ideas through effective use of words, numbers and other symbols.

□ that it is our responsibility to provide learning experiences to assure students shall achieve a working knowledge of the communication skills with the ability to identify, discriminate and comprehend.

□ that all types of growth proceed together and affect each other.

□ that a well-planned comprehensive physical education program is necessary for all children (K–6) that has as its foundation a common core of learning experiences that are basic motor skills.

□ be cognizant of national statements of aims of education made by prominent individuals and groups
□ evaluate national statements and select from those statements, revising as they deem necessary, the aims of education which they find acceptable
□ draw up a statement of educational aims to which they subscribe or, alternately, incorporate the aims they have selected into a statement of philosophy

In respect to the philosophical dimension of Component I, curriculum workers should be able to

□ identify principal beliefs of leading schools of educational philosophy
□ analyze statements of philosophy and identify the schools to which they belong
□ analyze and clarify their own educational philosophies
□ write a statement of philosophy for their schools

BOX 6-2   cont'd.

☐ that a flexible program of interdisciplinary skill experiences in social studies, social sciences, health, safety, art, music and physical education will develop respect for others, accept differences, develop favorable attitudes, habits and practices necessary for responsible citizenship in the home, school, community and country.

☐ that learning experiences should be planned that will guide the student in the development of moral and ethical sensitivity which values the goals and processes of a free society.

☐ that all students, levels (3–6), shall have an opportunity to become bilingual in our school.

☐ it is our responsibility to plan a wide variety of learning experiences utilizing available human and financial resources; visitations to public facilities and from community agencies, utilize all available educational media, multi-media in classrooms, open library, printed and unprinted materials and learning centers; area specialists, such as math, reading, guidance, music, art, physical education, other resource personnel and volunteer personnel.

☐ that an ongoing evaluation in all phases of our curriculum is necessary to strengthen the entire program.

☐ that to provide for maximum growth for each child it is important to have parental involvement, home visitations, parent-teacher conferences, parent-teacher meetings and parent-teacher planned special functions for students.

SOURCE: Henry M. Flagler Elementary School, Dade County, Florida. Reprinted by permission.

SUMMARY

A holistic approach to curriculum development begins with an examination of the aims of education in our society. Aims are perceived as the broad purposes of education that are national, and on occasion, international in scope.

Over the years a number of prominent individuals and groups expressed their positions on the appropriate aims of education for America. The curriculum worker should be able not only to formulate his or her own statement of aims but should also be knowledgeable about historic and significant statements of aims.

In this chapter we examined four philosophies of education — reconstructionism, progressivism, essentialism, and perennialism — two of which, essentialism and progressivism, are deemed to have special significance for our schools.

Essentialism with its emphasis on subject matter has been the prevailing philosophy of education throughout most of our country's history. Progressivism, however, with its emphasis on the child's needs and interests has had a profound impact on educational programs and practices. Curriculum workers are urged to clarify their own philosophies and to draw up a statement of their school's philosophy that can be communicated to other professionals and to the public. Samples of school philosophies are included in this chapter not as models of content, i.e., statements to be borrowed, but rather as examples of process. Curriculum developers should put together their own statement of beliefs in their own words. It is very likely that their statements will be eclectic in nature, borrowing from both essentialism and progressivism.

The development of a statement of aims of education and a school philosophy is seen as the first phase or component of a comprehensive model for curriculum development.

SUPPLEMENTARY EXERCISES

1. Demonstrate with appropriate references how the aims of education in the United States differ from those in the Soviet Union.
2. State at least three premises of each of the following schools of philosophy:
    a. reconstructionism
    b. progressivism
    c. perennialism
    d. essentialism
3. Write a report using appropriate references contrasting essentialism and progressivism.
4. Prepare a report on the educational beliefs of one of the following thinkers, citing quotations from one or more of that person's works:

William C. Bagley	William H. Kilpatrick
Jerome Bruner	Kurt Lewin
John Childs	Abraham H. Maslow
Arthur W. Combs	Johann Pestalozzi
James B. Conant	Jean Piaget
George S. Counts	Charles S. Pierce
John Dewey	Carl Rogers
Friedrich Froebel	Jean-Jacques Rousseau
Georg W. F. Hegel	Harold Rugg
Johann F. Herbert	B. F. Skinner
Robert M. Hutchins	Herbert Spencer
William James	Edward L. Thorndike
Immanuel Kant	John B. Watson
Earl Kelley	Max Wertheimer

5. Identify several practices in the schools that follow behavioristic principles.
6. Identify several practices in the schools that follow (a) experimentalist principles, (b) gestaltist principles, and (c) principles of perceptual psychology.

7. Demonstrate with appropriate references how particular learning theories are related to certain schools of philosophy.
8. Write a short paper with appropriate references on the place and use of memorization in the classroom.
9. Write a paper on reflective thinking and show how it can be applied in the field of specialization you know best.
10. Write a report summarizing the findings of the Eight-Year Study.
11. Summarize the major beliefs of the following schools of philosophy and draw implications, if any, for the curriculum:
    a. existentialism
    b. idealism
    c. realism
    d. scholasticism
    Identify by name at least one philosopher from each school.

BIBLIOGRAPHY

Aikin, Wilford M. *The Story of the Eight-Year Study.* New York: Harper & Row, 1942.

Bagley, William C. "An Essentialist's Platform for the Advancement of American Education," *Educational Administration and Supervision,* 24, no. 4 (April 1938): 241–256.

Bode, Boyd H., *How We Learn.* Boston: D. C. Heath, 1940.

———. "Pragmatism in Education," *New Republic* 121, no. 16 (October 17, 1949): 15–18.

Bossing, Nelson L. *Principles of Secondary Education.* Englewood Cliffs, N.J.: Prentice-Hall, 1949.

Brameld, Theodore. *Patterns of Educational Philosophy: A Democratic Interpretation.* Yonkers, New York: World Book Company, 1950.

———. *Patterns of Educational Philosophy: Divergence and Convergence in Culturological Perspective.* New York: Holt, Rinehart and Winston, 1971.

Combs, Arthur W. "A Perceptual View of the Adequate Personality," *Perceiving, Behaving, Becoming,* 1962 Yearbook. Alexandria, Va.: Association for Supervision and Curriculum Development, 1962, pp. 50–64.

Combs, Arthur W. and Snygg, Donald. *Individual Behavior: A Perceptual Approach to Behavior,* rev. ed. New York: Harper & Row, 1959.

Commission on the Reorganization of Secondary Education. *Cardinal Principles of Secondary Education.* Washington, D.C.: United States Office of Education, Bulletin 35, 1918.

Conant, James B. *The American High School Today.* New York: McGraw-Hill, 1959.

———. *The Comprehensive High School.* New York: McGraw-Hill, 1967.

———. *Recommendations for Education in the Junior High School Years.* Princeton, N.J.: Educational Testing Service, 1960.

Counts, George S. *Dare The School Build a New Social Order?* New York: The John Day Company, 1932.

Cremin, Lawrence A. *The Transformation of the School: Progressivism in American Education 1876–1975.* New York: Alfred A. Knopf, 1961.

Dewey, John. *The Child and the Cur-*

riculum. Chicago: The University of Chicago Press, 1902.

————. *Democracy and Education: An Introduction to the Philosophy of Education.* New York: Macmillan, 1916. Also, New York: Free Press, 1966.

————. *Interest and Effort in Education.* Boston: Houghton Mifflin Company, 1913.

————. *My Pedagogic Creed.* Washington, D.C.: Progressive Education Association, 1929.

Ebel, Robert L. "What Are Schools For?" *Phi Delta Kappan* 54, no. 1 (September 1972): 3–7.

Educational Policies Commission. *Moral and Spiritual Values in the Public Schools.* Washington, D.C.: National Education Association, 1951.

————. *The Unique Function of Education in American Democracy.* Washington, D.C.: National Education Association, 1937.

Eisner, Elliot W. and Vallance, Elizabeth, eds. *Conflicting Conceptions of Curriculum.* Berkeley, Cal.: McCutchen, 1974.

Harvard Committee on General Education. *General Education in a Free Society.* Cambridge, Mass.: Harvard University Press, 1945.

Hutchins, Robert M. *The Higher Learning in America.* New Haven, Conn.: Yale University Press, 1936.

————. *On Education.* Santa Barbara, Cal.: Center for the Study of Democratic Institutions, 1963.

Jelinek, James John, ed. *Improving the Human Condition: A Curricular Response to Critical Realities,* 1978 Yearbook. Alexandria, Va.: Association for Supervision and Curriculum Development, 1978.

Kilpatrick, William H., ed. *The Educational Frontier.* New York: Appleton-Century-Crofts, 1933.

McNeil, John D. "Philosophical Models," in *Designing Curriculum: Self-Instructional Modules.* Boston: Little, Brown, 1976, pp. 85–100.

Maslow, Abraham H. "Some Basic Propositions of a Growth and Self-Actualization Psychology," in *Perceiving, Behaving, Becoming,* 1962 Yearbook. Alexandria, Va.: Association for Supervision and Curriculum Development, 1962, pp. 34–49.

————. *Toward a Psychology of Being,* 2d ed. New York: Van Nostrand Reinhold, 1968.

Rickover, Hyman G. *Education for All Children: What We Can Learn From England: Hearings Before the Committee on Appropriations, House of Representatives, Eighty-Seventh Congress, Second Session.* Washington, D.C.: U.S. Government Printing Office, 1962.

Rugg, Harold, et al. *The Foundations and Technique of Curriculum-Construction,* 26th Yearbook of the National Society for the Study of Education. Part II, *The Foundations of Curriculum-Making,* edited by Guy Montrose Whipple. Bloomington, Ill.: Public School Publishing Company, 1926. Also, Arno Press and *The New York Times,* 1969.

Rugg, Harold, et al. *Foundations for American Education.* Yonkers, N.Y.: World Book Company, 1947.

Sizer, Theodore R. "Education and Assimilation: A Fresh Plea for Pluralism," *Phi Delta Kappan* 58, no. 1 (September 1976): 31–35.

Taba, Hilda. *Curriculum Development: Theory and Practice.* New York: Harcourt, Brace, Jovanovich, 1962.

Tanner, Daniel and Tanner, Laurel N. *Curriculum Development: Theory Into Practice,* 2d ed. New York: Macmillan. 1980.

Thayer, V. T. *The Role of the School in American Society.* New York: Dodd Mead, 1960.

Wiles, Jon and Bondi, Joseph, Jr. *Curriculum Development: A Guide to Practice.* Columbus, Ohio: Charles E. Merrill, 1979. Chapter 5.

7

Needs Assessment

After studying this chapter you should be able to:
1. Identify and describe major sources of curriculum content.
2. Outline levels and types of needs of students.
3. Outline levels and types of needs of society.
4. Show how needs are derived from the structure of a discipline.
5. Describe the steps in conducting a needs assessment.
6. Construct an instrument for conducting a curricular needs assessment.

You should also be able to formulate and give reasons for your views on the following issues:
1. The necessity of identifying needs of students, society, and subject matter as an early step in curriculum improvement.
2. The effectiveness of a needs assessment process for identifying curricular needs.

CATEGORIES OF NEEDS

In the beginning of the 1980s the following items of content among thousands of items were being taught at specified grades of at least one American school system:[1]

- First grade: Identify ordinal positions to the tenth.
- Second grade: Recognize words with prefix, suffix, plural, possessive, comparative, superlative, or tense changes.
- Third grade: Apply montage and mixed media techniques.
- Fourth grade: Develop acceptance criteria for food selection and patterns of eating.
- Fifth grade: Respond to poems about people and nature with original writing, art work, or body movement.
- Sixth grade: Do fifteen bent-knee sit-ups with partner holding feet.
- Seventh grade: Make specific measurements of length, mass, volume in metric units and of temperature on the Celsius scale.
- Eighth grade: Know how the system of checks and balances may be used to check the power of the executive, legislative, and judicial branches of the federal government.
- Ninth grade: Write a paragraph with connecting words or phrases that show relationships.
- Tenth grade: Determine the solution to real-world problems involving purchases and a rate of sales tax.
- Eleventh grade: Know conditions, personalities, and events affecting the course and outcome of the Mexican War.
- Twelfth grade: Perform the fifty yard dash in 6.8 seconds.

We could have listed hundreds of items that young people are called on to master in the course of their education from elementary through secondary school. For the moment, these twelve items will suffice for our purpose.

In reviewing these and other items, we could raise a number of questions. How did these particular items of content get there? Did they come about by tradition, by a superintendent's or faculty's decision or by a school board's or state legislature's mandate? Are they there because the current textbooks contain these items?

We should also ask: Are these items the same as last year or the year before? Will they be the same next year, the year after, or forever? What needs do the items fulfill? Have the right items been selected? What has been omitted that should have been included and what might be eliminated from the curriculum? How do we find out whether an item is filling a need? Which needs are being met satisfactorily and which are not being met? What kinds of needs are there to which curriculum planners must pay attention?

---

[1] Dade County Public Schools, *Instructional Objectives Grades 1–6; Grades 7–9; Grades 10–12* (Miami, Fla.: Dade County Public Schools, 1978).

In the preceding chapter it was seen that statements of educational aims and philosophy are based upon needs of students in general and needs of society. Needs of both students and society are evident in the following phrases drawn from statements of aims and philosophy:

- to promote the Judeo-Christian heritage
- to promote free enterprise
- to develop a well-rounded individual
- to develop a skilled worker
- to promote the pursuit of happiness
- to enrich the spirit
- to develop the ability to use the basic skills
- to develop the ability to think
- to develop a knowledgeable citizen
- to develop communication skills
- to develop respect for others
- to develop ethical values

Statements of aims and philosophy point to common needs of students and society and set a general framework within which a school or school system will function. In formulating curriculum goals and objectives for a particular school or school system, curriculum developers must give their attention not only to (1) the needs of students in general and (2) the needs of society but also to (3) the needs of particular students, (4) the needs of the particular community, and (5) the needs derived from the subject matter. The reader will recall that Tyler, in a similar vein, listed three sources from which tentative general objectives are derived: student, society, and subject.[2]

We could expand upon the needs of both students and society in a greater level of detail than is shown in the model for curriculum development. We may classify the needs of students and society into two broad categories — levels and types — thereby emphasizing points that curriculum planners should consider.

A Classification Scheme

To focus our thinking, we might develop the following four-part classification scheme:

- Needs of students by level
- Needs of students by type
- Needs of society by level
- Needs of society by type

Before analyzing each category, we must stress that the needs of the student cannot be completely divorced from those of society or vice versa. The

[2] See p. 156 of this text.

needs of one are intimately linked to those of the other. True, the two sets of needs sometimes conflict. For example, an individual's need may be contrary to society's when he or she shouts "Fire" to gain attention in a crowded theatre when there is no fire. An individual's desire to keep an appointment may result in his or her speeding on the highway and thereby endangering the lives of other members of society. In these two examples, the apparent needs of the person and those of society are antithetical.

The needs of the person and the needs of society are, fortunately, often in harmony. An individual's desire to amass wealth, if carried out legally and fairly, is compatible with a democratic, productive society. That wealth may benefit society in the form of investment or taxes. An individual's need for physical fitness is congruent with society's demand for physically fit people. The literate citizen is as much a need of society as literacy is a need of the individual. Consequently, it is sometimes difficult to categorize a particular need as specifically a need of the person or of society. That degree of refinement is not necessary. As long as the curriculum planner recognizes the need, its classification is a secondary matter.

As stated earlier, curriculum goals and objectives are derived from five sources (components I and II of the model for curriculum development).[3] Lest there be a misunderstanding, the needs of the particular student do not completely differ from those of students in general but do vary from those of other students who share the same general needs. Students manifest not only their own particular needs but the needs of young people generally in our society as the film *American Graffiti* so aptly demonstrates. The needs of a particular community do not completely vary from those of society in general but do differ from those of other communities that share the same general societal needs. The thousands of communities in the United States are, in spite of local distinctions of needs, resources, and cultural idiosyncrasies, parts of the total culture linked by mass media and transportation.

Interests and Wants

Before proceeding with our discussion of needs of students, we should say a word about the place of student *interests* and *wants* in curriculum development. By *interest* we mean attitudes of predisposition toward something, e.g., auto mechanics, history, dramatics, or basketball. By *want* we mean wishes, desires, or longings for something, e.g., the want for an automobile, spending money, or stylish clothes.

It has already been observed that none of the models of curriculum development in Chapter 5 builds into it either the interests or wants of students. The reasons why interests and wants of students are not shown in the proposed model for curriculum development are:

---

[3] See pp. 168–170 of this text.

1. The model would become unduly complex and burdensome were these facets of student behavior to be incorporated as well as needs.
2. Interests and wants can be immediate or long-range; serious or ephemeral. Immediate and ephemeral interests and wants have less relevance than long-range and serious interests and wants.
3. Both interests and wants may actually be the bases of needs. For example, an interest in the opposite sex, which may be derived from a basic human drive, may indicate a need for curriculum responses in the areas of human and social relationships. A want may actually be a need. The *want* to be accepted, for example, is, in fact, the psychological *need* to be accepted. Alternatively, the want for a pair of expensive, brand-name jeans, though some may possibly argue, is not a need. If, then, interests and wants can be the bases for needs and are sometimes needs themselves, it would be redundant for them to be shown separately in a model for curriculum improvement.
4. Needs are given higher priority in the grand scheme of curriculum development than interests and wants. The curriculum worker is on more solid ground when he or she seeks to give closer attention to needs than to interests or wants.

Curriculum workers and instructional personnel know full well, of course, that they cannot ignore interests and wants of students, for these can be powerful motivators. Certainly, as far as interests go, the literature is filled with admonitions for educators to be concerned with student needs and interests to the point where the three words seem to be one and the two concepts, needs and interests, are one blended concept, needs-and-interests.

Interests and wants of students must be continuously considered and sifted in the processes of both curriculum development and instruction. Whereas curriculum developers cannot cater to whimsical interests and wants of students, they cannot ignore legitimate and substantial interests and wants.

NEEDS OF STUDENTS: LEVELS

The levels of student needs of concern to the curriculum planner may be identified as (1) human; (2) national; (3) state or regional; (4) community; (5) school; and (6) individual.

Human

It is helpful for curriculum planners to ask themselves what the needs of students are as members of the human race and what the common needs are of all human beings on this globe. As examples of universal human needs, we might mention food, clothing, shelter, and good health. To the credit of the reconstructionist philosophers, they put the satisfaction of basic human needs at the top of their agenda.[4]

In his state of the union address to the U. S. Congress in 1941, Franklin D. Roosevelt iterated four universal needs of humanity, widely known as the Four Freedoms. These freedoms are: freedom from want, freedom from fear, freedom to worship God in one's own way, and freedom of speech and expression. The American student shares in common with brothers and sisters all over the world certain fundamental human needs. The curriculum planner must be a student of anthropology in order to recognize fundamental human needs.

National

At this level, the general needs of students in our society are assessed. Chapter 6 already presented efforts to identify nationwide needs of students through statements of aims of education. For example, the Educational Policies Commission posited that the central purpose of American education is to develop the ability to think.[5] We might identify as needs of students throughout our nation mastery of basic skills, preparation for a vocation or college, the ability to drive a car, consumer knowledge and skills, and a broad general knowledge. Some of the national needs we might identify are ones held in common by inhabitants of all nations. For example, few would argue that literacy education is not essential to the development and growth of any nation. In that sense literacy education is a worldwide but not a human need as men and women do not need to read or write to exist. Human beings, however, cannot exist without food and water or with overexposure to the elements.

To become aware of nationwide needs of students, it is essential for the curriculum planner to be well read and it is helpful for him or her to be well traveled. The curriculum planner should recognize changing needs of our country's youth. For example, contemporary young people must learn to live with the computer, to conserve dwindling natural resources, and to change some basic attitudes to survive in twenty-first century America.

State or Regional

It is important to determine if students have needs particular to a state or region. Whereas preparing for a vocation is a common need of all students in our society, preparing for specific vocations may be more appropriate in a particular community, state, or region. General knowledge and specialized training in certain fields, e.g., secretarial science, auto mechanics, woodworking, computer programming, and data processing may be applied throughout the country. Yet states or regions may require students to be equipped with specific knowledge and skills for their industrial and agricultural specializa-

---

[4] See p. 186 of this text.
[5] See p. 95 of this text.

tions. Construction workers may be needed, for example, in growing areas of the sunbelt. The needs of young people in Kansas are not completely identical to those in Louisiana. Students in the Navajo nation, white or black America, or Hispanic America all have different needs.

Community

The curriculum developer studies the community served by the school or school system and asks what students' needs are in this particular community. Students growing up in a mining town in West Virginia have some demands that differ from those of students living among the cherry orchards of Michigan. In some urban communities with their mélange of races, creeds, colors, and national origins, one of the greatest needs of students may be to learn to get along with one another. Students who finish school and choose to remain in their communities will need knowledge and skills sufficient for them to earn a livelihood.

School

The curriculum planner typically probes and excels at analyzing the needs of students in a particular school. These needs command the attention of curriculum workers to such an extent that sometimes the demands of the individual student are obscured. The need for remedial reading and mathematics is obvious in schools designated as "deficient" by some school systems. The need for the English language may be pressing in a school with a large percentage of children with another native language. Recently integrated or multiethnic school populations show, as a rule, the need for opening communication among groups. Some schools, for example, secondary schools specializing in science, the performing arts, or the building trades reflect the built-in needs of their student body.

Individual

Finally, the needs of individual students in a particular school must be examined. Can it be that the needs of individual students go unattended while we focus on the needs of the many? Have we taken care of the needs of the average, the gifted, the academically talented, the slow, the retarded, the diabetic, the hyperactive, the withdrawn, the aggressive, the antisocial, and the creative pupil, to mention but a few categories of individual behavior? We must ask to what extent the philosophical pledges to serve the needs of individuals are being carried out.

Each level of student needs builds upon the preceding level and makes, in effect, a cumulative set. Thus, the individual student presents needs that emanate from his or her (1) individuality, (2) membership in the school, (3) residence in the community, (4) living in the state or region, (5) residing in the United States, and (6) belonging to the human race.

NEEDS OF STUDENTS: TYPES

Another dimension is added when the curriculum planner analyzes the needs of students as to types. Three broad types can be established: physical, sociopsychological, and educational.

Physical

Biologically determined, the physical needs of young people are common within the culture and generally constant across cultures. Students need movement, exercise, rest, proper nutrition, and adequate medical attention. On leaving the childhood years, students need help with the transition from puberty to adolescence. In the adolescent years they must learn to cope with their developing sexuality. Providing for the physically handicapped is a growing concern in our society. A sound curriculum aids students to understand and meet their physical needs not only during the years of schooling but into adulthood.

Sociopsychological

Some curriculum developers might divide this category into social and psychological needs. Yet, it is often difficult to distinguish between the two. For example, an individual's need for affection is certainly a psychological need. Affection, however, is sought from other individuals and in that context becomes a social need. At first glance, self-esteem seems a purely psychological need. If we believe perceptual psychologists like Earl Kelley, however, the self is formed through relationships with others:[6]

> The self consists, in part at least, of the accumulated experiential background, or backlog, of the individual.... This self is built almost entirely, if not entirely, in relationship to others.... Since the self is achieved through social contact, it has to be understood in terms of others.[7]

Among the common sociopsychological needs are affection, acceptance and approval, belonging, success, and security. Furthermore, each individual, both in school and out, needs to be engaged in meaningful work. The lack of significant work may well account, at least in part, for the notorious inefficiency of some nations' bloated governmental bureaucracies.

The needs of the mentally and emotionally exceptional child fit more clearly into the psychological category. Attention must be paid to the wide range of exceptionalities: the gifted, the creative, the emotionally disturbed, the mildly retarded, and the severely retarded. Curriculum workers must be able to identify sociopsychological needs of students and to incorporate within the curriculum ways to meet these needs.

---

[6] See pp. 194–195 of this text.
[7] Earl C. Kelley, "The Fully Functioning Self," *Perceiving, Behaving, Becoming,* 1962 Yearbook (Alexandria, Va.: Association for Supervision and Curriculum Development, 1962), pp. 9, 13.

Educational

Curriculum planners view their task of providing for the educational needs of students as a primary concern. The educational needs of students shift as our society changes and as we learn more about the physical and sociopsychological aspects of child growth and development. Historically, we have gone from emphasizing a classical and theocratic education to a vocational and secular education. We have sought to meet the educational needs of young people through general education, sometimes interpreted as the liberal arts and sciences and sometimes as the study of contemporary problems of students and/or society. We have featured in our educational history "life adjustment" courses and career education. The basic skills are today featured as the curricular pièce de résistance. It is important for the curriculum worker to keep in mind that educational needs do not exist outside the context of students' other needs and society's.

Developmental Tasks

Robert J. Havighurst made popular the concept of a "developmental task," which he viewed as a task that had to be completed by an individual at a particular time in his or her development if that individual is to experience success with later tasks.[8] He traced the developmental tasks of individuals in our society from infancy through later maturity describing the biological, psychological, and cultural bases as well as the educational implications of each task.

Found between individual needs and societal demands, developmental tasks do not fall neatly into the schemes developed in this chapter for classifying the needs of students and the needs of society. These tasks are in effect personal-social needs that arise at a particular stage of life and that must be met at that stage. In middle childhood, for example, youngsters must learn to live, work, and play harmoniously with each other. In adolescence, individuals must learn to become independent, responsible citizens.

Havighurst addressed the question of the usefulness of the concept of developmental tasks in the following way:

> There are two reasons why the concept of developmental tasks is useful to educators. First, it helps in discovering and stating the purposes of education in the schools. Education may be conceived as the effort of society, through the school, to help the individual achieve certain of his developmental tasks.
>
> The second use of the concept is in the timing of educational efforts. When the body is ripe, and society requires, and the self is ready to achieve a certain task, the teachable moment has come. Efforts at teaching which would have been largely wasted if they had come earlier, give gratifying

---

[8] See Robert J. Havighurst, *Developmental Tasks and Education,* 3rd ed. (New York: Longman, 1972).

results when they come at the *teachable moment,* when the task should be learned.[9]

NEEDS OF SOCIETY: LEVELS

The curriculum worker not only looks at the needs of students in relation to society but also at the needs of society in relation to students. These two levels of needs sometimes converge, diverge, or mirror each other. When we contemplate the needs of students as the focal point, we gain a perspective that may differ from that accorded us in studying the needs of society. In analyzing the needs of society, the curriculum planner must bring a different set of skills to the task. Grounding in the behavioral sciences is the most important skill for analyzing the needs of the individual whereas training in the social sciences is pivotal to analyzing the needs of society.

As we did in the case of assessing students' needs, let's construct two simple taxonomies of the needs of society, first, as to level and second, as to type. We can classify the levels of needs of society from the broadest to the narrowest: human, international, national, state, community, neighborhood.

Human

What needs, we might ask, do human beings throughout the world have as a result of their membership in the human race? Men and women as a species possess the same needs as individual human beings — food, clothing, and shelter. Collectively, humankind has a need for freedom from want and from fear. As a civilized society, presumably thousands of years removed from the Stone Age, human beings have the need to live in a state of peace. Human society, by virtue of its position at the pinnacle of evolutionary development, has a continuing need to maintain control over subordinate species of the animal kingdom. When we see the devastation wrought by earthquakes, volcanoes, floods, tornadoes, and drought, we are constantly reminded of the need for humankind to strive to understand and control the forces of nature. Some of the needs — or demands, if you will — of society are common to the human race.

International

It is important to consider what needs cut across national boundaries and exist not so much because they are basic needs of humanity but because they arise from our loose confederation of nations. The study of foreign languages, for example, is a response to the need for peoples to communicate with each other. The nations of the world need to improve the flow of trade across their borders. They need to work out more effective means of solving mutual problems and conflicts. They need to develop better means of sharing expertise and discov-

---

[9] Havighurst, 1st ed. (Chicago: The University of Chicago Press, 1948), p. 8.

eries for the benefit of all nations. The more fortunate nations can assist the less fortunate to meet their developmental needs by sharing the fruits of their good fortune. The people of each nation continually need to try to understand more about the culture of other nations.

Several years ago I attempted to define a number of understandings that appeared to be essential for American youth to know about the world.[10] Few of these understandings have changed with the passing of time except in some cases the negative aspects may be more pronounced. With the possible exception of the last item in the following list, the same understandings are relevant to the people of every nation, not only Americans.

All American youth need to understand that

1. the world's population is rapidly outstripping its resources.
2. there is more poverty in the world than riches.
3. more than one-third of the world's population is illiterate.
4. there are more "colored" people in the world than white.
5. there are more nonChristians in the world than Christians.
6. our actions at home are sources of propaganda abroad.
7. nationalism is on the march as never before.
8. most of the nations of the world are struggling for technical advances.
9. you can reach by air any point on the globe within thirty-six hours.
10. in spite of our problems at home, thousands of foreigners abroad want to migrate to the land of the free and the home of the brave.

Thus, contemporary curriculum development takes into consideration international needs.

National

The curriculum planner must be able to define with some degree of lucidity the needs of our nation. Certainly, our form of government rests upon the presence of an educated and informed citizenry. Education for citizenship is to a great extent the function of the school. One means of identifying national needs is to examine the social and economic problems faced by our country. The United States has an urgent need, for example, to solve the problem of unemployment. One solution is to train or retrain persons in occupations that appear to be growing rather than declining. If we look into the *Occupational Outlook Handbook,* we can find a list of the fields subject to growth. New opportunities for employment will be created for: scientists, engineers, technicians, medical professionals, health services staff, business managers, quick-service grocers, fast-food restauranteurs, operators of office machines, people in construction trades, service workers, clerical workers, truck drivers, and salespersons. Posi-

10 Peter F. Oliva, "International Problems and the Schools," *Journal of the Florida Education Association* 35, no. 7 (March 1958): 14–15. Also in *Social Education* 23, no. 6 (October 1959): 266–268.

tions for railroad repairers, textile operators, and farm workers, however, will decline.[11] An oversupply of persons may be found at the present time among lawyers, teachers, entertainers, airline pilots, college professors, and oceanographers.[12]

Of course, a nation's employment needs change from time to time as the economy changes and as new technology appears. A curriculum worker must stay tuned to changing needs. The curriculum worker must recognize that even within generally crowded fields opportunities for employment are possible. For example, although openings for teachers in the elementary and secondary school are less numerous than in past years, certain fields of specialization offer greater opportunities for employment than others. Teachers of vocational subjects, mathematics, and the natural and physical sciences have had much less difficulty in finding positions.[13] Further, as an indication of changing needs, a modest increase in pupil enrollments in school in future years might create an increase in the need for teachers.[14]

Our nation faces a critical need to develop alternate sources of energy to replace the costly and diminishing supplies of fuel oil. Engineers and technicians will be required in emerging fields such as solar energy, synthetic fuels, and conversion of organic wastes.

As the nation strives to achieve full employment, it needs employees who feel secure in their work and who do not fear that the competitive free enterprise system will force them into the ranks of the unemployed. In Japan the worker feels a close identity with his or her company and is protected against arbitrary dismissals. To a far greater extent than in America, the Japanese worker is retained in his or her job on a lifelong basis. Could the collective feeling of security among Japanese workers account at least in part for the phenomenal success of Japanese industry throughout the world? Does this feeling of security contribute to a feeling of pride in the organization which, in turn, translates into efficiency and quality performance?

The United States Congress responded to a national need — and caused the schools to respond as well — by enacting Public Law 94–142, The Education for All Handicapped Children Act of 1975. Through this and similar legislation, the Congress said that the country could not afford to waste the talents of a sizable segment of the population.

The presence of programs in basic skills, and in citizenship, consumer, global, career, and sex education in schools across the country is indicative of curriculum planners' responding to national needs.

---

[11] United States Department of Labor, *Occupational Outlook Handbook,* 1978–79 Edition (Washington, D. C.: Superintendent of Documents, U.S. Government Printing Office, 1978), pp. 19–27.

[12] United States Department of Labor, pp. 23, 147–148, 210–219.

[13] United States Department of Labor, p. 215.

[14] United States Department of Labor, p. 213. See also Beverly T. Watkins, "A 'Critical' Shortage of Schoolteachers Likely by 1985, Education Dean Warns," *The Chronicle of Higher Education* 22, no. 5 (March 23, 1981): 1, 10.

It is apparent that national needs differ or are perceived to differ from country to country. Certain needs exist in some countries that do not exist in others. Nations of the Third World, for example, have great need for improving methods of agriculture and for balancing their agriculture with industry. Many countries, particularly some in Asia and Latin America, need to implement population controls.

Whereas some needs are common to many, most, or even all nations, other needs, as perceived by a nation's government or people, are clearly unacceptable to nations with differing philosophies. The government of South Africa, for example, apparently perceives a need to continue the policy of apartheid. The government of the Soviet Union presumably has a continuing need for skilled social and economic planners to manage their controlled, socialistic economy. Most people of the capitalist nations, on the other hand, reject the notion of an economic system that does not permit some degree of private enterprise.

The United States has many needs from improving its educational system to solving its ethnic problems to providing for full employment to meeting the health needs of its population to maintaining its military strength. The curriculum worker must be a student of history, sociology, political science, economics, and current events to perceive the needs of the nation.

State

States also have special needs. When the sale of automobiles declines, the state of Michigan experiences special difficulties. When drought parches the corn or wheat belt, the producers of corn and wheat in mid-America suffer. When frost strikes the citrus crop, Florida's economy is hurt. When whole industries move from the cold and expensive Northeast to sunnier climes where labor and other costs are lower, the abandoned states feel the loss.

The continuing trend of population from the North and Midwest to the South, Southwest, and West has brought with it an array of needs not only in the states whose populations are growing but also in the states that people are deserting. Migratory waves of citizens, including those from Puerto Rico, and of noncitizens from Cuba, Viet Nam, Mexico, and Haiti have had a great impact on some states and, of course, on the nation as a whole.

State needs are made apparent when pupils in schools of some states consistently score below the median of national norms in basic skills and knowledge. Consequently, many states have been moving to instituting tests of minimal competence for receipt of the high school diploma.

Job opportunities, needs for training of specialized workers, and types of schooling needed differ from state to state and pose areas of concern for curriculum workers.

Community

Curriculum workers are more frequently able to identify the needs of a community as they are usually aware of significant changes in its major businesses and industries. They know very well, as a rule, whether the community's economy is stagnant, depressed, or booming. On the other hand, changes are sometimes so gradual that schools neglect to adapt their programs to changing community needs. For example, it is possible to find schools offering programs in agriculture although their communities have shifted to small business and light industry. Or, we find schools training pupils for particular manufacturing occupations when the type of manufacturing in the area has changed or factories have converted to automation. More subtle and more difficult to respond to are needs produced by the impersonality of large urban areas and their deteriorating quality of life. Urban dwellers need to break through the facade of impersonality and to develop a sense of mutual respect. They also need to become aware of possible contributions to improving life in the big city.

Schools know full well the differences in communities' abilities to raise taxes to support public education. As the Serrano versus Priest case in California clearly demonstrated, wealthier communities with their ability to raise funds through taxes on property can provide a higher quality of education than can communities with a poorer tax base.[15] In this respect community need becomes a state need since education, through the Tenth Amendment to the U. S. Constitution, is a power reserved to the states.

Schools cannot, of course, solve these societal problems by themselves. On the other hand, they can make — and cannot avoid the obligation to make — an impact on the future citizens of the community whom they are educating by making them aware of the problems and equipping them with skills and knowledge that will help them resolve some of the problems.

Neighborhood

Are there needs, the curriculum developer must ask, peculiar to the neighborhood served by the school? The answer is obvious in most urban areas. The people of the inner-city have needs of which the people of the golden ghettos are scarcely aware except through the press and television. Crime and use of drugs are more common in some neighborhoods than in others. The needs of people in areas housing migrant workers are much different from those of people in areas where executives, physicians, and lawyers reside. Children in lower socioeconomic levels achieve less well in their neighborhood schools than more affluent children do in theirs. Families of children in the more fortunate schools are able to afford cultural experiences that children in the less fortunate schools seldom encounter.

The curriculum worker must be perceptive to changes in neighborhoods. For example, city dwellers who moved to suburbia in search of the good life are finding after some years in a housing development, often a tract variety with a sameness of architectural design, that the good life has eluded them. They have become disenchanted with wall-to-wall housing (which some so-

---

[15] *Serrano v. Priest,* 5 Cal. 3rd 584, 487 P. 2nd 1241 (1971).

ciologists predict as our future) and with block after block of shopping centers. Grass, trees, and unpolluted air have given way to the bulldozer, the cement mixer, and, in spite of the cost of gasoline and the development of unleaded fuel, a superabundance of air-polluting automobiles.

As a result, some suburban dwellers have continued the trek on to exurbia, even further away from the city's core than suburbia. Some of the suburban settlements have joined the central city in experiencing blight and decay and the host of allied problems that accompany these conditions. On the other hand, we have begun to see a small reversal in the movement of people within the metropolitan areas. A small trickle of persons has been returning to the central city where properties are depressed and therefore cheap. Renovation of old homes promises to make some formerly depressed central city locations once again choice places to inhabit.

The curriculum specialist must develop plans that show an understanding of the needs of society on all of the foregoing levels.

NEEDS OF SOCIETY: TYPES

The curriculum planner must additionally look at the needs of society from the standpoint of types. For example, each of the following types of societal needs has implications for the curriculum:

□ political
□ social
□ economic
□ educational
□ environmental
□ defense
□ health
□ moral and spiritual

A curriculum council studying the needs of society would be well advised to try its hand at generating its own system for classifying these needs. It might then compare its classification system with some of those found in the literature. The Seven Cardinal Principles and the Ten Imperative Needs, mentioned in Chapter 3, were efforts to identify needs of students as a function of the needs of society.

Social Processes

Numerous attempts have been made throughout the years to identify societal needs or demands under the rubrics of social processes, social functions, life activities, or social institutions. As we review several of the better known efforts to specify these needs, we should recall the student-society duality of needs. "Making a home," for example, is both a societal and a personal need. The person has a need for the skills of making a home while the society has a need for persons who possess homemaking skills. Curriculum specialists who seek to delineate social processes or functions do so in order to identify individual needs that have social origins. It might be argued, parenthetically, that all personal needs, except purely biological ones, are social in origin.

Zais credited Herbert Spencer for the beginning of the practice of studying society empirically.[16] In 1859 Spencer recommended that students be prepared for "the leading kinds of activity which constitute human life."[17] He classified these activities in order of importance as follows:

1. those activities which directly minister to self-preservation.
2. those activities which, by securing the necessaries of life, indirectly minister to self-preservation.
3. those activities which have for their end the rearing and discipline of offspring.
4. those activities which are involved in the maintenance of proper social and political relations.
5. those miscellaneous activities which make up the leisure part of life, devoted to the gratification of the tastes and feelings.[18]

The 1934 Virginia State Curriculum Program has been identified as one of the better known attempts to organize a curriculum around life processes.[19] O. I. Frederick and L. J. Farquear reported the following nine areas of human activity that the state of Virginia incorporated into the curriculum of its schools:

1. Protecting life and health
2. Getting a living
3. Making a home
4. Expressing religious impulses
5. Satisfying the desire for beauty
6. Securing education
7. Cooperating in social and civic action
8. Engaging in recreation
9. Improving material conditions[20]

The Wisconsin State Department of Education *Guide to Curriculum Building* has been highly regarded for its social functions approach. The Wis-

---

[16] Robert S. Zais, *Curriculum: Principles and Foundations* (New York: Harper & Row, 1976), p. 301.

[17] Herbert Spencer, "What Knowledge Is Of Most Worth?" in *Education: Intellectual, Moral, and Physical* (New York: John B. Alden, 1885). Reprinted from 1963 ed. (Paterson, N.J.: Littlefield, Adams, 1963), p. 32.

[18] Spencer, p. 32.

[19] Hilda Taba, *Curriculum Development: Theory and Practice* (New York: Harcourt, Brace, Jovanovich, 1962), p. 398.

[20] O. I. Frederick and L. J. Farquear, "Areas of Human Activity," *Journal of Educational Research* 30, (May 1937): 672–679.

consin State Department of Public Instruction listed the following social functions in its guide for a core curriculum[21] at the junior high school level:

- ☐ To keep the population healthy.
- ☐ To provide physical protection and guarantee against war.
- ☐ To conserve and wisely utilize natural resources.
- ☐ To provide opportunity for people to make a living.
- ☐ To rear and educate the young.
- ☐ To provide wholesome and adequate recreation.
- ☐ To enable the population to satisfy aesthetic and spiritual values.
- ☐ To provide sufficient social cement to guarantee social integration.
- ☐ To organize and govern in harmony with beliefs and aspirations.[22]

Florence B. Stratemeyer, Hamden L. Forkner, Margaret G. McKim, and A. Harry Passow proposed a plan for organizing curriculum experiences around activities of human beings, as shown below.

Situations Calling for Growth in Individual Capacities
Health
  A. Satisfying physiological needs
  B. Satisfying emotional and social needs
  C. Avoiding and caring for illness and injury
Intellectual power
  A. Making ideas clear
  B. Understanding the ideas of others
  C. Dealing with quantitative relationships
  D. Using effective methods of work
Moral choices
  A. Determining the nature and extent of individual freedom
  B. Determining responsibility to self and others
Aesthetic expression and appreciation
  A. Finding sources of aesthetic satisfaction in oneself
  B. Achieving aesthetic satisfactions through the environment

Situations Calling for Growth in Social Participation:
Person-to-person relationships
  A. Establishing effective social relations with others
  B. Establishing effective working relations with others
Group membership
  A. Deciding when to join a group
  B. Participating as a group member
  C. Taking leadership responsibilities
Intergroup relationships
  A. Working with racial, religious, and national groups
  B. Working with socioeconomic groups
  C. Dealing with groups organized for specific action

---

[21] For discussion of the core curriculum see Chapter 9 of this text.
[22] Wisconsin State Department of Public Instruction, *Guide to Curriculum Building,* Bulletin No. 8 (Madison, Wisc.: State Department of Education, January, 1950), p. 74.

Situations Calling for Growth in Ability to Deal with Environment Factors and Forces:

　　Natural phenomena
　　A. Dealing with physical phenomena
　　B. Dealing with plant, animal and insect life
　　C. Using physical and chemical forces
　　Technological resources
　　A. Using technological resources
　　B. Contributing to technological advance
　　Economic-social-political structures and forces
　　A. Earning a living
　　B. Securing goods and services
　　C. Providing for social welfare
　　D. Molding public opinion
　　E. Participating in local and national government[23]

Taba pointed out the strength of the Stratemeyer, Forkner, McKim, and Passow scheme:

> This . . . scheme seems to be an effort to correct one deficiency of the social-process approach, the disregard for the learner. In effect this approach combines the concepts of common activities, needs, and life situations with an awareness of the learner as a factor in curriculum design and uses both to find a unifying scheme.[24]

In sum, the curriculum worker must analyze both the needs of learners and of society. The study of both "sources," as they are called by Ralph Tyler, provides clues for curricular implementation and organization.

NEEDS DERIVED FROM THE SUBJECT MATTER

One major source of curriculum objectives remains for us to consider — needs as derived from the subject matter or, as Jerome Bruner and others would say, from the "structure of a subject." [25] Bruner refers to the structure of a subject as the "basic ideas" [26] or "fundamental principles." [27] "Grasping the structure of a subject," said Bruner, "is understanding it in such a way that permits many other things to be related to it meaningfully. To learn structure, in short, is to learn how things are related." [28]

---

[23] Florence B. Stratemeyer, Hamden L. Forkner, Margaret G. McKim, and A. Harry Passow, Chapter 6, "The Scope of Persistent Life Situations and Ways in Which Learners Face Them," in *Developing a Curriculum for Modern Living,* 2d ed. (New York: Teachers College Press, Columbia University, 1957), pp. 146–172.

[24] Taba, p. 399.

[25] Jerome S. Bruner, *The Process of Education* (Cambridge, Mass.: Harvard University Press, 1977), p. 6.

[26] Bruner, pp. 12–13.

[27] Bruner, p. 25.

[28] Bruner, p. 7.

As examples of elements of the structure of disciplines, Bruner mentioned tropism in the field of biology; commutation, distribution, and association in mathematics; and linguistic patterns in the field of language.[29] Each subject bears within it certain essential areas or topics (the bases for determining the scope of a course) which, if the learner is to achieve mastery of the field, must be taught at certain times and in a logically prescribed order (sequence). The sequence could be determined by increasing complexity (as in mathematics, foreign languages, English grammar, science), by logic (as in social studies programs that begin with the child's immediate environment — the home and school — and expand to the community, state, nation, and world), or psychologically (as in vocational education programs that start with immediate interests of learners and proceed to more remote ones).

New Programs in the Disciplines

The subject matter areas remained essentially the same except for updating until the 1950s with the advent of the "new math," the "new science," the "new linguistics," and the widespread development of the audio-lingual method of teaching foreign languages. The scholarly ferment of the 1950s, propelled by National Defense Education Act funds, gave birth to such new definitions of the structures of the disciplines as, for example, the three versions of a course in biology (blue, green, and yellow) developed by the Biological Sciences Curriculum Study (BSCS). Each version presented principles of biology with a different central focus and organization. The structure of this field of science as prescribed in the green version, considered the easiest of the three, centered around the topics of evolution and ecology. The blue version, considered the most difficult, stressed biochemistry and physiology and the yellow version concentrated on genetics and the development of organisms.

Two additional projects illustrate the type of planning going on in the field of science in the midfifties and early sixties. The Physical Sciences Study Committee, which began its work in 1956, just three years before the Biological Sciences Curriculum Study was initiated, unified a high school course in physics under the following four topics:[30]

1. the universe, which includes time, space, matter, and motion.
2. optics and waves, which involves a study of optical phenomena.
3. mechanics, which concerns dynamics, momentum, energy, and the laws of conservation.
4. electricity, which includes electricity, magnetism, and the structure of the atom.

---

[29] Bruner, pp. 7–8.

[30] Peter F. Oliva, *The Secondary School Today,* 2d ed. (New York: Harper & Row, 1972), p. 151.

In the early 1960s the Earth Science Curriculum Project developed an earth-science course with the following ten unifying themes:[31]

1. Science as inquiry
2. Comprehension of scale
3. Prediction
4. Universality of change
5. Flow of energy in the universe
6. Adjustment to environmental change
7. Conservation of mass and energy in the universe
8. Earth systems in time and space
9. Uniformity of process
10. Historical development and presentation

While the scientists were overhauling the curriculum of their specialties, the foreign language curriculum people were breaking out of the mold of the old reading-translation objectives dominating foreign language study for generations. Calling attention to the change in objectives of foreign language study, I wrote:

> The objectives, in order of priority, among foreign language teachers are: (a) aural comprehension, (b) speaking, (c) reading, and (d) writing. . . . The four above-mentioned linguistic objectives are integrated with the general cultural objective, understanding of the foreign customs and foreign peoples.[32]

Foreign language study provides an excellent illustration of a sequenced structure, for language students will learn a foreign language more readily when, for example, the concept of singular is presented before the concept of plural, when regular verbs precede irregular, when the first person singular is mastered before other persons, when the present tense is perfected before other tenses, when simple tenses come before compound, and when the indicative mood is taught before the subjunctive.

Many state departments of education and local boards of education have published syllabi, courses of study, and curriculum guides[33] developed by teacher-specialists in each field. These publications outline the structure of a subject, including topics to be covered, their order of presentation, and the appropriate grade level for each topic. The Board of Education of Newark, New Jersey, for example, issued a course of study with a suggested sequence for Algebra II. Topics suggested in this guide were:[34]

---

[31] Oliva, *The Secondary School Today,* p. 152.

[32] Peter F. Oliva, *The Teaching of Foreign Languages* (Englewood Cliffs, N.J.: Prentice-Hall, 1969), p. 11.

[33] For discussion of curriculum products, see Chapter 15 of this text.

[34] Martin Moskowitz, Irving Seid, and Morton Seltzer, *Algebra II* (Newark, N.J.: Board of Education, 1968), pp. ii–vi.

    I. Variables, sets, and the number line.

    II. Sentences — equations and inequalities of the first degree.

    III. Systems of linear open sentences.

    IV. Multiplication, division and factoring of polynomials.

    V. Rational expressions.

    VI. Relations and functions.

    VII. Irrational numbers.

    VIII. The second degree polynomial function (the quadratic function).

    IX. The second degree polynomial equation (the quadratic equation).

    X. Second degree relations and systems (quadratic relations and systems).

    XI. Logarithms.

    XII. Complex numbers (in the form of $a + bi$).

    XIII. Progressions.

Optional

    XIV. The binomial theorem.

    XV. Permutations and combinations.

The Arizona State Department of Public Instruction produced a guide for high school health programs in which it recommended six basic areas:[35]

    □ Nutrition

    □ Fatigue and Tension

    □ Diseases

    □ Eyes, Skin, and Teeth

    □ Alcohol, Addicting Drugs, Tobacco

    □ Family Relationships

Minimal Competencies

In more recent years the structures of the disciplines have been communicated to learners in terms of competencies written in the form of behavioral objectives. The state of Florida, for example, has established minimum performance standards in reading, writing, and mathematics for students completing grades three, five, eight, and eleven.[36] As an illustration of attempts to set forth the structure of a discipline in the form of performance standards or competencies, let's look at Florida's minimum performance standards in writing, grade five. With these competencies are basic skills stated in the form of behavioral objectives or subcompetencies that delimit the performance standards.

The standards reveal basic principles of the discipline. In keeping with sound procedures of curriculum development, curriculum specialists of the Florida State Department of Education collaborated with school district cur-

---

[35] Arizona State Department of Public Instruction, *Health Guide, Secondary Schools of Arizona* (Phoenix, Ariz.: State Department of Public Instruction, 1966), pp. 8–45.

[36] Florida State Dept. of Education, *Minimum Student Performance Standards for Florida Schools, 1977–78, 1978–79, 1979–80, Grades 3, 5, 8, and 11. Reading, Writing & Mathematics* (Tallahassee, Fla.: State Dept. of Education, 1977).

riculum specialists, classroom teachers, and lay persons in the development of the minimum standards. Interestingly, the state's manual advises: "The standard statements are written primarily to communicate with the general public. Skill statements are written primarily for teachers and curriculum specialists." [37] The writing guidelines for beginning grade five call for ten standards and twenty-nine basic skills, as shown in Table 7-1.

As an illustration at the secondary school level, we show in Table 7-2 the twenty-two standards and thirty-six basic skills for mathematics, grade eleven.

Curriculum workers who are specialists in a field may either attempt to define the structure of a discipline as they view it or make use of studies of the discipline that have already been done. Some of the studies that identify the elements of a discipline have utilized the talents of recognized experts in a subject area. Consequently, the use of predetermined national, regional, and state analyses of structure may prove a wiser course of action for curriculum planners than making their own analyses from scratch.

The purpose of the discussion of needs to this point is to direct the curriculum developers to consider three major sources of needs — the learner, the society, and the subject matter. Whereas Ralph Tyler discusses these three sets of needs as sources from which tentative general objectives are derived [38] — a sound procedure — they are examined and illustrated here as a preface to a systematic procedure for studying needs and identifying those not met by the school's curriculum. Such a procedure is usually referred to in the literature as a needs assessment.

NEEDS ASSESSMENT

In its simplest defintion a *needs assessment* is a process for identifying programmatic needs that must be addressed by curriculum planners. Fenwick W. English and Roger A. Kaufman offered several interpretations of the term needs assessment. They described the process in the following ways:

> Needs assessment is a process of defining the desired end (or outcome, product, or result) of a given sequence of curriculum development. . . .
>
> Needs assessment is a process of making specific, in some intelligible manner, what schooling should be about and how it can be assessed. Needs assessment is not by itself a curricular innovation, it is a method for determining if innovation is necessary and/or desirable.
>
> Needs assessment is an empirical process for defining the outcomes of education, and as such it is then a set of criteria by which curricula may be developed and compared. . . .
>
> Needs assessment is a process for determining the validity of behav-

---

[37] Florida State Dept. of Education, *Minimum Student Performance Standards*, p. iii.

[38] See p. 156 of this text.

ioral objectives and if standardized tests and/or criterion-referenced tests are appropriate and under what conditions.

Needs assessment is a logical problem-solving tool by which a variety of means may be selected and related to each other in the development of curriculum.

Needs assessment is a tool which formally harvests the gaps between current results (or outcomes, products) and required or desired results, places these gaps in priority order, and selects those gaps (needs) of the highest priority for action, usually through the implementation of a new or existing curriculum or management process.[39]

The objectives of a needs assessment are twofold: (1) to identify needs of the learners not being met by the existing curriculum and (2) to form a basis for revising the curriculum in such a way as to fulfill as many unmet needs as possible. The conduct of a needs assessment is not a single, one-time operation but a continuing and periodic activity. Some curriculum workers perceive a needs assessment as a task to be accomplished at the beginning of an extensive study of the curriculum. Once the results are obtained from this initiatory needs assessment, these planners believe that further probing is deemed unnecessary for a number of years.

Since the needs of students, society, and the subject matter change over the years and since no curriculum has reached a state of perfection in which it ministers to all the educational needs of young people, a thorough needs assessment should be conducted periodically — at least every five years — with at least minor updating annually.

A needs assessment is also not time-specific in that it takes place only at the beginning of a comprehensive study of the curriculum. A needs assessment is a continuing activity that takes place (a) before specification of curricular goals and objectives, (b) after identification of curricular goals and objectives, (c) after evaluation of instruction, and (d) after evaluation of the curriculum.[40] English and Kaufman pointed out that most school systems require six months to two years to complete a full-scale needs assessment.[41] Not all school systems, of course, conduct full-scale needs assessments. The scope of assessments varies from simple studies of perceived needs to thorough analyses using extensive data.

Perceived Needs Approach

Some schools limit the process of assessing needs to a survey of the needs of learners as perceived by (1) teachers, (2) students, and (3) parents. Instead

---

[39] Fenwick W. English and Roger A. Kaufman, *Needs Assessment: A Focus for Curriculum Development* (Alexandria, Va.: Association for Supervision and Curriculum Development, 1975), pp. 3–4.

[40] See components of the suggested model for curriculum improvement, p. 169 of this text.

[41] English and Kaufman, p. 14.

TABLE 7-1   Beginning grade 5

WRITING STANDARDS	BASIC SKILLS – THE STUDENT WILL:
A — *The student will compose grammatically correct sentences.*	1. Identify singular forms of nouns.
	2. Identify the correct forms of regular verbs in context.
	3. Identify regular plural forms of nouns.
	4. Write the plural form of nouns by adding "s" or "es" to the base word.
	5. Write declarative sentences using appropriate English word order.
	6. Write interrogative sentences using appropriate English word order.
B — *The student will organize objects and information into logical groupings and orders.*	7. Classify words naming objects with similar characteristics under appropriate headings.
	8. Organize three segments of a story into an appropriate sequential order.
C — *The student will write a paragraph expressing ideas clearly.*	9. Arrange four sentences into a meaningful paragraph.
	10. Write at least two related sentences which expand a specified topic sentence.
D — *The student will write for the purpose of supplying necessary information.*	11. List information (who, what, when, and where) of a given message.
E — *The student will write letters and messages using commonly accepted formats.*	12. Write a friendly note.
	13. Address an envelope.
F — *The student will fill out common forms.*	14. Complete forms requesting name, age, address, and telephone number.
G — *The student will spell correctly.*	15. Spell words from a selected high-frequency list of those words needed in writing through grade four.
	16. Spell words correctly in independent work.
	17. Spell his/her own complete address.
	18. Use guide words to locate specified words in a dictionary.

TABLE 7-1 continued

WRITING STANDARDS	BASIC SKILLS — THE STUDENT WILL:
H — *The student will punctuate correctly.*	19. Use a question mark to complete an interrogative sentence he/she has written. 20. Use a period to complete abbreviations of common titles (Mr., Ms., Mrs., Dr.). 21. Use a comma to separate names of states from names of cities in an address. 22. Use a comma to separate the year from the day of the month in a date. 23. Use a comma in the greeting and in the closing of a friendly letter. 24. Use an apostrophe to form contractions.
I — *The student will capitalize correctly.*	25. Capitalize proper nouns which name persons, days of the week, months of the year, and names of streets, cities, states, and countries. 26. Capitalize simple greeting and closing of a letter. 27. Capitalize common titles (Mr., Mrs., Dr., Ms.).
J — *The student will write legibly.*	28. Write legibly in manuscript and cursive. 29. Space sentences to form a legible paragraph.

Source: Florida State Dept. of Education, *Minimum Student Performance Standards for Florida Schools,* 1977-78, 1978-79, 1979-80, Grades 3, 5, 8 and 11, *Reading, Writing & Mathematics* (Tallahassee, Fla.: State Dept. of Education, 1977). Reprinted by permission.

TABLE 7-2   Beginning grade 11

MATHEMATICS STANDARDS	BASIC SKILLS – THE STUDENT WILL:
A – *The student will count quantities.*	(Skills mastered at previous progression levels are expected to be maintained with more difficult materials appropriate for this grade level.)
B – *The student will read and write numerals.*	(Skills mastered at previous progression levels are expected to be maintained with more difficult materials appropriate for this grade level.)
C – *The student will round numbers.*	1. Round a number less than 100 with no more than three decimal places to any designated place. 2. Round a mixed number with a whole number component less than 100 to the nearest whole number.
D – *The student will put numbers in order.*	3. Put in order any three whole numbers through millions.
E – *The student will determine equivalent forms of fractions, decimals, and percents.*	4. Identify an improper fraction that is equivalent to a mixed number having a whole number component less than 100. 5. Identify a mixed number having a whole number component less than 100 that is equivalent to an improper fraction. 6. Identify a decimal or percent that is equivalent to a proper fraction having a denominator of 2, 3, 4, 5, 20, 25, 50, or 1,000.
F – *The student will add whole numbers.*	(Skills mastered at previous progression levels are expected to be maintained with more difficult materials appropriate for this grade level.)
G – *The student will subtract whole numbers.*	(Skills mastered at previous progression levels are expected to be maintained with more difficult materials appropriate for this grade level.)

TABLE 7-2 continued

MATHEMATICS STANDARDS	BASIC SKILLS – THE STUDENT WILL:
H — *The student will multiply whole numbers.*	7. Multiply two 3-digit numbers.
I — *The student will divide whole numbers.*	8. Divide a 5-digit number by a 2-digit number.
J — *The student will add and subtract fractions.*	9. Add two mixed numbers having whole number components less than 100, with denominators of 2, 3, 4, 5, 6, 8, or 10. 10. Subtract a whole number and a mixed number with denominators of 2, 4, 6, 8, and 10. 11. Subtract two mixed numbers with denominators of 2, 4, 6, 8, and 10.
K — *The student will multiply fractions.*	12. Multiply a whole number and a mixed number.
L — *The student will add and subtract decimals.*	(Skills mastered at previous progression levels are expected to be maintained with more difficult materials appropriate for this grade level.)
M — *The student will multiply and divide decimals.*	13. Multiply two numbers, each having no more than two decimal places. 14. Divide two numbers, each having no more than two decimal places.
N — *The student will find percentages.*	15. Multiply a whole number and a whole number percent less than 100. 16. Multiply a number with no more than two decimal places and a whole number percent less than 100.

Table continues on next page.

TABLE 7-2 continued

MATHEMATICS STANDARDS	BASIC SKILLS — THE STUDENT WILL:
O — *The student will measure time, temperature, distance, capacity, and weight.*	17. Determine the elapsed time between two events stated in seconds, minutes, hours, days, weeks, months, or years. 18. Determine length, width, or height by measuring objects to the nearest millimeter or 1/8 inch. 19. Estimate the length, width, or height of an object in millimeters, centimeters, feet, or inches. 20. Determine capacity by measuring quantities in milliliters. 21. Estimate capacity in milliliters, liters, cups, or quarts. 22. Estimate mass/weight in grams, kilograms, ounces, or pounds. 23. Identify the freezing and boiling points of water, normal body temperature, and comfortable room temperature in Celsius or Fahrenheit.
P — *The student will identify geometric figures and shapes.*	(Skills mastered at previous progression levels are expected to be maintained with more difficult materials appropriate for this grade level.)
Q — *The student will identify the value of coins and bills.*	24. Determine equivalent amounts of up to one hundred dollars using coins and paper currency.
R — *The student will determine the information needed to solve a problem.*	25. In solving a real-world problem having two steps, determine whether insufficient, sufficient, or extraneous information is given.
S — *The student will estimate solutions by rounding.*	26. Estimate the solution to a real-world problem by rounding to the appropriate place. 27. Estimate the solution to a real-world multiplication problem involving two 2-digit numbers rounded to the nearest ten and/or two 3-digit numbers rounded to the nearest hundred.

TABLE 7-2 continued

MATHEMATICS STANDARDS	BASIC SKILLS — THE STUDENT WILL:
	28. Estimate the solution to a real-world division problem involving a 2-digit whole number divisor and a 3-digit whole number dividend, each rounded to the nearest ten.
T — *The student will solve real-world problems involving whole numbers.*	29. Determine the solution to a real-world problem involving averages of no more than ten numbers and no more than two distinct operations. 30. Determine the solution to real-world problems involving one or two distinct whole number operations.
U — *The student will solve real-world problems involving fractions, decimals, and percents.*	31. Determine the solution to real-world problems involving addition or subtraction of proper fractions with unlike denominators of 2, 3, 4, 5, 6, 8, or 10. 32. Determine the solution to real-world problems involving decimal fractions or percents and one or two distinct operations.
V — *The student will solve money problems.*	33. Determine the solution to real-world problems involving comparison shopping. 34. Determine the solution to real-world problems by finding the amount of simple interest. 35. Determine the solution to real-world problems involving purchases and a rate of sales tax. 36. Determine the solution to real-world problems involving purchases and a rate of discount given in fraction or percent form.

Source: Florida State Dept. of Education, *Minimum Student Performance Standards for Florida Schools, 1977-78, 1978-79, 1979-80. Grades 3, 5, 8 and 11, Reading, Writing & Mathematics* (Tallahassee, Fla.: State Dept. of Education, 1977). Reprinted by permission.

of turning to objective data, curriculum planners in these schools pose questions to one or more of these groups. Parents, for example, are asked questions like:

□ How well do you feel your child is doing in school?
□ Is your child experiencing any difficulty in school? If so, please explain.
□ What content or programs do you believe the school should offer that are not now being offered?
□ What suggestions do you have for improving the school's program?
□ Are you satisfied with the programs that the school is offering your child? If you are dissatisfied with any programs, please specify which ones and your reasons.

Teachers and students may be asked to respond to similar questions in order to gain their perceptions of the school's curriculum and of needed improvements. The perceived needs approach, however, is but a first cut at the process. It is advantageous in that it is a simple process, requires relatively little time and effort, and is relatively inexpensive to conduct. It also provides an opportunity for the various groups to express their views about what is needed in the curriculum. In using the technique with parents, the perceived needs approach is an effective public relations device; it says, in effect, that the school cares to know what parents think about the school's programs and gives the parents a chance to make some suggestions. As a first step, the perceived needs approach is worthwhile.

On the other hand, the perceived needs approach is limited. By its very nature, it is concerned with perceptions rather than facts. Although the curriculum planner must learn the perceptions of various groups, he or she must also know what the facts are. The needs of learners as perceived by the various groups may be quite different from needs as shown by more objective data. Consequently, the needs assessment must be carried beyond the gathering of perceptions of needs.

Data Collection

Those charged with conducting a needs assessment should gather data about the school and its programs from whatever sources the data are available. Necessary data include background information about the community, the student body, and the staff. Curriculum planners will need information on programs offered and facilities available. It will be necessary for them to have access to all test data on the achievement of students in the school. Data may be obtained from various sources, including student records; data from school district offices; surveys of attitudes of students, teachers, and parents; classroom observations; and examination of instructional materials. Data such as these are necessary for making decisions about the selection of fields and topics to be encountered by the students and for specifying the goals of the curriculum. The data will provide clues as to the necessity for curriculum change. All these data should be put together in a coherent fashion so they can be analyzed and decisions can be made about revising the curriculum.[42]

A needs assessment is customarily carried out when pressure is felt by personnel in schools seeking accreditation by their regional accrediting association. Schools seeking regional accreditation must conduct a full-scale self-study and be visited by a full committee every ten years; they must also conduct an interim study every five years. The standards used, entitled *Evaluative Criteria,* provide for a comprehensive needs assessment. These *Criteria* call for a statement of the school's philosophy and objectives, a report on the school and community, data on each staff member, information on school facilities, and evaluations of all phases of the school's curriculum.[43]

Steps in Conducting a Needs Assessment

English and Kaufman proposed one of the most detailed plans for conducting a needs assessment. Their plan included fourteen generic and seven post needs assessment steps.[44] Following each step is a brief explanation in my own words.

Generic Steps of Needs Assessment

1. *Planning to plan: charting means and ends* — Preparations need to be made for the needs assessment, including decisions about time allotted, resources available, who will be participating, etc.
2. *Goal derivation* — Knowledgeable persons are asked to state outcomes of education that they feel to be desirable.
3. *Goal validation* — Face validity is determined by asking citizens, both educators and noneducators, whether the goals are appropriate.
4. *Goal prioritization* — A large sampling of citizens, including students, educators, and school board members, is asked to rank the goals in order of importance.
5. *Goal translation* — Statements of goals are converted into measurable performance standards.
6. *Validation of performance objectives* — The groups that validated the goals now validate the performance standards (objectives) as to the accuracy of translating the goals into performance objectives and as to whether all the necessary objectives have been specified.
7. *Goal reprioritization* — Goals are reconsidered as a result of a second sampling of students, staff, and community repeating step number two. Step three and following steps may also be repeated, if desired.

---

42 See Jon Wiles and Joseph Bondi, Jr., *Curriculum Development: A Guide to Practice* (Columbus, Ohio: Charles E. Merrill, 1979), pp. 242–243, for a suggested outline of needs assessment data.

43 The *Evaluative Criteria* are more fully discussed in Chapter 13 of this text. National Study of School Evaluation, *Evaluative Criteria* (Falls Church, Va.: National Study of School Evaluation). Periodically. Separate criteria for elementary, junior high/middle school, and secondary schools.

44 English and Kaufman, pp. 12–48.

8. *Futuristic input in goal ranking* — Future-oriented objectives are included. The Delphi Technique by which informed persons are asked to predict future directions (in this case for education) may be used to generate and validate educational goals from which performance objectives are then derived.[45]

9. *Rerank goals* — Goals are reranked using research and predictive studies such as the Delphi Technique.

10. *Select testing instruments or evaluative strategies for assessing the current state.* Testing instruments are selected and administered to ascertain current levels of student performance, to learn whether student achievement meets the desired defined levels.

11. *Collate data gathered* — Data collected must be put into tables, charts, graphs, etc. English and Kaufman reminded us that "a needs assessment is the process of formulating gaps or discrepancies between two sets of criteria, a list of future desired conditions and results, and a list of current, existing (not necessarily desired) conditions and results."[46] Thus, in presenting the data "the most detailed information should be provided to those by whom decisions must ultimately be made about what to do with the 'gaps' as the primary consideration."[47]

12. *Develop initial gap or "need statements"* — A list of needs — gaps in student performance between what is desired and what is performed — is drawn up.

13. *Prioritize gap statements according to step four* — Gaps are clustered around the educational goals to which they relate and are ranked by the degree of difference between desired levels of student achievement and actual performance.

14. *Publish list of gap statements* — At this point the needs assessment is complete.

Post Needs Assessment Steps

1. *Interpolate gaps by program and level* — Needs that are identified — the gaps — are located by program and level.

2. *Conduct diagnostic/planning sessions to develop implementation strategies to meet identified needs* — The responsible curriculum group tries to find out the reasons for the gaps and makes plans for closing them.

3. *Budget for implementation strategies* — The cost of each implementation strategy is calculated and budgeted.

4. *Fund strategies* — Depending on availability of funds, all strategies or only top strategies are funded.

---

[45] For discussion of the Delphi Technique see Olaf Helmer, "Analysis of the Future: The Delphi Method," in James R. Bright, ed., *Technological Forecasting for Industry and Government: Methods and Applications* (Englewood Cliffs, N.J.: Prentice-Hall, Inc., 1968), pp. 116–122.

[46] English and Kaufman, p. 35.

[47] English and Kaufman, p. 39.

5. *Implement strategies* — Strategies are put into operation either in existing or new programs.

6. *Reassess gaps via feedback* — Both formative and summative data are gathered and analyzed to see if the gaps have actually been closed.

7. *Repeat steps of needs assessment process* — English and Kaufman recommended that generic steps one through nine be repeated periodically and generic steps ten through fourteen continually.[48]

It should be observed that the process recommended by English and Kaufman goes beyond a simple needs assessment. The process incorporates the generation of goals and performance objectives as well as implementation and evaluation phases.

A District-wide Assessment

The Madison, Wisconsin Public Schools conducted an extensive needs assessment in two of its geographical attendance areas (Memorial and Lafollette). Following their own eleven-step process, their efforts furnish an excellent illustration of a district-wide needs assessment.[49] Figure 7-1 shows the eleven steps in the Madison model. As in the needs assessment model suggested by English and Kaufman, the Madison Public Schools also sought to determine the discrepancies (gaps) between what exists in the current program and what results should be obtained. The Madison schools set forth the purposes of the Memorial Area Needs Assessment Program as follows:

GOALS OF THE MEMORIAL AREA NEEDS ASSESSMENT PROGRAM

1. Identify what parents, students, teachers, administrators and other people in the Memorial Area expect their schools to accomplish.

2. Establish a set of ranks or priorities for the identified expectations.

3. Evaluate the current educational program in the Memorial Area in terms of all the priority stated goals or of the high priority goals, and thus identify discrepancies or needs.

4. Generate possible strategies for resolving these discrepancies so as to provide Memorial Area students with the best possible learning environment.

5. Provide a vehicle for the community citizens for their input into the educational decision-making process.

6. Develop teamwork in the total educational process including planning, implementation, and evaluation.

7. Provide positive feedback to the community relative to the identified strengths of the educational program.

---

[48] English and Kaufman, p. 47.

[49] Theodore J. Czajkowski and Jerry L. Patterson, *School District Needs Assessment: Practical Models for Increasing Involvement in Curriculum Decisions* (Madison, Wisc.: Madison Public Schools, 1976). A paper presented at the national conference of the Association for Supervision and Curriculum Development, Miami Beach, Florida, March, 1976.

FIGURE 7-1   The Madison model for planning needs assessments

---

1.0 DEVELOP PLAN OF ACTION

1.1 Reach decisions for strategies to be used in subsequent steps

2.0 GENERATE GOALS

2.1 Adapt currently available lists to district needs

3.0 VALIDATE GOALS

3.1 Use representative committee to validate goals

4.0 RANK GOALS

4.1 Indicate most important and least important items

5.0 CONDUCT CURRICULUM ANALYSIS

5.1 Coordinate curriculum to reduce discrepancies

6.0 PREPARE PERFORMANCE INDICATORS

6.1 Use appropriate staff expertise

7.0 DEVELOP INSTRUMENTS

7.1 Use various types of assessment tools

8.0 COLLECT DATA

8.1 Use sampling techniques to collect test data (along with supplementary data) at designated grade levels

9.0 ANALYZE DATA FOR DISCREPANCIES

9.1 Compare performance and expectations

10.0 DETERMINE PROBABLE REASONS FOR DISCREPANCIES

10.1 Evaluate possible confounding variables

10.2 Re-examine expectations

10.3 Conduct in-depth analysis

11.0 ACT ON DISCREPANCIES

11.1 Determine priority areas for improvement

11.2 Establish program responsibility for priority areas

11.3 Generate commitment for reducing discrepancies

11.4 Develop plan of action

The Memorial Attendance Area of the Madison schools generated its own goals through three needs assessment instruments that were developed by a steering committee composed of parents, teachers, principals, and students and distributed to a representative sample of the community. One instrument contained thirty-nine educational goals; one, forty; and one, seventy-nine.

As a result of the surveys the educational goals were reduced to thirteen, which the community was then asked to rank by means of the instrument shown in Box 7-1.

BOX 7-1   Ranking of educational goals

DIRECTIONS

Listed below are thirteen broad educational goals. Each of these goals is important to a child's development. These goals are the shared responsibility of many agencies, including the family, the schools, the church, the community and the media. We need your help in sorting out the schools' educational priorities for our children. To which of these goals should our SCHOOLS give the most attention.

Step 1: Read the enclosed brochure explaining Memorial Area Priorities (MAP)

Step 2: Now read each goal statement carefully. Using the blanks on the left, rank the goal statements in order of importance for our SCHOOLS. Assign a "1" to the goal you consider the most important for the schools, a "2" to the second most important, a "3" to the next one . . . and a "13" to the goal you consider the least important for the schools. Give each statement only one number. No number may be used twice; therefore, there should be no ties.

Step 3: If you are interested in actively participating in phase two of MAP, please fill in the participation blank in the brochure. Enclose this in the return envelope.

Step 4: When you have finished, place the survey in the return envelope and drop it in the mail.

_____ *Interpersonal relations*
Interpersonal relations means getting along with others. Students should appreciate, respect and have concern for all people.

_____ *Self-realization*
People grow when they know who they are and feel that they are important. People should grow both mentally and emotionally.

_____ *Fundamental learning skills*
Students should learn skills, such as reading, writing, and math. They should learn these skills to the best of their abilities. Therefore, students should explore and learn the best possible ways to use basic skills.

Box continues on next page.

BOX 7-1   continued

_____ *Citizenship and political understanding*
Good citizenship means taking part in local, state, national, and world communities. Students should learn their roles, rights and duties within government.

_____ *Self-discipline*
Self-discipline is reached when people control themselves without outside force. Students should learn inner controls to do the things they do not always want to do, but must do.

_____ *Physical environment*
Students should protect our physical environment. They should know how to conserve our natural resources.

_____ *Career education and occupational competence*
In our society, jobs change; some new jobs appear and other jobs go out of date. Students should be prepared for occupational, academic and/or vocational programs after high school.

_____ *Family life and human sexuality*
Family life and sex are important at every stage of a person's life. Students should have knowledge and develop the attitudes which will enrich the quality of family life and human sexuality.

_____ *Individual values*
Each person has values and morals which guide personal decisions. Thus, each student should develop basic individual values. Each should appreciate and respect the values of others.

_____ *Critical thinking*
Critical thinking means a person should be able to deal with changes in life. One should use imagination and creativity to work out problems. Students should learn skills to help them to think and act in an intelligent way.

_____ *Economic understanding*
A person lives within the American economy as a consumer and producer of goods and services. A student should know what affects individual economic life and the national and international economy.

_____ *Physical health*
For a healthy society, each person must develop and stay physically fit. With an increase in leisure time, each person must have many ways of using that time. Students should develop physical skills and leisure time activities to live up to their own potential.

_____ *Cultural appreciation*
Art, drama, and music are a few of the many ways that people have found to tell about themselves and their lives. To help them know people better, students should have a chance to value and do creative things.

BOX 7-1   continued

DO YOU HAVE ANY COMMENTS TO MAKE ABOUT THE SCHOOLS? If so, write them below:

PLEASE GIVE US THE FOLLOWING INFORMATION. (Check those that apply.)

Parents

_____ have school age children
_____ have pre-school children
_____ children have graduated

Faculty

_____ elementary staff
_____ middle school staff
_____ high school staff

Non-parents

_____ have no children

Students

_____ middle school student
_____ high school student

Your sex: M _____   F _____

Your age: 18–29 _____   30–39 _____   40–49 _____   50–59 _____   60– _____

If you are a parent, check any schools in which your children are *presently* enrolled:

MEMORIAL ATTENDANCE AREA SCHOOLS

_____ Crestwood Elementary
_____ Falk Elementary
_____ Huegel Elementary
_____ Jefferson Middle
_____ Madison Memorial
_____ Muir Elementary

_____ Orchard Ridge Elementary
_____ Orchard Ridge Middle
_____ Spring Harbor Elementary
_____ Stephens Elementary
_____ Other schools (list)

_____

SOURCE: Madison, Wisconsin Public Schools. Reprinted by permission.

The priorities of the community in respect to the thirteen goals are clearly shown in Table 7-3. After identifying goals, the Madison Public Schools set into motion a plan for reducing the gaps. The Madison assessment plan flows in the following manner as shown in its eleven-step model:

goals → curriculum analysis → testing → detection

of discrepancies → action on discrepancies

We can see that a thorough needs assessment is more than a "quick-and-dirty" survey of perceived needs. When done properly, it is a time-consuming process requiring the commitment of human and material resources sufficient

TABLE 7-3 Memorial area priorities — statistical summary of population responses

	TOTAL SAMPLE N = 3222		ALL CITIZENS (MAILED RETURNS) N = 1581		STUDENTS (GRADES 8-12) N = 1187		ALL STAFF N = 318	
	RANK	MEAN	RANK	MEAN	RANK	MEAN	RANK	MEAN
Fundamental Learning Skills	1	3.31	1	2.24	1	4.72	1	2.94
Interpersonal Relations	2	5.36	4	5.57	2	5.29	2	4.42
Self-Discipline	3	5.60	3	5.50	3	5.81	5	5.01
Critical Thinking	4	5.73	2	5.19	7	6.68	4	4.98
Self-Realization	5	5.90	5	5.92	4	6.03	3	4.67
Career Education	6	6.57	6	6.58	5	6.25	7	8.23
Individual Values	7	6.61	7	6.94	6	6.30	6	6.31
Physical Health	8	8.13	9	8.46	8	7.58	8	8.32
Citizenship and Political Understanding	9	8.18	8	7.92	11	8.44	9	8.62
Economic Understanding	10	8.64	10	8.67	10	8.39	12	9.77
Physical Environment	11	8.68	12	9.45	9	7.64	10	8.81
Cultural Appreciation	12	9.08	11	9.02	13	9.15	11	8.93
Family Life and Human Sexuality	13	9.19	13	9.51	12	8.74	13	9.80

Rank   = On a scale of 1 to 13, 1 means most important and 13 least important for the schools.
Mean   = Average score.
Total N = 3338 responses (106 responses could not be tabulated).

to accomplish the job. A systematic process for discovering learners' needs that are not being met is an essential step in curriculum improvement.

SUMMARY

Curriculum planners must attend to the needs of students and society. These needs may be classified as to level and type. Various attempts have been made to identify the social processes, functions, and institutions that have import for the curriculum.

Each discipline has its own unique set of elements or structure that affects decisions about scope and sequence. The structure of a subject is shown by exposition of the basic ideas, fundamental principles, broad generalizable topics, competencies, or performance objectives.

In addition to studying empirically the needs of students, society, and the disciplines, curriculum workers should conduct systematic needs assessments to identify gaps — discrepancies between desired and actual student performance. Identified unmet needs should play a major role in curriculum revision.

SUPPLEMENTARY EXERCISES

1. Give an illustration of at least one need of students at the following levels:
   human
   national
   state or regional
   community
   school
   individual
2. Give an illustration of at least one student need of the following types:
   physical
   sociopsychological
   educational
3. Analyze Robert J. Havighurst's developmental tasks of middle childhood or adolescence (see bibliography) and judge whether you feel each task is still relevant. Give reasons for your position on each task that you feel is no longer relevant.
4. Confer with appropriate personnel in a school system you know well and see if the school system has conducted a curriculum needs assessment in recent years. Report on instrumentation and results if a needs assessment has been conducted.
5. Conduct a simple study using the Delphi Technique. (See Olaf Helmer reference in the bibliography.)
6. Describe the process of goal validation as explained by English and Kaufman (see bibliography).
7. Examine the report of the school-and-community committee of a school that has undergone regional accreditation and summarize the data contained therein.
8. Identify needs that the following content is supposed to fulfill:
   income tax
   Jacksonian democracy
   principle of leverage
   Beowulf
   adding mixed fractions
   Latin declensions
   building cabinets
   typing
9. Read and report in detail on Henry C. Morrison's description of social institutions (see bibliography).
10. Create your own list of social processes or functions and compare this list with one found in the professional literature.

11. Read and report on Herbert Spencer's description of life activities (see bibliography).
12. Explain how you would go about identifying needs of students.
13. Explain how you would go about identifying needs of society.
14. Identify several of the basic ideas (structure) of a discipline you know well.

BIBLIOGRAPHY

Arizona State Department of Public Instruction. *Health Guide, Secondary Schools of Arizona.* Phoenix, Ariz.: State Department of Public Instruction, 1966.

Association for Supervision and Curriculum Development. *What Are the Sources of the Curriculum? A Symposium.* Alexandria, Va.: Association for Supervision and Curriculum Development, 1962.

Banathy, Bela H. *Instructional Systems.* Belmont, Cal.: Fearon Publishers, 1968.

Bruner, Jerome S. *The Process of Education.* Cambridge, Mass.: Harvard University Press, 1977.

Combs, Arthur W., ed. *Perceiving, Behaving, Becoming,* 1962 Yearbook. Alexandria, Va.: Association for Supervision and Curriculum Development, 1962.

Dade County Public Schools. *Instructional Objectives Grades 1–6; Grades 7–9; Grades 10–12.* Miami, Fla.: Dade County Public Schools, 1978.

English, Fenwick W. and Kaufman, Roger A. *Needs Assessment: A Focus for Curriculum Development.* Alexandria, Va.: Association for Supervision and Curriculum Development, 1975.

Florida State Department of Education. *Minimum Student Performance Standards for Florida Schools, 1977–78, 1978–79, 1979–80, Grades 3 and 5, Grades 8 and 11, Reading, Writing & Mathematics.* Tallahassee, Fla.: State Department of Education, 1977.

Frederick, O.I. and Farquear, L.J. "Areas of Human Activity," *Journal of Educational Research* 30 (May 1937): 672–679.

Harap, Henry, ed. *The Changing Curriculum.* New York: Appleton-Century-Crofts, 1937.

Havighurst, Robert J. *Developmental Tasks and Education,* 3rd ed. New York: Longman, 1972.

Helmer, Olaf. "Analysis of the Future: The Delphi Method," in *Technological Forecasting for Industry and Government: Methods and Applications.* Edited by James R. Bright. Englewood Cliffs, N.J.: Prentice-Hall, 1968, pp. 116–122.

Kaufman, Roger A. *Educational System Planning.* Englewood Cliffs, N.J.: Prentice-Hall, 1972.

———. *Identifying and Solving Problems: A System Approach,* 2d ed. San Diego: University Associates, 1979.

Kaufman, Roger and English, Fenwick W. *Needs Assessment: Concept and Application.* Englewood Cliffs, N.J.: Educational Technology Publications, 1979.

Kaufman, Roger and Stakenas, Robert G. "Needs Assessment and Holistic Planning," *Educational Leadership* 38, no. 8 (May 1981): 612–616.

Kaufman, Roger and Thomas, Susan. *Evaluation Without Fear.* New York: Franklin Watts, 1980.

Kelley, Earl C. "The Fully Functioning Self," *Perceiving, Behaving, Becoming,* 1962 Yearbook. Alexandria, Va.: Association for Supervision and Curriculum Development, 1962, pp. 9–20.

McNeil, John D. "The Needs Assessment Approach to Selecting Educational Objectives," *Designing Curriculum: Self-Instructional Modules.* Boston: Little, Brown, 1976, pp. 79–84.

Morrison, Henry C. *The Curriculum*

of the Common School. Chicago: University of Chicago Press, 1940.

Moskowitz, Martin; Seid, Irving; and Seltzer, Morton. *Algebra II.* Newark, N.J.: Board of Education, 1968.

National Study of School Evaluation. *Elementary School Evaluative Criteria,* 2d ed. Falls Church, Va.: National Study of School Evaluation, 1981.

————. *Evaluative Criteria,* 5th ed. Falls Church, Va.: National Study of School Evaluation, 1978.

————. *Middle School/Junior High School Evaluative Criteria.* Falls Church, Va.: National Study of School Evaluation, 1979.

New Orleans Public Schools. *Guidelines for Mathematics Grades 7–9.* New Orleans, La.: Division of Instruction, New Orleans Public Schools, 1969.

Oliva, Peter F. *The Secondary School Today,* 2d ed. New York: Harper & Row, 1972.

Smith, B. Othanel; Stanley, William O.; and Shores, J. Harlan. *Fundamentals of Curriculum Development,* rev. ed. New York: Harcourt, Brace, Jovanovich, 1957.

Spencer, Herbert. *Education: Intellectual, Moral, and Physical.* New York: John B. Alden, Publisher, 1885. Also, Paterson, N.J.: Littlefield, Adams, 1963.

Stratemeyer, Florence B.; Forkner, Hamden L.; McKim, Margaret G; and Passow, A. Harry. *Developing a Curriculum for Modern Living,* 2d ed. New York: Bureau of Publications, Teachers College Press, Columbia University, 1957.

Taba, Hilda. *Curriculum Development: Theory and Practice.* New York: Harcourt, Brace, Jovanovich, 1962.

Tyler, Ralph W. *Basic Principles of Curriculum and Instruction.* Chicago: University of Chicago Press, 1949.

United States Department of Labor. *Occupational Outlook for College Graduates, 1978–79 ed.* Bulletin 1956. Washington, D. C.: Bureau of Labor Statistics, U.S. Department of Labor, 1978.

————. *Occupational Outlook Handbook, 1978–79 ed.* Bulletin 1955. Washington, D. C.: Superintendent of Documents, U.S. Government Printing Office, 1978.

Wiles, Jon and Bondi, Joseph, Jr. *Curriculum Development: A Guide to Practice.* Columbus, Ohio: Charles E. Merrill, 1979.

Wisconsin State Department of Public Instruction. *Guide to Curriculum Building,* Bulletin No. 8. Madison, Wisc.: State Department of Education, January, 1950.

Zais, Robert S. *Curriculum: Principles and Foundations.* New York: Harper & Row, 1976.

FILMSTRIP-TAPE PROGRAM

Deciding on Defensible Goals via Educational Needs Assessment, 1971. Vimcet Associates, P.O. Box 24714, Los Angeles, California 90024.

8

Curriculum Goals and Objectives

After studying this chapter, you should be able to:
1. Distinguish between goals and objectives.
2. Distinguish between aims of education and curriculum goals and objectives.
3. Distinguish between curriculum goals and objectives and instructional goals and objectives.
4. Specify and write curriculum goals.
5. Specify and write curriculum objectives.

You should also be able to formulate and give reasons for your views on the following issues:
1. The value of distinguishing between goals and objectives.
2. The importance of identifying needs prior to writing curriculum goals and objectives in this chapter.

HIERARCHY OF OUTCOMES

Following the model for curriculum improvement suggested in Chapter 5, let's see how far we have come. We have:

- □ analyzed needs of students in general in our society
- □ analyzed needs of American society
- □ reviewed aims of education and affirmed those with which we are in agreement
- □ written our philosophy of education
- □ initiated a needs assessment by surveying needs of students in the community and school and by surveying needs of the community
- □ conducted a needs assessment and identified unmet needs

All of these steps are a prelude to the next phase. They provide a framework; they set the stage. They furnish data that are vital to making curricular decisions. The planning of the curriculum is now about to begin.

In Chapter 6 we defined the terms "aims of education," "curriculum goals," "curriculum objectives," "instructional goals" and "instructional objectives" as used in this text. We also established a hierarchy of purposes of education from the broadest to the narrowest. Let's review that hierarchy; it is essential both to this chapter on curriculum goals and objectives and to Chapter 10 on instructional goals and objectives. We might chart this hierarchy as shown in Figure 8-1.

FIGURE 8-1   Hierarchy of outcomes

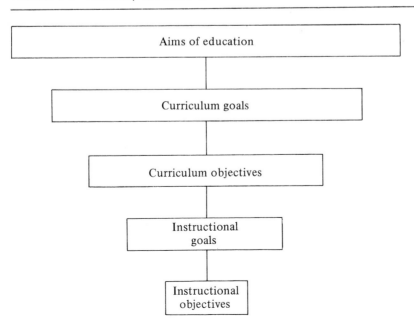

It sometimes seems that the educational literature is surfeited with discussions of goals and objectives. In spite of these many commentaries, I have included three chapters in this text (Chapters 6, 8, and 10) on aims, goals, and objectives for the following reasons:

1. They are essential components in a comprehensive model for curriculum improvement.
2. These various terms for purpose are used loosely and interchangeably in some of the literature, leading to possible confusion.
3. Some of the recommendations in the literature on the writing of goals and objectives are helpful; other recommendations seem less helpful.

Aims, Goals, and Objectives

Several problems can be found if we research the literature on aims, goals, and objectives. First, aims of education are often equated with goals, which, in a lexical sense, of course, they are. John W. Gardner in *Goals for Americans* was really describing aims of education when he wrote:

> Our deepest convictions impel us to foster individual fulfillment. We wish each one to achieve the promise that is in him. We wish each one to be worthy of a free society, and capable of strengthening a free society. ... Ultimately, education serves all of our purposes — liberty, justice, and all our other aims — but the one it serves most directly is equality of opportunity.
>
> [The] ... tasks of producing certain specially needed kinds of educated talent ... should not crowd out the great basic goals of our educational system: to foster individual fulfillment and to nurture the free, rational and responsible men and women without whom our kind of society cannot endure. Our schools must prepare *all* young people, whatever their talents, for the serious business of being free men and women.[1]

In this case the problem of equating aims of education with goals is minor since Gardner communicates to the reader that he is consistently discussing broad goals or aims. The problem arises when discussions of aims, curriculum goals and objectives, and instructional goals and objectives are intermingled. There is little difficulty when a single meaning for a term is used in a single context or when an author clearly defines how he or she uses a term. That, however, does not always happen.

Second, the terms "educational goals" and "educational objectives" are used in the profession with varying meanings. Some use these terms in the same way other people speak of aims of education or educational aims. Some perceive educational goals as curriculum goals and educational objectives as

---

[1] John W. Gardner, "National Goals in Education," in *Goals for Americans: Programs for Action in the Sixties.* The Report of the President's Commission on National Goals, Henry M. Wriston, Chairman (New York: The American Assembly, Columbia University, 1960), pp. 81, 100.

curriculum objectives. Some substitute educational goals for instructional goals and educational objectives for instructional objectives.

Third, as we shall see in examples of school statements of goals and objectives, goals are equated with objectives and the terms are used synonymously. Yet, if we believe what we read, there are two entities — one called goals and another objectives — as numerous schools have prepared statements of goals and objectives. Unless we choose to believe the problem is one of redundancy, which I do not, goals are different from objectives.

W. James Popham and Eva L. Baker used the terms interchangeably when they wrote:

> We have given considerable attention to the topic of instructional objectives because they represent one of the most important tools available to the teacher.... There is undoubtedly a positive relationship between a teacher's clarity of instructional goals and the quality of his teaching.[2]

Robert F. Mager used goals and objectives synonymously in *Preparing Instructional Objectives*. Mager commented:

> ...an instructor ... must then select procedures, content, and methods that ... measure or evaluate the student's performance according to the objectives or goals originally selected.... Another important reason for stating objectives sharply relates to the evaluation of the degree to which the learner is able to perform in the manner desired ... unless goals are clearly and firmly fixed in the minds of both parties, tests are at best misleading....[3]

Two widely followed taxonomies of educational objectives bear the subtitle, *The Classification of Educational Goals*.[4] In some of the literature goals *are* objectives and vice versa.

Fourth, some curriculum specialists do not distinguish curriculum goals and objectives from instructional goals and objectives or they use these two sets of terms synonymously. If curriculum and instruction are two different entities — the position taken in this text — then curriculum goals and objectives are different from instructional goals and objectives. Only if we choose a curriculum-instruction model in which the two are mirror images can curriculum goals and objectives be identical to instructional goals and objectives. I hold, however, the view that the two are separate but related entities.

These observations are not meant to criticize the positions, definitions, or

---

[2] W. James Popham and Eva L. Baker, *Systematic Instruction* (Englewood Cliffs, N.J.: Prentice-Hall, 1970), p. 43.

[3] Robert F. Mager, *Preparing Instructional Objectives* (Belmont, Cal.: Fearon Publishers, 1962), pp. 1, 3–4.

[4] Benjamin S. Bloom, ed., *Taxonomy of Educational Objectives: The Classification of Educational Goals: Handbook I: Cognitive Domain* (New York: Longman, 1956) and David R. Krathwohl et al., *Taxonomy of Educational Objectives: The Classification of Educational Goals: Handbook II: Affective Domain* (New York: Longman, 1964).

approaches of other curriculum specialists. As Decker F. Walker aptly stated in an enlightening discussion of writings on curriculum:

> Our barnstorming tour of curriculum writing has revealed an extremely varied pattern. Curriculum is clearly an iffy subject. It belongs to Aristotle's "region of the many and variable" where certain knowledge is not possible, only opinion — multiple and various, more or less considered, more or less adequate, but never clearly true or false.[5]

My remarks about the differences in use of curriculum terms convey, as mentioned in Chapter 1, that the language of curriculum is somewhat imprecise and can lead to confusion. Curriculum specialists, unfortunately, do not agree among themselves on terminology. As a result, the practitioner who seeks to carry out curriculum development following principles established by the experts must first understand these terms and the contexts within which they appear.

To prevent confusion, I have made distinctions between curriculum goals and objectives and instructional goals and objectives in order to help practitioners facilitate the natural flow of curriculum development from general aims of education to precise instructional objectives. Specifying curriculum goals and objectives, then, is viewed as an intermediate planning step between these two poles. We will first define the terms curriculum goals and objectives, present some examples, and then develop some guidelines for writing them.

DEFINING GOALS AND OBJECTIVES

Curriculum Goals

A *curriculum goal* is a purpose or end stated in general terms without criteria of achievement. Curriculum planners wish students to accomplish it as a result of exposure to segments or all of a program of a particular school or school system. For example, the following statement meets this definition of a curriculum goal: "Students shall acquire those attributes necessary for functioning, on a daily basis, as good citizens in their own school and community setting." [6]

We have already seen in Chapter 3 examples of curriculum goals. The Seven Cardinal Principles — health, command of fundamental processes, worthy home membership, vocation, citizenship, worthy use of leisure, and ethical character — are examples of curriculum goals, albeit in a form of shorthand.[7] The Commission on the Reorganization of Secondary Education

---

[5] Decker F. Walker, "A Barnstorming Tour of Writing on Curriculum," *Considered Action for Curriculum Improvement,* 1980 Yearbook (Alexandria, Va.: Association for Supervision and Curriculum Development, 1980), p. 81.

[6] Dade County Public Schools, *District Comprehensive Educational Plan,* 1974–79 (Miami, Fla.: Dade County Public Schools, 1974), p. 8.

[7] Commission on the Reorganization of Secondary Education, *Cardinal Principles of Secondary Education* (Washington, D.C.: United States Office of Education, Bulletin No. 35, 1918).

could have expanded these principles into forms like:

- ☐ The school will promote the physical and mental health of the students.
- ☐ Students will achieve a command of the fundamental processes.
- ☐ A goal of the school is to foster worthy home membership.

The Ten Imperative Needs of Youth, listed by the Educational Policies Commission, are a set of curriculum goals, which, as noted earlier, included such statements as:

> All youth need to develop salable skills.
> All youth need to develop and maintain good health, physical fitness, and mental health.
> All youth need to grow in their ability to think rationally, to express their thoughts clearly, and to read and listen with understanding.[8]

The Educational Policies Commission pointed to four purposes or aims of education in American democracy. As previously mentioned, they identified these aims as self-realization, human relationships, economic efficiency, and civic responsibility.[9] These purposes might be modified by a particular school or school system and turned into curricular goals, stated in a variety of ways, as follows:

- ☐ The school's program provides experiences leading to self-realization.
- ☐ Our school seeks to promote human relationships.
- ☐ A goal of the school is development of skills of learners that will lead to their country's and their own economic efficiency.
- ☐ Students will develop a sense of civic responsibility.

Many variations are used for expressing these four purposes. This chapter will later present a preferred form for writing goals and objectives. For now, these four goals are shown only as examples of substance, not of form.

Aims of education can become curriculum goals when applied to a particular school or school system. The distinction drawn between aims of education and curriculum goals is one of generality (or looking at it from the other end of the telescope, specificity). "To transmit the cultural heritage" and "to overcome ignorance" are aims of all school programs. No single program or school can accomplish these extremely broad purposes. A school can, of course, contribute to transmitting the cultural heritage and to overcoming ignorance and, stated with those qualifications, educational aims can become curriculum goals. The expression "to contribute to the physical development of the individual" can be both an educational aim of our society and a curriculum goal of a particular school or school system.

---

8 Educational Policies Commission, *Education for All American Youth* (Washington, D.C.: National Education Association, 1944), pp. 225–226.
9 Educational Policies Commission, *The Purposes of Education in American Democracy* (Washington, D.C.: National Education Association, 1938).

Curriculum Objectives

Curriculum goals are derived from a statement of philosophy, defined aims of education, and assessment of needs. From curriculum goals, we derive curriculum objectives. We may define a curriculum objective in the following manner: A *curriculum objective* is a purpose or end stated in specific, measurable terms. Curriculum planners wish students to accomplish it as a result of exposure to segments or all of a program of the particular school or school system.

Earlier in this chapter the following example of a curriculum goal was presented: "Students shall acquire those attributes necessary for functioning, on a daily basis, as good citizens in their own school and community setting." From that curriculum goal this curriculum objective can be derived: During the election of student government officers, 90 percent of the student body will cast ballots. Note how the curriculum objective refines the curriculum goal. Many curriculum objectives can emanate from a single curriculum goal.

Examples of Curriculum Goals

Many illustrations of statements of curriculum goals and objectives are reproduced in this chapter. Although the statements may not conform to distinctions between curriculum goals and objectives advocated and presented in this text, they are representative samples of faculty efforts. Three examples of curriculum goals are provided: (1) those formulated by St. Lucie County (Florida) Public Schools (see Box 8-1) for the entire school district (their statement of philosophy appeared in Chapter 6); (2) those established by Carol City (Florida) Junior High School (Box 8-2); and (3) those created by Miami Palmetto Senior High School (Box 8-3). Note that these statements are couched in terms of what the schools seek to do rather than what students will do.

LOCUS OF CURRICULUM GOALS AND OBJECTIVES

As the statements of the Seven Cardinal Principles and the Ten Imperative Needs of Youth demonstrated, curriculum goals are infrequently written on a national basis by individuals and groups as proposals for consideration by schools throughout the country. Curriculum objectives, however, as just defined, are too specific to emanate from national sources.

Curriculum goals and objectives are regularly written at the state, school-district, and individual school level with the expectation that they will be followed within the jurisdiction of each level. State pronouncements apply to all public schools in the state; school-district statements apply district-wide; and individual school specifications, school-wide.

The illustrations from school systems that we have seen so far come from the school-district or individual school level. For the most part, curriculum goals and objectives developed for nationwide consideration or state, district, and school implementation cut across disciplines. A school's statement, for example, applies generally throughout the school. It is possible, however, for grades and departments to develop curriculum goals and objectives that do not apply generally throughout the school but to a particular group of students, that is, those within a particular grade or subject area.

Let us suppose, by way of example, that the following statement is a curriculum goal of the school: All children need to develop skill in working with numbers. The fourth-grade teachers could create a grade-level goal by simply reiterating the school goal, as: Fourth graders need to develop skill in working with numbers. On the other hand, the fourth-grade teachers might choose to interpret the school's curriculum goal and create a grade-level curriculum objective, as follows: This year's fourth graders will excel last year's by an average of five percentile points on the same standardized test of arithmetic.

Another example of a school-wide curriculum goal is: Students will improve their scores on state assessment tests. One of the school's curriculum objectives derived from this goal might be: At least 85 percent of the students will achieve passing scores on the statewide assessment tests. The eleventh-grade faculty might set as its objective: Ninety percent of the juniors will pass the state assessment test this year.

We encounter a similar case with a twelfth-grade faculty when the school seeks to accomplish the following curriculum goal: Students will develop self-discipline and self-reliance. A twelfth-grade faculty might spell out the following curriculum goal: Seniors will demonstrate skills of independent study. The twelfth-grade teachers might be more specific by following up this curriculum goal with a curriculum objective, as follows: At least 70 percent of the seniors will seek to improve their self-discipline, self-reliance, and self-study techniques by engaging in independent research projects at least one hour of the school day three hours a week.

Teachers of foreign language may furnish us with an example of curriculum goals and objectives found within a discipline. They might, for example, consider the school's curriculum goal: Students will develop the ability to relate to ethnic and national groups different from their own. The foreign language teachers might also note one of the school's curriculum objectives, in this case applying to the students generally but aimed at a particular field: Seventy-five percent of the student body will elect a foreign language.

The foreign language teachers might decide on the following curriculum goal: Students will initiate a number of requests for advanced courses in a foreign language. They might identify as a curriculum objective: Fifty percent of the students who are taking or who have taken a foreign language will enroll in a second foreign language.

In all cases, the grade or departmental level's and the school's curriculum goals and objectives must relate to one another. In the same manner, a school's

BOX 8-1

EDUCATIONAL GOALS
OF
ST. LUCIE COUNTY SCHOOLS

The public schools should help each student to develop his personal knowledge, skills, competence, and creative ability, to the maximum of his capacity, and to learn behavior patterns which will enable him to become a responsible member of society. Each student, according to his ability, should achieve in the following areas:

I *Health*

  A. Knowledge about health concepts essential to the maintenance of optimal health.

  B. Some skill in sports and other forms of recreation which will permit life-long employment of physical exercise.

  C. Competence in recognizing and preventing environmental health problems.

II *Fundamental Processes*

  A. Knowledge of the traditionally accepted fundamental skills, such as reading, writing, and arithmetic essential to the later learning of concepts in such areas as higher mathematics, science, language arts, social sciences and the arts.

  B. Skill in the logical processes of search, analysis, evaluation and problem solving.

  C. Competence and motivation for continuing self-evaluation, self-instruction and adaptation to a changing environment.

III *Citizenship*

  A. Knowledge about comparative political systems and comparative economic systems with emphasis on democratic institutions, the heritage and the responsibilities and privileges of citizenship.

---

curriculum goals and objectives must be compatible with a district's, and both an individual school's and district's must be coordinated with the state's.

State Curriculum Goals and Objectives

The state, through its department of education, may exert curriculum leadership by circulating a statement of curriculum goals and sometimes of curriculum objectives to all its schools. The state of Florida, for example, has identified seven goal areas of student development with a number of specific goals within each area (see Box 8-4). These areas and their accompanying goals are reproduced.

The state of Florida has followed up its specification of goals and devel-

BOX 8-1   cont'd.

B. Skill for participating in the process of public, private, and political organizations and for influencing decisions made by such organizations.

C. Competence in judging the merits of competing political ideologies and candidates for political position.

IV *Vocation*

A. Knowledge of the opportunities for successful participation in our nation's economic system.

B. Career vocational knowledge and skills to enter and advance in the economic system.

C. Competence in the application of fundamental economic skills.

V *Cultural and Aesthetic Values*

A. Knowledge of art, music, literary and drama forms and their place in the cultural heritage.

B. Skill in the creative use of leisure time.

C. Competence in the evaluation of cultural offerings and opportunities.

VI *Personal and Social Relations*

A. Knowledge about basic psychological and sociological factors affecting human behavior.

B. Skills in interpersonal and group relations and in formation of ethical and moral standards of behavior.

C. Competence for adjusting to change in personal status and social patterns.

SOURCE: St. Lucie County, Florida Public Schools. Reprinted by permission.

---

oped a set of performance standards, a requirement mandated by the Florida legislature.[10] We have already seen some of these performance standards in Chapter 7 where they were introduced to show needs derived from the subject matter. In its document, *Goals for Education in Florida,* the state explained how to conceptualize goals:

> ... the goals of education can be conceived in terms of the life activities of human adults in modern society. These activities may generally be placed in three categories: occupational, citizenship, and self-fulfillment. By constructing such a framework, it becomes possible to state the kinds of

---

[10] Florida Statute 229.053(2)(a), *Florida School Laws,* 1979, p. 11.

BOX 8-2

EDUCATIONAL GOALS AND OBJECTIVES OF THE CAROL CITY (FLORIDA) JUNIOR HIGH SCHOOL

Goals

1. To give students an opportunity to discover, propose, and create by making the most of potential powers by encountering challenge.

2. To provide students with real opportunities for constant practice and use, to develop personal abilities through systematically planned curriculum.

3. To give students an opportunity to develop a positive attitude toward work and occupations.

4. To enable students to find immediate and saleable occupations upon completing high school.

5. To make students become experienced in discerning fact from opinion, objectivity from bias.

6. To help students form effective interpersonal relations that are dependent on a sensitivity to the needs and interests of others; adequately developed communication skills, and the ability to cope with conflict and authority.

7. To help students to increase ability in the clarification and weighing of values to contribute to student's feeling of competence and sense of identity.

8. To provide activities which contribute to the student's perception of teachers as fellow inquirers.

9. To provide the reservoir of data, ideas, concepts, generalizations and theories which, in combination with thinking, valuing and social participation, can be used by the student to function rationally and humanely.

Objectives

1. To expand the effort now being made to individualize the educational process and to personalize the experiences within a climate conducive to learning for all students.

2. To provide a variety of programs to meet the student's needs.

3. To help the student recognize that his efforts are essential in realizing his potentials.

4. To create an atmosphere where learning can be an enjoyable, meaningful and challenging experience.

5. To stimulate the student to acquire the knowledge and skills to cope with the changes of his present and future world.

6. Leading the students to develop an attitude for inquiry, problem solving, and decision making.

7. Providing a curriculum where students can develop those occupational competencies consistent with their interest, aptitudes, and abilities.

8. Assisting the students in finding and developing their life interests.

SOURCE: Carol City Junior High School, Dade County, Florida Public Schools. Reprinted by permission.

BOX 8-3

EDUCATIONAL OBJECTIVES OF THE MIAMI PALMETTO SENIOR HIGH SCHOOL

1. To teach the pupil to think logically, to express his ideas more clearly in speaking and writing, and to listen with a critical mind.

2. To stimulate a desire within the pupil to acquire and maintain sound mental and physical health.

3. To provide instruction and materials to encourage the slow, stimulate the average, and guide the gifted learner.

4. To achieve an understanding of scientific principles through the study of factual and experimental evidence.

5. To help him prepare for further study.

6. To orient students in the effective use of the library: to encourage reading widely in search of facts upon which intelligent opinions may be based; to provide a rich variety of books and non-print media for students, and thus stimulate the purposeful use of all library resources.

7. To develop specific interests, cooperative attitudes, and to experience self-satisfaction in co-curricular activities.

8. To guide the pupil in developing manipulative skills and in understanding the conditions conducive to successful family living.

9. To help the student to distinguish between reasoned and emotional opinion; to discuss rather than argue; and to see the relationship between cause and effect.

10. To develop a keener insight and appreciation of other cultures, as well as his own.

11. To help students acquire an understanding of the principles and processes of the American free enterprise system, and to expand the occupational skills program.

12. To research and make available to students the resources of the community and the school.

13. To actively encourage courtesy, friendliness, and cooperation throughout the school.

SOURCE: Miami Palmetto Senior High School, Dade County, Florida Public Schools. Reprinted by permission.

---

performance which should equip adults to function effectively in society — the *objectives* of education.[11]

---

[11] Florida Department of Education, *Goals for Education in Florida* (Tallahassee, Fla.: State Department of Education, c. 1972), p. 4.

BOX 8-4

GOALS FOR STUDENT DEVELOPMENT

Goal Area I. *Communication and Learning Skills.* All students shall acquire, to the extent of their individual, physical, mental, and emotional capacities, a mastery of the basic skills required in obtaining and expressing ideas through the effective use of words, numbers, and other symbols.

   a. All students shall achieve a working knowledge of reading, writing, speaking, and arithmetic during the elementary school years, accompanied by gradual progress into the broader fields of mathematics, natural science, language arts, and the humanities.

   b. All students shall develop and use skills in the logical processes of search, analysis, evaluation, and problem-solving, in critical thinking, and in the use of symbolism.

   c. All students shall develop competence and motivation for continuing self-evaluation, self-instruction, and adaptation to a changing environment.

Goal Area II. *Citizenship Education.* All students shall acquire and continually improve the habits and attitudes necessary for responsible citizenship.

   a. All students shall acquire knowledge of various political systems with emphasis on democratic institutions, the American heritage, the contributions of our foreign antecedents, and the responsibilities and privileges of citizenship.

   b. All students shall develop the skills required for participation in the processes of public and private political organizations and for influencing decisions made by such organizations, including competence in judging the merits of competing political ideologies and of candidates for public office.

Goal Area III. *Occupational Interests.* All students shall acquire a knowledge and understanding of the opportunities open to them for preparing for a productive life, and shall develop those skills and abilities which will enable them to take full advantage of those opportunities — including a positive attitude toward work and respect for the dignity of all honorable occupations.

   a. All students shall acquire knowledge of and develop an understanding of the fundamental economic structure and processes of the American system, together with an understanding of the opportunities and requirements for individual participation and success in the system.

   b. All students shall develop those occupational competencies consistent with their interests, aptitudes, and ability which are prerequisite to entry and advance in the economic system, and/or academic preparation for acquisition of technical or professional skills through post-high school training.

   c. All students shall develop competence in the application of economic knowledge to practical economic functions (such as planning and budgeting for the investment of personal income, calculating tax obligations, financing major purchases, and obtaining desirable employment).

Goal Area IV. *Mental and Physical Health.* All students shall acquire good health habits and an understanding of the conditions necessary for the maintenance of physical and emotional well-being.

BOX 8-4   cont'd.

a. All students shall develop an understanding of the requirements of personal hygiene, adequate nutrition, and physical exercise essential to the maintenance of physical health, and a knowledge of the dangers to mental and physical health from addiction and other aversive practices.

b. All students shall develop skills in sports and other forms of recreation which will permit life-long enjoyment of physical exercise.

c. All students shall develop competence in recognizing and preventing environmental health problems.

d. All students shall acquire a knowledge of basic psychological and sociological factors affecting human behavior and mental health, and shall develop competence for adjusting to changes in personal status and social patterns.

Goal Area V. *Home and Family Relationships.* All students shall develop an appreciation of the family as a social institution.

a. All students shall develop an understanding of their roles and the roles of others as members of a family, together with a knowledge of the requirements for successful participation in family living.

b. All students shall understand the role of the family as a basic unit in the society.

Goal Area VI. *Aesthetic and Cultural Appreciations.* All students shall develop understanding and appreciation of human achievement in the natural sciences, the social sciences, the humanities and the arts.

a. All students shall acquire a knowledge of major arts, music, literary and drama forms, and their place in the cultural heritage.

b. All students shall be active in one or more fields of creative endeavor, and develop skills in the creative use of leisure time.

c. All students shall acquire competence in the critical evaluation of cultural offerings and opportunities.

Goal Area VII. *Human Relations.* All students shall develop a concern for moral, ethical, and spiritual values and for the application of such values to life situations.

a. All students shall acquire the greatest possible understanding of and appreciation of themselves as well as of persons belonging to social, cultural, and ethnic groups different from their own, and of the worthiness of all persons as members of society.

b. All students shall develop skill in interpersonal and group relationships, and shall recognize the importance of and need for ethical and moral standards of behavior.

SOURCE: Florida Department of Education, *Goals for Education in Florida* (Tallahassee, Fla.: State Department of Education, c. 1972), pp. 6–9. Reprinted by permission.

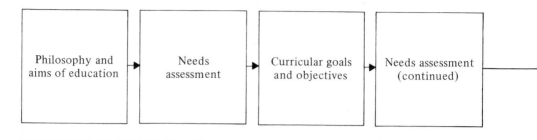

FIGURE 8-2   The sequence of goal specification and needs assessment

This statement recalls the method described in Chapter 7 of analyzing society's needs by spelling out social processes, functions, or life activities.

Characteristics of Goals. Florida helped curriculum developers when it explained the characteristics of goals, providing them with useful guidelines when attempting to write curriculum goals. It summarized the characteristics of goals as follows:

1. Goals are statements of ultimate desired outcomes; they specify conditions desired for the population in general.
2. Goals are timeless, in the sense that no time is specified by which the goals must be reached.
3. Goals do not specify criteria for achievement, but provide a direction for system improvement.
4. Goals are not permanent. Feedback from the entire evaluation/ decision-making process is used to assess progress in the direction specified by the goals, and goals may be modified wherever necessary or desirable.
5. Goals are of equal importance.[12]
6. Goals are stated broadly enough to be accepted at any level of the educational enterprise: state, district, or local school. They thus represent the conceptual framework upon which the education enterprise depends.[13]

The Florida publication on goals commented: "While it is necessary to know current status in order to specify educational needs and to assign priorities for satisfaction of these needs, the statements of desired outcomes are logically a prerequisite to establishing needs." [14] Let's refer for a moment to Chapter 7 where I made this comment on the timing of needs assessment and goal specification:

---

[12] Some may question this point.
[13] *Goals for Education in Florida*, pp. 5–6.
[14] *Goals for Education in Florida*, p .5.

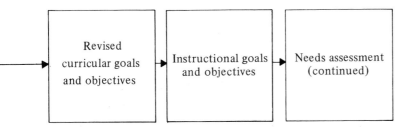

A needs assessment is a continuing activity that takes place (a) before specifying curricular goals and objectives, (b) after identifying curricular goals and objectives, (c) after evaluating instruction, and (d) after evaluating the curriculum.[15]

To clarify the sequence of goal writing and needs assessment, we may refer to Figure 8-2.

Once curriculum goals and objectives have been spelled out, the needs assessment process proceeds to determine unmet needs. Once identified, these needs will result in more curriculum goals and objectives and/or a modification of those already specified.

In summary, a state may formulate both broad aims and curriculum goals (and also curriculum objectives, instructional goals, and instructional objectives) for all schools and all students in that state.

School districts and individual schools may accept the states' formulation verbatim or, if the state permits, as in Florida, may independently develop their own statement. In either case, however, the statements of the school districts and individual schools must be in harmony with the state's. We have already seen an illustration of one school district, St. Lucie County, Florida, which drafted its own statement of the goals of its school system. The Dade County Public Schools adopted and expanded the Florida goal areas. For example, the state's Goal Area V, Home and Family Relationships, contained two goals whereas Dade County's included a third, reflecting, perhaps, a sensitivity to its multiethnic population: It reads:

GOAL AREA V

Home and Family Relationships. Students shall develop an appreciation of the family as a social institution.

a) Students shall develop an understanding of their roles and the roles of others as members of a family, together with a knowledge of the requirements for successful participation in family living.

b) Students shall develop an understanding of the role of the family as a basic unit in our society.

---

15 See p. 229 of this text.

c) Students shall develop an awareness of the diversity of family patterns and the value of the contributions of the individuals to family and community living.[16]

CONSTRUCTING STATEMENTS OF CURRICULUM GOALS

The examples of curriculum goals suggest a variety of forms of expression. Some schools phrase goals to stress the role of the curriculum or of the school, as:

□ to give students the opportunity to develop a positive attitude toward work and experience (Carol City Junior High School)
□ to teach the child to think logically, to express his ideas more clearly in speaking and writing, and to listen with a critical mind (Miami Palmetto Senior High School)

Although stressing the role of the school is common, an alternate form featuring the student seems preferable for many reasons:

1. Philosophically, this form is more in keeping with progressive doctrine that places the pupil at the center of learning — a sound principle.
2. It is in keeping with modern instructional design that focuses on the achievements of the learner rather than the performance of the teacher or school.
3. It parallels common practice, as we shall see in Chapter 10, in writing instructional goals and objectives. Thus, curriculum goals may be better understood and the process of curriculum development better integrated.
4. It is easier to design evaluation processes when we know what is expected of students as opposed to what is expected of the teacher or school.

Writing curriculum goals in a form that starts with the students, we might revise the previous illustrations in the following manner:

□ Students will develop a positive attitude toward work and experience.
□ Students will develop skills of thinking logically, expressing their ideas clearly in speaking and writing, and listening with critical minds.

Characteristics of Curriculum Goals

The characteristics of curriculum goals as conceptualized in this text may be summarized as follows:

1. They relate to the educational aims and philosophy.
2. They are programmatic. Although they speak to one or more areas of the curriculum, they do not delineate specific courses or specific items of content.
3. They refer to the accomplishment of groups (as, all students, students in general, most students) rather than the achievement of individual students.

---

[16] Dade County Public Schools, *District Comprehensive Educational Plan*, p. 10.

4. They are stated in general terms that provide directions for curriculum development.
5. They are broad enough to lead to specific curriculum objectives.

CONSTRUCTING STATEMENTS OF CURRICULUM OBJECTIVES

Like curriculum goals, curriculum objectives relate to the educational aims and philosophy, are programmatic in nature, and refer to accomplishments of groups. Unlike curriculum goals, curriculum objectives are stated in specific and measurable terms.

Elements of Curriculum Objectives

Curriculum objectives are refinements of the curriculum goals. They specify the performance standards for the students for whom the curriculum is designed. We can turn a curriculum goal into a curriculum objective by adding the following three elements that we will see again when discussing instructional objectives:

□ performance or behavioral terms, i.e., those skills and knowledge that students are expected to be able to demonstrate
□ the degree of mastery desired by the curriculum planners
□ conditions under which the performance will take place, if not readily understood

Let's analyze the following curriculum objective for these three elements:

> On completion of the first testing, 75 percent of the eleventh graders will have successfully passed the state's functional literacy test; by completion of the second testing, 90 percent will have passed.

Are all three elements present in this two-part objective? Yes, they are. The performance expected is successfully passing the state's functional literacy test. The degrees of mastery desired are 75 and 90 percent. Completion of the first and second testings is the condition.

To accomplish the transition from curriculum goal to curriculum objective, it is helpful to jot down several indicators of student performance that will serve as guides for writing the objectives. Let's take another look at the illustrative curriculum goal mentioned earlier:

> Students shall acquire those attributes necessary for functioning, on a daily basis, as good citizens in their own school and community setting.[17]

What are some indicators of learner performance that reveal good citizenship in the school and community? We might look for such behaviors as:

□ care of school building and grounds
□ less fighting among students
□ orderliness in school assemblies

---

[17] Dade County Public Schools, *District Comprehensive Educational Plan*, p. 8.

    □ participation in community youth organizations like church groups, scout groups, etc.
    □ contribution of labor or money to some worthy cause
    □ keeping informed on current events
    □ refraining from littering the school and community
    □ serving on committees of the school

We could turn the first performance indicator — care of school building and grounds — into a curriculum objective in the following manner:

> By the end of April students will have demonstrated care of the building to the extent that there will be a 95 percent reduction in the number of graffiti on the walls.

It is apparent that from this one curriculum goal on good citizenship we can generate many curriculum objectives and that from the first performance indicator alone we can create a number of objectives.

When conducting their needs assessment, the Madison, Wisconsin Public Schools carried out a detailed procedure for converting curriculum goals into objectives. The Madison schools spelled out major curriculum goals, divided these into subgoals, established performance indicators, and then specified the curriculum objectives. A sample of the Madison process for changing major goals into objectives is shown in Table 8-1. The curriculum objectives are identified in this process under the column labeled "Performance Conditions."

The generation of curriculum goals and objectives is a highly creative exercise. The curriculum goals and objectives set the direction for the subsequent organization and development of the curriculum. The curriculum goals and objectives place their seal upon the activities that will take place in the many classrooms of the school.

VALIDATING AND PRIORITIZING GOALS AND OBJECTIVES

As stated earlier, the assessment of curriculum needs is a continuing process that starts after a school formulates its philosophy and clarifies its aims of education. The needs of society, of students in general, and of the particular students, community, and subject matter give rise to initial statements of curriculum goals and objectives. After these goals and objectives are identified, the needs assessment process is continued to determine if any needs have not been met. When unmet needs are exposed, a revised list of curriculum goals and objectives is prepared. These goals and objectives require validation and prioritization.

Validation is the process of determining whether the goals and objectives are accepted as appropriate or "right" for the school system proposing them. *Prioritization* is the placing of the goals and objectives in order of relative importance to the students of the school system. Groups concerned with the progress of the school should be enlisted to help identify suitable goals and objectives and to set priorities.

The needs assessment process both advocated by English and Kaufman[18] and followed by the Madison Public Schools[19] includes a step for validating goals. The English and Kaufman model requires as an additional step validating performance standards, which are analogous to objectives.

Some school systems seek to validate both goals and objectives; others limit the process to validating goals on the presumption that once the goals are identified, a representative committee can handle the task of making the goals specific, i.e., turning them into objectives.

Function of Curriculum Committee

The validation process, whether carried out by the state, district, or school, assumes forming a curriculum committee or council charged with the task. The curriculum committee will submit the goals by means of a questionnaire or opinionnaire to groups who are concerned with the progress of the school(s). English and Kaufman recommended that the goals and performance standards be submitted to lay people, educators, and students for their review, validation, and prioritization. The Madison Public Schools presented their goals to a representative committee for its decision on the validity of the goals.

It is a good practice to submit curriculum goals and any already identified accompanying curriculum objectives to a broad sampling of groups: lay persons (including parents), students, teachers, administrators, and curriculum experts (on the staffs of public school systems or on the faculties of teacher education institutions). The effort should be made to learn whether there is widespread acceptance of the goals formulated by the curriculum planners and what the groups' priorities will be. Curriculum objectives that are developed after a broad sampling of opinion has been gathered can be submitted to either a more limited sampling of the same groups or to the curriculum committee for validation and prioritization.

Data should be gathered and interpreted preferably by a curriculum committee representative of the various groups polled. Such a committee will be called on to make judgments that will tax its collective wisdom. It cannot treat the data in a simplistic fashion, tallying responses from all groups, and simply following the majority's opinions. It needs to analyze discrepancies of opinion, if any, among the various groups surveyed, and discuss the discrepancies among themselves and with members of the various groups.

---

18 Fenwick W. English and Roger A. Kaufman, *Needs Assessment: A Focus for Curriculum Development* (Alexandria, Va.: Association for Supervision and Curriculum Development, 1975).

19 Theodore J. Czajkowski and Jerry L. Patterson, *School District Needs Assessment: Practical Models for Increasing Involvement in Curriculum Decisions* (Madison, Wisc.: Madison Public Schools, 1976).

TABLE 8-1   Changing goals into objectives

MAJOR GOALS: Generated through the needs assessment process	SUBGOAL: Generated by the steering committee	PERFORMANCE INDICATORS: Generated via community meetings	PERFORMANCE INDICATORS: Refined by measurement specialists	PERFORMANCE CONDITIONS: Established by measurement specialists
Fundamental Learning Skills Student should learn skills such as reading, writing, and math. They should learn these skills to their abilities. Therefore, students should explore and learn the best possible ways to use basic skills.	Seek to know by asking questions	a) feel confident and comfortable in asking questions b) use probing questions c) be motivated to ask questions d) take advantage of an opportunity to ask questions and know when to question e) know and use available resources, including opinions, to find answers on his own f) apply answers g) follow a pattern of questioning and build from initial questions h) ask questions at a variety of levels i) use various communication skills in asking questions j) encourage questioning by others and demonstrate tolerance for and respect of opinions and questions of others k) question, understand and evaluate one's own value system l) know how to obtain and apply answers to questions to help one function in society	a) Voluntarily ask questions within a classroom setting b) Ask questions at least 50% of which elicit thinking beyond the fact-memory level	Given three different defined classroom situations, lasting at least 30 minutes each, ____ % of a stratified random sample of 50 twelfth graders will voluntarily ask at least ____ questions, ____ % of which elicit thinking beyond the fact-memory level. (1a, 1b)

Note:
a) Sample will be generated by stratifying sex, grade point average, and curricular area. Percentages sampled in each stratum will be proportionate to the population in that stratum.
b) Defined classroom situations can include: guest speaker, class discussion in small groups, or class discussion in large groups.
c) Observation of students asking questions can be gathered in one or more of the following ways: classroom teacher notes, questions asked by target student, carefully selected student in small classroom |

			shadows target student, trained parent observers sit in classroom and shadow target student, class is audio-taped and content analyzed. d) Classroom situations will be selected across subject areas to include: language arts, math, science, and social studies.
		a) Spell correctly b) Construct sentences correctly (grammar, syntax) c) Capitalize and punctuate correctly d) Write legibly e) Organize (logical sequence) f) Choose appropriate vocabulary in writing	Given the assignment of preparing a critique of their high school experience, ___ % of a stratified random sample of 50 twelfth graders will prepare a written composition of not less than ___ words which meet the following criteria: a) No more than ___ misspelled words per 500 words of written prose. b) No more than ___ usage errors per 500 words of written prose as agreed to by three out of four independent judges of rhetoric. c) No more than ___ punctuation and/or capitalization errors per 500 words of written prose.
Express ideas, facts, and feelings in writing	a) spell correctly b) construct sentences correctly (grammar, syntax) c) capitalize and punctuate correctly d) write legibly e) organize (logical sequence) f) translate to appropriate form for purpose g) use appropriate form for purpose h) write a summary i) use effective word choice j) write at various levels of thinking		

Table continues on next page.

TABLE 8-1 continued

MAJOR GOALS: Generated through the needs assessment process	SUBGOAL: Generated by the steering committee	PERFORMANCE INDICATORS: Generated via community meetings	PERFORMANCE INDICATORS: Refined by measurement specialists	PERFORMANCE CONDITIONS: Established by measurement specialists
				d) A score on cursive style of ___ or better on a 9-point scale, from illegible to very readable, as agreed to by three out of four independent judges.
				e) No more than ___ words per 500 words of written prose that failed to meet the expected semiformal tone of the assignment as agreed to by three out of four independent judges.
	Organize a given set of ideas and/or facts into a framework	a) convey ideas/facts to someone else in writing and verbally b) construct an outline c) make a succinct statement of an idea and support it with facts and logical reasoning in written or verbal form d) given a problem situation, can generate methods of attack to a problem e) compare/contrast ideas, fact or evidence	a) Make a succinct statement of an idea in written or verbal form b) Given a problem situation, can generate methods of attack to a problem c) Compare/contrast ideas facts, or evidence	Three out of four independent judges can underline the statement(s) which serve to identify each writer's thesis. Three out of four independent judges will identify techniques of logical organization which each writer used to support his thesis and will judge them appropriate to the situation.

f) classify or arrange in logical order a set of ideas/facts/events/tasks

g) adjust presentation of information/ideas to level of audience

h) reach (and state) a conclusion (position) based on accumulated evidence

i) take notes and use them for study

j) identify the key idea in a paragraph or passage

Given a passage of at least 1000 words, ____ % of a stratified random sample of 50 twelfth graders will correctly outline the thesis, supporting assertions, and development to three levels of abstraction. (I, A, 1)

Source: Theodore J. Czajkowski and Jerry L. Patterson, *School District Needs Assessment: Practical Models for Increasing Involvement in Curriculum Decisions.* (Madison, Wisc.: Madison Public Schools, 1974), Appendix F. A paper presented at the National Conference of the Association for Supervision and Curriculum Development, Miami Beach, Florida, March 1976. Reprinted by permission.

Weighting Opinions. As a general rule, the wishes of students, for example, should not hold the same priority as the beliefs of parents and other lay people. The opinions of groups small in number, like curriculum specialists or college professors, cannot be treated in the same light as the attitudes of large numbers of residents of the community. Nor, for that matter, should the opinions of a few school administrators, in spite of their status, be given as great a weight as those of large numbers of teachers and parents.

Since the committee interpreting the data may not find consensus on goals and objectives among the various groups, it has the heavy responsibility of reconciling differing positions and reaching consensus among its own members. Utilizing the opinions of the groups that have been polled, the curriculum committee must decide which goals are valid and which should be assigned priority. To prioritize is to say that some goals are more important than others and deserve more time, attention, and emphasis in the curriculum.

It is clear that the goals of a state, district, or school should be validated and prioritized by submission to sizable numbers of educators and noneducators. It is debatable, however, whether curriculum goals and objectives of grades or departments need or should be submitted to persons beyond the school or school-district personnel. It would be somewhat impractical, redundant, expensive, and time-consuming for curriculum goals and objectives of the grades and departments to be submitted to significant numbers of the school system's constituents. The faculties of the grade and departmental levels may satisfy their responsibilities for validation and prioritization of goals and objectives by submitting their statements to the curriculum committee for its review and endorsement.

The process of validation and prioritization may be repeated as often as the curriculum committee finds necessary with modifications and reprioritization made as a result of each survey and prior to a subsequent survey. After the curriculum goals and objectives have been validated and prioritized, the curriculum planners now turn to the next phase in the curriculum development process — putting the goals and objectives into operation.

SUMMARY

State school systems, school districts, and individual schools engage in the task of specifying curriculum goals and objectives. Curriculum goals and objectives are derived from the developers' philosophy and educational aims.

Curriculum goals are programmatic statements of expected outcomes without criteria of achievement. They apply to students as a group and are often interdisciplinary or multidisciplinary.

Curriculum objectives are specific, measurable, programmatic statements of outcomes to be achieved by students as a group in the school or school system.

Curriculum goals and objectives are essential for:

1. conducting a complete needs assessment to identify unmet needs
2. carrying out subsequent phases of the suggested model for curriculum improvement
3. generating instructional goals and objectives
4. providing a basis for evaluating the curriculum
5. giving direction to the program

It is recommended that curriculum goals and objectives be phrased in terms of anticipated accomplishments of students. Curriculum objectives, which are more specific than curriculum goals, should stipulate expected degrees of mastery and the conditions under which students can master the desired behaviors. Curriculum goals and objectives should be validated and prioritized by the school's curriculum committee after review by representatives of the various constituencies that the school serves.

SUPPLEMENTARY EXERCISES

1. Define and give *two* examples of
   a. aims of education
   b. curriculum goals
   c. curriculum objectives
2. Following definitions in this text, explain both the relationship and difference between
   a. an aim of education and a curriculum goal
   b. a curriculum goal and a curriculum objective
3. Explain the relationship of curriculum goals and objectives to needs assessment.
4. Respond to the following questions showing your position on each:
   a. Is it necessary to write an educational philosophy in order to specify curriculum goals and objectives?
   b. Is it necessary to list educational aims to specify curriculum goals and objectives?
   c. Is it necessary to specify both educational aims and curriculum goals and objectives?
   d. Is it necessary to specify curriculum goals to identify curriculum objectives?
5. Locate and report on illustrations of curriculum goals in either education textbooks or in curriculum materials of any school or school system in the U. S.
6. Locate and report on illustrations of curriculum objectives in either education textbooks or in curriculum materials of any school or school system in the U. S.

7. Obtain and, following principles advocated in this chapter, critique the statement of:
   a. curriculum goals of a school that you know well
   b. curriculum objectives of a school that you know well
   c. curriculum goals and/or objectives of a school district that you know well
   d. curriculum goals and/or objectives of one of the fifty states
8. Recast one of the statements of curriculum goals and/or curriculum objectives of one of the schools found in this chapter following guidelines suggested by the author.

BIBLIOGRAPHY

Bloom, Benjamin S., ed. *Taxonomy of Educational Objectives: The Classification of Educational Goals: Handbook I: Cognitive Domain.* New York: Longman, 1956.

Commission on the Reorganization of Secondary Education. *Cardinal Principles of Secondary Education.* (Washington, D.C.: United States Office of Education, Bulletin No. 35, 1918).

Czajkowski, Theodore J. and Patterson, Jerry L. *School District Needs Assessment: Practical Models for Increasing Involvement in Curriculum Decisions.* Madison, Wisc.: Madison Public Schools, 1976.

Dade County Public Schools. *District Comprehensive Educational Plan,* Fiscal Years 1974–79. Miami, Fla.: Dade County Public Schools, 1974.

Doherty, Victor W. and Peters, Linda B. "Goals and Objectives in Educational Planning and Evaluation," *Educational Leadership* 38, no. 8 (May 1981): 606–611.

Doll, Ronald C. *Curriculum Improvement: Decision Making and Process,* 4th ed. Boston: Allyn and Bacon, 1978.

Educational Policies Commission. *Education for All American Youth.* Washington, D.C.: National Education Association, 1944.

————. *The Purposes of Education in American Democracy.* Washington, D.C.: National Education Association, 1938.

Florida Department of Education. *Goals for Education in Florida.* Tallahassee, Fla.: State Department of Education, c. 1972.

Foshay, Arthur W., ed. *Considered Action for Curriculum Improvement.* Alexandria, Va.: Association for Supervision and Curriculum Development, 1980.

Krathwohl, David R., Bloom, Benjamin S., and Masia, Bertram B. *Taxonomy of Educational Objectives: The Classification of Educational Goals: Handbook II: Affective Domain.* New York: Longman, 1964.

Mager, Robert F. *Preparing Instructional Objectives.* Belmont, Cal.: Fearon Publishers, 1962. 2nd ed., Belmont, Cal.: Pitman Learning, Inc., 1975.

Popham, W. James and Baker, Eva L. *Establishing Instructional Goals.* Englewood Cliffs, N.J.: Prentice-Hall, 1970.

————. *Systematic Instruction.* Englewood Cliffs, N.J.: Prentice-Hall, 1970.

Pratt, David. *Curriculum: Design and Development.* New York: Harcourt, Brace, Jovanovich, 1980.

President's Commission on National Goals. *Goals for Americans: Programs for Action in the Sixties.* New York: The American Assembly, Columbia University, 1960.

Saylor, J. Galen, Alexander, William M., and Lewis, Arthur J. *Curriculum Planning for Better Teaching and Learning,* 4th ed. New York: Holt, Rinehart and Winston, 1981.

Saylor, J. Galen and Alexander, William M. *Planning Curriculum for Schools.* New York: Holt, Rinehart and Winston, 1974.

Tyler, Ralph W. *Basic Principles of Curriculum and Instruction.* Chicago: University of Chicago Press, 1949.

Wiles, Jon and Bondi, Joseph, *Curriculum Development: A Guide to Practice.* Columbus, Ohio: Charles E. Merrill, 1979.

FILMSTRIP-TAPE PROGRAMS

Vimcet Associates, P.O. Box 24714, Los Angeles, California 90024:

#1 *Educational Objectives,* 1967.

#3 *Selecting Appropriate Educational Objectives,* 1967.

#25 *Deciding on Defensible Goals via Educational Needs Assessment,* 1971.

9

Organizing and Implementing the Curriculum

After studying this chapter, you should be able to:
1. Describe and state strengths and weaknesses of the following plans for organizing the curriculum: open education and open space, nongraded schools, middle schools, flexible scheduling, comprehensive high schools, the activity curriculum, differentiated staffing/team teaching, and the core curriculum.
2. Relate each organizational arrangement discussed in this chapter to (a) the psychological and sociological circumstances of the public school and (b) the achievement of one or more aims of education or curriculum goals at each of the three school levels: elementary, junior/middle, and senior high.
3. Specify several curriculum goals for the elementary, junior high/middle school, or senior high school level; choose or design, and defend a curriculum organization plan that you believe will most satisfactorily result in accomplishing these goals.

You should also be able to formulate and give reasons for your views on the following issues:
1. The appropriateness and feasibility of each major organizational plan discussed in this chapter.
2. The relationship you believe should exist between school and curriculum organization and the needs of both learners and society.
3. The durability of the graded school and the subject matter curriculum.
4. The question of whether you see a need for reform in elementary or secondary education.

NECESSARY DECISIONS

A Hypothetical Setting

Imagine, if you will, a building complex of three schools — an elementary school of six grades plus kindergarten, a junior high school of three grades, and a senior high school of three grades — constructed in the early days of Franklin D. Roosevelt and situated on a twenty-block square tract of land. We could place this complex in a small town in any state where the three schools serve all the children of a particular school district. Or, we could locate it in a sector of a large urban area where the three schools are a part of the local school system.

Let's create in our own minds the administrative offices of the superintendent (or area superintendent) and school board across the street from this complex. From a second floor conference room we can look out on the children at play in the elementary school yard; we can see awkward teenyboppers of the junior high school up the street to our right; and we can observe the senior high school Harrys and Janes spinning out in their gasoline chariots from the parking lot in the background.

On a particular day in September a group of curriculum planners has gathered in the conference room. It is 4:00 p.m. and for a moment they stand at the window looking over the complex across the way. Activity at the elementary school has virtually ceased for the day, has just about tapered off at the junior high school, and continues apace at the senior high school. Only two cars remain in the elementary school parking lot — the principal's and the custodian's.

Making up the curriculum group are the district supervisor (director of curriculum) and the chairpersons of the district curriculum steering committee and the curriculum councils of each of the three schools. In front of them are in finished form, neatly typed and packaged, (1) the report of the needs assessment that revealed gaps in the school district's curricula, and (2) a set of both district and individual school curriculum goals and objectives that they laboriously hammered out with the help of many faculty members, students, administrators, supervisors, and lay citizens.

Hypothetical Steps

The task of this curriculum group now is to decide on next steps. What do they do with the curriculum goals and objectives now that they are finished? Shall they duplicate, distribute, and then forget them? Shall they take the position that the process of defining the goals and objectives was sufficient or should the process lead to further action? Shall they file the goals and objectives with the superintendent and principals to be pulled out on special occasions such as visits of parent groups, accrediting committees, or others? How shall they meet the discrepancies shown by the needs assessment and the curriculum goals and objectives developed as a result of that assessment?

The curriculum planners of the district, whose leadership is represented by this committee, must decide how to go about putting the goals and operations into effect and how to go about organizing the curriculum in such a way that the goals and objectives can be achieved. They must decide what structure will be the most conducive to successfully accomplishing the goals and objectives and to fulfilling learner needs. They must ask themselves and their cohorts how best to go about implementing the curriculum decisions that they have made up to this point.

Assessing Curriculum Organization

The question is often posed to curriculum workers: "How shall we go about organizing the curriculum?" The literature on curriculum organization often appears to make one of two assumptions: (1) curriculum planners regularly have the opportunity to initiate a curriculum in a brand new school (or perhaps in a deserted old school) for which no curriculum patterns yet exist or (2) curriculum developers automatically have the freedom to discard that which now exists and supplement it with patterns of their own choosing.

Both assumptions are likely to be erroneous. It is not an everyday occurrence for curriculum planners to be charged with the responsibility of developing an original curriculum for a brand new school (or more accurately, for an upcoming new school, since planning must precede construction). It is true, of course, that new schools are built to meet growths and shifts in population and to replace decrepit structures, which, like old soldiers, slowly fade away. The development of a curriculum for a brand new school does provide an opportunity for curriculum planning from the ground floor, so to speak. But even that planning must be carried out within certain parameters, including local traditions, state and district mandates, and the curricula of other schools of the district. The programs of the new school must be compatible with others in the district.

It is also unlikely that curriculum planners can simply substitute as they wish new patterns of curriculum organization for old. Again we face certain parameters: student needs, teacher preferences, administrators' values, community sentiment, physical restrictions, and financial resources.

Our fictitious curriculum group is talking about possible ways of reorganizing the curriculum to meet pupil needs and to provide the best possible structure for attaining the district's and each school's curriculum goals and objectives. The group decides that one way of approaching this task is to consider the schools' past, present, and future ideas for curriculum organization. They will identify patterns that have been tried and those that might be feasible or successful in the immediate and distant future.

The committee decides to clarify at this meeting what they mean by curriculum organization. They agree to talk with their colleagues on their schools' curriculum councils and others and come to the next meeting of this group prepared to trace the historical development of the curricular organizations of the three schools. Each will provide an overview of the more significant patterns of curriculum organization that have been studied and implemented, studied and rejected, and considered for future implementation.

Before adjourning this meeting, the committee agrees as to what they will include under the rubric of curriculum organization. They define curriculum organization as those patterns of both a curricular and administrative nature by which learners are confronted with the subject matter. Thus, it includes not only broad plans for programmatic offerings, such as the subject matter curriculum, but also delivery systems, which possess an administrative dimension, such as team teaching.

Several weeks later when the committee reassembles, exhilarated by its research on the history of curriculum developments in their schools, it expresses a newfound admiration for previous curriculum planners. Whereas the aging facades of the buildings might convey to the outside world that "the more things change, the more they stay the same," inside, innovation and change have been key words. The committee spends several sessions sharing its discoveries and studying what the experts say about the structures it uncovered. The committee is sure that by examining past patterns, projecting future arrangements, and comparing both past practices and future possibilities with present structures, it can come up with more effective ways of implementing the curriculum.

This hypothetical committee's discoveries are significant enough to be shared with you. Since the experience of this one curriculum group is symbolic of what has taken place in American education in general, we will generalize its findings.

Our discussion will be organized into three major parts: the past (Where We Have Been), the present (Where We Are), and the future (Where We Are Going). For each period we describe some major plans in school and curriculum organization at each of three levels: elementary, junior high/middle school, and senior high school.

Remember that axiom 3 in Chapter 2 postulates that changes do not, as a rule, start and stop abruptly but overlap. Axiom 3 applies to our hypothetical community as it does elsewhere. Consequently, when we discuss the graded school, for example, as a place where we have been, we do not imply that it has necessarily disappeared from the present or that it will not exist in the future.

We are aware that curricular arrangements are not always confined to one level. The subject matter curriculum, the graded school, the nongraded school, team teaching, and flexible scheduling exist or have existed at more than one level. By placing a curricular arrangement at a particular level, we are not saying that it could not be found or could not have been found either at the same time or at another time at other levels even in the hypothetical community we use for illustrative purposes. You would tire, however, if, for example, we repeated a discussion of the subject matter curriculum at each of the three levels. Therefore, I have placed the arrangements, perhaps arbitrarily, at levels where the arrangements were particularly strong, significant, or common. Unless a curricular arrangement had particular significance for more than one level and possessed distinctive characteristics for each level, as in the case of the nongraded elementary school and the nongraded high school, a particular plan is discussed at only one level.

WHERE WE HAVE BEEN

THE ELEMENTARY SCHOOL

The Graded School

Historians tell us that the concept of the graded school started in Prussia, a land famed for discipline and regimentation, and migrated across the ocean to the New World.[1] The Quincy Grammar School of Boston, which opened in 1848, is credited as the first school in the United States to become completely graded. With enough youngsters for several groups, it took not a quantum leap but a simple bit of ingenuity to reason that youngsters might be taught more efficiently if they were sorted and graded. Instead of being mixed, they could be divided largely on the basis of chronological age.

The graded school has become the standard model not only for the United States but for the world. As our country steadily grew in population, expanded westward, and became industrialized, the number of grades provided for children by the numerous school districts of the nation increased in proportion.

By the early twentieth century twelve grades were made available and were considered as sufficient education for most American boys and girls. School systems grew, providing the opportunity for young people to receive not ten, nor eleven, but twelve full years of education at public expense. For one reason or another many children and youth in early days and to a decreasing extent today have not been able to complete the twelve grades of elementary and secondary education even in communities that offer twelve grades. We could add in passing that both public and private community junior colleges and senior institutions have been established to offer youth opportunities for further learning, but that's another story in itself.

Twelve Years As Norm. Administrators, curriculum experts, teachers, and the public have accepted the twelve years as a norm for most of our young people and have adjusted the component levels as the situation seemed to demand. Thus, until rather recently the most common organizational plan for schools across the country was the eight-four plan (eight years of elementary school and four of secondary school). Under this plan grades seven and eight were considered as parts of the elementary rather than the secondary school.

---

[1] William J. Shearer, *The Grading of Schools* (New York: H. P. Smith Publishing Company, 1898).

As the junior high school began to emerge after the first decade of the twentieth century, the six-two-four plan (six elementary, two junior high, and four senior high grades) offered a variant to the eight-four.

Communities of moderate size showed a fondness for the six-six plan (six elementary, six secondary), which, although clearly attaching junior high school to secondary education, also buries its identity in that of the senior high school. Larger communities expressed a preference for the six-three-three plan with three years of junior high school between the elementary and senior high school. The three-year junior high school combining grades seven, eight, and nine replicated the structure of the first junior high schools that came into existence in 1910 in Berkeley, California and Columbus, Ohio. Other variations have been suggested such as the six-three-five plan and the six-three-three-two plan, which would extend public secondary education through grades thirteen and fourteen. But those last two years have clearly become identified with college age. As it is, grades eleven and twelve are normally beyond the age of sixteen, the usual limit for compulsory school attendance. The rearrangement of the twelve years of public schooling has continued to the present, as we shall see later when we discuss the development of the middle school.

The concomitant outgrowth of the graded school was the self-contained classroom — a heterogeneous group of youngsters of approximately the same age, in multiples of twenty-five to thirty-five, under the direction of one teacher. Primary school teachers of the graded school were no longer required to master all disciplines of all grades like their counterparts in the one-room school but only to master all disciplines at the particular grade level. The group of children assigned to a teacher in a self-contained, graded elementary school spent the entire day under the watchful eye of that teacher. It has taken militant action of teacher organizations in recent years to pry loose some breathing time for elementary school teachers during the school day.

The concept of the graded school, aided by the measurement movement in education, has firmly established the principle that certain learnings should be accomplished by pupils not at certain general periods of growth and development but by the end of certain grade levels. Syllabi, courses of study, and, lately, minimal competencies have been determined for each grade level. In the graded school material is tailored to fit the confines of fixed times during the customary ten months of the school year. Thus, by means of a standardized test of reading, for example, we can state that a third grade child in April (the eighth month of the school year) whose test score placed him or her at the grade norm of 3.2 (second month of the third grade year) was reading at a level six months below the norm for that grade.

When we speak of the self-contained classroom, we normally think of the elementary school. We sometimes forget that the self-contained classroom has been the prevailing pattern in the secondary school except for a brief period when core programs — discussed later — were popular.

Like the junior and senior high school, the elementary school adopted an organizational framework that stressed the mastery of subject matter. This framework, commonly referred to as the subject matter curriculum, will be examined shortly.

Typical Schedule. A typical week in a self-contained, subject-oriented elementary school calls for separate subjects scheduled at specific and regular times during the day. Little or no effort is made to integrate these diverse areas. Some elementary schools, of course, have never departed from this model whereas others departed for a time and then swung back in recent years.

In the late 1920s, through the 1930s, and into the 1940s, many elementary schools, warmed by the glow of the progressive movement that championed the child over subject matter, abandoned the subject matter curriculum for the activity or experience curriculum.

The Activity Curriculum

The activity (or experience) curriculum was an attempt by educators to break away from the rigidity of the graded school. It is of historical interest that the activity curriculum was a contribution of two of the better known laboratory schools — the Laboratory School founded by John Dewey at the University of Chicago and the University Elementary School directed by J. L. Meriam at the University of Missouri. The activity curriculum came about as an effort to translate progressive beliefs into the curriculum. As such, it captured the imaginations of elementary school educators in the first quarter of the twentieth century.

Disenchanted with the subject matter curriculum promoted by the essentialist philosophers and curriculum makers, Dewey and others sought to free the learner from the confines of a subject-centered curriculum and to create an environment that catered to learner needs and interests.

Human Impulses. Smith, Stanley, and Shores observed that Dewey's Laboratory School curriculum was based on the following four human impulses, which Dewey referred to as "uninvested capital:"

> . . . the *social impulse,* which is shown in the child's desire to share his experiences with the people around him; the *constructive impulse,* which is manifested at first in play, in rhythmic movement, in make-believe, and then in more advanced form in the shaping of raw materials into useful objects; the *impulse to investigate and experiment,* to find out things, as revealed in the tendency of the child to do things just to see what will happen; and the *expressive or artistic impulse,* which seems to be a refinement and further expression of the communicative and constructive interests.[2]

---

[2] B. Othanel Smith, William O. Stanley, and J. Harlan Shores, *Fundamentals of Curriculum Development,* rev. ed. (New York: Harcourt, Brace, Jovanovich, 1957), p. 265.

Dewey's curriculum eschewed the usual subjects and focused on occupations in which all men and women engaged — carpentry, cooking, and sewing.

Human Activities. The University Elementary School at the University of Missouri followed principles advocated by Junius L. Meriam and structured its program not around subjects but around human activities of observation, play, stories, and handwork.[3] The California State Curriculum Commission outlined a daily program for an activity curriculum as shown in Table 9-1. As these two examples reveal, the content of the activity curriculum is centered around projects or experiences that are of immediate interest to the learners. The various subjects, including the basic skills, are used as a means of promoting learning rather than as ends or centers of learning for themselves.

Subject Matter From Child's World. Here the curriculum is developed by the teacher in cooperation with the pupils. The subject matter evolves from the child's world rather than from the adult world. Whereas the teacher can suggest activities or problems to the learners, the children's interests become the dominant factor. William H. Kilpatrick advocated pupil activities that he referred to as projects (ergo, the "project method") and took the position that the child should do his or her own thinking and planning.

Problem-solving — Dewey's "reflective thinking" — is the instructional method par excellence. Experience in the process of problem-solving is perceived by those who espouse progressive thought as more important than attaining the solutions to the problems. A great effort is made to integrate subject matter, using any and all content as needed without regard to discipline boundaries for the solution of problems or carrying out of projects.

By its very nature, the activity curriculum cannot be fully planned in advance. Consequently, the activity curriculum can be described only after it has been completed, for the teacher cannot be sure in advance where the interests of the students will lead them.

The unit method of organizing instruction (a unit of work centered around a single topic or problem) lends itself well to the goal of problem-solving. Units are designed by the teacher in cooperation with the pupils to include a sufficient variety of activities to provide for individual differences among pupils. A series of units can provide a skeletal framework for a given grade level.

Drill, if needed, is carried out in meaningful terms, not in isolated rote fashion. With the social orientation of the progressivists, the activity curriculum calls for the socialization of the learners and the use of the community as a learning laboratory.

Scheduling is flexible with time allotments variable depending on the activities under way. Pupils are grouped according to interests and abilities,

---

[3] See Junius L. Meriam, *Child Life and the Curriculum* (Yonkers, New York: World Book Company, 1920), p. 382.

TABLE 9-1 Schedule for an activity curriculum

TIME	ACTIVITIES
9:00	(Monday through Friday) Informal greetings, reports, observations, rhymes, music, events of current interest, informal activities designed to create a mental set conducive to a happy, profitable day.
9:15	*Arithmetical Enterprises* (Monday through Friday) Playstores, banking activities, handling of school supplies, etc. Although rich in arithmetical content through which the child is trained in skills and abilities, such units also yield abundantly in group and individual situations which develop initiative, responsibility, and co-operation. The flexible period provides opportunity for individual instruction.
10:00	*Healthful Living Enterprises* (Monday through Friday) Physical education enterprises, free play, the nutrition program, and adequate relief periods are provided for daily; units of work such as: "the study of milk," "a balanced meal," etc., provide enterprises which have heathful living as a center of interest but provide situations developmental of social and civic attitudes as well.
10:50	*Language Arts* (Monday through Friday) Oral and written composition, spelling and writing develop from activities rich in opportunities for expression, as the writing of a play to be presented in the auditorium period, puppet shows, the school newspaper, etc. The period should provide opportunity for literary discrimination and original expression; the long period provides for concentration of effort and attention according to individual interest and need.
12:00	(Monday through Friday) Lunch, rest and directed playground activities.

obviating the need for fixed grade levels. Some schools have tossed out marks, report cards, and the assumption that certain learnings have to be mastered at each grade level.

The teacher of the activity curriculum finds his or her role not as subject matter specialist and expert-in-residence but rather as a guide and facilitator of learning. Key concepts that the progressivists wove into the activity curriculum are the active rather than passive role of the learner and the sharing of students' experiences with the teacher and each other.

The activity curriculum, like progressive education itself, left its indelible imprint on American education. Flexible scheduling, unit teaching, problem solving, project method, nongraded schools, and open education owe a debt to the activity curriculum. Nevertheless, the activity curriculum lost popularity

TABLE 9-1 continued

TIME	ACTIVITIES

1:00   *Avocational Activities*

(Monday)
Music; activities, music appreciation, rhythm, harmonica, band, orchestra, etc.

(Tuesday)
Nature Club, school museum, aquarium, gardens, terrarium.

(Friday)
Civics Club committees responsible for various phases of school life.

(Wednesday)
Creative art and constructive activities in pottery, weaving, painting, drawing.

(Thursday)
Use of auditorium for music, dancing, dramatics, projects, stagecraft, related to class activities.

1:50   (Monday through Friday) Recreation and rest.

2:00   *Reading Groups: Library Activities*
(Monday through Friday) Group organization on the basis of reading ability provides opportunity for remedial work with children having reading deficiencies and library guidance to superior readers. The quiet reading period may contribute to the development of information needed in the class activities related to social science, avocational, or health or other interests.

2:50   (Monday through Friday) Recreation and rest.

3:00
(Monday)
Social studies activities

(Tuesday)
Social studies activities

(Wednesday)
Free creative work period

(Thursday)
Social studies activities

(Friday)
Shop enterprises

Source: Ruth Manning Hockett, ed., *Teachers' Guide to Child Development: Manual for Kindergarten and Primary Teachers* (Sacramento, Calif.: California Department of Education, 1930), pp. 355–356. Reprinted by permission.

and died out as a viable organizational pattern for the public elementary school. There are many reasons for its demise.

With the activity curriculum the needs of society and the needs of the adult world took a back seat to the needs of immature youngsters. Progressive, i.e., activity-oriented schools, projected an unfavorable image to the public who felt that subject matter learning was being neglected and too much stress was being placed on the immediate interests of immature learners.

Excesses on the part of some progressive schools led to cynical jokes like the following:

The teacher asks: Is the earth round or flat?
The pupil answers: I don't know. Let's vote on it.

Or, during a unit on redbirds the primary school teacher used every device possible to work redbirds into English, science, mathematics, social studies, etc. At the end of a hard day something struck the outside of the classroom window. The teacher, startled asked, "What was that?" A pupil in the back responded, "Aw, it was just that damn redbird." Or, a classic put-down of the progressive school: The teacher enters the room in the morning and asks the class, "O.K., kids, what do you want to learn today?" and the children complain, "Do we have to do what we want to do today?"

It was not commonly understood that teachers of the activity curriculum had to be more knowledgeable and better trained not only in subject matter but also in techniques of guiding learning. The activity curriculum also required for its success resources and facilities that exceeded those of the typical elementary school. Further, more flexible administrators and teachers were needed for successful operation of a program of this type. The secondary schools also complained when receiving products of the activity curriculum with a great range of knowledge and skills and glaring gaps in their education.

The Nongraded Elementary School

The nongraded elementary school, following plans that permit continuous progress, evolved as an alternative to the graded school. The nongraded or continuous progress school was a reaction to increasing rigidity of the graded school, which was an innovation designed to provide a more efficient education for children.

Persons unfamiliar with the concept of the nongraded school are sometimes confused by the term and interpret it to signify a school without a formal marking system. When we speak of the nongraded school, we refer to schools that have abandoned grade level designations rather than marks.

In a nongraded school typical grade levels and standards for those levels are absent. Children are grouped for instruction according to their particular needs and progress through the program at their own speed. Effort is made to individualize, some say personalize, instruction. The nongraded concept has made its greatest headway at the elementary school level. However, as we shall see when we discuss developments in secondary education later in this chapter, nongradedness is possible in the high school as well.

John I. Goodlad and Robert H. Anderson, proponents of the nongraded elementary school, saw nongradedness as a reaction to the Procrustean bed of the graded school.[4] "The realities of child development defy the rigorous ordering of children's abilities and attainments into conventional graded structures," observed Goodlad and Anderson.[5]

[4] John I. Goodlad and Robert H. Anderson, *The Nongraded Elementary School,* rev. ed. (New York: Harcourt, Brace, Jovanovich, 1963), p. 1.

[5] Goodlad and Anderson, p.3.

Herbert I. Von Haden and Jean Marie King explained some of the principles underlying the nongraded school in the following way:

> Nongrading is a philosophy of teaching and learning which recognizes that children learn at different rates and in different ways and allows them to progress as individuals rather than classes. Such designations as grade one or grade three are eliminated. Flexible groupings allow the pupil to proceed from one level of work to another whenever he is ready. Thus, the child's progress is not dependent upon that of others in the room. His own readiness, interest, and capacity set the pace for each pupil. . . . Flexible grouping permits each child to move ahead with other children of approximately the same level of ability. Groupings are different for each subject area and can be changed at any time. Failure, retention, and skipping of grades are replaced by continuous progress as the pupil proceeds at his own rate. Slower children are not forced to go on with the class group before they are ready. Faster workers are not compelled to wait for the others. Individualization and continuous progress are the key elements of nongrading.[6]

Growth of Nongraded Schools. The nongraded movement began in earnest in the 1930s, grew in intensity through the 1940s and 1950s, and leveled off in the 1960s. Among the nongraded schools of the thirties and forties were those in Western Springs, Illinois; Richmond, Virginia; Athens, Georgia; Youngstown, Ohio; and Milwaukee, Wisconsin.[7] In the 1950s and 1960s nongraded schools were started in Bellevue, Washington; Appleton, Wisconsin; Chicago, Illinois; and Southern Humboldt Unified School District, California.[8]

School personnel of Appleton, Wisconsin, compared the graded school with the continuous progress school, as shown in Table 9-2. The nongraded school seeks to eliminate failure and retention by permitting children to proceed through the program at their own pace. Programs of the nongraded school are organized primarily around reading levels and to a lesser extent around mathematics levels rather than around the traditional chronological age-grade levels.

Reading is used as the nucleus for grouping of youngsters in the nongraded school. Hillson explained:

> The present-day nongraded elementary schools, for the most part, rely on levels of accomplishment in reading as the bases for advancement and assignment in a program of vertical progression through the six years of the elementary school organization. Current nongraded plans, with some

---

[6] Herbert I. Von Haden and Jean Marie King, *Educational Innovator's Guide* (Worthington, Ohio: Charles A. Jones, 1974), pp. 30–31.

[7] Von Haden and King, p. 33. See also p. 38 for list of schools where nongraded plans were tried.

[8] David W. Beggs III and Edward G. Buffie, eds., *Nongraded Schools in Action: Bold New Venture* (Bloomington, Ind.: Indiana University Press, 1967).

TABLE 9-2 Comparison of the graded and continuous progress schools

GRADED STRUCTURE	CONTINUOUS PROGRESS
1. It is assumed that all children of the same chronological age will develop to the same extent in a given period of time.	1. It is assumed that each child has his own pattern and rate of growth and that children of the same age will vary greatly in their ability and rate of growth.
2. A child who does not measure up to certain predetermined standards of what should be accomplished in nine months is called a failure.	2. No child is ever considered a failure. If he does not achieve in proportion to his ability, we study the cause and adjust his program to fit his needs and problems.
3. If a child fails, he is required to repeat the grade in which he did not meet the standards.	3. A child never repeats. He may progress more slowly than others in the group, but individual records of progress make it possible to keep his growth continuous.
4. A decision as to grade placement must be made after each nine months.	4. Decisions as to group placement can be made at any time during the three-year period (for social or emotional adjustment, an additional year if needed, etc.).
5. Grade placements are based too largely upon academic achievement.	5. Group placement is flexible, based upon physical, mental, social, and emotional maturity.
6. Fixed standards of achievement within a set time put pressures upon teachers and children which cause emotional tensions and inhibit learning.	6. Elimination of pressures produces a relaxed learning situation conducive to good mental health.

Source: Royce E. Kurtz and James N. Reston, "Continuous Progress in Appleton, Wisconsin," in David W. Beggs III and Edward G. Buffie, eds., *Nongraded Schools in Action: Bold New Venture* (Bloomington, Ind.: Indiana University Press, 1967), p. 139. Reprinted by permission.

rare but exciting departures, accept the format of an attempted homogeneous grouping based on factors attendant to reading achievement.[9]

To form reading groups attention is paid to many factors, including intelligence, achievement, motivation, readiness, and maturity.

Hillson elaborated on the salient features of nongraded plans:

Briefly, then, many of the present nongraded schools are ones in which grades are replaced by levels which a child accomplishes at his own speed.

---

[9] Maurie H. Hillson, "The Nongraded School: A Dynamic Concept," in Beggs and Buffie, p. 34.

No grade designators are used. These levels of experience are clearly described and without the fear of retention or, conversely, without the fear of encroachment upon material reserved for a next higher grade, the child progresses through them as competency is achieved. . . . The rapid learner may accomplish a three-year nongraded program in two years. . . . The slow learner may take four years to accomplish three.[10]

Problems Encountered. Nongraded plans encountered problems that led to a tapering off in their popularity. Nongraded programs are much more complex than the traditional, graded organization. They require continuous flexibility, more time by the faculty, greater resources, and a style of teaching different from that in typical graded schools. Careful diagnosis must be made of the learners' needs.

Nongraded schools could become as inflexible as the graded school if teachers and administrators merely substituted reading levels for chronological grades. Continuous progress plans concentrated to a great degree on reading and to a much lesser degree on mathematics, generally leaving the other subjects in the curriculum much as they were before — traditionally organized without well-planned sequencing of levels.

Nongraded plans excelled in vertical organization of the reading curriculum and sometimes the mathematics curriculum but failed to work out relationships at any level among the various disciplines. Further, the transition from a continuous progress elementary school to a graded junior high school could be rather abrupt for the learners when the junior high school was less concerned with personalized learning.

Tanner and Tanner spoke of the shortcomings of the nongraded school as follows:

> Although the proponents of nongrading claimed that it provided for pupil differences and fostered a longitudinal concept of curriculum, or vertical curriculum articulation, the nongraded approach presented its own difficulties. For example, many nongraded schools had replaced the so-called graded lockstep with mechanical criteria for establishing the level of pupil placement in their studies, namely, standardized achievement test scores. Moreover, although it was claimed that the nongraded approach allowed for greater attention being given to vertical curriculum articulation, it also tended to mitigate against horizontal curriculum articulation or the interrelationships between the various studies that constitute the total curriculum.
>
> Finally, the claim that nongraded arrangements provide for superior pupil achievement over graded patterns has not been substantiated by research.[11]

---

10 Hillson, p. 45.
11 Daniel Tanner and Laurel N. Tanner, *Curriculum Development: Theory Into Practice,* 2d ed. (New York: Macmillan, 1980), p. 453.

THE JUNIOR HIGH SCHOOL

The School in the Middle

Ever since its inception the junior high school has been an institution in search of an identity. Today, the junior high school normally consists of grades seven, eight, and nine. Grade nine has always held a precarious position. It is both the first year of the senior high school and the last year of the junior high school. Grades seven and eight have also had a waiflike existence, appended, as already noted, to either the elementary or secondary school.

Educators' perceptions of the role of the junior high school have varied considerably. Is it an upward projection of the elementary school? Is it a downward extension of the senior high school? Is its purpose primarily exploratory, serving learners in a transition period between puberty and adolescence, or is it a preparatory school for the senior high? Should it be housed in the same building with the senior high school or located in a separate building? The mission of this level of schooling is still changing as the newer organizational and curricular patterns of many middle schools reveal.

The subject matter curriculum, discussed more fully in the senior high school section, has been the dominant pattern in elementary, junior high, and senior high programs. Proponents of essentialism have urged both the junior high and senior high schools to give their curricula a strong academic orientation.

Conant's Recommendations. In Chapter 6 we discussed the studies of the junior and senior high school conducted by James B. Conant. Since Conant's recommendations were so favorably received, we should be remiss not to examine some and to discern their nature. Among Conant's fourteen recommendations for the junior high school are:[12]

> REQUIRED SUBJECTS FOR ALL PUPILS IN GRADES 7 AND 8.
> The following subjects should be required of all pupils in grades 7 and 8: English (including heavy emphasis on reading skills and composition), social studies (including emphasis on history and geography), mathematics (arithmetic except as noted . . .) and science.
>
> In addition, all pupils should receive instruction in art, music, and physical education. All girls should receive instruction in home economics and all boys instruction in industrial arts. . . .
>
> NEW DEVELOPMENTS IN MATHEMATICS AND FOREIGN LANGUAGES.
> A small fraction of pupils should start algebra (or one of the new brands of mathematics) in grade 8. Some, if not all, pupils should start the study

---

[12] Conant, *Recommendations for Education in the Junior High School Years* (Princeton, N.J.: Educational Testing Service, 1960). It should be observed that Conant's recommendations regarding home economics and industrial arts are of 1960 vintage.

of a modern foreign language on a conversational basis with a bilingual teacher in grade 7.

BASIC SKILLS.

Instruction in the basic skills begun in the elementary school should be continued as long as pupils can gain from the instruction. This statement applies particularly to reading and arithmetic. Pupils with average ability should read at or above grade level; superior pupils considerably above grade level. By the end of grade 9 even the poorest readers (except the mentally retarded) should read at least at the sixth-grade level.

BLOCK-TIME AND DEPARTMENTALIZATION.

Provisions should be made to assure a smooth transition for the young adolescent from the elementary to the secondary school.

FLEXIBILITY IN SCHEDULE.

The daily class schedule should be sufficiently flexible to avoid the necessity for pupils to make choices between, for example, science and foreign languages.

PROGRAM IN GRADE 9.

In the ninth grade, the curriculum should provide for the usual sequential elective program as well as the continuation of the required courses in general education.

COORDINATION OF SUBJECT-MATTER INSTRUCTION.

Whatever the organization of a school system, there should be careful coordination in each one of the subject areas in grades K–12.

Many schools reviewed, reaffirmed, or modified their curricula in light of the Conant recommendations and our hypothetical junior high school was no exception.

ASCD Proposals. At about the same time Conant was recommending increased emphasis on the academics, the Commission on the Education of Adolescents of the Association for Supervision and Curriculum Development (ASCD) was presenting a different point of view on the function and programs of the junior high school.[13] Writing for the ASCD, Jean D. Grambs and others, acknowledging that the junior high school was under pressure, advocated variations in lengths of class periods, programs planned explicitly for the junior high school years, ungraded programs, and a block-of-time program offered each year for the three years of junior high school. As we will see, a block-of-time program usually runs for two or three hours of a school day.

Whereas Conant's proposals for the school in the middle were more subject-centered, the ASCD proposals were more learner-centered. However, proponents of both points of view agree on the necessity for adequate facilities

13 Jean D. Grambs, Clarence G. Noyce, Franklin Patterson, and John Robertson, *The Junior High School We Need* (Alexandria, Va.: Association for Supervision and Curriculum Development, 1961).

and resources, a professionally trained staff, a moderate and manageable size of school, and ample guidance.

The Core Curriculum

Basic education, common learnings, core curriculum, and general education are terms, like goals and objectives, that are tossed about rather loosely in the profession. These terms are used by educators to describe programs that are almost at opposite poles. To some, basic education, common learnings, and general education signal a set of courses or subjects that are required of all students — the earmark of the subject matter curriculum, grounded in essentialistic philosophy. In this vein, the Harvard Committee stated its interpretation of general education:

> Clearly, general education has somewhat the meaning of liberal education [p. 52]. . . . General education, we repeat, must consciously aim at these abilities: at effective thinking, communication, the making of relevant judgments, and the discrimination of values [p. 72]. . . . It therefore remains only to draw the scheme of general education that follows from these premises. At the center of it . . . would be the three inevitable areas of man's life and knowledge . . . : the physical world, man's corporate life, his inner visions and standards [p. 98]. . . . In school, in our opinion, general education in these three areas should form a continuing core for all. taking up at least half a student's time [p. 99]. . . . Accepting the course-unit system as established, at least for the present, despite its grave weaknesses dwelt on earlier, that would amount to some eight units, preferably spaced by means of half-courses over the four years of school rather than compressed into two or three. The common and desirable division within these eight units would probably be three in English, three in science and mathematics, and two in the social studies. But — and this is the important point — this half of the schoolwork to be spent on general education would seem the barest minimum, either for those not going on to college or for those who are [p. 100].[14]

James B. Conant, President of Harvard University at the time the Harvard Committee issued its report, took a similar position when he recommended general education programs consisting of required courses at both the junior and senior high school levels.

At the other end of the spectrum, from the camps of the pragmatic and reconstructionist philosophers, come those who hold a quite different conception of general education. They frequently refer to their plans for common learnings or general education as a "core curriculum." Unlike the "continuing core for all" recommended by the Harvard Committee, the core curriculum at its inception was a radically new departure in curriculum organization.

---

[14] Harvard Committee, *General Education in a Free Society* (Cambridge, Mass.: Harvard University Press, 1945), pp. 52–100.

John H. Lounsbury and Gordon F. Vars noted that many curriculum specialists regarded core as a truly innovative development.[15]

What is the core curriculum? Lounsbury and Vars defined core — short for core curriculum — as follows:

> Specifically, core is a form of curriculum organization, usually operating within an extended block of time in the daily schedule, in which learning experiences are focused directly on problems of significance to students.[16]

Unification of Subject Matter. The core curriculum gained momentum in the 1930s and 1940s but its roots go back to the nineteenth century. In a presentation made by Emerson E. White to the National Department of Superintendents in 1896, White discussed one of the basic principles of core: the unification of subject matter.

> Complete unification is the blending of all subjects and branches of study into one whole, and the teaching of the same in successive groups or lessons or sections. When this union is effected by making one group or branch of study in the course the center or core, and subordinating all other subjects to it, the process is properly called the concentration of studies.[17]

Smith, Stanley, and Shores credited Ziller, founder of the Herbartian school at the University of Leipzig and Colonel Francis W. Parker, Superintendent of Schools, Quincy, Massachusetts, in 1875 and later principal of the Cook County (Chicago) Normal School as proponents of the principle of unification of subject matter.[18]

The core concept received a significant boost in the 1930s when the curriculum committees of a number of states sought to plan a curriculum around social functions of living and turned for assistance to Hollis L. Caswell, then of George Peabody College for Teachers and later of Teachers College, Columbia University. The Virginia State Curriculum Program pioneered in establishing the core curriculum — the content of which centered on societal functions.[19]

The core curriculum is in philosophy and intent the secondary school counterpart of the activity curriculum of the elementary school. Espoused

---

[15] See John H. Lounsbury and Gordon F. Vars, *A Curriculum for the Middle School Years* (New York: Harper & Row, 1978), p. 57.

[16] Lounsbury and Vars, p. 56.

[17] Emerson E. White, "Isolation and Unification as Bases of Courses of Study," *Second Yearbook of the National Herbart Society for the Scientific Study of Teaching* (now the National Society for the Study of Education) (Bloomington, Ill.: Pantograph Printing and Stationery Co., 1896), pp. 12–13.

[18] Smith, Stanley, and Shores, pp. 312–313.

[19] State of Virginia, *Tentative Course of Study for the Core Curriculum of Virginia Secondary Schools* (Richmond, Va.: State Board of Education, 1934).

as a concept for both the junior and senior high schools, the core curriculum made its greatest inroads at the junior high school level. The core concept was especially popular in the state of Maryland. Yet, Lounsbury and Vars pointed out that core, like many programs which are different, did not meet with universal acceptance even at the junior high school level.[20]

Characteristics of Core. While varying in structure and focus, core curricula, as described in this chapter, possess the following characteristics:

1. They constitute a portion of the curriculum that is required for all students.
2. They unify or fuse subject matter, usually English and social studies.
3. Their content centers around problems that cut across the disciplines; the primary method of learning is problem-solving, using all applicable subject matter.
4. They are organized into blocks of time, usually two to three periods under a "core" teacher and with possible use of additional teachers and others as resource persons.
5. They encourage teachers to plan with students.
6. They provide pupil guidance.

Types of Core. Harold B. Alberty and Elsie J. Alberty distinguished five types of core.[21] The first two are core in the Harvard Committee's use of the term — subjects required of all — and as such fall into the classification of the subject matter curriculum. Alberty and Alberty classified types of core as follows:

Type 1: Separate subjects are taught separately with little or no effort to relate them to each other.

Type 2: Two or more subjects are correlated. Although subjects remain discrete and are taught separately, effort is made to relate one to the other. The history teacher, for example, may work with the English teacher to show students relationships between topics which they happen to be studying in the two courses.

Type 3: Two or more subjects are fused. The majority of core programs in schools fall into this classification. English and social studies are fused or integrated and scheduled in a block of time, usually two to three periods. Not a complete departure from traditional subject matter organization, this type of core organizes content around contemporary social problems or around historic or cultural epochs. Several experimental schools of the Eight-

---

[20] Lounsbury and Vars, p. 57.

[21] Harold B. Alberty and Elsie J. Alberty, *Reorganizing the High-School Curriculum,* 3rd ed. (New York: Macmillan, 1962), pp. 199–233. It is of interest to note that in previous editions Alberty and Alberty distinguished six types of core. They included a type of correlation related to Type 2, in which teachers of separate courses agreed on a joint theme to be taught in their respective courses.

Year Study of the Progressive Education Association used Types 2 and 3 cores.[22]

Type 4: A block of time is established to study adolescent and/or social problems, such as school living, family life, economic problems, communication, multicultural relationships, health, international problems, conservation, and understanding the self. This type of core requires a complete departure from the typical subject matter curriculum and a thorough reorganization of the curriculum.

Type 5: Teacher-student planned activities are developed without regard to formal structure. Teachers and students are free to pursue whatever interests or problem areas they desire. This core program resembles the unstructured experience curriculum of the elementary school.

Core curricula tend to consume a block of time consisting of two to three periods of the school day. The remaining periods are devoted to specialized interests of students. "Block-time classes" is a term sometimes equated with "core." However, they may or may not be core classes.[23] They may simply be subjects scheduled in a block of time but taught separately, as in the cases of Types 1 and 2 of the Alberty and Alberty classification. Block-time classes can be core classes, however, if they meet the characteristics of a core as just outlined.

Reporting on a survey of block-time classes and core programs in junior high schools, Grace S. Wright listed four types of programs in block-time classes as follows:[24]

> *Type A* — Each subject retains its identity in the block-time class, that is, separate subjects are taught (1) with consciously planned correlation, (2) with no planned correlation.
>
> *Type B* — Subjects included in the block-time class are unified or fused around a central theme or units of work or problems stemming from one or more of the subject fields in the block-time class.
>
> *Type C* — Predetermined problem areas based upon the personal-social needs of adolescents — both needs that adolescents themselves have identified and needs as society sees them determine the scope of the core program. Subject matter is brought in as needed in working on the problems. Pupils may or may not have a choice from among several of these problem areas; they will, however, have some responsibility for suggesting and choosing activities in developing units of study.
>
> *Type D* — The scope of the core program is not predetermined. Pupils

---

[22] See Wilford M. Aikin, *The Story of the Eight-Year Study* (New York: Harper & Row, 1942).

[23] See William Van Til, Gordon F. Vars, and John H. Lounsbury, *Modern Education for the Junior High School Years,* 2d ed. (Indianapolis: Bobbs-Merrill, 1967), pp. 181–182.

[24] Grace S. Wright, *Block-Time Classes and the Core Program in the Junior High School,* Bulletin No. 6, 1958 (Washington, D.C.: U.S. Office of Education, 1958), p. 9.

and teacher are free to select the problems upon which they wish to work. Subject matter content is brought in as needed to develop or to help solve the problems.

Note the points of agreement between the Wright and the Alberty and Alberty classifications.

Illustrative Schedule.[25] The organizational plan of the core and its relationship to other subject areas are illustrated by the plan for grades seven through twelve at the P. K. Yonge Laboratory School in Gainesville, Florida (see Figure 9-1). In a six-period day a block of four periods is devoted to core in the seventh grade, three periods in the eighth, and two periods each succeeding year.

Although core programs may still be found, particularly in junior high schools, they have declined in popularity. They have never been fully understood by the public "What is core?" asks the average citizen. What does an "A" in core mean to parents, to college admissions officers? Informed persons will admit that the ripples caused by the Eight-Year Study, which allowed for innovative plans like the core, generally lost their force, and colleges went back to demanding high school credit in subjects they understood.

Core teaching is a demanding task requiring skills that take special training. Teachers' colleges, by and large, neglected the preparation of core teachers. The perceived threat from the Russians in 1957 renewed demand for the "hard" subjects — science, mathematics, and foreign language — and brought about a reaction to unusual programs like core.

Conant, who commanded a considerable audience, was less than ecstatic with core. He recommended that core be limited to a block of time (two to three periods) in grade seven only. Even in that block of time Conant took the position that instruction need not be integrated. Said Conant:

> To my mind, there should be a block of time set aside, at least in grade 7, in which one teacher has the same pupils for two or more periods, generally in English and social studies. Otherwise, grades 7, 8, and 9 should be departmentalized; that is to say, pupils should have specialist teachers in each of the subject-matter fields. . . . The block-time teaching I am discussing need not break down subject-matter lines.[26]

Tanner and Tanner assessed the core curriculum, observing:

> The core idea never gained the widespread acceptance that was expected of it by progressive educators. Not only was it countered by the discipline-centered curriculum reforms of the 1950's and 1960's but it has met with other difficulties over the years. . . . teachers are products of

---

[25] For a widely cited theoretical model of a senior high school schedule with a "common learnings" core see Educational Policies Commission, *Education for All American Youth* (Washington, D.C.: National Education Association, 1944), p. 244.

[26] Conant, *Recommendations for Education in the Junior High School Years,* pp. 22–23.

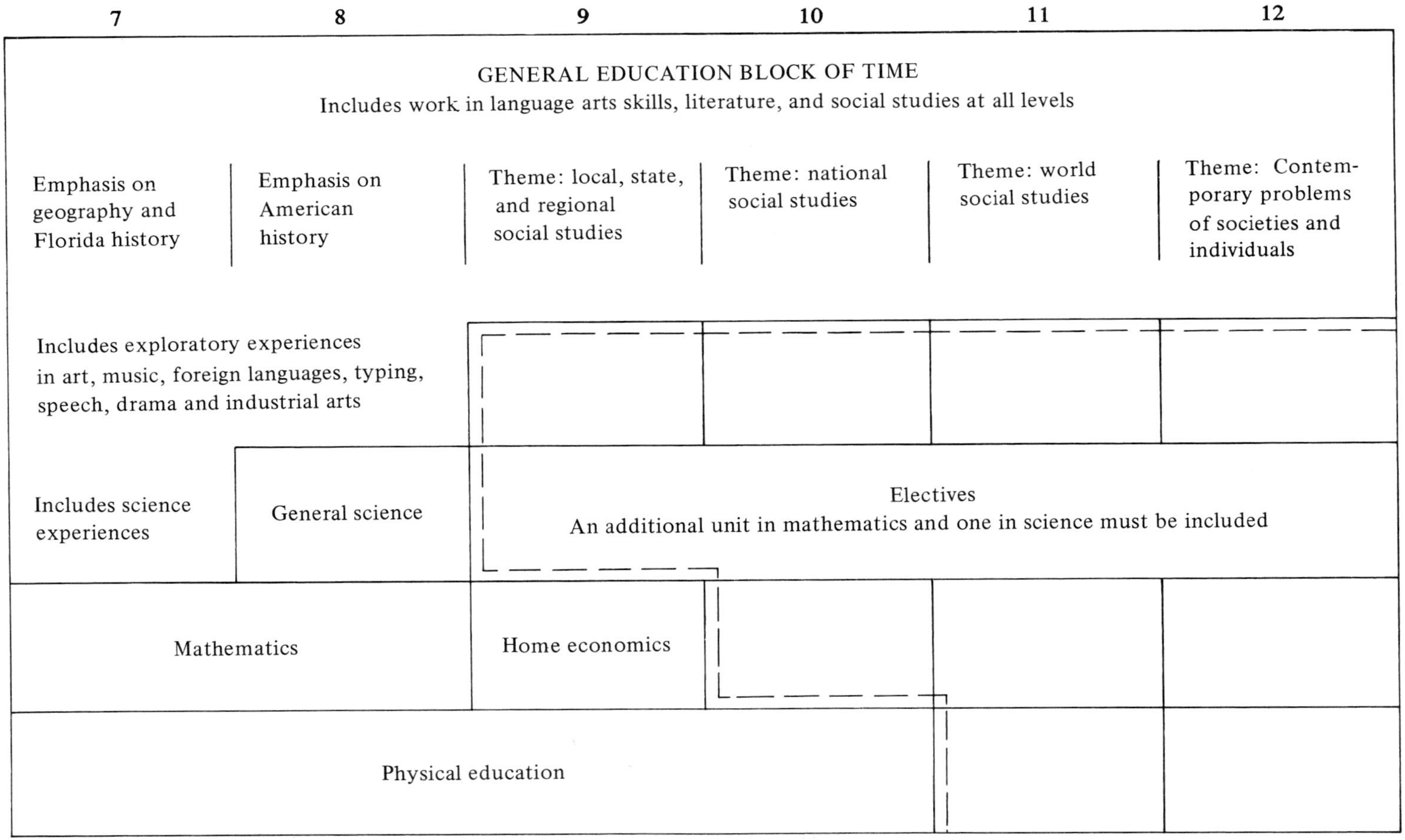

GENERAL EDUCATION BLOCK OF TIME
Includes work in language arts skills, literature, and social studies at all levels

7	8	9	10	11	12

Emphasis on geography and Florida history

Emphasis on American history

Theme: local, state, and regional social studies

Theme: national social studies

Theme: world social studies

Theme: Contemporary problems of societies and individuals

Includes exploratory experiences in art, music, foreign languages, typing, speech, drama and industrial arts

Includes science experiences

General science

Mathematics

Home economics

Electives

An additional unit in mathematics and one in science must be included

Physical education

FIGURE 9-1   Secondary curriculum — P. K. Yonge Laboratory School, University of Florida, Gainesville, Florida

disciplined-centered curricula in the colleges and universities, and so they tend to be oriented toward the subject curriculum. Textbooks and other curriculum materials are geared to the subject curriculum. . . . Without extensive resource materials the core class is unable to attack problems in any great breadth and depth of treatment. The core curriculum requires enormous teacher resourcefulness. . . . The core curriculum requires teachers to have considerable breadth and depth of background in general education. Yet, the colleges have been largely allowing their own curricula in general education to erode in favor of specialism and special-interest studies.

Perhaps the most serious problem, aside from the national trend toward disciplinary studies over a period of almost two decades, was the unrealistic expectation that teachers should develop their own curriculum materials under conditions where resources are lacking.[27]

THE SENIOR HIGH SCHOOL

The Subject Matter Curriculum

The subject matter curriculum has been the most prevalent form of curriculum organization at all levels of education ever since the Boston Latin School, the first Latin Grammar School in the United States, opened in 1635. The subject matter curriculum remains the most common pattern of organization throughout most of the world. Whereas other forms of curriculum organization have asserted themselves in the United States from time to time, the subject matter curriculum has continued strong and has gained renewed strength in recent years with the stress placed on developing the basic skills. The subject matter curriculum has existed at all levels of schooling but has been particularly entrenched at the senior high and college levels.

Smith, Stanley, and Shores pointed out in the following passage that the subject matter curriculum dates back to antiquity:

> The subject is the oldest and most widely accepted form of curriculum organization. Perhaps the earliest example of this organization is the Seven Liberal Arts, which were present in an incipient form in the schools of ancient Greece and Rome, and which were offered in a more advanced stage of development in the monastery and cathedral schools of the Middle Ages. The Seven Liberal Arts consisted of two divisions: the trivium, which was comprised of grammar, rhetoric, and dialectic (logic); and the quadrivium, which consisted of arithmetic, geometry, astronomy, and music. . . . In the modern period the trivium was further divided to include literature and history as distinct subjects; and the quadrivium, to include algebra, trigonometry, geography, botany, zoology, physics, and chemistry. In the last half century the number of subjects offered in the public schools increased by leaps and bounds, so that by 1930 there were over three hun-

---

[27] Tanner and Tanner, p. 485.

dred distinct subjects of instruction. Despite this enormous multiplication of subjects the Seven Liberal Arts are still the nucleus of the subject curriculum, as a casual survey of required courses will reveal.[28]

As the name implies, the subject matter curriculum is an organizational pattern that breaks the school's program into discrete subjects or disciplines. The seventeenth century Latin Grammar School stressed classical subjects, including Greek, Latin, Hebrew, mathematics, history, and *The Bible*. Notably absent from this early school were English and science, which were considered too functional or too frivolous for scholars of this period. With the opening of Benjamin Franklin's Philadelphia Academy and Charitable School in 1751 English, science, and modern languages were added to the curriculum. Today's secondary schools offer a potpourri, some say smorgasbord, of courses.

Essentialistic in outlook, the subject matter curriculum seeks to transmit the cultural heritage. The subjects or disciplines organize knowledge from the adult world in such a way that it can be transmitted to the immature learner.

As we saw in Chapter 6 when we discussed the philosophy of essentialism, the subject matter curriculum has not been at a loss for spokespersons. Max Rafferty left no doubt of his position regarding the subject matter curriculum when he voiced the following:

> What *is* significant for the children — what the people want for their children and mean to get — is subject matter that is systematic, organized, and disciplined and that is taught effectively and interestingly as subject matter. . . . Stress subject matter, *all* subject matter.[29]

Whereas the subject matter curriculum is found at both the elementary and secondary school levels, it has had its greatest impact at the secondary level. Elementary school faculties have been more prone to experiment and to try out new patterns of organization that depart from subject matter emphasis. Secondary school teachers and administrators have consistently tended to be more subject-centered than their counterparts at the elementary school level.

Advantages. The subject matter curriculum presents to its followers certain distinct advantages. It is the easiest organizational pattern to structure. On the elementary school level, it is simply a matter of allocating a certain number of minutes for each subject during the course of the day. On the secondary school level, subject matter is organized into "courses" that are designated as either required subjects (constants) or electives. Typically every subject of the secondary school is scheduled for the same amount of time. The recommendations of two well-known groups helped to imprint the model of equal time for each subject in the secondary schools.

---

[28] Smith, Stanley, and Shores, pp. 229–230.
[29] Max Rafferty, *What They Are Doing to Your Children* (New York: New American Library, 1964), pp. 43–44.

At the tail end of the nineteenth century the National Education Association's Committee of Ten proposed:

> ... every subject which is taught at all in a secondary school should be taught in the same way and to the same extent to every pupil so long as he pursues it, no matter what the probable destination of the pupil may be, or at what point his education is to cease. Thus, for all pupils who study Latin, or history, or algebra, for example, the allotment of time and the method of instruction in a given school should be the same year by year. Not that all pupils should pursue every subject for the same number of years; but so long as they do pursue it, they should all be treated alike.[30]

The Carnegie Unit. A few years later, in 1906, the Carnegie Foundation for the Advancement of Teaching created the Carnegie unit, which standardized the amount of time to be spent in each subject in high school for purposes of college admission. To most people today the concept is known simply as a "unit," the Carnegie modifier having been lost in the corridors of time. The Carnegie Foundation for the Advancement of Teaching defined a unit as satisfactory completion of a subject that met five days per week, a minimum of forty minutes per period, and a minimum of 120 clock hours for the school year. In addition, the Carnegie Foundation stipulated that a secondary school pupil should amass a total of sixteen units for graduation. These two recommendations of the Carnegie Foundation for the Advancement of Teaching were universally adopted by American secondary schools and have continued in force with infrequent modifications.

The content of the subject matter curriculum is, unlike that of the experience curriculum, planned in advance by the teacher or, more accurately, by the writers of the adopted textbooks or curriculum guides that the teacher follows. The needs and interests of learners play little part in the curriculum that is organized around the disciplines.

Unlike the activity or experience curriculum and the core curriculum, which have been discussed earlier in this chapter, the subject matter curriculum is well understood by the public, students, and the profession and for the most part has met with general favor. The methodology followed in the subject matter curriculum is rather straightforward. The teacher is the expert in the field and is likely to pursue a set of procedures that some instructional specialists refer to as the "assign-study-recite-test" method. William H. Burton succinctly described these procedures:

> The learning situation is organized around materials and experiences which are assigned by the teacher. The pupils then study in various ways. The results of their studying are presented and shared during a recitation

---

[30] National Education Association, *Report of the Committee of Ten on Secondary School Studies* (New York: American Book Company, 1894), p. 17.

period. Testing of results occurs at the conclusion of a series of assignments and may occur at stated times within the sequence.[31]

Writing in 1962 Burton stated, "The assign-study-recite-test formula will be used for many years to come." [32] What he might have said is that the assign-study-recite-test formula has been used for generations and is likely to continue for more to come. This approach is what many people both within and without the profession call "teaching."

Cognitive Emphasis. The subject matter curriculum, which in days of old was imbedded in the quagmire of faculty psychology or mental discipline, has found behavioristic psychology compatible with its objectives. Student achievement is rather easily assessed, since evaluation is limited to measuring cognitive objectives by teacher-made or standardized tests. Some effort is made to measure performance in the psychomotor domain but the perceptual motor skills are treated more or less as appendages to the cognitive domain. As testimony, most high schools that have separate tracks of curricula — such as general, commercial, industrial, and college preparatory — regard the most cognitive, the college preparatory track, as the most prestigious.

In the subject matter curriculum little effort is made to gauge performance of students in the affective domain. Evaluation of feelings and values is not only extremely difficult but also proponents of the subject matter curriculum, essentialist as they are, do not accept the affect as a primary concern of the school. The approach to individual differences and needs of students in the subject matter curriculum lies more in the provision of elective or special interest subjects from among which the students may choose. The breadth or scope of the subject matter curriculum and its sequence are revealed in the textbooks that are adopted for use in the classroom.

Conant's Proposals. Conant's studies of both the American high and junior high schools strengthened advocates of the subject matter curriculum. To sense the overall impact of the Conant report on the high school, which preceded the report on the junior high, we will cite several of the twenty-one recommendations proffered in this report.

One wonders if the titles of Conant's two reports have political significance. His 1959 report on the high school was labeled "a first report to interested citizens" whereas his 1960 junior high school report was subtitled "a memorandum to school boards." Conant made the following proposals for the high school:[33]

---

[31] William H. Burton, *The Guidance of Learning Activities,* 3rd ed. (New York: Appleton-Century-Crofts, 1962), p. 289.
[32] Burton, p. 289.
[33] Conant, *The American High School Today* (New York: McGraw-Hill, 1959).

REQUIRED PROGRAMS FOR ALL.

A. General Education.

The requirements for graduation for all students should be as follows: four years of English, three or four years of social studies — including two years of history (one of which should be American history) and a senior course in American problems or American government — one year of mathematics in the ninth grade (algebra or general mathematics), and at least one year of science in the ninth or tenth grade, which might well be biology or general physical science. By a year, I mean a course is given five periods a week throughout the academic year or an equivalent amount of time. This academic program of general education involves nine or ten courses with homework to be taken in four years and occupies more than half the time of most students, whatever their elective programs.

B. The Elective Program.

The other requirement for graduation should be successful completion of at least seven more courses, not including physical education. All students should be urged to include art and music in their elective programs. All students should be advised to have as the central core of their elective programs significant sequences of courses, either those leading to the development of a marketable skill or those of an academic nature.

C. Standards for Pass and Failure.

... the teachers of the advanced academic *elective* courses — foreign languages, mathematics, and science — should be urged to maintain high standards. They should be told not to hesitate to fail a student who does not meet the minimum level of performance they judge necessary for mastery of the subject in question. ... On the other hand, for the *required* courses another standard should be applied. Since these courses are required of all, irrespective of ability, a student may be given a passing grade if he has worked to full capacity whether or not a certain level of achievement has been reached.

ABILITY GROUPING.

In the required subjects and those elected by students with a wide range of ability, the students should be grouped according to ability, subject by subject. ... This type of grouping is not to be confused with across-the-board grouping according to which a given student is placed in a particular section in *all* courses.

ENGLISH COMPOSITION.

The time devoted to English composition during the four years should occupy about half the total time devoted to the study of English. Each student should be required to write an average of one theme a week. Themes should be corrected by the teacher ... no English teacher should be responsible for more than one hundred pupils.

To test the ability of each student in English composition, a schoolwide composition test should be given in every grade; in the ninth and eleventh grades, these composition tests should be graded not only by the teacher but by a committee of the entire school. Those students who do not obtain a grade on the eleventh-grade composition test commensurate with their ability as measured by an aptitude test should be required to take a special course in English composition in the twelfth grade.

DIVERSIFIED PROGRAMS FOR THE DEVELOPMENT OF MARKETABLE SKILLS. Programs should be available for girls interested in developing skills in typing, stenography, the use of clerical machines, home economics. . . . Distributive education should be available. . . . If the community is rural, vocational agriculture should be included. . . . For boys, depending on the community, trade and industrial programs should be available. Half a day is required in the eleventh and twelfth grades for this vocational work.

SPECIAL CONSIDERATION FOR THE VERY SLOW READERS. Those in the ninth grade of the school who read at a level of the sixth grade or below should be given special consideration. These pupils should be instructed in English and the required social studies by special teachers. . . . Remedial reading should be part of the work, and special types of textbooks should be provided. The elective programs of these pupils should be directed toward simple vocational work. . . .

THE PROGRAMS OF THE ACADEMICALLY TALENTED. . . . the elective programs of academically talented boys and girls [the top 15 percent] should [include] . . . as a minimum: Four years of mathematics, four years of one foreign language, three years of science, in addition to the required four years of English and three years of social studies; a total of eighteen courses with homework to be taken in four years. This program will require at least fifteen hours of homework each week.

HIGHLY GIFTED PUPILS. For the highly gifted pupils [the top 3 percent] some type of special arrangement should be made. . . . If enough students are available to provide a special class, these students should take in the twelfth grade one or more courses which are part of the Advanced Placement Program.

ORGANIZATION OF THE SCHOOL DAY. The school day should be so organized that there are at least six periods in addition to the required physical education and driver education. . . . A seven- or eight-period day may be organized with periods as short as forty-five minutes . . . laboratory periods as well as industrial arts should involve double periods.

The thrust of the Conant recommendations for the high school reaffirmed the subject matter curriculum with special emphasis on the needs of the academically talented. As such, albeit in more modern trappings, it reinforced and expanded the Harvard Report that preceded it by almost fifteen years. Whereas many secondary schools rushed to implement some of Conant's recommendations, particularly those for the academically talented, they gave up on others. English teachers still wistfully hope for a maximum of one hundred pupils. Schools still dream of a full-time counselor for every 250 to 300 pupils; the normal ratio is often one counselor to 500 or more. Finally, grouping students by ability, although implemented widely, remains enmeshed in controversy.

The subject matter curriculum has been popular with many curriculum planners for it lends itself well to a mechanical type of curriculum development: dropping, adding, or splitting courses, rearranging or extending sequences, updating topics, and changing textbooks.

Broad-Fields Curriculum

In the early part of the twentieth century a pattern of curriculum organization appeared that became — on the surface at least — a standard feature of both elementary and secondary schools. Called the broad-fields curriculum, this form of curriculum organization is a modification of the strict subject-matter curriculum. Effort is made to unify and integrate content of related disciplines around broad themes or principles. History A (ancient), history B (modern) and history C (American) for example, as existed in the secondary school curriculum of New York State schools well into the 1930s, were converted into broad fields and designated simply tenth grade social studies, eleventh grade social studies, and twelfth grade social studies.

"In the broad-fields approach," said Tanner and Tanner, "the attempt is made to develop some degree of synthesis or unity for an entire branch of knowledge. . . . it may even go so far as to synthesize two or more branches of knowledge into a new field. Ecology represents such a synthesis." [34] "Courses in the broad-fields curriculum," explained Smith, Stanley, and Shores, "have various appellations. . . . In the college, they are called 'survey' or 'comprehensive' courses, and sometimes 'general courses.' At the high school level they are called 'fusion courses' or 'general courses,' or else they are simply designated by course titles as in the elementary school." [35]

Thus, we find the various elements of English (reading, writing, grammar, literature, speech, etc.) brought together under the rubric of language arts. The various social science fields (history, political science, government, economics, anthropology, sociology, etc.) were combined to become the social studies. Art, music, architecture, and literature became the humanities. Principles of physical and natural science were unified into a course in general science. The industrial arts tied together various aspects of vocational education. Physical education included health and safety. General mathematics offered experiences drawn from arithmetic, algebra, geometry, etc.

Zais spoke about the advantages of the broad-fields curriculum as follows:

> Two main advantages are claimed for the broad-fields design. First, because it is ultimately based on the separate subjects, it provides for an orderly and systematic exposure to the cultural heritage. This advantage it shares with the subject curriculum. But it also integrates separate subjects,

---

[34] Tanner and Tanner, pp. 473, 474.
[35] Smith, Stanley, and Shores, p. 257.

thereby enabling learners to see relationships among various elements in the curriculum. This second advantage is the special strength that the broad-fields design claims over the subject curriculum.[36]

He warned, however:

> With respect to the integration claimed for the broad-fields design, it is worth noting that in practice, combining subjects into a broad field often amounts to little more than the compression of several separate subjects into a single course with little actual unification taking place.[37]

In a true broad-fields approach, teachers select certain general themes or principles to be studied at each year of the sequence of a discipline, e.g., social studies. Obviously, not all curricula labeled broad fields are truly of that genre.

Zais addressed the question of common criticisms of the broad-fields curriculum:

> ... opponents of the broad-fields curriculum claim that it lacks depth and cultivates superficiality by providing students with only a smattering of information from a variety of subjects. ... Aside from the criticism that it lacks depth, the broad-fields design is subject to the same general criticisms as the other subject-centered designs: to one degree or another, it, too, is fragmented insofar as it does not provide for integration between broad fields (e.g., between general social studies, general science, general arts, etc.). It is by its nature divorced from the real world, is weak in providing for the experience and interests of students, and does not adequately account for the psychological organization by which learning takes place. Finally, though less so than the subject curriculum, the broad-fields design tends to stress the goals of content coverage and acquisition of information, offering little opportunity for the achievement of either cognitive or affective process goals.[38]

Proponents of the broad-fields curriculum would respond to these criticisms by saying that if the curriculum were properly planned and carried out, these deficiencies would be overcome. What appears to have happened in many schools is that the rubric of broad fields has been retained but the curricula themselves have reverted to the separate disciplines of the subject matter curriculum.

The majority of boys and girls in American schools, both elementary and secondary, have been and continue to be educated under the subject matter curriculum. Admittedly, some modifications have been made, but by and large the subject matter curriculum has proved to be a comfortable plan that is widely accepted in our culture. The subject matter curriculum at the senior high school level has been favored by college admissions officers and regional

---

[36] Robert S. Zais, *Curriculum: Principles and Foundations* (New York: Harper & Row, 1976), p. 407.
[37] Zais, p. 407.
[38] Zais, pp. 407–408.

accrediting associations, for it is much easier to understand and evaluate than more experimental types of curricula. And, we must add that the subject matter curriculum has met with considerable success.

Team Teaching

While Conant was conducting his surveys of the senior and junior high schools, the National Association of Secondary School Principals was in 1956 seeking ways to cope with increased enrollments in the schools, a teacher shortage, and the introduction of new curricula in various disciplines — phenomena all quite different from today's scene. Under the leadership of J. Lloyd Trump, Associate Secretary of the National Association of Secondary School Principals, a Commission on Curriculum Planning and Development was launched that developed a proposal for new ways of utilizing staff through teaming of faculty.

Funded by the Ford Foundation's Fund for the Advancement of Education, team teaching enjoyed a brief flurry of popularity across the nation from Newton, Massachusetts to Evanston, Illinois to San Diego, California. The National Association of Secondary School Principals proceeded to appoint a Commission on the Experimental Study of the Utilization of the Staff in the Secondary School with J. Lloyd Trump as its director and charged it with the task of promoting the cause of team teaching. Harvard University's Graduate School of Education and Claremont Graduate School (California) took a special interest in this innovative organizational plan.

J. Lloyd Trump and Delmas F. Miller defined team teaching as follows:

> The term "team teaching" applies to an arrangement in which two or more teachers and their assistants, taking advantage of their respective competencies, plan, instruct, and evaluate in one or more subject areas a group of elementary or secondary students equivalent in size to two or more conventional classes, using a variety of technical aids to teaching and learning through large-group instruction, small-group discussion, and independent study.[39]

Ira J. Singer described team teaching in this way:

> Team teaching may be defined as an arrangement whereby two or more teachers, with or without teacher aides, cooperatively plan, instruct, and evaluate one or more class groups in an appropriate instructional space and given length of time, so as to take advantage of the special competencies of the team members.[40]

---

[39] J. Lloyd Trump and Delmas F. Miller, *Secondary School Curriculum Improvement: Meeting Challenges of the Times,* 3rd ed. (Boston: Allyn and Bacon, 1979), p. 410.

[40] Ira J. Singer, "What Team Teaching Really Is," in David W. Beggs III, ed., *Team Teaching: Bold New Venture* (Bloomington, Ind.: Indiana University Press, 1964), p. 16.

Singer pointed out that the major factors in a team teaching plan are:

- cooperative planning, instruction, and evaluation.
- student grouping for special purposes (large group instruction, small group discussion, independent study).
- flexible daily schedule.
- use of teacher aides.
- recognition and utilization of individual teacher talents.
- use of space and media appropriate to the purpose and content of instruction.[41]

The purpose of team teaching was to capitalize on the strengths of teachers, utilizing their varying expertise in different ways. Teams were organized within subject areas and across subject fields.

A particular variant of team teaching came to be known as the Trump Plan. J. Lloyd Trump and Dorsey Baynham postulated three ingredients for an effective organizational structure that would capitalize on teacher assets and provide better opportunities for the learners. The school week, according to Trump and Baynham, should provide opportunities for pupils to attend large-group instruction, to interact in small groups, and to carry out independent study. Prophesied Trump and Baynham:

> The school of the future will schedule students in class groups an average of only 18 hours a week. The average student at the level of today's tenth grade will spend about 12 of the 18 hours in *large-group instruction* and six in *small-group discussion*.
>
> In addition, students will spend, on an average, 12 hours each week in school in individual *independent study*.[42]

These figures convert to 40 percent of a student's time in large-group instruction, 20 percent in small-group discussion, and 40 percent in independent study.

Singer contrasted schedules of two history teachers under a conventional plan and under a team teaching plan that incorporates the three ingredients: large-group instruction (LG), small-group discussion (SG), and independent study (IS) (See Table 9-3.).

Differentiated Staffing. Team teaching offered a creative answer to utilizing limited faculty and resources more effectively. More elaborate school-wide staffing patterns were developed incorporating the principle of differentiated assignment. The North Miami Beach Senior High School (Florida) developed

---

[41] Singer, p. 16.
[42] J. Lloyd Trump and Dorsey Baynham, *Focus on Change: Guide to Better Schools* (Chicago: Rand McNally, 1961), p. 41.

TABLE 9-3 Comparison of two types of schedules

(a) CONVENTIONAL SCHEDULE				
TIME	MONDAY	TUESDAY	WEDNESDAY	THURSDAY	FRIDAY
8:00– 8:50	Hist. 10A Hist. 10B	Hist. 10A Hist. 10B	Hist. 10A Hist. 10B	Hist. 10A Hist. 10B	Hist. 10A Hist. 10B

(b) SINGLE-DISCIPLINE TEAM SCHEDULE				
TIME	MONDAY	TUESDAY	WEDNESDAY	THURSDAY	FRIDAY
8:00– 8:50	History 10AB (LG)	History 10AB1* (SG) History 10AB2 (SG) History 10AB3 (SG)	History 10AB (LG)	History 10AB1* (SG) History 10AB2 (SG) History 10AB3 (SG)	History 10AB (IS) Project work in library, laboratory, music room, art studio, etc.

(60 students, 2 teachers, 1 instruction assistant)

*One History 10AB-SG can be supervised by an instruction assistant, student teacher or student leader. LG = large group, SG = small group, IS = independent study.

Source: Ira J. Singer, "What Team Teaching Really Is," in David W. Beggs III, ed., *Team Teaching. Bold New Venture* (Bloomington, Ind.: Indiana University Press, 1964), p. 17. Reprinted by permission.

a set of categories of personnel for its differentiated staffing plan.[43] These included:

□ *Community Relations Specialist.* Coordinates activities involving school and community.
□ *Human Relations Specialist.* Seeks to create harmonious climate within the school.
□ *In-Service Coordinator.* Coordinates the training and development program of the professional and paraprofessional staff.
□ *Psychologist.* Counsels students on emotional problems.
□ *School Social Worker.* Helps students to function adequately in school; a behavioral consultant.
□ *Media Specialist.* Supervises and develops media program.

[43] North Miami Beach Senior High School, Dade County, Florida Public Schools.

- *Media Technician.* Provides skilled technical assistance to staff and students.
- *Coordinating Librarian.* Supervises library resources.
- *Teaching Designer.* Assists teachers in improving instruction and evaluating effectiveness.
- *Teaching Prescriber.* Provides assessment, diagnosis, and prescription for each student's program through observation, testing, and individual and/or group conferences.
- *Resource Specialist.* Gathers, coordinates, and disseminates materials for helping solve specific learning situations.
- *Facilitating Teacher.* Guides students through learning; teaches specific courses.
- *Instructional Intern.* Assists a directing teacher; a college junior, senior, or graduate student who serves for a full school year in the high school.
- *Instructional Aide.* Assists by performing paraprofessional responsibilities.
- *Clerical Aide.* Performs clerical duties.

In recent years secondary schools have turned away from the concepts of team teaching and differentiated staffing. However, team teaching is a prominent feature of most plans for middle and open-space schools. Results were not always as anticipated. In some cases teachers found themselves incompatible, unable to cooperate effectively. Cooperative planning requires a high degree of interpersonal skill that some team members lacked.

Some administrators bought into the large-group instruction aspect of team teaching for the convenience and economy of scheduling large numbers of students and omitted the important companion features of small-group discussion and independent study. Large-group instruction by itself deprives students of interaction with the teacher and with each other. When coupled with instructional television, also attempted at this period, students became inattentive and bored.

Schools experienced varying degrees of success with independent study. In some cases it became apparent that not all students are capable of self-directed learning. Plans for large-group instruction, small-group discussion, and independent study call for special facilities and resources that were missing in some schools that attempted this type of organization.

The very complexity of staffing and scheduling under team teaching patterns confused parents, teachers, and students. Tradition, therefore, lent its weight to uniform time blocks, completely supervised study, and individual, rather than team teaching assignments.

Flexible Scheduling

With but a few significant departures from traditional practice, high schools have continued to schedule subjects in the conventional mode, one period per day, five days per week. The Carnegie unit, Conant's recommendations that each course meet five times a week for the academic year, and customary standards of the regional accrediting associations have added to the pressures to maintain traditional scheduling.

Yet, it is difficult to find a logical reason why all subjects must be taught for the same period of time. Some disciplines are by their very nature more difficult than others and require more time for mastery. Some courses are most effectively taught when accompanied by a laboratory that requires extra time. Some subject matter is simply not as relevant as other subject matter and, therefore, should be accorded less time.

There is also not a logical reason why equal amounts of time must be allotted to every subject every day of the week. Some days and some weeks more time is needed to explore a topic in depth. Some days it is apparent to the teacher that youngsters have not comprehended the lesson and need to revisit the territory or undergo remedial work.

There is also not a sufficient reason why the instructional mode must be standardized every period of every day. Variation should be possible for lecture, mediated instruction, laboratories, seminars, field trips, independent study, and other modes.

Efforts were made in the sixties to break out of the mold of the standard schedule. These efforts are subsumed in a movement referred to as flexible scheduling. Donald C. Manlove and David W. Beggs III described the concept of flexible scheduling as follows:

> . . . the flexible schedule is an organization for instruction which:
> 1. calls for classes of varying size within and between courses. (Students sometimes may meet in large assembly classes, and at other times in small inquiry classes. In addition, part of the day will be spent in individual or independent study.)
> 2. provides for instructional groups which meet at varying frequencies for varying lengths. (Some classes may meet every day of the week, others will not. Some instructional sessions will be for a short duration, others for an extended period of time.)
> 3. makes team teaching possible in any content area or for any group of students in the school. (The use of a teaching team, two or more teachers working with a given group of students on a common instructional problem, is suggested in this model.)
> 4. requires countless professional decisions by teachers about students, content, and teaching methods.[44]

Types of Schedules. Flexible schedules have taken varying forms; some are minor departures from traditional plans, others radical changes. Among the varieties of flexible scheduling are the following:

1. Two or more periods are simply combined as in the case of core classes.

---

[44] Donald C. Manlove and David W. Beggs III, *Flexible Scheduling: Bold New Venture* (Bloomington, Ind.: Indiana University Press, 1965), pp. 22–23.

2. Subjects are scheduled for both double and single periods in the same week. For example, some classes may meet two periods on Monday and Thursday, other classes two periods on Tuesday and Friday, but all only one period on Wednesday. Teachers can thus use the larger blocks of time in ways not permitted by the constraints of the single period schedule.
3. Classes are rotated during the week. Trump and Miller supplied diagrams of rotating schedules with standard periods and with periods varying in length (see Table 9-4).
4. Instead of typical forty-five to fifty-five minute periods, the schedule is

TABLE 9-4 Rotating schedules

ROTATION OF CLASSES — STANDARD PERIODS				
TIME	MONDAY	TUESDAY	WEDNESDAY	THURSDAY	FRIDAY
8:00	1	1	1	1	2
9:00	2	2	2	3	3
10:00	3	3	4	4	4
11:00	4	5	5	5	5
12:00			Lunch		
12:30	6	6	6	6	7
1:30	7	7	7	Special	Special

ROTATION OF CLASSES — PERIODS VARY IN LENGTH				
TIME	MONDAY	TUESDAY	WEDNESDAY	THURSDAY	FRIDAY
8:55–10:26	1	2	4	5	6
10:30–11:26	2	4	5	6	1
11:30–12:26	3	3	3	3	3
12:26–1:04			Lunch		
1:04–2:30	4	5	6	1	2
2:34–3:30	5	6	1	2	4

Note: Numbers indicate different subjects.
Source: J. Lloyd Trump and Delmas F. Miller, *Secondary School Curriculum Improvement: Meeting Challenges of the Times,* 3rd ed. (Boston: Allyn and Bacon, 1979), p. 400. Reprinted by permission.

broken into modules, which, by faculty agreement, may be multiples of fifteen, twenty, thirty, or more minutes. Modular scheduling can be described as follows:

> Modular scheduling, or flexible-modular scheduling . . . requires complete abandonment of the division of the school schedule into equal amounts of time for each course. . . . Some subjects are scheduled for two or three modules (conceivably, even for a single module) per day. Those which require a great deal of time are scheduled in multiple modules. . . .
>
> The duration of the module is purely a matter for decision, ordinarily made by the faculty of the school at the time a modular schedule is introduced. Fifteen-minute modules are common. A school day based on fifteen-minute modules would encompass approximately twenty-five modules. Schools which follow the Stanford School Scheduling System use modules of twenty-two minutes; twenty modules make up the day. The Indiana Flexible Schedule uses fifteen modules per day of thirty minutes each. Ridgewood High School, Norridge-Harwood Heights, Illinois (as one example) has a school day made up of twenty modules of twenty minutes plus an additional ten-minute module for homeroom period.[45]

Trump and Miller provided an illustration of a modular schedule using fifteen-minute modules, as shown in Table 9-5.

5. Class schedules are set frequently, even daily. This "scheduling on demand" is the ultimate goal of flexible scheduling, allowing, as J. Lloyd Trump observed, teachers and students the greatest possible latitude in determining their instruction and learning. Trump told how this process was accomplished at the Brookhurst Junior High School in Anaheim, California:

> Individual members of teaching teams determine three days in advance what students they want to teach, in what size groups, for what length of time, in what places, and with what technological aids. Teacher job-specification forms containing this information are turned in to their team leaders. The team leaders then assemble to make a master schedule for the day, a procedure that takes approximately twenty minutes each day. The master schedule is then duplicated and made available to the students and their counselors. In a daily 20-minute meeting, with the advice and consent of their counselor (twenty minutes to a counselor), each student makes his schedule. A student noting, for example, that the schedule calls for a large-group presentation on a given subject and deciding that he already knows that material, may elect rather to spend his time in independent study in the art room or library or some place else. The counselor either approves or rejects this decision. Then the student makes out his own schedule for the

---

[45] Oliva, *The Secondary School Today,* 2d ed. (New York: Harper & Row, 1972), p. 196.

TABLE 9-5 15 minute modules — same schedule every day

TIME	SUBJECT
8:00	
8:15	Mathematics
8:30	
8:45	
9:00	Speech correction
9:15	
9:30	
9:45	Science
10:00	
10:15	
10:30	
10:45	Music
11:00	
11:15	Spanish
11:30	
11:45	Music practice
12:00	Lunch
etc.	

Source: J. Lloyd Trump and Delmas F. Miller, *Secondary School Curriculum Improvement: Meeting Challenges of the Times,* 3rd ed. (Boston: Allyn and Bacon, 1979), p. 398. Reprinted by permission.

day in quadruplicate. One copy is for himself, one for the office, one for the counselor, and one for his parents.[46]

Traditional versus Flexible Scheduling. Flexible scheduling is an essential aspect of newer plans for curriculum organization such as team teaching, which calls for large-group instruction, small-group instruction, and independent study. Traditional schedules have forced teachers to utilize the same amounts of time for all activities.

Manlove and Beggs contrasted the traditional and the flexible schedule in Table 9-6. They summarized the advantages and disadvantages of flexible scheduling to teachers, making the comparisons shown in Table 9-7.

Trump and Miller also warned of a danger inherent in modular scheduling — or in any innovation for that matter — "once a change is made, the new

---

[46] J. Lloyd Trump, "Flexible Scheduling — Fad or Fundamental?" *Phi Delta Kappan,* 44, no. 8 (May, 1963): 370.

TABLE 9-6   Characteristics of traditional and flexible schedules

ELEMENT	TRADITIONAL SCHEDULE	FLEXIBLE SCHEDULE
Content	Assumes each course is equivalent in requirements for mastery to all others	Assumes requirements for mastery of content vary from course to course
Facilities	Use is set by schedule	Use is determined sometimes by student needs
Groups	All class groups are nearly equal size	Class groups differ in size depending on the instructional task
Scheduling unit	The day; each day in the week has the same order as every other day	The week; each day in the week has different order
Students	Students should be in a class group or supervised study	Students may be in a class group or be working independently
Teachers	All have equal numbers of classes or assignments and demands on their time	Number of classes vary from teacher to teacher and demands on time vary
Time	Usually equal for all subjects	Usually different for various subjects

Source: Donald C. Manlove and David W. Beggs III, *Flexible Scheduling: Bold New Venture* (Bloomington, Ind.: Indiana University Press, 1965), p. 26. Reprinted by permission.

schedule can become almost as rigid as the one it replaced." [47] The complexity of operation; a structure that shifts from day to day; the high degree of planning required on the part of students, teachers, and administrators; and the decline in popularity of the team teaching concept have mitigated against flexible scheduling and caused some schools to pull back to more traditional and more commonly understood forms of scheduling.

The Nongraded High School

During the sixties when the elementary schools were experimenting with continuous progress plans, eliminating grades as we know them, several high schools were attempting to develop ungraded patterns of organization. Prominent among these high schools were Nova High School (Broward County, Florida) and Melbourne High School (Brevard County, Florida).

In the mid-1960s Nova High School and Melbourne High School were the epitome of innovation. Nova High School was established amidst what was at that time a semirural tract of now populous Broward County (Fort Lau-

---

[47] Trump and Miller, p. 308.

TABLE 9-7   Advantages and disadvantages of flexible scheduling

ADVANTAGES FOR TEACHERS	DISADVANTAGES FOR TEACHERS
1. Provides a means for pacing the instruction to an individual student's needs	1. Danger of not giving enough time to one subject
2. Allows teachers to make decisions about the length and frequency of learning activities	2. Requires more time and cooperative effort of teachers in making the schedule
3. Gives teachers time to work with small groups and individuals	3. Possibility of too little identification of a student with his teachers
4. Takes unnecessary repetition out of the teacher's day	4. Is difficult to schedule
5. Places increased responsibility on students for learning	5. Requires teachers to change their teaching patterns
6. Provides the opportunity to use resource experts for a large group of students in an economical way for the resource person	6. Is not understood by the public or even by all teachers

Source: Donald C. Manlove and David W. Beggs III, *Flexible Scheduling: Bold New Venture* (Bloomington, Ind.: Indiana University Press, 1965), p. 67. Reprinted by permission.

derdale) as the first facility in a projected complex that came to embrace elementary schools, a junior high, and a junior college as well as the high school — all publicly supported. A private institution of higher learning, Nova University, is a next-door neighbor.

Nova High School utilized teaching teams complete with clerical assistants and teacher aides. Organized on a trimester plan, Nova High School incorporated closed circuit television, a photographic laboratory, data processing equipment, and learning resource centers equipped with tape recorders, microfilm readers, and teaching machines.

A schedule was devised consisting of five periods per day of eighty minutes each with an optional sixth period of one hour's duration. Speaking to the nongraded feature of Nova High School, Arthur B. Wolfe, Director of the K–12 Center, set forth the Nova Plan in these terms:

> The Nova Plan will eliminate grade designation and will establish a far wider range of learning levels through which each student may progress at a rate commensurate with his interests and abilities. Each of the established levels will be only slightly advanced over the level below, thereby enabling the student to move from one level to the next at any given time during the school year. This process will be applicable to the program of each student and to each separate subject area, thereby placing a realistic evaluation on

each student's progress on an individual basis, one not entirely related to the sum total of his progress. . . .

Following the enrollment of new students, records will be examined and a series of tests will be administered. The faculty will place students in an achievement group that will provide a smooth transition to a new learning environment. This process will be followed for each of the subject areas in which students may be enrolled. It will be necessary in some cases to move students forward or back until an achievement level has been found in which they will feel comfortable.[48]

Nova, like Melbourne, sought to put into action some of the more significant innovations of the day.

Situated in the stimulating setting of the then bustling space-oriented Brevard County with Cape Canaveral practically in its backyard, Melbourne High School, under its principal, B. Frank Brown, achieved widespread recognition in both the professional and lay periodicals. Melbourne High School was, as its stationery proclaimed, the school "Where the library is bigger than the gymnasium." Melbourne High was host to so many visitors from all over the country that at one time it set up monthly briefing sessions.

Like Nova High School, Melbourne High School ventured to try out many new ideas. Stress on the academics could be seen in its library with carrels, resembling a college installation; in its six foreign languages (including Russian and Chinese); and in its stress on independent study particularly for the academically talented. Melbourne's chief claim to fame lay in its nongraded organizational plan. In the Melbourne Plan students are grouped not by ability as measured by tests of intelligence or scholastic aptitude but on the basis of achievement tests, subject by subject. A tenth grade student, therefore, might be enrolled in Algebra 1, Phase 2 and English, Phase 4. Some subjects, such as typing and physical education, are neither graded nor phased. Melbourne's schedule of course offerings described each of its seven phases:[49]

- Phase 1: Subjects are designed for students who need special assistance in small classes.
- Phase 2: Subjects are designed for students who need more emphasis on the basic skills.
- Phase 3: Courses are designed for students who have an average background of achievement.
- Phase 4: Subject matter is designed for extremely well prepared students desiring education in depth.
- Phase 5: Courses are available to students who are willing to assume responsibility for their own learning and pursue college level courses while still in high school.
- Phase Q: Students whose creative talents are well developed should

[48] Arthur B. Wolfe, *The Nova Plan for Instruction* (Fort Lauderdale, Fla.: Broward County Board of Public Instruction, 1962), pp. 14–15.
[49] Melbourne High School, Brevard County, Florida Public Schools.

give consideration to the Quest phase of the curriculum. This is an important dimension of the phased organization designed to give thrust in the direction of individual fulfillment. In this phase a student may research an area in which he is deeply and broadly curious either to develop creative powers or in quest of knowledge.

□ Phase X: Subjects which do not accommodate student mobility; e.g., typing, physical education, are ungraded but unphased.

To show the full scope of the phased organizational plan of Melbourne High School a recent schedule is reproduced in Figure 9-2. To conserve space, names of faculty and room assignments have been omitted from this reproduction.

Brown referred to the ungraded concept implemented at Melbourne High School not only as the nongraded school [50] but also the multiphased school.[51] Brown gave particular attention to the independent study or quest phase of the program. He referred to the quest phase as both "Education by Appointment" [52] since students see their teachers by appointment in the tutorial fashion and "Education by Agreement" since he recommended that schools emulate the Dalton plan by drawing up an agreement form or contract specifying the independent study that a student plans to do.[53]

Although a noble experiment in curriculum reorganization, nongradedness has not reached the goal that Brown predicted, namely, that within a few years after its inception, "every intellectually respectable high school will have some degree of nongraded education." [54]

Over the decades a number of curricular arrangements have been tried out with varying degrees of success in both our hypothetical community and elsewhere.

WHERE WE ARE

THE ELEMENTARY SCHOOL

Open Education and Open Space

Some six years ago the hypothetical elementary school that we created at the beginning of this chapter caught on to the tail-end of a movement known as the open-space school. The interior walls between classrooms came tumbling

---

[50] B. Frank Brown, *The Nongraded High School* (Englewood Cliffs, N.J.: Prentice-Hall, 1963).

[51] B. Frank Brown, *The Appropriate Placement School: A Sophisticated Nongraded Curriculum* (West Nyack, N.Y.: Parker Publishing Company, 1965).

[52] B. Frank Brown, *Education by Appointment/New Aproaches to Independent Study* (West Nyack, N.Y.: Parker Publishing Company, 1968), p. 61.

[53] For information on the Dalton (Massachusetts) Plan see Helen Parkhurst, *Education on the Dalton Plan* (New York: E. P. Dutton, 1922).

[54] Brown, *The Nongraded High School*, p. 44.

FIGURE 9-2   Schedule of course offerings at Melbourne High School

MELBOURNE HIGH SCHOOL
SCHEDULE OF COURSE OFFERINGS

DEPARTMENT	PERIOD 1 7:30 - 8:30	PHASE	PERIOD 2 8:35 - 9:30	PHASE
ENGLISH Recommendation: Phase 3-5, 10th year students take American Literature All students must take one English class each semester. *Means semester only.*	World Literature	4	AP Literature	5
	British Literature	4	Writing*	3-4
	British Literature	3	British Literature	3
	American Literature	5	Speech*	3-4
	World Literature	3	Plan	
	American Literature	3	American Literature	3
	World Literature	3	World Literature	3
			Contemporary Literature*	3-4
			American Literature	3
	American Literature	3	American Literature	4
	Career English	3	Communications II	1-2
SOCIAL STUDIES All students must earn credit in American History and C.P.S. Plus ½ additional credit *Means semester only.*	Communications I	1-2	Communications I	1-2
	American History	4	American History	4
	American History	3	American History	3
	C.P.S.*	2	Problems of Today*	2
	C.P.S.*	3	C.P.S.*	4
	American History	3	American History	3
	Geography*	3-4		
SCIENCE 1 credit required	Biology	4	Biology	4
	Chemistry I	3	Chemistry I	3
	Biology	3	Biology	3
	Physical Science	2	Plan	
	Marine Science	3	Biology	3
	Biology	2	Biology	2
MATHEMATICS 2 credits required (One must be 10th year) *Means semester only.*	Physics I	3	Physics I	4
	Geometry	3	Geometry	3
	Algebra II	3	Geometry	4
	Individual Math	1-2	Plan	
	Algebra I	3	Algebra I	3
	Consumer Math	3	Consumer Math	3
	Calculus	5	Computer Math	4-5
	Math Analysis	4	Trigonometry*	4
			Plan	
	Plan			
	Consumer Math	3		

PERIOD 3 9:35 -10:30	PHASE	PERIOD 4 10:35 - 12:00	PHASE	PERIOD 5 12:05 -1:00	PHASE	PERIOD 6 1:05 -.2:00	PHASE
AP British Literature	5	World Literature	4	World Literature	4	Plan	
British Literature	4	British Literature	4	Plan		British Literature	4
British Literature	3	Plan		British Literature	3	Annual	X
Plan		American Literature	4	American Literature	4	American Literature	4
World Literature	4	World Literature	3	World Literature	4	World Literature	3
Plan		British Literature	3	American Literature	3	American Literature	3
World Literature	3						
Humanities I	3	Humanities I	4				
American Literature	3						
American Literature	4	American Literature	3	Mystery Literature*	3	Plan	
Communications II	1-2	Plan		Communications III	1-2	Career English	3
		Bulldog Bark	X				
Plan		Career English	2				
Plan		American History	4-5	Law in Action*	3-4	American History	4
American History	3	Plan		American History	4	C.P.S.*	4
Plan		American History	1-2	American History	2	American History	2
C.P.S.*	3	C.P.S.*	3	Plan		European History	3-4
Problems of Today*	3-4	American History	3	Problems of Today*	3-4	Plan	
		Plan		American History	3	American History	3
Humanities I	3	Humanities I	4				
Biology	4	Microbiology	4	Plan		Science Research	Q
Chemistry I	4	Chemistry	4	Plan		Biology	4
Plan		Chemistry I	3	Chemistry I	3	Chemistry I	3
Ecology	3	Biology	3	Biology	3	Biology	3
Biology	3	Plan		Physiology	4	Physiology	4
Biology	1	Biology	2	Biology	3	Plan	
				Aviation	3	Aviation	3
Physics I	4	Plan				Science Research	Q
Geometry	3	Geometry	3	Plan		Advanced Algebra*	3
Algebra II	3	Algebra II	3	Algebra II	3	Plan	
Algebra I	3	Algebra I	3	Algebra I	3	Algebra I	3
Algebra I	3	Plan					
				Math Daily Living	3	Math Daily Living	3
Plan		Algebra II	4-5	Computer Math	4-5	Algebra II	4
Trigonometry*	3	Trigonometry*	3	Plan		Trigonometry*	4
		Plan		Geometry	4		
				Individual Math	1-2	Individual Math	1-2
Math Daily Living	3						
				Plan		Consumer Math	3
				Consumer Math	3		

FIGURE 9-2   Melbourne High School (*continued*)

DEPARTMENT	PERIOD 1 7:30 - 8:30	PHASE	PERIOD 2 8:35 - 9:30	PHASE
FOREIGN LANGUAGES	Spanish III	4	Spanish II	3-4
	French I	3-4	French II	3-4
PHYSICAL EDUCATION	Aquatics	X	Co-ed Team	X
	Conditioning (Co-ed)	X	Conditioning (Co-ed)	X
			Plan	
	Dance	X	Advance Dance	X
	Aquatics	X		
FINE ARTS	Instru. Tech.	X	Concert Band	X
	Plan		Art I	X
AIR FORCE ROTC	AE I	X	AE II	X
	ROTC Administration and Athletic Business Management			
DRIVER EDUCATION *Means semester only.*			Plan	
	Driver Education*	X	Plan	
BUSINESS EDUCATION VOCATIONAL *Means semester only.*	Clerical Occ.	X	Fundamentals of Business	X
	Plan		Secretarial Occ.	X
	Fundamentals of Business	X	Plan	
LIBRARY SCIENCE	Library Science	X	Library Science	X
	Library Science	X	Library Science	X
INDUSTRIAL TRADES & INDUSTRIAL ARTS	Building Trades I	X	Building Trades I	X
	Auto Mechanics I	X	Auto Mechanics I	X
	Electronics II			X
	Commercial Art	X	Commercial Art	X
	Drafting III	X	Drafting II	X
	Engineering Drawing I	X	Engineering Drawing II	X
HOME ECONOMICS	Family Living*	X	Fundamentals of Foods	X
	Plan		Child Care	X
	Clothing Management, Production & Services			X
CO-OP ED. D.E. D.C.T.	Marketing & Merchandizing I	X	Marketing & Merchandizing II	X
	DCT	X	DCT (Employment Skills)	X
JOB ENTRY	Job Entry	X	Job Entry	X
INDEPENDENT STUDY	Independent Study	Q	Independent Study	Q
SPECIAL EDUCATION E.H./S.L.D.	EH	X	EH	X
	SLD	X	SLD	X
ALTERNATIVE ED.	Alt. Education	X	Alt. Education	X
COMPENSATORY ED.	Math	X	Math	X
CETA	Math	X	Math	X

PERIOD 3 9:35 -10:30	PHASE	PERIOD 4 10:35 - 12:00	PHASE	PERIOD 5 12:05 -1:00	PHASE	PERIOD 6 1:05 -.2:00	PHASE
Spanish I	3-4	Plan		Spanish II	3-4	Spanish I	3-4
		German I	3-4	Plan		German II	3-4
French III	3-4						
Co-Ed Individual Sports	X	Co-Ed Individual Sports	X	Plan		Conditioning (Co-ed)	X
Conditioning (Co-ed)	X	Conditioning (Co-ed)	X	Conditioning (Co-ed)	X	Plan	
Co-ed Team	X	Co-ed Team	X	Co-ed Team	X	Conditioning (Co-ed)	X
Choreography	X	Plan		Dance	X	Dance	X
Instru. Tech.	X	Symphonic Band	X	Jazz Band	X	Plan	
Chorale	X			Plan		Solos & Ensembles	X
Crafts	X	Crafts	X	Crafts	X	Art I	X
		Plan		Drawing & Painting	X	Drawing & Painting	X
AE III	X	AE II	X	AE I	X	Plan	
Driver Education*	X	Driver Education*	X	Driver Education*	X	Driver Education*	X
Fundamentals of Business	X	Plan		Fundamentals of Business	X	Consumer Math	3
Math Daily Living	3	Fundamentals of Business	X	Fundamentals of Business	X	Fundamentals of Business	X
Accounting Occ.	X	Accounting Occ.	X	Individual Math	2	Individual Math	2
Library Science	X	Library Science	X	Library Science	X	Library Science	X
Library Science	X	Library Science	X	Library Science	X	Library Science	X
Building Trades III			X	Plan		Building Trades II	X
Auto Mechanics II & III			X	Auto Mechanics I	X	Plan	
Electronics I	X	Electronics I	X			Plan	
Commercial Art	X	Plan		Drawing & Painting	X	Drawing & Painting	X
Drafting II	X	Drafting I	X	Drafting I	X	Plan	
Architectural Drawing	X	Engineering Drawing I	X	Plan		Engineering Drawing I	X
Food Production & Services			X	Fundamentals of Food	X	Plan	
Child Care II	X	Child Care	X	Child Care II	X	Child Care II	X
Plan	X	Health*	X	Fundamentals of Clothing	X	Fundamentals of Clothing	X
Fashion Mrkt-Merchandising*	X	Plan		DE Marketing Occ. Experience			X
DCT	X	Plan		DCT Supervision			X
Job Entry	X	Job Entry	X	Job Entry	X	Job Entry	X
Independent Study	Q	Independent Study	Q	Search	Q	Independent Study	Q
Plan		SLD	X	SLD	X	SLD	X
Plan		SLD	X	SLD	X	SLD	X
Alt. Education	X	Alt. Education	X	Alt. Education	X	Alt. Education	X
Math	X	Math	X	Plan			
Math	X	Math	X	Plan		Athletic Office	

down or as many walls as possible in a building constructed as a graded school many years ago. The purpose in eliminating barriers between classes was to permit innovative approaches such as flexible grouping, individualized instruction, nongradedness, and team teaching.

Open-space or *open-area education* is an architectural response to a broader philosophical and organizational concept called open education, the open classroom, or, simply, the open school. In practice, the terms are often interchanged. An *open classroom,* for example, might signal a classroom operated according to principles of *open education.* At the same time, this classroom might be an *open area,* although open space is not a prerequisite to open education. An *open school* might be a school that implements the open-education concept or it might be an open-space school in which all classrooms are without walls.

C. M. Charles and others commented: "Many people think that open space and open education are synonymous. They are not. In fact, they can be (but don't have to be) quite opposite." [55] Charles and others defined an open school not as an open-space school but as a school with several open classrooms following principles of open education.[56] Open-space schools normally subscribe to at least some of the principles of open education, whereas open schools, as defined by Charles and coworkers may or may not be open-space schools.

In the ensuing discussion we will use the terms open school, open classroom, and open education when we speak of the broad concept and open space or open area when we talk about the architectural arrangement of classrooms without walls.[57] The open-space concept was illustrated in Chapter 3 with patterns two and three of team/grade level organization.

Imported from Great Britain the open-classroom concept was designed as a curricular and organizational response to formal, traditional schools. Charles and others briefly described open education as follows:

> Open education refers to organization and management that allow much student choice and self-direction. The teacher helps, but dominates neither the planning nor the learning activities. Instead, the teacher "facilitates" student learning. This facilitation is done through talking, exploring, suggesting options, helping find resources, and deciding on ways of working that suit the group. Emphasis falls continually on maintaining relationships, interacting positively with others, fostering a sense of personal

[55] C. M. Charles, David K. Gast, Richard E. Servey, and Houston M. Burnside, *Schooling, Teaching, and Learning: American Education* (St. Louis: The C. V. Mosby Company, 1978), p. 118.

[56] Charles et al., pp. 118–119.

[57] To complicate the matter further, classrooms without walls are not the same as schools without walls. Schools without walls operate without their own school buildings, sending their students wherever they need to be sent in the area to receive the education they need. Thus, the students may be studying in agencies of the community or may be enrolled in other schools.

and group worth, and providing for the development of individual potential.[58]

Louis Rubin described the philosophical basis for the open classroom as
follows:

> The basic ideology is rooted in the notion that children have a natural
> interest and desire in learning. Thus, when there is a conducive environ-
> ment, and when the learning structure does not inhibit individuality, good
> education invariably will occur. What we have come to call relevance, as
> a result, is built into the fundamental philosophy itself; the curriculum, in
> short, is derived almost entirely from student interests and needs.[59]

Rubin went on to contrast the traditional and open classrooms, saying:

> The critical distinctions between open and traditional education are
> that the goals are different, their means of attainment vary, and different
> outputs are yielded by each. A traditional program, for example, requires
> that a prescribed course of study be followed, leaving little leeway for
> accommodation to individual student interests. Its chief virtue, therefore,
> is that we can determine in advance, to a very sizable extent, what the
> child will and will not learn. But in the open education climate precisely
> the opposite condition prevails; since the child's own intellectual interests
> serve as the educational point of departure, predetermined objectives must
> defer to individual whim, and specified learning outcomes cannot be
> guaranteed.[60]

Common sights in the elementary school today are large expanses of
classroom space, groups of one hundred or more pupils spread out and
engaged in a variety of activities at many stations within the areas, and teams
of teachers working with individuals, small groups, and large groups of
learners.

Beliefs Underlying Open-Space Schools. Proponents of the open classroom
stress active learning and the affective domain. John H. Proctor and Kathryn
Smith stated six beliefs to which the faculty and administration of Oliver
Ellsworth School (Windsor, Connecticut), a modified open-area elementary
school, subscribe. These are:

1. We believe learning should be an active process; therefore, both the
   children and the teacher are actively involved in learning and teaching.
2. We believe children develop at different rates and have different
   strengths and weaknesses; therefore, different assignments and groupings are used by the teachers and students to meet these needs.

---

[58] Charles et al., p. 119.
[59] Louis Rubin, "Open Education: A Short Critique," in Louis Rubin, ed., *Curriculum Handbook: The Disciplines, Current Movements, and Instructional Methodology*
(Boston: Allyn and Bacon, 1977), p. 375.
[60] Rubin, pp. 375–376.

3. We believe children learn best what they are interested in; therefore, a wide variety of activities is provided.

4. We believe that children should learn to function as cooperative members of a group; therefore we provide for constant group interaction.

5. We believe children function best under conditions of trust, support, encouragement, and success; therefore, we emphasize the positive aspects of behavior and work, rather than the coercive, negative factors.

6. We believe children should learn how to learn and make decisions; therefore we emphasize both skills and processes.[61]

"The primary advantage of open space," said Proctor and Smith, "is the increased communication and interaction of teacher to teacher, teacher to student, and student to student." [62] Significant features of the open-space concept are the flexibility of grouping and the use of concrete materials that appeal to the interests and maturity level of the learners. Whereas many open elementary schools are organized into clusters or teams of a single grade level, e.g., first grade, others, like Oliver Ellsworth, are nongraded and organized into multiunits. The pattern for this school with its four units or teams is shown in Figure 9-3.[63]

The open-education/open-space movements appear at this time to have crested. Many schools that removed or built walls just for an open-area model are reinstalling walls or partitions to recreate smaller, self-contained units. What happened to this seemingly promising movement within the short space of some ten years?

Pratt offered one reason for difficulties incurred by the open-space school when he observed:

> The attempt to transplant the architectural aspect (of open-area schools in England) to North America has not been universally successful. Frequently, the innovation consisted of building schools with fewer interior walls, an environment into which teachers were introduced who had neither participated in, approved of, or been trained for the open environment. Continuing to teach in a conventional way, they found the absence of walls merely an audible and visible distraction. Bookcases, screens, and miniature palm trees were quickly turned into makeshift barriers between the teaching areas. Small wonder that the research evidence shows, at best, disappointing performance by students in open classrooms, not only in academic subjects but also in creativity, and an increased anxiety level.[64]

---

[61] John H. Proctor and Kathryn Smith, "IGE and Open Education: Are They Compatible?" *Phi Delta Kappan* 55, no. 8 (April 1974): 564.

[62] Proctor and Smith, p. 565.

[63] Proctor and Smith, p. 565.

[64] David Pratt, *Curriculum: Design and Development* (New York: Harcourt, Brace, Jovanovich, 1980), p. 384.

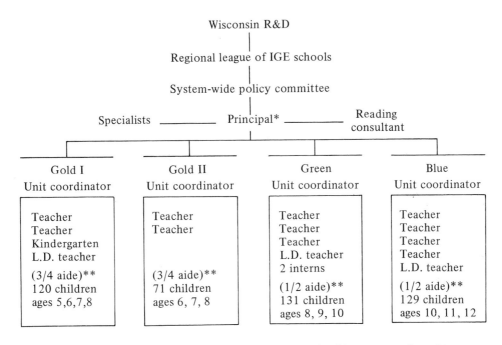

Wisconsin R&D

Regional league of IGE schools

System-wide policy committee

Specialists _____ Principal* _____ Reading consultant

Gold I	Gold II	Green	Blue
Unit coordinator	Unit coordinator	Unit coordinator	Unit coordinator
Teacher	Teacher	Teacher	Teacher
Teacher	Teacher	Teacher	Teacher
Kindergarten		Teacher	Teacher
L.D. teacher		L.D. teacher	Teacher
(3/4 aide)**	(3/4 aide)**	2 interns	L.D. teacher
120 children	71 children	(1/2 aide)**	(1/2 aide)**
ages 5,6,7,8	ages 6, 7, 8	131 children	129 children
		ages 8, 9, 10	ages 10, 11, 12

*The principal and unit coordinators make up the Instructional Improvement Committee.
**All units use parent volunteers.

FIGURE 9-3   Organization chart for Oliver Ellsworth School

The audible and visual distractions have been, in my judgment, erroneously minimized. Visits to open classrooms rather consistently reveal a noise level that is not conducive to learning. Harried teachers must consistently keep elevating their voices to make themselves understood. When ardent proponents of the open classroom are questioned about the noise, their response is often: "What noise?" or "Some noise is necessary for learning to take place." Perhaps, we can attribute some of the fault for these distractions to the lack of fit between program and architecture.

Rubin pointed out that, contrary to the claims of some advocates of open education, traditional education is not necessarily as bad as some people paint it. He commented:

In fairness, it must be acknowledged that the proponents of open education have sometimes built their case upon a straw man. Traditional education — although formalized and structured — need not be depressing nor debilitating of the learner's spirit. In point of fact, there is abundant reason to believe that some learners thrive better in a traditional setting than in an open one. To wit, children sometimes find a lack of structure uncomfortable and large doses of freedom anxiety provoking. Similarly, provisions for the affective components of education, for the emotional feelings of students, can be made in both a traditional and an open format. As a result, one cannot in good conscience claim that an unstructured, open curriculum is necessarily more "humanistic" than a structured, traditional one.

Nor, to extend the point further, can one claim that an open curriculum automatically teaches the child to think more than a traditional one, or that multiage grouping cannot exist in either situation, or that prescribed programs of instruction must, inevitably, prohibit individualization. Put another way, a large number of benefits habitually claimed by champions of one approach or the other can, in reality, be used with equal effectiveness in both.[65]

In regard to the success of open-space and open-education plans, Charles and coworkers observed: "In many cases, open space has not produced the results that were hoped for.... There is little evidence, however, to support open education on the grounds of academic achievement." [66]

THE JUNIOR HIGH SCHOOL

A School in Transition

The hypothetical junior high school that we visualized up the street from the equally fictitious school board office is largely subject-centered. Comprising grades seven, eight, and nine, it is not much different from its 7,000 or so counterparts elsewhere in the country. The fictitious curriculum committee meeting in the school board office is painfully aware that finding the "right" curriculum for the junior high school is a task yet to be realized.

The goals of the junior high school are exceedingly ambitious. It expects to continue the students' development of the basic skills, provide a solid cognitive program, offer exploratory experiences so children can sharpen their interests, prepare pupils for high school, help boys and girls as they grow socially and biologically from puberty to adolescence, serve as a guidance center, and help children develop affective competencies.

Junior High School Standards. One of the members of our hypothetical curriculum committee — a teacher at the junior high school — thumbs through a copy of *The Junior High School We Need,* a brief report issued by the Association for Supervision and Curriculum Development in 1961.[67] Looking at the chapter entitled "The Junior High School Today," the teacher muses, "I wonder whether we meet these standards even now," and proceeds to read the

[65] Rubin, p. 376.
[66] Charles et al., pp. 118–119.
[67] Grambs et al., *The Junior High School We Need.*

standards to the other members of the curriculum committee. Her comments (in quotes) follow each standard.

The good junior high school of today should:

1. Be of moderate size.

"We meet that standard, albeit we've actually lost a few students with declining enrollment. We're in the 500 to 800 category recommended."

2. Have a well-stocked library staffed by a professional librarian-teacher.

"A ratio of 10 or more books per student is recommended. We're close."

3. Provide ample guidance services.

"We have two guidance counselors for our 600+ children, which could be called sufficient but certainly not ample."

4. Offer block-of-time instruction each year for the three years so that one teacher will have a group of children for a substantial period.

"We dropped our block-time organization a few years ago."

5. Maintain flexibility of scheduling.

"We have a conventional single period schedule."

6. Be staffed with teachers prepared for junior high school teaching and devoted to junior high school age students.

"We try to fill vacancies with teachers who wish to work in the junior high school. No doubt, however, some are marking time until an opening arises in the senior high school. Unfortunately, a secondary teaching certificate in this state qualifies for both junior and senior high school. There is no certificate for junior high school per se. As a matter of fact, no special courses on the junior high school are required as part of the secondary certificate."

7. Provide help for teachers by principals, by supervisory staff, and by clerical personnel.

"We have reasonably adequate clerical help and instructional materials and equipment. Each teacher has a planning period."

8. Provide a modern instructional program in subject areas.

"I'd say we do this as well as any junior high school. We try to articulate the program with the elementary and senior high school. We provide both remedial and developmental programs in the basic skills. Our guidance counselors do their best to assist the pupils with school problems."

9. Have adequate physical education programs.

"We do well in this area."

10. Have ample laboratory and workshop facilities.

"We have adequate facilities in industrial arts, homemaking, and music. We need additional space for art and science. We have no foreign language laboratory but are not sure that we need it."

11. Have an established, reasonable teacher load.

"Each teacher teaches five periods per day. The teachers' union successfully defeated two attempts of the school board in recent years to increase the teachers' loads to six periods per day."

In spite of a more or less positive assessment, however, the faculty of this hypothetical junior high school has been dissatisfied with the program for quite some time. For that reason, they have been shaping up a proposal that will be ready for the curriculum committee in the near future. We shall see what they propose later in this chapter.

THE SENIOR HIGH SCHOOL

A Comprehensive High School

Marching band? They can put on a razzle-dazzle spectacular at half-time with the best. They have been invited to participate in parades of the major bowls in the United States.

Football? Basketball? Try baseball, golf, and tennis. The showcase in front of the principal's office is crammed with shiny trophies won by students of this school. We should not be unkind enough to mention that most of the trophies have been won by boys. School officials are moving rapidly to eliminate vestiges of sex discrimination.

Typing? Classes of fifty students pound away at relatively new electric typewriters. Skill in typing is encouraged for all.

Art? Come to the annual art show put on by the school's art students to appreciate the excellence of their work.

Vocational education? Wood shop, metals shop, electricity, and auto mechanics are all available. Each shop has ample space and is well equipped.

The academics? Students from this school regularly achieve high scores on national standardized tests of achievement in the subject areas; graduates are placed in colleges and universities without difficulty; science students yearly win recognition at the science fairs; foreign language students bring home prizes from state competitions in their field; many students are enrolled in advanced placement courses; the student body as a whole is well above the norm in reading and mathematics.

What we are describing here is a high quality, traditional, comprehensive high school. As such, it meets the definition of a comprehensive high school given by James B. Conant who saw the comprehensive high school as "a high school whose programs correspond to the educational needs of *all* youth in the community." [68] Personnel of this school concur with the Association for Supervision and Curriculum Development (ASCD) and with Conant as to the objectives of the school. The ASCD maintains:

> The secondary school should be a comprehensive school. If a major task of the public school system in America is to develop the basic values of a free society, and mutual respect for the range of persons and groups within our diverse culture, students must have an opportunity to live and work together. The comprehensive secondary school is an essential element

---

[68] Conant, *The American High School Today,* p. 12.

in the development of a common viewpoint sufficiently strong to hold our nation together.[69]

Conant cited three main objectives of a comprehensive high school:

> . . . *first,* to provide a general education for all the future citizens; *second,* to provide good elective programs for those who wish to use their acquired skills immediately on graduation; *third,* to provide satisfactory programs for those whose vocations will depend on their subsequent education in a college or university.[70]

This school shows up well on criteria suggested by both Conant and the ASCD. Conant listed the following points to be considered in evaluating a comprehensive school:

A. Adequacy of general education for all as judged by:
    1. Offerings in English and American literature and composition
    2. Social studies, including American history
    3. Ability grouping in required courses
B. Adequacy of nonacademic elective program as judged by:
    4. The vocational programs for boys and commercial programs for girls
    5. Opportunities for supervised work experience
    6. Special provisions for very slow readers
C. Special arrangements for the academically talented students:
    7. Special provisions for challenging the highly gifted
    8. Special instruction in developing reading skills
    9. Summer sessions from which able students may profit
    10. Individualized programs (absence of tracks or rigid programs)
    11. School day organized into seven or more instructional periods
D. Other features:
    12. Adequacy of the guidance services
    13. Student morale
    14. Well-organized homerooms
    15. The success of the school in promoting an understanding between students with widely different academic abilities and vocational goals (effective social interaction among students)[71]

ASCD Recommendations. Our hypothetical secondary school would meet not only the criteria as set forth by Conant but also the standards recommended by the Association for Supervision and Curriculum Development. Kimball Wiles and Franklin Patterson, writing for the ASCD's Commission on the

---

[69] Kimball Wiles and Franklin Patterson, *The High School We Need* (Alexandria, Va.: Association for Supervision and Curriculum Development, 1959), pp. 5–6.
[70] Conant, *The American High School Today,* p. 17.
[71] Conant, *The American High School Today,* pp. 19–20.

Education of Adolescents, made recommendations for the comprehensive high school, some of which are cited here:

> Certain types of growth must be promoted in all youth who attend the secondary school. Each youth should develop increased understanding of self and his responsibilities in society, commitment to democratic values, economic understanding, political acumen, and ability to think. . . .
>
> The program for each individual must contain general education and specialized education. . . . One-third to one-half of each student's program should be devoted to general education . . . the required courses and activities . . . essential for competent citizenship. . . . One-half to two-thirds of each student's program should be used to develop his talents and to further his personal goals within the framework that the community is willing and able to support. . . .
>
> Choices among the various offerings of the curriculum should be made jointly by the pupil, parents and staff members of the school in terms of the pupil's purposes, aptitude and level of achievement. . . .
>
> Each student should have one staff member who guides him throughout his high school career. . . .
>
> Each high school student should be a member of at least one home base group with which he has a continuing relationship. . . .
>
> Students should be grouped in various ways in different phases of their high school experience . . . the general education phase of an individual's schedule should be in classes that are heterogeneously grouped. . . . In the portion of the student's program that is elective, the grouping should be homogeneous in terms of two factors: the pupil's intensity of purpose and his level of achievement. . . .[72]

When Conant came out with his follow-up study, officials of our hypothetical senior high school were pleased that their school compared favorably with the better comprehensive high schools. They surely enrolled more than 750 pupils; they graduated at least 100 pupils each year; they offered calculus and four years of a modern foreign language (two languages, to be exact); the ratio of counselors to students was within the recommended range of 250 to 300; students were grouped homogeneously in the elective subjects and heterogeneously in the required courses; they offered courses in business education, homemaking, and industrial arts; and they required two years of social studies (making three with ninth-grade social studies) and three years of English.[73] This school well met the tests of comprehensiveness.

---

[72] Wiles and Patterson, pp. 6–17.
[73] See Conant, *The Comprehensive High School* (New York: McGraw-Hill, 1967).

WHERE WE ARE GOING

THE ELEMENTARY SCHOOL

Return to Traditional Modes

With the accountability movement still strong, we may expect to see the elementary school intensifying its emphasis on the basic skills. The public, through its state legislatures, has given its strong endorsement to programs of state assessment — the testing of youngsters in a number of subject areas, but especially in reading and mathematics.

Our hypothetical elementary school is restoring its walls as rapidly as possible, reverting to the self-contained classroom model. Reorganization plans, which we will soon describe in connection with the junior high school, will affect both the elementary school and the senior high school.

The broad-fields approach will continue to predominate but teachers will give more attention to preplanning. Minimal competencies in the various disciplines will be spelled out so the direction of the school's program will be more evident. The elementary school will attempt to curb the flight of pupils to private and parochial schools by becoming more traditional.

While remaining conscious of the affective needs of the learners, teachers will demand more of classroom behavior, known as deportment in older times. Children will be given the opportunity to participate in decision making to the extent of their abilities and maturity. Once decisions are made, pupils will be expected to follow through. Teachers will behave much as William Glasser implies: "Teachers who care accept no excuses." [74]

The elementary school of the immediate future will be a sophisticated elementary school of the past, basically essentialistic in character, but with progressive overtones.

THE JUNIOR HIGH SCHOOL

The Middle School

Something substantial is clearly afoot in our hypothetical junior high school. Dramatic changes are in the wind that will make an impact on the neighboring elementary and senior high schools. The elementary school will lose a grade in the process and the high school will gain or, more accurately, regain a grade. Representatives of these three schools have been working together for two years now to reorganize the structure of their system with the junior high school as the focal point. Next year, assuming approvals are obtained from the faculties, school administrators, district curriculum committee, and

---

[74] William Glasser, *Schools Without Failure* (New York: Harper & Row, 1969), p. 23.

parent advisory groups, a major change will be effected. The junior high school will be converted from its present status with grades seven, eight, and nine to a middle school housing grades six, seven, and eight. The elementary school will then encompass grades one through five besides kindergarten, and the three-year high school, an innovation in its own day, will reincorporate the ninth grade.

It became clear to educators that the needs of a special group of youngsters — adolescents or early adolescents or, in the newest terminology, "transescents" — were not being met by either the elementary school or the high school structure. These preadolescents were children in the middle.

Special Needs of Students. Some other countries have recognized the needs of middle students for a long time, as in Germany with its *mittelschule*. Boys and girls of the pre- and early adolescent years, ages ten to fourteen as a rule, evidence special needs. They are too mature to be treated as primary school children and too immature to be considered high schoolers. They evidence a host of physical, social, and emotional growth needs as well as educational demands. Their career and life interests are just beginning to take shape. They need time to explore, to adjust, to socialize as well as to study.

As a result, the junior high school spun off from the other levels as a separate institution and literally mushroomed. From two identified separate junior high schools with grades seven, eight, and nine in 1910, the junior highs now number more than 7,000. Their number, however, is declining as they undergo the metamorphosis from junior high to middle school.

Lounsbury and Vars characterized the junior high school as a significantly successful development in American education.[75] Whereas the seven-eight-nine pattern was the most common for the junior high school, other relatively common patterns were seven-eight, six-seven-eight, seven through ten, and eight through ten. Despite this variety, as the years passed dissatisfaction with the junior high school began to set in. It was argued that this intermediate school had become a carbon copy of the senior high school with all the trappings — interscholastic athletics, band, high school subjects, etc.

Junior high school students were changing not only physically but also socially in response to new, unexpected social values. L. J. Chamberlin and R. Girona described the more recent drives that affect early adolescents in the following manner:

> Today's young child is motivated by drives that a few years ago affected only youths ten years his or her senior. Traits such as straining against parental authority, desire for greater freedom, and extreme loyalty to peer groups that once characterized the late teen years, now are often encountered in much younger children.[76]

---

[75] See Lounsbury and Vars, p. 15.

[76] L. J. Chamberlin and R. Girona, "Our Children Are Changing," *Educational Leadership*, 33, no. 4 (January 1976): 303.

As a result of these changes and of society's new demands on adolescents, the program for these years was revised and updated. A new organizational pattern grouped grades five or six through eight into a middle school with its own unique program, and a four-four-four system or five-three-four system began to emerge. Although the ninth grade is generally considered as "belonging" to the high school, there is some uncertainty amongst middle-school specialists as to whether the fifth grade should be attached to the elementary school or to the middle school.

Phenomenal Growth. The middle school has experienced a phenomenal growth. In 1965 the Educational Research Service of the National Education Association conducted a nationwide survey and found 63 middle schools.[77] William M. Alexander in a 1967–68 survey reported 1101 middle schools, and Mary F. Compton accounted for 3723 middle schools in 1974.[78] Kenneth Brooks identified 4,060 middle schools operating in 1978.[79] Observed Brooks:

> The number of schools has grown significantly in every state except Nebraska and in the District of Columbia, which are still without any middle schools. The more populous states — Florida, Illinois, Michigan, New York, Ohio, Pennsylvania, Texas, and Virginia — account for over half of the middle schools.[80]

Alexander and others saw the middle school as an emerging institution and defined it in the following manner:

> To us, it is *a school providing a program planned for a range of older children, preadolescents, and early adolescents that builds upon the elementary school program for older childhood and in turn is built upon by the high school's program for adolescence.* . . . Thus, the emergent middle school may be best thought of as *a phase and program of schooling bridging but differing from the childhood and adolescent phases and programs.*[81]

Transformation of the junior high school into a middle school should not be perceived as a reorganization of but one level of the school system. Alexander and others pointedly remarked, ". . . the new middle school should be seen more as an effort to reorganize the total school ladder than just one of its levels." [82]

Recommendations for the Middle School. Thomas E. Gatewood and Charles A. Dilg, speaking for the Association for Supervision and Curriculum Devel-

---

[77] Lounsbury and Vars, pp. 22–23.
[78] Lounsbury and Vars, pp. 22–23.
[79] Kenneth Brooks, "The Middle Schools—A National Survey," *Middle School Journal* 9, no. 1 (February, 1978): 6–7.
[80] Brooks, p. 6.
[81] William M. Alexander et al., *The Emergent Middle School,* 2d, enlarged edition (New York: Holt, Rinehart and Winston, 1969), p. 5.
[82] Alexander et al., p. 4.

opment's Working Group on the Emerging Adolescent Learner, made a series of recommendations for the middle school.[83] Let's examine a few. Speaking of the physical characteristics of transescents they recommended:

> A program for the emerging adolescent that is adapted to the ever-changing physical needs of this learner. . . .
>
> Instruction related to growth of the body so that one can better understand changes in himself or herself and in others and be prepared for future changes and problems.[84]

Speaking of mental and intellectual growth, Gatewood and Dilg made the following recommendations:

> Learning experiences for transescents at their own intellectual levels, relating to immediate rather than remote academic goals.
>
> A wide variety of cognitive learning experiences to account for the full range of students who are at many different levels of concrete and formal operations. . . .
>
> Opportunities for the development of problem-solving skills, reflective-thinking processes, and awareness for the order of the student's environment.
>
> Cognitive learning experiences so structured that students can progress in an individualized manner. However, within the structure of an individualized learning program, students can interact with one another. . . .
>
> A common program in which areas of learning are combined and integrated to break down artificial and irrelevant divisions of curriculum content. . . .
>
> Methods of instruction involving open and individually directed learning experiences. The role of the teacher should be more that of a personal guide and facilitator of learning than of a purveyor of knowledge.[85]

Speaking of personality development characteristics, Gatewood and Dilg recommended:

> Administrative arrangements to ensure that personality development has continuity both in breadth and in depth. Thus continuous, cooperative curriculum planning is essential among elementary, middle, and secondary school personnel.
>
> A comprehensive, integrated series of learning encounters to assist learners to develop a self which they realize, accept, and approve. . . .
>
> Classroom instruction, counseling, and extra-class activities that take into account the social-emotional needs of transescents.
>
> An approach in working with emerging adolescents that will have consistency with basic democratic principles.[86]

---

[83] Thomas E. Gatewood and Charles A. Dilg, *The Middle School We Need* (Alexandria, Va.: Association for Supervision and Curriculum Development, 1975).

[84] Gatewood and Dilg, p. 8.

[85] Gatewood and Dilg, pp. 11–12.

[86] Gatewood and Dilg, p. 16.

Gatewood and Dilg have called attention to the broad range of physical, intellectual, and personal characteristics of middle school students. In their recommendations they have presented guidelines for meeting various needs of the emerging adolescent.

Proposed Design. A curriculum design for the middle school has been proposed by Lounsbury and Vars, consisting of three main components: core, continuous progress (nongraded learning experiences), and variable.[87]

Core in their conception is "a problem-centered block-time program." [88] The continuous progress (nongraded) component consists of "those skills and concepts that have a genuine sequential organization." [89] Science, for example, may overlap with the core along with its placement in the nongraded component. The variable component is comprised of "the activities and programs that have proven their worth in schools . . . neither so highly sequential as to be placed exclusively in the nongraded component nor so essentially problem-centered as to fit entirely within the core." [90] The middle-school curriculum as proposed by Lounsbury and Vars is shown schematically in Figure 9-4.[91]

Our hypothetical junior high school, changing as it will to a pattern which has been in successful operation throughout the country for almost twenty years now, is catching onto the coattails of a promising development in education for the preadolescent years.

THE SENIOR HIGH SCHOOL

Some Alternatives

The comprehensive high school, which we discussed in some detail, was conceived as a unique American response to the needs of youth. Every young person would find in this institution programs necessary to his or her present and future success in our society. The comprehensive high school was a reaction to specialized high schools that cared for specific segments of our student population. This institution would accommodate boys and girls from every social strata and ethnic group. They would live, work, and play together thus breaking down barriers between them. The comprehensive high school was a democratic response to education in a democratic society.

Yet, from the 1960s the comprehensive high school came under attack. The National Panel on High Schools and Adolescent Education claimed that the comprehensive high school reinforced social class and race stratification

---

[87] Lounsbury and Vars, pp. 45–48.

[88] Lounsbury and Vars, p. 46.

[89] Lounsbury and Vars, p. 47.

[90] Lounsbury and Vars, p. 47.

[91] Gordon F. Vars, "New Knowledge of the Learner and His Cultural Milieu: Implications for Schooling in the Middle Years." Paper presented at the Conference on the Middle School Idea, College of Education, University of Toledo, November 1967. ERIC Document No. ED 016 267 CG 901400, p. 14. See also Lounsbury and Vars, p. 45.

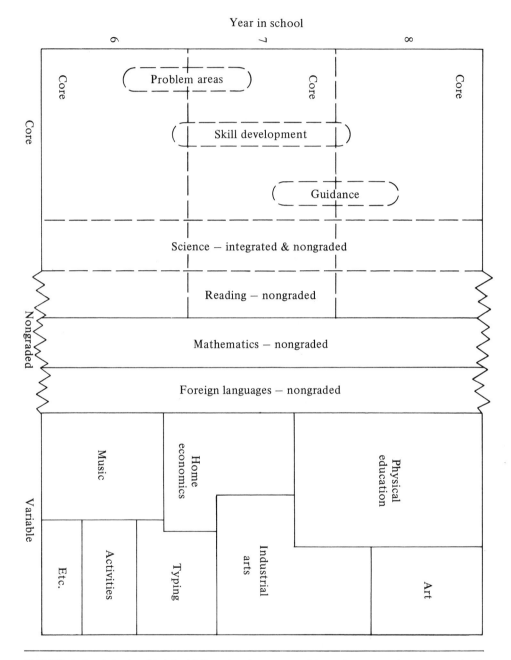

FIGURE 9-4   A junior high/middle school program. Note that core classes are scheduled back to back to facilitate cross-graded grouping on a temporary basis whenever appropriate.

rather than diminished it.[92] The comprehensive high school was criticized for a number of reasons. Some felt it deemphasized the academics; others felt the opposite and claimed it deemphasized the affective domain. Some believed it was too structured; others, that it was not structured enough. Some maintained it was taking on too many responsibilities; some, that it was not assuming enough. Some accused the comprehensive high school of slighting career education; others were not satisfied with the students' achievement in the cognitive domain.

Call for Reform. In recent years we have heard the clarion cry for "reform" in secondary education. John Henry Martin, author of *The Education of Adolescents,* the report of the National Panel on High Schools and Adolescent Education of the United States Office of Education, for example, expressed the belief that the Seven Cardinal Principles were too inclusive and were "inflated statements of purpose." [93] He argued that the Seven Cardinal Principles were much too broad, stating:

> Among the unfortunate consequences of the sweeping language of the Seven Cardinal Principles has been our assumption that the schools could reform all of society's ills. Schools have undertaken burdens that they have neither the resources nor the talents to overcome.[94]

Martin took the position that schools cannot be responsible for all aspects of life, that goals of the school (that is, the high school) must be redefined, and that aims more modest than those of the Seven Cardinal Principles must be set.

Martin perceived the community as sharing responsibility for the education of youth. He advised as follows:

> Redefining the goals of schools and building new relationships between youth and adults requires that the comprehensive high school be replaced with a comprehensive program of community-based education. Such a design for the education of adolescents should delineate those purposes of education that would remain the primary responsibility of the high school, those that might better be shifted to other and new community agencies, and those that would be served by a cooperative sharing of resources.[95]

---

92 See John Henry Martin, *The Education of Adolescents,* Report of the National Panel on High Schools and Adolescent Education (Washington, D.C.: U.S. Office of Education, 1976).

93 John Henry Martin, "Reconsidering the Goals of High School Education," *Educational Leadership* 37, no. 4 (January, 1980): 280.

94 Martin, "Reconsidering the Goals of High School Education," p. 279.

95 Martin, "Reconsidering the Goals of High School Education," p. 281. See also "High School Goals: Responses to John Henry Martin," *Educational Leadership* 37, no. 4 (January 1980): 286–298.

A. Harry Passow discussed proposals of five national groups looking at secondary education.[96] In addition to the National Panel on High Schools and Adolescent Education, the American public has received reports from the National Association of Secondary School Principals,[97] the National Commission on the Reform of Secondary Education (referred to as the Kettering Commission),[98] the Panel on Youth of the President's Science Advisory Committee,[99] and Educational Facilities Laboratories and I/D/E/A.[100]

Among the proposals coming out of these national groups were calls for:

☐ a reduced school day with more time being spent in work experience programs in the community
☐ educational options, i.e., alternative forms of schooling to be selected by students and parents
☐ a lowering of the age of compulsory attendance to fourteen years of age
☐ establishment of specialized high schools in the European tradition
☐ an emphasis on career education
☐ restriction of the function of the high school to cognitive learning

It is clear that if some of these proposals were seriously considered and adopted, the comprehensive high school, which Tanner and Tanner describe as "the institutional ideal of the American social conscience," [101] would be greatly altered or might even disappear. It is an anomaly that some of America's educators advocate alternative and specialized schools as a response to the democratization of education whereas England's planners, for example, long experienced with separate schools, are looking to comprehensive secondary schools to keep their people unified.

Educational Options. Responding to some of the current criticisms of public education, alternative schools have been popping up around the country at both the elementary and secondary level. Kenneth G. Michaels reported:

> It is estimated that there are some 2,000 alternatives presently in operation in 35 states in communities of all sizes and economic status. State

---

[96] A. Harry Passow, "Reforming America's High Schools," *Phi Delta Kappan* 56, no. 9 (May 1975): 587–590. Also in Glen Hass, *Curriculum Planning: A New Approach,* 3rd ed. (Boston: Allyn and Bacon, 1980), pp. 380–384.

[97] National Association of Secondary School Principals, National Committee on Secondary Education, *American Youth in the Mid-Seventies* (Reston, Va.: National Association of Secondary School Principals, 1972).

[98] National Commission on the Reform of Secondary Education, *The Reform of Secondary Education: A Report to the Public and the Profession* (New York: McGraw-Hill, 1973).

[99] James S. Coleman, Chairman, Panel on Youth of the President's Science Advisory Committee, *Youth: Transition to Adulthood* (Washington, D.C.: Superintendent of Documents, U.S. Government Printing Office, 1973). Also (Chicago: University of Chicago Press, 1974).

[100] Ruth Weinstock, *The Greening of the High School* (New York: Educational Facilities Laboratories, 1973).

[101] Tanner and Tanner, p. 605.

departments of education in Connecticut, Massachusetts, Delaware, California, Illinois, New Jersey, New York, Pennsylvania, and Washington are actively encouraging school systems to explore and develop alternatives within the system. . . . the Minneapolis School Board voted unanimously to try to offer alternative educational styles to all elementary students. . . . Since 1972, all families in the Berkeley, California school district could choose from 23 alternatives. The new Quincy, Illinois high school offers five alternative forms of education to its students, one of which is, of course, traditional school.[102]

Alternative education is also known as education by choice or educational options. The following statements suggest the rationale for developing and supporting alternative public secondary education. Some, perhaps many, cannot profit from the established high school; they cannot learn effectively in a structured setting. The impact of agencies outside the school — families, peer groups, churches, businesses, and industries — on learners is far greater than that of the school; these agencies should therefore be tapped. In a democratic society families should have a choice as to the type of education they wish their children to receive. Unless the public schools make changes from within, young people will either drop out physically, stay in and drop out mentally, or transfer to private schools.

What, we may ask, is an alternative school? The National Consortium for Options in Public Education defined an alternative school as "any school (or minischool) within a community that provides alternative learning experiences to the conventional school program and is available by choice to every family within the community at no extra cost." [103]

Free schools, street academies, storefront schools, and schools without walls are illustrations of alternative education. Among the better known options are the Parkway Program in Philadelphia, which dates back to 1969, and Metro High School in Chicago, which began its program in 1970. In programs of this type, the community, in effect, becomes the school. The school system enlists the cooperation of business, cultural, educational, industrial, and social institutions to serve in the education of young people. The school system draws on the talents of knowledgeable and experienced persons in the community to serve as instructors.

Education by choice, however, is possible in the more typical school *with* walls. Parents may be accorded the option of placing their children in open-space schools, bilingual schools, or even traditional basic skills schools.

The concept of choice in education is certainly appealing and is in the best democratic tradition. On the other hand, if young high school people, for

---

[102] Kenneth G. Michaels, "A Statement on Behalf of Education by Choice," *The FASCD Journal* 1, no. 1 (February 1979): 16–17.

[103] National Consortium for Options in Public Education, *The Directory of Alternative Public Schools,* Robert D. Barr, ed. (Bloomington, Ind.: Educational Alternatives Project, Indiana University, 1975), p. 2. The 1975 Directory is out of print and no longer available.

example, are siphoned off to other educational settings, the comprehensive high school will be fractured and rendered impotent without an accompanying guarantee that alternative forms of schooling will yield a superior education.

The American public, concerned that children achieve the fundamentals, that they have access to higher education, and that economy of operation is maintained, is unlikely to support radical departures from the established forms of schooling. The public is not likely to heed proposals for deschooling or for turning loose fourteen-year-olds on the precarious job market. On the other hand, it may well support reasonable alternatives within the existing framework.

What Is in the Distant Future?

A growing number of individuals both inside and outside of the academic world are being identified by the rather ambiguous label of "futurist." One of the better known persons in this group is Alvin Toffler, whose books, *Future Shock* and *The Third Wave,* provoked many of us to contemplate problems of the future and to begin considering ways to solve them.[104] High on the agenda of any futurist are problems like population control, health needs, air and water pollution, housing needs, adequate food supplies, demands for energy, and the use of technology.

The futurists' scenario inevitably calls our attention to the invention of tiny semiconductor chips that have made possible new electronic marvels for leisure (home video equipment, electronic games) and for business (microcomputers, data banks). Futurists who concern themselves with educational problems see computer literacy as a needed basic skill.[105]

Some educational futurists view the new technology as aiding the teacher and administrator to provide a more effective education within the school setting. Others predict what amounts to a type of deschooling. Peter Sleight, for example, reported on the type of deschooling that might be effected by the computer age, stating:

> It may be that children won't attend schools at all, but attend classes in their own homes, taking lessons through the computer, with the teacher talking to them through a video image.
>
> Through the same network, the teacher will know whether a student is tuned in and can take "attendance" in the old-fashioned sense.
>
> Homework for the children will also be changed. No longer will they be bringing home textbooks and doing assignments on paper. Instead, they may plug into the school data base to receive their assignments, execute

---

[104] Alvin Toffler, *Future Shock* (New York: Random House, 1970); *The Third Wave* (New York: William Morrow, 1980).

[105] See Arthur J. Lewis, "Educational Basics to Serve Citizens in the Future," *The FASCD Journal* 1, no. 1 (February 1979): 5.

them on the computer screen at home and "send" it to their teacher via the computer hook-up.[106]

When or if this day comes, what will happen to the notion of interactive learning, i.e., interaction between teacher and students and student and student? How will students learn to socialize with each other? What will happen to multicultural, multiethnic education? How will boys and girls learn to live in a pluralistic society? Perhaps, we might wish to conceptualize this type of computerized schooling as consuming only a portion of the day with alternative forms of education in the community taking the remaining portion.

SUMMARY

Before curriculum planners can proceed with their task of developing the curriculum, they must decide on the organizational structure within which programs will be implemented. At the beginning of this chapter, we visualized as illustrative examples three schools — elementary, junior high, and senior high — which like their counterparts in other areas of the country have undergone numerous internal changes.

We traced some of the past organizational patterns at each level, described current organizational structures, and went on to discuss some immediate and apparent long-range future developments. On the elementary level we reviewed the graded school, the activity curriculum, and the continuous progress plans. At the junior high school level we looked at the core curriculum. Several organizational plans at the senior high level were revisited, including the subject matter curriculum, the broad-fields curriculum, team teaching, flexible scheduling, and the nongraded high school.

The elementary school was currently engaged in a plan utilizing the open-space concept. The junior high school was in the midst of revamping its curricular organization and the senior high exemplified a quality comprehensive high school.

It is anticipated that in the near future the elementary school will move away from the open-space concept and revert to a traditional, subject-centered, basic skills school, though maintaining some of the fundamental overtones of child-centeredness. The junior high school is definitely headed toward transformation into a middle school, which will, of course, affect the programs of both the elementary and the senior high schools as well as its own. The comprehensive high school will adjust to recent criticisms and demands for the reform of secondary education by adopting some alternative forms of schooling offered within and under supervision of the public school system.

The ubiquitous computer could conceivably revolutionize education at all levels, and curricula could be expected to respond, perhaps organizationally

---

[106] Peter Sleight, "Information Services: Possibilities Are Endless," *Fort Lauderdale News and Sun-Sentinel,* July 27, 1980, Section H, p. 3.

and, more certainly, substantively, to emerging social problems of growing concern to our people.

SUPPLEMENTARY EXERCISES

1. Prepare a written report on British open schools.
2. Write a paper summarizing some of the research on the achievement of learners in open-space schools.
3. Look up the Eight-Year Study and write a report summarizing its methodology and findings.
4. Describe one or more core programs from either the professional literature or from a school with which you have had firsthand experience.
5. Prepare a paper on the topic: "Shall We Group Pupils?" If so, how? Whether the answer is "yes" or "no," reasons must be stated.
6. Play the role of futurist and predict what may happen in curriculum organization fifteen years hence.
7. Write a paper citing at least three references, accounting for the current reversion to emphasis on the basic skills.
8. Write a paper on the question of the placement of fifth grade in the educational system — in elementary school or middle school?
9. Write a paper on the question of the placement of ninth grade in the educational system — in middle school or high school?
10. From the literature or from firsthand knowledge, describe several options in education, i.e., alternative forms of schooling.
11. State pros and cons of specialized versus comprehensive high schools and show your position.
12. Write a paper on the topic "Junior High School or Middle School — Which?"
13. Explain what is meant by a broad-fields curriculum. Critique this approach.
14. Write a paper on the question "Why did the decade from 1955 to 1965 produce so many curricular innovations?"
15. Explain what is meant by the activity curriculum. Critique this approach.
16. Read the report of one of the national groups mentioned in this chapter that spoke to the question of reform in secondary education.
17. State whether you believe the school (any level) should limit itself to cognitive learning. Give reasons for the position taken.
18. Write a paper on the applications of the computer to in-school education.

BIBLIOGRAPHY

Aikin, Wilford M. *The Story of the Eight-Year Study*. New York: Harper & Row, 1942.

Alberty, Harold B. and Alberty, Elsie J. *Reorganizing the High-School Curriculum,* 3rd ed. New York: Macmillan, 1962.

Alexander, William M., et al. *The Emergent Middle School,* 2d, enlarged edition. New York: Holt, Rinehart and Winston, 1969.

————. "Guidelines for the Middle Schools We Need Now," *The National Elementary School Principal* 51, no. 3 (November 1971): 79–89.

Beggs, David W., III, ed. *Team Teaching: Bold New Venture.* Bloomington, Ind.: Indiana University Press, 1969.

———— and Buffie, Edward G., eds. *Nongraded Schools in Action: Bold New Venture.* Bloomington, Ind.: Indiana University Press, 1967.

Brooks, Kenneth. "The Middle Schools — A National Survey," *Middle School Journal* 9, no. 1 (February 1978): 6–7.

Brown, B. Frank. *Education by Appointment: New Approaches to Independent Study.* West Nyack, N.Y.: Parker Publishing Co., 1968.

————. *The Appropriate Placement School: A Sophisticated Nongraded Curriculum Study.* West Nyack, N.Y.: Parker Publishing Co., 1965.

————. *The Nongraded High School.* Englewood Cliffs, N.J.: Prentice-Hall, 1963.

Buffie, Edward G. and Jenkins, John M. *Curriculum Development in Nongraded Schools: Bold New Venture.* Bloomington, Ind.: Indiana University Press, 1971.

Burton, William H. *The Guidance of Learning Activities,* 3rd ed. New York: Appleton-Century-Crofts, 1962.

Bush, Robert N. and Allen, Dwight W. *A New Design for High School Education: Assuming a Flexible Schedule.* New York: McGraw-Hill, 1964.

Calvin, Allen D., ed. *Programmed Instruction: Bold New Venture.* Bloomington, Ind.: Indiana University Press, 1969.

Chamberlin, L. J. and Girona, R. "Our Children Are Changing," *Educational Leadership* 33, no. 4 (January 1976): 301–305.

Coleman, James S., Chairman, Panel on Youth of the President's Science Advisory Committee. *Youth: Transition to Adulthood.* Washington, D.C.: Superintendent of Documents, U.S. Government Printing Office, 1973. Also, Chicago: University of Chicago Press, 1974.

Commission on the Reorganization of Secondary Education. *Cardinal Principles of Secondary Education.* Bulletin 35. Washington, D.C.: U.S. Office of Education, 1918.

Conant, James B. *The American High School Today.* New York: McGraw-Hill, 1959.

————. *The Comprehensive High School.* New York: McGraw-Hill, 1967.

————. *Recommendations for Education in the Junior High School Years.* Princeton, N.J.: Educational Testing Service, 1960.

Costello, Lawrence F. and Gordon, George H. *Teach With Television.* New York: Hastings House, 1961.

Educational Policies Commission. *Education for All American Youth.* Washington, D.C.: National Education Association, 1944.

Eurich, Alvin C., ed. *High School 1980.* New York: Pitman Publishing Corp., 1970.

Fantini, Mario, ed. *Alternative Education: A Source Book for Parents, Teachers, and Administrators.* Garden City, N.Y.: Anchor Books, 1976.

————. "Alternatives Within Public Schools," *Phi Delta Kappan* 54, no. 7 (March 1973): 444–448.

————. *Public Schools of Choice: Alternatives in Education.* New York: Simon and Schuster, 1973.

————. "The What, Why, and Where of the Alternatives Movement," *The National Elementary Principal* 52, no. 6 (April 1973): 14–22.

Faunce, Roland C. and Bossing, Nelson L. *Developing the Core Curriculum.* Englewood Cliffs, N.J.: Prentice-Hall, 1951.

Foshay, Arthur W. *Curriculum for the 70's: An Agenda for Invention.* Washington, D.C.: National Education Association, Center for the Study of Instruction, 1970.

Fry, Edward B. *Teaching Machines and Programmed Instruction: An Introduction.* New York: McGraw-Hill, 1963.

Gatewood, Thomas E. and Dilg, Charles A. *The Middle School We Need.* Alexandria, Va.: Association for Supervision and Curriculum Development, 1975.

Gibbons, Maurice, Chairman, Phi Delta Kappa Task Force on Compulsory Education and Transitions for Youth. *The New Secondary Education: Task Force Report.* Bloomington, Ind.: Phi Delta Kappa, 1976.

Glasser, William. *Schools Without Failure.* New York: Harper & Row, 1969.

Goodlad, John I. and Anderson, Robert H. *The Nongraded Elementary School,* rev. ed. New York: Harcourt, Brace, Jovanovich, 1963.

Grambs, Jean D., Noyce, Clarence G., Patterson, Franklin, and Robertson, John. *The Junior High School We Need.* Alexandria, Va.: Association for Supervision and Curriculum Development, 1961.

Hansen, John H. and Hearn, Arthur C. *The Middle School Program.* Chicago: Rand McNally, 1971.

Harvard Committee. *General Education in a Free Society.* Cambridge, Mass.: Harvard University Press, 1945.

Hass, Glen. *Curriculum Planning: A New Approach,* 3rd ed. Boston: Allyn and Bacon, 1980.

Hassett, Joseph D. and Weisberg, Arline. *Open Education: Alternatives Within Our Tradition.* Englewood Cliffs, N.J.: Prentice-Hall, 1972.

Hillson, Maurie and Bongo, Joseph.

Continuous-Progress Education: A Practical Approach. Palo Alto, Cal.: Science Research Associates, 1971.

Hunkin, Francis P. *Curriculum Development: Program Planning and Improvement.* Columbus, Ohio: Charles E. Merrill, 1980.

Illich, Ivan. *Deschooling Society.* New York: Harper & Row, 1971.

Kilpatrick, William H. *Foundations of Method: Informal Talks on Teaching.* New York: Macmillan, 1925.

Kindred, Leslie W., Wolotkiewicz, Rita J., Mickelson, John M., Coplein, Leonard E., and Dyson, Ernest. *The Middle School Curriculum: A Practitioner's Handbook.* Boston: Allyn and Bacon, 1976.

Kohl, Herbert R. *The Open Classroom: A Practical Guide to a New Way of Teaching.* New York: New York Review, distributed by Random House, 1969.

Lewis, Arthur J. "Educational Basics to Serve Citizens in the Future," *The FASCD Journal* 1, no. 1 (February 1979): 1–8.

Lounsbury, John H. and Vars, Gordon F. *A Curriculum for the Middle School Years.* New York: Harper & Row, 1978.

McNeil, John D. *Curriculum Administration: Principles and Techniques of Curriculum Development.* New York: Macmillan, 1965.

Manlove, Donald C. and Beggs, David W., III. *Flexible Scheduling: Bold New Venture.* Bloomington, Ind.: Indiana University Press, 1965.

Martin, John Henry. *The Education of Adolescents,* Report of the National Panel on High Schools and Adolescent Education. Washington, D.C.: United States Office of Education, 1976.

Meriam, Junius L. *Child Life and the Curriculum.* Yonkers, N.Y.: World Book Co., 1920.

Michaels, Kenneth G. "A Statement

on Behalf of Education by Choice," *The FASCD Journal* 1, no. 1 (February 1979): 16–20.

Miller, Richard I., ed. *The Nongraded School: Analysis and Study.* New York: Harper & Row, 1967.

Moss, Theodore C. *Middle School.* Boston: Houghton Mifflin, 1969.

Murray, Evelyn M. and Wilhour, Jane R. *The Flexible Elementary School: Practical Guidelines for Developing a Nongraded Program.* West Nyack, New York: Parker Publishing Company, 1971.

National Association for Core Curriculum. *Core Today: Rationale and Implications.* Kent, Ohio: National Association for Core Curriculum, 1973.

National Association of Secondary School Principals, National Committee on Secondary Education. *American Youth in the Mid-Seventies.* Reston, Va.: National Association of Secondary School Principals, 1972.

National Commission on the Reform of Secondary Education. *The Reform of Secondary Education: A Report to the Public and the Profession.* New York: McGraw-Hill, 1973.

National Consortium for Options in Public Education. *The Directory of Alternative Public Schools.* Bloomington, Ind.: Educational Alternatives Project, Indiana University, 1975.

National Education Association. *Report of the Committee of Ten on Secondary School Studies.* New York: American Book Co., 1894.

Oliva, Peter F. *The Secondary School Today,* 2d ed. New York: Harper & Row, 1972.

Parkhurst, Helen. *Education on the Dalton Plan.* New York: E. P. Dutton, 1922.

Passow, A. Harry, ed. *Curriculum Crossroads.* New York: Teachers College, Columbia University, 1962.

———. "Reforming America's High Schools," *Phi Delta Kappan* 56, no. 9 (May 1975): 587–596.

Phenix, Philip H. *Realms of Meaning: A Philosophy of the Curriculum for General Education.* New York: McGraw-Hill, 1964.

Popper, Samuel H. *The American Middle School: An Organizational Analysis.* Waltham, Mass.: Blaisdell Publishing Co., 1967.

Pratt, David. *Curriculum Design and Development.* New York: Harcourt, Brace, Jovanovich, 1980.

Proctor, John H. and Smith, Kathryn. "IGE and Open Education: Are They Compatible?" *Phi Delta Kappan* 55, no. 8 (April 1974): 564–566.

Rafferty, Max. *What They Are Doing to Your Children.* New York: New American Library, 1964.

Rogers, Vincent R. "English and American Primary Schools," *Phi Delta Kappan* 51, no. 2 (October 1969): 71–75.

Rollins, Sidney P. *Developing Nongraded Schools.* Itasca, Ill.: F. E. Peacock Publishers, 1968.

Rubin, Louis, ed. *Current Movements and Instructional Technology.* Boston: Allyn and Bacon, 1977.

Shane, Harold G. *Curriculum Change Toward the 21st Century.* Washington, D.C.: National Education Association, 1977.

Shearer, William J. *The Grading of Schools.* New York: H. P. Smith Publishing Co., 1898.

Smith, B. Othanel, Stanley, William O., and Shores, J. Harlan. *Fundamentals of Curriculum Development,* rev. ed. New York: Harcourt, Brace, Jovanovich, 1957.

Stephens, Lillian S. *The Teacher's Guide to Open Education.* New York: Holt, Rinehart and Winston, 1974.

Tanner, Daniel and Tanner, Laurel N. *Curriculum Development: Theory Into*

Practice, 2d ed. New York: Macmillan, 1980.

Toffler, Alvin. *Future Shock.* New York: Random House, 1970.

————. *The Third Wave.* New York: William Morrow, 1980.

Trump, J. Lloyd. "Flexible Scheduling—Fad or Fundamental?" *Phi Delta Kappan* 44, no. 8 (May 1963): 370.

———— and Baynham, Dorsey. *Focus on Change: Guide to Better Schools.* Chicago: Rand McNally, 1961.

———— and Miller, Delmas F. *Secondary School Curriculum Improvement: Meeting the Challenges of the Times,* 3rd ed. Boston: Allyn and Bacon, 1979.

Tyler, Ralph W. "Curriculum Development Since 1900," *Educational Leadership* 38, no. 8 (May 1981): 598–601.

Van Til, William, Vars, Gordon F., and Lounsbury, John H. *Modern Education for the Junior High School Years,* 2d ed. Indianapolis, Ind.: Bobbs-Merrill, 1967.

Vars, Gordon F., ed. *Common Learnings; Core and Interdisciplinary Team Approaches.* Scranton, Pa.: International Textbook Company, 1969.

Von Haden, Herbert I. and King, Jean Marie. *Educational Innovator's Guide.* Worthington, Ohio: Charles A. Jones, 1974.

Weinstock, Ruth. *The Greening of the High School.* New York: Educational Facilities Laboratories, 1973.

Wiles, Kimball. *The Changing Curriculum of the American High School.* Englewood Cliffs, N.J.: Prentice-Hall, 1963.

———— and Patterson, Franklin. *The High School We Need.* Alexandria, Va.: Association for Supervision and Curriculum Development, 1959.

Wolfe, Arthur B. *The Nova Plan for Instruction.* Fort Lauderdale, Fla.: Broward County Board of Public Instruction, 1962.

Wright, Grace S. *Block-Time Classes and the Core Program in the Junior High School,* Bulletin 1958, no. 6. (Washington, D.C.: U.S. Office of Education, 1958.

Zais, Robert S. *Curriculum: Principles and Foundations.* New York: Harper & Row, 1976.

FILMS

And No Bells Ring. Parts I and II. Total time: 57 minutes. Sound. Black and white. Reston, Va.: National Association of Secondary School Principals, 1960. Hugh Downs narrates this film on team teaching. Film depicts large-group instruction, small-group discussion, and independent study. J. Lloyd Trump is shown in the film.

Make a Mighty Reach. 28 minutes. Sound. Color. Melbourne, Fla.: Institute for Development of Educational Activities, 1967. Shows a variety of innovations, including ungraded programs, flexible scheduling, and computer-assisted instruction.

RECORD/FILMSTRIP

Focus on Change. 23 minutes. Washington, D.C.: National Education Association, 1962. Howard K. Smith narrates this recording on large-group instruction, small-group discussion, and independent study. Filmstrip in color.

FILMSTRIP-TAPE PROGRAM

Vimcet Associates, P.O. Box 24714, Los Angeles, California 90024:

Opening Classroom Structure, 1972.

10

Instructional Goals and Objectives

After studying this chapter you should be able to:
1. Identify the three major domains of learning.
2. List the major categories of learnings from one taxonomy of each of the three domains.
3. Explain the relationships between curriculum goals and objectives and instructional goals and objectives.
4. Distinguish between instructional goals and objectives.
5. Be able to identify and write instructional goals in each of the three domains.
6. Be able to identify and write instructional objectives in each of the three domains.

You should also be able to formulate and give reasons for your views on the following issues:
1. Your feelings about the task of writing nonbehavioral instructional goals.
2. Your feelings about the task of writing instructional (behavioral) objectives.
3. Your agreements or disagreements with the taxonomies of the three domains featured in this chapter.

PLANNING FOR INSTRUCTION

With the curriculum decisions made, the broad territory known as instruction looms before us. In some ways it is a familiar land whose landmarks — lesson plans, teaching strategies, and tests — are recognized by administrators, teachers, students, and parents. As we enter the area of instruction, decision making remains a major responsibility, only, this time, the responsibility falls directly on the classroom teacher. Up to this point persons identified as curriculum planners, among whose number are classroom teachers, have been engaged in making decisions of a programmatic nature. Now classroom teachers will become occupied in making decisions of a methodological nature. They will be answering questions like:

- □ What are the objectives to be accomplished as a result of instruction?
- □ What topics will we cover?
- □ What procedures are best for directing the learning?
- □ How do we evaluate instruction?

At this stage the teacher must decide whether to designate topics or specify competencies; whether to feature the teacher's objectives or the pupils'; whether to seek mastery of content or simply exposure to the material; whether to aim instruction at groups or at individuals.

Planning for instruction includes specifying instructional goals and objectives (discussed in this chapter), selecting instructional strategies (considered in Chapter 11), and choosing techniques to evaluate instruction (treated in Chapter 12).

To put our next task in perspective, let's review the steps we have taken so far. We have:

- □ surveyed needs of students in general
- □ surveyed needs of society
- □ clarified our philosophy of education and stated general aims
- □ identified curriculum goals and objectives
- □ determined needs of students in the school, needs of the community, and needs as shown by the subject matter
- □ reaffirmed plans for organizing the curriculum or selected and implemented plans for reorganizing the curriculum

Having completed these steps, we are ready to undertake planning, presenting, and evaluating instruction. The instructional phases of the curriculum-instruction continuum are shown as a subset of the model for curriculum development suggested in Chapter 5.[1] The subset consists of six components (VI, VII, VIII; IX A and B; X, XI), shown in Figure 10-1. In Chapter 5 we diagrammed these instructional components in such a way that they

---

[1] See p. 169 of this text.

could be removed from the overall model for curriculum development. Yet, we posited in Chapter 1 an intimate relationship between curriculum and instruction, concluding that the two could be separated for purposes of analysis but the existence of one could not be meaningful without the other.

The Instructional Model

Figure 10-1 represents a model of instruction that, for simplicity, we will refer to as the Instructional Model. This Instructional Model is broken into two major phases: the planning phase and the operational phase. The operational phase is divided into two parts: the implementation or presentation of instruction and the evaluation of instruction.

The planning phase of the Instructional Model consists of four components: component VI—the identification of instructional goals; component VII—the specification of instructional objectives; component VIII—the teacher's plans for instructional strategies or choice of weapons, we might say; and component IX, which consists of both a preliminary and a final phase of planning for the evaluation of instruction.

Where, then, and how does the teacher begin to plan for instruction? Let's look at several approaches to planning for instruction. Teacher A comes into the class without a preconceived notion of what he or she will cover and pulls a theme out of the air as the spirit moves him or her. Given the profession's penchant for turning rubrics into seeming substance, some might call this approach instantaneous planning. Others, less kind, might term it nonplanning.

Teacher B takes the textbook, divides the number of chapters by the number of weeks in the school year, lists the topics of each chapter by week and from there takes any one of a number of directions. For each topic in its turn the teacher might:

☐ jot down some questions for class discussion
☐ prepare notes for a lecture
☐ design individual and group assignments for clarifying points in the chapters

Teacher C selects topics for study during the year, using all kinds of materials related to the topic, including the textbook, and creates a succession of units of work for the class.

Teacher B's most likely course of action is the Assign-Study-Recite-Test approach, mentioned in the preceding chapter. Teacher C will follow what is commonly called the unit method of teaching, a problem-solving approach.

All three teachers may or may not relate their plans to the predetermined curriculum goals and objectives. All three may or may not specify the instructional goals and objectives that pupils are expected to accomplish. It is my position that both of these actions should be taken by teachers.

Of course, these three illustrations of types of teachers are exaggerated.

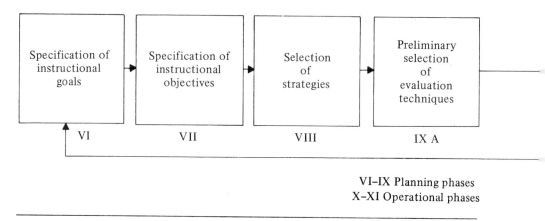

VI–IX Planning phases
X–XI Operational phases

FIGURE 10-1   The instructional model

Eclectic as teachers are and, perhaps should be, they are not likely to fall into any one consistent mold. Too, these are but three illustrations of an almost infinite variety of teacher models. Yet, the illustrations are general enough to represent a significant number of teachers. The thesis of this chapter is that, regardless of the teacher's model or style of teaching, curriculum goals and objectives are more likely to be accomplished and students more likely to demonstrate mastery of learning if instructional goals and objectives are specified before starting instruction.

INSTRUCTIONAL GOALS AND OBJECTIVES DEFINED

Before we tackle the central mission of this chapter — selecting and writing instructional goals and objectives — let's see what instructional goals and objectives are. An *instructional goal* is a statement of performance expected of each student in a class, phrased in general terms without criteria of achievement. The term instructional goal is used in this text like Norman E. Gronlund's *general instructional objective*[2] and Tyler's term *tentative general objective*.[3] "The student will show an understanding of the stock market" is an example of an instructional goal. It indicates the performance expected of the learner, but that performance is not stated in such a fashion that its attainment can be readily measured. As a curriculum goal pointed the direction to curriculum objectives, an instructional goal points the way to instructional objectives.

---

[2] Norman E. Gronlund, *Stating Objectives for Classroom Instruction,* 2d ed. (New York: Macmillan, 1978).

[3] Ralph W. Tyler, *Basic Principles of Curriculum and Instruction* (Chicago: University of Chicago Press, 1949).

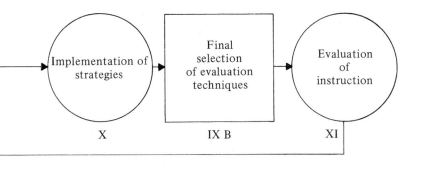

An *instructional objective* is a statement of performance to be demonstrated by each student in the class, derived from an instructional goal, phrased in measurable and observable terms. We may equate this term with Gronlund's *specific learning outcome* and Tyler's *precise instructional objective*. The following statement is an example of an instructional objective: "The student will convert the following fractions to percentages with 100 percent accuracy: 1/4, 1/3, 1/2, 2/3, 3/4." Instructional objectives are also known as behavioral objectives, performance objectives, or competencies.

Stating Objectives

Whereas teachers have consistently been urged to specify objectives, they have only been encouraged relatively recently to state these objectives in terms of expected pupil behavior. Tyler discussed four ways that instructors state objectives.[4] Objectives are:

1. things that the instructor will do. Tyler gave as examples, "to present the theory of evolution," "to demonstrate the nature of inductive proof," "to present the Romantic poets," and "to introduce four-part harmony."
2. topics, concepts, generalizations, or other elements of content that are to be dealt with in the course or courses. Tyler's examples are: "the Colonial period" and "matter can be neither created nor destroyed."
3. generalized patterns of behavior that fail to indicate more specifically the area of life or the content to which the behavior applies. Tyler identified illustrations of this type of objective: "to develop critical thinking," "to develop appreciation," and "to develop social attitudes."
4. terms that identify both the kind of behavior to be developed in the student and the content or area of life in which this behavior is to operate. Tyler's examples are: "to write clear and well-organized reports of social studies projects" and "to develop an appreciation of the modern novel."

---

4 Tyler, pp. 44–47.

Of the four types of objectives outlined by Tyler, the fourth is preferable. As the next section reveals, current methodology advocates specifying instructional objectives in terms of expected, specific student behavior, not as actions of the teacher, as topics, or as generalized patterns of behavior.

THE USE OF BEHAVIORAL OBJECTIVES

Whether to use behavioral objectives or not is a debate that has raged among educators for years. Supporters of behavioral objectives argue that this approach to instruction

- forces the teacher to be precise about what is to be accomplished
- enables the teacher to communicate to pupils what they must achieve
- simplifies evaluation
- makes accountability possible
- makes sequencing easier

W. James Popham, in support of behavioral objectives, wrote:

> Measurable instructional objectives are designed to counteract what is to me the most serious deficit in American education today, namely, a preoccupation with the process without assessment of consequences.... There are at least three realms in which measurable objectives have considerable potential dividends: in curriculum (what goals are selected); in instruction (how to accomplish those goals); and in evaluation (determining whether objectives of the instructional sequence have been realized). ... It is perhaps because I am a convert to this position that I feel viscerally, as well as believe rationally, that measurable objectives have been the most significant instructional advance in the past 10 years.[5]

The opponents of behavioral objectives hold that writing behavioral objectives

- is a waste of time
- is dehumanizing
- restricts creativity
- leads to trivial competencies

James D. Raths voiced his opposition to behavioral objectives as follows:

> ... consider the long range implications a teacher and his students must accept once it has been decided that all students are to acquire a specific instructional objective. The teacher's task becomes at once difficult and tedious. He must inform his students of the objective to which they are expected to aspire; he must convince them of the relevance of this

---

[5] W. James Popham, "Practical Ways of Improving Curriculum Via Measurable Objectives," *The Bulletin of the National Association of Secondary School Principals* 55, no. 355 (May 1971): 76.

objective to their lives; he must give his students the opportunity to practice the behavior being taught; he must diagnose individual differences encountered by members of his group; he must make prescriptions of assignments based on his diagnosis and repeat the cycle again and again. . . . Yet even if all programs could be set up on the basis of behavioral objectives and even if strict training paradigms could be established to meet the objectives, who could argue that such a program would be other than tedious and ultimately stultifying? [6]

Problems With Behavioral Objectives

While the yeasayers and naysayers argued with each other, the behavioral objectives camp itself added to the difficulty of convincing teachers to use behavioral objectives. Some, perhaps overenthusiastic about the behavioral objectives movement, turned off teachers by:

1. assuming a rather dogmatic approach that seemed to rule out all other methodologies. Although I am favorably disposed toward the use of behavioral objectives, I would be hard-pressed to come up with solid experimental data to show that students exposed to a behavioral-objectives approach consistently show higher achievement than students taught by other approaches.

    What some of the research reveals is that behavioral objectives can be useful as preinstructional strategies, that objectives work better if they pertain to the particular instructional task, that objectives are more effective with certain kinds of instruction than with others, that objectives are useful in accomplishing learning at higher levels of the cognitive taxonomy, and that students of average ability, male students of high socioeconomic background, and both the more independent and less conscientious students benefit from behavioral objectives.[7]

2. resorting to formulae, which tended to make the writing of behavioral objectives mechanical rather than creative, as, for example, "Given the _____, the student will _____ in _____ minutes with a score of _____."

3. downplaying affective objectives — a primary concern among opponents of behavioral objectives — and sometimes implying that it is as easy to write behavioral objectives in the affective domain as in the cognitive and psychomotor domains.

In spite of the hubbub over behavioral objectives, I believe that with a reasoned approach, the practice of identifying and writing both instructional goals and objectives has considerable merit. The writing of instructional ob-

---

6 James D. Raths, "Teaching Without Specific Objectives," *Educational Leadership* 28, no. 7 (April 1971): 715.

7 See James Hartley and Ivor K. Davies, "Preinstructional Strategies: The Role of Pretests, Behavioral Objectives, Overviews, and Advance Organizers," *Review of Educational Research* 46, no. 2 (Spring 1976): 239–265.

jectives forces the teacher to identify the outcomes he or she seeks. The specification of instructional objectives simplifies the selection of instructional strategies and resources. When stated in behavioral terms, instructional objectives provide a basis for measurement and they communicate to all — students, parents, and other professionals — exactly what it is students are expected to demonstrate.[8]

GUIDELINES FOR PREPARING INSTRUCTIONAL GOALS AND OBJECTIVES

To pursue the task of selecting and writing instructional goals and objectives, it will be helpful to establish several guidelines to be followed. Instructional goals and objectives should:

- □ relate to the already specified curriculum goals and objectives
- □ be specified for three domains of learning — the cognitive, affective, and psychomotor, whenever applicable
- □ be identified at both low and high levels of learning with greater emphasis on the higher
- □ follow a few simple rules for writing

We shall consider each of these guidelines.

Relationship to Curriculum Goals and Objectives

Instructional goals and objectives should relate to curriculum goals and objectives. Unless the classroom teacher participated in drafting the curriculum goals and objectives, he or she must become familiar with them. The instructional goals and objectives are derived from the curriculum goals and objectives. Let's show this relationship by choosing a *curriculum goal* for the fifth grade, as: Students will during the course of the year appreciably improve their skills in reading. From this general goal we may deduce the following *curriculum objectives:* (1) By the end of the eighth month, 75 percent of the students will have increased their ability to comprehend a selected set of words in English by 25 percent and (2) By the end of the academic year all students will have met or exceeded the grade norm of 5.9 in reading comprehension.

The curriculum objectives are derived from the curriculum goals, apply to the program and to groups of students, and are stated in measurable terms. The formulation of *instructional goals* follows and bears a direct relationship to the curriculum goals and objectives, as seen in the following examples: (1) The student will demonstrate his or her ability to read silently at sight

---

[8] Leslie J. Briggs cited twenty-one reasons for writing instructional objectives, for which please see Leslie J. Briggs, *Handbook of Procedures for the Design of Instruction* (Washington, D.C.: American Institutes for Research, 1970), pp. 17–18.

without great difficulty and (2) The student will demonstrate his or her ability to read orally at sight without difficulty.

Both of the foregoing statements are expectations of each pupil. The statements are couched in general terms and include no criteria of mastery. For each of the instructional goals we may create *instructional objectives*. To promote the goal of reading silently, for example, the teacher might design the following objectives: (1) The student will read silently a passage from the fifth grade reader and then summarize orally without appreciable error in comprehension each of its four major points and (2) The student will read silently a passage from the fifth grade reader and then respond correctly in writing to eight out of ten written questions provided by the teacher.

To further the goal of reading orally, the teacher might identify the following objectives: (1) The student will read orally from a classroom library book and make no more than four mistakes in pronunciation in a passage of about one hundred words and (2) The student will read orally a passage from a classroom library book and then summarize orally without appreciable error in comprehension each of the three main points of the passage.

Unless an instructional objective is differentiated for a particular subgroup of students, e.g., bright, slow, or handicapped, it is expected that every student will master the objective. When instructional objectives are aimed at all students in a given class, they may be called minimal competencies. State testing programs are designed to assess students' mastery of the minimal competencies, as, for example, competencies to be achieved in all or selected disciplines at the end of, say, fourth, eighth, or eleventh grade.

Some confusion may exist between curriculum and instructional goals and objectives for, in one sense, they may both be designed for all students. The curriculum goals and objectives are broader in nature, aimed at all students as a group or groups, frequently jump across grade boundaries, often cut across disciplines, and many times are relevant to more than one teacher either within a discipline or among disciplines.

Yet, there are times when a curriculum objective may be congruent with an instructional objective or, put another way, an instructional objective may repeat a curriculum objective. When we, as curriculum planners, designate as a curriculum objective improving the scores of all students on a standardized achievement test in mathematics by ten percentile points, we will be pleased that the mathematics curriculum (program) is functioning to that degree. When we as classroom teachers stipulate that all pupils score ten percentile points higher on a standardized test of mathematics, we will be pleased with each student who functions that well and may refer to our own instruction as effective if many students achieve that objective.

Though we may state them slightly differently, curriculum and instructional goals and objectives may converge. One is the alter ego of the other, so to speak. Conversely, curriculum and instructional goals and objectives may diverge. When we as curriculum planners desire that 80 percent (even 100 percent) of the seniors with quantitative aptitude test scores at the 75 percentile elect calculus, we are talking about program, not instruction.

The distinctions between curriculum and instructional goals and objectives matter only to the extent that neither of the two sets is overlooked. If an instructional objective repeats a curriculum objective, so be it; it is a perfect fit. On the other hand, instructional objectives by their very nature tend to be more specific than the curriculum goals and objectives, focus on what takes place in the classroom, and come to pass as a result of the individual instructor's efforts. Whatever the degree of congruence, there is a direct and natural progression from curriculum goal to instructional objective.

Domains of Learning

The instructional goals and objectives should be specified for three domains of learning — the cognitive, the affective, and the psychomotor, whenever applicable. Note these three illustrations of different types of learning:

- □ knowledge of the system of election primaries
- □ enjoyment in reading
- □ skill in laying bricks

These examples are illustrative of the three major areas (domains) of learning. Knowledge of the primary system falls into the cognitive domain, enjoyment in reading in the affective domain, and skill in laying bricks in the psychomotor domain.

Cognitive Domain. Bloom and associates defined the cognitive domain as including objectives that "deal with the recall or recognition of knowledge and the development of intellectual abilities and skills." [9] Cognitive learnings, which involve the mental processes, range from memorization to the ability to think and solve problems.

Affective Domain. Krathwohl and others defined the affective domain as including objectives that "emphasize a feeling tone, an emotion, or a degree of acceptance or rejection." [10] Affective learnings encompass the emotions, feelings, beliefs, attitudes, and values.

Psychomotor Domain. Robert J. Armstrong and others defined the psychomotor domain as including behaviors that "place primary emphasis on neuro-muscular or physical skills and involve different degrees of physical dex-

---

[9] Benjamin S. Bloom, ed., *Taxonomy of Educational Objectives: The Classification of Educational Goals: Handbook I: Cognitive Domain* (New York: Longman, 1956), p. 7.
[10] David R. Krathwohl, Benjamin S. Bloom, and Bertram B. Masia, *Taxonomy of Educational Objectives: The Classification of Educational Goals: Handbook II: Affective Domain* (New York: Longman, 1964), p. 7.

terity." [11] Sometimes referred to as "perceptual-motor skills," psychomotor learnings include bodily movements and muscular coordination.

Ordinarily, schools assume responsibility for student achievement in all three broad areas. Although we might visualize the three horses — Cognitive, Affective, and Psychomotor — in the form of a Russian troika, racing three abreast, they are hitched more like a lead horse followed by two abreast. More often than not, Cognitive is in the forefront. On occasion, depending on the mood of the profession and the public, Cognitive is overtaken by Affective or Psychomotor.

The battle over which domain is the most important has endured for many years. With the exception of work by people like Rousseau, Froebel, Pestalozzi, and Neil (Summerhill School, England) most of the rest of the world, if we may generalize on such a vast scale, marches to the beat of the cognitive drummer. Although many fine opportunities for vocational education are provided by many countries, the cognitive domain remains the prestige category and is the entrée to institutions of higher learning. If our horses were pitted in an international race, Affective would come in a poor third.

Judging from the popularity of books critical of public education, the accountability movement in education, the flight to private schools, and the push for national and state assessment in the fundamental disciplines, we might conclude that the American public is partial to the cognitive domain. Recent Gallup Polls of the Public's Attitudes Toward the Public Schools confirm this conclusion. Table 10-1 shows the twelfth Annual Gallup Poll findings regarding priorities that the public would assign to the new federal department of education. The cognitive domain (basic education) tops the list; vocational training (psychomotor) follows closely; affective priorities come third.

Only a year before, the public ranked mathematics and English grammar and composition (cognitive areas) as top priorities; physical education (psychomotor) ranked lower but ahead of affective-like studies such as interdependence of nations, foreign relations, music and art,[12] which stress attaining affective objectives. This book encourages each teacher to identify and write instructional goals and objectives in all three domains, whenever possible, making allowances for the nature of the subject matter.

Normally, the domains overlap; each possesses elements of the other, even when one is obviously dominant. Thus, it is often difficult to categorize learnings as falling precisely into one domain. We can identify learnings, for example, that are primarily psychomotor (running a football play) and second-

---

11 Robert J. Armstrong, Terry D. Cornell, Robert E. Kraner, and E. Wayne Roberson, *The Development and Evaluation of Behavioral Objectives.* (Worthington, Ohio: Charles A. Jones, 1970), p. 22.
12 George H. Gallup, "The 11th Annual Gallup Poll of the Public's Attitudes Toward the Public Schools," *Phi Delta Kappan* 61, no. 1 (September 1979): 40.

TABLE 10-1 Priorities the public would assign to the U.S. Department of Education

PRIORITY	NATIONAL TOTALS
Basic education (reading, writing, arithmetic)	69%
Vocational training (training students for jobs)	56%
Developing individual educational plans for every child	33%
International education	19%
Improving opportunities for women and minorities	18%

Source: George H. Gallup, "The 12th Annual Gallup Poll of the Public's Attitudes Toward the Public Schools," *Phi Delta Kappa* 62, no. 1 (September 1980): 41–42. Reprinted by permission.

arily cognitive and affective. We can give examples of learning that are primarily cognitive (civil rights legislation) and secondarily affective. We can offer examples of learnings that are primarily affective (honesty) and secondarily cognitive. We have learnings that are primarily cognitive (constructing an equilateral triangle) and secondarily affective and psychomotor.

Many learnings will obviously fall into single categories. If we discount the bit of affective pleasure a student may or may not feel in knowing the right answer, the formula for finding the area of a right triangle (½ base x height) is pretty much a cognitive experience. Doing sit-ups, which are psychomotor exercises, requires very little cognition and may even evoke an undesired affective response. Faith in one's fellow man or woman is primarily an affective goal, secondarily cognitive, and usually not psychomotor.

The classroom teacher should identify and write instructional goals and objectives in all three domains, if indeed all three are relevant. It might be asked, "From what cloth do we cut the instructional goals and objectives?" We might respond by saying, "From the same cloth from which we cut the curriculum goals and objectives — the three sources: the needs of the student, of society, and of the subject matter — with the curriculum goals and objectives themselves serving as inspiration."

TAXONOMIC LEVELS

Instructional goals and objectives should be identified at both high and low levels of learning with greater emphasis being placed on the higher. It is obvious that some learnings are more substantive, complex, and important than others. Note, for example, the following learning outcomes, all in the cognitive domain, to see the differences in complexity:

☐ The student will name the first president of the United States.
☐ The student will read Washington's first inaugural address and summarize the major points.
☐ The student will show how some of Washington's ideas apply or do not apply today.
☐ The student will analyze Washington's military tactics in the Battle of Yorktown.
☐ The student will write a biography of Washington.
☐ The student will evaluate Washington's role at the Continental Congress.

The knowledge and skills required for naming the first president of the United States are at a decidedly lower level than those for each of the subsequent objectives. Each succeeding item is progressively more difficult, requiring greater cognitive powers. What we have is a hierarchy of learning outcomes from low to high.

Or take the following illustrations from the affective domain:

☐ The student will listen while others express their points of view.
☐ The student will answer a call for volunteers to plant trees in a public park.
☐ The student will express appreciation for the contributions of ethnic groups other than his or her own to the development of our country.
☐ The student will choose nutritious food over junk food.
☐ The student will habitually abide by a set of legal and ethical standards.

As with the examples in the cognitive domain, each objective is progressively more substantial than the preceding one.

Finally, let's look at a set of objectives from the psychomotor domain:

☐ The student will identify a woolen fabric by its feel.
☐ The student will demonstrate how to hold the reins of a horse while cantering.
☐ The student will imitate a right-about-face movement.
☐ The student will mix a batch of mortar and water.
☐ The student will operate a 16mm projector.
☐ The student will arrange an attractive bulletin board.
☐ The student will create an original game requiring physical movements.

The first example from the psychomotor domain — simple identification of the texture of a fabric — is at a much lower level of skill than the creation of an original game involving physical activity.

Cognitive Taxonomy

Benjamin S. Bloom and others developed an extensive taxonomy for classifying educational objectives in the cognitive domain.[13] Of all classification systems, the Bloom taxonomy of the cognitive domain is perhaps the best known and most widely followed. It categorizes the types of cognitive learning outcomes that are featured at all levels of the educational system. Bloom and his associates classified cognitive learnings in six major categories: knowledge, comprehension, application, analysis, synthesis, and evaluation. Let's take each of these categories, refer back to the example previously given, and place it in the appropriate category, as follows:

- □ *Knowledge level:* The student will name the first president of the United States.
- □ *Comprehension level:* The student will read Washington's first inaugural address and summarize the major points.
- □ *Application level:* The student will show how some of Washington's ideas apply or do not apply today.
- □ *Analysis level:* The student will analyze Washington's military tactics in the Battle of Yorktown.
- □ *Synthesis level:* The student will write a biography of George Washington.
- □ *Evaluation level:* The student will evaluate Washington's role at the Continental Congress.

This taxonomy shows learning objectives as classified in a hierarchical fashion from the lowest (knowledge) to the highest (evaluation). A central premise of professional educators is that the higher levels of learning should be stressed. The ability to think, for example, is fostered not through low level recall of knowledge but through application, analysis, synthesis, and evaluation.

Objectives in the cognitive domain are, of the three domains, the easiest to identify and the simplest to evaluate. They are drawn primarily from the subject matter and are readily measurable, usually by written tests and exercises.

Affective Taxonomy

Shortly after the appearance of the cognitive taxonomy, David R. Krathwohl and others, including Benjamin Bloom, developed a taxonomy of objectives in the affective domain, which consisted of five major categories.[14] We may categorize the affective examples given earlier in the following manner:

- □ *Receiving* (attending): The student will listen while others express their points of view.

---

[13] Bloom et al., *Taxonomy of Educational Objectives: Cognitive Domain.*
[14] Krathwohl et al., *Taxonomy of Educational Objectives: Affective Domain.*

- *Responding:* The student will answer a call for volunteers to plant a tree in a public park.
- *Valuing:* The student will express appreciation for the contributions of ethnic groups other than his or her own to the development of our country.
- *Organization:* The student will choose nutritious food over junk food.
- *Characterization by value or value complex:* The student will habitually abide by a set of legal and ethical standards.

The affective domain poses a serious problem for educators. Controversy swirls around this domain. Historically, parents and educators have viewed the school's mission as cognitive learning. Not until rather recent times has affective learning come to be considered by many as a province of the school. As we have seen elsewhere in this text, the affective domain is still not accepted by some educators as a legitimate focus of the school. On the other hand, some educators feel that affective outcomes are more important than others.

Combs, for example, stated the case for affective education, tying it to the development of adequate personalities, as follows:

> For many generations education has done an excellent job of *imparting* information. . . . Our greatest failures are those connected with the problems of helping people to behave differently as a result of the information we have provided them. . . . Adequate persons are, among other factors, the product of strong values. The implication seems to be clear, then, that educators must be interested in and concerned with values. Unfortunately, this is not the case in many schools and classrooms today. The emphasis is too often on the narrowly scientific and impersonally objective. . . . Education must be concerned with the values, beliefs, convictions, and doubts of students. These realities as perceived by an individual are just as important, if not more so, as the so-called objective facts.[15]

Bloom attested to the neglect of instruction for affective learning when he said:

> Throughout the years American education has maintained that among its most important ideals is the development of such attributes as interests, desirable attitudes, appreciation, values, commitment, and willpower. However, the types of outcomes which in fact receive the highest priorities in our schools, to the detriment of these affective goals, are verbal-conceptual in nature.[16]

---

[15] Arthur W. Combs, ed., *Perceiving, Behaving, Becoming: A New Focus for Education,* 1962 Yearbook (Alexandria, Va.: Association for Supervision and Curriculum Development, 1962), p. 200.

[16] Benjamin S. Bloom, J. Thomas Hastings, and George F. Madaus, *Handbook on Formative and Summative Evaluation of Student Learning* (New York: McGraw-Hill, 1971), p. 225.

Bloom identified these reasons for the neglect of affective learning:

> Our system of education is geared to producing people who can deal with the words, concepts, and mathematical or scientific symbols so necessary for success in our technological society.[17]

> Standardized tests used by the schools . . . lay stress on intellectual tasks.[18]

> Characteristics of this kind, unlike achievement competencies, are considered to be a private rather than a public matter.[19]

Some hold that affective outcomes are the province of the home and the church and that instruction in the affective domain smacks of indoctrination. "One of the reasons for the failure to give instructional emphasis to affective outcomes is related to the Orwellian overtones which attitudinal and value-oriented instruction often conjures up in the minds of teachers and the public," said Bloom and coauthors.[20]

Whose values should be taught? Are white, Anglo-Saxon, Protestant, middle-class values the ones to be promoted? Whence come the values to be selected? If you agree with me that affective learnings should be taught, identifying common values is an essential task for the curriculum planners. Affective objectives are both difficult to identify and extremely difficult — often impossible — to measure, which constitutes another reason why teachers tend to shy away from the affective domain. In Chapter 12 we will discuss some approaches to the evaluation of student performance in the affective domain.

Psychomotor Taxonomies

For some reason difficult to fathom, the development of a taxonomy in the psychomotor domain has not been given as much attention as the cognitive and affective domains. Taxonomies of the psychomotor domain do exist but they have been developed by fewer individuals rather than by broad participation as in the case of the Bloom and Krathwohl taxonomies. The psychomotor taxonomies are also not as widely known as the other two.

The examples from the psychomotor domain given earlier follow the classification system developed by Elizabeth Jane Simpson.[21] Following her taxonomy, we categorize these illustrations as follows:

□ *Perception:* The student will identify a woolen fabric by its feel.
□ *Set:* The student will demonstrate how to hold the reins of a horse when cantering.

---

17 Bloom et al., p. 225.
18 Bloom et al., p. 226.
19 Bloom et al., p. 227.
20 Bloom et al., p. 226.
21 Elizabeth Jane Simpson, "The Classification of Educational Objectives in the Psychomotor Domain," *The Psychomotor Domain,* Vol. 3 (Washington, D.C.: Gryphon House, 1972), pp. 43–56.

□ *Guided response:* The student will imitate a right-about-face movement.

□ *Mechanism:* The student will mix a batch of mortar and water.

□ *Complex overt response:* The student will operate a 16mm projector.

□ *Adaptation:* The student will arrange an attractive bulletin board display.

□ *Origination:* The student will create an original game requiring physical movements.

Anita J. Harrow provided a clarifying description for each of the categories of the Simpson taxonomy and proposed a taxonomy of the psychomotor domain.[22]

The use of the taxonomies of the three domains as guidelines can lead to more effective instruction. The taxonomies direct attention to the three major domains of learning and to the subdivisions of each. Arranged in a hierarchical fashion, the taxonomies should serve to stimulate teachers to move their learners from the lower to the higher and more enduring levels of learning in each domain.

RULES FOR WRITING

Instructional goals and objectives should follow a few simple rules for writing. Early in this chapter we distinguished instructional goals from instructional objectives. Instructional goals defined student performance in general terms whereas instructional objectives defined it in more specific and measurable terms.

Instructional goals are often poorly stated instructional objectives. For example, "The student will know names of the first five presidents of the United States" is an instructional goal as it is not written in measurable and observable terms. We might change this instructional goal into an instructional objective by writing: "The student will name correctly and in order the first five presidents of the United States."

On the other hand, an instructional goal may serve the purpose of pointing the direction that leads to instructional objectives. For example, the instructional goal, "The student will develop an awareness of the energy crisis," could lead to a multitude of instructional objectives, as, for example, "The student will identify the five leading oil-producing countries," "The student will identify three sources of energy that are alternatives to oil," "The student will determine how much the price of imported oil has risen in the last ten years," and "The student will propose and describe three ways Americans can conserve energy."

An instructional goal may thus be written in rather broad, imprecise terms. Or it may be stated simply as a topic, for example, "The Organized

---

22 See Anita J. Harrow, *A Taxonomy of the Psychomotor Domain: A Guide for Developing Behavioral Objectives* (New York: Longman, 1972), p. 27.

Labor Movement." Implied in the topic is the instructional goal, "The student will develop an understanding of the organized labor movement."

Though variations in style of formulating instructional goals and objectives are certainly possible, I incline to starting instructional goals and objectives with "The student . . ." (in the singular) in order to (1) signal the meaning "each student" and (2) help distinguish from curriculum goals and objectives, which I begin with "Students . . ." (in the plural) to convey the meaning of "students in general." Although it is preferable for all plans to be committed to paper, it is possible for teachers to keep the instructional goals in mind and to move directly to the writing of instructional objectives.

It may be well to caution once again that some educators use the term goals and objectives interchangeably whereas others prefer the word goals in place of objectives. Walter Dick and Lou Carey, for example, use the term instructional goal for what I identify as an instructional objective. They define an instructional goal as "a statement that describes what . . . students will be able to do after they have completed instruction." [23]

The term instructional goals in this text is used in the same sense as Dick and Carey's term "nonbehavioral goal statements." Although I feel non-behavioral statements are helpful, Dick and Carey recommend they be avoided, if possible, since they cannot be directly observed and are difficult to measure.[24]

Three Elements of an Instructional Objective

When writing an instructional (behavioral) objective, it is generally recommended that three elements or components be included:

1. the behavior expected of the student
2. the conditions under which the behavior is to be demonstrated
3. the degree of mastery required [25]

Specifying Behavior. When specifying behavior, instructors should choose, as often as possible, action verbs that are subject to measurement and observation. Action words in particular distinguish instructional objectives from instructional goals. The verb "understand," for example, is unsuitable in an instructional objective because it is neither measurable nor observable. Thus, "The student will understand his or her rights under the first ten amendments to the U. S. Constitution," is an instructional goal, not an instructional objective. If "understand" is changed to a performance-oriented verb, we can create an instructional objective, such as, "The student will write summaries

---

[23] Walter Dick and Lou Carey, *The Systematic Design of Instruction* (Glenview, Ill.: Scott, Foresman, 1978), p. 14.

[24] Dick and Carey, p. 18.

[25] For helpful discussion on writing instructional objectives, see Robert F. Mager, *Preparing Instructional Objectives,* 2d ed. (Belmont, Cal.: Fearon Publishers, 1975).

of the first ten amendments to the U. S. Constitution." This cognitive objective at the comprehension level can be raised to the evaluation level by modifying the statement as, "The student will write a paper listing the principal rights in the first ten amendments to the U. S. Constitution and will evaluate the importance of each right to us today." The instructional objective, therefore, must include behavior expected of the learner as a result of exposure to instruction.

To help with the writing of instructional objectives, the teacher may wish to develop lists of behaviorally-oriented verbs that can be used for each category of the three domains. Examples are shown in Table 10-2.

Specifying Conditions. The conditions under which the learner demonstrates the behavior should be specified, if they are necessary and not obvious. In the objective, "Given a list of needs of this community, the student will rank them in order of priority," "Given a list of needs of this community" is the condition under which the behavior is performed. It is an essential part of the objective. Or, as an additional illustration, in the objective "On the classroom wall map the student will point out the People's Republic of China," "On the classroom wall map" is the necessary condition. However, if students are to point out several countries on the same wall map, it becomes redundant and therefore unnecessary to repeat "On the classroom wall map" for each instructional objective. What the instructor should do in this case is write one instructional objective: "On the classroom wall map the student will point out . . . ," then list all the geographical features to be pointed out.

To conserve the instructor's valuable time, conditions, if obvious, need not be specified; they are simply understood. There is no need, for example, for the teacher to waste time placing before an objective, "Given paper and pen, the student will write an essay on the work of Mark Twain." Unless the use of paper and pen has some special significance and is not routine, it probably should not be specified. Adding routine and obvious conditions to instructional objectives can border on the ridiculous and can create an adverse reaction to the writing of instructional objectives at all. If we may exaggerate to stress the point, we do not wish to see the objective; "Given a tennis ball, a tennis racket, a tennis court, a net, a fair day, proper dress, and preferably an opponent also equipped with ball, racket, and proper dress, the student will demonstrate how to serve a tennis ball." "The student will demonstrate how to serve a tennis ball" is sufficient *ad diem,* as the lawyers say.

Specifying the Criterion. The statement of the instructional objective should include the acceptable standard or criterion of mastery of the behavior if it is not obvious. For example, a French teacher might write the following statement: "The student will translate the following sentences." There is no need to write the condition, "from French to English"; the students can see that. There is no need to specify the criterion "into good English" (which should

TABLE 10-2   Behaviorally oriented verbs for the domains of learning

COGNITIVE DOMAIN (BLOOM TAXONOMY)

LEVEL	VERBS
Knowledge	identify, specify, state
Comprehension	explain, restate, translate
Application	apply, solve, use
Analysis	analyze, compare, contrast
Synthesis	design, develop, plan
Evaluation	assess, evaluate, judge

AFFECTIVE DOMAIN (KRATHWOHL TAXONOMY)

LEVEL	VERBS
Receiving	accept, demonstrate awareness, listen
Responding	comply with, engage in, volunteer
Valuing	express a preference for, show appreciation by stating, show concern by stating
Organization	adhere to, defend, synthesize
Characterization by value or value complex	demonstrate empathy, express willingness to be ethical, modify behavior

PSYCHOMOTOR DOMAIN (SIMPSON TAXONOMY)

LEVEL	VERBS
Perception	distinguish, identify, select
Set	assume a position, demonstrate, show
Guided response	attempt, imitate, try
Mechanism	make habitual, practice, repeat
Complex overt response	carry out, operate, perform
Adaptation	adapt, change, revise
Origination	create, design, originate

Note: For a useful listing of verbs in the affective, cognitive, and psychomotor domains, see Gronlund, pp. 26–34, 69–72. For a useful listing of verbs and direct objects applicable to the Bloom and Krathwohl Taxonomies, see Newton S. Metfessel, William B. Michael, and Donald A. Kirsner, "Instrumentation of Bloom's and Krathwohl's Taxonomies for the Writing of Educational Objectives," *Psychology in the Schools* VI, no. 3 (July 1969): 227–231.

be routinely expected behavior) or "with 100 percent accuracy" or "with no errors." Unless a criterion is specified, it can be assumed that the teacher wishes students to achieve 100 percent accuracy.

Some objectives require more elaborate criteria than others. For example, let's go back to the illustration, "The student will write an essay on the work of Mark Twain." We could embellish this objective with various criteria, some of which are and are not essential. "In legible handwriting" or "free of typographical errors" should be normal expectations and, therefore, do not have to appear in every instructional objective. On the other hand, if the instructor desires an essay with no more than three spelling errors, with no more than three grammatical errors, and with all the footnotes and bibliographical entries in correct form, that information should be conveyed to the students. The criteria are particularly important if the objective is being used as a test item. It is a necessary and sound principle of evaluation that students be informed by what standards they will be evaluated.

Robert H. Davis, Lawrence T. Alexander, and Stephen L. Yelon listed six types of standards and gave examples of each, as follows:

1. When mere OCCURRENCE of the behavior is sufficient, describe the behavior. Example: The knot will be tied loosely as in the photograph.
2. When ACCURACY is important, provide a statement of acceptable range or deviation. Example: The answer must be correct to the nearest whole number.
3. If the number of ERRORS is important, state the number. Example: with a maximum of one error.
4. If TIME or SPEED is important, state the minimal level. Example: within five seconds; five units per minute.
5. If a KNOWN REFERENCE provides the standard, state the reference. Example: Perform the sequence of steps in the same order as given in the text.
6. If the CONSEQUENCES of the behavior are important, describe them or provide a model. Example: Conduct the class so that all students participate in the discussion.[26]

Novice instructors sometimes ask how the teacher decides on the criterion. How do you decide whether to permit three or four errors or whether a student should complete the task in ten rather than five minutes? These decisions are based on past experience of teachers with students and on the teacher's professional and, if you will, arbitrary judgment. After a few years, the teacher begins to sense what is possible for students to accomplish and proceeds on that knowledge. Certain traditions may also guide the teacher. For example, 70 percent is considered by most students, teachers, and parents

---

[26] Robert H. Davis, Lawrence T. Alexander, and Stephen L. Yelon, *Learning System Design: An Approach to the Improvement of Instruction* (New York: McGraw-Hill, 1974), pp. 39–40.

as so-so; 80 percent is considered not bad; 90 percent is considered good. Thus, criteria in the 70 to 100 percent range often show up in statements of instructional objectives.

Although it is relatively simple to specify objectives in the cognitive and psychomotor domain, specifying criteria in the affective domain is enough to tax one's soul. We shall wrestle with the problem of establishing criteria for affective objectives in Chapter 12. At this point, however, we should mention that it is usually impossible to specify criteria for objectives in the affective domain. What criteria, for example, should we append to this objective: "The student will express a sense of pride in his or her country?" Should the student's response be fervent?, passionate? The affective domain presents its unique instructional problems.

To the standards component Davis, Alexander, and Yelon added a stability component, i.e., the number of opportunities the student will be given and the number of times he or she must succeed in demonstrating the behavior.[27] We may illustrate the stability component with this example: "The student will type at least fifty words per minute on each of three successive tries." Analyzing this objective shows that to type is the behavior; the conditions are understood (a typewriter, paper, desk, chair, typewriter ribbon); the performance criterion is at least fifty words per minute; and the stability component is on each of three successive tries.

Generally speaking, instructional objectives should consist of at least three components: the behavior (often called the terminal behavior), the conditions, and the criterion.

VALIDATING AND PRIORITIZING INSTRUCTIONAL GOALS AND OBJECTIVES

Instructional goals and objectives should be validated and prioritized. Teachers should know whether the instructional goals and objectives are appropriate and which are the more important.

In practice, it is far simpler to validate and prioritize instructional than curriculum goals and objectives. Instructional goals and objectives are not normally submitted to lay groups or students for this process nor to administrators with any regularity. This practice is appropriate as instructional goals and objectives are content-specific. To make a judgment on their validity and to decide which are essential calls for a foundation both in the subject matter being taught and in the methods for teaching that subject matter. The subject matter is often technical and beyond the knowledge and skills of lay persons and students. Instructional matters are the prerogative of persons trained in their fields of specialization.

As a result, far fewer persons need be involved in validating instruc-

---

[27] Davis et al., p. 41.

tional goals and objectives. It often appears that no other persons are involved beyond the classroom teacher or the teacher and his or her close grade-level or department colleagues.

Validating and prioritizing instructional goals and objectives are usually accomplished by referring to the adopted textbooks, reference books, and curriculum guides. The authors of these materials serve as the validators and prioritizers. This method of validating and prioritizing instructional goals and objectives is, by far, the most common.

The classroom teacher can also seek help with validating and prioritizing instructional goals and objectives from members of his or her team, grade-level, or department; other knowledgeable faculty members; curriculum consultants; and supervisors. Consultants and supervisors trained and experienced in special fields should also be able to help the classroom teacher decide which instructional goals and objectives are appropriate to the subject and to the learners and which ones should be stressed. Finally, teachers may seek advice from acknowledged experts in the subject area outside the school system as well as from specialists in other school systems or in higher education institutions.

SUMMARY

Instructional goals and objectives are directly related to the previously specified curriculum goals and objectives. Instructional goals provide direction for specifying instructional objectives.

Learning outcomes may be identified in three major domains: the cognitive, the affective, and the psychomotor. The cognitive domain is the world of the intellect; the affective, the locale of the emotions, beliefs, and attitudes; and the psychomotor, the territory of perceptual-motor skills.

Taxonomies for each domain classify objectives in a hierarchical fashion from the lowest to the highest level of learning. Taxonomies are useful in revealing the types of learnings encompassed in each domain and in guiding instructors toward placing greater emphasis on learnings at the higher levels.

Instructional goals are statements written in nonbehavioral terms without criteria of mastery. With the possible exception of outcomes in the affective domain, instructional objectives should be written in measurable and observable terms.

It is recommended that whenever practical and necessary, instructional objectives consist of three components: the behavior that learners will demonstrate, the conditions under which the behavior is to be demonstrated, and the criterion of mastery of the behavior.

Instructional goals and objectives are validated and prioritized by referring to text materials written by experts and by seeking the judgments of knowledgeable colleagues, supervisors, and consultants from both within and without the school system.

SUPPLEMENTARY EXERCISES

1. Define "cognitive," "affective," and "psychomotor."
2. Define the word "taxonomy."
3. Distinguish between a nonbehavioral goal and a behavioral objective.
4. Consult the Bloom taxonomy of the cognitive domain and prepare a list of verbs that might be used for writing objectives in each category.
5. Consult the Krathwohl taxonomy of the affective domain and prepare a list of verbs that might be used for writing objectives in each category.
6. Consult the Harrow or Simpson taxonomies of the psychomotor domain and prepare a list of verbs that might be used for writing objectives in each category.
7. Write one instructional objective for each of the six major categories of the Bloom taxonomy of the cognitive domain.
8. Write one instructional objective for each of the five major categories of the Krathwohl taxonomy of the affective domain.
9. Write one instructional objective for each of the major categories of either the Simpson or the Harrow taxonomy of the psychomotor domain.
10. State the three components of an instructional objective.
11. List and give examples of six types of standards of performance that may be included in an instructional objective.
12. Describe what is meant by "stability component" and give an example.
13. Classify the following instructional objectives as to the principal domain and major category according to Bloom, Krathwohl, or Simpson. (Answers to this exercise follow.) This exercise is taken from a workshop prepared for the Dade-Monroe County (Florida) Teacher Education Center.
   The student will:
   a. solve ten multiplication problems in twenty minutes and achieve a score of eight correct.
   b. cut and splice a strip of film.
   c. spell fifteen words correctly.
   d. respond to a call to serve on an environmental clean-up committee.
   e. using the financial pages of the daily newspaper, study the closing prices of several common stocks on one day of a particular week and tell whether the value of the stocks has gone up or down or remained the same the next day of that same week.
   f. using a wall map and pointer trace the path of the Mississippi River from source to mouth.
   g. demonstrate an awareness that school spirit must be improved.
   h. write a paper of ten pages, typed double-spaced, on the topic, *Traveling in Space*. The paper must be scientifically accurate and in good English. It must contain at least two footnotes and a bibliography of at least five references.

i. with a compass draw a circle that has a two-inch diameter.

j. express admiration for skills shown by a famous actor or actress.

k. identify a living American author whose works he or she believes will become classics and by referring to the author's works support his or her choice of author.

l. design and make a pair of earrings out of black coral.

m. demonstrate the proper way to hold the bowling ball before beginning the approach.

n. using a musical instrument convert a classical theme to a rock or disco beat.

o. regularly donate money or goods to a charity.

p. explain reasons for his or her preference for a political party.

q. apply epoxy glue to join two pieces of wood together following directions on the label.

r. identify the smell of baking bread.

ANSWERS TO EXERCISE 13

a. cognitive-application

b. psychomotor-complex overt response

c. cognitive-knowledge

d. affective-responding

e. cognitive-analysis

f. cognitive-comprehension

g. affective-receiving

h. cognitive-synthesis

i. psychomotor-mechanism

j. affective-valuing

k. cognitive-evaluation

l. psychomotor-origination

m. psychomotor-set

n. psychomotor-adaptation

o. affective-characterization by value or value complex

p. affective-organization

q. psychomotor-guided response

r. psychomotor-perception

14. Choose one curriculum goal and write two curriculum objectives for it. Then write one instructional goal for one of the curriculum objectives and two instructional objectives for the instructional goal.

15. In the following items, put a CG if you believe the item is a curriculum goal, CO for a curriculum objective, IG for an instructional goal, and IO for an instructional objective (answers follow).

_____a. Students will develop an awareness of major social and economic problems of the community.

_____b. Without using a calculator, the student will solve the following division problem, carrying out the answer to two places: 6859 ÷ 27.

_____c. Students will increase their use of the school library as evidenced by a 10 percent rise in the circulation of library books over the previous year.

_____d. The student will develop an appreciation for *Macbeth*.

_____e. By the end of the year all students will have engaged in at least one community service project.

_____f. The student will understand why the United States entered the Viet Nam War.

_____g. The student will distinguish between the sounds of ă and ā.

_____h. Students will improve their skills in aesthetic expression.

_____ i. The student will know the functions of the executive, legislative, and judicial branches of the government.

_____ j. Students will improve their skills in composition.

Answers to 15:   a. CG   b. IO   c. CO   d. IG   e. CO   f. IG   g. IO   h. CG   i. IG   j. CG

BIBLIOGRAPHY

Armstrong, Robert J., Cornell, Terry D., Kraner, Robert E., and Roberson, E. Wayne. *The Development and Evaluation of Behavioral Objectives.* Worthington, Ohio: Charles A. Jones, 1970.

Bloom, Benjamin S., ed. *Taxonomy of Educational Objectives: The Classification of Educational Goals: Handbook I: Cognitive Domain.* New York: Longman, 1956.

Bloom, Benjamin S., Hastings, J. Thomas, and Madaus, George F. *Handbook on Formative and Summative Evaluation of Student Learning.* New York: McGraw-Hill, 1971.

Briggs, Leslie J. *Handbook of Procedures for the Design of Instruction.* Washington, D.C.: American Institutes for Research, 1970.

Burton, William H. *The Guidance of Learning Activities,* 3rd ed. New York: Appleton-Century-Crofts, 1962.

Combs, Arthur W., ed. *Perceiving, Behaving, Becoming?: A New Focus for Education,* 1962 Yearbook. Alexandria, Va.: Association for Supervision and Curriculum Development, 1962.

Davies, Ivor K. *Objectives in Curriculum Design.* London: McGraw-Hill (UK), Ltd., 1976.

Davis, Robert H., Alexander, Lawrence T., and Yelon, Stephen L. *Learning System Design: An Approach to the Improvement of Instruction.* New York: McGraw-Hill, 1974.

Dick, Walter and Carey, Lou. *The Systematic Design of Instruction.* Glenview, Ill.: Scott, Foresman, 1978.

Dillman, Caroline Matheny and Rahmlow, Harold F. *Writing Instructional Objectives.* Belmont, Cal.: Fearon Publishers, 1972.

Gagné, Robert M. and Briggs, Leslie J. *Principles of Instructional Design.* New York: Holt, Rinehart and Winston, 1974.

Gallup, George H. "The 12th Annual Gallup Poll of the Public's Attitudes Toward the Public Schools," *Phi Delta Kappan* 62, no. 1 (September 1980): 33–46.

Gronlund, Norman E. *Stating Objectives for Classroom Instruction,* 2d ed. New York: Macmillan, 1978.

Harrow, Anita J. *A Taxonomy of the Psychomotor Domain: A Guide for Developing Behavioral Objectives.* New York: Longman, 1972.

Kibler, Robert J., Barker, Larry L., and Miles, David T. *Behavioral Objectives and Instruction.* Boston: Allyn and Bacon, 1970.

Kibler, Robert J., Cegala, Donald J., Miles, David T., and Barker, Larry L. *Objectives for Instruction and Evaluation.* Boston: Allyn and Bacon, 1974.

Krathwohl, David R., Bloom, Benjamin S., and Masia, Bertram B. *Taxonomy of Educational Objectives: The Classification of Educational Goals: Handbook II: Affective Domain.* New York: Longman, 1964.

McNeil, John D. "Deriving Objectives," in *Designing Curriculum: Self-Instructional Modules.* Boston: Little, Brown, 1976, pp. 45–61.

Mager, Robert F. *Preparing Instructional Objectives,* 2d ed. Belmont. Cal.: Fearon Publishers, 1975.

Oliva, Peter F. *The Secondary School Today,* 2d ed. New York: Harper & Row, 1972.

————. *Supervision for Today's Schools.* New York: Harper & Row, 1976.

Orlosky, Donald E. and Smith, B. Othanel. *Curriculum Development: Issues and Insights.* Chicago: Rand McNally, 1978.

Popham, W. James. "Practical Ways of Improving Curriculum Via Measurable Objectives," *The Bulletin of the National Association of Secondary School Principals* 55, no. 355 (May 1971): 76–90.

———— and Baker, Eva L. *Establishing Instructional Goals.* Englewood Cliffs, N.J.: Prentice-Hall, 1970.

————. *Systematic Instruction.* Englewood Cliffs, N.J.: Prentice-Hall, 1970.

Raths, James D. "Teaching Without Specific Objectives," *Educational Leadership* 28, no. 7 (April 1971): 714–720.

Simpson, Elizabeth Jane, "The Classification of Educational Objectives in the Psychomotor Domain," in *The Psychomotor Domain,* Vol. 3, Washington, D.C.: Gryphon House, 1972, pp. 43–56.

Tyler, Ralph W. *Basic Principles of Curriculum and Instruction.* Chicago: University of Chicago Press, 1949.

Westinghouse Learning Press. *Behavioral Objectives: A Guide to Individualizing.* Sunnyvale, Cal.: Westinghouse Learning Press, 1977. 4 volumes.

————. *Learning Objectives for Individualized Instruction.* Sunnyvale, Cal.: Westinghouse Learning Press, 1977. 4 volumes.

SOURCES OF OBJECTIVES

Florida Catalog of Objectives, Panhandle Area Educational Cooperative, Chipley. Florida.

Instructional Objectives Exchange, P.O. Box 24095, Los Angeles, California 90024.

FILMSTRIP-TAPE PROGRAMS

Vimcet Associates, P.O. Box 24714, Los Angeles, California 90024:

Educational Objectives, 1967.

Selecting Appropriate Educational Objectives, 1967.

Defining Content for Objectives, 1969.

Identifying Affective Objectives, 1969.

Humanizing Educational Objectives, 1972.

TRAINING PACKAGE

Objectives for Instructional Programs. Insgroup, Inc., 16052 Beach Boulevard, Huntington Beach, California 92647. Program on how to develop objectives, create instructional plans, and measure results. Filmstrip, audio cassette, response forms, programmed textbook, reference pamphlet, reference chart, and coordinator's guide.

11

Selecting and Implementing Strategies of Instruction

After studying this chapter you should be able to:
1. Define style, model, method, and skills of teaching and state how each relates to the selection of instructional strategies.
2. Distinguish between generic and specific teaching skills.
3. Present a rationale for using a unit plan.
4. Relate daily lesson planning to long-range planning.

You should also be able to formulate and give reasons for your views on the following issues:
1. Your feelings about one or more different styles of teaching.
2. Your preferred model(s) of teaching.

DECIDING ON INSTRUCTIONAL STRATEGIES

It's the planning period. The twelfth grade American history teacher just left the teachers' lounge where she consumed a cup of coffee and chatted with her colleagues. She is seated now at a carrel in the teachers' work room, curriculum guide and history textbook before her. The topic to be studied by the students is World War II — the European Theatre. Conscientious planner that she is, she asks herself, "What is the best way to go about teaching this topic?" "What methods shall I use?" "What strategies are possible, suitable?" "How do I put together plans for instruction?" "Which suggestions from the curriculum guide shall I adopt?' She jots down a number of approaches that she might use in creating a learning unit on the topic.

- ☐ Have the students read the appropriate chapters and come to class prepared to discuss them.
- ☐ Devise some key questions to give the class and let them find the answers as they read the chapter.
- ☐ Lecture to the class, adding points not covered in the text.
- ☐ Have each student write a paper on selected aspects of the war such as the invasion of Normandy, the Battle of the Bulge, the crossing of the Rhine, etc.
- ☐ Have each student select a related but different topic, e.g., the opposing military leaders, and present an oral report to the class.
- ☐ Show the film *The Longest Day* on the invasion of Normandy; then follow it up with small group discussion and independent study on topics of interest to the students.
- ☐ Have the students draw charts of the tactics of both sides in selected major battles.
- ☐ Have the students read chapters in the textbook and give them quizzes in class the next day.
- ☐ Using a large classroom wall map of Europe or a small map with an opaque projector, point out the most significant geographical features of the area.
- ☐ Write a number of objective test items that will be incorporated in the end-of-unit test and drill the students on the answers as the topic is discussed.
- ☐ Invite a veteran of the war in Europe to come to class to recount his experiences.
- ☐ Have students choose books on the topic from the school or public library, read them, and present oral reports to the class, comparing what they have read in the library books with accounts in the textbook.
- ☐ Make comparisons between World War I and World War II as to causes, numbers of combatants, number of casualties, battle tactics, and aftermath.

The teacher must decide how many days she will devote to the topic; whether she will use any or all of the approaches considered; which approaches she will use first; and how she will put the selected approaches together.

If we refer back to the diagram shown in Chapter 10, we will note that selecting strategies is the next step called for in the Instructional Model. In this text strategy broadly encompasses the methods, procedures, and techniques the teacher uses to confront students with the subject matter and to bring about effective outcomes. A strategy ordinarily includes multiple procedures or techniques. Lecturing, for example, can include procedures like handing out charts and calling for evaluations at the end of the lecture. It may also include techniques like set induction and closure, which are generic teaching skills.

Among the common instructional strategies are the lecture, small group discussion, independent study, library research, mediated instruction, repetitive drill, and laboratory. To this list we might add tutoring, testing, and field trips. We might include the inquiry or discovery, inductive, and deductive methods. We could add programmed instruction, problem solving, and questioning. Suffice it to say that the teacher has at his or her disposal a great variety of strategies for implementing instruction.

How does the teacher decide which strategy or strategies to use? The teacher may be fortunate enough to find a curriculum guide that will detail not only strategies to be used but also objectives, suggested resources, and suggested evaluation techniques.

Unfortunately, curriculum guides do not always exist for topics that the teacher wishes to emphasize and often when they do exist and are accessible, they do not fit the teacher's and students' purposes. Consequently, the teacher must exercise his or her own professional judgment and choose the strategies to be employed. Selecting strategies becomes a less difficult problem when the teacher recognizes that instructional strategies are derived from five major sources. Let's briefly examine each of these sources.

SOURCES OF STRATEGIES

Objectives as Source

The choice of strategies is limited at the onset by the specified instructional objectives. Although an almost infinite number of techniques for carrying out instruction may exist, only a finite number apply to any particular objective. For example, how many alternatives does the teacher have to teach the number fact that $2 \times 2 = 4$? He or she may tell the students; have them repeat again and again the 2× table; use flash cards for drill purposes; give a chalk talk using the blackboard; have students practice using a workbook; use an abacus; use a slide rule; have students practice the Korean system *chisenbop;* let pupils use a calculator; or let pupils use a printed multiplication table. We are rapidly exhausting the possibilities. Of course, not all of the possible courses of action will be suitable or acceptable to the teacher or the students, which limits the range of possibilities even more.

How many techniques suggest themselves to accomplish the following objectives? The student will:

- □ purify water by boiling
- □ write an editorial
- □ sew a zipper into a garment
- □ demonstrate a high jump
- □ help keep his or her school clean

Sometimes the strategy is obvious. There is no practical alternative; in essence, as "the medium is the message," to use Marshall McLuhan's words, the objective *is* the strategy. The student will demonstrate a high jump, for example, by performing that act. No amount of "teaching about" high jumping will permit the students to demonstrate that they can perform the high jump.

Subject Matter As Source

Subject matter provides a source of instructional strategies. With some subject matter, selecting strategies is relatively simple. If we are teaching a course in television repair, certain operations must be mastered, such as checking the circuits, replacing the picture tube, replacing the solid state components, and adjusting the color.

The teacher must zero in on the subject matter determining what principal facts, understandings, attitudes, appreciations, and skills must be mastered by the learners. Whereas some subject areas have a reputation for being harder *to learn,* e.g., calculus, chemistry, and physics, others are more difficult *to teach.* Although learners may have difficulty balancing chemical equations, the strategies for teaching this content are fairly straightforward: lecture-demonstration followed by ample practice, followed by testing. Less apparent, however, are strategies for teaching the dictum "Thou shalt not cheat." What would be the most effective methods for inculcating an attitude of disapproval of cheating? How would the teacher test for mastery of this affective outcome?

Teaching about a subject as opposed to teaching a subject is an approach that even experienced teachers must guard against. We have alluded to this practice in the instance of teaching students to high jump. But we can find other illustrations. For example, teachers who require students to commit grammar rules to memory often test only a knowledge of these rules rather than an ability to apply them. Rather than use the library, students are sometimes confined to studying the Library of Congress cataloguing system only in the English classroom. Again, students are permitted to verbalize what a balanced meal is but are not required to pick out or prepare one.

It is easy to be trapped into teaching about desired outcomes in the affective domain. Students read about democracy as a way of life but are not given the opportunity — sometimes inadvertently, sometimes deliberately — to practice democracy in the school. Students are lectured on the importance of self-discipline but are not allowed an opportunity to demonstrate it.

Teaching about content can lead to verbalism — the ability to describe a behavior but the inability to carry it out. Verbalism results when students are placed in a passive mode. Whenever possible, the learners should be actively involved in the instructional process; they should be placed in real situations or, barring that, in simulated ones.

These comments are not meant to rule out vicarious learning, far from it. We would be lost without it and life would be much bleaker. It is not possible, of course, for pupils to always be involved in real situations. History must be learned vicariously, for example. Until the day when the science fiction writer's dreams become reality, we cannot project ourselves backward in time, propel ourselves physically into the future, or project ourselves spatially into a co-existent present. Most of us can sail up the Amazon, for example, only through words and pictures of someone who has performed the feat and written of his or her exploits in publications like *The National Geographic Magazine*. We can only experience directly the here and now in our own little corner of the universe.

Vicarious experience is more efficient in cases too simple for direct experiencing by every student. Valuable time would be wasted, for example, by having each student in an automotive program demonstrate changing an air filter on an automobile. A presentation by the instructor should suffice for learning this uncomplicated skill. Vicarious experience is the only option, however, when (1) resources are lacking, as, in the case of using the latest model of a self-correcting typewriter when only earlier models are available; (2) facilities are lacking, as in learning to inspect an automobile's brakes when a school does not have an auto shop; and (3) the experience is too complicated, as in preparing a gourmet meal of bouillabaisse, coq au vin, and chocolate mousse.

To conclude, whether personal or vicarious in nature, instructional strategies may emerge from the subject matter.

Student As Source

Instructional strategies must be appropriate for the students. The teacher will not send the average third grader to the library to gather information from the *Encyclopedia Britannica* on the Galápagos Islands. Conversely, the teacher will not attempt to engage junior or senior high school boys and girls in a rousing game of *London Bridge* or *Ring Around the Rosie*. Elementary Spanish is inappropriate for students ready for the intermediate level. Highly abstract, verbal approaches to content do not fit the needs of the mentally retarded or slow learners. Independent study is applicable only to those students with enough self-discipline and determination to profit from it.

Teachers who underestimate the ability of learners and talk down to them or who overestimate the aptitude of learners and talk over their heads follow approaches that do not recognize the pupil as a source of strategy. It may be deduced that unless the teacher is careful, one source of strategy may conflict with another. A particular methodology may relate perfectly to the objectives, may be right on target as to the subject matter, but may be completely inappropriate from the standpoint of the learner. We may generalize, therefore, that any particular strategy must not run counter to any of the sources of strategies.

The teacher should enlist the aid of students in both long-range and short-range planning for instruction. The teacher cannot assume, for example, that his or her purposes are identical to the students' purposes in studying a subject and must, therefore, make an effort to discover student purposes.

When initiating a topic, the teacher should help students identify their personal reasons, if any, for studying the material. Students should be asked to state their objectives in their own words. The teacher may wish students to study the Viet Nam War, for example, so (1) they can complete a section of the textbook, (2) they can fulfill a requirement of a course in American history, (3) they can become familiar with that segment of our history, and (4) they might become interested enough in history to continue it in college. The students, on the other hand, may wish to study the Viet Nam War in order to (1) understand books, television programs, and films concerned with this topic, (2) learn what friends and relatives experienced there, and (3) find out what got us into the war, why there was so much student protest, and how we can avoid getting into such a situation again.

Students may effectively participate in planning by (1) choosing among equally acceptable topics, (2) helping identify the instructional objectives, (3) suggesting appropriate strategies, (4) choosing individual and group assignments, (5) selecting materials, and (6) structuring learning activities.

Community As Source

The desires of parents, the type of community, tradition, and convention all play a part in determining classroom strategies. Sex education, for example, alarms persons in many communities. Some oppose the school's venturing into this area on religious grounds; others feel it is the prerogative of the home. Consequently, examining various contraceptives, for example, might be considered by many in the community as inappropriate at any level.

A survey of drug habits among youth of a community might be rejected by some citizens who feel a negative image of the community might be the result. Counseling techniques that probe into a pupil's family life, psychological and personality tests, and sensitivity training may disturb parents.

Learning activities that stimulate excessive competition among students in the classroom and on the athletic field may meet with community disapproval. The use of outdated methodologies like the overuse of memorization can disturb parents as can procedures that call for behaviors either beyond the pupils' capacities or below their abilities.

Community efforts to censor materials and methods occur frequently in some localities. Although teachers may experience some difficulties with the community over their choice of techniques or content, they need not abandon a course of action for this reason alone. Yet, as discussed early in this text, involving members of the community in the process of curriculum development is desirable. Learning about community needs, beliefs, values, and mores may be necessary before the teacher can gain support for using techniques he or she believes are most effective. Through advisory committees, parent volunteer aides, parent-school organizations, and civic groups, community opinions about the school and its curriculum can be gathered.

Teacher As Source

Instructional strategies must conform to (1) the teacher's personal style of teaching and (2) the model or models of instructing the teacher follows. Large-group instruction, for example, will not appeal to the teacher who prefers to work closely with students. A teacher who regularly follows an inductive model of teaching is not likely to be content with using a deductive model. It is incumbent upon teachers to analyze the particular style of teaching they project and the models they find most suitable for their particular styles. Teachers should seek to expand their repertoires by developing more than a single model of teaching.

Guidelines for Selecting Strategies

To help teachers choose instructional strategies, I have drawn up some guidelines.[1] The guidelines suggest that a strategy must be right for:

□ the learners. It must meet their needs and interests and be in keeping with their learning styles.

□ the teacher. The strategy must work for the individual teacher.

□ the subject matter. Artificial respiration, for example, is taught more effectively by demonstration and practice than by lecturing.

□ the time available. A scientific experiment requiring an extended period of several days, for example, is not possible if sufficient time is not available.

□ the resources available. Reference materials must be available if students are required to carry out research projects that necessitate their use.

□ the facilities. Dividing a class into small groups for discussion purposes,

---

[1] Peter F. Oliva, *Supervision for Today's Schools* (New York: Harper & Row, 1976), pp. 103–105.

for example, may be impractical if the room is small, if acoustics are poor, and if the furniture is not moveable.

- □ the objectives. The strategies must be chosen to fulfill the instructional objectives.

STYLES OF TEACHING

A style of teaching is a set of personal characteristics and traits that clearly identify the individual as a unique teacher. Personal factors that make one teacher different from another include:

- □ dress
- □ language
- □ voice
- □ gestures
- □ energy level
- □ facial expressions
- □ motivation
- □ interest in people
- □ dramatic talent
- □ intellect
- □ scholarship

Teachers consciously or unconsciously adopt certain styles. The teacher as helper, disciplinarian, actor, friend, father or mother image, autocrat, artist, big brother or sister, and as expounder are examples of teaching styles. Barbara Bree Fischer and Louis Fischer defined teaching style as "a pervasive quality in the behavior of an individual, *a quality that persists though the content may change.*" [2] Teachers differ in teaching style, they observed, in much the same way that U. S. presidents, for example, varied in speaking style, famous painters differed in artistic style, or well-known tennis players demonstrated unique playing styles.

The teacher with a high, squeaky voice had best not rely heavily on the lecture as a methodology. The teacher who is formal and proper in dress and manner will probably rule noisy games out of his or her repertoire. The teacher who lacks confidence in his or her management skill may not feel comfortable with a freewheeling, open-ended discussion. If a teacher of low energy level or low motivation refuses to read carefully students' assigned essays or term papers, there is little point in using such strategies.

The teacher with a penchant for scholarship will likely include among his or her methods various forms of research. The teacher with an interest in people will choose procedures in which he or she and the students are not only interacting with each other but with people both inside and outside the school.

The teacher who is confident about his or her work will invite visitors to the classroom, use resource persons, and permit audio and video taping of classroom activities. The teacher who is democratically-oriented will design

---

[2] Barbara Bree Fischer and Louis Fischer, "Styles in Teaching and Learning," *Educational Leadership* 36, no. 4 (January 1979): 245.

activities that permit students to participate in decision making. Unflappable individuals will be more inclined to try out innovative techniques that might result in failure whereas less intrepid individuals will tend to stick to the tried-and-true.

Some teachers reject the use of audiovisual techniques because they do not feel competent enough to use the equipment or they harbor the attitude that the use of media is somehow a waste of valuable time. In the judgment of these teachers, Guttenberg provided the definitive answer to instructional media — the printed page.

Fischer and Fischer identified a number of styles of teaching, including:

> *The Task-Oriented* — These teachers prescribe the materials to be learned and demand specific performance on the part of the students. Learnings to be accomplished may be specified on an individual basis, and an explicit system of accounting keeps track of how well each student meets the stated expectations.
>
> *The Cooperative Planner* — These teachers plan the means and ends of instruction with student cooperation. . . . Opinions of the learners are not only listened to, but are respected. These teachers encourage and support student participation at all levels.
>
> *The Child-Centered* — This teacher provides a structure for students to pursue whatever they want to do or whatever interests them. . . . This style is not only extremely rare, it is almost impossible to imagine in its pure form because the classroom, with its adult-child ratio and adult-responsible environment, automatically encourages some interests and discourages others.
>
> *The Subject-Centered* — These teachers focus on organized content to the near exclusion of the learner. By "covering the subject," they satisfy their consciences even if little learning takes place.
>
> *The Learning-Centered* — These teachers have equal concern for the students and for the curricular objectives, the materials to be learned. They reject the over-emphasis of both the "child-centered" and "subject-centered" styles, and instead help students, whatever their abilities or disabilities, develop toward substantive goals as well as in their autonomy in learning.
>
> *The Emotionally Exciting and Its Counterpart* — These teachers show their own intensive emotional involvement in teaching. They enter the teaching-learning process with zeal and usually produce a classroom atmosphere of excitement and high emotion.[3]

You and I no doubt find some teaching styles more appealing and more acceptable than others. We might identify some styles as negative (e.g., undemocratic behavior) and some as positive (concern for students). Human beings that we are, we will probably give our approval to styles of learning

---

[3] Fischer and Fischer, p. 251.

that emulate our own. Fischer and Fischer made their position clear in unequivocable terms:

> We do not consider all styles of teaching and learning to be equally valid. All too often, indefensible practices are justified with the claim, "Well, that's my style. I have mine, you have yours, and each is as good as the other. . . . Since the very idea of style is based on a commitment to individualization of instruction and the development of learner autonomy, styles that encourage undue conformity and dependence are not acceptable to us.[4]

STYLES OF LEARNING

The teacher's style obviously bears some relationship to the pupils' styles of learning. Some pupils are:

- □ samovars
- □ eager beavers
- □ mules
- □ self-starters

- □ plodders
- □ shining stars
- □ skeptics

Some express themselves better orally than in written form. Some can deal with abstractions; others can learn only with concrete materials. Some learn more effectively from aural and visual techniques than through reading. Some can work under pressure; others cannot. Some need much direction; others, little. Pupils are as different in learning styles as teachers are in teaching styles.[5] In fact, they are more different since there are more of them. Teachers must be aware that their teaching styles can have a strong impact on student achievement and that their styles can at times be at cross-purposes to their pupils'.

A teaching style cannot be selected in the same way an instructional strategy can. Style is not something that can be readily switched on and off. It is not simple to change from a task-oriented to a child-centered approach. Only with considerable difficulty, if at all, can a nonemotionally exciting teacher become an emotionally exciting one. Two questions must be asked about teaching styles: Can a teacher change his or her style? Should a teacher change his or her style?

Given a willingness to change, appropriate training, counseling, or therapy, if need be, a teacher can change his or her style. Contrary to ancient beliefs about the impossibility of changing a person's behavior, human beings can and do change. Sometimes personality change is modeled on the behavior of another person who is in some way important to an individual. Sometimes

---

4 Fischer and Fischer, p. 246.
5 For analysis of students' learning styles see Rita Dunn and Kenneth Dunn, *Teaching Students Through Their Individual Learning Styles: A Practical Approach* (Reston, Va.: Reston Publishing Company, 1978).

a crisis or trauma effects personality change. All religions share the basic premise that individuals can change their behavior. Thus, change is possible, though it may not be easy.

Perhaps a larger question is whether a teacher should change his or her style. Three answers are given to this question, one of which presupposes a teacher's ability to change style. First, one school of thought holds that a teacher's learning style should match the pupils'. Consequently, we would attempt to analyze the styles of the teacher and pupils respectively, then group pupils and teachers with compatible styles. The pupils and teachers would then follow their own styles.

At first glance, ignoring the complexities of analyzing styles and grouping the pupils with compatible teachers, this position seems to be very sound and logical. Rapport between teacher and pupils would most likely be high and the classroom climate would be conducive to learning. Herbert A. Thelen supported the concept of matching teachers with teachable students: "We remain convinced that any grouping which does not in some way attempt to 'fit' students and teachers together can have only accidental success." [6]

Perhaps there is some merit, holds a second school of thought, in exposing students to a great variety of personal styles during their schooling so they will learn how to interact with different types of people. Although some students might prefer the less structured, informal, relaxed approach while they are in school, a legion of high school graduates compliment their task-oriented, subject-centered teachers for having "held their feet to the fire" and thereby helped them to succeed after graduation in spite of themselves.

Richard L. Turner took this second position when he commented:

> A key feature of virtually all school organizations is that little effort is made to control the variability of teaching styles and learning styles. Schools rarely attempt to match the styles of learners to styles of teachers. Therein lies much of the strength and durability of the school as a social entity.
>
> Among any group of students, some will adapt more readily to the style of a particular teacher than others will. The strength of the school as a collective lies in the fact that over long periods of time students are exposed to many different teaching styles. By virtue of this variation, all but a few students are exposed to several teaching styles to which they readily adapt, and to some with which they must struggle. [7]

A third response to the question of whether a teacher should change his or her style holds that a teacher should be flexible, utilizing more than one style with the same group of students or with differing groups of students.

---

[6] Herbert A. Thelen, *Classroom Grouping for Teachability* (New York: John Wiley, 1967), p. 186.

[7] Richard L. Turner, "The Value of Variety in Teaching Styles," *Educational Leadership* 36, no. 4 (January 1979): 257–258.

This answer combines features of both the first and second responses. Teachers vary their styles, if they can, for particular groups of learners and by the same token, the pupils are exposed to a variety of styles. Whatever the strategy chosen, it must conform to the teacher's inimitable style. That is why it is so important for teachers to know who they are, what they are, and what they believe. Rita S. Dunn and Kenneth J. Dunn spoke about the effect of the teacher's attitudes and beliefs on teaching style as follows:

> The attitudes teachers hold toward various instructional programs, methods, and resources as well as the kinds of youngsters they prefer working with constitute part of their "teaching style." It is true, however, that some teachers believe in specific forms of instruction that they do not practice (administrative constraints, inexperience, lack of resources, or insecurity) and that others practice methods in which they do not believe (administrative or community mandates, inability to change or to withstand pressures). It is also true that teachers may prefer students different from those they are actually teaching.[8]

Style and method are used rather loosely in the professional literature and often interchangeably. Fischer and Fischer caution us, "style is not to be identified with method, for people will infuse different methods with their own styles. For example, lecturing is not a style, in our conception, for people with distinctive styles will infuse their respective lectures with their own unique qualities." [9]

MODELS OF TEACHING

Whereas style of teaching is a personalized set of teacher behaviors, a model of teaching is a generalized set of behaviors that emphasize a particular strategy or set of strategies. Lecturing, for example, is an instructional strategy or method. One whose predominant strategy is lecturing is fulfilling the model of lecturer. The contrast between model and style can readily be seen by a person who attends presentations given by two different lecturers.

Bruce Joyce and Marsha Weil defined a model of teaching in this way: "A model for teaching is a plan or pattern that can be used to shape curriculums (long-term courses of studies), to design instructional materials, and to guide instruction in the classroom and other settings." [10] The model or instructional role that the teacher displays guides the teacher's choice of strategies. In one sense, the model or role is the method or strategy. When the teacher plays the role of questioner, for example, questioning is the instruc-

---

[8] Rita S. Dunn and Kenneth J. Dunn, "Learning Styles/Teaching Styles: Should They . . . Can They . . . Be Matched?", *Educational Leadership* 36, no. 4 (January 1979): 241.

[9] Fischer and Fischer, p. 245.

[10] Bruce Joyce and Marsha Weil, *Models of Teaching,* 2d ed. (Englewood Cliffs, N.J.: Prentice-Hall, 1980), p. 1.

tional strategy or methodology. If the teacher writes learning activity packages (LAP's), the use of LAP's is the methodology. On the other hand, if the teacher acts as a facilitator — a much broader role — a number of instructional strategies or methods may be employed. Students may choose their own materials, make up their own questions, and critique their own work, all under the general facilitating supervision of the teacher.

Susan S. Ellis clarified the meaning of a model of teaching when she wrote:

> Models of teaching are strategies based on the theories (and often the research) of educators. psychologists, philosophers, and others who question how individuals learn. Each model consists of a rationale, a series of steps (actions, behaviors) to be taken by the teacher and the learner, a description of necessary support systems, and a method for evaluating the learner's progress. Some models are designed to help students grow in self-awareness or creativity; some foster the development of self-discipline or responsible participation in a group; some models stimulate inductive reasoning or theory-building; and others provide for mastery of subject matter.[11]

In preservice teacher education, students usually gain familiarity and some limited experience with several of the more common models of teaching, including expository teaching, group discussion, role playing, demonstration, simulation, discovery, learning laboratories, programmed instruction, tutoring, problem solving, and mediated instruction. The assumption teacher education institutions make is that students will gain proficiency in one or more of the models (methodologies) and identify those with which they will feel most comfortable. Given the limited time at their disposal, teacher education institutions can only introduce students to the many instructional models, encourage students to identify their favorites, and help students to develop a degree of skill in carrying out various models.

Bruce Joyce identified twenty-five models of teaching.[12] In their book, *Models of Teaching,* Joyce and Weil elaborated on twenty-four models grouped under four major categories or families: (1) social models, e.g., Byron Massialas and Benjamin Cox's social inquiry model and the National Training Laboratory's T-Group Model; (2) information-processing models, e.g., Hilda Taba's inductive model and J. Richard Suchman's inquiry training model; (3) personal models, e.g., Carl Rogers' nondirective teaching and William Glasser's classroom meeting model; and (4) behavioral models, e.g., contingency management and the self-control model.[13]

When we speak of models rather than methods of teaching, we convey the

---

[11] Susan S. Ellis, "Models of Teaching: A Solution to the Teaching Style/Learning Style Dilemma," *Educational Leadership* 36, no. 4 (January 1979): 275.

[12] Bruce Joyce, *Selecting Learning Experiences: Linking Theory and Practice* (Alexandria, Va.: Association for Supervision and Curriculum Development, 1978).

[13] Joyce and Weil, *Models of Teaching.*

concept that a model is a generalized pattern of behavior that can be learned and imitated. Although teachers may develop their own enduring personal styles, which they may not be able to change easily or desire to change, they may develop skills inherent in a variety of models. Thus, we might ask the same questions about models that we asked about styles: Can teachers change their models of teaching? Should they change them?

To the first question, the answer must be "Yes." Were this not so, a significant portion of preservice and inservice teacher education would not be valuable. To the second question, a change of model is desirable if the teacher's stock in trade is limited to one particular model, no matter how successfully the teacher carries it out.

Need for Variety

Variety of modeling is essential to successful teaching. Constant exposure to a single model can lead to restlessness and boredom on the part of students. Let us fabricate a very unlikely situation. A male teacher develops a successful model that his colleagues admire. In their search for the "right" and "best" method, they begin to emulate their colleague to the point where every teacher in the school adopts his model. Can you imagine what school would be like if every teacher were enthusiastic about the discovery method, for example? Life could be extremely dull for both students and teachers alike.

Of course, the use of a single, consistent model by all teachers is not sound pedagogy; a model must be compatible with both the teacher's style and the students' styles of learning. Deductive thinking — in which a rule is given first, then many opportunities for applying it — is less time-consuming and more efficient with some learners than inductive thinking, in which the applications are given first and the learners determine the rule from them.

The use of a uniform model by all teachers is unlikely, fortunately. Yet, we can detect sentiment among some educators that there is both a "best" style and a "best" model of teaching. Some models are proposed by their creators to supplant rather than supplement others.

Turner saw the quest for the best style of teaching as a pervasive problem, stating:

> It is important, then, that all teachers be skilled, and it is critical that they vary in style. A widespread problem in school districts, in schools of education, and in educational research is the idea that there is a single best style of teaching and that teachers should be highly skilled in that style. A more fruitful conception is that there are many effective styles of instruction and that every teacher should be skilled in at least one, preferably in several.[14]

---

[14] Turner, p. 258.

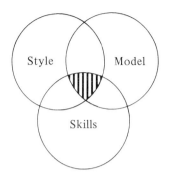

FIGURE 11-1   Teachers' approach

Joyce and Weil viewed the search for the best model of teaching to be a fallacy and noted that the research does not champion one model over another.[15]

TEACHING SKILLS

Up to this point we have been discussing styles and models of teaching, both of which are germane to selecting particular strategies or methods. We should add a third dimension that bears upon selecting instructional strategies — teaching skills. A word is needed to signify the interrelationship between style, model, and skills of teaching. "Method" is a tempting word except it already conveys the meanings of both "strategy" and "model," e.g., the strategy of lecturing = the method of lecturing. For want of a better term, the coining of which we will leave to others, we will use the ambiguous word "approach" to signify the interrelationship among the triumvirate of style, model, and skills. We might chart this relationship in the form of a diagram in which the shaded area represents the teacher's approach (see Figure 11-1).

Let's take a simple illustration of this relationship and see how the three aspects of the teacher's approach come together. Let's choose programmed instruction for our example. The teacher who plays the role of programmer (model) is likely to be a person who is subject-centered, has a penchant for detail, believes pupils learn best in graduated bits (style), and who has skill in selecting content, sequencing, writing programs, and testing (skills). At the risk of redundancy, we might say that programming is the teacher's method (or model) and the use of programs with the learners is the teacher's instructional strategy (or method).

---

[15] Joyce and Weil, p. 1.

What skills are pertinent to a particular approach? For example, what skills are required for lecturing — a method used at some time or other by most teachers? We might list the following:

- ability to enunciate
- ability to project one's voice
- ability to use proper grammar and sentence structure
- ability to "read" student facial expressions
- ability to select content to be used in lectures
- ability to sustain interest
- ability to relate content to past and future experiences of learners
- ability to speak to level of audience
- ability to deal with individuals causing distractions
- ability to stimulate thinking
- ability to organize thoughts

All of these abilities are generic teaching skills. We may define generic teaching skills as those instructional skills that are general in nature and can be employed by teachers in any field and at any level. The converse, special teaching skills, are specific abilities that must be demonstrated by teachers in a particular field or level. The foreign language teacher, for example, must be skillful in varying stimuli, a generic skill, while also adept at projecting specific stimuli unique to the language being taught. Skill in interpreting one language into another is a special skill of a foreign language teacher, not a talent that must be evidenced by every teacher.

Generic Competencies

Educators in recent years have taken an interest in identifying generic teaching skills (competencies). The state of Florida, for example, identified twenty-three generic competencies. Since July 1, 1980 all persons seeking state teacher certification must demonstrate a mastery of these generic skills on the Florida Teacher Certification Examination. The twenty-three skills are presented in Box 11-1. Dwight Allen and Kevin Ryan also compiled a well-known list of fourteen generic teaching skills common to all levels.[16]

The state of Georgia assesses beginning teacher performance by means of a criterion-referenced test of fourteen generic competencies under three major categories: classroom procedures, interpersonal skills, and teaching plans and materials.

---

[16] See Dwight Allen and Kevin Ryan, *Microteaching* (Reading, Mass.: Addison-Wesley, 1969).

BOX 11-1   Florida's 23 essential generic competencies

COMMUNICATION SKILLS

1. Demonstrate the ability to orally communicate information on a given topic in a coherent and logical manner.

2. Demonstrate the ability to write in a logical, easily understood style with appropriate grammar and sentence structure.

3. Demonstrate the ability to comprehend and interpret a message after listening.

4. Demonstrate the ability to read, comprehend, and interpret professional material.

BASIC KNOWLEDGE

5. Demonstrate the ability to add, subtract, multiply, and divide.

6. Demonstrate the ability to comprehend patterns of physical, social, and academic development in students, and to counsel students concerning their needs in these areas.*

TECHNICAL SKILLS

7. Diagnose the entry knowledge and/or skill of students for a given set of instructional objectives using diagnostic tests, teacher observations, and student records.

8. Identify long-range goals for a given subject area.

9. Construct and sequence related short-range objectives for a given subject area.

10. Select, adapt, and/or develop instructional materials for a given set of instructional objectives and student learning needs.

11. Select, develop, and sequence related learning activities appropriate for a given set of instructional objectives and student learning needs.

12. Establish rapport with students in the classroom by using verbal and/or visual motivational devices.

With appropriate training, teachers can learn to master the generic teaching skills. Although generic teaching skills may be employed by all teachers at all levels, it does not follow that any teacher at any level or in any field can use any generic skill in any situation. Although every teacher should possess skill in asking probing questions, for example, each teacher will need to decide when the nature of the content and the learning styles of the pupils will make probing questions appropriate.

Whether the skills are generic or specific, teachers must demonstrate a variety of instructional skills that can be adapted to their own styles and models. Research on teacher behaviors, such as Allen and Ryan's, suggests that teaching skills can be imitated, learned, modified, and adopted.

BOX 11-1   cont'd.

---

13. Present directions for carrying out an instructional activity.

14. Construct or assemble a classroom test to measure student performance according to criteria based upon objectives.

ADMINISTRATIVE SKILLS

15. Establish a set of classroom routines and procedures for utilization of materials and physical movement.

16. Formulate a standard for student behavior in the classroom.

17. Identify causes of classroom misbehavior and employ a technique(s) for correcting it.

18. Identify and/or develop a system for keeping records of class and individual student progress.

INTERPERSONAL SKILLS

19. See competency number 6.

20. Identify and/or demonstrate behaviors which reflect a feeling for the dignity and worth of other ethnic, cultural, linguistic, and economic groups.

21. Demonstrate instructional and social skills which assist students in developing a positive self-concept.

22. Demonstrate instructional and social skills which assist students in interacting constructively with their peers.

23. Demonstrate teaching skills which assist students in developing their own values, attitudes, and beliefs.

* Competencies 6 and 19 were combined into one competency by statute.
SOURCE: Florida Department of Education, *The Florida Teacher Certification Exam Effective July 1, 1980* (Tallahassee, Fla.: Office of Preservice Teacher Education, 1980). Reprinted by permission.

The teachers' personal styles, the models they follow, and the teaching skills they have mastered all affect their design for instruction. Teachers select strategies, for example, that match their personal styles. They follow models to which they are receptive and choose strategies for which they have the requisite teaching skills.

ORGANIZING FOR INSTRUCTION

Planning for instruction involves selecting the following components:

- goals
- objectives

▫ strategies
▫ learning resources
▫ evaluation techniques

We discussed selecting instructional goals and objectives in Chapter 10 and considered selecting strategies and, indirectly, the resources needed to carry them out in this chapter. We will treat choosing evaluation techniques in Chapter 12.

Somehow the teacher must bring all the separate components together into a cohesive plan. Both long-range and short-range planning are required. We will examine some long-range plans in Chapter 15. Let's look now at the more immediate types of plans: the short-range unit plan and the even shorter-range daily plan.

Unit Plans

The unit plan, also called a "learning unit," "teaching unit," or simply, "unit," is a means of organizing the instructional components for teaching a particular topic or theme. Burton defined a unit as follows:

> A unit is any combination of subject-matter content and outcomes, and thought processes, into learning experiences suited to the maturity and needs (personal and social) of the learners, all combined into a whole with internal integrity determined by immediate and ultimate goals.[17]

The unit plan ordinarily covers a period from several days to several weeks. A series of units might actually constitute a particular course. The daily plan organizes the instructional components of the lesson(s) of the day. A unit serves as a source of a number of daily plans. Ordinarily, instructional planning progresses from course to unit to daily plans.

The writing of unit and daily lesson plans is a key skill that teacher education institutions seek to develop in preservice teachers. Some institutions insist on a degree of meticulousness and thoroughness in writing plans that is rarely seen in practice in the classroom.

We find considerable variation in the structure of unit plans.[18] Burton offered a detailed outline for a unit plan, as follows:

▫ *Title.* Attractive, brief, and unambiguous.
▫ *The Overview.* Brief statement of the nature and scope of the unit.
▫ *The Teacher's Objectives.* Understandings (generalizations), attitudes, appreciations, special abilities, skills, behavior patterns, facts.
▫ *The Approach.* A brief account of the most probable introduction.
▫ *The Pupil's Aim or Objective.* The major objective which it is hoped the learners will develop or accept.

---

[17] William H. Burton, *The Guidance of Learning Activities,* 3rd ed. (New York: Appleton-Century-Crofts, 1962), p. 329.

[18] See, for example, Kenneth T. Henson, *Secondary Teaching Methods* (Lexington, Mass.: D. C. Heath, 1981), p. 197.

- □ *The Planning and Working Period.* Learning activities with desired outcomes for each activity.
- □ *Evaluation Techniques.* How evidence will be gathered showing that the objectives of the unit have been developed.
- □ *Bibliographies.* Books useful to the teacher and books useful to the learners.
- □ *Audio-Visual Materials and Other Instructional Aids, with Sources.*[19]

Analysis of various unit outlines shows that a unit plan should contain the title, the level or course for which it is intended, and the amount of time to be devoted to the following minimum essentials:

- □ instructional goals
- □ instructional objectives (cognitive, affective, psychomotor)
- □ instructional procedures (learning activities)
- □ evaluation techniques (preassessment, formative, summative — about which, more later)
- □ resources (human and material)

Many teachers choose to include in their unit outlines of the content a budget of time for each portion of the unit and tentative outlines of daily lesson plans.

Units are written to be used; they are living documents and should be followed where helpful, and augmented, diminished, revised, and discarded when inappropriate. They are not meant as attractive products to be neatly packaged, filed, or tossed onto a shelf where they may gather dust. Box 11-2 provides an illustration of a unit plan.

Lesson Plans

Lesson plans chart the daily instruction. Conceivably, lesson plans could (and sometimes are) written without reference to any unit plan. Yet on strictly logical grounds, higher quality, better organized, and more complete lesson plans are achieved with than without unit plans. Creating units is essential to holistic planning.

Like unit planning, lesson planning is an individual exercise. According to Laurence J. Peter, "a lesson plan is simply an outline prepared in advance of teaching, so that time and materials will be used efficiently."[20] Peter pointed out that "various types of lessons require different kinds of lesson plans."[21] We might add, on a philosophical level, "various types of teachers require different kinds of lesson plans" and "various types of learners require different kinds of lesson plans." On a practical level, "various types of administrators and supervisors require different kinds of lesson plans."

---

[19] Burton, pp. 372–374.
[20] Laurence J. Peter, *Competencies for Teaching: Classroom Instruction* (Belmont, Cal.: Wadsworth, 1975), p. 194.
[21] Peter, p. 194.

BOX 11-2   Illustrative unit plan

Title: Financing Our Community's Public Schools
Level: Senior high school — Problems of American Democracy
Time: Five days

A. Instructional Goals

1. The student will understand that quality education is costly.

2. The student will understand that ignorance is more costly than education.

3. The student will become aware of sources of funding for the schools.

4. The student will become familiar with problems of financing education in our community.

B. Instructional Objectives

Cognitive

1. The student will describe the role and extent of local involvement in financing the schools.

2. The student will describe the role and extent of state involvement in financing the schools.

3. The student will describe the role and extent of federal involvement in financing the schools.

4. The student will explain the process by which public moneys are expended for the schools.

5. The student will explain what our public moneys buy for the schools.

6. The student will compare salaries of teachers in our community's schools with salaries paid outside of teaching.

Affective

1. The student will take a position on the property tax: necessary, too high, too low? Reasons must be stated for the position taken.

2. The student will take a position on the statement: Teachers are underpaid. Reasons must be stated for the position taken.

3. The student will take a position on federal aid to education: pro or con? Reasons must be stated for the position taken.

4. The student will take position on the statements: The schools cost too much. There are too many frills in education. Reasons must be stated for the positions taken.

Psychomotor

None

C. Instructional Procedures

1. Read the district superintendent's annual report and discuss the revenues and expenditures.

BOX 11-2 cont'd.

2. Read last year's school budget and compare with proposed budget for next year. Account for changes in the total amounts each year.

3. Draw a chart of the percentages of money spent by the locality, state, and federal government for support of the community's schools.

4. Prepare a bar graph showing the total number of dollars expended this past year by the locality, state, and federal government for the community's schools.

5. Report on your family's school tax and show how it was calculated.

6. Invite a school principal to class and interview him or her about expenditures and revenues for his or her school.

7. Invite the superintendent or one of his or her staff or a member of the school board to class and interview him or her about expenditures and revenues for the school district.

8. Report on the costs of one federally supported program in our community's schools.

9. Consult and discuss publications of the state department of education on financing schools in the state.

10. Compare amounts of money raised throughout the state by property taxes and by sales, income, and other taxes.

11. Compare salaries of teachers in our community with salaries of (1) teachers in other communities in the state, (2) teachers in other states, and (3) persons outside of teaching.

12. Account for variations in amounts of money raised for the support of education by localities of the state and in the total amounts of money available to these localities.

13. Account for variations in amounts of money raised for the support of education by the various states.

14. Compile a list of average annual costs of selected items for which schools must pay, including instructional supplies, equipment, heat, lights, water, salaries of all personnel, insurance, and maintenance.

15. Compute the costs of vandalism in our community's schools for a one-year period.

16. Write a report advocating either greater or lesser funding for our community's schools. In your report show what is to be added or cut.

17. Suggest improved ways of funding the schools.

D. Evaluation Techniques

1. Preassessment
Construct and administer a pretest to assess students' entry knowledge and skills. Sample questions might include:
a. Estimate the total amount of money spent for the public schools of our community this past year. *(continued on next page)*

BOX 11-2   cont'd.

b. How is the property tax determined?
c. Which spends more money on our community's schools: the locality, the state, or the federal government?

2. Formative evaluation
   a. Daily oral questioning of the students by the teacher on the more difficult aspects of the lessons.
   b. Daily summarizations by students and teacher at the end of each lesson.
   c. Teacher's evaluation of student products, as charts, graphs, etc.

3. Summative evaluation
   a. Quiz on the day following conclusion of the unit. Sample test items may include questions similar to those of the pretest plus additional items. A combination of objective and essay test items may be used. Sample test items might include:
      (1) Essay: Explain the process by which our community raises money locally for the schools.
      (2) Objective: In reference to taxation, a mill is written as:
          (a) .01
          (b) 1.0
          (c) .001
          (d) .0001

E. Resources

Human

☐ School principal.
☐ School superintendent, member of his or her staff, or member of the school board.

Material

☐ Publications of the local school board.
☐ Publications of the state department of education.
☐ Publications of the U. S. Department of Education, including:

Dearman, Nancy B. and Pliske, Valena White. *The Condition of Education: Statistical Report,* 1980 ed. Washington, D. C.: U. S. Department of Education, National Center for Education Statistics, 1980.

Grant, W. Vance and Eiden, Leo J. *Digest of Education Statistics,* 1980. Washington, D. C.: U. S. Department of Education, National Center for Education Statistics, 1980.

U. S. Bureau of the Census. *Statistical Abstract of the United States.* Washington, D. C.: Superintendent of Documents, U. S. Government Printing Office, annually.

The World Almanac and Book of Facts. New York: Newspaper Enterprise Association, annually.

NOTE: This illustrative learning unit is based on the illustrative resource unit shown in Chapter 15.

A six-part outline for a lesson plan that can be used generically follows:

A. Objectives
B. Activities
C. Assignment
D. Evaluation Techniques
E. Bibliography
F. Instructional Aids and Sources[22]

A sample lesson plan based on the illustrative unit plan is shown in Box 11-3.

The less experience a teacher has, the more complete his or her unit and lesson plans should be. It is desirable for both experienced and inexperienced teachers to prepare complete unit plans to fully communicate their ideas. Yet, experienced teachers will discover ways to simplify and shorten lesson plans. This practice is to be encouraged as long as the lesson plans remain serviceable to both themselves and substitute teachers. Once the unit and lesson plans have been made, the teacher can begin to demonstrate his or her style, model, and skills.

SUMMARY

Selecting instructional strategies is one of the final steps in planning for instruction. Instructional strategies are derived from a number of sources, including: the objectives, the subject matter, the pupil, the community, and the teacher.

Teachers vary in style, model, and skills of teaching. By style we mean the unique, personal qualities that a teacher develops over the years to distinguish himself or herself from all other teachers. Mr. Chips, of *Goodbye Mr. Chips* and Henry Higgins of *Pygmalion,* for example, have distinct, memorable styles.

When we speak of models of teaching, we mean a generalized role, a pattern of methods, as discussion leader, television instructor, or foreign language informant. The so-called Socratic method of stimulating thinking is, in effect, a model. Jesus's sermons to the people are examples of a model (preacher) as well as a method (sermonizing).

By skills of teaching we mean those generic and specific abilities necessary to design and carry out instruction. Lesson planning, for example, is a generic skill, i.e., pertinent to all teachers at all levels. The ability to teach pupils to perform the division of whole numbers is a specific skill. Both the models and skills must be compatible with the teacher's style. Instructional strategies must be appropriate to the teacher's style, model, and skill.

It should be emphasized that instructional strategies, styles of teaching,

---

22 Peter F. Oliva, *The Secondary School Today,* 2d ed. (New York: Harper & Row, 1972), p. 313.

BOX 11-3   Illustrative lesson plan

First Day
Unit: Financing Our Community's Schools
Fifty minutes

A. Objectives

Cognitive

1. The student will list three sources of funding for the schools.
2. The student will describe the source(s) of local funding for the schools.
3. The student will define "property tax," "assessed valuation," and "mill."

Affective

1. The student will take positions, giving reasons, on whether the property tax is necessary, too high, or too low.
2. The student will express an opinion and give reasons as to whether he or she believes expenditures for schools in the community are more than adequate, adequate, or inadequate.

B. Activities

1. Set induction: Students will listen to the teacher read a recent editorial from the local newspaper on the needs of local schools. The class will discuss its perceptions of the accuracy of the editorial (eight minutes).

2. Using an overhead projector, the teacher will show transparencies of charts selected from the district superintendent's annual report to the school board. Students will respond to teacher's questions asking for interpretation of the charts (ten minutes).

3. Using the same data, students will prepare original charts and/or graphs showing sources and amounts of funds for the community's schools this past year. Copies of the superintendent's report will also be available for students' use (ten minutes).

4. Students will listen to teacher's description of sources of local funding. Key points: property tax, assessed evaluation, tax assessor, exemptions, and millage (ten minutes).

---

and teaching skills are all selected, adopted, and implemented to promote accomplishing instructional goals and objectives. The ultimate purpose of all strategies, styles, models, and skills is fostering student achievement.

The various instructional components should be organized into, among other types of plans, short-term unit plans and daily lesson plans. Although teachers may design their own formats for unit and lesson plans, generic outlines are suggested. As teachers gain experience, less detail in planning is possible. However, *some* planning is always necessary.

BOX 11-3   cont'd.

5. Students will calculate amount of school tax to be paid on the following properties (five minutes):
   a. A house assessed at $60,000; no exemptions; millage rate of 8.5 mills.
   b. A house assessed at $50,000; homestead exemption of $5,000; millage rate of 6.52 mills.
   c. A house assessed at $75,000; homestead exemption of $5,000 plus senior citizen exemption of $5,000; millage rate of 7.15 mills.

6. Closure: Teacher will ask students questions such as: Which level of government spends most on the education of young people in the community? Approximately how much money was raised locally for schools last year? What percentage of funding came from the state? What percentage of funding came from the federal government? What is the current millage rate? (five minutes)

C. Assignment (two minutes)
   1. See if you can find any articles in the local newspapers about costs of education in the community, state, or nation.
   2. Ask your parents how much school tax they paid last year and, if they do not object, report to the class how much it was and how it was calculated. Ask your parents also whether they believe the property tax is too high or low or about right.

D. Evaluation Techniques
   1. Spot-check students' work at seats on charts and calculations of property tax.
   2. Ask students to respond to teacher's oral questions at the end of the lesson.

E. Bibliography
   1. Copies of the district superintendent's annual report to the school board.
   2. Editorial from local newspaper.

F. Instructional Aids and Sources
   Overhead projector and transparencies.

SUPPLEMENTARY EXERCISES

1. Select an instructional objective and design at least three strategies for accomplishing it.
2. Observe several teachers, describe their styles, and tell what makes each teacher unique.
3. Select one of the models of teaching described by Bruce Joyce and Marsha Weil (see bibliography) and describe it to the class.

4. Describe with examples how a teacher's style affects selection of instructional strategies.

5. Observe several teachers and try to identify the models they are using.

6. Select one of the generic skills described by Dwight Allen and Kevin Ryan (see bibliography), demonstrate it in class or videotape your demonstration of the skill and critique it in class.

7. Search the literature on instruction, find several outlines for unit plans, compare them, and select an outline you would use, stating reasons.

8. Search the literature on instruction, find several outlines of lesson plans, compare them, and select an outline you would use, stating reasons.

9. List several specific teaching skills for a teaching field you know well.

10. Write an essay with appropriate references in support of or opposed to training in generic teaching skills for all teachers.

11. Critique the twenty-three Florida Generic Teaching Competencies and decide whether you agree they are essential skills for very teacher.

12. Take a position, stating reasons, on testing of teacher competency.

13. Design a five-to-ten-day-long unit plan appropriate for teaching and learning toward a specific instructional goal.

14. Design a lesson plan for one day based on the unit plan that you prepared for exercise thirteen.

BIBLIOGRAPHY

Allen, Dwight and Ryan, Kevin. *Microteaching.* Reading, Mass.: Addison-Wesley, 1969.

Berenson, David H., Berenson, Sally R., and Carkhuff, Robert B. *The Skills of Teaching: Lesson Planning Skills.* Amherst, Mass.: Human Resource Development Press, 1978.

———. *The Skills of Teaching: Content Development Skills.* Amherst, Mass.: Human Resource Development Press, 1978.

Berenson, Sally R., Berenson, David H., and Carkhuff, Robert R. *The Skills of Teaching: Teaching Delivery Skills.* Amherst, Mass.: Human Resource Development Press, 1979.

Brooks, Douglas M. "Ethnographic Analysis of Instructional Method," *Theory Into Practice* 19, no. 2 (Spring 1980): 144–147.

Burton, William H. *The Guidance of Learning Activities,* 3rd ed. New York: Appleton-Century-Crofts, 1962.

Carkhuff, Robert R. *The Art of Helping III.* Amherst, Mass.: Human Resource Development Press, 1977.

———, Berenson, David H., and Pierce, Richard M. *The Skills of Teaching: Interpersonal Skills.* Amherst, Mass.: Human Resource Development Press, 1977.

Cooper, James, et al. *Classroom Teaching Skills: A Handbook.* Lexington, Mass.: D. C. Heath, 1977.

Dunn, Rita S. and Dunn, Kenneth J. "Learning Styles/Teaching Styles: Should They . . . Can They . . . Be Matched?" *Educational Leadership* 36, no. 4 (January 1979): 238–244.

———. *Teaching Students Through Their Individual Learning Styles: A Practical Approach.* Reston, Va.: Reston Publishing Company, 1978.

Ellis, Susan S. "Models of Teaching: A Solution to the Teaching Style/Learning Style Dilemma," *Educational Leadership* 36, no. 4 (January 1979): 274–277.

Fischer, Barbara Bree and Fischer, Louis. "Styles in Teaching and Learning," *Educational Leadership* 36, no. 4 (January 1979): 245–254.

Gage, N. L., ed. *The Psychology of Teaching Methods,* 75th Yearbook of the National Society for the Study of Education, Part I. Chicago: University of Chicago Press, 1976.

Henson, Kenneth T. *Secondary Teaching Methods.* Lexington, Mass.: D. C. Heath, 1981.

Hyman, Ronald T. *Strategic Questioning.* Englewood Cliffs, N.J.: Prentice-Hall, 1979.

Joyce, Bruce. *Selecting Learning Experiences: Linking Theory and Practice.* Alexandria, Va.: Association for Supervision and Curriculum Development, 1978.

Joyce, Bruce and Weil, Marsha. *Models of Teaching,* 2d ed. Englewood Cliffs. N.J.: Prentice-Hall, 1980.

Oliva, Peter F. *The Secondary School Today,* 2d ed. New York: Harper & Row, 1972.

Orlich, Donald C., et al. *Teaching Strategies: A Guide to Better Instruction.* Lexington, Mass.: D. C. Heath, 1980.

Peter, Laurence J. *Competencies for Teaching: Classroom Instruction.* Belmont, Cal.: Wadsworth, 1975.

Thelen, Herbert A. *Classroom Grouping for Teachability.* New York: John Wiley, 1967.

Turner, Richard L. "The Value of Variety in Teaching Styles," *Educational Leadership* 36, no. 4 (January 1979): 257–258.

Weil, Marsha and Joyce, Bruce. *Information Processing Models of Teaching: Expanding Your Teaching Repertoire.* Englewood Cliffs, N.J.: Prentice-Hall, 1978.

―――. *Social Models of Teaching: Expanding Your Teaching Repertoire.* Englewood Cliffs, N.J.: Prentice-Hall, 1978.

―――, and Kluwin, Bridget. *Personal Models of Teaching: Expanding Your Teaching Repertoire.* Englewood Cliffs, N.J.: Prentice-Hall, 1978.

FILMSTRIP-TAPE PROGRAMS

Vimcet Associates, P.O. Box 24714, Los Angeles, California 90024:

Systematic Instructional Decision-Making, 1967.

Appropriate Practice, 1967.

Perceived Purpose, 1967.

Analyzing Learning Outcomes, 1969.

Knowledge of Results, 1969.

Teaching Units and Lesson Plans, 1969.

Individualizing Instruction, 1971.

Instructional Tactics for Affective Objectives, 1971.

12

Evaluating Instruction

After studying this chapter you should be able to:
1. Define preassessment, formative evaluation, and summative evaluation, and describe the purposes of each.
2. Explain the differences between norm-referenced and criterion-referenced measurement and state the purposes for which each is intended.
3. Design test questions in the major categories of each of the three domains of learning.

You should also be able to formulate and give reasons for your views on the following issues:
1. The extent of problems that accompany evaluating instruction.
2. The importance of clear objectives for the purposes of evaluation.
3. The value of different approaches to evaluation.

ASSESSING INSTRUCTION

Assessing Student Achievement

She holds her head in her hands, staring at the top of the desk, transfixed. She looks with displeasure at the pile of examinations in front of her, each filled with red marks indicating errors. She has administered the acid test — the examination on the unit on elections: local, state, and federal. Four weeks' work wasted! On a scale of one to one hundred and a passing grade of seventy, only twelve out of thirty-six pupils achieved the passing mark. Why? she asks herself. What went wrong? A potpourri of reasons floods her brain:

- □ The students are all blithering idiots who would flunk any test no matter how simple.
- □ They did not pay attention when she was going over the material.
- □ They do not study; they are more interested in drugs and sex than in the electoral process.
- □ They are too careless in answering the questions.
- □ Their parents do not force them to do their homework.

After several moments of indulging in recrimination and blaming the poor results on the students, she begins to take a look at the situation more rationally. What are some hypotheses, she asks herself, for such a high percentage of failures? After some serious reflection, she begins to wonder:

- □ Were the objectives appropriate? Were they pertinent to the subject matter? Were they within the learning abilities of the pupils? Were they relevant to the students?
- □ Did the pupils possess the prerequisite competencies before we began the unit on which they did so poorly? How do I know?
- □ Did I use the right instructional techniques? Did the strategies I chose fit the learning styles of the students?
- □ Did I make periodic checks along the way? What did they reveal?
- □ Did I alert them to the type of exam?
- □ Did the exam questions relate to the objectives? Were they clear?
- □ Did the pupils have sufficient time to respond to all the questions? Were the classroom conditions suitable for exam taking?
- □ Were the pupils at fault for their failures? Did I fail the pupils in my role as instructor? Or was there a blending of responsibilities for the low scores?
- □ Did I really find out what the students did or did not learn?
- □ And what do I do now? How shall I treat the exam results? What effect should their scores have on the next report card? How will I explain low scores to the principal, to the pupils, to the parents?

Curriculum planner that she is, the teacher realizes that if the examination results are poor, the instructional objectives have not been achieved; if the instructional objectives have not been met, neither have the instructional goals; if the instructional goals have not been accomplished, neither have the curriculum objectives; and if the curriculum objectives have not been achieved, neither have the curriculum goals.

Evaluating instruction tells us about both the pupils' accomplishments and the instructor's success. When we speak of evaluating instruction in this text, we are concerned with the teacher's techniques for assessing student achievement. We shall not discuss the methods for evaluating the *instructor* — his or her classroom performance. Though extremely important, evaluating the instructor is quite another tale beyond the scope of this text.[1]

Cycle Within a Cycle

Instruction in the model for curriculum development followed in this text is a cycle within the curriculum cycle (see Figure 12-1). Let's once again pull out the instructional chain which makes up the Instructional Model. It is a submodel of the model for curriculum development presented in Chapter 5 (see Figure 12-2). To keep our original model for curriculum development uncluttered, the feedback line for this submodel was depicted simply. It proceeds from the terminal component of the instructional chain — the Evaluation of Instruction — directly to the beginning of the instructional model — the Specification of Instructional Goals.

Note that the feedback line from Evaluation of Instruction to Instructional Goals demonstrates a cycle and indicates that modification in the system can be made in sequence, However, this figure would be more accurate if it showed the feedback lines to *each* component since evaluation results may reveal needed modifications in components anywhere in the system. The instructional submodel with all feedback lines is shown in Figure 12-3.

As we have seen, the instructional chain begins with specifying the goals. This cycle is not complete until we learn whether or not the instructional goals and objectives have been achieved. The problem before us now is one of evaluating the instruction that has taken place.

AN ERA OF ASSESSMENT

Evaluation. Assessment. Measurement. Testing. Accountability. These words are heard with great frequency today in both public and professional circles. Specialists in measurement and evaluation are in great demand, for we have entered the Era of Assessment. Although this era began some time ago, its tempo began to increase considerably in the midseventies. In the past few years, the movement's emphasis and the sources of its impetus have changed somewhat.

---

[1] For discussion of teacher evaluation see Peter F. Oliva, *Supervision for Today's Schools* (New York: Harper & Row, 1976), Chapter 9.

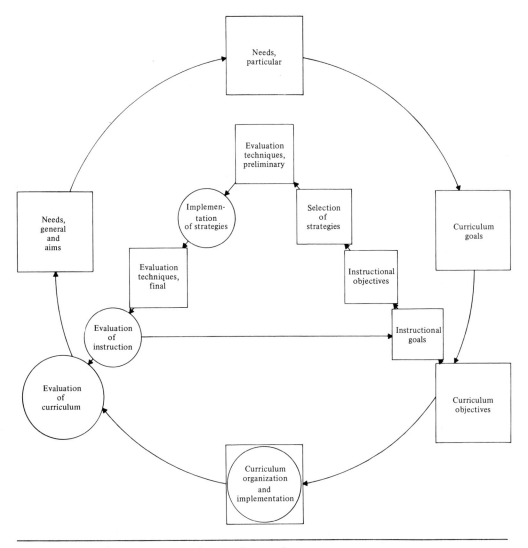

FIGURE 12-1   The instruction and curriculum cycles

We are all familiar with the phenomenon of mass testing that has dominated America ever since Edward L. Thorndike conceptualized the first standardized tests. The standardized SAT and GRE tests are household words in
the United States in much the same way the nonstandardized baccalaureate
tests are in France.

William H. Whyte, Jr., Martin Gross, and Banesh Hoffman were pointing
to the dangers of mass testing in the late fifties and early sixties. Whyte and

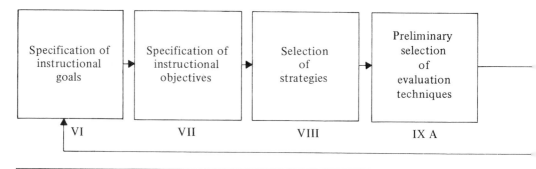

FIGURE 12-2   Instructional model with one feedback line

Gross were particularly concerned about personality testing, and Hoffman was critical of typical standardized multiple-choice tests.[2]

The National Assessment of Educational Progress

The National Assessment of Educational Progress (NAEP), a program funded by the National Center for Education Statistics of the U. S. Department of Education, has been instrumental in promoting the cause of assessment of student achievement throughout the country. In 1964, with the backing of the Carnegie Corporation, Ralph W. Tyler and the Committee on Assessing the Progress of Education began to develop criterion-referenced tests for nationwide assessment. Testing by NAEP began in 1969 and eventually encompassed ten areas: art, citizenship, literature, mathematics, music, occupational development, reading, science, social studies, and writing. Data in these areas have been collected from samples of children, ages nine, thirteen, and seventeen, and from young adults, twenty-six to thirty-five. Data have been reported by geographical region, size and type of community, educational level of parents of pupils, sex, age, and ethnic group (black and white). Although not identifying either individuals or schools, the NAEP has made the public and school systems aware of deficiencies in the various subject areas tests. Curriculum planners throughout the country have, in the light of NAEP data, re-examined their own school systems' programs to determine whether they have deficiencies and, if necessary, to plan ways to overcome them.

State Assessment Programs

In recent years the assessment spotlight has moved from the national arena to the state level. Several factors motivated state legislators and educators to

---

[2] William H. Whyte, Jr., *The Organization Man* (New York: Simon and Schuster, 1956); Martin L. Gross, *The Brain Watchers* (New York: Random House, 1962); Banesh Hoffman, *The Tyranny of Testing* (New York: Crowell-Collier Press, 1962).

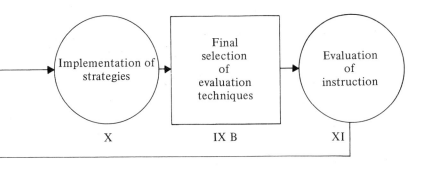

establish minimal competencies for student achievement at various grade levels and for graduation from high school. They disliked the results reported by the National Assessment for Educational Progress; they felt dissatisfied with the "products" their schools were turning out; and they heard the public clamor for a return to the basic skills and for accountability of teachers for their pupils' achievements. Assessment tests, therefore, became necessary for determining whether students had achieved the competencies. By 1978 some thirty-six states had set minimum standards of performance for students in their schools.

Assessment is, of course, an expected and necessary part of the curriculum-instructional process. It is imperative that teachers determine the extent to which pupils have attained the objectives. The intensity of assessment, however, is relatively new to the educational scene. The push for assessment is a companion to the drive for basic skills.

Definition of Terms

At this point, let's clarify the meaning of the main terms used in this chapter. These are: evaluation, assessment, measurement, and testing. "Evaluation," said Davis, Alexander, and Yelon, "is a continuous process of collecting and interpreting information in order to assess decisions made in designing a learning system." [3] *Evaluation* and *assessment* are used interchangeably in this text to denote the general process of appraisal. Measurement and testing are subsumed under the general classifications of evaluation and assessment.

Measurement is the means of determining the degree of achievement of a particular competency. *Testing* is the use of instruments for measuring achievement. Measurement and testing are thus ways of gathering evaluation and assessment data. However, we have means other than testing to evaluate student performance. When we speak of evaluating a student's performance of a com-

---

[3] Robert H. Davis, Lawrence T. Alexander, and Stephen L. Yelon, *Learning System Design* (New York: McGraw-Hill, 1974), p. 81.

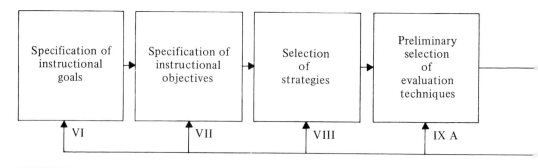

FIGURE 12-3   Instructional model with all feedback lines

petency, we may or may not measure that performance. Measurement implies a degree of precision and observable behavior.

In this chapter, we will not fully explore measurement, evaluation, testing techniques, and the byproducts of evaluating instruction — marking and reporting.[4] We will seek instead to develop some basic understandings about evaluating instruction, including a limited number of principles of measurement and testing.

STAGES OF PLANNING FOR EVALUATION

You will note, in referring to the proposed model for curriculum development,[5] that component IX on the selection of evaluation techniques is divided into two parts: IXA, Preliminary Selection of Evaluation Techniques and IXB, Final Selection of Evaluation Techniques. This separation is made in order to convey the understanding that planning of evaluation techniques takes place both before and after instruction. However, this dual separation is an oversimplification. To be more precise, we should show planning for evaluation techniques interspersed at each stage of the Instructional Model. An expanded diagram of instruction showing the many stages of planning for evaluation is presented in Figure 12-4.

Expanded Model of Instruction

What the expanded model indicates is that the selection of evaluation techniques, including test items, is a continuous process. This concept of planning for evaluation differs from the practice of many teachers who wait until the end of the instruction (called "treatment" by some educators), then prepare

---

[4] See L.R. Gay, *Educational Evaluation & Measurement: Competencies for Analysis and Application* (Columbus, Ohio: Charles E. Merrill, 1980).
[5] See p. 169 of this text.

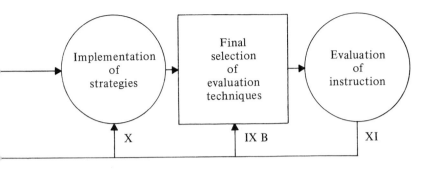

and administer an end-of-treatment test. Evaluation techniques should be jotted down at each of the five stages shown in the expanded model. Three of these stages are prior to instruction; one, midinstruction; and one, post-instruction. Test items should be recorded when they occur to the teacher while the content is fresh in mind. Continuous accumulation of test items and other evaluation techniques can simplify end-of-treatment evaluation.

Three Phases of Evaluation

The teacher needs to be able to demonstrate skills in three phases of evaluation:

- □ preassessment
- □ formative evaluation
- □ summative evaluation

These terms are technical words to connote evaluation that takes place *before* instruction (preassessment), *during* instruction (formative), and *after* instruction (summative).

Preassessment. *Preassessment* possesses a dual nature. Walter Dick and Lou Carey described two types of tests that precede instruction.[6] These two types are an entry-behaviors test and a pretest. The *entry-behaviors test* is "a criterion-referenced test designed to measure skills which the instructor has identified as being critical to beginning the instructional materials."[7] This type of preassessment is conducted to determine whether students possess the pre-requisite knowledge that will enable them to proceed with the new treatment. The *pretest* is "criterion-referenced to objectives which the designer intends to teach in the module."[8] A "module" is essentially the same as a "unit." "Criterion-referenced" tests, discussed later in this chapter, measure students'

---

[6] Walter Dick and Lou Carey, *The Systematic Design of Instruction* (Glenview, Ill.: Scott, Foresman, 1978), p. 79.

[7] Dick and Carey, p. 79.

[8] Dick and Carey, p. 79.

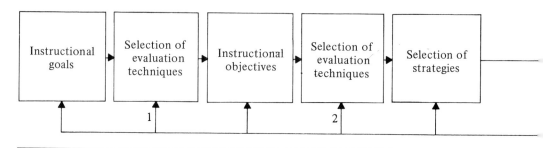

FIGURE 12-4   Stages of planning for evaluation

achievement not by how they compare with their classmates but by how well they master predetermined instructional objectives.

The entry-behaviors (or entry skills) test covers preceding (prerequisite) learnings whereas the pretest covers subject matter to be learned. A pretest alone is not sufficient, for if students do poorly on a pretest (as they should, if future instruction is really new to them), the instructor cannot tell whether the students did poorly because they did not know the material to come (acceptable) or did not have the prerequisite knowledge or skills (not acceptable). Some means of judging possession of prerequisite skills is essential. Lack of prerequisite skills calls for remedial instruction and repetition of instruction instead of proceeding with new content.

Formative Evaluation. *Formative evaluation* consists of those techniques of a formal and informal nature, including testing, that are used during the period of instruction. Progress tests are an illustration of formative evaluation. Bloom, Hastings, and Madaus advised instructors to "break a course or subject into smaller units of learning" and to administer "brief diagnostic progress tests." [9] Dick and Carey advocated "an embedded test," which they described as follows: "This is not necessarily a single test, but rather represents clusters of criterion-referenced test items which are interspersed throughout the module.[10]

Through formative evaluation teachers may diagnose student difficulties and take remedial action to help them overcome their difficulties before they

---

[9] Benjamin S. Bloom, George F. Madaus, and J. Thomas Hastings, *Handbook on Formative and Summative Evaluation of Student Learning* (New York: McGraw-Hill, 1971), p. 53.
[10] Dick and Carey, p. 79.

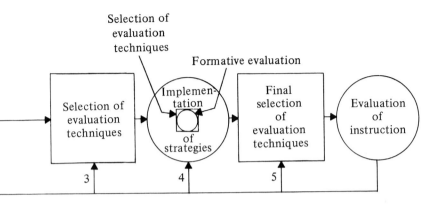

are confronted with the *terminal (summative) evaluation*. Formative evaluation enables teachers to monitor their instruction so that they may keep it on course.

Summative Evaluation. *Summative evaluation* is the assessment that takes place at the end of a course or unit. A final examination (*posttest*) is a means used for the summative evaluation of instruction. Its major purpose is to find out whether the students have mastered the preceding instruction. The astute teacher utilizes results of summative evaluation to revise his or her program and methodology for subsequent groups.

NORM-REFERENCED AND CRITERION-REFERENCED MEASUREMENT

Norm-Referenced Measurement

Two divergent concepts of measurement compete for the attention and loyalty of instructors. *Norm-referenced measurement* is the classic approach to assessment in which a student's performance on a test is compared to the performance of other students who took the test. Following this principle, standardized tests of achievement are administered and norms — standards of performance — are calculated for various groups who took the tests. The scores made by students who subsequently take the tests are compared to those made by the population on whom the test was standardized.

Classroom teachers follow the same principle whenever they measure the achievement of one student against or in relationship to that of other students in class. As a gross example of this approach to measurement, the teacher will administer a test, calculate the scores, rank the scores from highest to lowest, find the middle score, which becomes a C grade, then grade all other tests in relationship to that middle grade. In this nonstandardized situation, students are rated in relationship to performance of that particular group on that particular test.

Criterion-Referenced Measurement

Since the norm-referenced approach to measurement is so common and so universally practiced, it might be asked, "What other approach is there?" *Criterion-referenced measurement* is the alternative to norm-referenced measurement. In this approach the performance of students on a test is compared to criteria that were established in the instructional objectives. A student's success on a criterion-referenced test depends on demonstrated mastery of the objectives and not on his or her performance as related to others in the class.

Although it is true that the two approaches to measurement have their distinct uses and that both forms of measurement can be found in the schools, norm-referenced measurement seems to retain the edge.[11] With its long history of usage the norm-referenced approach is reasonably well understood by teachers, students, and parents. Further, imbued with a sense of competition, many parents invite the kinds of comparisons that are made under a norm-referenced system.

Among the proponents of norm-referenced testing are the standardized testmakers; those who advocate competitive grading; and those who have a need to screen or select persons, as, for example, college admissions officers; those who draw up honor rolls; admission committees of honorary societies; and those who award scholarships. Norm-referenced testing is necessary when a limited number of places are to be filled from a pool of applicants in excess of the number of places and when only a limited number of awards are to be distributed among a group of aspirants. It is problematic whether this condition prevails in the classroom. Among the practitioners of criterion-referenced measurement are the instructional-design specialists and the district, state, and national assessment people. These persons desire to know whether students achieve mastery of specified objectives. If we may use the analogy of the smiling or nonsmiling face, the norm-referenced tester frowns when all students pass an exam as it does not discriminate between high and low achievers. The criterion-referenced tester wears a broad smile when all students pass an exam, since students have mastered the objectives on which they were tested.

The emergence of criterion-referenced measurement is relatively new. Dick and Carey made reference to this phenomenon when they observed:

> During the last ten years, classroom testing has taken a very different turn. . . . As more and more emphasis has been placed on statements of ex-

---

[11] See Myron H. Dembo, *Teaching For Learning: Applying Educational Psychology in the Classroom* (Santa Monica, Cal.: Goodyear Publishing Co., 1977), p. 346.

plicit behaviors which students must demonstrate, it has been increasingly obvious that a fair and equitable evaluation system is one that measures those specific behaviors. That is, after students have been told what they have to do to be successful on a learning unit, they should be tested accordingly.[12]

Comparison of the Two Types of Measurement

Mary-Jeanette Smythe, Robert J. Kibler, and Patricia W. Hutchings have made a comparison of general characteristics of norm-referenced and criterion-referenced measurement systems, as shown in Table 12-1.

Kibler, Cegala, Miles, and Barker listed the following four ways that criterion-referenced tests may be used:

□ for preassessment purposes
□ for formative testing . . . that is, testing that is used concurrently with instruction for the purpose of checking the progress of students so that assistance may be provided when necessary
□ to determine whether components of the instructional model . . . need modification
□ to determine whether students have achieved the criterion levels of objectives[13]

W. James Popham described a major distinction between the purposes of norm-referenced and criterion-referenced measurement when he explained:

> Since norm-referenced measures permit comparisons among people, their primary purpose is to make decisions about *individuals*. Which pupils should be counseled to pursue higher education? Which pupils should be advised to attain vocational skills? . . .
>
> Criterion-referenced tests make decisions both about *individuals* and *treatments*. In decisions regarding individuals, we might use a criterion-referenced test to determine whether a learner had mastered a criterion skill considered prerequisite to a new training program. In decisions regarding treatments, we might design a criterion-referenced measure which reflected a set of instructional objectives supposedly achieved by a replicable instructional sequence. By administering the criterion-referenced measure to appropriate learners who had completed the instructional sequence, we could decide the effectiveness of the sequence.[14]

On the surface, norm-referenced tests look no different from criterion-referenced tests. However, Dick and Carey spoke of differences in construction of the two types of measures as follows:

> . . . criterion-referenced tests include only test items that are based on specified behavioral objectives. Each item requires students to demonstrate

---

12 Dick and Carey, p. 78.
13 Robert J. Kibler, Donald J. Cegala, David T. Miles, and Larry L. Barker, *Objectives for Instruction and Evaluation* (Boston: Allyn and Bacon, 1974), p. 116.
14 W. James Popham, *Evaluating Instruction* (Englewood Cliffs, N.J.: Prentice-Hall, 1973), pp. 25–26.

TABLE 12-1 Comparison of norm-referenced and criterion-referenced measurement

NORM-REFERENCED MEASUREMENT	CRITERION-REFERENCED MEASUREMENT
1. The main function of norm-referenced measurement is to ascertain the student's relative position within a normative group.	1. The main function of criterion-referenced measurement is to assess whether the student has mastered a specific criterion or performance standard.
2. Either general conceptual outcomes (usually done) or precise objectives may be specified when constructing norm-referenced measurement.	2. Complete behavioral objectives (i.e., planning objectives) are specified when constructing criterion-referenced measurement.
3. The criterion for mastery is not usually specified when using norm-referenced measurement.	3. The criterion for mastery must be stated (i.e., planning objectives) for use in criterion-referenced measurement.
4. Test items for norm-referenced measurement are constructed to discriminate among students.	4. Test items for criterion-referenced measurement are constructed to measure a predetermined level of proficiency.
5. Variability of scores is desirable as an aid to meaningful interpretation.	5. Variability is irrelevant; it is not a necessary condition for a satisfactory criterion-referenced measurement.
6. The test results from norm-referenced measurement are amenable to transposition to the traditional grading system (A, B, C, D, F).	6. The test results from criterion-referenced measurement suggest the use of a binary system (i.e., satisfactory-unsatisfactory; pass-fail). However, criterion-referenced measurement test results can be transposed into the traditional grading system by following a set of specifically constructed rules.

Source: Mary-Jeanette Smythe, Robert J. Kibler, and Patricia W. Hutchings, "A Comparison of Norm-Referenced and Criterion-Referenced Measurement with Implications for Communication Instruction," *The Speech Teacher* 22, no. 1 (January 1973): 4. Reprinted by permission.

the performance stated in an objective. Standards for acceptable performance on the test are based upon criteria stated in the objectives.

Norm-referenced tests are constructed differently. It is usually unnecessary for the exact performance desired to be described in behavioral terms prior to item or test construction. Test items are not necessarily based on instruction students receive or on skills or behaviors that are identified as relevant for student learning. Items that are developed from a given domain for norm-referenced tests are administered to a variety of students from the target population. Those items that cause the greatest spread or range in students' responses are selected for inclusion on a norm-referenced test. The range of scores is usually expected to resemble a normal or bell-shaped curve, hence the name "norm-referenced." [15]

Popham saw differences in the construction of items for the two types of tests as a matter of "set." Said Popham:

> The basic differences between item construction in a norm-referenced framework and item construction in a criterion-referenced framework is a matter of "set" on the part of the item writer. . . . When an individual constructs items for a norm-referenced test, he tries to produce *variant* scores so that individual performances can be contrasted. . . . He disdains items which are "too easy" or "too hard." He avoids multiple choice items with few alternative responses. He tries to increase the allure of wrong answer options. He does all of this to develop a test which will produce different scores for different people. . . .
>
> The criterion-referenced item designer is guided by a different principle. His chief purpose is to make sure the item accurately reflects the criterion behavior. Difficult or easy, discriminating or indiscriminate, the item has to represent the class of behaviors delimited by the criterion.[16]

The Instructional Model suggested in this text places the specification of instructional objectives in a central position and, therefore, inclines to a criterion-referenced approach to classroom testing. This point of view, however, does not eliminate the use of standardized tests in the school or the use of norm-referenced teacher-made tests for purposes they can fulfill. It does eliminate the use of a norm-centered approach to classroom testing that permits teachers to adopt the philosophy of the normal curve and to generate scores that result in a normal distribution of grades ranging from A through F on every test. Such a practice violates the philosophy of the normal curve, which holds that traits are distributed at random throughout the general population. No single class is a random sample of the general population. Therefore, to hold A's to a mere handful, to condemn some students automatically to F's, and to assign about two-thirds of a class to the so-called average or C grade is not a defensible practice.

EVALUATION IN THREE DOMAINS

Objectives, as we have noted, fall into three domains — the cognitive, the affective, and the psychomotor. Teachers face the task of assessing pupils' performance in the various domains. They may choose any of the numerous types of tests: actual performance, essay, or one or more objective tests —

---

[15] Dick and Carey, p. 88.
[16] Popham, *Evaluating Instruction*, p. 30.

multiple-choice, alternate response, completion, matching, or rearrangement.[17]

Each domain presents its unique evaluation problems. Let's look at some illustrations of test items for the major categories of each domain.

Psychomotor Domain

Objectives in the psychomotor domain are best evaluated by actual performance of the skill being taught. For example, if we wish students to be able to swim one hundred yards without stopping, we require that they hop into the water and show us that they can do it. The students fail, we might say, if they sink to the bottom.

We may wish to qualify the performance by requiring students to swim one hundred yards in x number of minutes. To pass the test students would have to satisfy that criterion.

The teacher has some judgmental calls to make when students are asked to demonstrate perceptual-motor skills. Form and grace might be considered in the one hundred yard swim as well as completion or speed of completion. Evaluative judgments are made when students are asked to demonstrate the ability to make a mobile in art class, to build a bookcase in woodshop, to create a blouse in homemaking, to drive a golf ball in physical education class, or to administer artificial respiration in the first aid course.

Beyond the simple dichotomy — performance or nonperformance (pass-fail, satisfactory-unsatisfactory) — of a skill lie such factors as speed, originality, and quality. The teacher may choose to include these criteria as part of the assessment process. When judgmental criteria are to be used, they should be communicated to the students in advance. It is helpful for the teacher to identify as many indicators of the criteria as possible. For example, in the case of the mobile made in art class, indicators of quality might be durability, precision of construction, neatness, and detail.

There are times when teachers settle for a cognitive recounting of how the student demonstrates a perceptual-motor skill. Ideally, psychomotor skills should be tested by actual performance. Yet, because of lack of time or facilities, it is not always possible for every pupil to demonstrate every skill. For example, a group of students in homemaking working together may have baked bread. A final examination question might be, "List the steps you would take in making white bread." Although not altogether satisfactory from a pedagogical point of view — most of us can talk a better game than we can play — this technique may be used. We suspect, of course, that many a forlorn loaf of bread will be turned out by the inexperienced bakers before the skill is perfected.

Test Items of the Psychomotor Domain. Here are examples of test items for each of the seven major categories of the psychomotor domain.

---

[17] For discussion of types of tests and test items see Peter F. Oliva, *The Secondary School Today,* 2d ed. (New York: Harper & Row, 1972), Chapter 19.

1. Perception: Distinguish between an s sound and a z sound.
2. Set: Demonstrate how to hold a fishing pole.
3. Guided response: Make half-notes following the teacher's explanation.
4. Mechanism: Saw a six-foot two-by-four into three pieces of equal size.
5. Complex overt response: Perform an auto tune-up.
6. Adaptation: Sketch a new arrangement for the furniture of a living room.
7. Origination: Paint an original landscape in watercolors.

All of these test items call for actual performance. Observe that all seven could equally be instructional objectives. We have, therefore, a perfect match between the objectives and the test items. On the other hand, let's take the following psychomotor objective. Is this objective at the same time a test item?

Objective for high school physical education: The pupil will demonstrate skill in swimming. This objective is broad, complex, and without a stipulated degree of mastery. Although it is an objective desired by the physical education instructor, it is difficult to convert into a test item, as is. It would help to establish a series of subobjectives from which we could derive the test items. For example, the sudent will demonstrate how to:

- dive into the pool
- tread water
- float on his or her stomach
- float on his or her back
- do the breast stroke
- do the crawl
- swim under water the width of the pool

The instructor might limit appraisal of the pupils' performance in these skills to "satisfactory" or "unsatisfactory."

Cognitive Domain

Achievement in the cognitive domain is ordinarily demonstrated in school by pupil performance on paper and pencil tests administered to a group, usually, but not always, an entire class. To administer individual written or oral tests on a regular basis requires an excessive amount of time. The teacher should seek to evaluate student achievement in all six levels of the cognitive domain as appropriate, using both essay and objective test items.

Test Items of the Cognitive Domain. Whereas objective items sample knowledge of content on a broad scale, essay tests sample limited content and provide information about the student's ability to organize his or her thoughts, write coherently, and use English properly. The following test items show several ways objectives in the cognitive domain can be evaluated:

1. Knowledge
   Essay: Explain how Samuel Clemens got the name Mark Twain.
   True-False: A whale is a warm-blooded mammal.

Completion: The United States, the Soviet Union, Great Britain, France, and _____ hold permanent seats on the U. N. Security Council.

2. Comprehension

Essay: What is meant when a person says, "Now you've opened Pandora's box?"

Multiple-Choice: A catamaran is a:

   a. lynx
   b. boat
   c. fish
   d. tool

3. Application

Essay: Describe, giving at least three current illustrations, how the law of supply and demand works.

Multiple-Choice: $4 \div \frac{1}{2} =$

   a. 2
   b. 4
   c. 6
   d. 8

4. Analysis

Essay: Analyze the school board's annual budget as to categories of funds, needs of the schools, and sources of funds.

Multiple-Choice: A survey of parents showed 90 percent believe schools are too lax in discipline; 5 percent too strict; and 5 percent undecided. We might conclude that these parents:

   a. favor looser discipline
   b. favor smaller classes
   c. favor stricter teachers
   d. favor higher taxes
   e. favor all of the above

5. Synthesis

Essay: Describe the origin and significance of the Thanksgiving Day holiday.

Since synthesis and the highest category of the cognitive domain — evaluation — require extensive narration, they are best evaluated through use of essay test items.

6. Evaluation

Essay: Read the following planks from the platform of the Democratic Party and give your reasons for whether you believe the planks fulfill current needs in the country. Identify evidence to support your reasons.

Selecting the types of test items depends on the teacher's purpose and the amount of time that can be devoted to the test. As a general rule, a combination of test items provides variety and thereby stimulates interest. If essay items are used either alone or in conjunction with objective items, sufficient time needs to be provided for students to organize their answers and to respond fully to the essay questions. The passing score should always be communicated to the learners before they take a test.

Cognitive objectives, like psychomotor, are often suitable test items. For example, if we choose the objective, "The student will be able to list the steps by which a federal bill becomes a law," the teacher has a ready-made test item, "List the steps by which a federal bill becomes a law." However, if the objective is a general competency like, "The student will be able to divide whole numbers by fractions," the teacher must create specific test items that permit students to demonstrate the competency.

Affective Domain

We should refrain from using the terms "testing" and "measurement" in reference to the affective domain. As stated earlier, student achievement in the affective domain is difficult and sometimes impossible to assess. Attitudes, values, and feelings can be deliberately concealed; learners have the right to hide personal feelings and beliefs, if they so choose. Affective learnings may not be visible in the school situation at all.

The achievement of objectives in the affective domain, therefore — though important in our educational system — cannot be measured or observed like objectives in the cognitive and psychomotor domains. For that reason, students should not be graded on an A through F or percentage system for their lack or possession of affective attributes. Except for a few affective objectives like conduct (provided it can be defined and observed), these types of learning should probably not be graded at all, even with different symbols.

We attempt evaluating affective outcomes when we encourage students to express their feelings, attitudes, and values about the topics discussed in class. We can observe students and may find obvious evidence of some affective learnings. For example, a child who cheats has not mastered the value of honesty. The bully who picks on smaller children has not learned concern for other people. The child who expresses a desire to suppress freedom of speech has not learned what democracy means. The normal child who habitually feels that he or she cannot do the work has developed a low self-concept.

Thus, some affective behaviors are apparent. Teachers can spot them and through group or individual counseling can perhaps bring about a change in behavior. On the other hand, children are at school only six or seven hours per day. They are constantly demonstrating affective behaviors — positive and negative — outside of school, where the teacher will never have occasion to observe them. Are the students helpful at home? Are they law-abiding in the community? Do they protect the environment? Do they respect other people? Who can tell for sure without observing the behavior? Students may profess to behave in certain ways to please the teacher or others and then turn around and behave far differently.

Let's look at some affective objectives that contain ways for evaluating their achievement.

1. Receiving
The student expresses in class an awareness of friction among ethnic groups in this school.
2. Responding
The student volunteers to serve on a human relations committee in the school.
3. Valuing
The student expresses a desire to achieve a positive school climate.
4. Organization
The student controls his or her temper when driving.
5. Characterization by value or value complex
The student expresses and exemplifies in his or her behavior a positive outlook on life.

Assessment Items of the Affective Domain. The Progressive Education Association in its evaluation of the Eight-Year Study assessed students' preference for newspaper reading (an objective within the affective category Receiving) by presenting them with a list of sections of the newspaper and asking them to mark each section with a U if they usually read it, an O if they read it occasionally, and an R if they read it rarely.[18] Whether students found pleasure in science activities (category Responding) was evaluated by the Progressive Education Association by a list of scientific activities for each of which the students indicated satisfaction, uncertainty of their reaction, or dissatisfaction. In addition, students were asked if they had ever performed the activity.[19]

To assess the appreciation of economic factors in people's lives (category Valuing) the Progressive Education Association created descriptions of economic problems. For each problem a number of courses of action were presented for students to indicate approval, disapproval, or uncertainty.[20]

Box 12-1 illustrates assessment items for the affective categories of Organization and Characterization by value or value complex.

Observe that some instruments are titled "tests" by their makers. The agree-disagree attitude inventory is a frequent means used to determine achievement of affective objectives. These types of questions reveal a basic problem in teaching for affective learning. If the teacher or testmaker has preconceived notions of the "correct" responses, he or she is operating in a twilight zone between achievement of affective outcomes and indoctrination.

---

[18] David R. Krathwohl, Benjamin S. Bloom, and Bertram B. Masia, *Taxonomy of Educational Objectives: The Classification of Educational Goals: Handbook II: Affective Domain* (New York: Longman, 1964), p. 116.
[19] See Krathwohl, p. 138.
[20] See Krathwohl, p. 144.

Further, remember that students can and do respond to attitudinal type questions as they believe the teacher or testmaker wishes them to respond rather than the way they actually feel.

Attaining affective objectives is discerned by instruments such as opinionnaires or attitude inventories, by observation of the behavior of students, and by essay questions that ask pupils to state their beliefs, attitudes, and feelings about a given topic. Perhaps, instead of thinking of using instruments that seek to discover students' attitudes and values through an accumulation of items administered test-fashion, we should think more of asking frequent value-laden questions and listening to students' responses. Instead of leveling a continuous barrage of factual questions, teachers can interject questions like: How do you feel about . . . ? What do you believe about . . . ? Would you be interested in . . . ? Are you in agreement with . . . ?

OTHER MEANS OF EVALUATION

Although we normally equate the word "test" with "examination" and usually think of a test in a summative context at the end of instruction, we should remember that it is really an attempt to demonstrate mastery of objectives in whatever domain. Students can demonstrate achievement both during and at the end of instruction through means other than typical examinations. For example, synthesis in the cognitive domain can be tested by means of essay items. Competency in this skill can also be tested by written reports during the period of instruction or by term papers at the end of instruction.

A skilled instructor can tell a great deal about pupils' success just by observing their classroom performance. Individual and group oral reports may be assigned for a variety of purposes, including testing ability to speak, knowledge of the subject, and, in the case of group activities, the ability to work together. Numerous techniques exist for evaluating student achievement. Teachers should seek to develop competency in the use of a wide range of evaluative techniques.[21]

Feedback

Evaluation yields data that provide feedback about student achievement and the instructional program. It is not sufficient for evaluative data to be used solely for the purpose of measuring pupil achievement. If pupils do poorly, teachers need to find out what caused the poor showing. Teachers need to ask themselves what they must do so that subsequent groups of students — or even the same group, if repetition of the instruction appears necessary — will not encounter the same difficulties. Teachers must know what needs to be changed, and the evaluation results provide them with this evidence.

Even if pupils do extremely well, teachers should use the data to re-

---

21 For discussion of means of evaluation other than testing, see Oliva, *The Secondary School Today,* Chapter 20.

BOX 12-1   Items for organization and characterization by value or value complex

Gordon W. Allport, Philip E. Vernon, and Gardner Lindzey created the following items that fall in the affective category Organization.

Category: Organization
Subcategory: Organization of a value system
Objective: Begins to develop dominant values

Item: *Directions:* Each of the following situations or questions is followed by four possible attitudes or answers. Arrange these answers in the order of your personal preference by writing, in the appropriate box at the right, a score of 4, 3, 2, or 1. To the statement you prefer most give 4, to the statement that is second most attractive 3, and so on.

In your opinion, can a man who works in business all week best spend Sunday in

a. trying to educate himself by reading serious books?
b. trying to win at golf, or racing?
c. going to an orchestral concert?
d. hearing a really good sermon?

Viewing Leonardo da Vinci's painting, "The Last Supper," would you tend to think of it

a. as expressing the highest spiritual aspirations and emotions?
b. as one of the most priceless and irreplaceable pictures ever painted?
c. in relation to Leonardo's versatility and its place in history?
d. the quintessence of harmony and design?

Paul L. Dresser and Lewis B. Mayhew showed examples of items which assess objectives at the highest level of the affective domain: characterization by value or value complex.

SOURCE: From Gordon W. Allport, Philip E. Vernon, and Gardner Lindzey, *Study of Values,* 3rd ed. (Boston: Houghton Mifflin Company, 1960), pp. 8, 10. In Krathwohl et al., pp. 163–164. Reprinted by permission of The Riverside Publishing Company.

examine the process. The instructional goals and objectives may have been too simple; students may have been capable of achieving higher objectives. If a test was administered, the test itself may not have been valid. The questions may have been too simple; they may not have measured all the objectives. At the implementation stage, the instructor may have omitted some crucial points and thereby left some objectives unachieved. The results of evaluation provide evidence for making changes in the instructional process.

SUMMARY

Although evaluating instruction is generally perceived as an activity taking place at the end of the instructional process, teachers should begin selecting

BOX 12-1 cont'd.

Category: Characterization by value or value complex
Subcategory: Generalized set
Objective: Respect for the worth and dignity of human beings

Item:

1. Tom and Bob who know each other only slightly were double-dating two girls who were roommates. A sudden storm made it impossible to go to the beach as planned. Tom suggested going to a movie. After making the suggestion, he realized that Bob was without funds. As Tom, what would you do?

   a. Pay for the party.
   b. Lend Bob money.
   c. Leave it up to the girls.
   d. Get Bob to suggest something.
   e. Apologize to Bob for making the suggestion.

2. Your social organization has pledged a student who is not liked by some of the members. One of your friends threatens to leave the social organization if this person is initiated. What would you do?

   a. Talk to your friend.
   b. Do not initiate the prospective member.
   c. Get more members to support the prospective member.
   d. Vote on the prospective member.
   e. Postpone the vote until the matter works itself out.

SOURCE: From *Problems in Human Relations Test.* Cited by Paul L. Dresser and Lewis B. Mayhew, *General Education: Explorations in Evaluation* (Washington: American Council on Education, 1954), p. 233. In Krathwohl et al., p. 170. Reprinted by permission of the American Council on Education.

---

evaluation techniques as soon as they identify their instructional goals. Two types of preassessment are suggested: one to evaluate the pupils' possession of prerequisite knowledge and/or skills to begin study of the new subject matter, the other to determine whether pupils have already mastered the subject matter to be presented.

Evaluation that takes place during the progress of instruction is referred to as formative evaluation and is necessary to monitor both pupil progress and the ongoing success of the instructional program. Summative evaluation is evaluation that comes at the end of instruction, as represented in a final examination.

Distinction is made between norm-referenced measurement in which a student's achievement on tests is compared to other students and criterion-referenced measurement in which a student's achievement is compared to a predetermined criterion of mastery. Norm-referenced tests are used when selection must be made from among a group of persons. Criterion-referenced tests are used to determine whether students achieved the objectives specified in advance.

The major purpose of evaluating instruction is to determine whether or not students accomplished the objectives. Instructors should design means of evaluating pupil performance in the three domains of learning — cognitive, psychomotor, and affective — whenever possible. Tests in the cognitive domain are normally written essay or objective tests administered to an entire class. Discovery of psychomotor outcomes is best carried out by means of tests of actual performance of the skill being taught. Although we may speak of measurement and testing in the cognitive and psychomotor domains, we should use the more general term, evaluation, in reference to the affective domain. Though evaluating affective achievement is difficult and normally imprecise, teachers should engage in this activity. At times, evaluation of affective objectives will not be apparent at all. Nevertheless, affective learning is an important dimension of education, and instructors should strive to determine, the best way they can, the extent to which students have achieved the desired objectives.

Instructors should keep in mind that there are numerous techniques other than testing for evaluating pupil performance. Good pedagogy calls for a diversity of evaluation techniques, as appropriate.

Feedback is an important feature of the Instructional Model. On the basis of evaluative data, instructors revise the preceding components of the model for subsequent instruction. Evaluation is perceived as a continuous, cyclical process.

SUPPLEMENTARY EXERCISES

1. Distinguish between evaluation, measurement, and testing.
2. Select a unit you will teach and prepare a pretest for it.
3. Search the literature on tests and measurement and prepare a set of guidelines for writing (a) essay, (b) multiple-choice, (c) alternate-response, (d) matching, (e) rearrangement, (f) completion items.
4. State the purposes for which essay test items are designed; state the purposes for objective test items.
5. Write a report on the use of test results.
6. Write an essay-test item and an objective-test item for each of the major categories of the cognitive domain.
7. Write a test item for each of the major categories of one of the taxonomies of the psychomotor domain.
8. Design some techniques for evaluating objectives in each of the major categories of the affective domain.

9. Deliver an oral report to the class on whether affective objectives can and should be evaluated.
10. Define formative evaluation and give some examples for a unit you are teaching or will teach.
11. Define summative evaluation and describe how you will conduct the summative evaluation for a unit that you are teaching or will teach.
12. Describe procedures you would use to evaluate:
   a. oral reports
   b. group work
   c. products created by students (give examples)
   d. term papers
   e. dramatic presentations

BIBLIOGRAPHY

Bloom, Benjamin S., ed. *Taxonomy of Educational Objectives: The Classification of Educational Goals: Handbook I: Cognitive Domain.* New York: Longman, 1956.

Bloom, Benjamin S., Hastings, J. Thomas, and Madaus, George F. *Evaluate to Improve Learning.* New York: McGraw-Hill, 1981.

————. *Handbook on Formative and Summative Evaluation of Student Learning.* New York: McGraw-Hill, 1971.

Davis, Robert H., Alexander, Lawrence T., and Yelon, Stephen L. *Learning System Design.* New York: McGraw-Hill, 1974.

Dembo, Myron H. *Teaching for Learning: Applying Educational Psychology in the Classroom.* Santa Monica, Cal.: Goodyear Publishing Co., 1977.

Dick, Walter and Carey, Lou. *The Systematic Design of Instruction.* Glenview, Ill.: Scott, Foresman, 1978.

Gay, L.R. *Educational Evaluation and Measurement: Competencies for Analysis and Application.* Columbus, Ohio: Charles E. Merrill, 1980.

Gronlund, Norman E. *Constructing Achievement Tests,* 2d ed. Englewood Cliffs, N.J.: Prentice-Hall, 1977.

Gross, Martin L. *The Brain Watchers.* New York: Random House, 1962.

Harrow, Anita J. *A Taxonomy of the Psychomotor Domain: A Guide for Developing Behavioral Objectives.* New York: Longman, 1972.

Hoffman, Banesh. *The Tyranny of Testing.* New York: Crowell-Collier Press, 1962.

Kibler, Robert J.; Cegala, Donald J.; Miles, David T.; and Barker, Larry L. *Objectives for Instruction and Evaluation.* Boston: Allyn and Bacon, 1974.

Krathwohl, David R.; Bloom, Benjamin S.; and Masia, Bertram B. *Taxonomy of Educational Objectives: The Classification of Educational Goals: Handbook II: Affective Domain.* New York: Longman, 1964.

Mager, Robert F. *Preparing Instructional Objectives.* Belmont, Cal.: Fearon Publishers, 1962.

Oliva, Peter F. *The Secondary School Today,* 2d ed. New York: Harper & Row, 1972.

————. *Supervision for Today's Schools.* New York: Harper & Row, 1976.

Popham, W. James. *Evaluating Instruction.* Englewood Cliffs, N.J.: Prentice-Hall, 1973.

Simpson, Elizabeth Jane. "The Classification of Educational Objectives in the Psychomotor Domain." In *The Psycho-*

Motor Domain, Vol. 3. Washington, D.C.: Gryphon House, 1972, pp. 43–56.

Smythe, Mary-Jeanette; Kibler, Robert J.; and Hutchings, Patricia W. "A Comparison of Norm-Referenced and Criterion-Referenced Measurement with Implications for Communication Instruction," *The Speech Teacher* 22, no. 1 (January, 1973): 1–17.

Whyte, William H., Jr. *The Organization Man.* New York: Simon and Schuster, 1956.

FILMSTRIP-TAPE PROGRAMS

Vimcet Associates, P.O. Box 24714, Los Angeles, California 90024:

Establishing Performance Standards, 1967.
Evaluation, 1967.
Modern Measurement Methods, 1969.
Writing Tests Which Measure Objectives, 1972.

13

Evaluating the Curriculum

After studying this chapter you should be able to:
  1. Explain the major features of at least two models of curriculum evaluation.
  2. Describe how one or more models of curriculum evaluation can be used by curriculum planners.
  3. Create your own model of curriculum evaluation.

You should also be able to formulate and give reasons for your views on the following issues:
  1. The question of whether evaluation is essential to the curriculum process.
  2. The question of whether evaluation can and should be planned.

PURPOSES AND PROBLEMS OF CURRICULUM EVALUATION

Years ago in a college foreign language class, the instructor lured his students into a grammatical frame of mind by promising to reveal to them "the secrets of the subjunctive." In this chapter we will disclose some of the secrets of curriculum evaluation. We shall make this revelation right now. The secrets of evaluation are:

- □ to ask questions
- □ to ask the *right* questions
- □ to ask the *right* questions of the *right* people

Depending on the problems, questions might be addressed to teachers, administrators, pupils, laypeople, parents, other school personnel, and experts in various fields, including curriculum.

As is often necessary in pedagogical discourse, we must first clarify our terms before we can talk about them. We find numerous articles and textbooks on educational, instructional, and curriculum evaluation. The broadest of these terms — *educational evaluation* — is used in this text to encompass all kinds of evaluations that come under the aegis of the school. It includes evaluation not only of curriculum and instruction but also of the grounds, buildings, administration, supervision, personnel, transportation, etc.

Instructional evaluation, discussed in the preceding chapter, is an assessment of (1) pupils' achievement, (2) the instructor's performance, and (3) the effectiveness of a particular approach or methodology. *Curriculum evaluation* includes instructional evaluation. Recall that the Instructional Model is a submodel of the comprehensive curriculum development model. Curriculum evaluation also goes well beyond the purposes of instructional evaluation into assessment of the program and related areas. Albert I. Oliver listed five areas of concern that call for evaluation — "the five P's," as he terms them, of program, provisions, procedures, products, and processes.[1]

The axiom was advanced early in this text that change is inevitable not only in education but also outside of education. As curriculum planners, we wish changes in education to take place for the better. Since the creations of mortals are always less than perfect, we can always seek improvement. Evaluation is the means for determining what needs improvement and for providing a basis for effecting that improvement.

Problems in Evaluation

It is generally conceded that one place where we are vulnerable in education is in evaluating the programs we have instituted. Our evaluation is often spotty

---

[1] Albert I. Oliver, *Curriculum Improvement: A Guide to Problems, Principles and Processes,* 2d ed. (New York: Harper & Row, 1977), p. 306.

and frequently inconclusive. We should be able to demonstrate, for example, whether:

- open-space education results in higher student achievement than the self-contained classroom
- second language learning helps in learning one's native language
- nongraded schools are more effective than graded
- the *McGuffey Reader* is a better tool to teach reading than some of the more modern materials
- specifying minimal competencies improves student performance
- one series of biology texts results in greater student achievement in biology than another series
- an inductive or deductive approach is more effective in teaching grammar
- class size makes a difference in pupil achievement
- specifying instructional objectives leads to improved pupil performance

Many of the conclusions we have reached in education about the success of innovations have been based on very limited evidence. The lack of systematic evaluation may be attributed to a number of causes. Careful evaluation can be very complicated. It requires know-how on the part of the evaluators, which means that training in evaluation is essential. Further, it is time- and energy-consuming. It is safe to say that we do not, as a rule, do a thorough job of evaluation and what we do is often not too helpful.

Daniel L. Stufflebeam and others observed that evaluation was ill and suffered from the following symptoms:[2]

1. The avoidance symptom. Because evaluation seems to be a painful process, everyone avoids it unless absolutely necessary.
2. The anxiety symptom. . . . anxiety stems primarily from the ambiguities of the evaluation process.
3. The immobilization symptom. . . . schools have not responded to evaluation in any meaningful way.
4. The skepticism symptom. . . . many persons seem to argue that there is little point in planning for evaluation because "it can't be done anyway."
5. The lack-of-guidelines symptom. . . . among professional evaluators . . . is the notable lack of meaningful and operational guidelines.
6. The misadvice symptom. Evaluation consultants, many of whom are methodological specialists in educational research, continue to give bad advice to practitioners.
7. The no-significant-difference symptom. . . . evaluation . . . is so often incapable of uncovering any significant information.
8. The missing-elements symptom. [There] is a lack of certain crucial ele-

---

[2] Daniel L. Stufflebeam et al., *Educational Evaluation & Decision Making* (Itasca, Ill.: F. E. Peacock Publishers, 1971), pp. 4–9.

ments needed if evaluation is to make significant forward strides. The most obvious missing element is the lack of adequate theory.

Revising the Curriculum Model. As in our analysis of evaluating instruction, we will develop some general understandings about curriculum evaluation and will discuss a limited number of evaluation procedures. Let's begin by taking a look at the Curriculum Model shown in Figure 13-1, which is a submodel of the proposed model for curriculum improvement.

The Curriculum Model is conceptualized as consisting of four components — Curriculum Goals, Curriculum Objectives, Organization and Implementation of the Curriculum, and Evaluation of the Curriculum. A feedback line connects the Evaluation component with the Goals component, making the model cyclical in nature. We should redefine the Curriculum Model in two ways. First, as with the Instructional Model, we should show the feedback line as affecting more than just the Curriculum Goals. Although the impact on Curriculum Goals is felt through all subsequent components, evaluative data should feed back to each of the components of the Curriculum Model. A more precise rendering of the feedback concept would show lines from Evaluation of the Curriculum not only to Curriculum Goals but also to Curriculum Objectives and to Organization and Implementation of the Curriculum, as shown in Figure 13-2.

Second, we should make clear that evaluation of the curriculum is not something done solely at the end of a program's implementation but is an operation that takes place before, during, and at the end of the implementation. Figure 13-3 shows the continuous nature of curriculum evaluation in a manner similar to the way we showed the continuous nature of instructional evaluation. Circles within boxes indicate that curriculum evaluation is going on while evaluation procedures are being planned.

FIGURE 13-1   Curriculum model with one feedback line

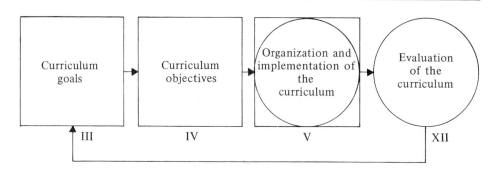

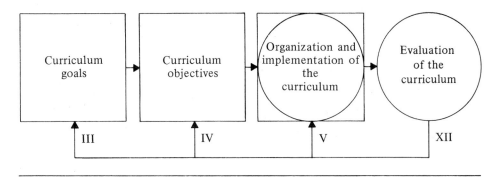

FIGURE 13-2   Curriculum model with all feedback lines

DELIMITING EVALUATION

Differences Between Instructional and Curriculum Evaluation

Some instructors and curriculum planners believe that assessing the achievement of instructional objectives constitutes curriculum evaluation. Thus, if students achieve the cognitive, affective, and psychomotor learnings, the curriculum is considered effective. To follow that line of reasoning, we would add all the evaluations of instruction together in a one plus one fashion to presumably determine the success of the curriculum. This position makes the mistake of equating curriculum with instruction. If such were the case, separate components for the Evaluation of Instruction and Evaluation of the Curriculum would not be shown on the Curriculum Development Model.

However, instruction and curriculum are not the same. The instructional process may be very effective whereas the curriculum, like the times, may be out of joint. In Aldous Huxley's *Brave New World,* the society runs very efficiently but few would opt to live there. Instructional evaluation may reveal that pupils are achieving the instructional objectives very well. On the other hand, unless we evaluate the curriculum — the programs — we may be teaching all the wrong things very effectively. If we may exaggerate to make our point, we could do a beautiful job teaching young people:

□ The earth is flat.
□ The earth is the center of the universe.
□ One ethnic group is inherently superior to another.
□ All children can be doctors and lawyers.
□ White collar workers always earn more money than blue collar workers.
□ There is no energy crisis.
□ All scientific advancements are the result of American ingenuity.
□ Illnesses are caused by the evil eye.

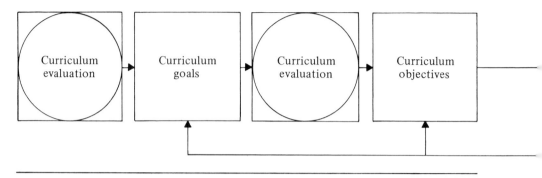

FIGURE 13-3   Continuous nature of curriculum evaluation

The primary purpose of curriculum evaluation is, of course, to determine whether the curriculum goals and objectives are being carried out. But we want to answer other questions as well. We want to know if the goals and objectives are right to begin with. We want to learn whether the curriculum is functioning while in operation. We want to find out if we are using the best materials and following the best methods. We must learn whether the products of our schools are successful in higher education and in jobs, whether they can function in daily life and contribute to our society. We must also determine whether our programs are cost-effective — whether we are getting the most for our money.

Difference Between Evaluation and Research

Discussion of evaluation inevitably leads us into the area of research. Evaluation is the process of making judgments; research is the process of gathering data to make those judgments. Whenever we gather data to answer problems, we are engaged in research. However, the complexity and quality of research differ from problem to problem. We may engage in research ranging from simple descriptive research to complex experimental research. As an example of the former: How many library books does the school library possess per child? As an example of the latter: Do children with learning disabilities perform more effectively when they are in segregated classes or when they are mainstreamed? Most ambitious of all — and very rare — are longitudinal studies like the Eight-Year Study that compared the success in college of graduates from traditional high schools to that of graduates from experimental high schools.[3]

The field of evaluation often calls for the services of specialists in evalua-

---

[3] For an account of the Eight-Year Study see Wilford M. Aikin, *The Story of the Eight-Year Study* (New York: Harper & Row, 1942).

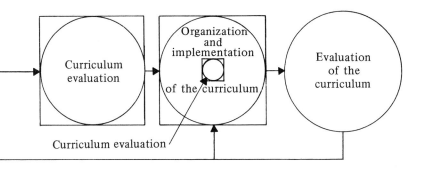

tion and research. Some large school systems are able to employ personnel to direct, conduct, and supervise curriculum evaluation for their school systems. These people bring to the task a degree of expertise not shared by most teachers and curriculum planners. Some school systems, which do not hire their own evaluation personnel, invite in outside consultants to help with particular curriculum problems and research. Yet, most evaluative studies must be and are conducted by the local curriculum planners and the teachers. The shortage of trained personnel plus the costs of employing specialists are prohibitive for many school systems. Even in large systems that employ curriculum evaluators, many curriculum evaluation tasks are performed by teachers and curriculum planners.

EVALUATION MODELS

Models have been developed showing types of evaluation that schools should carry out and the processes they should follow.[4] As in the case of models of instruction and of curriculum development, evaluation models differ in detail and the points which their creators choose to include. We will now look at two comprehensive evaluation models — the Saylor and Alexander model, a rather easily understood model that shows the scope and nature of curriculum eval-

---

[4] See the following models:

The Center for the Study of Evaluation, *Evaluation Workshop I: An Orientation* (Del Monte Research Park, Monterey, Cal.: CTB/McGraw-Hill, 1971).

Daniel L. Stufflebeam et al., *Educational Evaluation & Decision Making* (Itasca, Ill.: F.E. Peacock Publishers, 1971).

Malcolm Provus, *Discrepancy Evaluation for Educational Program Improvement and Assessment* (Berkeley, Cal.: McCutchan, 1971).

J. Galen Saylor and William M. Alexander, *Planning Curriculum for Schools* (New York: Holt, Rinehart and Winston, 1974). Chapter 7.

Robert E. Stake, "Language, Rationality, and Assessment," in *Improving Educational Assessment and An Inventory of Measures of Affective Behavior,* ed. Walcott H. Beatty (Alexandria, Va.: Association for Supervision and Curriculum Development, 1969).

uation, and the model of the Phi Delta Kappa National Study Committee on Evaluation, a more complex model in rather technical terms.[5]

The Saylor and Alexander Model

Figure 13-4 shows how Saylor and Alexander charted their model.[6] The Saylor and Alexander model calls for evaluating five components:

1. the goals, subgoals, and objectives
2. the program of schooling as a totality
3. the specific segments of the education program
4. instruction
5. evaluation program

The first, third, and fourth components contribute to the second — evaluating the program of schooling as a totality — by, among other ways, providing data that bear on the total program. In the figure these relationships are shown by the three arrows between the boxes, which point toward the second component. By including the fifth component — evaluation program — in their model, Saylor and Alexander suggested that it is necessary to evaluate the evaluation program itself. No arrow is shown from the box, Evaluation Program, since the evaluation of the evaluation program is perceived as an independent operation that has implications for the entire evaluation process. Perhaps we could embellish the Saylor and Alexander model by drawing four curved arrows leading out of the right-hand side of the box, Evaluation Program, to the right-hand side of each of the four boxes above it.

Once again, as we look at the model, we encounter the terms formative evaluation (evaluation that takes place during a component) and summative evaluation (evaluation that takes place at the end of a component). Saylor and Alexander's model calls attention to both formative and summative aspects of evaluation of each component.

Evaluation of Goals, Subgoals, and Objectives. Goals, subgoals, and objectives are evaluated (validated) in their formative stages by:

1. analysis of the needs of society
2. analysis of the needs of the individual
3. referring the goals, subgoals, and objectives to various groups
4. referring the goals, subgoals, and objectives to subject matter specialists
5. use of previous summative data

---

[5] See Stufflebeam, in preceding footnote.

[6] J. Galen Saylor and William M. Alexander, *Planning Curriculum for Schools* (New York: Holt, Rinehart and Winston, 1974), p. 311. This figure appears also in J. Galen Saylor, William M. Alexander, and Arthur J. Lewis, *Curriculum Planning for Better Teaching and Learning,* 4th ed. (New York: Holt, Rinehart and Winston, 1981), p. 334.

Curriculum planners must make their own analyses of whether a given goal, subgoal, or objective meets the needs of society and of the learners. They should seek the judgments of students (if they are mature enough), teachers, parents, and other lay people and should further consult subject matter specialists to determine whether a given goal, subgoal, or objective is appropriate to the particular discipline. Data gained from previous tryouts of the program should be used to revise goals, subgoals, and objectives prior to the next trial. For practical purposes, instead of referring every goal, subgoal, and objective to all the groups mentioned, the curriculum planner may elect to refer the goals for validation by all groups and the subgoals and objectives for validation by just the teachers, subject matter specialists, and other curriculum specialists.

To clarify this validation process, let's take as an example the prosaic objective mentioned in Chapter 12 — the baking of bread in homemaking class. Although we can certainly teach young people to bake bread and can evaluate their performance in this psychomotor skill, a more fundamental question must be answered: Should the baking of bread be included in the homemaking curriculum?

The question is not so simple to answer as it might first appear. A number of questions must be raised before this particular item of content can be validated. Some of these questions are as follows:

- Does society (the community, the home, the family) have any need for bread bakers?
- Is the skill of baking bread necessary or helpful to the individual?
- Does teaching the skill make sense in the light of comparison of costs of the home-baked bread versus "store-bought" bread?
- Does it require more energy to bake a loaf of bread at home or for commercial bakers to produce loaves for sale?
- Is there some overriding aesthetic or personal satisfaction in baking bread as opposed to purchasing it?
- Is home-baked bread more nutritious than store-bought bread?
- If baking bread is a content item, what other items were left out of the curriculum so that it could be included? Which items are the most important?
- Would experts in homemaking assert that this content item is essential to the homemaking curriculum?
- What percentage of families today bake their own bread?
- Is this skill something that can and should be taught in the home rather than in school?
- What has the success or failure of previous groups of students been in respect to this particular skill?

As we have seen, goals, subgoals, and objectives are established for the total program of the school. Although not diagrammed in the Saylor and

FIGURE 13-4　The Saylor and Alexander evaluation model

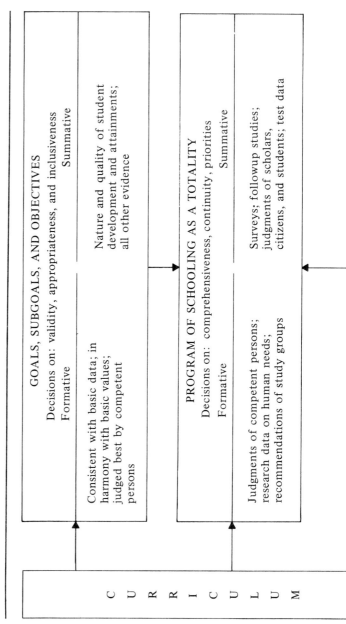

EVALUATION

SPECIFIC SEGMENTS OF THE EDUCATION PROGRAM

Decisions on: contribution to attainment of goals; coordination

Summative

Test data; judgments of knowledgeable persons; comparative data; measurements of outcomes

Formative

Tryouts; data from other similar schools; recommendations of national groups

INSTRUCTION

Decisions on: contributions to attainment of goals and objectives

Summative

All kinds of tests and measurements of achievement of goals; judgments; student reactions; success in further studies and career

Formative

Tryout of innovations and promising modes; experience of other teachers; recommendations of specialists

EVALUATION PROGRAM

Decisions on: effectiveness in providing needed data and findings

Summative

Judgments of decision makers; teachers' judgments; evidence of unanswered questions or inadequate data; reactions of citizens

Formative

Comparison with models of authorities; experience of other schools and agencies; judgments of consultants

The scope and nature of curriculum evaluation.

Alexander model, they are also established for specific program segments and for instruction. The accomplishment of curricular goals, subgoals, and objectives is revealed through an evaluation of the total program, the specific segments, and instruction.

Although Saylor and Alexander make the evaluation of the program of schooling as a totality "the second aspect of a full-scale program of curriculum evaluation," I would like to vary the sequence. Let's comment first on the two other components that impinge on "the total set of educational opportunities" — the evaluation of instruction and of the specific segments of the program.[7] We will return to the evaluation of the total program in a moment.

Evaluation of Instruction. We examined the question and procedures for evaluating instruction in some detail in Chapter 12. Saylor and Alexander recommended that after specifying and validating instructional goals and objectives, as part of the formative evaluation process, the context (antecedent) conditions should be examined — a process referred to by some evaluators as *context evaluation*. The characteristics of the learners, the classroom environment, the facilities, the resources, and the results of needs assessments are all evaluated and may affect the choice of instructional goals and objectives. The use of tests and other evaluative techniques provide summative data on the success of instruction.

Evaluation of Specific Segments. The specific segments of the program require evaluation. Saylor and Alexander included within their concept of specific segments the following: ". . . the plan for organizing curriculum domains, the design or designs of the curriculum for each domain, . . . courses offered, other kinds or sets of learning opportunities provided, extra-instructional activities sponsored, services provided students, community experiences under the direction of the school, and the kinds of informal relations that characterize the school climate." [8]

Assessment data from district, state, and national sources should be gathered by the curriculum planners for purposes of formative evaluation. At this stage data from the National Assessment of Educational Progress, for example, can prove helpful.[9] If, for example, the NAEP data revealed that nine-year-old children, either black or white, in comparable urban areas of the southeast United States are more deficient in reading skills than children in urban areas elsewhere in the country, intensive examination of the reading program of the particular school system is essential. State and district assessments, focusing as they do on children of the state and locality, may be even more meaningful in this respect.

Evaluative Criteria. At this stage too, the instruments of the *Evaluative*

---

[7] Saylor and Alexander, p. 316.
[8] Saylor and Alexander, p. 325.
[9] National Assessment of Educational Progress, Denver, Colorado.

Criteria of the National Study of School Evaluation may be used to gather empirical data about the segments for which there exist criteria.[10] These instruments assess specific areas of study and other specific segments of the program, such as student activities, learning media, and student services. Revised every ten years, this particular set of standards is used by regional associations of colleges and schools for accrediting institutions. Consisting of rating scales and direct questions, these *Criteria* permit faculties to analyze the principles related to the particular program, the evaluation techniques used, plans for improvement, and current status.

Curriculum planners must design summative measures to determine whether the curriculum goals and objectives of the specific segments have been achieved. If it was desired, for example, that 75 percent of the students in a senior high school be involved in at least one extraclass activity, a simple head count would reveal whether this objective has been realized. As when evaluating instruction, sometimes the objective itself is the evaluation item. On the other hand, if it is desired that a fourth-grade class whose members average two months below grade level in mathematics at the beginning of the year raise its scores to grade level by the end of the year, pretesting and posttesting will be necessary.

Evaluation of the Total Program. The functioning of the curriculum as a whole must be evaluated. The curriculum planners will wish to learn whether the goals and objectives of the total curriculum have been realized.

Studies of the needs of society and of young people speak to the question of the school's total program. Unless one limits the school's program to purely cognitive goals, some response should be made to some of the pressing problems of the day. These studies provide formative data for the curriculum planners. Surely problems like care of the environment, conservation of natural resources, discrimination of all types, and the misuse of chemical substances should be examined by young people.

Examining the objectives and the data in all curriculum areas furnished by the National Assessment of Educational Progress can provide clues in the many areas of the curriculum, including general areas like citizenship education and career and occupational development. Professional groups from the Committee of Ten on have made pronouncements concerning the school's curriculum. One of the more recent thrusts, for example, is in the area called global education. Aided by the report of the U. S. President's 1979 Commission on Foreign Languages and International Studies, which directed its attention primarily to the college level, internationalists and social studies educators have been promoting, with federal grants, the cause of global education in the schools.

---

[10] National Study of School Evaluation, *Evaluative Criteria* (Falls Church, Va.: National Study of School Evaluation), various levels. See bibliography.

Summative evaluation of the total program is conducted in several ways. Empirical data are gathered to determine if curriculum objectives have been accomplished. School-wide test data are analyzed. Follow-up studies reveal the success or lack of success of young people after leaving the school. Finally, surveys ask teachers, parents, students, and others to evaluate the school's program.

Evaluation of the Evaluation Program. The program for evaluating the curriculum should be continuously assessed. Judgments about how evaluation will be conducted should be made before an innovation or change is put into practice. The techniques for ongoing evaluation and final evaluation must be carefully planned and followed.

Sometimes it is beneficial to enlist the services of an evaluation specialist to review the evaluation techniques proposed by the curriculum planners. Questions must be answered as to the reliability and validity of the instruments to be used; whether or not the evaluation program is comprehensive, covering all the dimensions of the curriculum to be evaluated; whether the procedures are appropriate and possible. Reactions and suggestions about the evaluation procedures should be obtained from those who are most intimately exposed to them — the students and teachers.

If research studies are to be conducted, specialists inside or outside the system should review the proposed research techniques to determine whether they meet the standards of acceptable research.

When data are ultimately gathered, the planners may feel the need for requesting the help of evaluation specialists to treat and interpret the data. It must now be determined whether all the variables have been considered and appropriately controlled and whether the evaluation measures are designed to assess the appropriate objectives. For example, a cognitive test of American history will not assess student performance of citizenship skills. The ability to recite rules of grammar does not guarantee skill in writing.

When flaws are discovered in the evaluation program, changes should be made. Conclusions reached as a result of research and evaluation are often attacked not on their substance but on the evaluation processes by which they were reached.

Why is it, for example, that we can find skeptics for almost every curricular innovation ever tried? You name it — core curriculum, competency-based education, open education, team teaching, nongradedness, the once new, now old math, etc. — and we can find criticisms of it. Some who object do so because they are not convinced that the evaluation techniques purported to have been used actually proved the superiority of an innovation. Students of curriculum might well examine the processes for evaluating almost any program, change of program, or innovation in their school system — past or present — at any level to find out if curricula were evaluated rigorously or nonrigorously. Students are also likely to discover many innovations evaluated on the basis of perceived opinion of success (without adequate data), participants' feelings about the program (like/dislike), change of pace (variety as a spice), pleasure of being involved (Hawthorne effect), administrative assertion ("I say it works"), cost (if it was an expensive undertaking, it has to be good), public relations ("Look what we've done for your/ our young people"), and perceived leadership ("We're in the vanguard," also known as "on the cutting edge").

To conclude, Saylor and Alexander have illuminated the major evaluation components that confront curriculum planners in the process of curriculum development. Less technical than some models, the Saylor and Alexander model offers a comprehensive view of curriculum evaluation.

The CIPP Model

The Phi Delta Kappa National Study Committee on Evaluation, chaired by Daniel L. Stufflebeam, produced and disseminated a widely cited model of evaluation known as the CIPP (Context, Input, Process, Product) model.[11] Reference has already been made in Chapter 4 to two of the major features of the CIPP model: stages of decision making and types of decisions required in education.[12]

Comprehensive in nature, the model reveals types of evaluation, of decision settings, of decisions, and of change. In shaping their model, Stufflebeam and his associates defined evaluation in the following way: "Evaluation is the process of delineating, obtaining, and providing useful information for judging decision alternatives." [13]

Stufflebeam clarified what was meant by each of the parts of the definition as follows:

1. *Process.* A particular, continuing and cyclical activity subsuming many methods and involving a number of steps or operations.
2. *Delineating.* Focusing information requirements to be served by evaluation through such steps as specifying, defining, and explicating.
3. *Obtaining.* Making available through such processes as collecting, organizing, and analyzing, and through such formal means as statistics and measurement.
4. *Providing.* Fitting together into systems or subsystems that best serve the needs or purposes of the evaluation.
5. *Useful.* Appropriate to predetermined criteria evolved through the interaction of the evaluator and the client.
6. *Information.* Descriptive or interpretive data about entities (tangible or intangible) and their relationships.

---

11 Stufflebeam et al., pp. 218–235.
12 See pp. 123, 125 of this text.
13 Daniel L. Stufflebeam, an address given at the Eleventh Annual Phi Delta Kappa Symposium on Educational Research, Ohio State University, June 24, 1970. Quoted in Blaine R. Worthen and James R. Sanders, *Educational Evaluation: Theory and Practice* (Worthington, Ohio: Charles A. Jones, 1973), p. 129.

7. *Judging.* Assigning weights in accordance with a specified value framework, criteria derived therefrom, and information which relates criteria to each entity being judged.

8. *Decision Alternatives.* A set of optional responses to a specified decision question.[14]

"The evaluation process," said Stufflebeam, "includes the three main steps of delineating, obtaining, and providing. These steps provide the basis for a methodology of evaluation." [15] Before we begin to examine the various elements of which the CIPP model is composed, let's look at a figure of the entire model, shown in Figure 13-5.[16]

In flow chart form the model consists of rectangles (with small loops attached), hexagons, ovals, a circle, a fancy E, solid and broken lines with arrows, and three types of shading. Crosshatched, the hexagons show types of decisions; hatched, the ovals, the circle, and the big E depict activities performed; and mottled, the rectangles stand for types of evaluation.

Four Types of Evaluation. The Phi Delta Kappa Committee pointed to four types of evaluation: *Context, Input, Process,* and *Product,* hence the name of the model, CIPP. *Context evaluation* is "the most basic kind of evaluation," said Stufflebeam. "Its purpose is to provide a rationale for determination of objectives." [17] At this point in the model curriculum planner-evaluators define the environment of the curriculum, and determine unmet needs and reasons why the needs are not being met. Goals and objectives are specified on the basis of context evaluation.

Input evaluation is that evaluation the purpose of which is "to provide information for determining how to utilize resources to achieve project objectives." [18] The resources of the school and various designs for carrying out the curriculum are considered. At this stage the planner-evaluators decide on procedures to be used. Stufflebeam observed, "Methods for input evaluation are lacking in education. The prevalent practices include committee deliberations, appeal to the professional literature, the employment of consultants, and pilot experimental projects." [19]

Process evaluation is the provision of periodic feedback while the curriculum is being implemented. Stufflebeam noted, "Process evaluation has three main objectives — the first is to detect or predict defects in the procedural design or its implementation during the implementation stages, the second is to provide information for programmed decisions, and the third is to maintain a record of the procedure as it occurs." [20]

---

[14] Stufflebeam, in Worthen and Sanders, p. 129.
[15] Stufflebeam, in Worthen and Sanders, p. 129.
[16] Stufflebeam et al., p. 236.
[17] Stufflebeam, in Worthen and Sanders, p. 136.
[18] Stufflebeam, in Worthen and Sanders, p. 136.
[19] Stufflebeam, in Worthen and Sanders, p. 137.
[20] Stufflebeam, in Worthen and Sanders, p. 137.

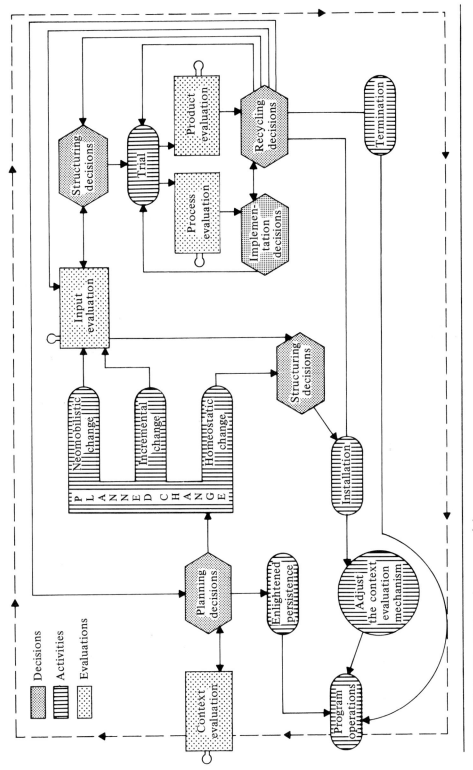

FIGURE 13-5   The CIPP evaluation model

Product evaluation, the final type, has as its purpose "to measure and interpret attainments not only at the end of a project cycle, but as often as necessary *during* the project term. The general method of product evaluation includes devising operational definitions of objectives, measuring criteria associated with the objectives of the activity, comparing these measurements with predetermined absolute or relative standards, and making rational interpretations of the outcomes using the recorded context, input, and process information." [21] Stufflebeam outlined the types of evaluation in respect to objectives, methods, and in relation to decision making in the change process, as shown in Table 13-1.

Four Types of Decisions. The hexagons represent four types of decisions, which were mentioned in Chapter 4: Planning, Structuring, Implementing, and Recycling. Note in Figure 13-5 that Planning Decisions follow Context Evaluation; Structuring Decisions follow Input Evaluation; Implementing Decisions follow Process Evaluation; and Recycling Decisions follow Product Evaluation.[22]

Decision making according to the Phi Delta Kappa Committee occurs in four different settings, as follows:[23]

a. small change with high information
b. small change with low information
c. large change with high information
d. large change with low information

Four Types of Changes. In these settings four types of changes may result: neomobilistic, incremental, homeostatic, and metamorphic. *Neomobilistic change* occurs in a setting in which a large change is sought on the basis of low information. These changes are innovative solutions based on little evidence. *Incremental changes* are a series of small changes based on low information. *Homeostatic change,* which is the most common in education, is a small change based on high information. Finally, *metamorphic change,* a large change based on high information, is so rare that it is not shown on the CIPP model.

The model plots the sequence of evaluation and decision making from context evaluation to recycling decisions. The Committee has touched up the model with small loops that look like light bulbs on the evaluation blocks to indicate that the general process of delineating, obtaining, and providing information is cyclical and applies to each type of evaluation.

The ovals, the circle, and the E in the model represent types of activities, types of change, and adjustment as a result of the evaluations made and decisions taken. The CIPP model presents a comprehensive view of the evaluation

---

[21] Stufflebeam, in Worthen and Sanders, p. 138.
[22] Stufflebeam et al., pp. 79–84.
[23] Stufflebeam et al., pp. 61–69.

TABLE 13-1 Four types of evaluation

	CONTEXT EVALUATION	INPUT EVALUATION	PROCESS EVALUATION	PRODUCT EVALUATION
OBJECTIVE	To define the *operating context*, to identify and assess *needs* and *opportunities* in the context, and to diagnose *problems* underlying the *needs* and *opportunities*.	To identify and assess *system capabilities*, available input *strategies*, and designs for implementing the strategies.	To identify or predict, in process, *defects* in the procedural design or its implementation, to provide information for the preprogrammed decisions, and to maintain a record of *procedural events* and *activities*.	To relate *outcome information* to objectives and to context, input, and process information.
METHOD	By describing the context; by comparing actual and intended inputs and outputs; by comparing probable and possible system performance; and by analyzing possible causes of discrepancies between actualities and intentions.	By describing and analyzing available human and material resources, solution strategies, and procedural designs for relevance, feasibility and economy in the course of action to be taken.	By monitoring the activity's potential procedural barriers and remaining alert to unanticipated ones, by obtaining specified information for programmed decisions, and describing the actual process.	By defining operationally and measuring criteria associated with the objectives, by comparing these measurements with predetermined standards or comparative bases, and by interpreting the outcomes in terms of recorded context, input and process information.
RELATION TO DECISION MAKING IN THE CHANGE PROCESS	For deciding upon the *setting* to be served, the *goals* associated with meeting needs or using opportunities, and the *objectives* associated with solving problems, i.e., for *planning* needed changes.	For selecting sources of *support*, solution *strategies*, and procedural designs, i.e., for *structuring* change activities.	For *implementing and refining the program design and procedure*, i.e., for effecting process control.	For deciding to *continue, terminate, modify,* or *refocus* a change activity, and for linking the activity to other major phases of the change process, i.e., for recycling change activities.

Source: Daniel L. Stufflebean, an address given at the Eleventh Annual Phi Delta Kappa Symposium on Educational Research, Ohio State University, June 24, 1970. Quoted in Blaine R. Worthen and James R. Sanders, *Educational Evaluation: Theory and Practice* (Worthington, Ohio: Charles A. Jones, 1973), p. 139. Reprinted by permission.

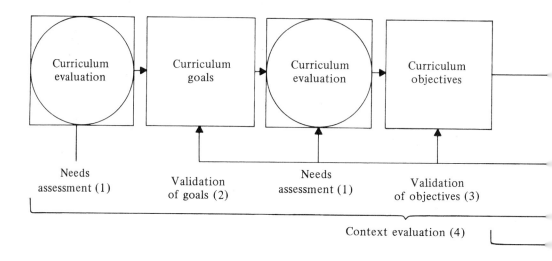

FIGURE 13-6   Sequence and types of evaluation

process. Like Saylor and Alexander, Stufflebeam and his associates also call for evaluation of the evaluation program. Said the Phi Delta Kappa Committee: "To maximize the effectiveness and efficiency of evaluation, *evaluation itself should be evaluated* . . . the criteria for this include internal validity, external validity, reliability, objectivity, relevance, importance, credibility, scope, pervasiveness, timeliness, and efficiency."[24]

Model with Types of Evaluation

To refine our concept of the necessary types of evaluation and to show what types are carried out at specific stages, we have rediagrammed our Curriculum Model in Figure 13-6. In this submodel of our earlier model for curriculum development, the types of evaluation are now numbered for easy reference.

Let's review each of the numbered elements.

1. The first step in the evaluation process is assessment of needs — a part of context evaluation.

---

[24] Stufflebeam et al., p. 239.

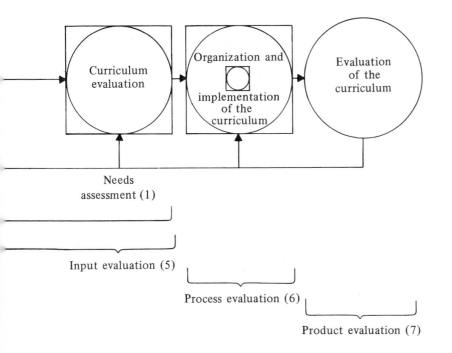

2. Curriculum goals are validated.
3. Curriculum objectives are validated.
4. Context evaluation begins with the needs assessment and continues up to the implementation stage.
5. Input evaluation takes place between specification of curriculum objectives and implementation of the curriculum.
6. Process evaluation is carried out during the implementation stage. Scriven described three types of process research: noninferential studies, investigations of causal claims about the process, and formative evaluation.[25]

  Noninferential studies are those observations and investigations of what is actually happening in the classroom. Investigation of causal claims is referred to by some educators as "action research." This type of research is a less than rigorous attempt to establish whether one teaching technique is better than another. Formative evaluation is assessment during the course of a treatment. To these three types of process research we might add the term "descriptive research," of which noninferential studies of teacher and student classroom behavior represent one form. The use of survey instruments and the application of such standards as

25 See Michael Scriven, "The Methodology of Evaluation," *AERA Monograph Series on Curriculum Evaluation: Perspectives of Curriculum Evaluation, no. 1* (Chicago: Rand McNally, 1967), pp. 49–51.

the previously mentioned *Evaluative Criteria* also fall into the category of descriptive research.

7. Product evaluation is summative evaluation of the entire process. This type of evaluation is sometimes referred to as outcome evaluation, product evaluation, or program evaluation. Program evaluation, however, is used not only in the sense of summative evaluation but also as a synonym for the entire process of curriculum evaluation. Thus, a model for curriculum evaluation might also be called a model for program evaluation.

The Saylor and Alexander model and the CIPP model provide us with two different ways of viewing the process of curriculum evaluation. The models are similar to the extent that they urge a comprehensive approach to evaluation. They are different in the terminology they use and the level of detail they depict. The Saylor and Alexander model is somewhat less complex than the CIPP model and may perhaps be more readily understood by curriculum workers generally. The CIPP model may be more appealing to specialists in curriculum evaluation.

Standards for Evaluation

The use of any evaluation model will be more effective and proper if the evaluators follow some agreed-upon standards. The Joint Committee on Standards for Educational Evaluation, chaired by Daniel Stufflebeam, identified four attributes of an evaluation: utility, feasibility, propriety, and accuracy.[26] This Committee proposed eight utility standards "to ensure that an evaluation will serve the practical information needs of given audiences." [27] They offered three feasibility standards "to ensure that an evaluation will be realistic, prudent, diplomatic, and frugal." [28] Eight propriety standards were advanced "to ensure that an evaluation will be conducted legally, ethically, and with due regard for the welfare of those involved in the evaluation, as well as those affected by its results." [29] Eleven accuracy standards were suggested "to ensure that an evaluation will reveal and convey technically adequate information about the features of the object being studied that determine its worth or merit." [30]

With evaluation of the curriculum, we conclude the model for curriculum development proposed in this text. However, we must stress that there is really no fixed end to the model; it is cyclical. Results of evaluation produce data for modifying earlier components. Without evaluation there can be no considered modifications and therefore little likelihood of improvement.

---

[26] Joint Committee on Standards for Educational Evaluation, *Standards for Evaluations of Educational Programs, Projects, and Materials* (New York: McGraw-Hill Book Company, 1981).

[27] Joint Committee on Standards for Educational Evaluation, p. 19.

[28] Joint Committee on Standards for Educational Evaluation, p. 51.

[29] Joint Committee on Standards for Educational Evaluation, p. 63.

[30] Joint Committee on Standards for Educational Evaluation, p. 97.

SUMMARY

Evaluation is a continuous process by which data are gathered and judgments made for the purpose of improving a system. Thorough evaluation is essential to curriculum development. Evaluation is perceived as the process of making judgments whereas research is perceived as the process of gathering data as bases for judgments.

Curriculum planners engage in various types of evaluation and research. Among the types of evaluation are context, input, process, and product evaluation. Among the types of research are action, descriptive, historical, and experimental research. In another vein curriculum planners engage in both formative (process or progress) evaluation and in summative (outcome or product) evaluation.

Two models of curriculum evaluation were reviewed in this chapter. The Saylor and Alexander model seeks evaluation of five components: the goals, subgoals, and objectives; the program of schooling as a totality; the specific segments of the education program; instruction; and the evaluation program. The CIPP model was designed by the Phi Delta Kappa National Study Committee on Evaluation, chaired by Daniel L. Stufflebeam. It is more complex and technical than the Saylor and Alexander model. The CIPP model combines ". . . three major steps in the evaluation process (delineating, obtaining, and providing), . . . three classes of change settings (homeostasis, incrementalism, and neomobilism), . . . four types of evaluation (context, input, process, and product), and . . . four types of decisions (planning, structuring, implementing, and recycling)." [31] The creators of both these models also urge an evaluation of the evaluation program.

Curriculum evaluators from both inside and outside are employed by school systems. Much of the burden for curriculum evaluation falls on teachers as they work in the area of curriculum development. Following a set of agreed-upon standards improves the evaluation process.

Evaluation of the curriculum is the culmination of the proposed model for curriculum improvement. Though placed at the end of the diagrammed model, evaluation connotes the end of one cycle and the beginning of the next. Improvements in the following cycle are made as a result of evaluation.

SUPPLEMENTARY EXERCISES

1. Define context, input, process, and product evaluation.
2. Report on evidence of any of the types of evaluation in exercise one carried out in a school system you know well.
3. Search the literature on evaluation, and locate and report on a model of evaluation different from either of the two models described in this chapter. Contrast the new model to the two presented.

---

[31] Stufflebeam et al., p. 238.

4. Look up and explain to the class what is meant by internal validity, external validity, reliability, objectivity, relevance, importance, credibility, scope, pervasiveness, timeliness, and efficiency as they relate to the evaluation of evaluation programs.

5. Distinguish between instructional and curriculum evaluation.

6. Define empirical data, descriptive research, action research, historical research, experimental research, and dynamic hypotheses.

7. Locate and present to the class a school system's job description for a curriculum evaluator.

8. Draw up a list of skills needed by a curriculum evaluator.

9. Write a position paper, using appropriate references, on the topic: When should outside consultants be used by the school systems?

10. Show with appropriate evidence that a school system you know well has used evaluative data to modify a curriculum.

11. Examine and critique the final evaluation (audit) of any state or federal program in a school system you know well.

12. Determine and provide evidence as to whether curriculum evaluation in a school system you know well suffers from any of the eight symptoms listed by the Phi Delta Kappa National Study Committee on Evaluation.

13. Locate in the professional literature on evaluation descriptions of "goal-based evaluation" and "goal-free evaluation." Compare these two approaches and state under what conditions each is appropriate.

14. This assignment is for four students. Refer to the publication of the Joint Committee on Standards for Educational Evaluation (see bibliography). Each of you should select one of the four attributes (utility, feasibility, propriety, and accuracy) of an evaluation and describe to the class the standards suggested for it. Critique the standards as to applicability and appropriateness.

BIBLIOGRAPHY

Aikin, Wilford M. *The Story of the Eight-Year Study.* New York: Harper & Row, 1942.

Apple, Michael W.; Subkoviak, Michael J.; and Luffler, Henry S., Jr., eds. *Educational Evaluation: Analysis and Responsibility.* Berkeley, Cal.: McCutchan, 1974.

California Evaluation Improvement Project. *Program Evaluator's Guide.* Princeton, N.J.: Evaluation Improvement Program, Educational Testing Service, 2nd ed., 1979.

The Center for the Study of Evaluation. *Evaluation Workshop I: An Orientation.* Del Monte Research Park, Monterey, Cal.: CTB/McGraw-Hill, 1971. Participant's Notebook and Leader's Manual.

Corey, Stephen M. *Action Research to Improve School Practices.* New York: Bureau of Publications, Teachers College, Columbia University, 1953.

"Curriculum Evaluation: Uses, Misuses, and Nonuses," *Educational Leadership* 35, no. 4 (January 1978): 243–297.

Eisner, Elliot W. *The Educational Imagination: On the Design and Evalua-*

tion of School Programs. New York: Macmillan, 1979.

————. "Educational Connoisseurship and Criticism: Their Form and Functions in Educational Evaluation," *The Journal of Aesthetic Education* 10, numbers 3–4 (July-October, 1976): 135–150.

Johnson, Mauritz Jr. *Intentionality In Education: A Conceptual Model of Curricular and Instructional Planning and Evaluation.* Albany, New York: Center for Curriculum Research and Services, 1977.

Joint Committee on Standards for Educational Evaluation. *Standards for Evaluations of Educational Programs, Projects, and Materials.* New York: McGraw-Hill, 1981.

Lewy, Arieh, ed. *Handbook of Curriculum Evaluation.* Paris: UNESCO, 1977; also New York: Longman, 1977.

Lindvall, C.M.; and Cox, Richard C.; with Bolvin, John O. *Evaluation as a Tool in Curriculum Development: The IPI Evaluation Program. American Educational Research Association Monograph* no. 5. Chicago: Rand McNally, 1970.

National Study of School Evaluation. *Elementary School Evaluative Criteria,* 2d ed. Falls Church, Va.: National Study of School Evaluation, 1981.

————. *Evaluative Criteria,* 5th ed. Falls Church, Va.: National Study of School Evaluation, 1978.

————. *Middle School/Junior High School Evaluative Criteria.* Falls Church, Va.: National Study of School Evaluation, 1979.

————. *Secondary School Evaluative Criteria: Narrative Edition.* Falls Church, Va.: National Study of School Evaluation, 1975.

Orlosky, Donald and Smith, B. Othanel, eds. *Curriculum Development: Issues and Insights.* Chicago: Rand McNally, 1978. Part V.

Payne, David A., ed. *Curriculum Evaluation: Commentaries on Purpose, Process, Product.* Lexington, Mass.: D.C. Heath, 1974.

Plakos, Marie; Plakos, John; and Babcock, Robert. *Workbook on Program Evaluation,* 2d ed. Princeton, N.J.: Educational Testing Service, 1978.

Popham, W. James. *Educational Evaluation.* Englewood Cliffs, N.J.: Prentice-Hall, 1975.

Provus, Malcolm. *Discrepancy Evaluation for Educational Program Improvement and Assessment.* Berkeley, Cal.: McCutchan, 1971.

Saylor, J. Galen and Alexander, William M. *Planning Curriculum for Schools.* New York: Holt, Rinehart and Winston, 1974.

Scriven, Michael. "The Methodology of Evaluation," *Perspectives of Curriculum Evaluation, AERA Monograph Series on Curriculum Evaluation no. 1.* Chicago: Rand McNally, 1967, pp. 39–83.

Stake, Robert E. "Language, Rationality, and Assessment." In *Improving Educational Assessment and An Inventory of Measures of Affective Behavior,* edited by Walcott H. Beatty. Alexandria, Va.: Commission on Assessment of Educational Outcomes, Association for Supervision and Curriculum Development, 1969.

Stufflebeam, Daniel L. "Educational Evaluation & Decision Making," an address to the 11th Annual Phi Delta Kappa Symposium on Educational Research, The Ohio State University, June 24, 1970.

———— et al. *Educational Evaluation and Decision Making.* Itasca, Ill.: F.E. Peacock Publishers, 1971.

Tyler, Ralph W. *Basic Principles of Curriculum and Instruction.* Chicago: University of Chicago Press, 1949.

————, ed. *Educational Evaluation: New Roles, New Means,* 68th Yearbook of the National Society for the Study of

Education. Chicago: University of Chicago Press, 1969.

————; Gagné, Robert M.; and Scriven, Michael. *Perspectives of Curriculum Evaluation, AERA Monograph Series on Curriculum Evaluation no. 1.* Chicago: Rand McNally, 1967.

Willis, George. "Democratization of Curriculum Evaluation," *Educational Leadership,* 38, no. 8 (May 1981): 630–632.

Worthen, Blaine R. and Sanders, James R. *Educational Evaluation: Theory and Practice.* Worthington, Ohio: Charles A. Jones, 1973.

FILMSTRIP-TAPE PROGRAMS

Vimcet Associates, P.O. Box 24714, Los Angeles, California 90024:

> *Current Conceptions of Educational Evaluation,* 1972.
> *Alternative Measurement Tactics for Educational Evaluation,* 1971.

KIT

Morris, Lyon Lyons, *Program Evaluation Kit* (Beverly Hills, Cal.: Sage Publications, 1978). The kit consists of the following volumes:

> *Evaluator's Handbook*
> *How to Deal With Goals and Objectives*
> *How to Design a Program Evaluation*
> *How to Measure Program Implementation*
> *How to Measure Attitudes*
> *How to Measure Achievement*
> *How to Calculate Statistics*
> *How to Present an Evaluation Report*

REPORTS OF THE NAEP

Reports of the National Assessment of Educational Progress are available from the Education Commission of the States, Suite 700, 1860 Lincoln Street, Denver, Colorado 80295.

Part IV

Curriculum Development: Problems and Products

14

Problems in Curriculum Development

After studying this chapter you should be able to:

1. Define "scope," "relevance," "balance," "integration," "sequence," "continuity," "articulation," and "transferability" and explain their significance to curriculum workers.
2. Identify current curriculum problems that are brought about by social and political forces and explain their significance for curriculum development.
3. Identify the impact of professional problems on the curriculum and explain their significance to curriculum planners.

You should also be able to formulate and give reasons for your views on the following issues:

1. The difficulty of developing the curriculum around sound principles.
2. The complexity of each problem of curriculum development discussed in this chapter.
3. The necessity for responding to curricular problems that are brought about by social and political forces.

454

CONTINUING PROBLEMS

Although a model for curriculum improvement may show us a process, it does not reveal the whole picture. It does not show us, for example, how we go about choosing from competing content, what we do about conflicting philosophies, how we assure articulation between levels, how we learn to live with change, how dependent we are upon effective leadership, what incentives motivate people to try out new ideas, how to go about finding the information we need to make intelligent decisions, and how we release human and material resources to do the job.

We already examined in Chapter 4 several major problems of curriculum development, including effecting change, group dynamics, interpersonal relationships, decision making, curriculum leadership, and communication skills. In this chapter we will consider: (1) a number of perennial or continuing problems that are central to the organization and implementation of the curriculum and (2) a number of current curricular problems on contemporary issues. We will first discuss eight perennial problems of curriculum development: relevance, balance, scope, sequence, continuity, articulation, integration, and transferability. Then we will examine seven contemporary curriculum issues and four professional problems that have an impact upon the curriculum.

The eight perennial problems to be discussed are not only problems of curriculum development but also are concepts that lead to principles of curriculum development. The provision of a well-functioning sequence, for example, is a continuing problem for the curriculum developer. At the same time, the curriculum developer must understand the concept of sequencing, which is essential to an effective curriculum. I will, therefore, refer to these eight problems as either concepts or principles.

All eight concepts are interrelated. We shall first examine four concepts closely related to each other: scope, relevance, balance, and integration. Relevance, balance, and integration are dimensions of scope; all four relate to the choice of goals and objectives.

We shall then consider three other closely interrelated concepts: sequence (or sequencing), continuity, and articulation. Continuity and articulation are dimensions of sequencing. Finally, we shall look at the concept of transferability, which is both a curricular and instructional problem.

Scope

Scope is usually defined as "the breadth" of the curriculum. The content of any course or grade level — identified as topics, learning experiences, activities, organizing threads or elements,[1] integrative threads,[2] or organizing cen-

---

[1] Ralph W. Tyler, *Basic Principles of Curriculum and Instruction* (Chicago: University of Chicago Press, 1949), p. 86.

[2] Benjamin S. Bloom, "Ideas, Problems, and Methods of Inquiry." In *The Integration of Educational Experiences,* 57th Yearbook, Part III, National Society for the Study of Education (Chicago: University of Chicago Press, 1958), pp. 84–85.

ters,[3] — constitutes the scope of the curriculum for that course or grade level. The summed content of the several courses or grade levels makes up the scope of the school curriculum. Saylor and Alexander defined scope in the following way: "By scope is meant the breadth, variety, and types of educational experiences that are to be provided pupils as they progress through the school program. Scope represents the latitudinal axis for selecting curriculum experiences." [4]

When teachers select the content that will be dealt with during the year, they are making decisions on scope. When curriculum planners at the district or state level set the minimum requirements for graduation from high school, they are responding to the question of scope.

We encounter a problem when we equate the activities or learning experiences with scope. It is true that the sum of all activities or learning experiences reveals the scope of the curriculum. Yet, the activities or learning experiences are the operational phases of the topics. For example, to make pupils confront the topic, The Renaissance, we can design many activities or learning experiences to teach that topic, including viewing photographs of works of art of the period, writing biographies of famous artists, reading novels about the period, reading histories of the period, writing reports on the roles of the church and state during this time, etc.

Organizing Centers or Threads. John Goodlad defined the elements of scope as ". . . the actual focal points for learning through which the school's objectives are to be attained." [5] He wanted to convey the meaning of these elements as one term for the following reason:

> Nowhere in the educational literature is there a term that conveys satisfactorily what is intended in these focal points. The words *activities* and *learning experiences* are used most frequently but are somewhat misleading. Under the circumstances there is virtue in using the technical term *organizing centers*. Although somewhat awkward, the term does permit the inclusion of such widely divergent focal points for learning as units of work, cultural epochs, historical events, a poem, a film on soil erosion, and a trip to the zoo. The *organizing center* for teaching and learning may be as specific as a book on trees or as general as press censorship in the twentieth century. *Organizing centers determine the essential character of the curriculum.*[6]

In a similar vein, Tyler advised those who are organizing the curriculum to identify the organizing threads or elements, that is, the basic concepts and

---

[3] John I. Goodlad, *Planning and Organizing for Teaching* (Washington, D. C.: National Education Association, 1963), Chapter 2.

[4] J. Galen Saylor and William M. Alexander, *Curriculum Planning for Better Teaching and Learning* (New York: Holt, Rinehart and Winston, 1954), p. 248.

[5] Goodlad, p. 28.

[6] Goodlad, p. 28.

skills to be taught.[7] Thus, curriculum planners must choose the focal points, the basic concepts and skills, and the knowledge that will be included in the curriculum. A central problem of this horizontal organization that we call scope is the delimitation of the concepts, skills, and knowledge to be included.

Explosion of Knowledge. Teachers must continuously wrestle with the problem of limiting subject matter. Knowledge, spurred on by emerging technology, increases at a fantastic — and sometimes alarming — rate. Humankind has no sooner begun to tame the computer than it has become involved in cloning, creating test-tube babies, and manufacturing new life forms. Humankind has journeyed through space but now worries about the debris floating around in our solar system. Humankind has harnessed the atom but has not learned to dispose of radioactive wastes safely. Arthur Lewis pointed up the problem that has been repeatedly referred to as "the explosion of knowledge" in the following words:

> If the information explosion continues at the present pace, by the time a child born today graduates from college, the amount of information in the world will have increased fourfold. By the time the child is 50 years old, information will have increased 32 times, and 97 percent of everything known in the world will have been learned since the child was born.[8]

When discussing the rapidity of change, Alvin Toffler spoke about the phenomenal increase in knowledge in this way:

> The rate at which man has been storing up useful knowledge about himself and the universe has been spiraling upward for 10,000 years. The rate took a sharp upward leap with the invention of writing. . . . The next great leap forward in knowledge-acquisition did not occur until the invention of movable type in the fifteenth century. . . . Prior to 1500, by the most optimistic estimates, Europe was producing books at the rate of 1000 titles per year. . . . By the mid-sixties, the output of books on a world scale, Europe included, approached the prodigious figure of 1000 titles per day. . . . Today the United States government alone generates 100,000 reports each year plus 450,000 articles, books and papers. On a worldwide basis, scientific and technical literature mounts at a rate of some 60,000,000 pages a year. The computer . . . has raised the rate of knowledge-acquisition to dumbfounding speeds.[9]

Clearly, the problem of limiting knowledge will only intensify in the future.

Aims Procedure. Somehow, some way, curriculum workers must select the concepts, skills, and knowledge to be incorporated into the curriculum. Many years ago Caswell and Campbell suggested a procedure for determining the

---

[7] Tyler, p. 86.

[8] Arthur J. Lewis, "Educational Basics to Serve Citizens in the Future," *FASCD Journal* 1, no. 1 (February 1979): 2.

[9] Alvin Toffler, *Future Shock* (New York: Random House, 1970), pp. 30–31.

scope of the curriculum. Referring to the process as the "aims procedure," they outlined the steps as follows:

> First, a general all-inclusive aim of education is stated. Second, this all-inclusive statement is broken up into a small number of highly generalized statements. Third, the statement of a small number of aims is divided to suit the administrative organization of the school [for the elementary, junior high, or senior high school divisions]. . . . Fourth, the aims of each division are further broken up by stating the objectives to be achieved by each subject. Fifth, the general objectives for the subjects in each division are analyzed into specific objectives for the several grades; that is, statements in as specific terms as possible are made of the part of the subject objectives to be achieved in each grade. The specific objectives for all the subjects in each grade represent the work to be carried forward in the respective grades and indicate the scope of work for the grades.[10]

Interestingly, Caswell and Campbell perceived the specific objectives — not learning experiences, focal points, topics, or organizing threads — as indicating the scope of the curriculum.

Necessary Decisions. With time so precious and the content burden so great, it must be demonstrated that every organizing center included in the curriculum is superior to those not included. Decisions as to the superiority of the selected elements are reached by group consensus, by expertise, or by both. Curriculum planners must answer questions to which there are no easy answers like:

□ What do young people need to succeed in our society?
□ What are the needs of our locality, state, nation, and world?
□ What are the essentials of each discipline?

Oliver highlighted the levels at which decisions on scope must be made, as follows:

> Scope operates [on] at least four levels. First, there must be decisions as to what to include in the curriculum as a whole, in the major areas within which the curriculum operates. Should we concern ourselves with sex education? Shall we offer driver education? German? Geometry? . . .
>
> Within this total pattern of elements selected to achieve the school's projected goals there is a second level — the scope of an area. Whether this be called a subject field, an interdiscipline or a domain, it is a subject within the total scope. What from the discipline of mathematics is appropriate for an elementary school, for a secondary school? . . .
>
> The third level of scope determination concerns the individual teacher

---

[10] Hollis L. Caswell and Doak S. Campbell, *Curriculum Development* (New York: American Book Company, 1935), p. 152.

within the broad framework of the curriculum. What theorems shall the teacher of geometry include? . . .

The fourth level relates to an individual lesson.[11]

Decisions on the scope of the curriculum are, as we see in Oliver's comments, multiple, relating to the curriculum as a whole, the various disciplines, courses or content within the disciplines, and the individual lesson. We might add an additional level before the individual lesson: the unit or module.

Curriculum workers must make decisions on scope not only within each of the three domains but also from among the domains. Within the domains they must raise questions such as:

□ Shall we include a course in geology as well as biology (cognitive)?

□ Shall we include development of charity as a value as well as the attitude of cooperation (affective)?

□ Shall we teach typing as well as automechanics (psychomotor)?

Curriculum planners and teachers may find the determination of scope within a domain, albeit taxing, easier to resolve than making decisions between domains. Which domain, it must be asked, is most important? This question resurrects philosophical arguments about the nature of knowledge, the nature and needs of learners and of society. The question brings us back to Herbert Spencer's classic query, "What knowledge is of most worth?" [12] Arno Bellack addressed the same question and concluded that schools should enable teachers to develop students' knowledge in the major disciplines.[13]

Others have stressed the domain of knowledge — the cognitive domain. Jerome Bruner wrote: ". . . the structure of knowledge — its connectedness and its derivations that make one idea follow another — is the proper emphasis in education;" [14] Robert L. Ebel championed cognitive learning;[15] and Philip H. Phenix said: "My thesis, briefly, is that *all* curriculum content should be drawn from the disciplines, or, to put it another way, that *only* knowledge contained in the disciplines is appropriate to the curriculum." [16]

Combs, Maslow, and others, on the other hand, looked beyond the realm of knowledge to the development of values and the self-concept as central to

---

[11] Albert I. Oliver, *Curriculum Improvement: A Guide to Problems, Principles and Processes*, 2d ed. (New York: Harper & Row, 1977), pp. 188–189.

[12] See p. 222 of this text.

[13] See Arno A. Bellack, "What Knowledge Is Of Most Worth?", *The High School Journal* 48 (February 1965): 318–322.

[14] Jerome Bruner, *On Knowing* (Cambridge, Mass.: Harvard University Press, 1962), p. 120.

[15] See Robert L. Ebel, "What Are Schools For?" *Phi Delta Kappan* 54, no. 1 (September 1972): 3–7.

[16] Philip H. Phenix, "The Disciplines as Curriculum Content," in *Curriculum Crossroads*, A. Harry Passow, ed. (New York: Teachers College Press, Columbia University, 1962), p. 57.

the educational process.[17] We shall not reopen the great debate between cognitive and affective learning but we should point out that the issue looms large in determining the scope of the curriculum.

Many teachers and curriculum planners, refusing to rely on their own judgment, leave decisions on scope to others — to curriculum consultants, to writers of curriculum guides, to the authors and publishers of textbooks. Thus, the scope consists, for example, of many pages of one or more texts, and the determination is made simply by dividing the number of pages by the number of days' schooling. Or, the number of topics and learning activities in a course of study are also divided by the number of days or weeks. Although this simplistic planning is better than none, the curriculum would be far more pertinent if planners through a systematic, cooperative process exercised their own combined professional judgment and selected from the entire field only those concepts, skills, and knowledge they deemed appropriate to their school, learners, society, state, region, and country.

Relevance

To assert that the curriculum must be relevant is to champion mom's blueberry pie. For who can disagree that mom's blueberry is one of the tastiest dishes ever concocted and is in the great American tradition? No one will stand up and argue for an irrelevant curriculum. Yet, the repeated demand for relevance in the curriculum — unless it is a strawperson — must be an indication of a lack of this essential characteristic in the curriculum.

Varying Interpretations. The difficulty of determining relevance lies in the multitude of interpretations of the word. What is considered relevant education for suburbia may not be for the inner city. What is considered relevant for the "Anglo" may not be for the Hispanic. What is relevant to the essentialists may not be to the progressivists. Relevance, like beauty, is in the eyes of the beholder. "Like the words 'relation' and 'relating,' " said Harry S. Broudy, " 'relevance' excludes virtually nothing, for everything mentionable is relevant in some sense to everything else that is mentionable." [18]

It is important that we stress the word *considered* in "what is considered relevant." Whether the curriculum *is* relevant or not may be beside the point. The consumers of the curriculum — the constituents and patrons of the school — will form attitudes toward relevance. Curriculum planners must deal first with perceptions of relevance before they can deal with the question of relevance itself.

Arguments about relevance swirl around immediate as opposed to remote needs and interests of learners. College and work, for examples, are psycho-

---

[17] See Arthur W. Combs, ed. *Perceiving, Behaving, Becoming,* 1962 Yearbook. (Alexandria, Va.: Association for Supervision and Curriculum Development, 1962).

[18] Harry S. Broudy, *The Real World of the Public Schools* (New York: Harcourt, Brace, Jovanovich, 1972), p. 179.

logically if not chronologically far into the future for most children. They feel a need for certain knowledge *now*. Like Scarlett O'Hara, they'll worry about remote needs tomorrow.

Disagreements arise over contemporary as opposed to historic content. There is some question as to how many students would enroll in history courses — with the possible exception of American history — if not required. History teachers constantly have trouble showing young people the value of history and the more ancient the history, the more difficulty they have.

Conflicts come about between the academic studies and the vocational curriculum. Preparation for careers is of extreme importance to young people. They can see the value in skill courses but often do not realize that the academic areas may (1) provide a grounding needed in every curriculum and (2) open new vistas toward other careers. English teachers, for example, must feel an increasing despair that, in spite of their best efforts, the American population — a more or less literate public in one of the most highly developed countries on earth — is not really a reading public. Further, what is read is not of the highest level. We can attribute the lack of reading in part to difficulties experienced by young people in learning to read in school. Children acquire early an aversion to reading.

We can also attribute the lack of reading to the American frontier mentality that equated reading with effete living and not with the macho men and pioneer women who tamed the West. Finally, television has delivered a blow to the printed word. Watching television is easier, more enjoyable to many, though perhaps less imaginative than reading.

Disagreements over relevance arise from conceptions of what *is* in society and what *should be*. The question becomes: Should curriculum planners educate young people for life as it is or as they think it should be? Should the curriculum develop the desire of citizens to read nonfiction, to subscribe to weighty journals, to listen to classical music, and to frequent art galleries? Or, should the curriculum teach young people how to make money and encourage them to read pop fiction, to enjoy rock and roll or disco music, and to artistically liven up their own homes. Or, should the curriculum remain neutral, abstain from all such value-laden content, or, conversely, expose the learners to both "high brow" and "low brow" content?

Arguments arise between the relative merits of the concrete versus the abstract. Some prefer to concentrate on content that can be experienced with the senses whereas others prefer to concentrate on developing the intellect through high level generalizations.

An Explanation of Relevance. B. Othanel Smith clearly explained relevance when he wrote:

> The teacher is constantly asked: 'Why should I learn that?' 'What is the use of studying history?' 'Why should I be required to take biology?' If the intent of these questions is to ask what use can one make of them

in everyday activities, only general answers are possible. We can and do talk about the relevance of subject matter to the decisions and activities that pupils will have to make. We know, among other things, that they must:

- choose and follow a vocation,
- exercise the tasks of citizenship,
- engage in personal relationships,
- take part in culture-carrying activities . . .

. . . the question of relevance boils down to the question of what is most assuredly useful.[19]

Smith admitted that it is difficult to show the utility of abstract subject matter:

> Unfortunately, the utility of this form of subject matter is much more difficult to demonstrate. . . . Perhaps the chief reason utility of abstract knowledge cannot be demonstrated to the skeptic is that a great deal of it functions as a second-order utility. A first-order utility is illustrated in the skills that we use in everyday behavior such as handwriting and reading. The second-order utility consists of a learning that shapes behavior, but which is not itself directly observable in behavior.[20]

Uses of Knowledge. Smith classified the uses of knowledge that are not directly observable as associative, interpretive, and applicative.[21] By associative Smith meant the learner's ability to relate knowledge freely, sometimes bringing about solutions to problems. With abstract knowledge individuals are helped to interpret their environment, which they cannot do without fundamental knowledge. Abstract subject matter enables learners to apply concepts to solve new problems.

Curriculum workers must, with considerable help from students and others, decide what is meant by relevance and then proceed to make the curriculum as relevant as possible.

Balance

Balance is an unusual curriculum concept that on the surface seems obvious but with some probing becomes somewhat cloudy. It is difficult to nail down a precise definition of balance. Many — perhaps most — educators feel that somehow the curriculum is in a state of imbalance. Observed Paul M. Halverson, "Curriculum balance will probably always be lacking because institutions

---

[19] B. Othanel Smith et al., *Teachers for the Real World* (Washington, D. C.: American Association of Colleges for Teacher Education, 1969), pp. 130–131.

See also Harry S. Broudy, B. Othanel Smith, and Joe R. Burnett, *Democracy and Excellence in American Secondary Education* (Chicago: Rand McNally, 1964), Chapter 3. Broudy, Smith, and Burnett discuss four uses of knowledge: replicative (repetition of a skill), associative, applicative, and interpretive.

[20] Smith et al., p. 131.

[21] Smith et al., pp. 131–133.

of all kinds are slow in adapting to new needs and demands of the culture except when social change is rapid and urgent in its implications for these institutions." [22] Balance, then, is something that schools do not have but apparently should. How would we know a balanced curriculum if we saw one? This is the key question for us to examine.

The search for a definition is complicated by differing interpretations of the word balance as it applies to the curriculum. Halverson spoke of balancing ends and means, as follows: "A balanced curriculum implies structure and order in its scope and sequence (means) leading to the achievement of educational objectives (ends)." [23]

John Goodlad would bring the learner-centered curriculum and the subject-centered curriculum into balance, commenting:

> Much recent and current controversy over the curriculum centers on the question of what kind and how much attention to give learners and subject matter, respectively. The prospect of stressing one to the exclusion of the other appears scarcely worthy of consideration. Nonetheless, the interested observer has little difficulty finding school practices emphasizing one component to the impoverishment of the other.[24]

Doll looked at balance from the learners' standpoint and described it as follows:

> If a learner enjoyed a balanced curriculum at a given time, this curriculum would completely fit him in terms of his particular educational needs at that time. It would contain just enough of each kind of subject matter to serve his purposes and speed his development. General balance in the curriculum can be partly achieved in the sense that certain kinds of experiences can be planned for large groups of learners according to what we know about them and about the subject matter they might learn. . . . Perhaps the best that can be done in working *toward* balance is by being clearer about what is valued for the growth of individual learners and then by applying these values in selecting curriculum content, grouping pupils for instruction, providing for articulation, and furthering guidance programs.[25]

In the foregoing comments Goodlad stressed the need for balance between the learner and the subject-centered curriculum whereas Doll emphasized the need for a curriculum fitting individuals through a judicious balance of group and individual experiences.

---

[22] Paul M. Halverson, "The Meaning of Balance," *Balance in the Curriculum,* 1961 Yearbook (Alexandria, Va.: Association for Supervision and Curriculum Development, 1961), p. 7.

[23] Halverson, p. 4.

[24] Goodlad, p. 29.

[25] Ronald C. Doll, *Curriculum Development: Decision Making and Process,* 4th ed. (Boston: Allyn and Bacon, 1978), pp. 138–139.

Sets of Variables. We can apply the principle of balance in a number of ways. Given the typical elementary, middle or junior high school, and a comprehensive senior high school, curriculum planners should seek balance between the following sets of variables:

1. The child-centered and the subject-centered curriculum. This variable presupposes a balance between the conflicting philosophies of progressivism and essentialism.
2. The needs of society and of the learner. The curriculum must not only be socially but personally oriented.
3. General and specialized education. Electives at the high school level should provide opportunities for learners in specialized areas. The Commission on the Education of Adolescents of the Association for Supervision and Curriculum Development advocated that one-third to one-half of each student's program in high school consist of general education and one-half to two-thirds, elective education.[26] Schools may still specialize, however, as in the case of New York City's Bronx High School of Science or Cooks' and Bakers' School. Balance can be achieved across a school system by having both general and specialized high schools. But there must be balance in schools claiming to be comprehensive in nature.

   It is obvious when we speak of proportions of one-third to two-thirds that we distort the mathematical concept of balance as equilibrium. In reference to the curriculum, however, we cannot and probably should not always seek to achieve a fifty-fifty balance. There are times when a one-third to two-thirds "balance" is defensible.
4. Breadth and depth. The curriculum can be so broad as to be superficial or conversely so profound as to limit learning. In either direction learning is restricted.
5. The three domains, if we may create a three-way balance. We cannot ignore either the cognitive, affective, or psychomotor domain. Each has its importance in the life of the individual. Youngsters cannot find their own balance when learning is limited to one domain.
6. Individualization and mass education. We must find some way to provide for individual differences, to individualize or personalize instruction within the context of a mass educational system. Many recommendations have been made to achieve individualization from programmed instruction to individually prescribed instruction to diagnostic-prescriptive teaching to independent study. However, of necessity, education remains largely a group process.
7. Innovation and tradition. Innovation cannot be incorporated at the drop of a hat. Tradition provides for stability and finds favor with the public.

---

[26] Kimball Wiles and Franklin Patterson, *The High School We Need* (Alexandria, Va.: Association for Supervision and Curriculum Development, 1959), pp. 9–10.

Constant innovation, often for its own sake, keeps faculties, students, and parents in a state of perpetual turmoil. We must pace innovations as to frequency and quantity in order to digest and evaluate changes taking place.

8. The logical and the psychological. These variables are equated in a philosophical context with the differences between essentialism and progressivism. Some content must be organized according to the logic of the subject matter; some to the logic of the learner.

9. The needs of the exceptional and the nonexceptional child. If intelligence is distributed at random among the population, some two-thirds of the students are in the "average" range. Curriculum planners must be careful that attention to the needs of special groups does not far outstrip attention to the needs of the average student.

10. The needs of the academically talented or gifted and the slow. In recent times if we have stressed either group, we have catered to the needs of slow learners. Perhaps we assumed that the academically talented and the gifted will teach themselves in spite of school. Or perhaps we were guided by statistics; there are more slow students than academically talented (the top 15 percent) and gifted (the top 3 percent). Awareness of the needs of the gifted is coming into vogue once again.

11. Methodologies, experiences, and strategies. Teachers should use a mixture of techniques, including audio and visual media. Some schools rely almost exclusively on the printed word, which runs counter to the population's addiction to mediated learning — films, television, and the computer. Educators are pointing out the lack of computer literacy, for example, and urging training in the use of the computer.

12. The immediate and the remote in both time and space. Some people would omit the study of ancient history (too remote) or the study of the non-Western world (too distant) and design only sparkling, new, contemporary, "with-it" curricula.

13. Work and play. At all levels youngsters need some balance between the academic work and leisure or physical activities. Play in the form of games, sports, and personal pursuits not only helps alleviate incipient boredom but can be an education in itself. Some of the avocations pursued by young people may become vocations or lifelong interests.

14. Different disciplines. Disciplines, especially elective ones in the secondary school, vie with each other for student enrollment. Occasionally, a school becomes known for an exceptionally strong department in some discipline. Although excellence is to be encouraged, this situation may imply less than excellence in the other disciplines. Curriculum planners should seek to foster excellence in all fields.

Achieving balance in the curriculum is an essential responsibility of the curriculum planner.

Integration

Curriculum workers should concern themselves with the problem of integrating subject matter. By integration we mean the blending, fusion, or unification of disciplines. Unlike determination of scope and sequence, which *must* be accomplished, the integration of disciplines is an optional and controversial undertaking. Whether or not curriculum planners choose to integrate subject matter hinges upon their philosophy of the nature of knowledge, the nature of learners, and the purposes of education. Generally speaking, educators support the conception of integrating subject matter. Tyler defined integration as "the horizontal relationship of curriculum experiences" and went on to say, "The organization of these experiences should be such that they help the student increasingly to get a unified view and to unify his behavior in relation to the elements dealt with." [27] Taba commented, "It is recognized that learning is more effective when facts and principles from one field can be related to another, especially when applying this knowledge." [28]

Yet, our schools have typically and traditionally behaved as if the integration of subject matter were not too important. The tenacity of the subject matter curriculum, which organizes subject matter into discrete disciplines, has been shaken only briefly by experiments like the activity curriculum and the core curriculum, discussed in Chapter 9. The activity curriculum on the elementary school level and the core curriculum on the secondary school level sought to break down the disciplinary barriers and to organize education around problems to be solved, utilizing whatever subject matter was applicable.

Subject matter may be organized on the basis of separate disciplines with their own time blocks. Another approach is to integrate it either on a schoolwide basis (as with the core curriculum) or on the classroom level (as with certain types of unit plans) without regard for disciplines.

Whether or not the curriculum is integrated and the degree to which it may be integrated are decided more on the basis of the curriculum planners' philosophies than on empirical data. It is impossible to prove without a doubt that integrating content necessarily leads to more productive, better educated citizens than organizing education into separate subjects.

It must be admitted that not all educators are advocates of integrating subject matter. Some believe that the various disciplines should be taught separately. Thus, they reject the broad-fields approach to curriculum organization and recommend that teachers and students concentrate on the separate disciplines.

The progressives felt with considerable logic that understanding is enhanced when the artificial barriers between disciplines are removed. It is true that human beings solve their problems by judiciously selecting whatever sub-

---

[27] Tyler, p. 85.
[28] Hilda Taba, *Curriculum Development: Theory and Practice* (New York: Harcourt, Brace, Jovanovich, 1962), p. 298.

ject matter is needed. Yet, whether a program to educate the immature learner must consist of integrated disciplines is debatable.

Two responses have been made over the years to reduce the separateness of disciplines. Subject matter has been both correlated and integrated. Curriculum planners have positioned themselves somewhere on a continuum which appears as follows:

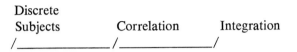

Discrete
Subjects　　　　Correlation　　Integration

Correlation of Subject Matter. Correlation is relating subjects to one another, while still maintaining their separateness. Relationships between subjects taught at a particular school level are shown to pupils, as in the cases of history and literature; math and science; art, music, and literature.

Subjects may be correlated horizontally across one grade level or vertically across two or more. As an example of the latter, ancient history, taught in the sophomore or junior year of high school, may be correlated with Latin, taught in the junior or senior year. The study of Latin is therefore enriched by this progression. If the courses are taken concurrently, the study of both disciplines is enhanced.

Correlation becomes integration when the subjects lose their identities. In the cultural-epoch core approach to curriculum organization, epochs of humankind's history provide the framework; the subjects — English, social studies, science, mathematics, art, music — are tapped to illuminate the cultural epochs. In the case of either correlation or integration, cooperative planning is necessary by all teachers affected.

Two Views of Integration. Taba offered two views of integration. The first view is the one we have been discussing: the horizontal relationship of subjects. In addition, said Taba, "integration is also defined as *something that happens to an individual.*" [29] If we follow the second view, "The problem, then, is that of developing ways of helping individuals in this process of creating a unity of knowledge. This interpretation of integration throws the emphasis from integrating subjects to locating the integrative threads." [30]

Regardless of whether the subject matter is presented to the learner in an integrated fashion by the teacher, the learner must integrate the knowledge into his or her own behavior. The distinction between an educated and an erudite person lies in the degree to which knowledge is integrated in the person. Taba remarked:

> Unification of subjects has been a theme in education ever since the Herbartians. By far the greatest number of experimental curriculum

---

[29] Taba, p. 299.
[30] Taba, p. 299.

schemes have revolved around the problem of unifying learning. At the same time we are far from achieving unification, partly because of fear of loss of disciplined learning if the study of specialized subjects is discarded, and partly because as yet no effective basis has been found for unifying school subjects.[31]

Curriculum planners must decide whether they will make a conscious effort either to correlate or to integrate subject matter and, if they plan to do either, what organizational structure they will create to do so.[32]

Sequence

Sequence is the order in which the organizing elements or centers are arranged by the curriculum planners. Whereas scope is referred to as "the what" of curriculum organization, sequence is referred to as "the when." Sequence answers the questions of when and where the focal points will be placed. Saylor and Alexander defined sequence as:

> . . . the order in which educational experiences are developed with pupils. Sequence refers to the "when" in curriculum planning. Determination of the sequence of educational experiences is a decision as to the most propitious time in which to develop those educational experiences suggested by the scope. If we think of scope as the latitudinal aspect of curriculum planning, sequence becomes the longitudinal axis.[33]

Once we identify the scope of the curriculum, we must put the elements into some kind of meaningful order. Let's take a simplified illustration from the reading curriculum. Suppose as reading teachers we wish students to be able to:

□ read novels
□ read words
□ read paragraphs
□ read sentences
□ recognize letters of the alphabet

Is there some particular order in which pupils learn those elements? The answer is obvious here. The student should recognize letters of the alphabet first, then proceed to reading words, sentences, paragraphs, and novels. Unless one is a Mozart-like prodigy, one does not normally begin to demonstrate reading skills by reading adult tomes.

---

[31] Taba, pp. 298–299.

[32] For discussion of types of integrated curricula see Gordon F. Vars, ed., *Common Learnings: Core and Interdisciplinary Team Approaches* (Scranton, Pa.: International Textbook Company, 1969).

[33] Saylor and Alexander, *Curriculum Planning for Better Teaching and Learning,* p. 249.

But take the following organizational threads in economics:

- □ insurance
- □ real estate
- □ banking
- □ stock market
- □ inflation
- □ recession
- □ foreign exchange

What is the sequence in this case? Is there a preferred sequence? What makes it preferred? Or, in what order should we study the American Revolution, the War of 1812, the Korean War, World War I, the Civil War, the VietNam War, World War II, and the Spanish-American War? The answer in this case is simple, you say. Simply place the wars in chronological order. But could there be any other defensible way of sequencing these items?

The problem of sequencing produces questions about:

- □ the maturity of the learners
- □ the interests of the learners
- □ the readiness of the learners
- □ the relative difficulty of the items to be learned
- □ the relationship between items
- □ the prerequisite skills needed in each case

Ways of Sequencing. How do curriculum workers decide which content comes first? Sequencing is accomplished in a variety of ways, including arranging the content:

1. From the simplest to the most complex. We must deal with tens, for example, before we work with one hundreds. Successful programmed instruction depends upon this approach.
2. In chronological order. History is most often taught in this fashion.
3. In reverse chronological order. Occasionally, a history teacher will start with the most recent events and work backward to the most ancient under the assumption that pupils' attention can be grasped quicker with more recent and therefore more familiar events. Themes that exist in the present may be seen repeated as they go backward in time.
4. From the geographically near to the geographically far. Some argue that it makes more sense to study phenomena and conditions close to home and to gradually expand the learner's horizons ultimately to the world and even the universe.
5. From the far to the near. This procedure focuses on distant lands and reserves study of the home environment — the pièce de résistance — until the end.
6. From the concrete to the abstract. The pupil learns to count blocks by

first manipulating them physically and only later manipulating them mentally.

7. From the general to the particular. This approach starts with the principle and proceeds to examples.
8. From the particular to the general. This approach starts with examples and proceeds to the principle.

When determining sequencing, there are times when the order of the units of content does not matter. When we are studying the works of twentieth century American authors, we might want to group writers of drama, short stories, novels, and nonfiction, but it is not likely to make a great deal of difference which grouping we study first.

There are times when we will deliberately violate a sequence. The class may be studying the political structure of ancient Rome, for example, when a landmark case affecting the country's political and social system is decided by the U. S. Supreme Court. The immediate case, which is significant content, is permitted to alter the planned sequence.

Prerequisite Skills. Frequently, pupils cannot engage in a unit of content until they master a preceding unit. The student of algebra is hard pressed without mastering arithmetic skills. The student cannot succeed in second year foreign language class without mastering the skills developed in the first year. For this reason the assessment of prerequisite skills is sound pedagogy. Teachers must know whether students have mastered the skills needed to proceed with the tasks before them.

Dubious Sequencing. Some curriculum planners in the past, following their own notions of what constitutes prerequisite skills, have instituted sequencing that is hard to defend on any solid grounds. For years high school students were required, for example, to take general science, biology, chemistry, and physics in that order. Actually, none is dependent upon the other. Each science depends more upon mastery of reading and mathematics than upon other sciences. We can find evidence of the same dubious sequencing in mathematics with the prescribed order: algebra I, geometry, algebra II, trigonometry, and calculus. Although it may be wise planning to start with algrebra I and hold calculus for the end, there is little reason to hold algebra II until after completion of geometry. Why is *Macbeth* invariably taught *after Julius Caesar*? Why does American history often come after world history? From a chauvinist point of view, we could argue that American history ought to come first in the senior high school sequence.

Conceptions of Sequencing. Donald E. Orlosky and B. Othanel Smith discussed three conceptions of sequencing: (1) sequencing according to need,

(2) macrosequencing, and (3) microsequencing. According to the first conception:

> ... the learner orders his own learning as he deals with a situation from moment to moment. He selects what he wants to know as the need arises. If he makes a mistake in the selection he simply goes through the process again until he finds that which satisfies his present need. This is an opportunistic notion of sequencing but those who advocate it maintain that it is psychologically sound.[34]

This perception of sequencing fits the views of some progressive educators and proponents of open education.

Macrosequencing follows principles of child development expounded by persons like Arnold Gesell, Frances L. Ilg, and Jean Piaget. Macrosequencing, said Orlofsky and Smith, is:

> ... the organization of knowledge and the formulation of instruction to coincide with the different stages of the individual's development. For a long time teachers have arranged the knowledge of instruction roughly in accordance with the development of the child. Examining the existing program of studies of almost any school proves that it corresponds roughly to the child's development.[35]

Microsequencing is the ordering of subject matter according to the prerequisite knowledge required of each unit of content. "This assumes," said Orlosky and Smith, "that for any learning task there is a hierarchy extending from the very simple to the more abstract and complex elements which lead to the attainment of a specified objective." [36]

Curriculum planners are called upon to make decisions on placement of content at the appropriate grade levels. Using the terms "sequence" and "grade placement" together, Smith, Stanley, and Shores observed:

> There are only two possible approaches to the solution of problems of grade placement and sequence. *The first* accepts the child as he is and adjusts the experience to his level of development while holding the instructional goals constant. ... *The second approach* assumes curriculum experiences to be located at a given grade level and provides learnings to adjust the child to these experiences — that is, to get him ready for the learning.[37]

Where to Begin. Disagreements over the process of sequencing center around whether curriculum planners should start with learners or subject matter. The

---

[34] Donald E. Orlosky and B. Othanel Smith, eds., *Curriculum Development: Issues and Insights* (Chicago: Rand McNally, 1978), p. 267.

[35] Orlosky and Smith, p. 251.

[36] Orlosky and Smith, p. 267.

[37] B. Othanel Smith, William O. Stanley, and J. Harlan Shores, *Fundamentals of Curriculum Development,* Rev. ed. (New York: Harcourt, Brace, Jovanovich, 1957), p. 171.

first demands choosing emphases in keeping with the learners' actual growth and development; the second, placing subject matter at the grade level at which it is assumed learners will be able to master it. The latter approach to sequencing has been the historic approach.

Smith, Stanley, and Shores advocated a blending of the two approaches, saying:

> To accept wholeheartedly the first approach, which emphasizes the nature of the child and regards the curriculum as always flexible enough at each grade level to be bent to the child's needs, is probably unrealistic. And just as unrealistic is the inflexibility of the second approach, which allows objectives and content to be so fixed at any one grade that lower grade experiences must always prepare for this hurdle and later experiences always build upon it. Probably neither of these approaches will be used without consideration for the other. . . .[38]

They counseled curriculum workers to take into account the maturation, experiential background, mental age, and interests of the learners and the usefulness and difficulty of the subject matter when developing a sequence.[39] The ordering of the organizing elements of the curriculum is one of the major tasks of the curriculum developer.

Continuity

Continuity is the planned repetition of content at successive levels, each time at an increased level of complexity. Tyler described continuity as follows:

> Continuity refers to the vertical reiteration of major curriculum elements. For example, if in the social studies the development of skills in reading social studies is an important objective, it is necessary to see that there is recurring and continuing opportunity for these skills to be practiced and developed. This means that over time the same kinds of skills will be brought into continuing operation. In similar fashion, if an objective in science is to develop a meaningful concept of energy, it is important that this concept be dealt with again and again in various parts of the science course. Continuity is thus seen to be a major factor in effective vertical organization.[40]

Spiral Curriculum. The principle of continuity is represented in what has been called the spiral curriculum.[41] Concepts, skills, and knowledge are introduced and reintroduced as, for example, the repetition of addition, study of democracy, writing, personal health, and conservation.

Expertise Needed. Planning a curriculum for continuity requires a high degree of expertise, which demands both knowledge of the subject field and of the

---

[38] Smith, Stanley, and Shores, p. 171.
[39] Smith, Stanley, and Shores, pp. 174–186.
[40] Tyler, pp. 84–85.
[41] Saylor, Alexander, and Lewis define sequence, continuity, and integration with slightly different interpretations from those in this text.

learners. To plan a mathematics sequence for twelve grades, for example, with appropriate scope, sequence, and continuity requires the combined skills of subject matter specialists and teachers. Continuity is not simply repetition of content but repetition with increasing levels of complexity and sophistication. Whereas elementary school youngsters, for example, may learn that democracy means government of the people, by the people, and for the people, secondary school students may wrestle with controversial and unresolved problems of democracy.

Experience will reveal to curriculum developers which units of content must be reintroduced and at what point. Preassessment, if only of the most rudimentary kind, is essential before each new organizing element is broached. Preassessment will uncover whether the learners are ready for (1) new content based on prior content and (2) prior content that will be repeated at a more complex level.

Articulation

If we view continuity as the spiralling of content upward through the grades of a particular school, we should view articulation as the meshing of organizing elements across school levels, i.e., across elementary and middle or junior high schools; across junior high or middle and senior high schools; and across senior high school and college. Like continuity, articulation is a dimension of sequencing.

Horizontal and Vertical. Oliver used the term "articulation" synonymously with "horizontal articulation" or "correlation." He equated the concept of "continuity" with "vertical articulation." [42] Regarding correlation as a halfway move toward integration, I agree with calling correlation horizontal articulation. Sequence, continuity, and articulation are all interrelated. I separate continuity from vertical articulation, defining continuity as a reintroduction of content at progressively more complex levels and articulation as the meshing of the curriculum of the various levels of the educational ladder to provide for smooth transition on the part of the learners. This meshing may or may not involve the reintroduction of units of content, progressively more difficult. When speaking of articulation, I am addressing the problem of vertical articulation.

It is unfortunate that efforts at articulation between levels are in many cases feeble and ineffective. Cooperative efforts are necessary among curriculum workers if articulated sequences are to be planned from kindergarten through twelfth grade and beyond.

We find considerable unplanned repetition of content among levels. This is neither articulation nor continuity but a laissez-faire attitude that permits

---

[42] Oliver, p. 222.

curriculum workers to develop their own programs without knowledge of what instructors at preceding and succeeding levels are teaching.

With our decentralized system of education, lack of articulation occurs frequently. Articulation is particularly difficult in some states where separate school districts exist side by side under separate administrators and separate school boards. Yet, even when all levels of schooling are centralized under a single administrator and school board, articulation remains a problem. Children may study Indians, as the cliché goes, from kindergarten through twelfth grade. They may learn more about Indians than they care to know.

We find cases where junior high schools permit the beginning of a sequence (first year German, let's say) when they know there is no follow-up level at the senior high school in which their junior high school pupils may enroll. We find situations in which seventh-grade mathematics is simply a rehash of sixth-grade math.

Gaps Between Levels. We often find great gaps between levels. The seventh-grade teacher (failing or refusing to preassess) assumes certain levels of mastery of knowledge when children enter from the elementary school; the senior high school teacher expects certain entry skills from youngsters who are promoted from the junior high school.

Personal Articulation. There is not only a need for planned articulation of subject matter but also for pupils' personal articulation. Schools are beginning to respond to students' varied capabilities. Some junior high school pupils, for example, are able to tackle senior high school subjects. Some senior high school pupils can perform ably in advanced placement courses given in the high school, junior college, or senior college courses in their area of residence. Some students can skip a year of high school and enter college early or can skip the lower division of college and enroll in the upper division.

Improved articulation eases the movement of pupils from one level to the next, which can be traumatic experiences for young people. With all the problems of social adjustment as they enter a higher level, they have little need for suffering either needless repetition, exposure to subject matter that is too easy for them, or, worse yet, grasping for learnings beyond their abilities and skills. Thus, curriculum planners cannot avoid the problem of articulation.

Let's recap what has been said about sequencing, continuity, and articulation. Continuity and articulation are dimensions of sequencing. Sequencing is the logical or psychological arrangement of units of content within lessons, units, courses, and grades. Continuity is the planned introduction and reintroduction of the same units of content through the grades of a school system at ever-increasing levels of complexity. Articulation is the planned sequencing of units of content across grade levels, i.e., from one grade level to the next to assure that the next grade level takes up where the previous grade level left off.

The three principles — sequence, continuity, and articulation — are interrelated and complement each other. Material must be appropriately sequenced at whatever level. Articulation must be observed to assure that there are no gaps in a sequence from one grade level to the next, whereas continuity must be sought to permit students to achieve greater depth in a subject. The implementation of any one of these three principles alone can lead to deficiencies in the curriculum.

Transferability

Whatever is taught in school should in some way possess transfer value. That is, learning in school should have applicability in either a broad or narrow sense outside of school and after school years. Education for education's sake — the mark of the learned person — is simply not sufficient as a goal of education. Education should in some way enrich the life of the individual.

The transfer of learning or transfer of training, as it is sometimes called, has been discussed at some length in the literature of educational psychology.[43] Transfer gives a permanence to learning beyond the moment of its first introduction into the classroom.

Vocational education possesses a built-in one-upsmanship in transferability. You can see the transfer; it's apparent. Skills learned in industrial arts and vocational education classes can be transferred to life situations. Teachers of psychomotor skills are particularly fortuitous as pupils have no difficulty seeing the transfer value of these areas of study. Students can and will use the skills they learn in such areas as music, art, physical education, typing, and homemaking. Transfer is paramount with most teachers of perceptual-motor skills. Physical educators tout the carry-over value of their activities, i.e., transfer.

Transfer in the affective and cognitive areas is more difficult to discern. Of course, we wish students to carry over values and positive attitudes into their daily living. We would like a student who demonstrates cooperation in the classroom to retain that behavior all his or her life. Transfer of cognitive learning is most often visible in student performance on assessment and standardized tests, in admission to and success in college, and in the evaluations employers place on the intellectual competence of their employees.

Proponents of faculty psychology (mental or formal discipline) maintained that rigorous subjects disciplined the mind; thus, such education was generally transferable. Some of the essentialists have held that education is the storing of data — computer-fashion — for use at a later date when the occasion arises. Unfortunately, disuse sets in; we forget; and when we need to retrieve the supposedly stored data, we find that they have slipped away.

It has generally been believed by many — a holdover of the formal dis-

---

[43] See Edward L. Thorndike, "Mental Discipline in High School Studies," *Journal of Educational Psychology* 15, no. 1 (January 1924): 1–22; continued in 15, no. 2 (February 1924): 83–98. Edward L. Thorndike, *The Principles of Teaching* (New York: Seiler, 1906). Sidney L. Pressey and Francis P. Robinson, *Psychology and the New Education,* Rev. ed. (New York: Harper & Row, 1944).

cipline days — that certain subjects lead to transfer more than other subjects. After an exhaustive study of over 8,000 students, Thorndike concluded:

> The expectation of any large difference in general improvement of the mind from one study rather than another seems doomed to disappointment. The chief reason why good thinkers seem superficially to have been made such by having taken certain school studies is that good thinkers have taken such studies, becoming better by the inherent tendency of the good to gain more than the poor from any study.[44]

Tanner and Tanner pointed out that the Eight-Year Study disproved the notion that certain subjects lead to transfer:

> But probably the most stunning attack (aside from Thorndike's 1924 study) on the idea that certain subjects have superior transfer to intelligence was delivered by the Progressive Education Association's Eight-Year Study. . . . the study proved that success in college is not dependent on credits earned in high school in prescribed subjects.[45]

Taba, however, explained the more current view on transfer as follows:

> . . . the recent ideas on transfer have returned to earlier assumptions of the possibility of fairly wide transfer, depending on the level of generalizing that takes place regarding either the content or the method of approach.[46]

Thus, if teachers wish to encourage transfer, they must stress general principles.

Current Beliefs. Let's summarize some of the current beliefs about transfer.

▢ Transfer is at the heart of education; it is a — if not the — goal of education.
▢ Transfer is possible.
▢ The closer the classroom situation is to the out-of-classroom situations, the greater is the transfer.
▢ Transfer can be increased and improved if teachers consciously teach for transfer.
▢ Transfer is greater when teachers help pupils to derive underlying generalizations and to make applications of those generalizations.
▢ Generally speaking, when the learner discovers knowledge for himself or herself, transfer is maximized. Bruner provided an example of children in a fifth grade class learning "a way of thinking about geography" as opposed to being dished out selected, unconnected geographical facts.[47]

---

[44] Thorndike, "Mental Discipline in High School Studies" (February 1924): 98.

[45] Daniel Tanner and Laurel N. Tanner, *Curriculum Development: Theory Into Practice,* 2d ed. (New York: Macmillan, 1980), p. 323.

[46] Taba, p. 124.

[47] Jerome S. Bruner, "Structures in Learning," *Today's Education* 52, no. 3 (March 1963): 26.

Bruner encouraged teachers to use a discovery approach, justifying it on the grounds of "increased intellectual potency, intrinsic rewards, useful learning techniques, and better memory processes." [48]

Guided Discovery. The jury is still out on the question of the extent of use of inquiry or discovery methods. David Ausubel pointed out that some discovery techniques can be an inefficient use of time.[49] Whatever the process used — discovery or other — enhancement of meaning during the process of instruction should increase the degree of transfer.

Transferability is a principle of both instruction and the curriculum. When we talk about methods of teaching for transferability, we are referring to the instructional process. When we analyze what the learner has transferred, we are in the area of curriculum. Curriculum developers should specify objectives, select content, and choose instructional strategies that will lead to maximum transfer. Further, plans for evaluating the curriculum should include means of judging the degree of transfer of the many segments of the curriculum.

Implications of the Continuing Curriculum Problems

Given the range and the many facets of curriculum problems covered, it is useful to briefly redefine them in the light of the curriculum workers' responsibilities. Curriculum workers attend to the problem of:

- □ *scope* when they select topics to be studied and specify the instructional objectives
- □ *relevance* when they "effect a congruence between the entire school system and the social order in which the young of today will spend their adult lives" [50]
- □ *balance* when they maintain each set of elements mentioned in this chapter in proportion
- □ *integration* when they make an effort to unify subject matter
- □ *sequence* when they determine the order in which subject matter will be made available to the students
- □ *continuity* when they examine the curriculum of each course and grade level to discover where units of content may fruitfully be repeated at increased levels of complexity
- □ *articulation* when they examine the curriculum of each discipline at each grade level to be sure the subject matter flows sequentially across grade-level boundaries
- □ *transferability* when they seek ways to achieve maximum transfer of learning

---

[48] Bruner, "Structures in Learning," p. 27.

[49] See David P. Ausubel, *Educational Psychology: A Cognitive View* (New York: Holt, Rinehart and Winston, 1968).

[50] Broudy, *The Real World of the Public Schools*, p. 193.

CURRENT CURRICULUM PROBLEMS

Several movements in recent years have had an impact on curriculum development. To gain a sense of the dimensions of these problems and their impact, let's briefly review some movements that have either changed the role of curriculum planners or caused modifications in the ways in which schools organize for curricular development.

Curriculum planners are buffeted by several strong social and political forces, some arising from pressure groups and some from the public in general. Some of the desires of both the pressure groups and the public generally have been enacted into law, primarily at the federal level.

Among the significant contemporary issues facing curriculum workers are (1) the back-to-basics movement, (2) the minimal competencies movement, (3) integration of the races, (4) sexist practices, programs, and content, (5) programs for the handicapped, (6) bilingual education, and (7) censorship.

The Back-to-Basics Movement

The call for a "return to the basic skills" is so strong at the present time that curriculum workers cannot ignore its existence.[51] Both elementary and secondary schools have resumed stress, if ever they had left it, on reading, writing, and arithmetic.

For several decades a movement has been building that criticizes schools for failing to teach youngsters to read. *Why Johnny Can't Read*[52] and publications of the Council on Basic Education have long censured the school program for inadequacies of students in the basic skills.

Although the Educational Policies Commission long ago advocated command of the fundamental processes, critics observed that it placed these skills at the bottom of a list of ten imperative needs of youth.[53] Champions of the back-to-basics movement see the shift as righting old excesses. It is part of the resurgence in essentialist doctrines in education and perhaps conservative doctrines in politics. More frequently today, we find unabashed advocacy of limiting the mission of schooling to cognitive learning.

Critics of the back-to-basics movement see the trend as defeating progressive doctrines that stressed the whole child and made room for affective education. Advocates of the movement perceive the basics as skills necessary for survival and feel that the failure of young people to find and hold satisfying occupations stems from their deficiencies in the fundamentals.

Back to basics is popular, too, in a day and age when economies are sought by the public. By limiting the role of the school, taxpayers can save

---

[51] See Ben Brodinsky, "Back to the Basics: The Movement and Its Meaning," *Phi Delta Kappan* 58, no. 7 (March 1977): 521–533.

[52] Rudolf Flesch, *Why Johnny Can't Read* (New York: Harper & Row, 1955).

[53] See pp. 94–95 of this text.

considerable sums of money, an appealing move in a time of inflation or recession.

The challenge for curriculum planners today is to meet the public's keen desires for citizens who can function at a literate level and to also preserve a curriculum that is broad enough to permit personal growth and development, to appeal to individual differences, and to expose young people to areas of study beyond the 3 R's. Sometimes it seems that the curriculum planner must be not only an educator but a magician.

Minimal Competencies

Many states, subscribing to the back-to-basics philosophy, have specified the particular standards or competencies students are expected to achieve at various grade levels and for graduation from high school.[54] The initial thrust has been to specify minimal competencies in the basic skill areas, though continuation of the process is almost certain to encompass all subject areas.

The movement to identify minimal competencies draws power from two related movements and begets another. The effort to specify minimal competencies is related to the *behavioral objectives movement* and is a response to the *accountability movement.*

Examples of minimal competencies in this text are shown as statements written in terms of performance expected of the learners.[55] The behavioral objectives movement provided a formula for drafting minimal competencies; competencies are simply behavioral objectives that have been determined by their authors as the sine qua non of education.

The minimal competencies movement is a natural outgrowth of the movement for accountability, that is, for holding teachers, administrators, and schools responsible for the education of the young. With the public clamoring for proof that its educational dollar is well spent, minimal competencies are seen as an efficient way to demonstrate accountability. The competencies are usually very specific items that can be measured. Thus, if we have minimal competencies, we must teach for their achievement and we must devise ways to assess their accomplishment by the learners. Hence, *the assessment movement* has arisen. Local, state, and national assessment of competencies, with criterion-referenced measures, has proceeded at a swift pace. In some cases, successful performance on the state assessment tests will be required for receiving the standard high school diploma.

The task of specifying minimal objectives is rather difficult initially for curriculum planners. Once localities, states, and the nation have developed a sufficiently large bank of competencies, the task becomes (or should become) simpler.[56] After all, there can only be so many competencies in the basic

---

[54] See articles in *Educational Leadership,* 35, no. 2 (November 1977).

[55] See pp. 230–233 of this text.

[56] Suggested instructional objectives in various fields can be obtained from Instructional Objectives Exchange, P. O. Box 24095, Los Angeles, California 90024.

skills. The competencies in the 3 R's are, hopefully, the same in Oregon as in North Carolina.

Minimal competencies tend to standardize the curriculum. Since their achievement is tied to accountability, teachers are shrewd enough to structure their teaching toward the competencies and therefore to the assessment tests. On these exams learners will demonstrate how successful not only they but their teachers have been.

Once the minimal competencies are identified and put into print, the role of the curriculum developer can be greatly diminished or changed. What needs to be developed when the dimensions of the curriculum have already been outlined? Curriculum planners may turn their attention to designing better ways of organizing the curriculum, devising learning activities to teach the competencies, and finding ways to remedy student deficiencies in particular competencies as revealed by the tests.

The previous history of curriculum movements may comfort curriculum planners. Movements that proceed to extremes will normally right themselves and move back to center. Although men and women cannot live well without the basic skills, they cannot live well with the basic skills alone. There must be room for the humanities and for developing a self-concept, social skills, and lifelong interests, all of which have been part of the school's curriculum for many decades.

Integration of the Races

Ever since the decision in the case of Brown versus the Board of Education of Topeka, Kansas[57] in which the United States Supreme Court ruled segregation of the races unconstitutional, efforts have been under way to eliminate vestiges of racial discrimination in the schools. Problem areas have ranged from curriculum materials that were slanted to white, middle-class culture to teaching, to testing, and to administrative practices such as busing, desegregation of faculties, and methods of discipline.

James S. Coleman, sociologist, surveyed some 4,000 elementary and secondary schools, 60,000 teachers, and 600,000 students to determine the extent and sources of inequality of educational opportunity among ethnic groups.[58] Authorized by the 1964 Civil Rights Act, the Coleman Report, which was issued in 1966, supported desegregation of schools.

Interestingly enough, Coleman concluded that achievement of students is influenced first by their social environment (families and peers); second, by their teachers, and third, by nonpersonal resources such as per pupil expenditures on education. A dozen years later, after observing the operation of schools that had been integrated, Coleman concluded that integration per se

---

[57] *Brown* v. *Board of Education of Topeka, Kansas,* 347 U.S. 483, 74 Sup. Ct. 686 (1954).

[58] See James S. Coleman et al., *Equality of Educational Opportunity* (Washington, D.C.: U.S. Office of Education, 1966).

does not necessarily increase the achievement of black students.[59] He remained committed to integration but was reported to maintain that parents should choose whether black students attend integrated schools.

One of the storm centers of the issue of discrimination revolves around assessment practices.[60] The state of Florida, for example, is a case in point. The state legislature in 1976 mandated administration of a functional literacy test to be taken by all eleventh graders. Receipt of the standard high school diploma was to be contingent upon passing the test. After initial administering of the test in 1977, suit was brought in the federal courts, charging that the test was discriminating against black children who had attended segregated schools and had not had the same educational opportunities as children of the majority. Although ruling that the test could be administered, the U. S. District Court in 1979 ordered the state department of education not to begin denying diplomas to students who failed the test until 1983.

The search to design curricula that will meet the needs of socio-economically disadvantaged children and youth of all ethnic groups is a continuing and as yet unsolved problem for curriculum planners. Funds from Title I of the Elementary and Secondary Education Act of 1965, provided by the U. S. Congress, have been utilized to provide improved programs for students in schools in socio-economically deprived areas.

Sexism

Title IX of the Educational Amendments of 1972 passed by the U. S. Congress caused school personnel to examine programs and to remove practices that discriminate between the sexes. Restricting homemaking to girls and industrial arts to boys, for example, is a sexist practice. Funding of interscholastic athletics, with the lion's share traditionally going to boys' athletics, has been challenged as sexist. The integration of females into male athletic teams has stirred controversy within the profession and outside. Questions have even been raised as to whether mother-daughter and father-son banquets can be sponsored by the school.

As noted earlier, Havighurst as recently as 1972 perceived achieving a masculine or feminine social role as one of the developmental tasks of adolescence.[61] The accomplishment of these roles is no longer simple, if it ever was. Though traditional attitudes toward the roles of men and women are still held by sizable segments of the public — especially in groups of certain nationalities, certain areas of the country, and certain religious groups — the distinctions in roles have been changing rapidly. What once appeared to be

---

[59] See *The Miami Herald,* September 24, 1978, p. 19-A.

[60] See Merle Steven McClung, "Are Competency Testing Programs Fair? Legal?" *Phi Delta Kappan* 59, no. 6 (February 1978): pp. 397–400.

[61] See Robert J. Havighurst, *Developmental Tasks and Education,* 3rd ed. (New York: Longman, 1972), pp. 23–25.

male occupations, like truck driving, construction work, police work, and even military service are no longer the exclusive province of the male.

Conversely, a "house-husband" is no longer unheard of and the female can be the family "breadwinner." Men can pursue careers and avocations that were formerly considered for women, such as nursing, elementary school teaching, and secretarial work. The unisex philosophy has shaken, if not toppled, some of the stereotypes of men and women.

Curriculum workers can experience great difficulties as they try to design curricula to eliminate sex discrimination. The role of curriculum planner can become uncomfortable when the planner is caught between legislation and community mores. Of course, the law takes precedence over local mores. Recognizing this fact, community groups have organized to pressure for the enactment of laws to counteract local mores and to speed social change. Some curriculum workers even secretly hope for legislation that will take them "off the hook" so they will not appear to violate local public sentiment.

Programs for the Handicapped

What curriculum planner has not yet encountered Public Law 94–142? This enactment of the U. S. Congress, titled The Education for All Handicapped Children Act of 1975, has sought to eliminate discrimination against the handicapped.[62] Schools must make special provision to assure that all handicapped children receive a "free and appropriate" education. To accomplish this goal, schools must develop an Individualized Educational Plan (IEP) for every handicapped child and must assure that each handicapped child will be placed in the "least restrictive environment." IEP's contain annual performance objectives for each child and must be reviewed every year. They require a considerable amount of the faculty's time. Determining the appropriate educational program and the best placement for each child requires difficult judgments by teachers and administrators.

It is expected that handicapped students will be "mainstreamed," i.e., taught in regular classrooms with nonhandicapped children unless their handicaps are so severe that they cannot be taught effectively in the regular classroom. Educators disagree as to whether handicapped youngsters are best taught by being in regular or special classes, in regular or special schools. Some educators see far-reaching consequences for school programs if parents of the nonhandicapped charge that their children are being discriminated against by not having individualized educational plans designed for them.

PL 94–142 furnishes an excellent illustration of the impact of sweeping federal legislation on the curriculum planner. Parenthetically, we should be mindful that federal legislation of which PL 94–142 is but one example is a

---

[62] See Robert W. Cole and Rita Dunn, "A New Lease on Life for the Handicapped: Ohio Copes with 94-142," *Phi Delta Kappan* 59, no. 1 (September 1977): 3–6 ff.

sometime thing which may deliver another kind of impact if and when funds are withdrawn.

Bilingual Education

As ethnic groups whose first language is other than English grow in size and power, more and more curriculum workers find themselves charged with the task of developing bilingual education programs. In 1967 Amendments to the Elementary and Secondary Education Act, the U. S. Congress provided support for bilingual education programs. In 1978 the Office of Bilingual Education of the U. S. Department of Education was spending $135 million to support 700 programs of bilingual education in 41 states and 5 territories.[63] Although bilingual education programs are offered in over 70 languages and dialects, the largest number of students in bilingual programs are Hispanic.

The U. S. Supreme Court's decision in the Lau v. Nichols case in 1974, which required San Francisco to provide English language instruction for Chinese-speaking students, advanced the cause of bilingual education. The efforts of Hispanic groups, now numbering about 9 percent of the U. S. population (compared with 12 percent blacks) have largely brought about the current emphasis on bilingual (and additionally, bicultural) education.

Bilingual education is an educational, linguistic, social, cultural, political, and economic issue. As such, it has become a controversial issue. Dade County (Florida) provides an example of public discord over this issue. In April 1973 Dade County, following the immigration of a large number of Spanish-speaking refugees from Cuba, was declared a bilingual community. Many "Anglos" took issue with the designation of the county as bilingual. This sentiment came to a head when county voters approved by a three to two vote an ordinance that forbade the county from using county funds "for the purpose of utilizing any language other than English, or promoting any culture other than that of the United States."

Although not likely to affect bilingual programs of the schools, the referendum signalled a divisiveness in the community within which curriculum planners must work. One of the problems that divides curriculum planners as well as the public is the exact definition of bilingual and its companion term bicultural.

Bilingual education may mean something as simple as setting up English classes for students whose native language is other than English. On the other hand, bilingual education is often extended to include these additional dimensions:

☐ Students are instructed in subject areas in their own native language, presumably until they have mastered enough English to study the subjects in English.

---

[63] See *Time,* February 13, 1978, p. 65.

☐ Native speakers of English are instructed in the foreign language, e.g., Spanish for English speakers. Ordinarily optional, this component of bilingual education is sometimes pushed by some lay people as a requirement.

☐ Efforts are made to perpetuate and promote the culture of the speakers of other languages, e.g., Cuba, Mexico, etc., through a variety of cultural experiences, including courses in the native language for speakers of the native language, e.g., Spanish for Spanish-speakers.

The U. S. Department of Education has until recently required schools that wished to receive bilingual education funds to provide instruction in the native language. When the U. S. Department of Education sought to force Fairfax County, Virginia to offer instruction to all students in their native language, Fairfax County brought suit on the grounds that its program of intensive English for speakers of other languages was successful as shown by their test scores. In late 1980, the U. S. Department of Education, on the strength of the success of Fairfax County students, decided not to force Fairfax County to provide instruction in the native language.

Censorship

Curriculum planners in a number of communities throughout the country have become enmeshed in a struggle over community groups' efforts to censor textbooks and school library books, to prohibit certain types of instruction, or conversely, to promote certain types of instruction. One organization, for example, in 1979 labeled a number of books in the school libraries of one South Florida county as pornographic and sought to have them removed. Another community group in the same state objected to sex education in the schools on the grounds that it violated the authority of parents.

Responding to community pressures, a school board in New York State removed several books from school libraries. Common charges against books are that they use obscene language, are irreligious, or are un-American. Sometimes the charge is made that books are anti-Christian, which raises the thorny issue of separation of church and state and whether the public schools can or should promote the values of one religion or any religion at all.

California, Indiana, North Dakota, New Jersey, West Virginia, and the state of Washington have all experienced efforts of community groups, often successful, to ban books.

Occasionally, efforts are made not to force the schools to cease certain practices but to incorporate content or programs. Although the U. S. Supreme Court ruled that reading *The Bible* for devotional purposes and reciting prayer in the school are unconstitutional,[64] efforts are still being made to reintroduce

---

[64] *Engle* v. *Vitale,* 370 U.S. 421, 82 Sup. Ct. 1261 (1962). Also, *School District of Abington Township* v. *Schempp* (and *Murray* v. *Catlett*), 374 U.S. 203, 83 Sup. Ct. 1560 (1963).

these sectarian practices. Another attempt to introduce content is proposed legislation to force schools to teach "scientific creationism," the theory that life appeared suddenly, as opposed to the theory of evolution, the idea that life evolved gradually.

As the previous examples suggest, efforts to censor or to promote particular programs and content complicate the curriculum developers' jobs. To respond to various social and political pressures, curriculum planners need not only professional knowledge and skills but also skills in public relations and working with community groups. They need to sprout antennae that alert them to community sentiments. When dealing with controversial issues in the curriculum, they should have channels for determining the seriousness of problems, the strength of community feelings, and the ways in which issues might be resolved before they become magnified and disproportionate.

THE IMPACT OF PROFESSIONAL PROBLEMS UPON CURRICULUM

Teacher Organizations

The power and influence of teachers' organizations have been increasing rapidly in recent years. Robert M. McClure spoke to the positive influence of teacher organizations on school improvement as follows:

> Unfortunately, the anti-establishment mystique in our society has drawn greater attention to teacher militancy and the struggle between the National Education Association and the American Federation of Teachers than to the considerable impact made by the professional associations on school improvement. The less conspicuous but major efforts of the NEA and its affiliates provide an impressive list of examples: the NEA Project on the Academically Talented Student; the NEA Project on Educational Implications of Automation; the Contemporary Music Project of the Music Educators National Conference (an NEA National Affiliate); the Staff Utilization Studies of the National Association of Secondary School Principals (an NEA Associated Organization); and the NEA Project on the Instructional Program of the Public Schools (Project on Instruction).[65]

Teachers' unions are prominent today and either directly or indirectly have an impact on the curriculum. When this happens, some of the decisions are made, not at the customary curriculum council table but at the bargaining table. Ordinarily, negotiations between teachers (labor) and administrators (management) are concerned with working conditions, rights of teachers, benefits, and the like. However, some items of negotiation impinge on the

---

[65] Robert M. McClure, "The Reforms of the Fifties and Sixties: A Historical Look at the Near Past," in *The Curriculum: Retrospect and Prospect,* 70th Yearbook of the National Society for the Study of Education, Part I (Chicago: University of Chicago Press, 1971), pp. 61–62.

curriculum. In communities in which school management and a teachers' union have effected a contract, the process for curriculum planning will likely need to be modified from that of school systems without union contracts.

For example, a recent contract between the United Teachers of Dade and Dade County (Florida) Public Schools provided task forces or councils reporting to the superintendent and school board. These councils were composed of equal representation by the union and the public schools. Three of the councils, which expired with submission of their reports to the superintendent, were clearly curriculum-oriented. The councils and their tasks were as follows:

> Curriculum Council — Composition shall be twelve (12) members. The task shall be to review and study the curriculum program of the Dade County Public Schools.
> Exceptional Child Task Force — Composition shall be ten (10) members. The task shall be to review and study the Dade County Public Schools' exceptional child program.
> Athletic and Physical Education Task Force — Composition shall be ten (10) members. The task shall be to review and study the Dade County Public Schools' athletic and physical education program.[66]

Ways need to be established to integrate efforts of the teacher organizations into the school district model for curriculum development. As members of the teachers' organizations themselves, curriculum planners can strive to enlist the teachers' organizations in the cause of continuous curriculum improvement.

Improved Dissemination

The curriculum workers' efforts would be greatly enhanced if we had improved means of disseminating results of research and experience of innovative programs. Though we have the Educational Resources Information Center (ERIC),[67] the National Diffusion Network,[68] regional education laboratories,[69] and many professional journals, the results of research and experimentation do not reach the classroom teacher to the degree they should. Curriculum decisions are still made on the basis of limited data and without all currently available data. Curriculum leaders must take special responsibility to stay informed of current research so that they can channel essential information to the classroom teacher and other curriculum workers.

---

[66] Contract between the Dade County Public Schools and the United Teachers of Dade, September 17, 1977–October 31, 1980, p. 49.
[67] See Appendix B.
[68] See Appendix C.
[69] See Appendix D.

Improved Research

Not only do the results of research need to be disseminated but both the quantity and quality of education research need to be expanded. The school systems need to be close partners with institutions of higher learning in the conduct of research. The profession is in particular need of more experimental research and more longitudinal studies. We have many status studies and surveys of opinions and practices but not enough controlled research or, for that matter, less controlled action research. Curriculum planners should encourage teachers to engage in unsophisticated action research to determine answers to simple problems that may be applicable only to their setting.

Improved Preparation

Better programs are needed to prepare curriculum leaders and planners. We might refer back to Chapter 1 on the areas of learning from which the field of curriculum is derived, to Chapter 3 on the multilevels and sectors of curriculum planning, and to Chapter 4 on the roles of various personnel in curriculum development to gain some perception of the preparation needed by curriculum developers. It would be reasonable for states to institute certificates in curriculum development. This certificate would parallel those in administration, supervision, guidance, and other specialties presently offered by professional education institutions. Such a certificate would go a long way toward establishing curriculum as a field of specialization in its own right.

Solutions to all of these problems could go a long way toward improving the efficacy of curriculum development.

SUMMARY

This chapter presented many perennial problems of curriculum development, several current curricular problems, and a few professional problems having an impact upon the curriculum.

Eight perennial or continuing problems were considered. Each was presented as a principle to which curriculum workers must give attention.

Scope is the breadth of the curriculum — the "what." The major task in planning the scope of the curriculum is the selection of units of content, organizing elements, organizing centers, or integrative threads from the wealth of possible choices.

Relevance is the usefulness of content to the learner. What makes determining the relevance of a curriculum difficult is the variety of perceptions of what is relevant. A consensus of the opinions of the various constituencies and patrons of the school should be sought by curriculum workers to determine what is of sufficient relevance to be included in the curriculum.

Curriculum planners should strive for balance among a number of variables. When a curriculum gives excessive attention to one dimension or to one group of students and ignores or minimizes attention to others, the curriculum may be said to be out of balance and in need of being brought into balance.

Integration is the unification of disciplines — the weakening or abandoning of boundaries between discrete subjects. Many educators feel that integrated content helps students in the task of problem solving. Relevance, balance, and integration are perceived as dimensions of scope.

Sequence is the "when," the ordering of the units of content. Attention must be paid to prerequisite learning requirements. Continuity is the planned introduction and reintroduction of content at subsequent grade levels and at ever increasing levels of complexity. This concept is at the heart of the "spiral curriculum."

Articulation is the meshing of subject matter and skills between successive levels of schooling to provide a smooth transition for boys and girls from a lower to a higher level. Sequence, continuity, and articulation are all related concepts. Continuity and articulation are perceived as dimensions of sequencing.

Transferability is that characteristic of learning which when realized in one setting permits it to be carried over into another. Although there is no proof that certain subjects per se enhance the transfer of learning, there is some evidence to support the thesis that teaching basic principles of a discipline and bringing out their application increases transfer. Transfer is a much desired goal of education.

We have examined seven current problems confronting curriculum planners. These problems, brought about by social and political forces, are the back-to-basics movement, the minimal competencies movement, integration, sexist practices, programs for the handicapped, bilingual education, and censorship. Curriculum workers must be aware of the dimensions of these problems as they attempt to develop curricula.

This chapter concluded with a brief discussion of four professional problems that have an impact upon the curriculum: the need to clarify the role of teacher organizations in respect to curriculum improvement, the need for better means of disseminating the results of curriculum research and experimentation, the need for more and better research, and the need for improved training programs for curriculum developers.

SUPPLEMENTARY EXERCISES

1. Outline the scope of a course you have taught or plan to teach.
2. Poll a number of teachers, students, and parents to find out what they feel is relevant in the curriculum and what relevant topics they think have been left out.
3. Determine in what ways a curriculum you know well appears to be in or out of balance. If you believe that the curriculum is out of balance, recommend ways to bring it into balance.

4. Report on any planned efforts you can find to correlate or integrate subject matter.

5. Outline and explain the rationale of the sequence of the topics or elements of a course you have taught or plan to teach.

6. Determine whether a school you know well has planned the curriculum keeping in mind the principle of continuity. Recommend improvements in continuity, if necessary.

7. Determine whether a school system you know well has planned the curriculum keeping in mind the principle of articulation. Recommend improvements in articulation, if necessary.

8. Show the transfer value of a discipline that you are certified to teach.

9. Write an analysis of J. Richard Suchman's Inquiry Training Model (see bibliography).

10. Write an analysis of David P. Ausubel's Advance Organizer Model (see bibliography).

11. Locate and summarize the content of at least one article or chapter of a book on one of the eight continuing curriculum problems discussed in this chapter.

12. Select one of the current curriculum problems facing curriculum workers, search the literature, review local practices, and document with references the degree to which it appears to be a problem both nationally and locally. Show your position on the problem and suggest ways for solving it.

13. Report on any activities of a teachers' association or union that have had an impact on the curriculum.

14. Select one of the professional problems having an impact on the curriculum, search the literature, review local practices, and document with references the degree to which it appears to be a problem both nationally and locally. Show your position on the problem and suggest ways of solving it.

15. Explain the purposes of the Educational Resource Information Center (ERIC) and show how the system works. Give illustrations (see Appendix B).

16. Write to the National Diffusion Network Facilitator for your state and report on exemplary programs that exist (see Appendix C).

17. Report on the work of one or more regional laboratories or research and development centers. Give illustrations of their impact on the curriculum (see Appendix D).

BIBLIOGRAPHY

Aikin, Wilford M. *The Story of the Eight-Year Study*. New York: Harper & Row, 1942.

Association for Supervision and Curriculum Development. *Balance in the Curriculum*, 1961 Yearbook. Alexandria, Va.: Association for Supervision and Curriculum Development, 1961.

Ausubel, David P. *Educational Psychology: A Cognitive View.* New York: Holt, Rinehart and Winston, 1968.

Bellack, Arno A. "What Knowledge Is Of Most Worth?" *The High School Journal* 48, no. 5 (February 1965): 318–332.

Berman, Louise M. *New Priorities in the Curriculum.* Columbus, Ohio: Charles E. Merrill, 1968.

Bloom, Benjamin S. "Ideas, Problems, and Methods of Inquiry." In *The Integration of Educational Experiences,* 57th Yearbook, Part III, National Society for the Study of Education. Chicago: University of Chicago Press, 1958, pp. 84–85.

Broudy, Harry S. *The Real World of the Public Schools.* New York: Harcourt, Brace, Jovanovich, 1972.

———, Smith, B. Othanel, and Burnett, Joe R. *Democracy and Excellence in American Secondary Education.* Chicago: Rand McNally, 1964.

Bruner, Jerome S. *On Knowing: Essays for the Left Hand.* Cambridge, Mass.: Harvard University Press, 1962.

———. *The Process of Education.* Cambridge, Mass.: Harvard University Press, 1977.

———. *The Relevance of Education.* New York: Norton, 1973.

———. "Structures in Learning," *Today's Education* 52, no. 3 (March, 1963): 26–27.

Caswell, Hollis L. and Campbell, Doak S. *Curriculum Development.* New York: American Book Company, 1935.

Coleman, James S., et al. *Equality of Educational Opportunity.* Washington, D.C.: U.S. Office of Education, 1966.

Combs, Arthur W., ed. *Perceiving, Behaving, Becoming,* 1962 Yearbook. Alexandria, Va.: Association for Supervision and Curriculum Development, 1962.

Doll, Ronald C. *Curriculum Development: Decision Making and Process,*

4th ed. Boston: Allyn and Bacon, 1978. 5th ed. 1982.

Gagné, Robert M. "Curriculum Research and the Promotion of Learning." In *Perspectives of Curriculum Evaluation,* AERA Monograph Series on Curriculum Evaluation #1. Chicago: Rand McNally, 1967, pp. 19–38.

Goodlad, John I. *Planning and Organizing for Teaching.* Washington, D.C.: National Education Association, 1963.

Halverson, Paul M. "The Meaning of Balance." In *Balance in the Curriculum,* 1961 Yearbook. Alexandria, Va.: Association for Supervision and Curriculum Development, 1961, pp. 3–16.

Hass, Glen. *Curriculum Planning: A New Approach,* 3rd ed. Boston: Allyn and Bacon, 1980.

Joyce, Bruce and Weil, Marsha. *Models of Teaching,* 2d ed. Englewood Cliffs, N.J.: Prentice-Hall, 1980.

Lewis, Arthur J. "Educational Basics to Serve Citizens in the Future," *FASCD Journal* 1, no. 1 (February 1979): 2–8.

McClure, Robert M., ed. *The Curriculum: Retrospect and Prospect,* 70th Yearbook of the National Society for the Study of Education, Part I. Chicago: University of Chicago Press, 1971.

Oliver, Albert I. *Curriculum Improvement: A Guide to Problems, Principles and Processes,* 2d ed. New York: Harper & Row, 1977.

Orlosky, Donald E. and Smith, B. Othanel, eds. *Curriculum Development: Issues and Insights.* Chicago: Rand McNally, 1978.

Phenix, Philip H. "The Disciplines as Curriculum Content." In *Curriculum Crossroads.* Edited by A. Harry Passow. New York: Teachers College Press, Columbia University, 1962, pp. 57–65.

Pressey, Sidney I. and Robinson, Frances P. *Psychology and the New Education,* Rev. ed. New York: Harper & Row, 1944.

Saylor, J. Galen and Alexander,

William M. *Curriculum Planning for Better Teaching and Learning.* New York: Holt, Rinehart and Winston, 1954. 4th ed. (with Arthur J. Lewis), 1981.

Short, Edmund C. and Marconnit, George D., eds. *Contemporary Thought on Public School Curriculum.* Dubuque, Iowa: William C. Brown, 1968.

Smith, B. Othanel, et al. *Teachers for the Real World.* Washington, D.C.: American Association of Colleges for Teacher Education, 1969.

Smith, B. Othanel; Stanley, William O., and Shores, J. Harlan. *Fundamentals of Curriculum Development,* Rev. ed. New York: Harcourt, Brace, Jovanovich, 1957.

Suchman, J. Richard. *The Elementary School Training Program in Scientific Inquiry,* Report of the U.S. Office of Education, Project Title VII, Project 216. Urbana, Ill.: University of Illinois Press, 1962.

Taba, Hilda. *Curriculum Development: Theory and Practice.* New York: Harcourt, Brace, Jovanovich, 1962.

Tanner, Daniel and Tanner, Laurel N. *Curriculum Development: Theory Into Practice,* 2d ed. New York: Macmillan, 1980.

Thorndike, Edward L. "Mental Discipline in High School Studies," *Journal of Educational Psychology* 15, no. 1 (January 1924): 1–22; Continued in 15, no. 2 (February 1924): 83–98.

———. *The Principles of Teaching: Based On Psychology.* New York: Seiler, 1906.

Toffler, Alvin. *Future Shock.* New York: Random House, 1970.

———. *The Third Wave.* New York: William Morrow, 1980.

Tyler, Ralph W. *Basic Principles of Curriculum and Instruction.* Chicago: University of Chicago Press, 1949.

Vars, Gordon F., ed. *Common Learnings: Core and Interdisciplinary Team Approaches.* Scranton, Pa.: International Textbook Company, 1969.

Wiles, Kimball and Patterson, Franklin. *The High School We Need.* Alexandria, Va.: Association for Supervision and Curriculum Development, 1959.

Zais, Robert S. *Curriculum: Principles and Foundations.* New York: Harper & Row, 1976.

15

Curriculum Products

After studying this chapter you should be able to:
1. Construct a curriculum guide.
2. Construct a resource unit.
3. Identify sources of curriculum materials.

You should also be able to formulate and give reasons for your views on the following issues:
1. The value of constructing and using curriculum guides.
2. The value of constructing and using resource units.
3. The desirability of sharing curriculum products.

TANGIBLE PRODUCTS

The Biblical expression "By their fruits ye shall know them" can certainly be applied to curriculum workers. Walk into the curriculum laboratory of any public school or university and you may be surprised, perhaps even overwhelmed, by the evidence of the productivity of those who travail in the vineyards of curriculum development. The products of their efforts are there for all to see — tangible, printed, often packaged in eye-catching style.

Curriculum workers have been turning out products for many years. Unfortunately, some curriculum developers view the creation of products as the terminal rather than the intermediate phase of curriculum improvement. The products are meant to be put into practice, tried out, revised, tried again, revised again.

Creating curriculum products not only has a functional value — the production of a plan or tool for implementing or evaluating the curriculum — but it gives the planners a great psychological boost. In producing tangible materials, they are able to feel some sense of accomplishment.

Throughout this text we have already seen a number of types of curriculum products. Chapter 6 contained examples of statements of philosophy and aims of education. Chapter 7 included needs assessment surveys and reports, sections of courses of study and curriculum guides, and portions of a state's statement of minimal standards. In Chapter 8 we saw statements of curriculum goals and objectives, subgoals, performance indicators, and performance conditions. Statements of instructional goals and objectives formed a part of Chapter 10. Unit and lesson plans were outlined in Chapter 11. Chapter 12 discussed instruments for evaluating instruction and Chapter 13, instruments for evaluating the curriculum.

Judging from the tasks that curriculum coordinators, consultants, directors, and other workers are called on to do in the schools, there is a healthy demand for training in the production of curriculum materials. In this chapter we will discuss the creation and use of several of the more common products found in the schools.

The content, the form, and the names by which curriculum materials are known are almost as varied as the number of groups that author them. We can find in the curriculum libraries of school systems materials called "curriculum bulletins," "curriculum guides," "courses of study," "syllabi," "resource units," and "source units."

Because curriculum materials are impermanent, nonstandardized products made primarily for local use, the variations among them are considerable. To put the creation of curriculum products into perspective, we must visualize curriculum committees and individuals in thousands of school districts all over the country constructing materials that they feel will be of most help to their teachers.

Terms for these types of curriculum materials may signal quite different products or may be used synonymously. A curriculum guide, for example, may be quite different from a course of study. On the other hand, what is called a curriculum guide in one locality may be called a course of study in another. For this reason it is difficult to predict what will be discovered in any particular curriculum product until it is examined.

The curriculum products that we will consider in this chapter are:

1. curriculum guides, courses of study, and syllabi
2. resource units

We will not discuss curriculum materials that have been adequately discussed in preceding chapters, such as modules or unit plans, lesson plans, and tests. All curriculum materials share the common purpose of serving as aids to teachers and planners in organizing, implementing, and evaluating curriculum and instruction.

CURRICULUM GUIDES, COURSES OF STUDY, AND SYLLABI

Three kinds of curriculum products are clearly related. These are (1) curriculum guides, (2) courses of study, and (3) syllabi. As already noted, some curriculum workers make no distinction among the three types. What is called a syllabus or course of study, for example, in one school system is called a curriculum guide in another. The following definitions of the terms are used in this chapter:

1. A *curriculum guide* is the most general of the three types of materials — guide, course of study, and syllabus. It may cover a single course or subject area at a particular grade level, e.g., ninth-grade English; all subjects at a particular grade level, e.g., ninth grade; a sequence in a discipline, e.g., language arts; or an area of interest applicable to two or more courses or grade levels, e.g., occupational safety. When a curriculum guide covers a single course, it may also be called a course of study. However, a curriculum guide is a teaching aid for a course of study rather than a complete course of study in itself.
2. A *course of study* is a detailed plan for a single course, including text materials (content). A well-known example of a curriculum product of this nature is *Man: A Course of Study,* which has been widely used in the schools and seen on television.[1] A course of study includes both what is to be taught (content) — in summary or in complete text — and suggestions for how to teach the course. A course of study usually specifies what

---

[1] See Jerome S. Bruner, *Man: A Course of Study* (Cambridge, Mass.: Educational Services, 1965).

must be taught, whereas a curriculum guide offers alternatives to the teacher.

3. A *syllabus* is an outline of topics to be covered in a single course or grade level.

Curriculum Guide

Let's look more closely at the creation of a curriculum guide. What is its purpose? What should be included? A curriculum guide provides many suggestions to teachers who choose to use it. In this sense it is a tool to ease the work of the teacher. The curriculum guide is one source from which teachers may derive ideas for developing their own resource units, learning units ,and lesson plans.

A curriculum guide may be written by a group of teachers or planners or by an individual. In the latter case, the guide is often reviewed by other specialists before it is disseminated within the school system. For those who write a curriculum guide, the process is almost as important as the product. The task of constructing a guide forces the writers to clarify their ideas, to gather data, to demonstrate creativity, to select content, to determine sequence, and to organize their thoughts.

Curriculum planners normally include the following components in a curriculum guide:

1. Introduction: The introduction includes the title of the guide, the subject or grade level for which the guide is designed, and any suggestions that might help users.
2. Instructional goals: In this section instructional goals (called general objectives by some planners) are stated in nonbehavioral terms.
3. Instructional objectives: Instructional objectives (called specific or performance objectives by some planners) of the course or for the subject area of a particular grade level should be stated in behavioral terms and should encompass all three domains of learning, if all are applicable.
4. Activities: Learning experiences that might be used by the teacher with pupils should be suggested and placed in preferred sequence.
5. Evaluation techniques: Suggestions should be given to teachers on how to evaluate student achievement. This section of the guide could include general suggestions on evaluating, sample test items, or even complete tasks.
6. Resources: Attention should be given to human resources — persons who might be called on to assist with the content developed by the guide — and to material resources, including books, media, and facilities.

Some writers of curriculum guides also include an outline of the content. Writers of guides should pay attention to format so that teachers can use them easily. Note the clear organization of the curriculum guide shown in Box 15-1.

BOX 15-1 A curriculum guide

STREET SAFETY
FOR
EARLY CHILDHOOD

Statistics show that accidents are the major cause of death and injury among the youth of our nation. These accidents can and must be reduced, as they entail the loss of life and financial resources that are irreplaceable.

Effectively incorporating our resources and knowledge into a safety education program in every grade throughout the school would seem to be the first step in a lifetime of preventive education. According to the National Safety Council, accidents in which a motor vehicle strikes a pedestrian or cyclist are the leading cause of death and personal injury. The Council therefore suggests that all safety programs be oriented to traffic safety for all — especially the young pedestrian.

Crossing the street is a very real problem in today's complex traffic system. Every child must understand exactly what behavior is expected of him/her at all times when he/she is walking outside. In bridging the gap between protection and self-reliance, schools must teach children to walk safely amid the many hazards and provide them with opportunities that are necessary to acquire this essential knowledge and skill.

A. Introduction

This curriculum guide is designed for teachers of Early Childhood Education. It provides the teacher with numerous objectives and activities geared at providing the pre-primary child with enriching educational experiences and opportunities to acquaint him/her with the necessary procedures for preventive street safety.

Safety education is a vital part of the early childhood program, since accidents threaten children's physical well-being; many take lives or cause people to be crippled for life. It is not enough to simply provide a room or playground safe and free from hazards — safety rules are necessary even in well-planned environments. The environment and the curriculum should complement each other in encouraging good attitudes toward safety rules and laws. In addition, it is the teacher's responsibility to find safe ways of releasing tension and pent-up energy in the child. Safety practices and measures are learned even as children go to and from school, or as they engage in work and play.

Preventive safety measures must be taught in the beginning days of school to prevent children from getting into accidents; safety instruction is the major theme for this guide. The activities are aimed at reaching every aspect of a child's daily life; they appeal to his/her everyday understanding so he/she may easily incorporate them, with almost no second thoughts. Safety measures must become instinctive.

The activities are designed around the media most attractive to a child's being. There is an emphasis on poems and songs — means through which young children are most readily able to communicate their thoughts and feelings. There is also a stress on being able to succeed easily in the activities, so the concepts presented will remain appealing and desirable for the children.

Through games, songs, poems, and creative expression, the child will be able to quickly accomplish the tasks and transfer them to his/her everyday life. He/she will be able to see the importance of safety precautions and will want to incorpo-

496

BOX 15-1   cont'd.

rate them in all of his/her activities — even to the point of telling the adult with him/her what to do! Such is the main goal of the program.

B. Instructional Goals

An essential component of street safety is knowing where to cross the street. It is when a child is heedless of these appropriate places that most accidents occur.

Children must know not to rush out into the street unheedingly. So often, oncoming traffic cannot see children when they rush out from between parked cars, or when they chase after a toy or pet.

A child must be aware of and understand the hazards involved in being a pedestrian. People versus the automobile has become a major crisis in our society. Too often a child feels a driver must watch out for a pedestrian; it is difficult to realize the motorist is too preoccupied with the manipulating of his vehicle, and of watching out for other vehicles to be aware of the unprotected pedestrian.

It is necessary to understand and obey the various traffic signs on the street. It may seem that these are primarily for the motorist to take heed of; however, a pedestrian needs to concern himself with these as well.

A traffic light is another essential object in correct traffic safety. A child must be able to recognize the purpose of the various lights in the traffic signal, and to know the appropriate procedure for each.

Just as important as the traffic light is the crossing signal at the traffic light or assigned pedestrian crossing. A child must be able to realize the association between the signal allowing him/her to cross and the traffic being required to stop. However, he must also be aware that some traffic may not obey the signal, and therefore careful crossing procedures must still be heeded.

A child needs to recognize the personnel involved in street life — the policeman, the crossing guard, etc. Often enough a signal is not to be heeded; rather the personnel involved are the ruling domain.

C. Instructional Objectives

Traffic Lights: The student will be able to:

- □ specify the three colors of the light (red, yellow/amber, green).
- □ demonstrate the correct positions on the light for each color.
- □ demonstrate the correct procedure to be followed for each color.
- □ state the dangers when lights are not obeyed.

Signs: The student will be able to:

- □ name specific traffic signs: (stop, crosswalk, railroad crossing, school crossing).
- □ identify the meaning of each sign.
- □ demonstrate what each sign requires him/her to do.
- □ state the hazards of disobeying the sign.

Crossing the Street: The student will be able to:

- □ identify the correct place to cross the street (corner, crosswalk).
- □ identify the incorrect place to cross the street (in the middle).

(continued on next page)

BOX 15-1 cont'd.

□ demonstrate the correct procedure to cross the street.

□ look both ways before crossing.

□ obey signals, signs, personnel for crossing the street.

Safety Hazards: The student will be able to:

□ describe the dangers told in many nursery rhymes.

□ relate safer ways to respond to those dangers.

□ dramatize the correct and incorrect actions in the nursery rhymes.

□ identify correct clothing for those conditions.

□ detect hazards at construction sites or in unsuitable neighborhoods.

□ refrain from talking to strangers.

□ refuse to get into a car with a stranger.

□ refuse gifts from strangers.

□ follow a designated route home.

□ walk facing traffic.

□ stay on the sidewalk or other appropriate walking area.

Personnel: The student will be able to:

□ identify personnel involved with street safety (crossing guard, policeman/ policewoman).

□ obey those people at all times.

D. *Activities*

□ Using colored masking tape, yarn, or string, make a road with intersections on the floor in the classroom. Have police officer or crossing guard direct children.

□ Add cardboard boxes as cars. Have the children dramatize being both motorist and pedestrian.

□ Cut out red, yellow, green circles. Have the children paste them in the correct position on another piece of construction paper. Or use yarn or colored macaroni.

□ Using large red, yellow, and green circles, have the children follow the meaning of each by 'driving' and obeying the circle which the teacher holds up.

□ "Red Light, Green Light, 1–2–3" — This game is played with one child standing at the front of the room/area with his back to the class. He/she says "Red Light, etc.," during which time the rest of the class must try to approach him stealthily. When he/she reaches "3," he/she turns around, trying to catch someone moving. Whoever is caught must go back to the beginning. The first one to reach the person at the front becomes the caller.

□ Have a police officer or crossing guard come to visit. Discuss: uniform, job function, why important, how they help, etc. Cut out paper hats like these workers' hats. Let children wear them.

498

BOX 15-1 cont'd.

□ Use figures with colored clothes to discuss appropriate apparel for night or bad weather walking. Paste correct colored apparel onto figures.

□ Paste black construction paper onto a milk carton. Onto side one, paste a red circle; side two, a yellow; side three, a green; side four, all. Place on a broom stick or long paper roll. Display sides separately and have children demonstrate correct action.

□ Use action pictures to discuss correct ways to cross the street; to walk along the street.

□ Use action pictures and/or dittos to trace correct areas for street crossing, etc.

□ Listen to selected poems and riddles.

□ Visit a police station.

E. Evaluation Techniques

□ Using action posters, ask questions which relate to the instructional objectives.

□ Using a flannel board, place red, yellow, and green circles in appropriate positions for a traffic light. Point to each circle, ask the color and what it means.

□ Dramatize stopping, looking, listening, waiting, crossing.

□ Tell a story about a child who makes mistakes in following safety rules. Ask pupils to tell what the mistakes are and how to correct them.

F. Resources

Books for Children

□ Birnbaum, A. *Green Eyes*. New York: Capitol Publishing, 1953.

□ Bright, Robert. *I Like Red*. New York: Doubleday, 1955.

□ Greene, Carla. *I Want To Be A Policeman*. Chicago: Children's Press, 1958.

□ Kessler, Leonard. *Mr. Pine's Mixed-Up Signs*. New York: Grossett & Dunlop, 1961.

□ Lattin, Anne. *Peter's Policeman*. Chicago: Follett Publishing, 1958.

□ Lenski, Lois. *I Went for a Walk*. New York: Walck, 1958.

□ McGinley, Phyllis. *All Around the Town*. Philadelphia, Pa.: J. B. Lippincott, 1962.

□ Nicholas, Charles. *How Do You Get From Here To There?* New York: Macmillan, 1962.

□ Pineo, Craig. *Peter Policeman*. New York: Golden Press, 1968, 1969.

□ Seuss, Dr. *And To Think I Saw It On Mulberry Street*. New York: Vanguard Press, 1937.

□ Stover, Jo Ann. *They Didn't Use Their Heads*. New York: McKay Co., 1963.

□ Walck, Henry. *The Little Auto*. New York: Golden Press, 1968.

□ Wokinska, W. *All By Myself*. New York: Holt, Rinehart and Winston, 1963.

(*continued on next page*)

BOX 15-1   cont'd.

Books for the Teacher

☐ Fournier, Raymond, and Presno, Vincent. *Advantage: A Program for Pre-School Children.* Englewood Cliffs, N.J.: Prentice-Hall, 1966.

☐ Pattison, William D. *Which Way?* New Jersey: Rand McNally, 1965.

☐ Presno, Vincent, and Preston, Gard. *People and Their Actions.* Chicago: Rand McNally, 1967.

☐ Senesh, Lawrence. *Our Working World — Neighbors At Work.* Chicago: Science Research Associates, 1965.

Film Strips
(from the County Board of Public Instruction)

☐ *Beginning Responsibility — Rules at School*

☐ *Helpers at Our School*

☐ *Let's Be Good Citizens in Our Town*

(from Walt Disney Studios Educational Marketing Co., 666 Busse Highway, Park Ridge Hill, Illinois 60068)

☐ *I'm No Fool as a Pedestrian*

☐ *Safety To and From School*

Action Posters and Pictures

☐ *Correct Ways of Walking Along the Street*

☐ *Correct Ways of Crossing the Street*

SOURCE: Written by Gilda Oran Ashbal, Hollywood, Florida, 1980. Abridged version. Reprinted by permission.

RESOURCE UNIT

A resource unit, called source unit by some curriculum persons, is "an arrangement of materials and activities around a particular topic or problem." [2] The resource unit is a curriculum product that falls somewhere between a teacher's learning unit and a course of study or curriculum guide. I explained elsewhere:

> . . . the resource unit is a source of information and ideas for teachers to use. . . . The major purpose of the resource unit is to provide ideas for a teacher who wishes to create his [or her] own learning unit on the same topic. . . . The resource unit contains a wealth of suggestions and information which will aid the teacher in supplementing material found in the basic textbook. The resource unit shortens the busy teacher's planning time

---

[2] Peter F. Oliva, *The Secondary School Today,* 1st ed. (Scranton, Pa.: International Textbook Company, 1967), p. 176.

and simplifies his [or her] work in the construction of learning units for his [or her] classes.[3]

In essence, the resource unit serves the same general purpose as a course of study or curriculum guide. The major distinction between these types of products is that the resource unit is much narrower in scope, focusing on a particular topic rather than on an entire year, course, subject area, or sequence. Although we may encounter a course of study or curriculum guide for eleventh-grade American history, for example, we may also find resource units on topics within American history, such as The Age of Jackson, the Great Depression, or The VietNam War.

The same outline that was suggested for a curriculum guide applies to the resource unit. An example of a resource unit is given in Box 15-2.

SOURCES OF CURRICULUM MATERIALS

These illustrations of curriculum products barely suggest the types that are available or can be constructed. In every state of the union curriculum committees have created a wide variety of useful materials.

Curriculum developers and others who are searching for curriculum materials beyond the textbooks and accompanying teachers' manuals may locate examples in several places: curriculum libraries of colleges and universities, particularly those of schools and departments of education: curriculum centers of the public school systems; teacher education centers; the offices of curriculum consultants; state departments of education and regional service centers of some state departments of education.

Professional organizations such as the Association for Supervision and Curriculum Development [4] and its state affiliates produce many helpful materials. Commercial firms are another source of curriculum materials that may be of use to the teacher. Many publishing firms display curriculum materials at major professional conferences.

Great variation can be found in both the format of printed curriculum materials and in the types of available materials. Beyond typical curriculum guides, we can find curriculum materials packaged into multimedia kits consisting of films, filmstrips, charts, tapes, records, etc.

SUMMARY

Curriculum planners and teachers frequently engage in developing curriculum products that will be of use to teachers in their school systems. In this chapter we looked at these types of products: curriculum guides, courses of study, syllabi; and resource units.

---

[3] Oliva, *The Secondary School Today,* 1st ed., p. 176.
[4] Association for Supervision and Curriculum Development, 225 N. Washington Street, Alexandria, Virginia 22314.

BOX 15-2   A resource unit

Grade Level/Course:
Senior High School/Problems of American Democracy
Topic: Education in the United States

A. Introduction

The enterprise of education in the United States consumes over 120 billion dollars per year. About 25 percent of the population is enrolled in schools from nursery through graduate level. In some way schooling touches the lives of every person in the country. Yet, schooling itself is rarely studied in the schools. Although most people have their own ideas about education, their data base is often limited or lacking. The purpose of this resource unit is to provide students with facts, insights, and understandings about our American educational system.

B. Instructional Goals

1. Cognitive

The student will become familiar with:

a. the purposes of education in the United States.
b. the general structure of education in the United States.
c. the ways in which education in the United States is administered and financed.
d. major differences between the U. S. system of education and systems of other countries.

2. Affective

The student will appreciate:

a. the complexity of the U. S. educational system.
b. our decentralized system of education.
c. the extent and complexity of problems facing education in the United States.
d. the achievements of American schools.

C. Instructional Objectives

1. Cognitive

The student will be able to:

a. identify sources of funding for education.
b. explain local, state, and federal responsibilities for education.
c. state purposes of levels of education: elementary, middle, junior high, senior high, community college, senior college, and university.
d. tell the strengths and weaknesses of our decentralized system of education.
e. explain how teachers are prepared and hired.
f. describe how the educational dollar is spent.
g. account for differences in the support of education by the various states.
h. identify problems facing the schools and tell what efforts are being made to solve them.
i. account for the growth of private schools.
j. compare the American system of education with the system in another country.

BOX 15-2 cont'd.

2. Affective

The student will:

  a. write a statement of purposes of education as he or she sees them.

  b. state what he or she feels constitutes a good education.

  c. state with reasons whether he or she believes compulsory education is desirable.

  d. describe how he or she feels education should be funded.

  e. take a position on whether public school education or private school education is better.

  f. take a position on whether American education or European (or Russian or Japanese) education is better.

  g. show his or her position by written reports on some controversial issues such as prayer in the schools, the teaching of the theory of evolution, censorship of textbooks and library books, busing of students for purposes of integrating the races, and bilingual education.

3. Psychomotor

None

D. Learning Activities

  1. Read provisions of the United States Constitution regarding education, especially the First, Tenth, and Fourteenth Amendments.

  2. Read provisions of the state constitution regarding education.

  3. Examine recent state and federal legislation on education.

  4. Prepare a chart showing the percentages of funding for education from local, state, and federal sources.

  5. Prepare a diagram showing overall dollars spent in any one year for education by local, state, and federal sources in the students' home state.

  6. Observe an elementary, middle/junior high, and secondary class in action and afterward compare such aspects as objectives, materials, methods of teaching, student conduct, etc.

  7. Visit a community college and interview one of the administrators on the purposes and programs of the community college.

  8. Invite a private school headmaster to come to class to talk on purposes and programs of his or her school.

  9. Invite a panel of public school principals at both elementary, middle/junior high, and secondary levels to come to class to talk on problems they face in administering their schools.

  10. Critique the requirements for a teacher's certificate in the students' home state.

  11. Gather and present data on the funding of higher education in both the United States and in the students' home state.

  12. Read and evaluate several statements of purposes of education.

  13. Read and evaluate a book or article critical of American public education.

(continued on next page)

BOX 15-2 cont'd.

14. Report on pressure groups that influence education.

15. Read a book or several articles on the educational system of one foreign country and describe major characteristics of that system.

16. Find out how teachers are trained, certified, and employed in the students' home state.

17. Find out how school administrators are trained, certified, and employed in the students' home state.

18. Attend a school board meeting and discuss it in class.

19. Visit the superintendent's office and hear the superintendent (or his or her deputy) explain the role of the superintendent.

20. Find out what the school tax rate is in the students' home community, how moneys are raised for the schools, and how much money is expended in the community for schools.

21. Find out how much teachers and administrators are paid in the students' home community and what fringe benefits they receive.

22. Examine the staffing patterns of an elementary or secondary school and determine types of employees needed to run the school.

23. Find out how serious the dropout problem is in the students' home community and what is being done to solve it.

24. Determine whether or not student achievement in schools of the students' home district is satisfactory. If not, account for reasons for unsatisfactory achievement and report on measures that are being taken to improve the situation.

25. Debate whether teachers should have the right to strike.

26. Choose a controversial educational issue and write a paper showing positions of several prominent persons and/or groups and the students' own position.

E. Evaluation Techniques

1. Give a pretest consisting of objective test items to survey students' factual knowledge about education in the United States.
   Sample test items:
   a. Responsibility for state control of education in the United States is derived from the U. S. Constitution's:
      (1) First Amendment
      (2) Fifth Amendment
      (3) Tenth Amendment
      (4) Fourteenth Amendment
   b. Policies for local school districts are promulgated by:
      (1) advisory councils
      (2) school boards
      (3) teachers' unions
      (4) school principals

2. Evaluate students' oral reports.

BOX 15-2   cont'd.

3. Evaluate students' written work — reports, charts, etc.

4. Observe students' reactions and comments in class discussion.

5. Give a posttest of objective items similar to those of the pretest.

F. Resources
    1. *Books*
       Allen, Dwight W. *The Teacher's Handbook*. Glenwood, Ill.: Scott, Foresman, 1971.

       Charles, C. M., Gast, David K., Servey, Richard E., and Burnside, Houston M. *Schooling, Teaching, and Learning: American Education*. Saint Louis: C. V. Mosby, 1978.

       Cremin, Lawrence A. *The Transformation of the School: Progressivism in American Education 1876–1957*. New York: Alfred A. Knopf, 1961.

       Dearman, Nancy B. and Plisko, Valena White. *The Condition of Education: Statistical Report*, 1980 ed. Washington, D. C.: U. S. Department of Education, National Center for Education Statistics, 1980.

       Education Commission of the States, Reports of the National Assessment of Educational Progress (various titles) Denver, Col.: Education Commission of the States, various dates.

       Ehlers, Henry. *Crucial Issues in Education*, 7th ed. New York: CBS College Publishing, 1981.

       Fain, Stephen M. and Shostak, Robert, with Bean, John F. *Teaching in America*. Glenwood, Ill.: Scott, Foresman, 1979.

       Grant, W. Vance and Eiden, Leo J. *Digest of Education Statistics 1980*. Washington, D. C.: U. S. Department of Education, National Center for Education Statistics, 1980.

       Joyce, Bruce R. and Morine, Greta G. *Creating the School: An Introduction to Education*. Boston: Little, Brown, 1976.

       King, Edmund J., *Other Schools and Ours: Comparative Studies for Today*, 4th ed. New York: Holt, Rinehart and Winston, 1973.

       Palardy, J. Michael. *Teaching Today: Tasks and Challenges*. New York: Macmillan, 1975.

       Silberman, Charles E., *Crisis in the Classroom*. New York: Random House, 1970.

       Tesconi, Charles A., Jr. *Schooling in America: A Social Philosophical Perspective*. Boston: Houghton Mifflin, 1975.

       Thayer, V. T. *The Role of the School in American Society*. New York: Dodd, Mead, 1960.

       United Nations Educational, Scientific, and Cultural Organization (UNESCO). *World Survey of Education*. Paris: UNESCO, periodically.

       United States Bureau of the Census, *Statistical Abstract of the United States*. Washington, D. C.: Superintendent of Documents, U. S. Government Printing Office, annually.

(continued on next page)

BOX 15-2   cont'd.

The World Almanac and Book of Facts. New York: Newspaper Enterprise Association, Inc., annually.

2. *Films*

The Difference Between Us. 60 min. Sound. Black and white. Bloomington, Ind.: National Educational TV, Inc., Indiana University, 1966. Compares secondary schools in England and the United States.

Education in America: The 17th and 18th Centuries. 16 min. Sound. Black and white/Color. Chicago: Coronet Instructional Films, 1958. Part of the History of Education in America series.

Education in America: The 19th Century. 16 min. Sound. Black and white/Color. Chicago: Coronet Instructional Films, 1958. Part of the History of Education in America series.

Education in America: The 20th Century. 16 min. Sound. Black and white/Color. Chicago: Coronet Instructional Films, 1958. Part of the History of Education in America series.

Make a Mighty Reach. 28 min. Sound. Color. Dayton, Ohio: Charles F. Kettering Foundation, 1967. Shows innovations in exemplary schools.

Meet Comrade Student. 54 min. Sound. Black and white. New York: American Broadcasting Company TV, 1962. Film on education in the Soviet Union.

Curriculum guides provide many suggestions to teachers for teaching a single course, a subject area at a particular grade level, an entire sequence, or an area of interest. Included in curriculum guides are suggested instructional goals, instructional objectives, activities, evaluation techniques, and resources. Sometimes an outline of the content is also included. Courses of study cover single courses and often contain a considerable amount of content material. Syllabi list topics to be covered.

Resource units are, in essence, minicurriculum guides for teaching particular topics or problems. Limited to single topics or problems, resource units offer types of suggestions similiar to those found in curriculum guides.

In the creation of curriculum materials, both the process and product are important. Examples of curriculum materials can be found in libraries of school systems, colleges and universities, and state departments of education. Professional organizations produce curriculum materials as do business and industrial concerns.

SUPPLEMENTARY EXERCISES

1. Suggest your own outline for writing (1) a curriculum guide and (2) a resource unit.

2. State values you see in various curriculum products.
3. State problems you see in various curriculum products.
4. Critique samples of curriculum guides, courses of study, syllabi, and resource units.
5. Survey opinions of teachers on the value of curriculum guides and other products listed in exercise four.
6. Locate and describe types of curriculum products other than those mentioned in this text.
7. Determine to what extent teachers in a school system you know well use their curriculum products. Account for their use or lack of use.
8. Locate and report on a curriculum product called a "scope and sequence chart."
9. Locate and list sources of curriculum materials available (1) in the school system, (2) in nearby colleges or universities, (3) from state departments of education or state service centers, (4) from professional associations, and (5) from business and industry.

BIBLIOGRAPHY

Kemp, Jerrold E. *Instructional Design: A Plan for Unit and Course Development.* Belmont, Cal.: Fearon Publishers, 1971.

Oliva, Peter F. *The Secondary School Today,* 1st ed. Scranton, Pa.: International Textbook, 1967. chapter 8.

Van Til, William, Vars, Gordon F., and Lounsbury, John H. *Modern Education for the Junior High School Years.* Indianapolis: Bobbs-Merrill, 1967. chapter 11.

Winters, Marilyn. *Designing Your Curriculum Guide: A Step-by-Step Approach.* Westlake, Calif.: Las Virgines Unified School District, 1980.

CURRICULUM GUIDES

Curriculum guides may be obtained from:
ERIC (see Appendix B of this text).
Pitman Learning, Inc., 6 Davis Drive, Belmont, California 94002. Guides on microfiche. See *The 1980 Curriculum Development Library,* Vols. 1–7.
University Microfilms International, P. O. Box 1307, Ann Arbor, Michigan 48106. Guides on microfiche.

KIT

Jerrold E. Kemp. *Instructional Design.* San Jose, Calif.: San Jose State University, 1977. Two books, ten audio cassettes, and five filmstrips.

Appendix A
Exit Competencies

After completing this course you should be able to demonstrate mastery of the following competencies:

1. To define curriculum development.
2. To distinguish between curriculum and instruction.
3. To describe roles of teachers, students, curriculum specialists, administrators, and parents in curriculum development.
4. To describe, giving examples, types of curriculum planning that are done at the local school, the school district, and the state levels.
5. To design and describe staff roles in a central curriculum office in a given school district.
6. To explain responsibilities and duties of a curriculum leader.
7. To list skills needed by a curriculum leader.
8. To explain, identifying appropriate principles, how to go about effecting change in the curriculum.
9. To demonstrate communication skills.
10. To draw and explain a model for curriculum improvement.
11. To demonstrate skills in leading a group.
12. To write a statement of aims of education.
13. To write a school philosophy.
14. To contrast major beliefs of essentialism and progressivism as they apply to the curriculum.
15. To conduct a curriculum needs assessment.
16. To write curriculum goals and objectives.
17. To develop a plan for organizing the curriculum of a school you know well, supporting the plan with appropriate references from the professional literature.

18. To write instructional goals and objectives in each of the three domains of learning.
19. To identify the most frequently used strategies of instruction and describe the strengths and weaknesses of each.
20. To write a learning unit plan.
21. To write a lesson plan.
22. To devise ways to preassess achievement of students.
23. To devise formative and summative methods of evaluating instruction.
24. To devise means of evaluating the curriculum.
25. To define and suggest ways to achieve each of the following: scope, relevance, balance, integration, sequence, continuity, articulation, and transferability.
26. To write a curriculum guide.
27. To write a resource unit.

Appendix B
ERIC Clearinghouses

Established in 1966, the Educational Resources Information Center (ERIC) is a national system for disseminating educational information. Now under the sponsorship of the National Institute of Education (created by the Educational Amendments Act of 1972), ERIC comprises not only Central ERIC at the National Institute of Education but also sixteen clearinghouses for information in specialized areas. The clearinghouses collect, abstract, and index documents, which may be obtained on hard copy or microfiche.

ERIC publishes *Resources in Education,* a monthly sourcebook that contains abstracts of reports.[1] Helpful to ERIC users are *Current Index to Journals in Education,* a monthly publication that contains annotations of articles and *Thesaurus of ERIC Descriptors,* a system for classifying ERIC documents.[2]

Following are the addresses of the current sixteen clearinghouses, Central ERIC, the ERIC Processing and Reference Facility, the ERIC Document Reproduction Service, and the Oryx Press.

---

[1] Available from the Superintendent of Documents, U.S. Government Printing Office.
[2] Available from Oryx Press.

510

ERIC NETWORK COMPONENTS [3]

There are currently sixteen (16) ERIC Clearinghouses, each responsible for a major area of the field of education. Clearinghouses acquire, select, catalog, abstract, and index the documents announced in *Resources in Education (RIE)*. They also prepare interpretive summaries and annotated bibliographies dealing with high interest topics and based on the documents analyzed for *RIE*; these information analysis products are also announced in *Resources in Education*.

ERIC CLEARINGHOUSES:

Adult, Career, and Vocational Education (CE)
Ohio State University
1960 Kenny Rd.
Columbus, Ohio 43210
Telephone: (614) 486-3655

Counseling and Personnel Services (CG)
University of Michigan
School of Education Building, Room 2108
East University & South University Sts.
Ann Arbor, Michigan 48109
Telephone: (313) 764-9492

Educational Management (EA)
University of Oregon
Eugene, Oregon 97403
Telephone: (503) 686-5043

Elementary and Early Childhood Education (PS)
University of Illinois
College of Education
Urbana, Illinois 61801
Telephone: (217) 333-1386

Handicapped and Gifted Children (EC)
Council for Exceptional Children
1920 Association Drive
Reston, Virginia 22091
Telephone: (703) 620-3660

Higher Education (HE)
George Washington University
One Dupont Circle, N. W., Suite 630
Washington, D. C. 20036
Telephone: (202) 296-2597

Information Resources (IR)
Syracuse University

School of Education
Syracuse, New York 13210
Telephone: (315) 423-3640

Junior Colleges (JC)
University of California at Los Angeles
Powell Library, Room 96
405 Hilgard Ave.
Los Angeles, California 90024
Telephone: (213) 825-3931

Educational Resources Information Center (Central ERIC)
National Institute of Education
Washington, D. C. 20208
Telephone: (202) 254-7934

ERIC Processing and Reference Facility
4833 Rugby Avenue, Suite 303
Bethesda, Maryland 20014
Telephone: (301) 656-9723

Languages and Linguistics (FL)
Center for Applied Linguistics
3520 Prospect Street, N. W.
Washington, D. C. 20007
Telephone: (202) 298-9292

Reading and Communication Skills (CS)
National Council of Teachers of English
1111 Kenyon Road
Urbana, Illinois 61801
Telephone: (217) 328-3870

Rural Education and Small Schools (RC)
New Mexico State University
Box 3 AP
Las Cruces, New Mexico 88003
Telephone: (505) 646-2623

---

[3] From *Resources in Education*.

Science, Mathematics, and Environmental Education (SE)
Ohio State University
1200 Chambers Road, Third Floor
Columbus, Ohio 43212
Telephone: (614) 422-6717

Social Studies/Social Science Education (SO)
Social Science Education Consortium, Inc.
855 Broadway
Boulder, Colorado 80302
Telephone: (303) 492-8434

Teacher Education (SP)
American Association of Colleges for Teacher Education
One Dupont Circle, N. W., Suite 616
Washington, D. C. 20036
Telephone: (202) 293-7280

Tests, Measurement, and Evaluation (TM)
Educational Testing Service
Princeton, New Jersey 08541
Telephone: (609) 921-9000

Urban Education (UD)
Teachers College
Columbia University
Box 40
New York, New York 10027
Telephone: (212) 678-3437

ERIC Document Reproduction Service
P.O. Box 190
Arlington, Virginia 22210
Telephone: (703) 841-1212

The ORYX Press
2214 North Central Avenue at Encanto
Phoenix, Arizona 85004
Telephone: (602) 254-6156

Appendix C
National Diffusion Network

The National Diffusion Network of the U. S. Department of Education provides technical assistance and training to school systems wishing to adopt programs developed throughout the country and deemed exemplary by the Joint Dissemination Review Panel. The goal of the National Diffusion Network is to bring about school improvements by disseminating programs that have proved successful. The National Diffusion Network provides funds for state facilitators whose job it is to help schools find out about, select, and adopt programs supported by the Network.

Following is a list of state facilitators.[1] Further information is available from the National Diffusion Network, Department of Education, Trans Point Building, Room B-448, Washington, D. C. 20202. The list of facilitators appears in the National Diffusion Network's catalog of *Educational Programs That Work* published by the Far West Laboratory for Educational Research and Development, 1855 Folsom Street, San Francisco, California 94103.

---

[1] 1980–81.

STATE FACILITATORS
NATIONAL DIFFUSION NETWORK, 1980–81

State Facilitators, located in 49 states, the District of Columbia and the Virgin Islands, assist public and private schools that are searching for ways to improve their education programs. State Facilitators can supply additional information about the NDN Developer/Demonstrators, put educators directly in touch with the programs for additional information and help arrange for adoptions of them.[2]

Alabama
R. Meade Guy
Alabama Facilitator Project
Alabama Information and Development
   System (AIDS)
Alabama Department of Education
Room 347, State Office Building
Montgomery, Alabama 36130
(205) 832-3138

Alaska
J. Kelly Tonsmeire
Alaska State Facilitator Project
Alaska Department of Education
Pouch F, State Office Building
Juneau, Alaska 99811
(907) 465-2814 or 2815

Arizona
L. Leon Webb
Arizona State Facilitator
Educational Diffusion Systems, Inc.
161 East First Street
Mesa, Arizona 85201
(602) 969-4880

Arkansas
Emil R. Mackey
Arkansas State Facilitator Project
Arkansas Department of Education
Communication and Dissemination
   Division
State Capitol Mall
Little Rock, Arkansas 72201
(501) 370-5038

Regional Facilitators
Mary B. Gunter
Arkansas State Facilitator Project
Region 1
Boston Mount Cooperation
P.O. Drawer 248
Prairie Grove, Arkansas 72753
(501) 846-2206

Ora Stevens
Arkansas State Facilitator Project
Region II
Marianna School District
P.O. Box 309
Marianna, Arkansas 72360
(501) 295-5291

California
Ira Barkman or Ginna Lurton
California State Facilitator
State Department of Education
Exemplary Program Replication Unit
721 Capitol Mall
Sacramento, California 95814
(916) 322-6797

Colorado
Duane C. Webb
Colorado State Facilitator
830 South Lincoln
Longmont, Colorado 80501
(303) 772-4420 or 442-2197

Connecticut
Carolyn McNally

---

[2] Produced by the ED Materials/Support Center, Far West Laboratory for Educational Research and Development, for the National Diffusion Network, October 1980. Further information about the National Diffusion Network and State Facilitator strategies may be found in: *NDN: A Success Story* (LEA Associates, 80 S. Main St., Concord, NH 03301, $1.50 prepaid) and *State Facilitator Profiles* (Far West Laboratory for Educational Research and Development, 1855 Folsom St., San Francisco, CA 94103).

Connecticut Facilitator Project (CFP)
Area Cooperative Educational Service
800 Dixwell Avenue
New Haven, Connecticut 06511
(203) 562-9967

Delaware
Peter Bachmann or Wilmer E. Wise
Delaware Facilitator Project
Planning, Research & Evaluation Division
State Department of Public Instruction
John G. Townsend Building, P.O. Box
    1402
Dover, Delaware 19901
(302) 736-4583

District of Columbia
Susan Williams
District Facilitator Project
Edmonds School
9th and D Streets, N.E.
Washington, D.C. 20002
(202) 547-8030

Florida
G. Michael Kuhn
State Facilitator for the Department of
    Education
Knott Building
Tallahassee, Florida 32301
(904) 487-1078

Georgia
India Lynn King or Mary Allison
Georgia Facilitator Center
226 Fain Hall
University of Georgia
Athens, Georgia 30602
(404) 542-3332

Hawaii
Kellett Min
Hawaii State Facilitator
Hawaii State Department of Education
P.O. Box 2360
Honolulu, Hawaii 96804
(808) 548-3425

Idaho
Ted L. Lindley
Idaho State Facilitator
Idaho State Department of Education

Len B. Jordan Office Building
Boise, Idaho 83720
(208) 334-2189

Illinois
Shirley M. Menendez
Illinois Statewide Facilitator
1105 East Fifth Street
Metropolis, Illinois 62960
(618) 524-2664

Indiana
Ted F. Newell
Indiana Facilitator Center
Logansport Community School Corp.
2829 George Street
Logansport, Indiana 46947
(219) 722-1754

Iowa
David C. Lidstrom
Iowa State Facilitator
Iowa Department of Public Instruction
Grimes State Office Building
Des Moines, Iowa 50319
(515) 281-3111

Kansas
James H. Connett
Kansas State Facilitator Project
KEDDS/LINK
1847 N. Chautauqua
Wichita, Kansas 67214
(316) 685-0271

Kentucky
John C. Padgett
Kentucky State Facilitator
State Department of Education
Capitol Plaza Tower Office Building
Frankfort, Kentucky 40601
(502) 564-4394

Louisiana
James R. Owens, Jr.
The Louisiana Facilitator Project
Louisiana State Department of Education
ESEA Title IV Bureau Office
P.O. Box 44064
Baton Rouge, Louisiana 70804
(504) 342-3375

Maine
Robert G. Shafto
Maine Facilitator Center
P.O. Box 1391
Gardiner, Maine 04345
(207) 582-7211 or 7212

Maryland
Raymond H. Hartjen
Maryland Facilitator Project/Educational
    Alternative Inc.
P.O. Box 265
Port Tobacco, Maryland 20677
(301) 934-2992

Massachusetts
John Collins
Massachusetts State Facilitator
The NETWORK, Inc.
290 South Main Street
Andover, Massachusetts 01810
(617) 470-1080

Michigan
Deborah Clemmons
Michigan State Facilitator
Michigan Department of Education
P.O. Box 30008
Lansing, Michigan 48909
(516) 373-1806

Regional Supplemental Centers
William Banach
Educational and Management Improve-
    ment Center
44001 Garfield Road
Mt. Clemens, Michigan 48043
(313) 286-8800

Ron Berg
Cheboygan-Otsego-Presque Isle ISD
Basic Regional Supplemental Center
6065 Learning Lane
Indiana River, Michigan 49749
(616) 238-9394

Richard D. Anderle
Kent Intermediate School District
Region 8 Supplemental Center
2650 East Beltline, S.E.
Grand Rapids, Michigan 49506
(616) 957-0250

Roy Butz
Oakland Intermediate School District
2100 Pontiac Lake Road
Pontiac, Michigan 48054
(313) 858-1940

Gerry Geik
Kalamazoo Valley Intermediate School
    District
Region 12 Supplemental Center
1819 E. Milham Road
Kalamazoo, Michigan 49002
(616) 381-4620 ext. 247

Bobbie Ann Robinson
Saginaw Intermediate School District
MERC (Mid-Eastern Regional Consor-
    tium)
6235 Gratiot Road
Saginaw, Michigan 48603
(517) 799-9071

Polly Friend
Marquette-Alger Intermediate School
    District
Lighthouse Schools
427 W. College Avenue
Marquette, Michigan 49855
(906) 228-9400

Olga Moir
Wayne County Intermediate School
    District
Project VALUE
33500 Van Born Road
Wayne, Michigan 48184
(313) 326-9300

Shirley Rappaport
Bay-Arenac Intermediate School District
Region 6 Supplemental Center
4228 Two Mile Road
Bay City, Michigan 48706
(517) 686-4410

Sylvia Ruscett
Ottawa Intermediate School District
13565 Port Sheldon Road
Holland, Michigan 49423
(616) 399-6940 ext. 359

Minnesota
Gene Johnson or James Christianson

Northern and Central Minnesota State
    Facilitator Project
Educational Cooperative Service Unit 5
102 N.E. Sixth Street
Staples, Minnesota 56479
(218) 894-1930

Diane Lassman
Southeast Minnesota Facilitator Project
The EXCHANGE
166 Peik Hall
University of Minnesota
Minneapolis, Minnesota 55455
(612) 376-5297

Richard L. Peterson
State Facilitator Project
ESCU Office
Southwest State University
Marshall, Minnesota 56258
(507) 537-1481

Mississippi
Jerome P. Brock
Mississippi Facilitator Project
Mississippi School Boards Association
P.O. Box 203
Clinton, Mississippi 39056
(601) 924-2001

Missouri
Jolene Schulz, Director
Missouri State Facilitator Center
310 North Providence Road
Columbia, Missouri 65201
(314) 443-2561 ext. 218/238 or 449-8622

Montana
Wayne Pyron
Montana State Facilitator Project
Office of Public Instruction
State Capitol
Helena, Montana 59601
(406) 449-2059

Regional Facilitators
Cliff Harmala
Montana Regional Facilitator
1011 N. River Avenue
Glendive, Montana 59240
(406) 365-4422 or 449-5643

Jim Palmer
Montana Regional Facilitator
P.O. Box 3836
Missoula, Montana 59806
(406) 251-4923

Jim Watkins
Montana Regional Facilitator
1325 Fourth Avenue North
Great Falls, Montana 59401
(406) 761-4144

Nebraska
Mary Lou Palmer
Nebraska State Facilitator Project
Nebraska State Department of Education
301 Centennial Mall
P.O. Box 94987
Lincoln, Nebraska 68509
(402) 471-2637

Nevada
Victor Hyden
Nevada State Facilitator Project
Nevada Department of Education
400 West King Street
Capitol Complex
Carson City, Nevada 89710
(702) 885-5700

New Hampshire
Jared Shady
New Hampshire Facilitator Center
80 South Main Street
Concord, New Hampshire 03301
(603) 224-9461

New Jersey
Joseph Picogna
New Jersey State Facilitator Project
Title IV Director
New Jersey State Department of
    Education
225 West State Street
Trenton, New Jersey 08625
(609) 292-5792 or 8736

New Mexico
Amy Atkins, Director, or
Susan Carter, Assistant Director
DEEP: Diffusing Exemplary Educational
    Practices in New Mexico

Department of Educational Foundations
College of Education
University of New Mexico
Albuquerque, New Mexico 87131
(505) 277-5204

New York
Robert N. King or Samuel Corsi, Jr.
New York State Facilitator Project
Office of Federal Demonstration Programs
Educational Building Annex, Room 860
New York State Education Department
Albany, New York 12234
(518) 474-1280

Regional Facilitators
John T. Donovan
OEP Representative
410 East Willow Street
Syracuse, New York 13203
(315) 425-4284

Grace Fairlie
Supervisor of Curriculum Development
756 St. Lawrence Avenue
Buffalo, New York 14216
(716) 833-5865

Evelyn Jones
Office of Special Projects
347 Baltic Street
Brooklyn, New York 11201
(212) 624-2273

Eleanor Peck
Program Analyst
City School District
Office of Urban Funded Programs
131 West Broad Street
Rochester, New York 14608
(716) 325-4560

Robert Raub
Madison-Oneida BOCES
Spring Road
Verona, New York 13478
(315) 363-8000

Richard Solomon
555 Warren Road
Ithaca, New York 14850
(607) 257-1555

Arthur Sullivan
Suffolk County BOCES III
507 Deer Park Road
Dix Hills, New York 11746
(516) 549-4900

Frank Thompson
Project Director
ECOS Training Institute
Box 369
Yorktown Heights, New York 10598
(914) 245-6919

Charles Weed
Regional Planning Center
1015 Watervliet-Shaker Road
Albany, New York 12205
(518) 456-9281

North Carolina
Henry A. Helms, Jr.
Division of Development
North Carolina Department of Public
    Instruction
Education Annex #1
Raleigh, North Carolina 27611
(919) 733-7018

Regional Facilitators
Glen Arrants
North Carolina Facilitator Center
Paton School
102 Old Clyde Road
Canton, North Carolina 28716
(704) 648-6960 ext. 31

Richard Barnes
North Central Regional Education Center
P.O. Box 21889
Greensboro, North Carolina 27402
(919) 379-5764

Maxine Brown
Northeast Regional Education Center
Box 1028
Williamston, North Carolina 27892
(919) 792-5166

Robert R. Byrd
North Carolina Facilitator Service
    Southwest Site
619 Wall Street

Albemarle, North Carolina 28001
(704) 983-2127

Brenda Dail
Central Regional Education Center
Box 549
Knightdale, North Carolina 27545
(919) 266-9282

Josephine Spaulding
South Central Regional Center
P.O. Box 786
Carthage, North Carolina 28327
(919) 947-5871

Joe Webb
Southeast Regional Facilitator Service
Education Center, Room 200
612 College Street
Jacksonville, North Carolina 28540
(919) 455-8100

James Sineon
Northwest Regional Center
303 "E" Street
North Wilkesboro, North Carolina 28659
(919) 667-2191

North Dakota
Hank Landeis
North Dakota State Facilitator
Department of Public Instruction
State Capitol
Bismarck, North Dakota 58505
(701) 224-2293

Ohio
Gordon Behm
Ohio Facilitator Center
The Ohio Department of Education
Division of Planning and Evaluation
65 South Front Street, Room 804
Columbus, Ohio 43215
(614) 466-3825

Oklahoma
Kenneth Smith
Oklahoma Statewide Facilitator Project
Edmond Public Schools
1216 South Rankin
Edmond, Oklahoma 73034
(405) 341-2246

Oregon
Dick Pedee
Oregon State Facilitator
Multnomah County Education Service
    District
220 S.E. 102nd Avenue
Portland, Oregon 97216
(503) 254-9925

Pennsylvania
Richard Brickley or Carolyn Trohoski
R.I.S.E. — Pennsylvania State Facilitator
198 Allendale Road
King of Prussia, Pennsylvania 19406
(215) 265-6056

Rhode Island
George McDonough
State Facilitator Center — R.I.S.F.C.
CIC Building
235 Promenade Street
Providence, Rhode Island 02908
(401) 277-3840 or 3841

South Carolina
James R. Buckner or Sharon Ray
South Carolina Facilitator Project
South Carolina State Department of
    Education
Office of Federal Programs
1429 Senate Street
Columbia, South Carolina 29201
(803) 758-3526

South Dakota
Gene K. Dickson
South Dakota State Facilitator
South Dakota Division of Elementary
    and Secondary Education
Richard F. Kneip Building
Pierre, South Dakota 57501
(605) 773-3395

Tennessee
Martin McConnell or Charles M. Achilles
Tennessee Statewide Facilitator Project
    (TSF)
College of Education/BERS
2046 Terrace Avenue
University of Tennessee
Knoxville, Tennessee 37916
(615) 974-4165 or 2272

Texas
William Scanell
Texas Education Agency
201 East 11th Street
Austin, Texas 78701
(512) 475-5601

George Franklin
Region I Education Service Center
    Diffusion Project
1900 West Schunior
Edinburg, Texas 78539
(512) 383-5611

Madalyn Cooke
Region II Education Service Center
209 North Water
Corpus Christi, Texas 78401
(512) 883-9288

Bill Powell
Region III Education Service Center
1905 Leary Lane
Victoria, Texas 77901
(512) 575-1471

Jake Parker
Region IV Education Service Center
P.O. Box 863
Houston, Texas 77001
(713) 868-1051

Edith Peacock
Region V Education Service Center
2295 Delaware Street
Beaumont, Texas 77703
(713) 835-5212

Everett Youngblood
Region VI Education Service Center
3332 Montgomery Road
Huntsville, Texas 77340
(713) 295-9161

Mike Owens
Region VII Education Service Center
P.O. Drawer 1622
Kilgore, Texas 75662
(214) 984-3071

Leroy Hendricks
Region VIII Education Service Center
100 North Riddle Street
Mt. Pleasant, Texas 75455
(214) 572-6676

Art Phillips
Region IX Education Service Center
301 Loop 11
Wichita Falls, Texas 76305
(817) 322-6928

Jacquelyn Harrison
Region X Education Service Center
400 East Spring Valley Road
P.O. Box 1300
Richardson, Texas 75080
(214) 231-6301

Mary F. Hull
Region XI Education Service Center
3001 North Freeway
Fort Worth, Texas 76106
(817) 625-5311

Rosemary Richards
Region XII Education Service Center
401 Franklin
Waco, Texas 76703
(817) 756-7494

Carrie Heim
Region XIII Education Service Center
7703 North Lamar
Austin, Texas 78752
(512) 458-9131

Robert E. Maniss
Region XIV Education Service Center
P.O. Box 3258
Abilene, Texas 79604
(915) 677-2911

Nancy Lowe
Region XV Education Service Center
P.O. Box 5199
San Angelo, Texas 76902
(915) 655-6551

Jack Shelton
Region XVI Education Service Center
1601 South Cleveland
P.O. Box 30600
Amarillo, Texas 79120
(806) 376-5521

Travis Brown
Region XVII Education Service Center
4000 22nd Place
Lubbock, Texas 79410
(806) 763-4127

Bill Whitfield
Region XVIII Education Service Center
P.O. Box 6020
Midland, Texas 79701
(915) 563-2380

George Chancellor
Region XIX Education Service Center
P.O. Box 10716
El Paso, Texas 79997
(915) 779-3737

Betty Child
Region XX Education Service Center
1550 N.E. Loop 410
San Antonio, Texas 78209
(512) 828-3551

Utah
Kenneth P. Lindsay
Utah State Facilitator Project
Utah State Office of Education
250 East Fifth South
Salt Lake City, Utah 84111
(801) 533-5431

Vermont
Joseph M. O'Brien
Vermont State Facilitator
Bennington-Rutland Supervisory Union
Manchester Center, Vermont 05255
(802) 362-2452

Virginia
J. B. Linder, Jr. or Robert Foster
Virginia State Facilitator
Educational Services, Inc.

2845 Rollingwood Road
Petersburg, Virginia 23803
(803) 536-5932 or (804) 732-3584

Washington
Keith Wright
Washington State Facilitator
Yakima Public Schools
104 North Fourth Avenue
Yakima, Washington 98902
(509) 575-3234

West Virginia
Kenny J. Smith
West Virginia State Facilitator
P.O. Box 1907
Elkins, West Virginia 26241
(304) 636-6918

Wisconsin
George R. Glasrud
Wisconsin State Facilitator
Department of Public Instruction
Instructional Services Division
125 South Webster
Madison, Wisconsin 53702
(608) 266-2101

Virgin Islands
Phyllis Betz
Virgin Islands State Facilitator
Virgin Islands Department of Education
P.O. Box 630
St. Thomas, Virgin Islands 00801
(809) 774-0807

Appendix D
Regional Educational Laboratories and Research and Development Centers

Regional educational laboratories and research and development centers came into being under Title IV of the Elementary and Secondary Education Act of 1965. The laboratories — private, nonprofit corporations and the university-based centers — conduct research, and develop and disseminate materials. The following is a current list of laboratories and research and development centers funded by the U. S. government.[1]

---

[1] See the National Institute of Education, *Institutional Profiles of Education Laboratories and R&D Centers* (Washington, D. C.: U. S. Department of Education, September, 1976).

Appalachia Educational Laboratory, Inc.
1031 Quarrier Street, P. O. Box 1348
Charleston, West Virginia 25325

Cemrel, Inc.
3120 59th Street
St. Louis, Missouri 63139

Center for Education Policy and Management
1472 Kincaid
Eugene, Oregon 97401

Center for the Study of Evaluation
UCLA Graduate School of Education
145 Moore Hall
Los Angeles, California 90024

Center for Social Organization of Schools
Johns Hopkins University
3505 North Charles Street
Baltimore Maryland 21218

Center for Vocational Education
The Ohio State University
1960 Kenny Road
Columbus, Ohio 43210

Far West Laboratory for Educational Research and Development
1855 Folsom Street
San Francisco, California 94103

Learning Research and Development Center
University of Pittsburgh
3939 O'Hara Street
Pittsburgh, Pennsylvania 15260

Mid-Continent Regional Educational Laboratory
7302 Pennsylvania Avenue
Kansas City, Missouri 64114

National Center for Higher Education Management Systems
P. O. Drawer P
Boulder, Colorado 80302

Northwest Regional Educational Laboratory
400 Lindsay Building
710 S. W. Second Avenue
Portland, Oregon 97204

Research for Better Schools, Inc.
1700 Market Street, Suite 1700
Philadelphia, Pennsylvania 19103

Research and Development Center for Teacher Education
University of Texas
Education Annex 3.203
Austin, Texas 78712

Southwest Educational Development Laboratory
211 East Seventh Street
Austin, Texas 78701

Southwest Regional Laboratory
4665 Lampson Avenue
Los Alamitos, California 90720

Stanford Center for Research and Development in Teaching
School of Education
Stanford University
Stanford, California 94305

Wisconsin Research and Development Center for Cognitive Learning
1025 West Johnson Street
Madison, Wisconsin 53706

CREDITS

(continued from page iv)

Prentice-Hall, Inc., Englewood Cliffs, N.J. Reprinted with permission. 17. From *The Secondary School Today*, 2nd ed. by Peter F. Oliva, p. 81. Copyright © 1972, 1967 by International Textbook Company. By permission of Harper & Row, Publishers, Inc.

Chapter 2. 4, 5. Joseph J. Schwab, *The Practical: A Language for Curriculum* (Washington, D.C.: National Education Association, Center for the Study of Education, 1970), pp. 2–3. Reprinted with permission. 10. Glen Hass, *Curriculum Planning: A New Approach*, 3rd ed. (Boston: Allyn and Bacon, 1980), pp. 40–42. Reprinted with permission. 12. David Turney, "Sisyphus Revisited," *Perspectives on Curriculum Development 1776–1976*, 1976 ASCD Yearbook (Alexandria, Va.: Association for Supervision and Curriculum Development, 1976), p. 232. Reprinted with permission of the Association for Supervision and Curriculum Development. Copyright © 1976 by the Association for Supervision and Curriculum Development. All rights reserved. 15. James B. Macdonald, "Curriculum Development in Relation to Social and Intellectual Systems," in *The Curriculum: Retrospect and Prospect*, ed. Robert M. McClure, 70th Yearbook, Part I, National Society for the Study of Education. (Chicago: University of Chicago Press, 1971), pp. 98–99. Reprinted with permission. 18. Jack R. Frymier and Horace C. Hawn, *Curriculum Improvement for Better Schools* (Worthington, Ohio: Charles A. Jones, 1970), p. 24. Reprinted with permission of Wadsworth Publishing Company. 19. Specified excerpt from *Curriculum Improvement: A Guide to Problems, Principles, and Process*, 2nd ed., by Albert I. Oliver, p. 37. Copyright © 1977 by Albert I. Oliver. By permission of Harper & Row, Publishers, Inc. 21. John R. Verduin, Jr., *Cooperative Curriculum Improvement*, p. 33. © 1967 by Prentice-Hall, Inc. Reprinted with permission. 22. Excerpt from *Curriculum Development: Theory and Practice* by Hilda Taba, p. 8, © 1962 by Harcourt, Brace and Jovanovich, Inc. and reprinted by permission of the publisher.

Chapter 3. 8. Figure 3-1. From *The Secondary School Today*, 2nd ed. by Peter Oliva, p. 280. Copyright © 1972 by Harper & Row, Publishers, Inc. Reprinted by permission. 13. Jack R. Frymier and Horace C. Hawn, *Curriculum Improvement for Better Schools* (Worthington, Ohio: Charles A. Jones, 1970), pp. 28–29. Reprinted with permission. 15, 16. From *Curriculum: Principles and Foundations* by Robert S. Zais (Thomas Y. Crowell, Inc.), pp. 18, 445, 448–449. Copyright © 1976 by Harper & Row, Publishers, Inc. By permission of Harper & Row, Publishers, Inc. 17. Amitai Etzioni, *Modern Organizations*, p. 81. © 1964 by Prentice-Hall, Inc., Englewood Cliffs, New Jersey. Reprinted with permission. 30. John D. McNeil, *Curriculum: A Comprehensive Introduction*, 2nd ed. (Boston: Little, Brown, 1981), p. 60. Reprinted with permission. 37. Educational Policies Commission,

Education for All American Youth (Washington, D.C.: National Education Association, 1944), pp. 225–226. Reprinted with permission. 45. Reprinted with permission of Macmillan Publishing Co., Inc. from *The Educational Imagination: On the Design and Evaluation of School Programs* by Elliot W. Eisner, p. 2. Copyright © 1979, Elliot W. Eisner.

Chapter 4. 1, 17. From *Planning Curriculum for Schools*, Third Edition, by J. Galen Saylor and William M. Alexander, pp. 59, 67–69. Copyright © 1974 by Holt, Rinehart and Winston. Reprinted by permission of Holt, Rinehart and Winston. 3, 4. Reprinted with permission of Macmillan Publishing Co., Inc. from *The Principalship* by William H. Roe and Thelbert L. Drake, pp. 11, 132. Copyright © 1980, Macmillan Publishing Co., Inc. 6. From *The New School Executive: A Theory of Administration*, 2nd ed. by Thomas J. Sergiovanni and Fred D. Carver, p. 49. Copyright © 1980 by Thomas J. Sergiovanni and Fred D. Carver. By permission of Harper & Row, Publishers, Inc. 8. John D. McNeil, *Curriculum: A Comprehensive Introduction*, 2nd ed. (Boston: Little, Brown, 1981), pp. 305–306. Reprinted with permission. 10. Ronald C. Doll, *Curriculum Improvement: A Guide to Problems, Principles, and Process*, 2nd ed. (Boston: Allyn and Bacon, 1978), p. 327. Reprinted with permission. 15, 16. Roald F. Campbell, Luvern L. Cunningham, Michael D. Usdan, and Raphael O. Nystrand, *The Organization and Control of American Schools*, 4th ed. (Columbus, Ohio: Charles E. Merrill, 1980), pp. 149, 377, 379. Reprinted with permission. 18. Reprinted from *Managerial Psychology: An Introduction to Individuals, Pairs, and Groups in Organizations*, 2nd ed. by Harold J. Leavitt by permission of The University of Chicago Press. © 1958, 1964 by The University of Chicago. 19, 26, 27, 28, 29. Robert G. Owens and Carl R. Steinhoff, *Administering Change in Schools*, pp. 60, 61–62, 142. © 1976 by Prentice-Hall, Inc., Englewood Cliffs, New Jersey. Reprinted with permission. 23, 24, 53. Robert J. Alfonso, Gerald R. Firth, and Richard F. Neville, *Instructional Supervision: A Behavior System*, 2nd ed. (Boston: Allyn and Bacon, 1981, pp. 283, 284, 175. Reprinted with permission. 32. Daniel L. Stufflebeam et al., *Educational Evaluation & Decision Making* (Itasca, Ill.: F. E. Peacock, 1971), pp. 80–84. © 1971 Phi Delta Kappa Educational Foundation. Reprinted with permission. 33. Kenneth D. Benne and Paul Sheats, "Functional Roles of Group Members," *The Journal of Social Issues* 4, no. 2 (Spring 1948): 43–46. Reprinted with permission. 34, 50. From *Emerging Patterns of Supervision: Human Perspectives* by Thomas J. Sergiovanni and Robert J. Starratt, pp. 199, 203. Copyright © 1971 by McGraw-Hill, Inc. Used with permission of McGraw-Hill Book Company. 44. Reprinted with permission of Macmillan Publishing Co., Inc. from *Educational Administration: An Introduction* by Ralph B. Kimbrough and Michael Y. Nunnery, p. 141. Copyright © 1976, Macmillan Publishing Co., Inc. 45, 46, 47. Morphet, Johns,

Reller, *Educational Organization and Administration: Concepts, Practices, and Issues*, 3rd ed. © 1974, pp. 106–108, 111–114, 117. Reprinted by permission of Prentice-Hall, Inc., Englewood Cliffs, N.J. 51. From *Administration of Public Education*, 3rd ed. by Stephen J. Knezevich, p. 87. Copyright © 1962, 1969, 1975 by Stephen J. Knezevich. By permission of Harper & Row, Publishers, Inc.

Chapter 5. 3, 21, 22, 23, 24, 25, 26, 27. Excerpts from *Curriculum Improvement: Theory and Practice* by Hilda Taba, pp. 11–12, 456–459, 345–379, 12, 458, 458–459. © 1962 by Harcourt, Brace and Jovanovich, Inc. and reprinted by permission of the publisher. 5, 9, 10, 11, 12, 14, 15. Reprinted from *Basic Principles of Curriculum and Instruction* by Ralph W. Tyler by permission of The University of Chicago Press, pp. 3, 33–36, 41, 38–39, 63, 68–82. Copyright 1949 by the University of Chicago. 13. Figure 5-1. W. James Popham and Eva L. Baker, *Establishing Instructional Goals*, p. 87. © 1970 by Prentice-Hall, Inc., Englewood Cliffs, N.J. Diagram of Tyler's curricular rationale. 17, 18. Reprinted with permission of Macmillan Publishing Co., Inc. from *Curriculum Development: Theory Into Practice* by Daniel Tanner and Laurel N. Tanner, p. 60. Copyright © 1975, Macmillan Publishing Co., Inc. 20. Figure 5-3. Mario Leyton Soto and Ralph W. Tyler, *Planeamiento Educacional* (Santiago, Chile: Editorial Universitaria, 1969). Reprinted with permission of Editorial Universitaria. 29. Figure 5-4. From *Planning Curriculum for Schools*, Third Edition, by J. Galen Saylor and William M. Alexander, p. 27. Copyright © 1974 by Holt, Rinehart and Winston, Inc. Reprinted by permission of Holt, Rinehart and Winston. 30, 31. From *Planning Curriculum for Schools*, Third Edition, by J. Galen Saylor and William M. Alexander, p. 24. Copyright © 1974 by Holt, Rinehart and Winston, Inc. Reprinted by permission of Holt, Rinehart and Winston. 39. Figure 5-5. From *Supervision for Today's Schools* by Peter F. Oliva, p. 232. Copyright © 1976 by Thomas Y. Crowell Company, Inc. By permission of Harper & Row, Publishers, Inc.

Chapter 6. 3. Educational Policies Commission, *Moral and Spiritual Values in the Public Schools* (Washington, D.C.: National Education Association, 1951), pp. 17–34. 7. Reprinted with permission of Macmillan Publishing Co., Inc. from *Democracy and Education: An Introduction to the Philosophy of Education* by John Dewey, pp. 49–51. Copyright © 1916, Macmillan Publishing Co., Inc., renewed 1944, John Dewey. 9. Educational Policies Commission, *The Unique of Education in American Democracy* (Washington, D.C.: National Education Association, 1937), p. 89. Reprinted with permission. 10. Harvard Committee on General Education, *General Education in a Free Society* (Cambridge, Mass.: Harvard University Press, 1945), p. 54. Reprinted with permission. 12. Educational Policies Commission, *The Central Purpose of American Education* (Washington, D.C.: National Education Association, 1961), p. 89. Reprinted with per-

mission. 14, 15, 29. Excerpts from *Curriculum Improvement: Theory and Practice* by Hilda Taba, pp. 23, 184, © 1962 by Harcourt, Brace and Jovanovich, Inc. and reprinted by permission of the publisher. 16, 28, 30. Theodore Brameld, *Patterns of Educational Philosophy: A Democratic Interpretation* (Yonkers-on-Hudson, New York: World Book Company, 1950), p. 477–478, 149, 103. Reprinted with permission. 17. Robert M. Hutchins, *On Education* (Santa Barbara, Calif.: Center for the Study of Democratic Institutions, 1963), p. 18. Reprinted with permission from "On Education," a publication of the Robert Maynard Hutchins Center for the Study of Democratic Institutions, Santa Barbara, California. 21. V. T. Thayer, *The Role of the School in American Society* (New York: Dodd, Mead, 1960), pp. 251–252. Reprinted with permission. 26. Reprinted from *The Child and the Curriculum* by John Dewey by permission of The University of Chicago Press, pp. 7–14. Copyright 1902 by The University of Chicago. 31. A. H. Maslow, "Some Basic Propositions of a Growth and Self-Actualization Psychology," *Perceiving, Behaving, Becoming*, 1962 Yearbook (Alexandria, Va.: Association for Supervision and Curriculum Development, 1962), p. 36. Reprinted with permission of the Association for Supervision and Curriculum Development. Copyright © 1962 by the Association for Supervision and Curriculum Development. All rights reserved. 32, 33, 34, 35. Arthur W. Combs, "A Perceptual View of the Adequate Personality," *Perceiving, Behaving, Becoming*, 1962 Yearbook (Alexandria, Va.: Association for Supervision and Curriculum Development, 1962), pp. 51, 51–62, 53. Reprinted with permission of the Association for Supervision and Curriculum Development. Copyright © 1962 by the Association for Supervision and Curriculum Development. All rights reserved. 37. From *The Secondary School Today*, 2nd ed. by Peter F. Oliva, p. 120. Copyright © 1972, 1967 by International Textbook Company. By permission of Harper & Row, Publishers, Inc. 38. John Dewey, *Interest and Effort in Education* (Boston: Houghton Mifflin Co., 1913), pp. 4–5. Reprinted with the permission of The Center for Dewey Studies, Southern Illinois University at Carbondale.

Chapter 7. 7. Earl C. Kelley, "The Fully Functioning Self," *Perceiving, Behaving, Becoming*, 1962 Yearbook (Alexandria, Va.: Association for Supervision and Curriculum Development, 1962), pp. 9, 13. Reprinted with permission of the Association for Supervision and Curriculum Development. Copyright © 1962 by the Association for Supervision and Curriculum Development. All rights reserved. 9. Robert J. Havighurst, *Development Tasks and Education* (Chicago: The University of Chicago Press, 1948), p. 8. Reprinted with permission. 20. O. I. Frederick and L. J. Farquear, "Areas of Human Activity," *Journal of Educational Research* 30, (May 1937): 672–679. Reprinted with permission. 23. Reprinted by permission of the publisher from Stratemeyer, Forkner, McKim, Passow, Chapter 6, "The Scope of Persistent Life

Situations and Ways in Which Learners Face Them," in *Developing a Curriculum for Modern Living* (New York: Teachers College Press. Copyright © 1957 by Teachers College, Columbia University. All rights reserved.), pp. 146–172. 24. Excerpt from *Curriculum Improvement: Theory and Practice* by Hilda Taba, p. 399, © 1962 by Harcourt, Brace and Jovanovich, Inc. and reprinted by permission of the publisher. 25, 26, 27, 28. Jerome S. Bruner, *The Process of Education* (Cambridge, Mass.: Harvard University Press, 1977), p. 6. Reprinted with permission. 30, 31. From *The Secondary School Today*, 2nd ed. by Peter F. Oliva, pp. 151, 152. Copyright © 1972, 1976 by International Textbook Company. By permission of Harper & Row, Publishers, Inc. 39, 44, 46, 47, 48. Fenwick W. English and Roger A. Kaufman, *Needs Assessment: A Focus for Curriculum Development* (Alexandria, Va.: Association for Supervision and Curriculum Development, 1975), pp. 3–4, 12–48, 35, 39, 47. Reprinted with permission of the Association for Supervision and Curriculum Development. Copyright © 1975 by the Association for Supervision and Curriculum Development. All rights reserved. 49, Table 7-3. Figure 7-1. Theodore J. Czajkowski and Jerry L. Patterson, *School District Needs Assessment: Practical Models for Increasing Involvement in Curriculum Decisions* (Madison, Wisc.: Madison Public Schools, 1976). Reprinted with permission.

Chapter 8. 1. John W. Gardner, "National Goals in Education," in *Goals for Americans: Programs for Action in the Sixties*, The Report of the President's Commission on National Goals, Henry M. Wriston, Chairman. © 1960 by The American Assembly, Columbia University, pp. 81, 100. 2. W. James Popham and Eva L. Baker, *Systematic Instruction*, p. 43. © 1970 by Prentice-Hall, Inc., Englewood Cliffs, N.J. Reprinted with permission. 3. From *Preparing Instructional Objectives*, First Edition by Robert F. Mager, pp. 1, 3–4. Copyright © 1962 by Fearon Publishers, Inc. Reprinted by permission of Pitman Learning, Inc., Belmont, California. 5. Decker F. Walker, "A Brainstorming Tour of Writing on Curriculum," *Considered Action for Curriculum Improvement*, 1980 Yearbook (Alexandria, Va.: Association for Supervision and Curriculum Development, 1980), p. 81. Reprinted with permission of the Association for Supervision and Curriculum Development. Copyright © 1980 by the Association for Supervision and Curriculum Development. All rights reserved. Table 8-1. Theodore J. Czajkowski and Jerry L. Patterson, *School District Needs Assessment: Practical Models for Increasing Involvement in Curriculum Decisions* (Madison, Wisc.: Madison Public Schools, 1976). Reprinted with permission.

Chapter 9. 2, 28, 35. B. Othanel Smith, William O. Stanley, and J. Harlan Shores, *Fundamentals of Curriculum Development*, rev. ed. (New York: Harcourt, Brace and Jovanovich, 1957), pp. 265, 229–230, 257. Reprinted with permission. 5. John I. Goodlad and Robert H. Anderson, *The Nongraded Elementary School*,

rev. ed. (New York: Harcourt, Brace and Jovanovich, 1963), p. 1. Reprinted with permission. 6. Herbert I. Von Haden and Jean Marie King, *Educational Innovator's Guide* (Worthington, Ohio: Charles A. Jones, 1974), pp. 30–31. Reprinted with permission of Wadsworth Publishing Company. 9, 10. Maurie H. Hillson, "The Nongraded School: A Dynamic Concept," in David W. Beggs III and Edward G. Buffie, eds., *Nongraded Schools in Action: Bold New Venture* (Bloomington, Ind.: Indiana University Press, 1967), pp. 34, 45. Reprinted with permission of Macmillan Publishing Company from *Curriculum Development: Theory Into Practice*, 2nd ed., by Daniel Tanner and Laurel N. Tanner, pp. 453, 485, 473, 474, 605. Copyright © 1980, Macmillan Publishing Co., Inc. 12, 26. James B. Conant, *Recommendations for Education in the Junior High School Years* (Princeton, N.J.: Educational Testing Service, 1960), pp. 16–34, 22–23. Reprinted with permission. 14. Harvard Committee, *General Education in a Free Society* (Cambridge, Mass.: Harvard University Press, 1945), pp. 52–100. Reprinted with permission. 16, 88, 89, 90, 91. Specified excerpts and chart (update) from *A Curriculum for the Middle School Years* by John H. Lounsbury and Gordon F. Vars, pp. 56, 46, 47, 48. Copyright © 1978 by John H. Lounsbury and Gordon F. Vars. By permission of Harper & Row, Publishers, Inc. 17. Emerson E. White, "Isolation and Unification as Bases for Courses of Study," Second Yearbook of the National Herbart Society for the Scientific Study of Teaching (now the National Society for the Study of Education) (Bloomington, Ill.: Pantograph Printing and Stationery Co., 1896), pp 12–13. Reprinted with permission. 21. Reprinted with permission of Macmillan Publishing Co., Inc. from *Reorganizing the High-School Curriculum*, 3rd ed. by Harold F. Alberty and Elsie J. Alberty, pp. 199–233. Copyright © 1962, Macmillan Publishing Co., Inc. 29. Max Rafferty, *What They Are Doing to Your Children* (New York: New American Library, 1964), pp. 43–44. Reprinted with permission. 30. National Education Association, *Report of the Committee of Ten on Secondary School Studies* (New York: American Book Company, 1894), p. 17. Reprinted with permission. 31, 32. William H. Burton, *The Guidance of Learning Activities: A Summary of the Principles of Teaching Based on the Growth of the Learner*, 3rd ed. © 1962, p. 289. Reprinted by permission of Prentice-Hall, Inc., Englewood Cliffs, N.J. 33, 68, 70, 71. From *The American High School Today* by James B. Conant, pp. 47–65, 12, 17, 19–20. Copyright © 1959 by James Bryant Conant. Used with permission of McGraw-Hill Book Company. 36, 37, 38. Specified excerpts from *Curriculum: Principles and Foundations* by Robert S. Zais (Thomas Y. Crowell, Inc.), pp. 407–408. Copyright © 1976 by Harper & Row, Publishers, Inc. By permission of Harper & Row, Publishers, Inc. 39, 47, Table 9-4, Table 9-5. J. Lloyd Trump and Delmas F. Miller, *Secondary School*

Scott, Foresman, 1978), pp. 79, 78, 88. Reprinted with permission. 9. From *Handbook on Formative and Summative Evaluation of Student Learning* by Benjamin S. Bloom, J. Thomas Hastings, and George F. Madaus, p. 53. Copyright © 1971 by McGraw-Hill, Inc. Used with permission of McGraw-Hill Book Company. 13. Robert J. Kibler, Donald J. Cegala, David T. Miles, and Larry L. Barker, *Objectives for Instruction and Evaluation* (Boston: Allyn and Bacon, 1974), p. 116. Reprinted with permission. 14, 16. W. James Popham, *Evaluating Instruction*, pp. 25–26, 30. © 1973 by Prentice-Hall, Inc., Englewood Cliffs, N.J. Reprinted with permission. Box 12-1. From Gordon W. Allport, Philip E. Vernon, and Gardner Lindzey. *Study of Values*, 3rd ed. (Boston: Houghton Mifflin Company, 1960), pp. 8, 10. Reprinted by permission of The Riverside Publishing Company, a subsidiary of Houghton Mifflin Company.

Chapter 13. 1. Specified excerpt from *Curriculum Improvement: A Guide to Problems, Principles, and Process*, 2nd ed. by Albert I. Oliver, p. 306. Copyright © 1977 by Albert I. Oliver. By permission of Harper & Row, Publishers, Inc. 2, 22, 23, 24, 31. Daniel L. Stufflebeam et al., *Educational Evaluation & Decision Making* (Itasca, Ill.: F. E. Peacock Publishers, 1971), pp. 4–9, 79–84, 61–69, 239, 238. © 1971, Phi Delta Kappa Educational Foundation. Reprinted with permission. 6. Figure 13-4. From *Planning Curriculum for Schools*, Third Edition, by J. Galen Saylor and William M. Alexander, p. 311. Copyright © 1974 by Holt, Rinehart and Winston, Inc. Reprinted by permission of Holt, Rinehart and Winston. 8. From *Planning Curriculum for Schools*, Third Edition, by J. Galen Saylor and William M. Alexander, p. 325. Copyright © 1974 by Holt, Rinehart and Winston, Inc. Reprinted by permission of Holt, Rinehart and Winston. 13, 14, 15, 17, 18, 19, 20, 21, Table 13-1. From an address given at the Eleventh Annual Phi Delta Kappa Symposium on Educational Research by Daniel L. Stufflebeam at Ohio State University, June 24, 1970. Quoted by permission of Daniel L. Stufflebeam. 16. Figure 13-5. From Daniel L. Stufflebeam et al., *Educational Evaluation & Decision Making* (Itasca, Ill.: F. E. Peacock Publishers, 1971), p. 236. © 1971, Phi Delta Kappa Educational Foundation. Reprinted with permission. 27, 28, 29, 30. From *Standards for Evaluation of Educational Programs, Projects, and Materials* by the Joint Committee on Standards for Educational Evaluation, pp. 19, 51, 63, 97. Copyright © 1981 by the Joint Committee on Standards for Educational Evaluation. Used with the permission of McGraw-Hill Book Company.

Chapter 14. 4, 33. From *Curriculum Planning for Better Teaching and Learning* by J. Galen Saylor and William M. Alexander, pp. 248, 249. Copyright © 1954 by J. Galen Saylor and William M. Alexander. Reprinted by permission of Holt, Rinehart and Winston. 5, 6, 24. John I. Goodlad, *Planning and Organizing for Teaching* (Washington, D.C.: National Education Association, 1963), pp. 28, 29. Reprinted with permission. 9. Alvin Toffler, *Future Shock* (New York: Random House, 1970), pp. 30–31. Reprinted with permission. 10. From Hollis L. Caswell and Doak S. Campbell, *Curriculum Development* (New York: American Book Company, 1935), p. 152. Reprinted with permission. 11. Specified excerpt from *Curriculum Improvement: A Guide to Problems, Principles, and Process*, 2nd ed. by Albert I. Oliver, pp. 188–189. Copyright © 1977 by Albert I. Oliver. By permission of Harper & Row, Publishers, Inc. 14. Jerome Bruner, *On Knowing* (Cambridge, Mass.: Harvard University Press, 1962), p. 120. Reprinted with permission. 16. From Philip H. Phenix, "The Disciplines as Curriculum Content," in A. Harry Passow, Editor, *Curriculum Crossroads*. (New York: Teachers College Press, 1962. Copyright © 1962 by Teachers College, Columbia University. All rights reserved.), p. 57. 18, 50. Harry S. Broudy, *The Real World of the Public Schools* (New York: Harcourt, Brace and Jovanovich, 1972), pp. 179, 193. Reprinted with permission. 19, 20. B. Othanel Smith, *Teachers for the Real World* (Washington, D.C.: American Association of Colleges for Teacher Education, 1969), pp. 130–131. Reprinted with permission. 22, 23. Paul M. Halverson, "The Meaning of Balance," *Balance in the Curriculum*, 1961 Yearbook (Alexandria, Va.: Association for Supervision and Curriculum Development, 1961), pp. 7, 4. Reprinted with permission of the Association for Supervision and Curriculum Development. Copyright © 1961 by the Association for Supervision and Curriculum Development. All rights reserved. 25. Ronald C. Doll, *Curriculum Improvement: Decision Making and Process*, 4th ed. (Boston: Allyn and Bacon, 1978), pp. 138–139. Reprinted with permission. 27, 40. Reprinted from *Basic Principles of Curriculum and Instruction* by Ralph W. Tyler by permission of The University of Chicago Press, pp. 84–85. Copyright 1949 by the University of Chicago. 28, 29, 30, 31, 46. Excerpts from *Curriculum Improvement: Theory and Practice* by Hilda Taba, pp. 298–299, 124. © 1962 by Harcourt, Brace and Jovanovich, Inc. and reprinted by permission of the publisher. 34, 35, 36. Donald E. Orlosky and B. Othanel Smith, *Curriculum Development: Issues and Insights*, pp. 267, 251. Copyright © 1978 Rand McNally College Publishing Company. Used by permission of Houghton Mifflin Company. 37, 38. B. Othanel Smith, William O. Stanley, and J. Harlan Shores, *Fundamentals of Curriculum Development*, rev. ed. (New York: Harcourt, Brace and Jovanovich, 1957), p. 171. Reprinted with permission. 45. Reprinted with permission of Macmillan Publishing Company from *Curriculum Development: Theory Into Practice*, 2nd ed. by Daniel Tanner and Laurel N. Tanner, p. 323. Copyright © 1980 by Macmillan Publishing Co., Inc. 48. Jerome S. Bruner, "Structures in Learning," *Today's Education* 52, no. 3 (March 1963): 26. Reprinted with permission. 65. Robert M. McClure, "The Reform of the Fifties and

Index

Academy, 33, 299

Accountability movement, 479

Activity curriculum, 282–286

Affective domain. *See* Domains of learning

Aikin, Wilford M., 196, 432n

Aims of education, 177–184, 250–252

Alberty, Elsie J., 294–295

Alberty, Harold B., 294–295

Alexander, Lawrence T., 367, 368, 407

Alexander, William M., 6, 106, 115–116, 164–167, 333, 436–441, 448, 449, 456, 468, 472n

Alfonso, Robert J., 120–121, 143

Allen, Dwight, 389

A-LM, 91

Alternatives in education. *See* Educational options

Anderson, Robert H., 286

Anderson, Vernon, 36

Arizona State Department of Public Instruction, 227

Articulation, 473–475

Ashbal, Gilda Oran, 496–500

Assessment, needs. *See* Needs assessment

Association for Supervision and Curriculum Development, 95, 291, 326–327, 328–330, 333–334, 501

Commission on the Education of Adolescents, 329–330, 464

The High School We Need, 329n

The Junior High School We Need, 326–327

The Middle School We Need, 334n

Working Group on the Emerging Adolescent Learner, 333–334

Ausubel, David P., 477

Back-to-basics movement, 478–479

Bagley, William C., 188

Baker, Eva L., 9, 158, 251

Balance, 462–465

Barker, Larry L., 413

Baynham, Dorsey, 307

Behavioral objectives. *See* Objectives, instructional

Beggs, David, III, 288, 310, 313, 314, 315

Behaviorism, 189–190

Bellack, Arno, 459

Benjamin, Harold, 24n

Benne, Kenneth D., 129–132, 133

Bennis, Warren G., 121, 133

Bestor, Arthur, 188

Bilingual education, 483–484

Biological Sciences Curriculum Study (BSCS), 92, 225

Block-time classes. *See* Core curriculum

Bloom, Benjamin S., 52–53, 251n, 356, 360, 361, 362, 410, 455n

Bobbitt, Franklin, 28

Bode, Boyd, 32, 190

Bondi, Joseph, Jr., 237n

Boston Latin School, 187, 298

Brameld, Theodore, 186, 191–192, 193

Broad-fields curriculum, 304

Brookhurst Junior High School (California), 312–313

Brooks, Kenneth, 333

Broudy, Harry S., 460, 477

Brown, B. Frank, 85, 316–317

Brown v. *Board of Education of Topeka, Kansas,* 480

Bruner, Jerome S., 53, 91, 224–225, 459, 476–477, 494n

Buffie, Edward G., 288
Burnside, Houston M., 322n
Burton, William H., 300–301, 392–393

California Department of Education, 284–285
Campbell, Doak S., 6, 457–458
Campbell, Roald F., 114–115
Cardinal Principles of Secondary Education, 92, 94, 221, 252, 337
Carey, Lou, 364, 409, 410, 412–415
Carnegie Corporation, 93, 406
Carnegie Foundation for the Advancement of Teaching, 300
Carnegie unit, 300
Carol City Junior High School (Florida), 258
Carver, Fred D., 109
Caswell, Hollis L., 6, 293, 457–458
Cegala, Donald J., 413
Censorship, 484–485
Chamberlin, L. J., 332–333
Change process, 119–125
Charles, C. M., 322
Childs, John, 190
Chin, Robert, 133
CIPP model of curriculum evaluation, 441–446, 449
Cognitive domain. See Domains of learning
Cole, Robert W., 482n
Coleman, James S., 480–481
Combs, Arthur W., 28, 193, 194, 195, 361, 459
Commission on the Reorganization of Secondary Education, 32, 92, 183, 252–253
Committee on Assessing the Progress of Education, 406
Commission on Foreign Languages and International Studies, 98, 439
Committee of Ten, 94, 300, 439
Communication skills, 141–147
Competencies, generic, 389–391
  Florida's, 389–391
  Georgia's, 389
Competencies, minimal, 227–228, 230–233, 479–480
Comprehensive high school, 328–330, 335–338
Compton, Mary F., 333
Conant, James B., 32, 53, 183, 188–189, 198, 290–291, 292, 296, 301–304, 328, 329, 330
  junior high school recommendations, 290–291
  senior high school recommendations, 301–304
Continuity, 472–473
Core curriculum, 292–298
Council for International Exchange of Scholars, 97
Council on Basic Education, 188
Counts, George S., 190
Curriculum axioms. See Curriculum principles
Curriculum changes, historical, 32–36
Curriculum committee, function of, 267–272
Curriculum, conceptions of, 4–10
Curriculum defined, 6–10
Curriculum development, 25, 103–147
  defined, 25
  role of administrator, 106–110
  role of adult citizens of community, 112
  role of curriculum leader, 118–147
  role of students, 110–112
  role of teachers, 117–118
Curriculum as a discipline, 14–18
Curriculum evaluation, 25, 428–449
  defined, 25
  models of, 433–448
  problems in, 428–429, 431
  standards for, 448
Curriculum goals. See Goals, curriculum
Curriculum guide, 494–500
Curriculum, interpretations of, 5–6
Curriculum model, 430, 431, 432, 446–447
Curriculum objectives. See Objectives, curriculum
Curriculum organization, 278–341
Curriculum planning
  levels of, 53–56, 58–89
  sectors of, 56–58, 89–99
Curriculum principles, 27–42
Curriculum, relationship to instruction, 10–14
Curriculum specialists, 18–19
Cycles of instruction and curriculum, 404–405
Czajkowski, Theodore J., 239n, 267

Dade County Public Schools (Florida), 202–203, 208, 263
Dalton plan, 317
Davis, Robert H., 367, 368, 407
Decision making, process of, 38–40, 123–125
Delphi Technique, 238
Developmental tasks, 215–216

Dewey, John, 32, 133, 182–183, 185, 187, 190–191, 197, 282
Dick, Walter, 364, 409, 410, 412–415
Differentiated staffing, 307–309
Dilg, Charles A., 333–335
Discipline, characteristics of a, 14–18
Doll, Ronald C., 7, 111, 463
Domains of learning, 356–363, 415–421
  affective, 356, 359, 360–362
  cognitive, 356, 359, 360
  psychomotor, 356–357, 359, 362–363
Drake, Thelbert L., 107, 108
Dunn, Kenneth J., 385
Dunn, Rita S., 385, 482n

Earth Science Curriculum Project, 226
Ebel, Robert L., 459
Education by choice. See Educational options
Education for All Handicapped Children Act, 218, 482–483
Educational Facilities Laboratories, 338
Educational options, 338–340
Educational Policies Commission, 32, 94–95, 181n, 183–184, 212, 253
Educational Resources Information Center (ERIC), 91, 487, 510–512
Eight-Year Study, 195–196, 294–295, 296, 420
Eisner, Elliot W., 96
Elementary school, 280–289, 317–326, 331
Ellis, Susan S., 386
English Classical School, 33
English, Fenwick W., 228–229, 237–239, 267
English High School. See English Classical School
Epperson v. Arkansas, 95n
Essentialism. See Philosophies of education
Etzioni, Amitai, 73
Evaluation of the curriculum. See Curriculum evaluation
Evaluation of instruction, 403–449
  definition of terms, 407–408
  formative evaluation, 410–411
  in three domains, 415–421, 422
  phases of, 409–412
  preassessment, 409
  summative evaluation, 411
Evaluative Criteria, 237, 438–439
Experience curriculum. See Activity curriculum
Experimentalist psychology, 193

Farquear, L. J., 222

Fiedler, Fred E., 133–134, 138
Firth, Gerald R., 94, 120–121, 143
Fischer, Barbara Bree, 381–383, 385
Fischer, Louis, 381–383, 385
Flanders, Ned A., 133
Flexible scheduling, 309–314
Florida State Department of Education, 227–228, 230–233, 260–261, 390–391
Ford Foundation, 97
Forkner, Hamden L., 223–224
Formal groups, 127
Foshay, Arthur W., 7
Franklin, Benjamin, 26, 32, 33, 299
Frederick, O. I., 222
Frymier, Jack R., 36–37, 71–72
Froebel, Friedrich, 188
Four freedoms, 212

Gagné, Robert M., 8
Gallup, George H., 357, 358
Gardner, John W., 250
Gast, David K., 322n
Gatewood, Thomas E., 333–335
Generic competencies. See Competencies, generic
Gestalt psychology, 193–194
Giles, H. H., 196
Girona, R., 332–333
Glasser, William, 331
Global awareness, 98
Goals, curriculum, 252–264, 354–356
  constructing statements of, 263–264
  state of Florida, 260–261
  validating and prioritizing, 266–267
Goals, instructional, 350, 354–356
  constructing statements of, 363–364
  validating and prioritizing, 368–369
Goodlad, John I., 286, 456, 463
Graded school, 280–282
Grambs, Jean D., 291
Gronlund, Norman, 350, 351
Groups, behavior of individuals in. See Interpersonal relations

Halverson, Paul M., 463
Harrow, Anita J., 363
Harvard Committee on General Education, 183, 292, 294, 303
Hass, Glen, 30
Hastings, J. Thomas, 410
Havighurst, Robert J., 215–216, 481
Hawn, Horace C., 36–37, 71–72
Hawthorne Effect, 17

Helmer, Olaf, 236
Henry M. Flagler Elementary School (Florida), 202–203
Henson, Kenneth T., 392n
Hillson, Maurie H., 287–289
Hockett, Ruth Manning, 284–285
Huebner, Dwayne, 4
Hutchings, Patricia W., 413, 414
Hutchins, Robert M., 187

Illich, Ivan, 31
Illinois ex rel McCollum v. *Board of Education,* 95n
Imperative needs of youth, 94–95, 221, 253
Informal groups, 127
Integration of subject matter, 466–468
Integration, racial, 480–481
Institute of International Education, 97
Instruction, relationship to curriculum, 10–14
Instructional goals. *See* Goals, instructional
Instructional model, 349–350, 406, 408–410, 415
Instructional objectives. *See* Objectives, instructional
Instructional strategies, 375–381
  guidelines for selecting, 380–381
  sources, 376–380
Interests and wants of students, 210–211
International Association for the Evaluation of Educational Achievement (IEA), 97–98
International Reading Association, 96
Interpersonal relations, 125–134
  roles of group members, 129–132

James, William, 193
Johns, Roe L., 136–137
Johnson, Mauritz, Jr., 8, 154n, 156–157
Joint Committee on Standards for Educational Evaluation, 448
Joyce, Bruce, 385, 386, 388
Judicial decisions, 88–89, 95
Junior high school, 290–298, 326–328, 331–335

Kaufman, Roger A., 228–229, 237–239, 267
Keats, John, 188
Kelley, Earl C., 52, 193, 214
Kellogg Foundation, 93, 107
Kettering Commission. *See* Commission on the Reform of Secondary Education
Kibler, Robert J., 413, 414

Kilpatrick, William H., 32, 190, 283
Kimbrough, Ralph B., 113n, 135
Kimpston, Richard D., 94
King, Jean Marie, 287
Knezevich, Stephen J., 139–140
Köhler, Wolfgang, 193
Koffka, Kurt, 193
Krathwohl, David R., 251n, 356, 360–361, 362, 420n
Kurtz, Royce E., 288

Latin Grammar School, 33
Lau v. *Nichols,* 51, 95n, 483
Leadership, 134–140
  approaches, 136–140
  skills, 134–135
  style, 136–140
  traits, 135–136
Learning styles. *See* Styles of learning
Leavitt, Harold J., 120
Legislative decisions, 87–88
Lewin, Kurt, 123, 133, 138, 193
Lewis, Arthur J., 457, 472n
Leyton Soto, Mario, 159–162
Likert, Rensis, 133
Lippitt, Ronald, 133, 138
Lounsbury, John H., 293, 332, 335, 336
Lovell, John T., 121
Lucio, William H., 120
Lynd, Albert, 188

McClure, Robert M., 485
McCutchen, S. P., 196
Macdonald, James B., 32–33
McGregor, Douglas M., 108–109
McKim, Margaret G., 223–224
McNeil, John D., 91, 110–111, 120
Madaus, George F., 410
Madison Public Schools (Wisconsin), 239–244, 266, 267, 268–271
Mager, Robert F., 251
Man: A Course of Study, 91
Management, school-based, 70–71
Manlove, Donald C., 310, 313, 314, 315
Mann, Horace, 32
Martin, John Henry, 337
Maslow, Abraham H., 109, 193, 194, 459
Measurement
  criterion-referenced, 412–415
  norm-referenced, 411–412, 413–415
Melbourne High School (Florida), 314, 316–317, 318–321
Meriam, J. L., 282

Miami Palmetto Senior High School (Florida), 259
Michaels, Kenneth G., 338–339
Middle school, 331–335
Miles, David T., 413
Miller, Delmas F., 306, 311, 312, 313–314, 315
Minimal competencies. *See* Competencies, minimal
Model of curriculum. *See* Curriculum model
Model of instruction. *See* Instructional model
Models of curriculum development, 154–171
    criteria for, 167–168
    Leyton Soto model, 159–162
    Oliva model (1976), 168
    Oliva model (1982), 168–171
    Saylor and Alexander model, 164–167
    Taba model, 161, 163–164
    Tyler model, 155–159
Models of curriculum evaluation. *See* Curriculum evaluation, models of
Models of the curriculum-instruction relationship. *See* Curriculum, relationship to instruction
Models of teaching, 385–388
Morphet, Edgar L., 136–137
Moskowitz, Martin, 226n

National Assessment of Educational Progress, 92–93, 406–407, 438, 439
National Association of Secondary School Principals, 338
National Center for Education Statistics, 406
National Commission on the Reform of Secondary Education, 338
National Consortium for Options in Public Education, 339
National Defense Education Act, 225
National Diffusion Network, 487, 513–521
National Education Association, 94, 180, 183–184, 300
National Institute of Education, 510
National Panel on High Schools and Adolescent Education, 335, 337, 338
National Science Foundation, 91, 92, 93
National Study Committee on Evaluation. *See* Phi Delta Kappa National Study Committee on Evaluation
National Study of School Evaluation, 198n, 439n
Needs assessment, 228–244
Needs derived from subject matter, 224–228

Needs of society, 216–224
    levels, 216–221
    types, 221–224
Needs of students, 209–215
    levels, 211–213
    types, 214–215
Neville, Richard F., 120–121, 143
Newark Board of Education (New Jersey), 226–227
Nongraded elementary school, 286–289
Nongraded high school, 314–317
North Miami Beach Senior High School (Florida), 307–308
Nova High School (Florida), 314–316
Nunnery, Michael Y., 113n, 135

Objectives, curriculum, 252–264
    constructing statements of, 264–266
    validating and prioritizing, 266–267
Objectives, instructional, 350–369
    rules for writing, 363–368
    validating and prioritizing, 368–369
Oliva, Peter F., 10, 20n, 53n, 54, 85n, 168, 196, 217, 225, 226, 312, 397n, 416n, 421n
Oliver, Albert I., 7, 37, 458–459, 473, 500–501
Oliver Ellsworth School (Connecticut), 323–325
Open-space education, 317–326
Organization of American States, 178
Orlosky, Donald E., 470–471
Owens, Robert G., 120, 122

Panel on Youth of the President's Science Advisory Committee, 338
Parker, Francis W., 293
Passow, A. Harry, 223–224, 338
Patterson, Franklin, 329–330, 464n
Patterson, Jerry L. 239n, 267n
Pavlov, Ivan, 189
Peddiwell, J. Abner. *See* Benjamin, Harold
Pestalozzi, Johann, 188
Peter, Laurence J., Jr., 135, 393
Perceptual psychology, 194
Perennialism. *See* Philosophies of education
Phenix, Philip H., 459
Phi Delta Kappa National Study Committee on Evaluation, 39n, 123, 434, 441–446, 448, 449
Philosophies, examples of school, 201–203

Philosophies of education, 184–198
  essentialism, 187–190
  perennialism, 186–187
  progressivism, 190–198
  reconstructionism, 185–186
Philosophy, formulating a, 198–200
Physical Science Study Committee (PSSC), 93, 225
Piaget, Jean, 32
Pierce, Charles C., 193
P. K. Yonge Laboratory School (Florida), 296–297
Planning for instruction, 348–369
Plans, lesson, 393, 397, 398–399
Plans, unit, 392–393, 394–396
Popham, W. James, 9, 158, 251, 352, 413, 415
Pratt, David, 324
Proctor, John H., 323–325
Professional organizations, 87
Programs for the handicapped, 482–483
Progressive Education Association, 188, 195–196, 295, 420
Progressivism. See Philosophies of education
Psychomotor domain. See Domains of Learning
Public Law 94-142. See Education for All Handicapped Children Act

Rafferty, Max, 188, 299
Raths, James D., 352–353
Reconstructionism. See Philosophies of education
Regional educational laboratories, 91, 487, 522–523
Relevance, 460–462
Reller, Theodore L., 136–137
Research and development centers, 522–523
Resource unit, 500–506
Reston, James N., 288
Rickover, Hyman G., 184
Roe, William H., 107, 108
Rogers, Carl, 193
Rousseau, Jean Jacques, 188, 190
Rubin, Louis, 323, 325–326
Rugg, Harold, 191n
Ryan, Kevin, 389

St. Lucie County Public Schools (Florida), 201, 256–257
Saylor, J. Galen, 6, 106, 115, 116, 164–167, 436–441, 448, 449, 456, 468, 472n

School District of Abington Township, Pa. v. Schempp & Murray v. Curlett, 95n
School Mathematics Study Group (SMSG), 92
Schwab, Joseph, 27–28
Scientific method, 192–193
Scope, 455–460
Scopes, John Thomas, 89
Scriven, Michael, 41n, 447n
Seid, Irving, 226n
Self-concept. See Perceptual psychology
Self-fulfilling prophecy, 195
Seltzer, Morton, 226n
Senior high school, 298–317, 328–330, 335–340
Sequence, 468–472
Sergiovanni, Thomas J., 109, 131, 139
Serrano v. Priest, 220
Servey, Richard E., 322n
Seven Cardinal Principles. See Cardinal Principles of Secondary Education
Sexism, 481–482
Sheats, Paul, 129–132
Shores, J. Harlan, 42n, 282, 293, 298–299, 304, 472
Silberman, Charles E., 53
Simpson, Elizabeth Jane, 362–363
Singer, Ira J., 306–307
Skills of teaching, 388–391
Skinner, B. F., 32, 189
Sleight, Peter, 340–341
Sloan Foundation, 93
Smith, B. Othanel, 42n, 282, 293, 298–299, 304, 461–462, 470–471, 472
Smith, Kathryn, 323–325
Smith, Mortimer, 188
Smythe, Mary-Jeanette, 413, 414
Snygg, Donald, 193
Southern States Cooperative Program in Educational Administration, 106–107
Spencer, Herbert, 222, 459
Stanley, William O., 42n, 282, 293, 298–299, 304, 472
Starratt, Robert J., 131, 139
State departments of education, 86–87
Steinhoff, Carl R., 120, 122
Stratemeyer, Florence B., 223–224
Stuart v. School District No. 1, Village of Kalamazoo, 88–89
Stufflebeam, Daniel L., 39n, 123, 133, 429, 434n, 441–446, 448, 449
Styles of learning, 383–385

Styles of teaching, 381–383
Subject matter curriculum, 298–304

Taba, Hilda, 7, 40, 155, 161, 163–164, 185, 192–193, 222n, 224, 466 467–468, 476
Tanner, Daniel, 7, 159, 289, 296, 298, 304, 338, 476
Tanner, Laurel N., 7, 159, 289, 296, 298, 304, 338, 476
Teacher organizations, impact of, 485–486
Teaching models. *See* Models of teaching
Teaching skills. *See* Skills of teaching
Teaching styles. *See* Styles of teaching
Team teaching, 306–307
Ten Imperative Needs of Youth. *See* Imperative needs of youth
Testing student achievement. *See* Evaluation of instruction, in three domains
Thayer, V. T., 189
Thelen, Herbert A., 384
Theory X, 108–109
Theory Y, 108–109
Thorndike, Edward L., 189, 405, 475n, 476
Title I, Elementary and Secondary Education Act, 90–91, 481
Title IX of the Educational Amendments of 1972, 51, 481
Toffler, Alvin, 340, 457
Transferability, 475–477
Trump, J. Lloyd, 306–307, 311, 312, 313–314
Trump Plan. *See* Trump, J. Lloyd
Turney, David, 31
Turner, Richard L., 384, 387–388
Tyler, Ralph W., 52, 155–160, 161, 196, 224, 228, 350, 351, 406, 455n, 456–457, 466, 472

United Nations Educational, Scientific, and Cultural Organization (UNESCO), 97, 178, 187

United States Department (Office) of Education, 52, 90–91, 92, 95, 97, 98, 183, 337, 406, 483, 484
United States Department of Labor, 218n
U.S.-U.S.S.R. Textbook Project, 98
University of Chicago Laboratory School, 190
University of Illinois Committee on School Mathematics (UICSM), 93

Validation of goals and objectives, 266–267, 368–369
Values, moral and spiritual, 180–182
Vars, Gordon F., 293, 332, 335, 336, 468n
Verduin, John R., Jr., 40
Virginia State Curriculum Program, 222
Von Haden, Herbert I., 287

Walker, Decker F., 252
Watson, John B., 189
Weil, Marsha, 385, 386, 388
Wertheimer, Max, 193
Western Electric researches, 16–17, 133
White, Ralph K., 133, 138
Wiles, Jon, 237n
Wiles, Kimball, 134, 329–330, 464n
Wisconsin State Department of Public Instruction, 223–224
Wolfe, Arthur B., 315
World Council for Curriculum and Instruction, 96–97
Wright, Grace S., 295

Yelon, Stephen L., 367, 368, 407

Zais, Robert S., 72, 222, 304–305
Zechiel, A. N., 196
Zorach v. *Clauson*, 95n